Emerging Research on Applied Fuzzy Sets and Intuitionistic Fuzzy Matrices

Amal Kumar Adak
Jafuly Deshpran High School, India

Debashree Manna
Damda Jr. High School, India

Monoranjan Bhowmik
Vidyasagar Teacher's Training College, India

A volume in the Advances in Computational Intelligence and Robotics (ACIR) Book Series

IGI GLOBAL
DISSEMINATOR OF KNOWLEDGE

www.igi-global.com

Published in the United States of America by
IGI Global
Information Science Reference (an imprint of IGI Global)
701 E. Chocolate Avenue
Hershey PA, USA 17033
Tel: 717-533-8845
Fax: 717-533-8661
E-mail: cust@igi-global.com
Web site: http://www.igi-global.com

Library of Congress Cataloging-in-Publication Data

Names: Adak, Amal Kumar, 1992- editor. | Manna, Debashree, 1987- editor. | Bhowmik, Manoranjan, editor.
Title: Emerging research on applied fuzzy sets and intuitionistic fuzzy matrices / Amal Kumar Adak, Debashree Manna, and Manoranjan Bhowmik, editors.
Description: Hershey PA : Information Science Reference, [2017] | Series: Advances in computational intelligence and robotics | Includes bibliographical references and index.
Identifiers: LCCN 2016033999| ISBN 9781522509141 (hardcover) | ISBN 9781522509158 (ebook)
Subjects: LCSH: Fuzzy sets, | Matrices.
Classification: LCC QA248.5 .E44 2017 | DDC 511.3/223--dc23 LC record available at https://lccn.loc.gov/2016033999

This book is published in the IGI Global book series Advances in Computational Intelligence and Robotics (ACIR) (ISSN: 2327-0411; eISSN: 2327-042X)

British Cataloguing in Publication Data
A Cataloguing in Publication record for this book is available from the British Library.

Advances in Computational Intelligence and Robotics (ACIR) Book Series

Ivan Giannoccaro
University of Salento, Italy

ISSN:2327-0411
EISSN:2327-042X

Mission

While intelligence is traditionally a term applied to humans and human cognition, technology has progressed in such a way to allow for the development of intelligent systems able to simulate many human traits. With this new era of simulated and artificial intelligence, much research is needed in order to continue to advance the field and also to evaluate the ethical and societal concerns of the existence of artificial life and machine learning.

The **Advances in Computational Intelligence and Robotics (ACIR) Book Series** encourages scholarly discourse on all topics pertaining to evolutionary computing, artificial life, computational intelligence, machine learning, and robotics. ACIR presents the latest research being conducted on diverse topics in intelligence technologies with the goal of advancing knowledge and applications in this rapidly evolving field.

Coverage

- Cyborgs
- Computational Intelligence
- Pattern Recognition
- Robotics
- Intelligent control
- Natural language processing
- Automated Reasoning
- Computational Logic
- Artificial Life
- Algorithmic Learning

IGI Global is currently accepting manuscripts for publication within this series. To submit a proposal for a volume in this series, please contact our Acquisition Editors at Acquisitions@igi-global.com or visit: http://www.igi-global.com/publish/.

The Advances in Computational Intelligence and Robotics (ACIR) Book Series (ISSN 2327-0411) is published by IGI Global, 701 E. Chocolate Avenue, Hershey, PA 17033-1240, USA, www.igi-global.com. This series is composed of titles available for purchase individually; each title is edited to be contextually exclusive from any other title within the series. For pricing and ordering information please visit http://www.igi-global.com/book-series/advances-computational-intelligence-robotics/73674. Postmaster: Send all address changes to above address.

Table of Contents

Preface xiii

Acknowledgment xvi

Chapter 1
Fuzzy Sets, Intuitionistic Fuzzy Sets: Separation of Generalized Interval-Valued Intuitionistic Fuzzy Sets 1
Monoranjan Bhowmik, Vidyasagar Teacher's Training College, India
Madhumangal Pal, Vidyasagar University, India

Chapter 2
Neutrosophic Sets and Logic 18
Mumtaz Ali, Quaid-i-Azam University Islamabad, Pakistan
Florentin Smarandache, University of New Mexico – Gallup, USA
Luige Vladareanu, Institute of Solid Mechanics of Romanian Academy, Romania

Chapter 3
Interval-Valued Intuitionistic Fuzzy Partition Matrices 64
Amal Kumar Adak, Jafuly Deshpran High School, India

Chapter 4
P-F Fuzzy Rings and Normal Fuzzy Ring: Fuzzy Ring 82
Manoj Kumar, International Engineering Services, India

Chapter 5
Intutionistic Fuzzy Difference Equation 112
Sankar Prasad Mondal, National Institute of Technology Agartala, India
Dileep Kumar Vishwakarma, National Institute of Technology Agartala, India
Apu Kumar Saha, National Institute of Technology Agartala, India

Chapter 6
Semiring of Generalized Interval-Valued Intuitionistic Fuzzy Matrices 132
Debashree Manna, Damda Jr. High School, India

Chapter 7
Classification Techniques in Data Mining: Classical and Fuzzy Classifiers 153
Ali Hosseinzadeh, Comprehensive Imam Hossein University, Iran
S. A. Edalatpanah, Ayandegan Institute of Higher Education, Tonekabon, Iran

Chapter 8
Multiobjective Optimization of Solar-Powered Irrigation System with Fuzzy Type-2 Noise Modelling 189
T. Ganesan, Tenaga Nasional Berhad - Research (TNBR), Malaysia
Pandian Vasant, Universiti Teknologi Petronas, Malaysia
I. Elamvazuthi, Universiti Teknologi Petronas, Malaysia

Chapter 9
Non-Linear Intuitionistic Fuzzy Number and Its Application in Partial Differential Equation.......... 215
Sankar Prasad Mondal, National Institute of Technology Agartala, India

Chapter 10
Use of Fuzzy Set Theory in DNA Sequence Comparison and Amino Acid Classification 235
Subhram Das, Narula Institute of Technology, India
Soumen Ghosh, Narula Institute of Technology, India
Jayanta Pal, Narula Institute of Technology, India
Dilip K. Bhattacharya, University of Calcutta, India

Chapter 11
On Bipolar Fuzzy B-Subalgebras of B-Algebras.. 254
Tapan Senapati, Padima Janakalyan Banipith High School, India

Chapter 12
Decision Making by Using Intuitionistic Fuzzy Rough Set.. 268
T. K. Das, VIT University, India

Chapter 13
An Efficient Method for Forecasting Using Fuzzy Time Series.. 287
Pritpal Singh, CHARUSAT University, India

Chapter 14
A Three-Level Supply Chain Model with Necessity Measure 305
Barun Das, Sidho-Kanho-Birsha University, India

Detailed Table of Contents

Preface xiii

Acknowledgment xvi

Chapter 1
Fuzzy Sets, Intuitionistic Fuzzy Sets: Separation of Generalized Interval-Valued Intuitionistic Fuzzy Sets 1
Monoranjan Bhowmik, Vidyasagar Teacher's Training College, India
Madhumangal Pal, Vidyasagar University, India

In this chapter, we define four separations of generalized interval-valued intuitionistic fuzzy sets (GIVIFSs). In fact, all interval-valued Intuitionistic fuzzy sets (IVIFSs) are GIVIFSs but all GIVIFSs are not IVIFSs. Also, we studied some properties of the four separated subsets of GIVIFSs.

Chapter 2
Neutrosophic Sets and Logic 18
Mumtaz Ali, Quaid-i-Azam University Islamabad, Pakistan
Florentin Smarandache, University of New Mexico – Gallup, USA
Luige Vladareanu, Institute of Solid Mechanics of Romanian Academy, Romania

Neutrosophic sets and Logic plays a significant role in approximation theory. It is a generalization of fuzzy sets and intuitionistic fuzzy set. Neutrosophic set is based on the neutrosophic philosophy in which every idea Z, has opposite denoted as anti(Z) and its neutral which is denoted as neut(Z). This is the main feature of neutrosophic sets and logic. This chapter is about the basic concepts of neutrosophic sets as well as some of their hybrid structures. This chapter starts with the introduction of fuzzy sets and intuitionistic fuzzy sets respectively. The notions of neutrosophic set are defined and studied their basic properties in this chapter. Then we studied neutrosophic crisp sets and their associated properties and notions. Moreover, interval valued neutrosophic sets are studied with some of their properties. Finally, we presented some applications of neutrosophic sets in the real world problems.

Chapter 3
Interval-Valued Intuitionistic Fuzzy Partition Matrices 64
Amal Kumar Adak, Jafuly Deshpran High School, India

If in an interval-valued intuitionistic fuzzy matrix each element is again a smaller interval-valued intuitionistic fuzzy matrix then the interval-valued intuitionistic fuzzy matrix is called interval-valued

intuitionistic fuzzy partion matrix (IVIFPMs). In this paper, the concept of interval-valued intuitionistic fuzzy partion matrices (IVIFPMs) are introduced and defined different types of interval-valued intuitionistic fuzzy partion matrices (IVIFPMs). The operations like direct sum, Kronecker sum, Kronecker product of interval-valued intuitionistic fuzzy matrices are presented and shown that their resultant matrices are also interval-valued intuitionistic fuzzy partion matrices (IVIFPMs).

Chapter 4
P-F Fuzzy Rings and Normal Fuzzy Ring: Fuzzy Ring 82
Manoj Kumar, International Engineering Services, India

In 1965, Zadeh introduced the concept of fuzzy subset. Since that time many papers were introduced in different mathematical scopes of theoretical and practical applications. In 1982, Liuformulated the term of fuzzy ring and fuzzy ideal of a ring R. In 2004, Hadi and Abou-Draeb, introduced and studied P-F fuzzy rings and normal fuzzy rings and now we are complete it. In this chapter, the concepts P-F fuzzy rings and normal fuzzy rings have been investigated. Several basic results related to these concepts have given and studied. The relationship between them has also been given. Moreover, some properties of t-pure fuzzy ideal of a fuzzy ring have been given which need it later.

Chapter 5
Intutionistic Fuzzy Difference Equation 112
Sankar Prasad Mondal, National Institute of Technology Agartala, India
Dileep Kumar Vishwakarma, National Institute of Technology Agartala, India
Apu Kumar Saha, National Institute of Technology Agartala, India

In this chapter we solve linear difference equation with intuitionistic fuzzy initial condition. All possible cases are defined and solved them to obtain the exact solutions. The intuitionistic fuzzy numbers are also taken as trapezoidal intuitionistic fuzzy number. The problems are illustrated by two different numerical examples.

Chapter 6
Semiring of Generalized Interval-Valued Intuitionistic Fuzzy Matrices 132
Debashree Manna, Damda Jr. High School, India

In this paper, the concept of semiring of generalized interval-valued intuitionistic fuzzy matrices are introduced and have shown that the set of GIVIFMs forms a distributive lattice. Also, prove that the GIVIFMs form an generalized interval valued intuitionistic fuzzy algebra and vector space over [0, 1]. Some properties of GIVIFMs are studied using the definition of comparability of GIVIFMs.

Chapter 7
Classification Techniques in Data Mining: Classical and Fuzzy Classifiers 153
Ali Hosseinzadeh, Comprehensive Imam Hossein University, Iran
S. A. Edalatpanah, Ayandegan Institute of Higher Education, Tonekabon, Iran

Learning is the ability to improve behavior based on former experiences and observations. Nowadays, mankind continuously attempts to train computers for his purpose, and make them smarter through trainings and experiments. Learning machines are a branch of artificial intelligence with the aim of reaching machines able to extract knowledge (learning) from the environment. Classical, fuzzy classification, as a

subcategory of machine learning, has an important role in reaching these goals in this area. In the present chapter, we undertake to elaborate and explain some useful and efficient methods of classical versus fuzzy classification. Moreover, we compare them, investigating their advantages and disadvantages.

Chapter 8
Multiobjective Optimization of Solar-Powered Irrigation System with Fuzzy Type-2 Noise Modelling 189
T. Ganesan, Tenaga Nasional Berhad - Research (TNBR), Malaysia
Pandian Vasant, Universiti Teknologi Petronas, Malaysia
I. Elamvazuthi, Universiti Teknologi Petronas, Malaysia

Design optimization has been commonly practiced for many years across various engineering disciplines. Optimization per se is becoming a crucial element in industrial applications involving sustainable alternative energy systems. During the design of such systems, the engineer/decision maker would often encounter noise factors (e.g. solar insolation and ambient temperature fluctuations) when their system interacts with the environment. Therefore, successful modelling and optimization procedures would require a framework that encompasses all these uncertainty features and solves the problem at hand with reasonable accuracy. In this chapter, the sizing and design optimization of the solar powered irrigation system was considered. This problem is multivariate, noisy, nonlinear and multiobjective. This design problem was tackled by first using the Fuzzy Type II approach to model the noise factors. Consequently, the Bacterial Foraging Algorithm (BFA) (in the context of a weighted sum framework) was employed to solve this multiobjective fuzzy design problem. This method was then used to construct the approximate Pareto frontier as well as to identify the best solution option in a fuzzy setting. Comprehensive analyses and discussions were performed on the generated numerical results with respect to the implemented solution methods.

Chapter 9
Non-Linear Intuitionistic Fuzzy Number and Its Application in Partial Differential Equation.......... 215
Sankar Prasad Mondal, National Institute of Technology Agartala, India

In this chapter the concept of non linear intuitionistic fuzzy number is addressed. Mainly the construction of non linear intuitionistic fuzzy number whose membership function is non linear function is taken here. Finally the number is taken with partial differential equation and solve the problem.

Chapter 10
Use of Fuzzy Set Theory in DNA Sequence Comparison and Amino Acid Classification 235
Subhram Das, Narula Institute of Technology, India
Soumen Ghosh, Narula Institute of Technology, India
Jayanta Pal, Narula Institute of Technology, India
Dilip K. Bhattacharya, University of Calcutta, India

This chapter describes the use of fuzzy set theory and intuitionistic fuzzy set theory in DNA sequence comparison. It also shows an indirect application of fuzzy set theory in comparing protein sequences. In fact, protein sequences consist of 20 amino acids. The chapter shows how such amino acids can be classified in six different groups. These groups are obtained purely from theoretical considerations. These are entirely different from the known groups of amino acids based on biological considerations. Also it is known how these classified groups of amino acids help in protein sequence comparison. The results

of comparison differ as the groups differ in number and their compositions. Naturally it is expected that newer results of comparison will come out from such newer classified groups of amino acids obtained theoretically. Thus fuzzy set theory is also useful in protein sequence comparison.

Based on the concept of bipolar fuzzy set, a theoretical approach of B-subalgebras of B-algebras are established. Some characterizations of bipolar fuzzy B-subalgebras of B-algebras are given. We have shown that the intersection of two bipolar fuzzy B-subalgebras is also a bipolar fuzzy B-subalgebra, but for the union it is not always true. We have also shown that if every bipolar fuzzy B-subalgebras has the finite image, then every descending chain of B-subalgebras terminates at finite step.

This chapter begins with a brief introduction of the theory of rough set. Rough set is an intelligent technique for handling uncertainty aspect in the data. This theory has been hybridized by combining with many other mathematical theories. In recent years, much decision making on rough set theory has been extended by embedding the ideas of fuzzy sets, intuitionistic fuzzy sets and soft sets. In this chapter, the notions of fuzzy rough set and intuitionistic fuzzy rough (IFR) sets are defined, and its properties are studied. Thereafter rough set on two universal sets has been studied. In addition, intuitionistic fuzzy rough set on two universal sets has been extensively studied. Furthermore, we would like to give an application, which shows that intuitionistic fuzzy rough set on two universal sets can be successfully applied to decision making problems.

Forecasting using fuzzy time series has been applied in several areas including forecasting university enrollments, sales, road accidents, financial forecasting, weather forecasting, etc. Recently, many researchers have paid attention to apply fuzzy time series in time series forecasting problems. In this paper, we present a new model to forecast the enrollments in the University of Alabama and the daily average temperature in Taipei, based on one-factor fuzzy time series. In this model, a new frequency based clustering technique is employed for partitioning the time series data sets into different intervals. For defuzzification function, two new principles are also incorporated in this model. In case of enrollments as well daily temperature forecasting, proposed model exhibits very small error rate.

In this chapter, a vertical information sharing in terms of inventory replenishment / requirement from the customer(s)→ retailer(s)→ producer→ supplier(s) has been done. The constant imprecise fuzzy

Preface

The concept of fuzzy set and intuitionistic fuzzy matrix (IFM) are one of the recent topics developed for dealing with the uncertainties present in most of our real life situations. The parameterizations tool of intuitionistic fuzzy matrix enhances the flexibility of its applications. Most of our real life problems in medical sciences, engineering, management, environment and social sciences often involve data which are not necessarily crisp, precise and deterministic in character due to various uncertainties associated with the problems. Such uncertainties are usually being handled with the help of the topics like probability, fuzzy sets, intuitionistic fuzzy sets, interval-valued intuitionistic fuzzy sets, etc.

This book will be very useful for the undergraduate students, post graduate students, decision makers and researchers in private sectors, universities and industries in the fields of various sciences and management. It is well known that uncertainty is invertible in every field of engineering, management and science. This book aims to become significant and very helpful for humankind.

The book is organized into 15 chapters. A brief description of each of the chapters is as follows:

Chapter 1 discusses four separations of generalized interval-valued intuitionistic fuzzy sets (GIVIFSs). Also, authos studied some properties of the four separated subsets of GIVIFSs.

Chapter 2 presents the notions of neutrosophic sets and logic. they studied neutrosophic sets with some of their basic properties and the hybrid structure neutrosophic crisp sets and their associated properties and notions have been studied.

Chapter 3 says that if in an interval-valued intuitionistic fuzzy matrix each element is again a smaller interval-valued intuitionistic fuzzy matrix then the interval-valued intuitionistic fuzzy matrix is called interval-valued intuitionistic fuzzy partion matrix (IVIFPMs). T concept of interval-valued intuitionistic fuzzy partion matrices (IVIFPMs) are introduced and defined different types of interval-valued intuitionistic fuzzy partion matrices (IVIFPMs).

Chapter 4 investigates the concepts P-F fuzzy rings and normal fuzzy rings. Several basic results related to these concepts have given and studied. The relationship between them has also been given. Moreover, some properties of t-pure fuzzy ideal of a fuzzy ring have been given which need it later.

Chapter 5 solves the difference equation with intutionistic fuzzy initial value. The all possible cases are defined and found the exact solution. The intutionistic fuzzy numbers are also taken are trapezoidal intutionistic fuzzy number. The problem are illustrated by two different numerical examples.

Chapter 6 introduces semiring of generalized interval-valued intuitionistic fuzzy matrices and shows that the set of GIVIFMs forms a distributive lattice. Also, prove that the GIVIFMs form a generalized interval valued intuitionistic fuzzy algebra and vector space over [0,1]. Some properties of GIVIFMs are studied using the definition of comparability of GIVIFMs.

Chapter 7 says that learning is the ability to improve behavior based on former experiences and observations. Nowadays, mankind continuously attempts to train computers for his purpose, and make them smarter through trainings and experiments. Learning machines are a branch of artificial intelligence with the aim of reaching machines able to extract knowledge (learning) from the environment. Classical, fuzzy classification, as a subcategory of machine learning, has an important role in reaching these goals in this area. In the present chapter, we undertake to elaborate and explain some useful and efficient methods of classical versus fuzzy classification. Moreover, we compare them, investigating their advantages and disadvantages.

Chapter 8 considers the sizing and design optimization of the solar powered irrigation system. This problem is multivariate, noisy, nonlinear and multi-objective. This design problem was tackled by first using the Fuzzy Type II approach to model the noise factors. Consequently, the Bacterial Foraging Algorithm (BFA) (in the context of a weighted sum framework) was employed to solve this multiobjective fuzzy design problem. This method was then used to construct the approximate Pareto frontier as well as to identify the best solution option in a fuzzy setting. Comprehensive analyses and discussions were performed on the generated numerical results with respect to the implemented solution methods.

Chapter 9 introduces non-linear intutionistic fuzzy number (NIFN). The arithmetic operation of this type number is also done here. All the operation is done by max-min principle. Finally we solve partial differential equation with NIFN. The defuzzification or crispification of the solution is done by max-min operator method.

In Chapter 10, measures of Intuitionistic fuzzy metric and fuzzy similarity do work satisfactorily as is evidenced from the results of S_1, S_2, and S_1, S_3. As supported biologically distance between the first pair should be less than the next pair and consequently the similarity of the first pair should be greater than the next pair. Actually this has happened in the present case for each value of α.The measures are of multiple choices. They vary as α varies. Again as α increases, distance measures increase and similarity measures decrease. This suggests that better is the result, larger is the value of α taken. Although the problem 1 is solved, normally it cannot be claimed that the metrics will behave equivalently for sequences other the ones used as counter examples. But as some value of the parameter θ is always involved in the calculations, so if some contradictory result appears at all, it is only apparent.

Chapter 11 gives some characterizations of bipolar fuzzy B-subalgebras of B-algebras. It is seen that the intersection of two bipolar fuzzy B-subalgebras is also a bipolar fuzzy B-subalgebra, but for the union it is not always true. We have also shown that if every bipolar fuzzy B-subalgebras has the finite image, then every descending chain of B-subalgebras terminates at finite step.

Chapter 12 defines the notions of fuzzy rough set and intuitionistic fuzzy rough (IFR) sets, and its properties are studied. Thereafter rough set on two universal sets has been studied. In addition, intuitionistic fuzzy rough set on two universal sets has been extensively studied. Furthermore, we would like to give an application, which shows that intuitionistic fuzzy rough set on two universal sets can be successfully applied to decision making problems.

Chapter 13 applies forecasting using fuzzy time series in several areas including forecasting university enrollments, sales, road accidents, financial forecasting, weather forecasting, etc. Recently, many researchers have paid attention to apply fuzzy time series in time series forecasting problems. In this paper, we present a new model to forecast the enrollments in the University of Alabama and the daily average temperature in Taipei, based on one-factor fuzzy time series.

Chapter 14 contains a vertical information sharing in terms of inventory replenishment / requirement from the customer(s)→ retailer(s)→ producer→ supplier(s) has been done. The constant imprecise fuzzy demands of the goods are made to the retailers by the customers. This chapter attempts to provide the reader a complete picture of supply chain management through a systematic literature review.

Chapter 15 gives an overview of computational iterative schemes for fuzzy system of linear equations. We also consider fully fuzzy linear systems (FFLS) and demonstrate a class of the existing iterative methods using the splitting approach for calculating the solution. Furthermore, the main aim in this work is to design a numerical procedure for improving this algorithm. Some numerical experiments are illustrated to show the applicability of the methods and to show the efficiency of proposed algorithm, we report the numerical results of large-scaled fuzzy problems.

Acknowledgment

This book is work on intuitionistic fuzzy matrices and intervalvalued intuitionistic fuzzy matrices. It would not be completed without the support of many people. I owe much to them and would like to take the opportunity to thank them for their encouragement and support.

At first we would like to record my gratitude to Prof. Madhumangal Pal, Department of Applied Mathematics with Oceanology and Computer Programming, Vidyasagar University, India for his supervision, advice and guidance from the very early stage of this work as well as giving us extraordinary experiences throughout the work.

Collective and individual acknowledgements with sincere appreciation are also owed to all our colleagues of Jafuly Deshpran High School (H.S.), Damda Jr. High School, V.T.T. College whose present somehow perpetually refreshed, continuous inspiration and co-operation helped me to complete the work.

We extend sincere appreciation and thanks to all the authors for having shared their knowledge and bright ideas with the academic and engineering community.

The book editors are very grateful to the editorial team and entire staff of IGI Global, for their confidence, interest, continuous guidance and support at all levels of preparation of this book.

We would like to thank everybody who was important to the successful realization of the book, as well as expressing our apology that we could not mention personally one by one.

Amal Kumar Adak
Jafuly Deshpran High School, India

Debashree Manna
Damda Jr. High School, India

Monoranjan Bhowmik
Vidyasagar Teacher's Training College, India

Chapter 1
Fuzzy Sets, Intuitionistic Fuzzy Sets:
Separation of Generalized Interval-Valued Intuitionistic Fuzzy Sets

Monoranjan Bhowmik
Vidyasagar Teacher's Training College, India

Madhumangal Pal
Vidyasagar University, India

ABSTRACT

In this chapter, we define four separations of generalized interval-valued intuitionistic fuzzy sets (GIVIFSs). In fact, all interval-valued Intuitionistic fuzzy sets (IVIFSs) are GIVIFSs but all GIVIFSs are not IVIFSs. Also, we studied some properties of the four separated subsets of GIVIFSs.

INTRODUCTION

It is well known that set theories play major role in various areas such as mathematics, physics, statistics, engineering, social sciences and many others. Several works on classical set theories are available in different journals even in books also. The set theories are so important that it has been placed in the school curriculum, college and university curriculum in different form and different degree of level all over world. But in all problems in daily as well as in different sectors and different subject discipline do not always involve crisp data. Recently fuzzy sets, vague set, rough set are used as the mathematical data for dealing with uncertainties. Zadeh (1965) first introduced the concept of fuzzy sets. In many real applications to handle uncertainty, fuzzy set is very much useful and in this one real value $MA(x) \in [0,1]$ is used to represent the grade of membership of a fuzzy set A defined on the universe of discourse X. After two decades the concept of interval-valued fuzzy set was introduced. Atanassov (1989) introduced several operations over interval-valued fuzzy set. It is true for some applications that it is not enough to satisfy to consider only one value to the membership-function to define the belongingness of an element in a fuzzy set. Using this conception Pal and Shyamal (2002a) introduced interval-valued fuzzy matrices

DOI: 10.4018/978-1-5225-0914-1.ch001

and have shown several properties of them. Again after two decades, Atanassov (1989 , 1994) introduced another type of fuzzy sets which is the generalization of fuzzy subset it is called intuitionistic fuzzy set which is more practical in real life situations. Intuitionistic fuzzy sets handle incomplete information i.e., the grade of membership function and non-membership function but not the indeterminate information and inconsistent information which exists obviously in belief system. Several authors present a number of results using intuitionistic fuzzy sets. By the concept of intuitionistic fuzzy sets, perhaps first time Pal (2001) introduced intuitionistic fuzzy determinant. Latter on Pal and Shyamal (2002b, 2005) introduced intuitionistic fuzzy matrices and distance between intuitionistic fuzzy matrices. Recently, Bhowmik and Pal(2008) studied some results on intuitionistic fuzzy matrices, intuitionistic circular fuzzy matrices and generalized intuitionistic fuzzy matrices. After three years of the work of Atanassov (1994) again Gargo and Atanassov (1989) introduced the interval-valued intuitionistic fuzzy sets. They have shown several properties on interval-valued intuitionistic fuzzy sets and shown applications over interval-valued intuitionistic fuzzy sets. Jana and Pal(2006) also studied some properties on interval-valued intuitionistic fuzzy sets. Bhowmik et al (2009) define generalized interval-valued intuitionistic fuzzy sets with some properties.

SOME DEFINITIONS AND PROPERTIES

We present two fundamental operators $\vee$ and $\wedge$ defined over fuzzy sets below:

On the interval [0,1] (where the fuzzy sets takes their elements) the following operations are defined for all x, y$\in$ [0,1]:

1. $x \vee y = \max(x, y)$,
2. $x \wedge y = \min(x, y)$.

We define a lattice $(L', \leq)$, where $L' = \{[x_1, x_2]: (x_1, x_2) \in [0,1]^2$ and $x_1 \leq x_2\}$, $[x_1, x_2] \leq [y_1, y_2] \Leftrightarrow (x_1 \leq y_1$ and $x_2 \leq y_2)$ *for all* $[x_1, x_2], [y_1, y_2] \in L'$.

Definition 1 (Fuzzy Set)

A fuzzy set A over X (universe of discourse) is an object having the form A=$\{\langle x, M_A(x)\rangle / x \in X\}$, where $M_A(x)$ denote the degree of membership of the element x to the set A and it can take any value from [0,1].

Some Properties of Fuzzy Set

Let A and B be two fuzzy sets of the form $A=\{\langle x, M_A(x)\rangle | x \in X\}$ and $B=\{\langle x, M_B(x)\rangle | x \in X\}$ Then

1. $A \subseteq B$ if and only if $M_A(x) \leq M_B(x)$; for all $x \in X$.
2. $\bar{A} = \{\langle x, 1 - M_A(x)\rangle \mid x \in X\}$;
3. $A \cap B = \{\langle x, M_A(x) \wedge M_B(x)\rangle \mid x \in X\}$;
4. $A \cup B = \{\langle x, M_A(x) \vee M_B(x)\rangle \mid x \in X\}$.

Definition 2 (Interval-Valued Fuzzy Set)

An interval-valued fuzzy set A over X (universe of discourse) is an object having the form A={⟨x, $M_A(x)$⟩| $x \in X$ }, where $M_A(x) = [M_{AL}(x), M_{AU}(x)]$ for all $x \in X$, X $\rightarrow D[0,1]$, where D[0,1] is the set of all subintervals of [0, 1]. The interval $M_A(x)$ denotes the intervals of the degree of membership.

Some Properties of Interval-Valued Fuzzy Set

Let A and B be two interval-valued fuzzy sets on X, where A= $\langle [M_{AL}(x), M_{AU}(x)]/x \in X \rangle$ and B =$\langle [M_{BL}(x), M_{BU}(x)]/x \in X \rangle$. Then

1. $A \leq B \Leftrightarrow \{M_{AL}(x) \leq M_{BL}(x)$ and $M_{AU}(x) \leq M_{BU}(x)\}$ for all $x \in X$.
2. $A \prec B \Leftrightarrow \{M_{AL}(x) \leq M_{BL}(x)$ and $M_{AU}(x) \leq M_{BU}(x)\}$ for all $x \in X$.
3. $A \subset_{\square} B$ iff $\{M_{AL}(x) \leq M_{BL}(x)$ and $M_{AU}(x) \leq M_{BU}(x)\}$ for all $x \in X$.
4. $A \subset_{\Diamond} B$ iff $\{N_{AL}(x) \geq N_{BL}(x)$ and $N_{AU}(x) \geq N_{BU}(x)\}$ for all $x \in X$.
5. $A \subseteq B$ iff $\{(M_{AU}(x) \leq M_{BU}(x)$ and $M_{AL}(x) \leq M_{BL}(x))$ for all $x \in X$.

Now, we define some unary and binary operations on interval-valued fuzzy sets:

1. $A \cap B = \left\{ \left\langle x, \min\left\{M_{AL}(x), M_{BL}(x)\right\}, \max\left\{M_{AU}(x), M_{BU}(x)\right\}\right\rangle \mid x \in X \right\}$.
2. $A \cup B = \left\{ \left\langle x, \max\left\{M_{AL}(x), M_{BL}(x)\right\}, \min\left\{M_{AU}(x), M_{BU}(x)\right\}\right\rangle \mid x \in X \right\}$.

Definition 3 (Intuitionistic Fuzzy Set)

An intuitionistic fuzzy set A over X (universe of discourse) is an object having the form A ={⟨x, $M_A(x)$, $N_A(x)$⟩| $x \in X$}, where $M_A(x)$ and $N_A(x)$ denote the degree of membership and degree of non-membership of the element x to the set A and take can any value form [0,1] for all $x \in X$, with the condition $0 \leq M_A(x) + N_A(x) \leq 1$.

Some Properties of Intuitionistic Fuzzy Set

Let A and B be two intuitionistic fuzzy sets of the form

A ={⟨x, $M_A(x)$, $N_A(x)$⟩| $x \in X$} and B ={⟨x, $M_B(x)$, $N_B(x)$⟩| $x \in X$}.

Then

1. $A \subseteq B$ if and only if $M_A(x) \leq M_B(x)$ and $N_A(x) \geq N_B(x)$;
2. $\bar{A} = \left\{ \left\langle x, N_A(x), M_A(x) \right\rangle \mid x \in X \right\}$;
3. $A \cap B = \left\{ \left\langle x, M_A(x) \wedge M_B(x), N_A(x) \vee N_B(x) \right\rangle \mid x \in X \right\}$;
4. $A \cup B = \left\{ \left\langle x, M_A(x) \vee M_B(x), N_A(x) \wedge N_B(x) \right\rangle \mid x \in X \right\}$.

Definition 4 (Interval-Valued Intuitionistic Fuzzy Set)

An interval-valued intuitionistic fuzzy sets A over X (universe of discourse) is an object having the form

$A = \{\langle x, M_A(x), N_A(x)\rangle | \, x \in X\}$,

where $M_A(x)$: $X \rightarrow D[0,1]$ and $N_A(x)$: $X \rightarrow D[0,1]$, where D[0,1] is the set of all subintervals of [0, 1]. The intervals $M_A(x)$ and $N_A(x)$ denote the intervals of the degree of membership and degree of non-membership of the element x to the set A, where

$M_A(x) = [M_{AL}(x), M_{AU}(x)]$

and

$N_A(x) = [N_{AL}(x), N_{AU}(x)]$,

for all $x \in X$, with the condition $0 \leq M_{AU}(x) + N_{AU}(x) \leq 1$.

Note 1: An element x of X is called significant with respect to a fuzzy subset A of X if the degree of membership $M_A(x) > 0.5$, otherwise, it is insignificant. We see that for a fuzzy subset A both the degrees of membership $M_A(x)$ and non- membership $N_A(x) = 1 - M_A(x)$ can not be significant. Further, for an intuitionistic fuzzy set

$A = \{\langle x, M_A(x), N_A(x)\rangle | \, x \in X\}$

it is observe that

$0 \leq M_A(x) + N_A(x) \leq 1$,

for all $x \in X$ and hence it is observed that $\min\{M_A(x), N_A(x)\} \leq 0.5$, for all $x \in X$.

Having motivated from the observation, perhaps first time we define generalized interval-valued intuitionistic fuzzy sets as follows:

Definition 5 (Generalized Interval-Valued Intuitionistic Fuzzy Set)

If the interval-valued intuitionistic fuzzy sets $A = \{\langle x, M_A(x), N_A(x)\rangle | \, x \in X\}$ satisfying with the condition

$$M_{AU}(x) \wedge N_{AU}(x) \leq 0.5$$

for all $x \in X$ then A is called generalized interval-valued intuitionistic fuzzy sets interval-valued intuitionistic fuzzy sets.

The condition

$$M_{AU}(x) \wedge N_{AU}(x) \leq 0.5$$

is called generalized interval-valued intuitionistic fuzzy condition. The maximum value of $M_{AU}(x)$ and $N_{AU}(x)$ is 1.0, therefore generalized interval-valued intuitionistic fuzzy sets Condition imply that

$0 \leq M_{AU}(x) + N_{AU}(x) \leq 1.5$.

It may be noted that all interval-valued intuitionistic fuzzy sets are generalized interval-valued intuitionistic fuzzy sets but the converse is not true.

We denote the set of all generalized interval-valued intuitionistic fuzzy sets on X by G(X).

Some Operations on Generalized Interval-Valued Intuitionistic Fuzzy Sets

Let A and B be two generalized interval-valued intuitionistic fuzzy sets on X, where A and B are the form of as follows:

$$A = \left\langle \left[M_{AL}(x), M_{AU}(X)\right], \left[M_{AL}(x), M_{AL}(x)\right] / \; x \in X \right\rangle$$

and

$$B = \left\langle \left[M_{BL}(x), M_{BU}(X)\right]\left[N_{BL}(x), N_{NL}(x)\right] / \; x \in X \right\rangle.$$

In the following we define some relational operations on generalized interval-valued intuitionistic fuzzy sets.

1. $A=B \Leftrightarrow M_A(x)=M_B(x)$ and $N_A(x)=N_B(x)$ for all $x \in X$.
2. $A \leq B \Leftrightarrow \{M_{AL}(x) \leq M_{BL}(x)$ and $M_{AU}(x) \leq M_{BU}(x)\}$ and $\{N_{AL}(x) \geq N_{BL}(x)$ and $N_{AU}(x) \geq N_{BU}(x)\}$, for all $x \in X$.
3. $A \prec B \Leftrightarrow \{M_{AL}(x) \leq M_{BL}(x)$ and $M_{AU}(x) \leq M_{BU}(x)\}$ and $\{N_{AL}(x) \leq N_{BL}(x)$ and $N_{AU}(x) \leq N_{BU}(x)\}$, for all $x \in X$.
4. $A \subset_{\Box} B$ iff $\{M_{AL}(x) \leq M_{BL}(x)$ and $M_{AU}(x) \leq M_{BU}(x)\}$.
5. $A \subset_{\Diamond} B$ iff $\{N_{AL}(x) \geq N_{BL}(x)$ and $N_{AU}(x) \geq N_{BU}(x)\}$.
6. $A \subseteq B$ iff $\{(M_{AU}(x) \leq M_{BU}(x)$ and $M_{AL}(x) \leq M_{BL}(x))\}$ and $(N_{AU}(x) \geq N_{BU}(x)$ and $N_{AL}(x) \geq N_{BL}(x))\}$.

Now, we define some unary and binary operations on generalized interval-valued intuitionistic fuzzy sets:

1.
$$\begin{aligned} A \cap B &= \{\langle [M_{A \cap B}(x), N_{A \cap B}(x)] \rangle \; / \; x \in X\} \\ &= \{\langle [\min M_{AL}(x), M_{BL}(x), \min(M_{AL}(x), M_{BU}(x))] \\ &= [\max(N_{AL}(x), N_{BL}(x), \max(N_{AU}(x), N_{BU}(x))] \rangle \; / \; x \in X\} \end{aligned}$$

$$A \cup B = \{\langle [M_{A\cup B}(x), N_{A\cup B}(x)] \rangle \,/\, x \in X\}$$

2. $$= \{\langle [\max M_{AL}(x), M_{BL}(x), \max(M_{AL}(x), M_{BU}(x))],$$
$$= [\min(N_{AL}(x), N_{BL}(x), \min(N_{AU}(x), N_{BU}(x))] \rangle \,/\, x \in X\}.$$

3. $\bar{A} = \{\langle [N_A(x), M_A(x)] \rangle \,/\, x \in X\}$.

The subset $\bar{A}$, A∩B and A∪B are all generalized interval-valued intuitionistic fuzzy sets.

SEPARATION OF GENERALIZED INTERVAL-VALUED INTUITIONISTIC FUZZY SETS

Definition 6

Let X be a non empty set. Let A be a generalized interval-valued intuitionistic fuzzy sets or interval-valued intuitionistic fuzzy sets on X. Then we separation X into the four subset of X as follows *:*

strong subset of $X = \vec{X}_A = \left\{x \in X : M_{AL} \in [0.5,1], N_{AU} \in [0,0.5]\right\}$

week subset *of* $X = \overleftarrow{X}_A = \left\{x \in X : M_{AL} \in [0,0.5], N_{AU} \in [0.5,1]\right\}$

intermediate subset $X = \tilde{X} = \{x \in X : M_{AU} \in [0,0.5], N_{AU} \in [0,1]$

or

$N_{AU} \in [0,0.5], M_{AU} \in [0,1]\}$,

Non generalized interval-valued intuitionistic fuzzy *subset of X*=

$\ddot{X}_A = \left\{x \in X : M_{AU} \in [0,0.5], N_{AU} \in [0,0.5]\right\}$.

Obviously

$X = \vec{X}_A \cup \overleftarrow{X}_A \cup \ddot{X}_A \cup \tilde{X}_A$.

Theorem 1

For any two generalized interval-valued intuitionistic fuzzy sets *A, B, on X:*

1. $\vec{X}_{A\cup B} = \vec{X}_A \cup \vec{X}_B$
2. $\overleftarrow{X}_{A\cup B} = \overleftarrow{X}_A \cap \overleftarrow{X}_B$
3. $\ddot{X}_{A\cup B} = \ddot{X}_A \cup \ddot{X}_B$
4. $\tilde{X}_{A\cup B} = \tilde{X}_A \cap \tilde{X}_B$

Proof

1. Let $x \in \vec{X}_{A \cup B} \Leftrightarrow x \in M_{A \cup B} \Rightarrow x \in \begin{bmatrix} \max\left\{M_{AL}(x), M_{BL}(x)\right\}, \\ \max\left\{M_{AU}(x), M_{BU}(x)\right\} \end{bmatrix}$

$\Leftrightarrow x \in$ either $M_{AL}(x)>0.5$ or $M_{BL}(x)>0.5\}$

$\Leftrightarrow$either $x \in \vec{X}_A$ or $x \in \vec{X}_B$

$\Leftrightarrow x \in \vec{X}_A \cup \vec{X}_B$.

2. The proof is similar to proof (i).
3. Let $x \in \ddot{X}_{A \cup B} \Leftrightarrow M_{A \cup B}(x) \leq 0.5$ and $N_{A \cup B}(x) \leq 0.5$

$\Rightarrow \max\{M_{AU}(x), M_{BU}(x)\} \leq 0.5$ and $\min\{N_{AU}(x), N_{BU}(x)\} \leq 0.5$

$\Rightarrow\{$either $M_{AU}(x) \leq 0.5$ or $M_{BU}(x) \leq 0.5$ and

$\{$either $N_{AU}(x) \leq 0.5$ or $N_{BU}(x) \leq 0.5\}$

$\Rightarrow$either$\{ M_{AU}(x) \leq 0.5$ and $N_{AU}(x) \leq 0.5\}$ or

either $\{ M_{BU}(x) \leq 0.5$ and $N_{BU}(x) \leq 0.5\}$

$\Rightarrow$either $x \in \ddot{X}_A$ or $x \in \ddot{X}_B$

$\Rightarrow x \in \ddot{X}_A \cup \ddot{X}_B$

So, $\ddot{X}_{A \cup B} \subseteq \ddot{X}_A \cup \ddot{X}_B$.

4. The proof is similar to proof (i).

Theorem 2

For any two generalized interval-valued intuitionistic fuzzy sets *A, B,* on *X:*

1. $\vec{X}_{A \cap B} = \vec{X}_A \cap \vec{X}_B$
2. $\overleftarrow{X}_{A \cap B} = \overleftarrow{X}_A \cup \overleftarrow{X}_B$
3. $\ddot{X}_{A \cap B} = \ddot{X}_A \cup \ddot{X}_B$
4. $\tilde{X}_{A \cap B} = \tilde{X}_A \cup \tilde{X}_B$

Proof

The proof is similar to Theorem 1.

Theorem 3

For any two generalized interval-valued intuitionistic fuzzy sets *A and B*

$\ddot{X}_{A\cap B} \cup \ddot{X}_{A\cup B} = \ddot{X}_A \cup \ddot{X}_B.$

Proof

By the Theorem 1, $\ddot{X}_{A\cup B} \subseteq \ddot{X}_A \cup \ddot{X}_B.$

And by the Theorem 2, $\ddot{X}_{A\cap B} \subseteq \ddot{X}_A \cup \ddot{X}_B.$

Then $\ddot{X}_{A\cap B} \cup \ddot{X}_{A\cup B} = \ddot{X}_A \cup \ddot{X}_B.$

Let $x \in \ddot{X}_A \cup \ddot{X}_B.$. Then without loss of generality, we know

$x \in \ddot{X}_A \Rightarrow x \in [M_{AU}(x) \leq 0.5$ and $N_{AU}(x) \leq 0.5]$.

But as B is generalized interval-valued intuitionistic fuzzy sets, we know

$\min\{M_{BU}(x), N_{BU}(x)\} \leq 0.5$

$\Rightarrow$ either $M_{AU}(x) \leq 0.5$ or $N_{BU}(x) \leq 0.5$

So either $\{M_{AU}(x) \leq 0.5$ and $N_{AU}(x) \leq 0.5$ and $M_{BU}(x) \leq 0.5\}$

or $\{M_{AU}(x) \leq 0.5$ and $N_{AU}(x) \leq 0.5$and $N_{BU}(x) \leq 0.5\}$

$\Rightarrow$either $\{\max(M_{AU}(x), M_{BU}(x)) \leq 0.5$ and $\min(N_{AU}(x) \leq 0.5, N_{BU}(x)) \leq 0.5\}$

or $\{\min(M_{AU}(x), M_{BU}(x)) \leq 0.5$ and $\max(N_{AU}(x) \leq 0.5, N_{BU}(x)) \leq 0.5\}$.

$\Rightarrow$either $x \in \ddot{X}_{A\cup B}$ or $x \in \ddot{X}_{A\cap B}$.

$\Rightarrow x \in \ddot{X}_{A\cup B}$ or $x \in \ddot{X}_{A\cap B}$.

So, $\ddot{X}_A \cup \ddot{X}_B = \ddot{X}_{A\cap B} \cup \ddot{X}_{A\cup B}.$

Hence, $\ddot{X}_A \cup \ddot{X}_B = \ddot{X}_{A\cap B} \cup \ddot{X}_{A\cup B}.$

SOME OPERATORS OF GENERALIZED INTERVAL-VALUED INTUITIONISTIC FUZZY SETS AND ITS PROPERTIES

Definition 7

For $\vec{X}_A, \overleftarrow{X}_A$, and $\ddot{X}_A$ of the generalized interval-valued intuitionistic fuzzy sets on X, we define the following subsets on [0,1] as follows:

$$\vec{K}_L = [\vec{K}_L, \vec{K}_U], \vec{L}_L = [\vec{L}_L, \vec{L}_U],$$

$$\overleftarrow{K}_L = [\overleftarrow{K}_L, \overleftarrow{K}_U], \overleftarrow{L}_L = [\overleftarrow{L}_L, \overleftarrow{L}_U],$$

$$\vec{k}_L = [\vec{k}_L, \vec{k}_U], \vec{l}_L = [\vec{l}_L, \vec{l}_U],$$

$$\overleftarrow{k}_L = [\overleftarrow{k}_L, \overleftarrow{k}_U], \overleftarrow{l}_L = [\overleftarrow{l}_L, \overleftarrow{l}_U],$$

$$\ddot{K} = [\ddot{K}_L, \ddot{K}_U], \ddot{L} = [\ddot{L}_L, \ddot{L}_U],$$

$$\ddot{k} = [\ddot{k}_L, \ddot{k}_U], \ddot{l} = [\ddot{l}_L, \ddot{l}_U].$$

where

$$\vec{K}_L = \max_{x \in \vec{X}_A} M_{AL}(X),$$

$$\vec{K}_U = \max_{x \in \vec{X}_A} M_{AU}(X),$$

$$\vec{L}_L = \min_{x \in \vec{X}_A} N_{AL}(X),$$

$$\vec{L}_U = \min_{x \in \vec{X}_A} N_{AU}(X),$$

$$\vec{k}_L = \min_{x \in \vec{X}_A} M_{AL}(X),$$

$$\vec{k}_U = \min_{x \in \vec{X}_A} M_{AU}(X),$$

$$\vec{l}_L = \max_{x \in \vec{X}_A} N_{AL}(X),$$

$$\vec{l}_U = \max_{x \in \vec{X}_A} N_{AU}(X),$$

$$\overleftarrow{K}_L = \max_{x \in \overleftarrow{X}_A} M_{AL}(X),$$

$$\overleftarrow{K}_U = \max_{x \in \overleftarrow{X}_A} M_{AU}(X),$$

$$\overleftarrow{L}_L = \min_{x \in \overleftarrow{X}_A} N_{AL}(X),$$

$$\overleftarrow{L}_U = \min_{x \in \overleftarrow{X}_A} N_{AU}(X),$$

$$\overleftarrow{k}_L = \min_{x \in \overleftarrow{X}_A} M_{AL}(X),$$

$$\overleftarrow{k}_U = \min_{x \in \overleftarrow{X}_A} M_{AU}(X),$$

$$\overleftarrow{l}_L = \max_{x \in \overleftarrow{X}_A} N_{AL}(X),$$

$$\overleftarrow{l}_U = \max_{x \in \overleftarrow{X}_A} N_{AU}(X),$$

$$\ddot{K}_L = \max_{x \in \ddot{X}_A} M_{AL}(X),$$

$$\ddot{K}_U = \max_{x \in \ddot{X}_A} M_{AU}(X),$$

$$\ddot{L}_L = \min_{x \in \ddot{X}_A} N_{AL}(X),$$

$$\ddot{L}_U = \min_{x \in \ddot{X}_A} N_{AU}(X),$$

$$\ddot{k}_L = \min_{x \in \ddot{X}_A} M_{AL}(X),$$

$$\ddot{k}_U = \min_{x \in \ddot{X}_A} M_{AU}(X),$$

$$\ddot{l}_L = \max_{x \in \ddot{X}_A} N_{AL}(X),$$

$$\ddot{l}_U = \max_{x \in \ddot{X}_A} N_{AU}(X).$$

Lemma 1

The following relations are obvious from above definition

1. $\vec{K} \geq \overleftarrow{K}, \vec{K} \geq \ddot{K}, \vec{K} \geq \vec{k}, \vec{K} \geq \overleftarrow{k}, \vec{K} \geq \ddot{k}$
2. $\overleftarrow{L} \geq \overleftarrow{L}, \quad \vec{L} \geq \ddot{L}$
3. $\vec{k} \geq \overleftarrow{k}, \vec{k} \geq \ddot{k}$
4. $\vec{l} \geq \overleftarrow{l}, \quad \vec{l} \geq \ddot{l}, \quad \vec{L} \geq \vec{l}, \quad \vec{L} \geq \overleftarrow{l}, \quad \vec{L} \geq \ddot{l}$

Proof

From Definition 5, $\vec{K} = [\vec{K}_L, \vec{K}_U], \overleftarrow{K} = [\overleftarrow{K}_L, \overleftarrow{K}_U]$.

Again

$$\vec{K}_L = \max_{x \in \vec{X}_A} M_{AL}(X)$$

and

$$\overleftarrow{K}_L = \max_{x \in \overleftarrow{X}_A} M_{AL}(X),$$

so by Definition 4

$0.5 < \vec{K}_L \leq 1.0$ and $0 \leq \overleftarrow{K}_L \leq 0.5$.

So, $\vec{K}_L \geq \overleftarrow{K}_L$. Similarly, $\vec{K}_U \geq \overleftarrow{K}_U$.
Hence, $\vec{K} \geq \overleftarrow{K}$.
Other Proofs are similar.

Definition 8

For every generalized interval-valued intuitionistic fuzzy sets A on X, we define the following subsets

1. $\vec{C}(A) = \{\langle[\vec{K}_L, \vec{K}_U], [\vec{L}_L, \vec{L}_U]\rangle\}$
2. $\overleftarrow{C}(A) = \{\langle[\overleftarrow{K}_L, \overleftarrow{K}_U], [\overleftarrow{L}_L, \overleftarrow{L}_U]\rangle\}$
3. $\ddot{C}(A) = \{\langle[\ddot{K}_L, \ddot{K}_U], [\ddot{L}_L, \ddot{L}_U]\rangle\}$
4. $\vec{I}(A) = \{\langle[\vec{k}_L, \vec{k}_U], [\vec{l}_L, \vec{l}_U]\rangle\}$
5. $\overleftarrow{I}(A) = \{\langle[\overleftarrow{k}_L, \overleftarrow{k}_U], [\overleftarrow{l}_L, \overleftarrow{l}_U]\rangle\}$
6. $\ddot{I}(A) = \{\langle[\ddot{k}_L, \ddot{k}_U], [\ddot{l}_L, \ddot{l}_U]\rangle\}$

Theorem 4

The subset defined in Definition 8 are all generalized interval-valued intuitionistic fuzzy sets.
We will prove the first-one and the proves of rest are similar.

Proof

1. We have to show $\vec{K}_U \wedge \vec{L}_U \leq 0.5$.

Clearly, if $\vec{K}_U \geq 0.5$, then there exist $x_1 \in X$ such that $M_{AU}(x_1) > 0.5$, as otherwise $x \in X \vee M_{AU}(x)$ cannot exceed 0.5. But then $M_{AU}(x_1) \leq 0.5$ and hence

$$\vec{L}_U = \min_{x \in X} M_{AU}(x) \leq M_{AU}(x_1) \leq 0.5.$$

So, $\vec{K}_U \wedge \vec{L}_U \leq 0.5$. Hence C(A) is generalized interval-valued intuitionistic fuzzy sets on X.

Theorem 5

For A∈G(X), $\vec{X}_A$, $\overleftarrow{X}_A$, and $\ddot{X}_A$, we have

1. $\vec{C}(A) \supseteq \overleftarrow{C}(A)$
2. $\vec{I}(A) \supseteq \overleftarrow{I}(A)$
3. $\vec{C}(A) \supseteq \vec{I}(A)$
4. $\overleftarrow{C}(A) \supseteq \overleftarrow{I}(A)$
5. $\ddot{C}(A) \supseteq \ddot{I}(A)$

Proof

From Lemma 1, we have $\vec{K} \geq \overleftarrow{K}$ and $\vec{L} \leq \overleftarrow{L}$.

Therefore obviously, $\vec{C}(A) \supseteq \overleftarrow{C}(A)$.

All other proofs are similarly by Lemma 1.

Theorem 6

For the strong separation subset of X of any two generalized interval-valued intuitionistic fuzzy sets A and B on X:

1. $\vec{C}(\vec{C}(A) = \vec{C}(A)$
2. $\vec{C}(\vec{I}(A) = \vec{I}(A)$
3. $\vec{I}(\vec{C}(A) = \vec{C}(A)$
4. $\vec{I}(\vec{I}(A) = \vec{I}(A)$
5. $\vec{C}(A \cup B) = \vec{C}(A) \cup \vec{C}(B)$
6. $\vec{I}(A \cap B) = \vec{I}(A) \cap \vec{I}(B)$
7. $\vec{C}(A \cap B) \subset \vec{C}(A) \cup \vec{C}(B)$
8. $\vec{I}(A \cup B) \supset \vec{I}(A) \cup \vec{I}(B)$

The proofs of the results of the theorem are simple. We will verify some results considering an example.

Example 1

Let A and B be two generalized interval-valued intuitionistic fuzzy sets X, where

A= {⟨x_1, [0.2, 0.4], [0.4, 0.6]⟩, ⟨x_2, [0.3, 0.5], [0.4, 0.8]⟩, ⟨x_3, [0.6, 0.8], [0.2, 0.3]⟩, ⟨x_4, [0.1, 0.4], [0.7, 0.9]⟩,⟨x_5,[0.7, 0.9], [0.1, 0.4]⟩, ⟨x_6,[0.2, 0.3], [0.6, 0.8]⟩, ⟨x_7, [0.1, 0.3], [0.2, 0.4]⟩, ⟨x_8, [0.2, 0.3], [0.1, 0.3]⟩}

B= {⟨x_1, [0.8, 1.0], [0.3, 0.5]⟩, ⟨x_2, [0.6, 0.9], [0.2, 0.4]⟩, ⟨x_3, [0.2, 0.4], [0.8, 1.0]⟩, ⟨x_4, [0.3, 0.5], [0.6, 0.9]⟩,⟨x_5, [0.2, 0.4], [0.0, 0.2]⟩, ⟨x_6, [0.2, 0.5], [0.1, 0.4]⟩, ⟨x_7, [0.3, 0.5], [0.4, 0.8]⟩, ⟨x_8, [0.1, 0.4], [0.3, 0.6]⟩}

A∪*B*={⟨x_1, [0.8, 1.0], [0.3, 0.5]⟩, ⟨x_2, [0.6, 0.9], [0.2, 0.4]⟩, ⟨x_3, [0.6, 0.8], [0.2, 0.3]⟩, ⟨x_4, [0.3, 0.5], [0.6, 0.9]⟩,⟨x_5, [0.7, 0.9], [0.0, 0.2]⟩, ⟨x_6, [0.2, 0.5], [0.1, 0.4]⟩, ⟨x_7, [0.3, 0.5], [0.2, 0.4]⟩, ⟨x_8, [0.2, 0.4], [0.1, 0.3]⟩}

A∩*B*={⟨x_1, [0.2, 0.4], [0.4, 0.6]⟩, ⟨x_2, [0.3, 0.5], [0.4, 0.8]⟩, ⟨x_3, [0.2 0.4], [0.8, 1.0]⟩, ⟨x_4, [0.1, 0.4], [0.7, 0.9]⟩,⟨x_5,[0.2, 0.4], [0.1, 0.4]⟩, ⟨x_6, [0.2, 0.3], [0.6, 0.8]⟩, ⟨x_7, [0.1, 0.3], [0.4, 0.8]⟩, ⟨x_8, [0.1, 0.3], [0.3, 0.6]⟩}

then

$$\vec{X}_A = \{x_3, x_5\}, \vec{X}_B = \{x_1, x_2\} \tag{1}$$

$$\overleftarrow{X}_A = \{x_4, x_6\}, \overleftarrow{X}_B = \{x_3, x_4\} \tag{2}$$

$$\ddot{X}_A = \{x_7, x_8\}, \ddot{X}_B = \{x_5, x_6\} \tag{3}$$

$$\tilde{X}_A = \{x_4, x_6\}, \tilde{X}_B = \{x_7, x_8\} \tag{4}$$

$$\vec{X}_{A\cup B} = \{x_1, x_2, x_3, x_5\}, \vec{X}_{A\cap B} = \phi \tag{5}$$

$$\overleftarrow{X}_{A\cup B} = \{x_4\}, \overleftarrow{X}_{A\cap B} = \{x_3, x_4, x_5\} \tag{6}$$

$$\ddot{X}_{A\cup B} = \{x_6, x_7, x_8\}, \ddot{X}_{A\cap B} = \{x_5\} \tag{7}$$

$$\tilde{X}_{A\cup B} = \varphi, \tilde{X}_{A\cap B} = \{x_1, x_2, x_7, x_8\} \tag{8}$$

Theorem 1 to 3 are verified by the equation 1 to 8 as follows.

$$\vec{C}(A) = \{\langle[0.7, 0.9], [0.1, 0.3]\rangle\}, \vec{I}(A) = \{\langle[0.6, 0.8], [0.2, 0.4]\rangle\}, \tag{9}$$

$$\overleftarrow{C}(A) = \{\langle[0.2, 0.4], [0.6, 0.8]\rangle\}, \overleftarrow{I}(A) = \{\langle[0.1, 0.3], [0.7, 0.9]\rangle\}, \tag{10}$$

$$\ddot{C}(A) = \{\langle[0.2, 0.3], [0.1, 0.3]\rangle\}, \ddot{I}(A) = \{\langle[0.1, 0.3], [0.2, 0.4]\rangle\}, \tag{11}$$

$$\tilde{C}(A) = \{\langle[0.3, 0.5], [0.4, 0.6]\rangle\}, \tilde{I}(A) = \{\langle[0.2, 0.4], [0.4, 0.8]\rangle\}, \tag{12}$$

Followed by the Equation 9 to 12, the Theorem 5 is verified.

$$\vec{C}(A \cup B) = \langle [0.8, 1.0], [0.0, 0.2]$$

$$\vec{C}(A \cap B) = \langle [0.3, 0.5], [0.1, 0.4]$$

$$\begin{aligned} \vec{C}(A) \cup \vec{C}(B) &= \langle [0.7, 0.9], [0.1, 0.3] \rangle \cup \langle [0.8, 1.0], [0.0, 0.2] \rangle \\ &= \langle [0.8, 1.0], [0.0, 0.2] \rangle \end{aligned}.$$

So,

$$\vec{C}(A \cup B) = \vec{C}(A) \cup \vec{C}(B).$$

and,

$$\vec{C}(A \cap B) \subset \vec{C}(A) \cup \vec{C}(B)$$

Note 2: For the other separation subsets i.e., week subset, intermediate subset and non generalized interval-valued intuitionistic fuzzy sets subset of X for any, two generalized interval-valued intuitionistic fuzzy sets A and B we will get the same expressions as Theorem 6.

Definition 9

For the generalized interval-valued intuitionistic fuzzy sets A on X, we define the following subsets:

1. $\vec{\ddot{C}}(A) = \{\langle [\vec{K}_L, \vec{K}_U], [\ddot{L}_L, \ddot{L}_U] \rangle\}$,
2. $\ddot{\vec{C}}(A) = \{\langle [\ddot{K}_L, \ddot{K}_U], [\vec{L}_L, \vec{L}_U] \rangle\}$,
3. $\overleftarrow{\ddot{C}}(A) = \{\langle [\overleftarrow{K}_L, \overleftarrow{K}_U], [\ddot{L}_L, \ddot{L}_U] \rangle\}$,
4. $\ddot{\overleftarrow{C}}(A) = \{\langle [\ddot{K}_L, \ddot{K}_U], [\overleftarrow{L}_L, \overleftarrow{L}_U] \rangle\}$,
5. $\vec{\ddot{I}}(A) = \{\langle [\vec{k}_L, \vec{k}_U], [\ddot{l}_L, \ddot{l}_U] \rangle\}$,
6. $\ddot{\vec{I}}(A) = \{\langle [\ddot{k}_L, \ddot{k}_U], [\vec{l}_L, \vec{l}_U] \rangle\}$,
7. $\overleftarrow{\ddot{I}}(A) = \{\langle [\overleftarrow{k}_L, \overleftarrow{k}_U], [\ddot{l}_L, \ddot{l}_U] \rangle\}$,
8. $\ddot{\overleftarrow{I}}(A) = \{\langle [\ddot{k}_L, \ddot{k}_U], [\overleftarrow{l}_L, \overleftarrow{l}_U] \rangle\}$.

Theorem 7

For the generalized interval-valued intuitionistic fuzzy set A on X:

1. $\ddot{\vec{C}}(A) \supseteq \ddot{\overleftarrow{C}}(A)$

2. $\ddot{\overleftarrow{C}}(A) \subseteq \vec{\ddot{C}}(A)$
3. $\vec{\ddot{I}}(A) \supseteq \ddot{\overleftarrow{I}}(A)$
4. $\vec{\ddot{I}}(A) \supseteq \overleftarrow{\ddot{I}}(A)$
5. $\overleftarrow{\ddot{C}}(A) \subseteq \vec{\ddot{C}}(A)$
6. $\ddot{\vec{I}}(A) \supseteq \ddot{\overleftarrow{I}}(A)$
7. $\ddot{\overleftarrow{I}}(A) \subseteq \ddot{\overleftarrow{C}}(A)$
8. $\overleftarrow{\ddot{I}}(A) \subseteq \overleftarrow{\ddot{C}}(A)$
9. $\vec{\ddot{I}}(A) \subseteq \vec{\ddot{C}}(A)$
10. $\ddot{\vec{I}}(A) \subseteq \ddot{\vec{C}}(A)$

Proof

We know from above definition

$$\ddot{\vec{C}}(A) = \{\langle [\ddot{K}_L, \ddot{K}_U], [\vec{L}_L, \vec{L}_U] \rangle\},$$

and

$$\ddot{\overleftarrow{C}}(A) = \{\langle [\ddot{K}_L, \ddot{K}_U], [\overleftarrow{L}_L, \overleftarrow{L}_U] \rangle\}.$$

It is fact $\ddot{K}_U = \ddot{K}_U$ and $\vec{L}_U \leq \overleftarrow{L}_U$ from Lemma 1, we have, therefore $\ddot{\vec{C}}(A) \supseteq \ddot{\vec{C}}(A)$.
All other proofs are similarly by Lemma 1.

CONCLUSION

In this chapter, we have introduced the concept of generalized interval-valued intuitionistic fuzzy sets and also the separation of generalized interval-valued intuitionistic fuzzy sets. We instigated some operations of generalized interval-valued intuitionistic fuzzy sets and proved some properties of generalized interval-valued intuitionistic fuzzy sets. Finally, we have verified the results with an example. In a subsequent paper we will try to make a relational properties of generalized interval-valued intuitionistic fuzzy sets i.e., symmetric, transitive and four types of reflexive and also we shall define Housdorff distance between two generalized interval-valued intuitionistic fuzzy sets.

REFERENCES

Atanassov, K. (1994). Operations over interval valued fuzzy sets. *Fuzzy Sets and Systems*, (64): 159–174. doi:10.1016/0165-0114(94)90331-X

Atanassov, K., & Gargo, G. (1989). Interval-valued intuitionistic fuzzy sets. *Fuzzy Sets and Systems*, *31*(1), 343–349. doi:10.1016/0165-0114(89)90205-4

Bhowmik, M., & Pal, M. (2008). Some results on Intuitionistic fuzzy matrices and intuitionistic circulant fuzzy matrices. *International Journal of Mathematical Sciences*, *7*(1-2), 81–96.

Bhowmik, M., & Pal, M. (2008). Generalized intuitionistic fuzzy matrices. *Far East Journal of Mathematics*, *29*(3), 533–554.

Bustince & Rillo. (1995). Intuitionistic fuzzy relation (part-I). *Mathware and Soft Computing*, (2), 5-38.

Gau, W. L., & Buehrer, D. J. (1993). Vague sets. *IEEE Transactions on Systems, Man, and Cybernetics*, *23*(2), 610–614. doi:10.1109/21.229476

Jana, N. K., & Pal, M. (2006). *Some operators defined over interval-valued intuitionistic fuzzy sets.*In S. Nanda (Ed.), *Fuzzy Logic and Optimization* (pp. 113–126). New Delhi, India: Narosa Publishing House.

Mondal, T. K., & Samanta, S. K. (2002). Generalizedintuitionistic fuzzy sets. *The Journal of Fuzzy Mathematics*, *10*(4), 839–862.

Pal. (2001). Intuitionistic fuzzy determinate. *V. U. J. Physical Sciences*, (7), 87-93.

Pal, M., Khan, S. K., & Shyamal, A. K. (2002a). Intuitionistic fuzzy matrices. *Notes on Intuitionistic Fuzzy Sets*, *8*(2), 51–62.

Panigrahi, M., & Nanda, S. (2006a). A comparison between intuitionistic fuzzy sets and generalized intuitionistic fuzzy sets. *The Journal of Fuzzy Mathematics*, *14*(2), 407–421.

Panigrahi, M., & Nanda, S. (2006b). *Generalized intuitionistic fuzzy sets and some new operators. In Fuzzy Logic and Optimization* (pp. 155–169). New Delhi, India: Narosa Publishing House.

Pawlak. (1982). Rough sets. *International J. Information and Computer Sciences*, (11), 341-356.

Shyamal & Pal. (2002). Distance between intuitionistics fuzzy matrices. *V.U.J. Physical Sciences*, (8), 81-91.

Shyamal & Pal. (2004). Two new operators on fuzzy matrices. *J. Applied Mathematics and Computing*, (15), 91-107.

Shyamal, A. K., & Pal, M. (2005). Distance between fuzzy matrices and its applications–I. *J. Nature. Physical Science (London)*, *19*(1), 39–58.

Zadeh, L. A. (1965). Fuzzy Sets. *Information and Control*, *8*(8), 338–353. doi:10.1016/S0019-9958(65)90241-X

Chapter 2
Neutrosophic Sets and Logic

Mumtaz Ali
Quaid-i-Azam University Islamabad, Pakistan

Florentin Smarandache
University of New Mexico – Gallup, USA

Luige Vladareanu
Institute of Solid Mechanics of Romanian Academy, Romania

ABSTRACT

Neutrosophic sets and Logic plays a significant role in approximation theory. It is a generalization of fuzzy sets and intuitionistic fuzzy set. Neutrosophic set is based on the neutrosophic philosophy in which every idea Z, has opposite denoted as anti(Z) and its neutral which is denoted as neut(Z). This is the main feature of neutrosophic sets and logic. This chapter is about the basic concepts of neutrosophic sets as well as some of their hybrid structures. This chapter starts with the introduction of fuzzy sets and intuitionistic fuzzy sets respectively. The notions of neutrosophic set are defined and studied their basic properties in this chapter. Then we studied neutrosophic crisp sets and their associated properties and notions. Moreover, interval valued neutrosophic sets are studied with some of their properties. Finally, we presented some applications of neutrosophic sets in the real world problems.

INTRODUCTION

The data in real life problems like engineering, social, economic, computer, decision making, medical diagnosis etc. are often uncertain and imprecise. This type of data is not necessarily crisp, precise and deterministic nature because of their fuzziness and vagueness. To handle this kind of data, (Zadeh, 1965). introduced fuzzy set sets Several types of approaches have been proposed which is based on fuzzy sets such as (interval valued fuzzy sets, 1986), (intuitionistic fuzzy sets, 1986), and so on. Researchers throughout the world have been successfully applied fuzzy sets in several areas like signal processing, knowledge representation, decision making, stock markets, pattern recognition, control, data mining, artificial intelligence etc.

DOI: 10.4018/978-1-5225-0914-1.ch002

Atanassov (1986) observed that there is some kind of uncertainty in the data which is not handled by fuzzy sets. Therefore, intuitionistic fuzzy sets were proposed (Atanassov, 1986), which became the generalization of fuzzy sets by inserting the non-membership degree to fuzzy sets. An intuitionistic fuzzy set has a membership function as well as a non-membership function. Intuitionistic fuzzy sets define more beautifully the fuzzy objects of the real world. A huge amount of research study has been conducted on intuitionistic fuzzy sets from different aspects. Intuitionistic fuzzy sets have been successfully applied in several fields such as modeling imprecision, decision making problems, pattern recognition, economics, computational intelligence, medical diagnosis and so on.

Smarandache (1995), coined the theory of neutrosophic sets and logic under the neutrosophy which is a new branch of philosophy that study the origin, nature, and scope of neutralities as well as their interactions with ideational spectra. A neutrosophic set can be characterized by a truth membership function T, an indeterminacy membership function I and falsity membership function F. Neutrosophic set is the generalization of fuzzy sets, intuitionistic fuzzy sets, paraconsistent set etc. Neutrosophic sets can treat uncertain, inconsistent, incomplete, indeterminate and false information. The neutrosophic sets and their related set theoretic operators need to be specified from scientific or engineering point of view. Indeterminacy are quantified explicitly in neutrosophic sets and T, I, and F operators are complementally independent which is very significant in several applications such as information fusion, physics, computer, networking, decision making, information theory etc.

In this chapter, we present the notions of neutrosophic sets and logic. In section 1, we presented a brief introduction. In section 2, we studied neutrosophic sets with some of their basic properties. In the next section 3, the hybrid structure neutrosophic crisp sets and their associated properties and notions have been studied. In section 4, interval valued neutrosophic sets have been studied. Section 5 is about to study some practical life applications of neutrosophic sets.

NEUTROSOPHIC SET, SIMILARITY MEASURES, NEUTROSOPHIC NORMS

In this section the notions of neutrosophic sets, some similarity measures of neutrosophic sets, neutrosophic norms respectively.

Neutrosophic Set

In this subsection the neutrosophic set is presented with their basic properties and notions with illustrative examples.

Definition 2.1.1

Let X be a universe of discourse and a neutrosophic set *A* on *X* is defined as

$$A=\left\{\left\langle x,T_A\left(x\right),I_A\left(x\right),F_A\left(x\right)\right\rangle,x\in X\right\}$$

where *T, I, F*: $X \to]^{-}0,1^{+}[$ and

$$^{-}0 \leq T_A(x) + I_A(x) + F_A(x) \leq 3^{+}.$$

From philosophical point of view, neutrosophic set takes the value in the interval [0,1], because it is difficult to use neutrosophic set with value from real standard or non-standard subsets of $]^{-}0,1^{+}[$ in real life application like scientific and engineering problems.

Definition 2.1.2

A neutrosophic set A is contained in another neutrosophic set B, if

$$T_A(x) \leq T_B(x), I_A(x) \leq I_B(x), F_A(x) \geq F_B(x)$$

for all $x \in X$.

Definition 2.1.3

An element x of U is called significant with respect to neutrosophic set A of U if the degree of truth-membership or falsity-membership or indeterminacy-membership value, i.e.,$T_A(x)$ or $F_A(x)$ or $I_A(x) \leq 0.5$.

Otherwise, we call it insignificant. Also, for neutrosophic set the truth-membership, indeterminacy-membership and falsity-membership all cannot be significant. We define an intuitionistic neutrosophic set by

$$A = \left\{ \left\langle x : T_{A(x)}, I_{A(x)}, F_{A(x)} \right\rangle, x \in U \right\},$$

where

$$\min\left\{ T_{A(x)}, F_{A(x)} \right\} \leq 0.5,$$

$$\min\left\{ T_{A(x)}, I_{A(x)} \right\} \leq 0.5,$$

$$\min\left\{ F_{A(x)}, I_{A(x)} \right\} \leq 0.5,$$

for all $x \in U$, with the condition

$$0 \leq T_{A(x)} + I_{A(x)} + F_{A(x)} \leq 2.$$

As an illustration, let us consider the following example.

Example 2.1.4

Assume that the universe of discourse U={x_1,x_2,x_3}, where x_1 characterizes the capability, x_2 characterizes the trustworthiness and x_3 indicates the prices of the objects. It may be further assumed that the values of x_1, x_2 and x_3 are in [0,1] and they are obtained from some questionnaires of some experts. The experts may impose their opinion in three components viz. the degree of goodness, the degree of indeterminacy and that of poorness to explain the characteristics of the objects. Suppose A is an intuitionistic neutrosophic set (IN S) of U, such that,

$$A = \left\{\langle x_1, 0.3, 0.5, 0.4\rangle, \langle x_2, 0.4, 0.2, 0.6\rangle, \langle x_3, 0.7, 0.3, 0.5\rangle\right\}$$

where the degree of goodness of capability is 0.3, degree of indeterminacy of capability is 0.5 and degree of falsity of capability is 0.4 etc.

Definition 2.1.5

Let X is a space of points (objects) with generic elements in X denoted by x. A neutrosophic set A in X is characterized by a truth-membership function $T_A(x)$, an indeterminacy membership function $I_A(x)$, and a falsity membership function $F_A(x)$ if the functions $T_A(x)$, $I_A(x)$, $F_A(x)$ are singletons subintervals/subsets in the real standard [0,1], i.e.

$$T_A(x) : X \to [0,1], I_A(x) : X \to [0,1], F_A(x) : X \to [0,1]$$

Then a simplification of the neutrosophic set A is denoted by

$$A = \left\{\left\langle x : T_A(x), I_A(x), F_A(x)\right\rangle, x \in X\right\}$$

Definition 2.1.6

Let X is a space of points (objects) with generic elements in X denoted by x. An SVNS A in X is characterized by a truth-membership function $T_A(x)$, an indeterminacy membership function $I_A(x)$ and a falsity-membership function $F_A(x)$, for each point

$x \in X$; $T_A(x)$, $I_A(x)$, $F_A(x) \in [0,1]$.

Therefore, a SVNS A can be written as

$$A_{SVNS} = \left\{\left\langle x : T_A(x), I_A(x), F_A(x)\right\rangle, x \in X\right\}.$$

For two SVNS,

$$A_{SVNS} = \{\langle x : T_A(x), I_A(x), F_A(x)\rangle, x \in X\}$$

and

$$B_{SVNS} = \{\langle x : T_B(x), I_B(x), F_B(x)\rangle, x \in X\},$$

the following expressions are defined in [2] as follows: $A_{NS} \subseteq B_{NS}$ if and only if

$$T_A(x) \le T_B(x), I_A(x) \ge I_B(x), F_A(x) \ge F_B(x).$$

$A_{NS}=B_{NS}$ if and only if

$$T_A(x) = T_B(x), I_A(x) = I_B(x), F_A(x) = F_B(x).$$

$$A^c = \langle x, F_A(x), 1 - I_A(x), T_A(x)\rangle.$$

For convenience, a SVNS A is denoted by $A=\langle T_A(x), I_A(x), F_A(x)\rangle$ for any $x \in X$ for two SVNSs A and B. Then,

1. $A \cup B = \langle \max(T_A(x), T_B(x)), \min(I_A(x), I_B(x)), \min(T_A(x), T_B(x))\rangle$,
2. $A \cap B = \langle \min(T_A(x), T_B(x)), \max(I_A(x), I_B(x)), \max(T_A(x), T_B(x))\rangle$.

Jaccard, Dice, and Cosine Similarity Measures of Neutrosophic Sets

The vector similarity measure is one of the most important techniques to measure the similarity between objects. In this subsection, the Jaccard, Dice and Cosine similarity measures between two vectors have been studied.

Definition 2.2.1

Let $X = (x_1, x_2, \ldots, x_n)$ and $Y = (y_1, y_2, \ldots, y_n)$ be the two vectors of length n where all the coordinates are positive. The Jaccard index of these two vectors is defined as

$$J(X,Y) = \frac{X \cdot Y}{X_2^2 + Y_2^2 + X \cdot Y} = \frac{\sum_{i=1}^{n} x_i \cdot y_i}{\sum_{i=1}^{n} x_i^2 + \sum_{i=1}^{n} y_i^2 - \sum_{i=1}^{n} x_i \cdot y_i},$$

where $X \cdot Y = \sum_{i=1}^{n} x_i \cdot y_i$ is the inner product of the vectors *X* and *Y*.

Definition 2.2.2

The Dice similarity measure is defined as

$$J(X,Y) = \frac{2X \cdot Y}{X_2^2 + Y_2^2} = \frac{2\sum_{i=1}^{n} x_i \cdot y_i}{\sum_{i=1}^{n} x_i^2 + \sum_{i=1}^{n} y_i^2}.$$

Cosine formula is defined as the inner product of these two vectors divided by the product of their lengths. This is the cosine of the angle between the vectors.

Definition 2.2.3

The cosine similarity measure is defined as

$$C(X,Y) = \frac{X \cdot Y}{X_2^2 \cdot Y_2^2} = \frac{\sum_{i=1}^{n} x_i \cdot y_i}{\sum_{i=1}^{n} x_i^2 \cdot \sum_{i=1}^{n} y_i^2}.$$

It is obvious that the Jaccard, Dice and cosine similarity measures satisfy the following properties

$$(P_1): 0 \le J(X,Y), D(X,Y), C(X,Y) \le 1,$$

$$(P_2): J(X,Y) = J(Y,X), D(X,Y) = D(Y,X) \text{ and } C(X,Y) = C(Y,X),$$

$$(P_3): J(X,Y) = 1, D(X,Y) = 1 \text{ and } C(X,Y) = 1 \text{ if } X = Y,.$$

i.e., $x_i = y_i\ (i = 1,2,\ldots,n)$ for every $x_i \in X$ and $y_i \in Y$ Also Jaccard, Dice, cosine weighted similarity measures between two SNSs A and B as discussed in [6] are

$$WJ(A,B) = \sum_{i=1}^{n} w_i \frac{T_A(x_i)T_B(x_i) + I_A(x_i)I_B(x_i) + F_A(x_i)F_B(x_i)}{\begin{gathered}(T_A(x_i))^2 + (I_A(x_i))^2 + (F_A(x_i))^2 \\ +(T_B(x_i))^2 + (T_A(x_i))^2 + (T_A(x_i))^2 + (T_A(x_i))^2 \\ -T_A(x_i)T_B(x_i) - T_B(x_i)T_C(x_i) - T_C(x_i)T_A(x_i)\end{gathered}},$$

$$WD(A,B)=\sum_{i=1}^{n} w_i \frac{2\left(T_A(x_i)T_B(x_i)+I_A(x_i)I_B(x_i)+F_A(x_i)F_B(x_i)\right)}{\left(T_A(x_i)\right)^2+\left(I_A(x_i)\right)^2+\left(F_A(x_i)\right)^2+\left(T_B(x_i)\right)^2+\left(T_A(x_i)\right)^2+\left(T_A(x_i)\right)^2+\left(T_A(x_i)\right)^2},$$

$$WC(A,B)=\sum_{i=1}^{n} w_i \frac{\left(T_A(x_i)T_B(x_i)+I_A(x_i)I_B(x_i)+F_A(x_i)F_B(x_i)\right)}{\sqrt{\left(T_A(x_i)\right)^2+\left(I_A(x_i)\right)^2+\left(F_A(x_i)\right)^2}\sqrt{\left(T_B(x_i)\right)^2+\left(T_A(x_i)\right)^2+\left(T_A(x_i)\right)^2+\left(T_A(x_i)\right)^2}}.$$

Neutrosophic N-Norms and Neutrosophic N-Conorms

In this subsection 2.3, neutrosophic norms and their related properties discussed by the authors.

Definition 2.3.1

$$N_n : \left(]^{-}0,1^{+}[\times]^{-}0,1^{+}[\times]^{-}0,1^{+}[\right)^2 \rightarrow \left(]^{-}0,1^{+}[\times]^{-}0,1^{+}[\times]^{-}0,1^{+}[\right)$$
$$N_n\left(x(T_1,I_1,F_1),y(T_2,I_2,F_2)\right)=\left(N_nT(x,y),N_nI(x,y),N_nF(x,y)\right)$$

where

$$N_nT(.,.),N_nI(.,.),N_nF(.,.)$$

are the truth /membership, indeterminacy, and respectively falsehood /nonmembership components. N_n have to satisfy, for any *x,y,z* in the neutrosophic logic/set *M*of the universe of discourse *U*, the following axioms:

- **Boundary Conditions:** $N_n(x,0)=0, N_n(x,1)=x$.
- **Commutativity:** $N_n(x,y)=N_n(y,x)$.
- **Monotonicity:** If $x \leq y, then\ N_n(x,z) \leq N_n(y,z)$.
- **Associativity:** $N_n\left(N_n(x,y),z\right)=N_n\left(x,N_n(y,z)\right)$.

N_n represent the and operator in neutrosophic logic, and respectively the intersection operator in neutrosophic set theory.

Example 2.3.2

A general example of N-norm would be this. Let $x\left(T_1, I_1, F_1\right)$ and $y\left(T_1, I_1, F_1\right)$ be in the neutrosophic set/logic M. Then:

$$N_n\left(x, y\right) = \left(T_1 \wedge T_2, I_1 \vee I_2, F_1 \vee F_2\right).$$

Definition 2.3.3

$$N_c : (]^-0,1^+[\times]^-0,1^+[\times]^-0,1^+[^2) \rightarrow (]^-0,1^+[\times]^-0,1^+[\times]^-0,1^+[)$$
$$N_c\left(x(T_1, I_1, F_1), y(T_2, I_2, F_2)\right) = \left(N_cT\left(x, y\right), N_cI\left(x, y\right), N_cF\left(x, y\right)\right),$$

where

$$N_cT\left(.,.\right), N_cI\left(.,.\right), N_cF\left(.,.\right)$$

are the truth /membership, indeterminacy, and respectively falsehood /non-membership components. N_c have to satisfy, for any *x,y,z* in the neutrosophic logic/set *M* of the universe of discourse *U*, the following axioms:

- **Boundary Conditions:** $N_c(x,0) = x, N_c(x,1) = 1$.
- **Commutativity:** $N_c\left(x, y\right) = N_c\left(y, x\right)$.
- **Monotonicity:** If $x \leq y, then\ N_c\left(x, z\right) \leq N_c\left(y, z\right)$.
- **Associativity:** $N_c\left(N_c\left(x, y\right), z\right) = N_c\left(x, N_c\left(y, z\right)\right)$.

Example 2.3.4

A general example of N-conorm would be this. Let $x\left(T_1, I_1, F_1\right)$ and $y\left(T_1, I_1, F_1\right)$ be in the neutrosophic set/logic M. Then:

$$N_c\left(x, y\right) = \left(T_1 \vee T_2, I_1 \wedge I_2, F_1 \wedge F_2\right)$$

where the "Λ" operator, acting on two (standard or non-standard) subunitary sets, is a N-norm (verifying the above N-norms axioms); while the "V" operator, also acting on two (standard or non-standard) subunitary sets, is a N-conorm (verifying the above N-conorms axioms). For example, Λ can be the Algebraic Product T-norm/N-norm, so T1ΛT2 = T1·T2; and V can be the Algebraic Product T-conorm/N-conorm, so T1VT2 = T1+T2-T1·T2. Or Λ can be any T-norm/N-norm, and V any T-conorm/N-conorm from the above and below; for example the easiest way would be to consider the min for crisp components (or inf for subset components) and respectively max for crisp components (or sup for subset components).

Theorem 2.3.5

For any s-norm s(x, y) and for all α≥1, we get the following s-norms and t-norms:

1. $S_{\alpha}^{s}(x,y)=\sqrt[\alpha]{s\left(x^{\alpha},y^{\alpha}\right)}$,
2. $T_{\alpha}^{s}(x,y)=1-\sqrt[\alpha]{s\left(\left(1-x\right)^{\alpha},\left(1-y\right)^{\alpha}\right)}$.

Theorem 2.3.6

For any t-norm t(x, y) and for all α>1, we get the following t-norms and s-norms:

1. $T_{\alpha}^{t}(x,y)=\sqrt[\alpha]{t\left(x^{\alpha},y^{\alpha}\right)}$,
2. $S_{\alpha}^{t}(x,y)=1-\sqrt[\alpha]{t\left(\left(1-x\right)^{\alpha},\left(1-y\right)^{\alpha}\right)}$.

Theorem 2.3.7

Let *f*, *g*:[0,1]→[0,1] be bijective functions such that *f*(0)=0, *f*(1)=1, *g*(0)=1 and *g*(1)=0. For any s-norm *s(x,y)* we get the following s-norm and t-norm:

1. $S_{f}^{s}\left(x,y\right)=f^{-1}\left[s\left(f\left(x\right),f\left(y\right)\right)\right]$,
2. $T_{g}^{s}(x,y)=g^{-1}\left[s\left(g\left(x\right),g\left(y\right)\right)\right]$.

Corollary 2.3.8

Let $f(x)=\sin\frac{\pi}{2}x$ and $g(x)=\cos\frac{\pi}{2}x$ then

1. $S_{\sin}^{s}\left(x,y\right)=\frac{2}{\pi}\sin^{-1}s\left(\sin\frac{\pi}{2}x,\sin\frac{\pi}{2}y\right)$ is an s-norm
2. $T_{\cos}^{s}(x,y)=\frac{2}{\pi}\cos^{-1}s\left(\cos\frac{\pi}{2}x,\cos\frac{\pi}{2}y\right)$ is a t-norm

Theorem 2.3.9

Let *f*, *g*:[0,1]→[0,1] be bijective functions such that *f*(0)=0, *f*(1)=1, *g*(0)=1 and *g*(1)=0. For any t-norm *t(x,y)* we get the following t-norm and s-norm:

1. $T_{f}^{t}\left(x,y\right)=f^{-1}\left[t\left(f\left(x\right),f\left(y\right)\right)\right]$,
2. $S_{g}^{t}\left(x,y\right)=g^{-1}\left[t\left(g\left(x\right),g\left(y\right)\right)\right]$.

Corollary 2.3.10

Let $f(x)= \sin\frac{\pi}{2}x$ and $g(x)= \cos\frac{\pi}{2}x$ then

1. $T^t_{\sin}\left(x,y\right)=\frac{2}{\pi}\sin^{-1}\left(t\left(\sin\frac{\pi}{2}x,\sin\frac{\pi}{2}y\right)\right)$ is a t-norm

2. $S^t_{\cos}\left(x,y\right)=\frac{2}{\pi}\cos^{-1}\left(t\left(\cos\frac{\pi}{2}x,\cos\frac{\pi}{2}y\right)\right)$ is an s-norm.

Definition 2.3.11

$$T_n : \left(]^-0,1^+[\times]^-0,1^+[\times]^-0,1^+[\right)^2 \rightarrow \left(]^-0,1^+[\times]^-0,1^+[\times]^-0,1^+[\right)$$
$$T_n\left(x(T,I,F),y(T,I,F)\right)=\left(t\left(x_T,y_T\right),s\left(x_I,y_I\right),s\left(x_F,y_F\right)\right)$$

where

$$t\left(x_T,y_T\right),s\left(x_I,y_I\right),s\left(x_F,y_F\right)$$

are the truth /membership, indeterminacy, and respectively falsehood /nonmembership components and *s* and *t* are the fuzzy s-norm and fuzzy t-norm respectively. T_n have to satisfy, for any *x,y,z* in the neutrosophic logic/set *M* of the universe of discourse *U*, the following axioms:

- **Boundary Conditions:** $T_n(x,0)=0, T_n(x,1)=x$.
- **Commutativity:** $T_n\left(x,y\right)=T_n\left(y,x\right)$.
- **Monotonicity:** If $x \leq y, then\ T_n\left(x,z\right) \leq T_n\left(y,z\right)$.
- **Associativity:** $T_n\left(T_n\left(x,y\right),z\right)=T_n\left(x,T_n\left(y,z\right)\right)$.

Definition 2.3.12

$$S_n : \left(]^-0,1^+[\times]^-0,1^+[\times]^-0,1^+[\right)^2 \rightarrow \left(]^-0,1^+[\times]^-0,1^+[\times]^-0,1^+[\right)$$
$$S_n\left(x(T,I,F),y(T,I,F)\right)=\left(s\left(x_T,y_T\right),t\left(x_I,y_I\right),t\left(x_F,y_F\right)\right)$$

where

$$s\left(x_T,y_T\right),t\left(x_I,y_I\right),t\left(x_F,y_F\right)$$

are the truth /membership, indeterminacy, and respectively falsehood /nonmembership components and s and t are the fuzzy s-norm and fuzzy t-norm respectively. S_n have to satisfy, for any x,y,z in the neutrosophic logic/set M of the universe of discourse U, the following axioms:

- **Boundary Conditions:** $S_n(x,0)=x, S_n(x,1)=1$.
- **Commutativity:** $S_n\left(x,y\right)=S_n\left(y,x\right)$.
- **Monotonicity:** If $x\le y, then\ S_n\left(x,z\right)\le S_n\left(y,z\right)$.
- **Associativity:** $S_n\left(S_n\left(x,y\right),z\right)=S_n\left(x,S_n\left(y,z\right)\right)$.

From now we use the following notation for N-norm and N-conorm respectively T_n–(x,y) and S_n–(x,y). We will use the following border 0(0,1,1) and 1(1,0,0).

Theorem 2.3.13

For any S_n–(x,y) and for all $\alpha\geq 1$, by using any fuzzy union s-norm we get the following Sn_(x,y)and Tn_(x,y):

1. $S^{\alpha}_{n_s}(x,y)=\left\langle\sqrt[\alpha]{s\left({x_T}^{\alpha},{y_T}^{\alpha}\right)},1-\sqrt[\alpha]{s\left(\left(1-x_I\right)^{\alpha},\left(1-y_I\right)^{\alpha}\right)},1-\sqrt[\alpha]{s\left(\left(1-x_F\right)^{\alpha},\left(1-y_F\right)^{\alpha}\right)}\right\rangle$ and
2. $T^{\alpha}_{n_s}(x,y)=\left\langle 1-\sqrt[\alpha]{s\left(\left(1-{x_T}^{\alpha}\right),\left(1-{y_T}^{\alpha}\right)\right)},\sqrt[\alpha]{s\left({x_I}^{\alpha},{y_I}^{\alpha}\right)},\sqrt[\alpha]{s\left({x_F}^{\alpha},{y_F}^{\alpha}\right)}\right\rangle$,

where s any s-norm (fuzzy union).

Proof

Axiom 1:

$$\begin{aligned}S^{\alpha}_{n_s}\left(0,x\right)&=\left\langle\sqrt[\alpha]{s(0^{\alpha},{x_T}^{\alpha})},1-\sqrt[\alpha]{s((1-1)^{\alpha},(1-x_I)^{\alpha})},1-\sqrt[\alpha]{s((1-1)^{\alpha},(1-x_F)^{\alpha})}\right\rangle\\&=x\left(x_T,x_I,x_F\right)\end{aligned}.$$

$$\begin{aligned}S^{\alpha}_{n_s}\left(1,x\right)&=\left\langle\sqrt[\alpha]{s(1^{\alpha},{x_T}^{\alpha})},1-\sqrt[\alpha]{s((1-0)^{\alpha},(1-x_I)^{\alpha})},1-\sqrt[\alpha]{s((1-0)^{\alpha},(1-x_F)^{\alpha})}\right\rangle\\&=1\left(1,0,0\right)\end{aligned}$$

Axiom 2:

$$\begin{aligned}S^{\alpha}_{n_s}(x,y)&=\left\langle\sqrt[\alpha]{s({x_T}^{\alpha},{y_T}^{\alpha})},1-\sqrt[\alpha]{s((1-x_I)^{\alpha},(1-y_I)^{\alpha})},1-\sqrt[\alpha]{s((1-x_F)^{\alpha},(1-y_F)^{\alpha})}\right\rangle\\&=\left\langle\sqrt[\alpha]{s({y_T}^{\alpha},{x_T}^{\alpha})},1-\sqrt[\alpha]{s((1-y_I)^{\alpha},(1-x_I)^{\alpha})},1-\sqrt[\alpha]{s((1-y_F)^{\alpha},(1-x_F)^{\alpha})}\right\rangle.\\&=S^{\alpha}_{n_s}(y,x)\end{aligned}$$

Axiom 3: Let

$$x\left(x_1, x_2, x_3\right) \leq y\left(y_1, y_2, y_3\right)$$

then

$$x_1 \leq y_1, x_2 \geq y_2, x_3 \geq y_3$$

and

$$s\left(x_1^{\alpha}, z_1^{\alpha}\right) \geq s\left(y_1^{\alpha}, z_1^{\alpha}\right)$$

which implies

$$\sqrt[\alpha]{s\left(x_1^{\alpha}, z_1^{\alpha}\right)} \geq \sqrt[\alpha]{s\left(y_2^{\alpha}, z_2^{\alpha}\right)}. \tag{1}$$

Also we have $(1-x_2)^{\alpha} \leq (1-y_2)^{\alpha}$ then

$$s\left(\left(1-x_2\right)^{\alpha}, \left(1-z_2\right)^{\alpha}\right) \leq s\left(\left(1-y_2\right)^{\alpha}, \left(1-z_2\right)^{\alpha}\right),$$

which implies that

$$1-\sqrt[\alpha]{s\left(\left(1-x_2\right)^{\alpha}, \left(1-z_2\right)^{\alpha}\right)} \geq 1-\sqrt[\alpha]{s\left(\left(1-y_2\right)^{\alpha}, \left(1-z_2\right)^{\alpha}\right)} \tag{2}$$

And we have $(1-x_3)^{\alpha} \leq (1-y_3)^{\alpha}$ then

$$s\left(\left(1-x_3\right)^{\alpha}, \left(1-z_3\right)^{\alpha}\right) \leq s\left(\left(1-y_3\right)^{\alpha}, \left(1-z_3\right)^{\alpha}\right),$$

which implies that

$$1-\sqrt[\alpha]{s\left(\left(1-x_3\right)^{\alpha}, \left(1-z_3\right)^{\alpha}\right)} \geq 1-\sqrt[\alpha]{s\left(\left(1-y_3\right)^{\alpha}, \left(1-z_3\right)^{\alpha}\right)} \tag{3}$$

From (1), (2) and (3) we have $S_{n_s}^{\alpha}\left(x, z\right) \geq S_{n_s}^{\alpha}\left(y, z\right)$.

Axiom 4:

$$S^{\alpha}_{\underset{s}{n}}\left(S^{\alpha}_{n}\left(x,y\right),z\right)=S^{\alpha}_{n}\left(\left\langle\sqrt[\alpha]{s(x_T{}^{\alpha},y_T{}^{\alpha})},1-\sqrt[\alpha]{s((1-x_I)^{\alpha},(1-y_I)^{\alpha})},1-\sqrt[\alpha]{s((1-x_F)^{\alpha},(1-y_F)^{\alpha})}\right\rangle,z\right)$$

$$=\left\langle\begin{array}{l}\sqrt[\alpha]{s\left(\left(\sqrt[\alpha]{s\left(x_T{}^{\alpha},y_T{}^{\alpha}\right)}\right)^{\alpha},z_T{}^{\alpha}\right)},1-\sqrt[\alpha]{s\left(\left(1-\left(1-\sqrt[\alpha]{s\left(\left(1-x_I\right)^{\alpha},\left(1-y_I\right)^{\alpha}\right)}\right)\right)^{\alpha},\left(1-z_I\right)^{\alpha}\right)},\\ 1-\sqrt[\alpha]{s\left(\left(1-\left(1-\sqrt[\alpha]{s\left(\left(1-x_F\right)^{\alpha},\left(1-y_F\right)^{\alpha}\right)}\right)\right)^{\alpha},\left(1-z_F\right)^{\alpha}\right)}\end{array}\right\rangle$$

$$=\left\langle\begin{array}{l}\sqrt[\alpha]{s\left(s\left(x_T{}^{\alpha},y_T{}^{\alpha}\right),z_T{}^{\alpha}\right)},1-\sqrt[\alpha]{s\left(s\left(\left(1-x_I{}^{\alpha}\right),\left(1-y_I{}^{\alpha}\right)\right),\left(1-z_I{}^{\alpha}\right)\right)},\\ 1-\sqrt[\alpha]{s\left(s\left(\left(1-x_F{}^{\alpha}\right),\left(1-y_F{}^{\alpha}\right)\right),\left(1-z_F{}^{\alpha}\right)\right)}\end{array}\right\rangle$$

$$=\left\langle\begin{array}{l}\sqrt[\alpha]{s\left(x_T{}^{\alpha},s\left(y_T{}^{\alpha},z_T{}^{\alpha}\right)\right)},1-\sqrt[\alpha]{s\left(\left(1-x_I{}^{\alpha}\right),s\left(\left(1-y_I{}^{\alpha}\right),\left(1-z_I{}^{\alpha}\right)\right)\right)},\\ 1-\sqrt[\alpha]{s\left(\left(1-x_F{}^{\alpha}\right),s\left(\left(1-y_F{}^{\alpha}\right),\left(1-z_F{}^{\alpha}\right)\right)\right)}\end{array}\right\rangle$$

$$=S^{\alpha}_{n}\left(x,S^{\alpha}_{\underset{s}{n}}\left(y,z\right)\right)$$

Therefore $S^{\alpha}_{\underset{s}{n}}\left(x,y\right)$ is an N-conorm.

Proof

The proof is similar to Proof 1.

Theorem 2.3.14

For any T_n–(*x*,*y*) and for all α≥1, by using any fuzzy intersection t-norm we get the following S_n–(*x*,*y*) and T_n–(*x*,*y*):

1. $S^{\alpha}_{\underset{t}{n}}\left(x,y\right)=\left\langle 1-\sqrt[\alpha]{t\left(\left(1-x_T{}^{\alpha}\right),\left(1-y_T{}^{\alpha}\right)\right)},\sqrt[\alpha]{t\left(x_I{}^{\alpha},y_I{}^{\alpha}\right)},\sqrt[\alpha]{t\left(x_F{}^{\alpha},y_F{}^{\alpha}\right)}\right\rangle$ and
2. $T^{\alpha}_{\underset{t}{n}}\left(x,y\right)=\left\langle\sqrt[\alpha]{t\left(x_T{}^{\alpha},y_T{}^{\alpha}\right)},1-\sqrt[\alpha]{t\left(\left(1-x_I{}^{\alpha}\right),\left(1-y_I{}^{\alpha}\right)\right)},1-\sqrt[\alpha]{t\left(\left(1-x_F{}^{\alpha}\right),\left(1-y_F{}^{\alpha}\right)\right)}\right\rangle$,

where *t* any t-norm (fuzzy intersection).

Proof

The proof is similar to Proof of theorem 3.3.

By these theorems we can generate infinitely many *N-norms* and *N-conorms* by using two bijective functions with certain conditions.

Theorem 2.3.15

Let *f*,*g*: [0,1]→[0,1] be bijective functions such that *f*(0)=0, *f*(1)=1, *g*(0)=1 and *g*(1)=0. For any S_n–(*x*,*y*) and by using any fuzzy union s-norm we get the following S_n–(*x*,*y*) *and* T_n–(*x*,*y*):

1. $\underset{f,g}{S_n^s}(x,y)=\left\langle f^{-1}\left[s\left(f\left(x_T\right),f\left(y_T\right)\right)\right],g^{-1}\left[s\left(g\left(x_I\right),g\left(y_I\right)\right)\right],g^{-1}\left[s\left(g\left(x_F\right),g\left(y_F\right)\right)\right]\right\rangle$, and
2. $\underset{f,g}{T_n^s}(x,y)=\left\langle g^{-1}\left[s\left(g\left(x_T\right),g\left(y_T\right)\right)\right],f^{-1}\left[s\left(f\left(x_I\right),f\left(y_I\right)\right)\right],f^{-1}\left[s\left(f\left(x_F\right),f\left(y_F\right)\right)\right]\right\rangle$.

Proof

Axiom 1:

$$\underset{f,g}{S_n^s}(x,0)=\left\langle f^{-1}\left[s\left(f\left(x_T\right),f\left(0\right)\right)\right],g^{-1}\left[s\left(g\left(x_I\right),g\left(1\right)\right)\right],g^{-1}\left[s\left(g\left(x_F\right),g\left(1\right)\right)\right]\right\rangle=x.$$

$$\underset{f,g}{S_n^s}(x,1)=\left\langle f^{-1}\left[s\left(f\left(x_T\right),f\left(1\right)\right)\right],g^{-1}\left[s\left(g\left(x_I\right),g\left(0\right)\right)\right],g^{-1}\left[s\left(g\left(x_F\right),g\left(0\right)\right)\right]\right\rangle=1(1,0,0).$$

Axiom 2:

$$\underset{f,g}{S_n^s}(x,y)=\left\langle f^{-1}\left[s\left(f\left(x_T\right),f\left(y_T\right)\right)\right],g^{-1}\left[s\left(g\left(x_I\right),g\left(y_I\right)\right)\right],g^{-1}\left[s\left(g\left(x_F\right),g\left(y_F\right)\right)\right]\right\rangle$$

$$=\left\langle f^{-1}\left[s\left(f\left(y_T\right),f\left(x_T\right)\right)\right],g^{-1}\left[s\left(g\left(y_I\right),g\left(x_I\right)\right)\right],g^{-1}\left[s\left(g\left(y_F\right),g\left(x_F\right)\right)\right]\right\rangle=\underset{f,g}{S_n^s}(y,x).$$

Axiom 3: Let *x*≤*y*. Since *f* is bijective on the interval [0,1] and by Axiom s3 we have

$$s\left(f\left(x_T\right),f\left(z_T\right)\right)\le s\left(f\left(y_T\right),f\left(z_T\right)\right)$$

then

$$f^{-1}\left[s\left(f\left(x_T\right),f\left(z_T\right)\right)\right]\le f^{-1}\left[s\left(f\left(y_T\right),f\left(z_T\right)\right)\right] \tag{1}$$

Also since g is bijective on the interval [0,1] and by Axiom t3 we have

$$s\left(g\left(x_I\right),g\left(z_I\right)\right) \geq s\left(g\left(y_I\right),g\left(z_I\right)\right)$$

then

$$g^{-1}\left[s\left(g\left(x_I\right),g\left(z_I\right)\right)\right] \geq g^{-1}\left[s\left(g\left(y_I\right),g\left(z_I\right)\right)\right] \tag{2}$$

and

$$s\left(g\left(x_F\right),g\left(z_F\right)\right) \geq s\left(g\left(y_F\right),g\left(z_F\right)\right)$$

then

$$g^{-1}\left[s\left(g\left(x_F\right),g\left(z_F\right)\right)\right] \geq g^{-1}\left[s\left(g\left(y_F\right),g\left(z_F\right)\right)\right] \tag{3}$$

From (1), (2) and (3) we have $\underset{f,g}{S_n^s}\left(x,z\right) \leq \underset{f,g}{S_n^s}\left(y,z\right)$

Axiom 4:

$$S_n^s\left(\underset{f,g}{S_n^s}\left(x,y\right),z\right) = \underset{f,g}{S_n^s}\left(\left\langle f^{-1}\left[s\left(f\left(x_T\right),f\left(y_T\right)\right)\right],g^{-1}\left[s\left(g\left(x_I\right),g\left(y_I\right)\right)\right],g^{-1}\left[s\left(g\left(x_F\right),g\left(y_F\right)\right)\right]\right\rangle,z\right)$$

$$=\left\langle \begin{array}{l} f^{-1}\left(f\left(f^{-1}\left[s\left(f\left(x_T\right),f\left(y_T\right)\right)\right]\right),f\left(z_T\right)\right),g^{-1}\left(g\left(g^{-1}\left[s\left(g\left(x_I\right),g\left(y_I\right)\right)\right]\right),g\left(z_I\right)\right), \\ g^{-1}\left(g\left(g^{-1}\left[s\left(g\left(x_F\right),g\left(y_F\right)\right)\right]\right),g\left(z_F\right)\right) \end{array} \right\rangle$$

$$=\left\langle \begin{array}{l} f^{-1}\left(s\left(f\left(x_T\right),f\left(y_T\right)\right),f\left(z_T\right)\right),g^{-1}\left(s\left(g\left(x_I\right),g\left(y_I\right)\right),g\left(z_I\right)\right), \\ g^{-1}\left(s\left(g\left(x_F\right),g\left(y_F\right)\right),g\left(z_F\right)\right) \end{array} \right\rangle$$

$$=\left\langle \begin{array}{l} f^{-1}\left(f\left(x_T\right),s\left(f\left(y_T\right),f\left(z_T\right)\right)\right),g^{-1}\left(g\left(x_I\right),s\left(g\left(y_I\right),g\left(z_I\right)\right)\right), \\ g^{-1}\left(g\left(x_F\right),s\left(g\left(y_F\right),g\left(z_F\right)\right)\right) \end{array} \right\rangle$$

$$= S_n^s\left(x,\underset{f,g}{S_n^s}\left(y,z\right)\right)$$

Therefore $\underset{f,g}{S_n^s}\left(x,y\right)$ is an S_n–(x,y).

Proof

The Proof is similar to Proof 1.

Corollary 2.3.16

Let $f(x)=\sin\frac{\pi}{2}x$ and $g(x)=\cos\frac{\pi}{2}x$ then

1. $$\underset{\sin,\cos}{S_n^s}\left(x,y\right)=\left\langle\begin{array}{c}\frac{2}{\pi}\sin^{-1}s\left(\sin\frac{\pi}{2}x_T,\sin\frac{\pi}{2}y_T\right),\\ \frac{2}{\pi}\cos^{-1}s\left(\cos\frac{\pi}{2}x_I,\cos\frac{\pi}{2}y_I\right),\\ \frac{2}{\pi}\cos^{-1}s\left(\cos\frac{\pi}{2}x_F,\cos\frac{\pi}{2}y_F\right)\end{array}\right\rangle$$ is an S_n–(x,y)

2. $$\underset{\sin,\cos}{T_n^s}\left(x,y\right)=\left\langle\begin{array}{c}\frac{2}{\pi}\cos^{-1}s\left(\cos\frac{\pi}{2}x_T,\cos\frac{\pi}{2}y_T\right),\\ \frac{2}{\pi}\sin^{-1}s\left(\sin\frac{\pi}{2}x_I,\sin\frac{\pi}{2}y_I\right),\\ \frac{2}{\pi}\sin^{-1}s\left(\sin\frac{\pi}{2}x_F,\sin\frac{\pi}{2}y_F\right)\end{array}\right\rangle$$ is a T_n–(x,y)

Theorem 2.3.17

Let f,g: $[0,1]\rightarrow[0,1]$ be bijective functions such that $f(0)=0$, $f(1)=1$, $g(0)=1$ and $g(1)=0$. For any T_n–(x,y) and by using any fuzzy intersection t-norm we get the following S_n–(x,y) *and* T_n–(x,y):

1. $\underset{f,g}{S_n^t}\left(x,y\right)=\left\langle g^{-1}\left[t\left(g\left(x_T\right),g\left(y_T\right)\right)\right],f^{-1}\left[t\left(f\left(x_I\right),f\left(y_I\right)\right)\right],f^{-1}\left[t\left(f\left(x_F\right),f\left(y_F\right)\right)\right]\right\rangle$, and
2. $\underset{f,g}{T_n^t}\left(x,y\right)=\left\langle f^{-1}\left[t\left(f\left(x_T\right),f\left(y_T\right)\right)\right],g^{-1}\left[t\left(g\left(x_I\right),g\left(y_I\right)\right)\right],g^{-1}\left[t\left(g\left(x_F\right),g\left(y_F\right)\right)\right]\right\rangle$.

Proof

The proof is similar to Proof of theorem 4.1.

Corollary 2.3.18

Let $f(x)=\sin\frac{\pi}{2}x$ and $g(x)=\cos\frac{\pi}{2}x$ then

1. $$S^{t}_{\substack{n\\ \sin,\cos}}\left(x,y\right)=\left\langle \begin{array}{l} \frac{2}{\pi}\cos^{-1}t\left(\cos\frac{\pi}{2}x_{T},\cos\frac{\pi}{2}y_{T}\right), \\ \frac{2}{\pi}\sin^{-1}t\left(\sin\frac{\pi}{2}x_{I},\sin\frac{\pi}{2}y_{I}\right), \\ \frac{2}{\pi}\sin^{-1}t\left(\sin\frac{\pi}{2}x_{F},\sin\frac{\pi}{2}y_{F}\right) \end{array}\right\rangle$$ is an S_n–(*x,y*)

2. $$T^{t}_{\substack{n\\ \sin,\cos}}\left(x,y\right)=\left\langle \begin{array}{l} \frac{2}{\pi}\sin^{-1}t\left(\sin\frac{\pi}{2}x_{T},\sin\frac{\pi}{2}y_{T}\right), \\ \frac{2}{\pi}\cos^{-1}t\left(\cos\frac{\pi}{2}x_{I},\cos\frac{\pi}{2}y_{I}\right), \\ \frac{2}{\pi}\cos^{-1}t\left(\cos\frac{\pi}{2}x_{F},\cos\frac{\pi}{2}y_{F}\right) \end{array}\right\rangle$$ is a T_n–(*x,y*).

We now generate some new S_n–(*x,y*) and T_n–(*x,y*)from existing S_n–(*x,y*) and T_n–(*x,y*)using the Generating Theorems and the Bijective Generating Theorems.

Example 2.3.19: Bounded Sum Generating Classes

New S_n–(*x,y*) and T_n–(*x,y*)from the bounded sum *s*-norm.

$$S^{\alpha}_{\substack{n\\ s}}(x,y)=\left\langle \begin{array}{l} \sqrt[\alpha]{\min(x_T{}^{\alpha}+y_T{}^{\alpha},1)},1-\sqrt[\alpha]{\min((1-x_I)^{\alpha}+(1-y_I)^{\alpha},1)}, \\ 1-\sqrt[\alpha]{\min((1-x_F)^{\alpha}+(1-y_F)^{\alpha},1)} \end{array}\right\rangle$$

and

$$T^{\alpha}_{\substack{n\\ bs}}(x,y)=\left\langle \begin{array}{l} 1-\sqrt[\alpha]{\min\left(\left(1-x_T\right)^{\alpha}+\left(1-y_T\right)^{\alpha},1\right)}, \\ \sqrt[\alpha]{\min\left(x_I{}^{\alpha}+y_I{}^{\alpha},1\right)},\sqrt[\alpha]{\min\left(x_F{}^{\alpha}+y_F{}^{\alpha},1\right)} \end{array}\right\rangle.$$

$$S^{bs}_{\substack{n\\ \sin,\cos}}\left(x,y\right)=\left\langle \begin{array}{l} \frac{2}{\pi}\sin^{-1}\left(\min\left(\left(\sin\frac{\pi}{2}x_T\right)+\left(\sin\frac{\pi}{2}y_T\right),1\right)\right), \\ \frac{2}{\pi}\cos^{-1}\left(\min\left(\left(\cos\frac{\pi}{2}x_I\right)+\left(\cos\frac{\pi}{2}y_I\right),1\right)\right), \\ \frac{2}{\pi}\cos^{-1}\left(\min\left(\left(\cos\frac{\pi}{2}x_F\right)+\left(\cos\frac{\pi}{2}y_F\right),1\right)\right) \end{array}\right\rangle$$

$$T_{\substack{n\\ \sin,\cos}}^{bs}\left(x,y\right)=\left\langle\begin{array}{l}\frac{2}{\pi}\cos^{-1}\left(\min\left(\left(\cos\frac{\pi}{2}x_T\right)+\left(\cos\frac{\pi}{2}y_T\right),1\right)\right),\\ \frac{2}{\pi}\sin^{-1}\left(\min\left(\left(\sin\frac{\pi}{2}x_I\right)+\left(\sin\frac{\pi}{2}y_I\right),1\right)\right),\\ \frac{2}{\pi}\sin^{-1}\left(\min\left(\left(\sin\frac{\pi}{2}x_F\right)+\left(\sin\frac{\pi}{2}y_F\right),1\right)\right)\end{array}\right\rangle.$$

Example 2.3.20: Algebraic Sum Generating Classes

New S_n–(x,y) and T_n–$(x,y)$from the algebraic sum *s*-norm.

$$S_{\substack{n\\ as}}^{\alpha}(x,y)=\left\langle\begin{array}{l}\sqrt[\alpha]{x_T{}^{\alpha}+y_T{}^{\alpha}-x_T{}^{\alpha}\cdot y_T{}^{\alpha}},1-\sqrt[\alpha]{\left(1-x_I\right)^{\alpha}+\left(1-y_I\right)^{\alpha}-\left(1-x_I\right)^{\alpha}\cdot\left(1-y_I\right)^{\alpha}},\\ 1-\sqrt[\alpha]{\left(1-x_F\right)^{\alpha}+\left(1-y_F\right)^{\alpha}-\left(1-x_F\right)^{\alpha}\cdot\left(1-y_F\right)^{\alpha}}\end{array}\right\rangle,$$

$$T_{\substack{n\\ as}}^{\alpha}(x,y)=\left\langle\begin{array}{l}1-\sqrt[\alpha]{\left(1-x_T\right)^{\alpha}+\left(1-y_T\right)^{\alpha}-\left(1-x_T\right)^{\alpha}\left(1-y_T\right)^{\alpha}},\\ \sqrt[\alpha]{x_I{}^{\alpha}+y_I{}^{\alpha}-x_I{}^{\alpha}\cdot y_I{}^{\alpha}},\sqrt[\alpha]{x_F{}^{\alpha}+y_F{}^{\alpha}-x_F{}^{\alpha}\cdot y_F{}^{\alpha}}\end{array}\right\rangle,$$

$$S_{\substack{n\\ \sin,\cos}}^{as}\left(x,y\right)=\left\langle\begin{array}{l}\frac{2}{\pi}\sin^{-1}\left(\left(\sin\frac{\pi}{2}x_T\right)+\left(\sin\frac{\pi}{2}y_T\right)-\left(\sin\frac{\pi}{2}x_T\right)\left(\sin\frac{\pi}{2}y_T\right)\right),\\ \frac{2}{\pi}\cos^{-1}\left(\left(\cos\frac{\pi}{2}x_I\right)+\left(\cos\frac{\pi}{2}y_I\right)-\left(\cos\frac{\pi}{2}x_I\right)\left(\cos\frac{\pi}{2}y_I\right)\right),\\ \frac{2}{\pi}\cos^{-1}\left(\left(\cos\frac{\pi}{2}x_F\right)+\left(\cos\frac{\pi}{2}y_F\right)-\left(\cos\frac{\pi}{2}x_F\right)\left(\cos\frac{\pi}{2}y_F\right)\right)\end{array}\right\rangle,$$

$$T_{\substack{n\\ \sin,\cos}}^{as}\left(x,y\right)=\left\langle\begin{array}{l}\frac{2}{\pi}\cos^{-1}\left(\left(\cos\frac{\pi}{2}x_T\right)+\left(\cos\frac{\pi}{2}y_T\right)-\left(\cos\frac{\pi}{2}x_T\right)\left(\cos\frac{\pi}{2}y_T\right)\right),\\ \frac{2}{\pi}\sin^{-1}\left(\left(\sin\frac{\pi}{2}x_I\right)+\left(\sin\frac{\pi}{2}y_I\right)-\left(\sin\frac{\pi}{2}x_I\right)\left(\sin\frac{\pi}{2}y_I\right)\right),\\ \frac{2}{\pi}\sin^{-1}\left(\left(\sin\frac{\pi}{2}x_F\right)+\left(\sin\frac{\pi}{2}y_F\right)-\left(\sin\frac{\pi}{2}x_F\right)\left(\sin\frac{\pi}{2}y_F\right)\right)\end{array}\right\rangle.$$

Example 2.3.21: Einstein Sum Generating Classes

New S_n–(x,y) and T_n–$(x,y)$from the Einstein sum *s*-norm.

$$S_{\underset{es}{n}}^{\alpha}(x,y)=\left\langle \sqrt[\alpha]{\frac{x_T^{\ \alpha}+y_T^{\ \alpha}}{1+x_T^{\ \alpha}y_T^{\ \alpha}}},1-\sqrt[\alpha]{\frac{(1-x_I)^{\alpha}+(1-y_I)^{\alpha}}{1+(1-x_I)^{\alpha}(1-y_I)^{\alpha}}},1-\sqrt[\alpha]{\frac{(1-x_F)^{\alpha}+(1-y_F)^{\alpha}}{1+(1-x_F)^{\alpha}(1-y_F)^{\alpha}}}\right\rangle,$$

$$T_{\underset{es}{n}}^{\alpha}(x,y)=\left\langle 1-\sqrt[\alpha]{\frac{\left(1-x_T\right)^{\alpha}+\left(1-y_T\right)^{\alpha}}{1+\left(1-x_T\right)^{\alpha}\left(1-y_T\right)^{\alpha}}},\sqrt[\alpha]{\frac{x_I^{\ \alpha}+y_I^{\ \alpha}}{1+x_I^{\ \alpha}y_I^{\ \alpha}}},\sqrt[\alpha]{\frac{x_F^{\ \alpha}+y_F^{\ \alpha}}{1+x_F^{\ \alpha}y_F^{\ \alpha}}}\right\rangle,$$

$$S_{\underset{\sin,\cos}{n}}^{bs}\left(x,y\right)=\left\langle \begin{array}{c} \frac{2}{\pi}\sin^{-1}\left(\frac{\left(\sin\frac{\pi}{2}x_T\right)+\left(\sin\frac{\pi}{2}y_T\right)}{1+\left(\sin\frac{\pi}{2}x_T\right)\left(\sin\frac{\pi}{2}y_T\right)}\right), \\ \frac{2}{\pi}\cos^{-1}\left(\frac{\left(\cos\frac{\pi}{2}x_I\right)+\left(\cos\frac{\pi}{2}y_I\right)}{1+\left(\cos\frac{\pi}{2}x_I\right)\left(\cos\frac{\pi}{2}y_I\right)}\right), \\ \frac{2}{\pi}\cos^{-1}\left(\frac{\left(\cos\frac{\pi}{2}x_F\right)+\left(\cos\frac{\pi}{2}y_F\right)}{1+\left(\cos\frac{\pi}{2}x_F\right)\left(\cos\frac{\pi}{2}y_F\right)}\right) \end{array}\right\rangle,$$

$$T_{\underset{\sin,\cos}{n}}^{bs}\left(x,y\right)=\left\langle \begin{array}{c} \frac{2}{\pi}\cos^{-1}\left(\frac{\left(\cos\frac{\pi}{2}x_T\right)+\left(\cos\frac{\pi}{2}y_T\right)}{1+\left(\cos\frac{\pi}{2}x_T\right)\left(\cos\frac{\pi}{2}y_T\right)}\right), \\ \frac{2}{\pi}\sin^{-1}\left(\frac{\left(\sin\frac{\pi}{2}x_I\right)+\left(\sin\frac{\pi}{2}y_I\right)}{1+\left(\sin\frac{\pi}{2}x_I\right)\left(\sin\frac{\pi}{2}y_I\right)}\right), \\ \frac{2}{\pi}\sin^{-1}\left(\frac{\left(\sin\frac{\pi}{2}x_F\right)+\left(\sin\frac{\pi}{2}y_F\right)}{1+\left(\sin\frac{\pi}{2}x_F\right)\left(\sin\frac{\pi}{2}y_F\right)}\right) \end{array}\right\rangle.$$

Example 2.3.22: Bounded Product Generating Classes

New S_n–(x,y) and T_n–$(x,y)$from the bounded product t-norm.

$$T_{\underset{bp}{n}}^{\alpha}(x,y)=\left\langle \begin{array}{l} \sqrt[\alpha]{\max\left(x_T{}^{\alpha}+y_T{}^{\alpha}-1,0\right)},1-\sqrt[\alpha]{\max\left(\left(1-x_I\right)^{\alpha}+\left(1-y_I{}^{\alpha}\right)-1,0\right)}, \\ 1-\sqrt[\alpha]{\max\left(\left(1-x_F\right)^{\alpha}+\left(1-y_F\right)^{\alpha}-1,0\right)} \end{array}\right\rangle,$$

$$S_{\underset{bp}{n}}^{\alpha}(x,y)=\left\langle \begin{array}{l} 1-\sqrt[\alpha]{\max\left(\left(1-x_T\right)^{\alpha}+\left(1-y_T\right)^{\alpha}-1,0\right)}, \\ \sqrt[\alpha]{\max\left(x_I{}^{\alpha}+y_I{}^{\alpha}-1,0\right)},\sqrt[\alpha]{\max\left(x_F{}^{\alpha}+y_F{}^{\alpha}-1,0\right)} \end{array}\right\rangle,$$

$$T_{\underset{\sin,\cos}{n}}^{bp}(x,y)=\left\langle \begin{array}{l} \frac{2}{\pi}\sin^{-1}\left(\max\left(\left(\sin\frac{\pi}{2}x_T\right)+\left(\sin\frac{\pi}{2}y_T\right)-1,0\right)\right), \\ \frac{2}{\pi}\cos^{-1}\left(\max\left(\left(\cos\frac{\pi}{2}x_I\right)+\left(\cos\frac{\pi}{2}y_I\right)-1,0\right)\right), \\ \frac{2}{\pi}\cos^{-1}\left(\max\left(\left(\cos\frac{\pi}{2}x_F\right)+\left(\cos\frac{\pi}{2}y_F\right)-1,0\right)\right) \end{array}\right\rangle,$$

$$S_{\underset{\sin,\cos}{n}}^{t}(x,y)=\left\langle \begin{array}{l} \frac{2}{\pi}\cos^{-1}\left(\max\left(\left(\cos\frac{\pi}{2}x_T\right)+\left(\cos\frac{\pi}{2}y_T\right)-1,0\right)\right), \\ \frac{2}{\pi}\sin^{-1}\left(\max\left(\left(\sin\frac{\pi}{2}x_I+\sin\frac{\pi}{2}y_I\right)-1,0\right)\right), \\ \frac{2}{\pi}\sin^{-1}\left(\max\left(\left(\sin\frac{\pi}{2}x_F+\sin\frac{\pi}{2}y_F\right)-1,0\right)\right) \end{array}\right\rangle.$$

Example 2.3.23: Einstein Product Generating Classes

New S_n–(x,y) and T_n–$(x,y)$from the Einstein product t-norm.

$$T_{\underset{ep}{n}}^{\alpha}(x,y)=\left\langle \begin{array}{l} \sqrt[\alpha]{\dfrac{x_T{}^{\alpha}y_T{}^{\alpha}}{2-\left(x_T{}^{\alpha}+y_T{}^{\alpha}-x_T{}^{\alpha}y_T{}^{\alpha}\right)}}, \\ 1-\sqrt[\alpha]{\dfrac{\left(1-x_I\right)^{\alpha}\left(1-y_I\right)^{\alpha}}{2-\left(\left(1-x_I\right)^{\alpha}+\left(1-y_I\right)^{\alpha}-\left(1-x_I\right)^{\alpha}\left(1-y_I\right)^{\alpha}\right)}}, \\ 1-\sqrt[\alpha]{\dfrac{\left(1-x_F\right)^{\alpha}\left(1-y_F\right)^{\alpha}}{2-\left(\left(1-x_F\right)^{\alpha}+\left(1-y_F\right)^{\alpha}-\left(1-x_F\right)^{\alpha}\left(1-y_F\right)^{\alpha}\right)}} \end{array}\right\rangle,$$

$$S_{\underset{ep}{n}}^{\alpha}\left(x,y\right)=\left\langle \begin{array}{l} 1-\sqrt[\alpha]{\dfrac{\left(1-x_T\right)^{\alpha}\left(1-y_T\right)^{\alpha}}{2-\left(\left(1-x_T\right)^{\alpha}+\left(1-y_T\right)^{\alpha}-\left(1-x_T\right)^{\alpha}\left(1-y_T\right)^{\alpha}\right)}}, \\ \sqrt[\alpha]{\dfrac{x_I^{\alpha}y_I^{\alpha}}{2-\left(x_I^{\alpha}+y_I^{\alpha}-x_I^{\alpha}y_I^{\alpha}\right)}}, \sqrt[\alpha]{\dfrac{x_F^{\alpha}y_F^{\alpha}}{2-\left(x_F^{\alpha}+y_F^{\alpha}-x_F^{\alpha}y_F^{\alpha}\right)}} \end{array}\right\rangle$$

$$T_{\underset{\sin,\cos}{n}}^{ep}\left(x,y\right)=\left\langle \begin{array}{l} \dfrac{2}{\pi}\sin^{-1}\left(\dfrac{\left(\sin\frac{\pi}{2}x_T\right)\left(\sin\frac{\pi}{2}y_T\right)}{2-\left(\left(\sin\frac{\pi}{2}x_T\right)+\left(\sin\frac{\pi}{2}y_T\right)-\left(\sin\frac{\pi}{2}x_T\right)\left(\sin\frac{\pi}{2}y_T\right)\right)}\right), \\ \dfrac{2}{\pi}\cos^{-1}\left(\dfrac{\left(\cos\frac{\pi}{2}x_I\right)\left(\cos\frac{\pi}{2}y_I\right)}{2-\left(\left(\cos\frac{\pi}{2}x_I\right)+\left(\cos\frac{\pi}{2}y_I\right)-\left(\cos\frac{\pi}{2}x_I\right)\left(\cos\frac{\pi}{2}y_I\right)\right)}\right), \\ \dfrac{2}{\pi}\cos^{-1}\left(\dfrac{\left(\cos\frac{\pi}{2}x_F\right)\left(\cos\frac{\pi}{2}y_F\right)}{2-\left(\left(\cos\frac{\pi}{2}x_F\right)+\left(\cos\frac{\pi}{2}y_F\right)-\left(\cos\frac{\pi}{2}x_F\right)\left(\cos\frac{\pi}{2}y_F\right)\right)}\right) \end{array}\right\rangle,$$

$$s_{\underset{\sin,\cos}{n}}^{ep}\left(x,y\right)=\left\langle \begin{array}{l} \dfrac{2}{\pi}\cos^{-1}\left(\dfrac{\left(\cos\frac{\pi}{2}x_T\right)\left(\cos\frac{\pi}{2}y_T\right)}{2-\left(\left(\cos\frac{\pi}{2}x_T\right)+\left(\cos\frac{\pi}{2}y_T\right)-\left(\cos\frac{\pi}{2}x_T\right)\left(\cos\frac{\pi}{2}y_T\right)\right)}\right), \\ \dfrac{2}{\pi}\sin^{-1}\left(\dfrac{\left(\sin\frac{\pi}{2}x_I\right)\left(\sin\frac{\pi}{2}y_I\right)}{2-\left(\left(\sin\frac{\pi}{2}x_I\right)+\left(\sin\frac{\pi}{2}y_I\right)-\left(\sin\frac{\pi}{2}x_I\right)\left(\sin\frac{\pi}{2}y_I\right)\right)}\right), \\ \dfrac{2}{\pi}\sin^{-1}\left(\dfrac{\left(\sin\frac{\pi}{2}x_F\right)\left(\sin\frac{\pi}{2}y_F\right)}{2-\left(\left(\sin\frac{\pi}{2}x_F\right)+\left(\sin\frac{\pi}{2}y_F\right)-\left(\sin\frac{\pi}{2}x_F\right)\left(\sin\frac{\pi}{2}y_F\right)\right)}\right) \end{array}\right\rangle.$$

Note that for the s-norms max and drastic sum and t-norms min, algebraic product and drastic product we get the same norms.

CRISP NEUTROSOPHIC SET, NEUTROSOPHIC CRISP NEIGHBORHOOD SYSTEMS, NEUTROSOPHIC CRISP LOCAL FUNCTIONS

In this section, crisp neutrosophic sets, neutrosophic crisp neighborhood systems and neutrosophic crisp local functions have been discussed.

Crisp Neutrosophic Set

In this subsection, the authors presented crisp neutrosophic sets and their related properties.

Definition 3.1.1

Let *X* be a non-empty fixed set. *A* neutrosophic crisp set (NCS for short) *A* is an object having the form $A = \langle A_1, A_2, A_3 \rangle$ where A_1, A_2, and A_3 are subsets of X satisfying $A_1 \cap A_2 = \varphi$, $A_1 \cap A_3 = \varphi$ and $A_2 \cap A_3 = \varphi$.

Definition 3.1.2

Let X be a nonempty set and $p \in X$ Then the neutrosophic crisp point p_N defined by $p_N = \left\langle \{p\}, \varphi, \{p\}^c \right\rangle$ is called a neutrosophic crisp point (NCP for short) in X, where NCP is a triple ({only one element in X}, the empty set,{the complement of the same element in X}).

Definition 3.1.3

Let X be a non-empty set, and $p \in X$ a fixed element in X. Then the neutrosophic crisp set $p_{N_N} = \left\langle \varphi, \{p\}, \{p\}^c \right\rangle$ is called "vanishing neutrosophic crisp point" (VNCP for short) in X, where VNCP is a triple (the empty set,{only one element in X},{the complement of the same element in X}).

Definition 3.1.4

Let $p_N = \left\langle \{p\}, \varphi, \{p\}^c \right\rangle$ be a NCP in X and $A = \langle A_1, A_2, A_3 \rangle$ a neutrosophic crisp set in X.

1. p_N is said to be contained in *A* ($p_N \in A$ for short) iff $p \in A_1$.
2. Let p_{NN} be a VNCP in X, and $A = \langle A_1, A_2, A_3 \rangle$ a neutrosophic crisp set in X. Then p_{NN} is said to be contained in *A* ($p_{NN} \in A$ for short) iff $p \notin A_3$.

Definition 3.1.5

Let X be non-empty set, and L a non–empty family of NCSs. We call a neutrosophic crisp ideal (NCL for short) on X if

1. $A \in L$ and $B \subseteq A \Rightarrow B \in L$ [heredity],
2. $A \in L$ and $B \in \mathrm{L} \Rightarrow A \vee B \in \mathrm{L}$ [Finite additivity].

A neutrosophic crisp ideal L is called a σ- neutrosophic crisp ideal if $\{M_j\}_{j\in \mathrm{N}} \leq L$, implies $\underset{j\in J}{\cup} M_j \in L$ (countable additivity). The smallest and largest neutrosophic crisp ideals on a non-empty set X are $\{\phi_N\}$ and the NSs on X. Also, NCL_f, NCL_c are denoting the neutrosophic crisp ideals (NCL for short) of neutrosophic subsets having finite and countable support of X respectively. Moreover, if A is a nonempty NS in X, then $\{B \in NCS : B \subseteq A\}$ is an NCL on X. This is called the principal NCL of all NCSs, denoted by NCL$\langle A\rangle$.

Proposition 3.1.6

Let $\{L_j : j \in J\}$ be any non - empty family of neutrosophic crisp ideals on a set X. Then $\bigcap_{j\in J} L_j$ and $\bigcup_{j\in J} L_j$ are neutrosophic crisp ideals on X, where

$$\underset{j\in J}{\cap} L_j = \left\langle \underset{j\in J}{\cap} A_{j_1}, \underset{j\in J}{\cap} A_{j_2}, \underset{j\in J}{\cup} A_{j_3} \right\rangle$$

or

$$\underset{j\in J}{\cap} L_j = \left\langle \underset{j\in J}{\cap} A_{j_1}, \underset{j\in J}{\cup} A_{j_2}, \underset{j\in J}{\cup} A_{j_3} \right\rangle$$

and

$$\underset{j\in J}{\cup} L_j = \left\langle \underset{j\in J}{\cup} A_{j_1}, \underset{j\in J}{\cup} A_{j_2}, \underset{j\in J}{\cap} A_{j_3} \right\rangle$$

or

$$\underset{j\in J}{\cup} L_j = \left\langle \underset{j\in J}{\cup} A_{j_1}, \underset{j\in J}{\cap} A_{j_2}, \underset{j\in J}{\cap} A_{j_3} \right\rangle.$$

Remark 3.1.7

The neutrosophic crisp ideal defined by the single neutrosophic set ϕ_N is the smallest element of the ordered set of all neutrosophic crisp ideals on X.

Proposition 3.1.8

A neutrosophic crisp set $A = \langle A_1, A_2, A_3\rangle$ in the neutrosophic crisp ideal L on X is a base of L iff every member of L is contained in A.

Neutrosophic Crisp Neighborhoods System

Definition 3.2.1

Let $A = \langle A_1, A_2, A_3 \rangle$, be a neutrosophic crisp set on a set X, then

$$p = \langle \{p_1\}, \{p_2\}, \{p_3\} \rangle,$$

$p_1 \neq p_2 \neq p_3 \in X$ is called a neutrosophic crisp point.
An NCP

$$p = \langle \{p_1\}, \{p_2\}, \{p_3\} \rangle$$

is said to be belong to a neutrosophic crisp set $A = \langle A_1, A_2, A_3 \rangle$, of X, denoted by $p \in A$, if may be defined by two types

Type 1: $\{p_1\} \subseteq A_1, \{p_2\} \subseteq A_2$ and $\{p_3\} \subseteq A_3$
Type 2: $\{p_1\} \subseteq A_1, \{p_2\} \supseteq A_2$ and $\{p_3\} \subseteq A_3$

Theorem 3.2.2

Let $A = \langle\langle A_1, A_2, A_3 \rangle\rangle$, and $B = \langle\langle B_1, B_2, B_3 \rangle\rangle$, be neutrosophic crisp subsets of X. Then $A \subseteq B$ iff $p \in A$ implies $p \in B$ for any neutrosophic crisp point p in X.

Proof

Let $A \subseteq B$ and $p \in A$. Then two types

Type 1: $\{p_1\} \subseteq A_1, \{p_2\} \subseteq A_2$ and $\{p_3\} \subseteq A_3$ or
Type 2: $\{p_1\} \subseteq A_1, \{p_2\} \supseteq A_2$ and $\{p_3\} \subseteq A_3$.

Thus $p \in B$. Conversely, take any x in X. Let $p_1 \in A_1$ and $p_2 \in A_2$ and $p_3 \in A_3$. Then p is a neutrosophic crisp point in X. and $p \in A$. By the hypothesis $p \in B$. Thus $p_1 \in B_1$, or

Type 1: $\{p_1\} \subseteq B_1, \{p_2\} \subseteq B_2$ and $\{p_3\} \subseteq B_3$ or
Type 2: $\{p_1\} \subseteq B_1, \{p_2\} \supseteq B_2$ and $\{p_3\} \subseteq B_3$. Hence $A \subseteq B$.

Theorem 3.2.3

Let $A = \langle A_1, A_2, A_3 \rangle$, be a neutrosophic crisp subset of X. Then $A = \cup \{p : p \in A\}$.

Proof

Since $\cup\{p : p \in A\}$ may be two types

Type 1: $\langle \cup\{p_1 : p_1 \in A_1\}, \cup\{p_2 : p_2 \in A_2\}, \cap\{p_3 : p_3 \in A_3\}\rangle$ or
Type 2: $\langle \cup\{p_1 : p_1 \in A_1\}, \cap\{p_2 : p_2 \in A_2\}, \cap\{p_3 : p_3 \in A_3\}\rangle$.

Hence $A = \langle A_1, A_2, A_3\rangle$.

Proposition 3.2.4

Let $\{A_j : j \in J\}$ is a family of NCSs in X. Then

(a_1) $p = \langle\{p_1\},\{p_2\},\{p_3\}\rangle \in \underset{j\in J}{\cap} A_j$ iff $p \in A_j$ for each $j \in J$.

(a_2) $p \in \underset{j\in J}{\cup} A_j$ iff $\exists j \in J$ such that $p \in A_j$.

Proposition 3.2.5

Let $A = \langle A_1, A_2, A_3\rangle$ and $B = \langle B_1, B_2, B_3\rangle$ be two neutrosophic crisp sets in X. Then

1. $A \subseteq B$ iff for each p we have $p \in A \Leftrightarrow p \in B$ and for each p we have $p \in A \Rightarrow p \in B$.
2. $A=B$ iff for each p we have $p \in A \Rightarrow p \in B$ and for each p we have $p \in A \Leftrightarrow p \in B$.

Proposition 3.2.6

Let $A = \langle A_1, A_2, A_3\rangle$ be a neutrosophic crisp set in X. Then
$A = \cup\langle\{p_1 : p_1 \in A_1\},\{p_2 : p_2 \in A_2\},\{p_3 : p_3 \in A_3\}\rangle$.

Definition 3.2.7

Let $f: X \to Y$ be a function and p be a nutrosophic crisp point in X. Then the image of p under f, denoted by $f(p)$, is defined by

$$f(p) = \langle\{q_1\},\{q_2\},\{q_3\}\rangle,$$

where $q_1 = f(p_1), q_2 = f(p_2)$ and $q_3 = f(p_3)$.

It is easy to see that $f(p)$ is indeed a NCP in Y, namely $f(p)=q$, where $q=f(p)$, and it is exactly the same meaning of the image of a NCP under the function f.

Neutrosophic Crisp Local Functions

Here, the author discussed neutrosophic crisp local functions.

Definition 3.3.1

Let p be a neutrosophic crisp point of a neutrosophic crisp topological space (X,τ). A neutrosophic crisp neighbourhood (NCNBD for short) of a neutrosophic crisp point p if there is a neutrosophic crisp open set(NCOS for short) B in X such that $p \in B \subseteq A$.

Theorem 3.3.2

Let (X,τ) be a neutrosophic crisp topological space (NCTS for short) of X. Then the neutrosophic crisp set A of X is NCOS iff A is a NCNBD of p for every neutrosophic crisp set $p \in A$.

Proof

Let A be NCOS of X . Clearly A is a NCBD of any $p \in A$. Conversely, let $p \in A$. Since A is a NCBD of p, there is a NCOS B in X such that $p \in B \subseteq A$. So we have

$$A = \cup\{p : p \in A\} \subseteq \cup\{B : p \in A\} \subseteq A$$

and hence

$$A = \cup\{B : p \in A\},$$

since each B is NCOS.

Definition 3.3.3

Let (X,τ) be a neutrosophic crisp topological spaces (NCTS for short) and L be neutrosophic crisp ideal (NCL, for short) on X. Let A be any NCS of X. Then the neutrosophic crisp local function $NCA^*(L,\tau)$ of A is the union of all neutrosophic crisp points(NCP, for short)

$$P = \left\langle \{p_1\}, \{p_2\}, \{p_3\} \right\rangle,$$

such that if $U \in N((p))$ and

$$NA^*(L,\tau) = \cup\{p \in X : A \wedge U \notin L \ for\ every\ U\ nbd\ of\ N(P)\},$$

$NCA^*(L,\tau)$ is called a neutrosophic crisp local function of A with respect to τ and L which it will be denoted by $NCA^*(L,\tau)$, or simply $NCA^*(L)$.

Example 3.3.4

One may easily verify that if

L= $\{\varphi_N\}$, then N $CA^*(L,\tau) = NCcl(A)$

for any neutrosophic crisp set $A \in NCSs$ on X.

If

$L = \{all\ NCSs\ on\ X\}$, then $NCA^*(L,\tau) = \varphi_N$

for any $A \in NCSs$ on X .

Theorem 3.3.5

Let (X,τ) be a NCTS and L_1,L_2 be two topological neutrosophic crisp ideals on X. Then for any neutrosophic crisp sets A, B of X. then the following statements are verified

1. $A \subseteq B \Rightarrow NCA^*(L,\tau) \subseteq NCB^*(L,\tau)$.
2. $L_1 \subseteq L_2 \Rightarrow NCA^*(L_2,\tau) \subseteq NCA^*(L_1,\tau)$.
3. $NCA^* = NCcl(A^*) \subseteq NCcl(A)$.
4. $NCA^{**} \subseteq NCA^*$.
5. $NC(A \cup B)^* = NCA^* \cup NCB^*$.
6. $NC(A \cap B)^*(L) \subseteq NCA^*(L) \cap NCB^*(L)$.
7. $\ell \in L \Rightarrow NC(A \cup \ell)^* = NCA^*$.
8. $NCA^*(L,\tau)$ is neutrosophic crisp closed set.

Proof

Since $A \subseteq B$, let

$$p = \langle\{p_1\},\{p_2\},\{p_3\}\rangle \in NCA^*(L_1)$$

then $A \cap U \notin L$ for every $U \in N(p)$. By hypothesis we get $B \cap U \notin L$, then

$$p = \langle\{p_1\},\{p_2\},\{p_3\}\rangle \in NB^*(L_1).$$

1. Clearly. $L_1 \subseteq L_2$ implies

$$NCA^*(L_2,\tau) \subseteq NCA^*(L_1,\tau)$$

as there may be other IFSs which belong to L_2 so that for GIFP

$$p = \langle \{p_1\}, \{p_2\}, \{p_3\} \rangle \in NCA^*(L_1)$$

but P may not be contained in $NCA^*(L_2)$.

2. Since $\{\varphi_N\} \subseteq L$ for any NCL on X, therefore by (2) and Example 3.1,

$$NCA^*(L) \subseteq NCA^*(\{O_N\}) = NCcl(A)$$

for any NCS A on X. Suppose

$$P_1 = \langle \{p_1\}, \{p_2\}, \{p_3\} \rangle \in NCcl(A^*(L_1)).$$

So for every $U \in NC(p_1)$, $NC(A^*) \cap U \neq \varphi_N$, there exists

$$P_2 = \langle \{q_1\}, \{q_2\}, \{q_3\} \rangle \in NCA^*(L_1) \cap U$$

such that for every V NCNBD of

$$P_2 \in N(P_2), A \cap U \notin L.$$

Since

$$U \wedge V \in N(p_2)$$

then

$$A \cap (U \cap V) \notin L$$

which leads to $A \wedge U \notin L$, for every $U \in N(p_1)$ therefore

$$P_1 \in NC(A^*(L))$$

and so

$$NCcl(NA^*) \subseteq NCA^*$$

While, the other inclusion follows directly. Hence

$NCA^* = NCcl(NCA^*)$.

But the inequality

$NCA^* \subseteq Ncl(NCA^*)$.

3. The inclusion

$NCA^* \cup NCB^* \subseteq NC(A \cup B)^*$

follows directly by (1). To show the other implication, let $p \in NC(A \cup B)^*$ then for every $U \in NC(p)$

$(A \cup B) \cap U \notin L$, i.e. $(A \cap U) \cup (B \cap U) \notin L$.

Then, we have two cases $A \cap U \notin L$ and $B \cap U \in L$ or the converse, this means that exist $U_1, U_2 \in N(P)$ such that

$A \cap U_1 \notin L$,

$B \cap U_1 \notin L$,

$A \cap U_2 \notin L$,

and

$B \cap U_2 \notin L$.

Then

$A \cap (U_1 \cap U_2) \in L$

and

$B \cap (U_1 \cap U_2) \in L$.

This gives

$(A \cup B) \cap (U_1 \cap U_2) \in L, U_1 \cap U_2 \in N(C(P))$

which contradicts the hypothesis. Hence the equality holds in various cases.

4. By (3), we have

$$NCA^{*^{*}} = NCcl(NCA^{*})^{*} \subseteq NCcl(NCA^{*}) = NCA^{*}$$

Let (X,τ) be a NCTS and L be NCL on X . Let us define the neutrosophic crisp closure operator

$$NCcl^{*}(A) = A \cup NC(A^{*})$$

for any NCS A of X. Clearly, let $NCcl^{*}(A)$ is a neutrosophic crisp operator. Let $NC\tau^{*}(L)$ be NCT generated by $NCcl^{*}$, i.e

$$NC\tau^{*}\left(L\right) = \left\{A : NCcl^{*}(A^{c}) = A^{c}\right\}.$$

Now

$$L = \left\{\varphi_{N}\right\} \Rightarrow NCcl^{*}\left(A\right) = A \cup NCA^{*} = A \cup NCcl\left(A\right)$$

for every neutrosophic crisp set A. So, $N\tau^{*}\left(\left\{\varphi_{N}\right\}\right) = \tau$. Again

$$L = \left\{all\ NCSs\ on\ X\right\} \Rightarrow NCcl^{*}\left(A\right) = A,$$

because $NCA^{*} = \varphi_{N}$, for every neutrosophic crisp set A so $NC\tau^{*}(L)$ is the neutrosophic crisp discrete topology on X. So we can conclude by Theorem 4.1.(2).

$$NC\tau^{*}\left(\left\{\varphi_{N}\right\}\right) = NC\tau^{*}\left(L\right) \text{i.e. } NC\tau \subseteq NC\tau^{*},$$

for any neutrosophic ideal L_1 on X. In particular, we have for two topological neutrosophic ideals L_1 and L_2 on X,

$$L_1 \subseteq L_2 \Rightarrow NC\tau^{*}\left(L_1\right) \subseteq NC\tau^{*}\left(L_2\right).$$

Theorem 3.3.6

Let τ_1,τ_2 be two neutrosophic crisp topologies on *X*. Then for any topological neutrosophic crisp ideal *L* on *X*, $\tau_1 \leq \tau_2$ implies

$$NA^{*}(L,\tau_2) \subseteq NA^{*}(L,\tau_1),$$

for every $A \in L$ then $NC\tau_1^{*} \subseteq NC\tau_2^{*}$

Proof

Clear. A basis $NC\beta(L,\tau)$ for $NC\tau^*(L)$ can be described as follows:

$$NC\beta(L,\tau) = \{A - B : A \in \tau, B \in L\}.$$

Then we have the following theorem.

Theorem 3.3.7

$$NC\beta(L,\tau) = \{A - B : A \in \tau, B \in L\}$$

forms a basis for the generated NT of the NCT(X,τ) with topological neutrosophic crisp ideal L on X.

The relationship between $NC\tau$ and $NC\tau^*(L)$ established throughout the following result which have an immediately proof.

Theorem 3.3.8

Let τ_1,τ_2 be two neutrosophic crisp topologies on X. Then for any topological neutrosophic ideal L on X, $\tau_1 \subseteq \tau_2$ implies $NC\tau_1^* \subseteq NC\tau_2^*$.

Theorem 3.3.9

Let (X,τ) be a NCTS and L_1,L_2 be two neutrosophic crisp ideals on X . Then for any neutrosophic crisp set A in X, we have

1. $NCA^*(L_1 \cup L_2,\tau) = NCA^*(L_1, NC\tau^*(L_1)) \wedge NCA^*(L_2, NC\tau^*(L_2))$.
2. $NC\tau^*(L_1 \cup L_2) = (NC\tau^*(L_1))^*(L_2) \wedge (NC\tau^*(L_2)^*(L_1)$.

Proof

Let $p \notin (L_1 \cup L_2,\tau)$, this means that there exists $U \in NC(P)$ such that $A \cap U_p \in (L_1 \cup L_2)$ i.e. There exists $\ell_1 \in L_1$ and $\ell_2 \in L_2$ such that $A \cap U \in (\ell_1 \vee \ell_2)$ because of the heredity of L_1, and assuming $\ell_1 \wedge \ell_2 = O_N$. Thus we have

$$(A \cap U) - \ell_1 = \ell_2$$

and

$$(A \cap U_p) - \ell_2 = \ell_1$$

therefore

$$\left(U - \ell_1\right) \cap A = \ell_2 \in L_2$$

and

$$\left(U - \ell_2\right) \cap A = \ell_1 \in L_1.$$

Hence

$$p \notin NCA^*\left(L_2, NC\tau^*\left(L_1\right)\right),$$

or

$$P \notin NCA^*\left(L_1, NC\tau^*\left(L_2\right)\right),$$

because p must belong to either ℓ_1 or ℓ_2 but not to both. This gives

$$NCA^*\left(L_1 \cup L_2, \tau\right) \geq NCA^*\left(L_1, NC\tau^*(L_1)\ \right) \cap NCA^*\left(L_2, NC\tau^*(L_2)\right).$$

To show the second inclusion, let us assume

$$P \notin NCA^*\left(L_1, NC\tau^*\left(L_2\right)\right).$$

This implies that there exist $U \in N(P)$ and $\ell_2 \in L_2$ such that $\left(U_p - \ell_2\right) \cap A \in L_1$. By the heredity of L_2, if we assume that $\ell_2 \subseteq A$ and define $\ell_1 = \left(U - \ell_2\right) \cap A$. Then we have

$$A \cap U \in \left(\ell_1 \cup \ell_2\right) \in L_1 \cup L_2.$$

Thus,

$$NCA^*\left(L_1 \cup L_2, \tau\right) \subseteq NCA^*\left(L_1, NC\tau^*(L_1)\ \right) \cap NCA^*\left(L_2, NC\tau^*(L_2)\right).$$

and similarly, we can get

$$NCA^*\left(L_1 \cup L_2, \tau\right) \subseteq NCA^*\left(L_2, \tau^*(L_1)\ \right)..$$

This gives the other inclusion, which complete the proof.

Corollary 3.3.10

Let (X,τ) be a NCTS with topological neutrosophic crisp ideal L on X. Then

1. $NCA^*(L,\tau) = NCA^*(L,\tau^*)$ and $NC\tau^*(L) = NC(NC\tau^*(L))^*(L)$.
2. $NC\tau^*(L_1 \cup L_2) = \left(NC\tau^*(L_1)\right) \cup \left(NC\tau^*(L_2)\right)$.

INTERVAL VALUED NEUTROSOPHIC SETS

In this section, we studied interval valued neutrosophic sets and their properties.

Definitions, Proofs, and Propositions

Definition 4.1

Let X be a space of points (objects) with generic elements in X denoted by x. An interval valued neutrosophic set (for short IVNS) A in X is characterized by truth-membership function $T_A(x)$, indeteminacy-membership function $I_A(x)$ and falsity-membership function $F_A(x)$. For each point x in X, we have that $T_A(x), I_A(x), F_A(x) \in [0, 1]$.

Definition 4.2

For two IVNS,

$$A_{INS} = \left\{ \left\langle x, \left[T_A^L(x), T_A^U(x)\right], \left[I_A^L(x), I_A^U(x)\right], \left[F_A^L(x), F_A^U(x)\right] \right\rangle \mid x \in X \right\}$$

and

$$B_{INS} = \left\{ \left\langle x, \left[T_B^L(x), T_B^U(x)\right], \left[I_B^L(x), I_B^U(x)\right], \left[F_B^L(x), F_B^U(x)\right] \right\rangle \mid x \in X \right\}$$

the two relations are defined as follows:

1. $A_{INS} \subseteq B_{INS}$ if and only if $T_A^L(x) \le T_B^L(x)$, $I_A^L(x) \ge I_B^L(x)$, $F_A^L(x) \ge F_B^L(x)$, $T_A^U(x) \le T_B^U(x)$, $I_A^U(x) \ge I_B^U(x)$, $F_A^U(x) \ge F_B^U(x)$.
2. $A_{INS} = B_{INS}$ if and only if $T_A^L(x) = T_B^L(x)$, $I_A^L(x) = I_B^L(x)$, $F_A^L(x) = F_B^L(x)$, $T_A^U(x) = T_B^U(x)$, $I_A^U(x) = I_B^U(x)$, $F_A^U(x) = F_B^U(x)$ for any x $\in$X.

Definition 4.3

Assume that there are two interval neutrosophic sets A and B in X $=\{x_1, x_2,\ldots,x_n\}$ Based on the extension measure for fuzzy sets, a cosine similarity measure between interval valued neutrosophic sets A and B is proposed as follows:

$$C_N(A,B)$$
$$=\frac{1}{n}\sum_{i=1}^{n}\frac{\Delta T_A(x_i)\Delta T_B(x_i)+\Delta I_A(x_i)\Delta I_B(x_i)+\Delta F_A(x_i)\Delta F_B(x_i)}{\sqrt{(\Delta T_A(x_i))^2+(\Delta I_A(x_i))^2+(\Delta F_A(x_i))^2}\sqrt{(\Delta T_B(x_i))^2+(\Delta I_B(x_i))^2+(\Delta F_B(x_i))^2}}$$

where

$$\Delta T_A(x_i)=T_A^L(x_i)+T_A^U(x_i),\Delta T_B(x_i)=T_B^L(x_i)+T_B^U(x_i),$$

$$T_A^L(x_i)+T_A^U(x_i),\Delta T_B(x_i)=T_B^L(x_i)+T_B^U(x_i),$$

$$\Delta I_A(x_i)=I_A^L(x_i)+I_A^U(x_i),\Delta I_B(x_i)=I_B^L(x_i)+I_B^U(x_i)$$

Proposition 4.4

Let A and B be interval valued neutrosophic sets then

1. $0\leq C_N(A,B)\leq 1$
2. $C_N(A,B)=C_N(B,A)$
3. $C_N(A,B)=1$ if A= B i.e $T_A^L(x_i)=T_B^L(x_i)$, $T_A^U(x_i)=T_B^U(x_i)$, $I_A^L(x_i)=I_B^L(x_i)$, $I_A^U(x_i)=I_B^U(x_i)$ and $F_A^L(x_i)=F_B^L(x_i)$, $F_A^U(x_i)=F_B^U(x_i)$ for i=1,2,…., n.

Proof

1. It is obvious that the proposition is true according to the cosine valued.
2. It is obvious that the proposition is true.
3. When A =B, there are $T_A^L(x_i)=T_B^L(x_i)$, $T_A^U(x_i)=T_B^U(x_i)$, $I_A^L(x_i)=I_B^L(x_i)$, $I_A^U(x_i)=I_B^U(x_i)$ and $F_A^L(x_i)=F_B^L(x_i)$, $F_A^U(x_i)=F_B^U(x_i)$ for i=1,2,…., n, So there is $C_N(A,B)=1$.

If we consider the weights of each element x_i, a weighted cosine similarity measure between IVNSs A and B is given as follows:

$$C_{WN}(A,B) = \frac{1}{n}\sum_{i=1}^{n} w_i \frac{\Delta T_A(x_i)\Delta T_B(x_i) + \Delta I_A(x_i)\Delta I_B(x_i) + \Delta F_A(x_i)\Delta F_B(x_i)}{\sqrt{(\Delta T_A(x_i))^2 + (\Delta I_A(x_i))^2 + (\Delta F_A(x_i))^2}\sqrt{(\Delta T_B(x_i))^2 + (\Delta I_B(x_i))^2 + (\Delta F_B(x_i))^2}}$$

where $w_i \in [0,1]$, i =1,2,…,n, and $\sum_{i=1}^{n} w_i = 1$.

If we take $w_i = \frac{1}{n}$, i =1,2,…,n, then there is $C_{WN}(A,B) = C_N(A,B)$.

Definition 4.5

The weighted cosine similarity measure between two IVNSs A and B also satisfies the following properties:

1. $0 \leq C_{WN}(A,B) \leq 1$
2. $C_{WN}(A,B) = C_{WN}(B,A)$
3. $C_{WN}(A,B) = 1$ if A= B i.e $T_A^L(x_i) = T_B^L(x_i)$, $T_A^U(x_i) = T_B^U(x_i)$, $I_A^L(x_i) = I_B^L(x_i)$, $I_A^U(x_i) = I_B^U(x_i)$ and $F_A^L(x_i) = F_B^L(x_i)$, $F_A^U(x_i) = F_B^U(x_i)$ for i=1,2,…., n

Proposition 4.6

Let the distance measure of the angle as d(A,B)= arcos $C_N(A,B)$,then it satisfies the following properties.

1. d(A, B) ≥ 0, if $0 \leq C_N(A,B) \leq 1$
2. d(A, B) = arcos(1) = 0, if $C_N(A,B) = 1$
3. d(A, B) = d(B, A) if $C_N(A,B) = C_N(B,A)$
4. d(A, C)≤ d(A, B) + d(B, C) if $A \subseteq B \subseteq C$ for any interval valued neutrosophic sets C.

Proof

Obviously, d(A,B) satisfies the (1) – (3). In the following, d(A,B) will be proved to satisfy the (4).

For any C = $\{x_i\}$, $A \subseteq B \subseteq C$ since Eq (7) is the sum of terms. Let us consider the distance measure of the angle between vectors:

$d_i(A(x_i), B(x_i))$ = arcos(C_N (A(x_i), B(x_i)),

$d_i(B(x_i), C(x_i))$= arcos(C_N (B(x_i), C(x_i)),

and

$d_i(A(x_i), C(x_i))$= arcos(C_N (A(x_i), C(x_i)), for i=1, 2, .., n,

where

$$C_N(A,B) = \frac{1}{n}\sum_{i=1}^{n}\frac{\Delta T_A(x_i)\Delta T_B(x_i)+\Delta I_A(x_i)\Delta I_B(x_i)+\Delta F_A(x_i)\Delta F_B(x_i)}{\sqrt{(\Delta T_A(x_i))^2+(\Delta I_A(x_i))^2+(\Delta F_A(x_i))^2}\sqrt{(\Delta T_B(x_i))^2+(\Delta I_B(x_i))^2+(\Delta F_B(x_i))^2}}$$

$$C_N(B,C) = \frac{1}{n}\sum_{i=1}^{n}\frac{\Delta T_B(x_i)\Delta T_C(x_i)+\Delta I_B(x_i)\Delta I_C(x_i)+\Delta F_B(x_i)\Delta F_C(x_i)}{\sqrt{(\Delta T_B(x_i))^2+(\Delta I_B(x_i))^2+(\Delta F_B(x_i))^2}\sqrt{(\Delta T_C(x_i))^2+(\Delta I_C(x_i))^2+(\Delta F_C(x_i))^2}}$$

$$C_N(A,C) = \frac{1}{n}\sum_{i=1}^{n}\frac{\Delta T_A(x_i)\Delta T_C(x_i)+\Delta I_A(x_i)\Delta I_C(x_i)+\Delta F_A(x_i)\Delta F_C(x_i)}{\sqrt{(\Delta T_A(x_i))^2+(\Delta I_A(x_i))^2+(\Delta F_A(x_i))^2}\sqrt{(\Delta T_C(x_i))^2+(\Delta I_C(x_i))^2+(\Delta F_C(x_i))^2}}$$

APPLICATIONS OF NEUTROSOPHIC SETS

In this section, the author gave some applications of neutrosophic sets in real life problems.

Multi-Criteria Group Decision-Making Methods Based on Hybrid Score-Accuracy Functions

In a multi-criteria group decision-making problem, let A= $\{A_1, A_2, \ldots, A_m\}$ be a set of alternatives and let C= $\{C_1, C_2, \ldots, C_n\}$ be a set of attributes. Then, the weights of decision makers and attributes are not assigned previously, where the information about the weights of the decision makers is completely unknown and the information about the weights of the attributes is incompletely known in the group decision-making problem. In such a case, we develop two methods based on the hybrid score-accuracy functions for multiple attribute group decision-making problems with unknown weights under single valued neutrosophic and interval neutrosophic environments.

Multi-Criteria Group Decision-Making Method in Single Valued Neutrosophic Setting

In the group decision process under single valued neutrosophic environment, if a group of t decision makers or experts is required in the evaluation process, then the kth decision maker can provide the evaluation information of the alternative A_i (i= 1, 2, …, m) on the attribute C_j (j= 1, 2, …, n), which is represented by the form of a SVNS:

$$A_i^k = \left\{\left\langle C_j, T_{A_i}^k(C_j), I_{A_i}^k(C_j), F_{A_i}^k(C_j)\right\rangle / C_j \in C\right\}.$$

Here,

$$0 \le T_{A_i}^k(C_j) + I_{A_i}^k(C_j) + F_{A_i}^k(C_j) \le 3,$$

$$T_{A_i}^k(C_j) \in [0,1],$$

$$I_{A_i}^k(C_j) \in [0,1],$$

$$F_{A_i}^k(C_j) \in [0,1],$$

for k = 1, 2, …., t, j=1, 2, …., n, i=1, 2, ….,m

For convenience, $a_{ij}^k = \langle T_{ij}^k, I_{ij}^k, F_{ij}^k \rangle$ is denoted as a SVNN in the SVNS. A_i^k (k= 1, 2, …t; i= 1, 2, …, m; j= 1, 2, …, n). Therefore, we can get the k-th single valued neutrosophic decision matrix $D^k = \left(A_{ij}^k\right)_{m\times n}$ (k= 1, 2, …, t).

Then, the group decision-making method is described as follows.

Step 1: Calculate Hybrid Score-Accuracy Matrix.

The hybrid score-accuracy matrix $Y^k = \left(Y_{ij}^k\right)_{m\times n}$ (k= 1, 2, …, t; i= 1, 2, …, m; j= 1, 2, …, n) is obtained from the decision matrix $D^k = \left(A_{ij}^k\right)_{m\times n}$ by the following formula:

$$Y_{ij}^k = \frac{1}{2}\alpha\left(1 + T_{ij}^k - F_{ij}^k\right) + \frac{1}{3}(1-\alpha)\left(2 + T_{ij}^k - I_{ij}^k - F_{ij}^k\right)$$

Step 2: Calculate the Average Matrix.

From the obtained hybrid score-accuracy matrices, the average matrix $Y_{ij}^* = (Y_{ij}^*)_{m\times n}$ (k= 1, 2, …, t; i= 1, 2, …, m; j= 1, 2, …, n) is calculated by $Y_{ij}^* = \frac{1}{t}\sum_{k=1}^{t}\left(Y_{ij}^k\right)$.

The collective correlation coefficient between Y^k (k= 1, 2, …, t) and Y* represents as follows:

$$e_k = \sum_{i=1}^{m} \frac{\sum_{j=1}^{n} Y_{ij}^k Y_{ij}^*}{\sqrt{\sum_{j=1}^{n}\left(Y_{ij}^k\right)^2}\sqrt{\sum_{j=1}^{n}\left(Y_{ij}^*\right)^2}}$$

Step 3: Determination Decision Maker's Weights.

In practical decision-making problems, the decision makers may have personal biases and some individuals may give unduly high or unduly low preference values with respect to their preferred or repugnant objects. In this case, we will assign very low weights to these false or biased opinions. Since the ''mean value'' is the ''distributing center'' of all elements in a set, the average matrix Y* is the maximum compromise among all individual decisions of the group. In mean sense, a hybrid score-accuracy matrix Y^k is closer to the average one Y*. Then, the preference value (hybrid score-accuracy value) of the k-th decision maker is closer to the average value and his/her evaluation is more reasonable and more important, thus the weight of the k-th decision maker is bigger. Hence, a weight model for decision makers can be defined as:

$$\lambda_k = \frac{e_k}{\sum_{k=1}^{t} e_k}, \text{ where } 0 \leq \lambda_k \leq 1, \sum_{k=1}^{t} \lambda_k = 1 \text{ for k=1, 2, ….,t.}$$

Step 4: Calculate Collective Hybrid Score-Accuracy Matrix.

For the weight vector $\lambda = \left(\lambda_1, \lambda_2, \cdots, \lambda_k\right)^T$ of decision makers obtained from eqation.(6), we accumulate all individual hybrid score-accuracy matrices of $Y^k = \left(Y_{ij}^k\right)_{m \times n}$ (k= 1, 2, …, t; i= 1, 2, …, m; j= 1, 2, …, n) into a collective hybrid score-accuracy matrix $Y = \left(Y_{ij}\right)_{m \times n}$ by the following formula:

$$Y_{ij} = \sum_{k=1}^{t} \lambda_k Y_{ij}^k$$

Step 5: Weight Model for Attributes.

For a specific decision problem, the weights of the attributes can be given in advance by a partially known subset corresponding to the weight information of the attributes, which is denoted by W. Reasonable weight values of the attributes should make the overall averaging value of all alternatives as large as possible because they can enhance the obvious differences and identification of various alternatives under the attributes to easily rank the alternatives. To determine the weight vector of the attributes Ye introduced the following optimization model:

$$\max W = \frac{1}{m} \sum_{i=1}^{m} \sum_{j=1}^{n} W_j Y_{ij}$$

Subject to,

$$\sum_{j=1}^{n} W_j = 1$$

where $W_j > 0$

This is a linear programming problem, which can be easily solved to determine the weight vector of the attributes $W = (W_1, W_2, \ldots, W_n)^T$

Step 6: Ranking Alternatives.

To rank alternatives, we can sum all values in each row of the collective hybrid score-accuracy matrix corresponding to the attribute weights by the overall weighted hybrid score-accuracy value of each alternative Ai (i= 1, 2, …, m):

$$M(A_i) = \sum_{j=1}^{n} W_j Y_{ij}$$

According to the overall hybrid score-accuracy values of $M(A_i)$ (i= 1, 2, …, m), we can rank alternatives Ai (i= 1, 2, …, m) in descending order and choose the best one.

Step 7: End.

Example of Teacher Recruitment Process

Suppose that a university is going to recruit in the post of an assistant professor for a particular subject.. After initial screening, five candidates (i.e. alternatives) A_1, A_2, A_3, A_4, A_5 remain for further evaluation. A committee of four decision makers or experts, D_1, D_2, D_3, D_4 has been formed to conduct the interview and select the most appropriate candidate. Eight criteria obtained from expert opinions, namely, academic performances (C_1), subject knowledge (C_2), teaching aptitude (C_3), research- experiences (C_4), leadership quality (C_5), personality (C_6), management capacity (C_7) and values (C_8) are considered for recruitment criteria. If four experts are required in the evaluation process, then the five possible alternatives A_i (i= 1, 2, 3, 4, 5) are evaluated by the form of SVNNs under the above eight attributes on the fuzzy concept "excellence". Thus the four single valued neutrosophic decision matrices can be obtained from the four experts and expressed, respectively, as shown in Tables 1, 2, 3, and 4.

Thus, we use the proposed method for single valued neutrosophic group decision-making to get the most suitable teacher. We take α= 0.5 for demonstrating the computing procedure of the proposed method. For the above four decision matrices, the following hybrid score-accuracy matrices are obtained by equation (3) (see Tables 5, 6, 7, 8).

From the hybrid score-accuracy matrices shown in Tables 5-8, by using equation (4) we can yield the average matrix Y* (see Table 9).

Table 1. Single valued neutrosophic decision matrix

$D_1=$

.	C_1	C_2	C_3	C_4	C_5	C_6	C_7	C_8
A_1	$\langle .8, .1, .1 \rangle$	$\langle .8, .1, .1 \rangle$	$\langle .7, .2, .1 \rangle$	$\langle .7, .2, .2 \rangle$	$\langle .7, .4, .1 \rangle$	$\langle .7, .4, .2 \rangle$	$\langle .7, .3, .1 \rangle$	$\langle .7, .4, .3 \rangle$
A_2	$\langle .8, .2, .2 \rangle$	$\langle .8, .2, .1 \rangle$	$\langle .7, .3, .2 \rangle$	$\langle .7, .3, .3 \rangle$	$\langle .7, .3, .2 \rangle$	$\langle .6, .4, .2 \rangle$	$\langle .7, .2, .2 \rangle$	$\langle .7, .3, .4 \rangle$
A_3	$\langle .8, .1, .2 \rangle$	$\langle .8, .3, .2 \rangle$	$\langle .7, .4, .3 \rangle$	$\langle .7, .3, .1 \rangle$	$\langle .7, .2, .3 \rangle$	$\langle .6, .3, .3 \rangle$	$\langle .7, .1, .3 \rangle$	$\langle .7, .3, .3 \rangle$
A_4	$\langle .8, .1, .0 \rangle$	$\langle .8, .2, .3 \rangle$	$\langle .7, .3, .4 \rangle$	$\langle .7, .1, .2 \rangle$	$\langle .7, .2, .2 \rangle$	$\langle .7, .2, .2 \rangle$	$\langle .7, .2, .3 \rangle$	$\langle .7, .2, .4 \rangle$
A_5	$\langle .8, .2, .2 \rangle$	$\langle .8, .3, .3 \rangle$	$\langle .7, .3, .4 \rangle$	$\langle .7, .2, .2 \rangle$	$\langle .7, .1, .3 \rangle$	$\langle .7, .1, .1 \rangle$	$\langle .7, .1, .2 \rangle$	$\langle .7, .1, .3 \rangle$

Table 2. Single valued neutrosophic decision matrix

	.	C_1	C_2	C_3	C_4	C_5	C_6	C_7	C_8
	A_1	$\langle .8, .2,.1\rangle$	$\langle .8,.1,.1\rangle$	$\langle .7,.2,.2\rangle$	$\langle .7,.1,.2\rangle$	$\langle .7,.4,.2\rangle$	$\langle .7,.4,.2\rangle$	$\langle .7,.3,.2\rangle$	$\langle .7,.3,.3\rangle$
	A_2	$\langle .8,.2,.2\rangle$	$\langle .8,.2,.2\rangle$	$\langle .7,.3,.3\rangle$	$\langle .7,.3,.3\rangle$	$\langle .7,.2,.2\rangle$	$\langle .6,.4,.3\rangle$	$\langle .7,.3,.2\rangle$	$\langle .7,.4,.4\rangle$
$D_2=$	A_3	$\langle .8,.2,.2\rangle$	$\langle .8,.3,.3\rangle$	$\langle .7,.3,.3\rangle$	$\langle .7,.3,.2\rangle$	$\langle .7,.3,.3\rangle$	$\langle .6,.3,.3\rangle$	$\langle .7,.2,.3\rangle$	$\langle .7,.2,.3\rangle$
	A_4	$\langle .8,.1,.0\rangle$	$\langle .8,.2,.2\rangle$	$\langle .7,.3,.4\rangle$	$\langle .7,.1,.2\rangle$	$\langle .7,.3,.2\rangle$	$\langle .7,.2,.2\rangle$	$\langle .7,.3,.3\rangle$	$\langle .7,.3,.4\rangle$
	A_5	$\langle .8,.1,.2\rangle$	$\langle .8,.2,.3\rangle$	$\langle .7,.3,.3\rangle$	$\langle .7,.2,.2\rangle$	$\langle .7,.2,.3\rangle$	$\langle .7,.1,.2\rangle$	$\langle .7,.2,.2\rangle$	$\langle .7,.2,.3\rangle$

Table 3. Single valued neutrosophic decision matrix

	.	C_1	C_2	C_3	C_4	C_5	C_6	C_7	C_8
	A_1	$\langle .8, .1,.0\rangle$	$\langle .8,.1,.1\rangle$	$\langle .7,.2,.2\rangle$	$\langle .7,.2,.1\rangle$	$\langle .7,.3,.1\rangle$	$\langle .7,.3,.2\rangle$	$\langle .7,.3,.2\rangle$	$\langle .7,.3,.3\rangle$
	A_2	$\langle .8,.2,.1\rangle$	$\langle .8,.2,.1\rangle$	$\langle .7,.3,.2\rangle$	$\langle .7,.2,.3\rangle$	$\langle .7,.3,.2\rangle$	$\langle .6,.4,.4\rangle$	$\langle .7,.3,.2\rangle$	$\langle .7,.3,.3\rangle$
$D_3=$	A_3	$\langle .8,.2,.2\rangle$	$\langle .8,.2,.2\rangle$	$\langle .7,.3,.3\rangle$	$\langle .7,.3,.2\rangle$	$\langle .7,.2,.2\rangle$	$\langle .6,.2,.3\rangle$	$\langle .7,.2,.3\rangle$	$\langle .7,.3,.4\rangle$
	A_4	$\langle .8,.1,.0\rangle$	$\langle .8,.2,.2\rangle$	$\langle .7,.3,.2\rangle$	$\langle .7,.1,.2\rangle$	$\langle .7,.2,.2\rangle$	$\langle .7,.2,.2\rangle$	$\langle .7,.2,.3\rangle$	$\langle .7,.2,.3\rangle$
	A_5	$\langle .8,.1,.2\rangle$	$\langle .8,.2,.3\rangle$	$\langle .7,.2,.4\rangle$	$\langle .7,.1,.2\rangle$	$\langle .7,.1,.3\rangle$	$\langle .7,.1,.2\rangle$	$\langle .7,.2,.2\rangle$	$\langle .7,.2,.3\rangle$

Table 4. Single valued neutrosophic decision matrix

	.	C_1	C_2	C_3	C_4	C_5	C_6	C_7	C_8
	A_1	$\langle .8, .2,.1\rangle$	$\langle .8,.2,.1\rangle$	$\langle .7,.2,.1\rangle$	$\langle .7,.2,.2\rangle$	$\langle .7,.3,.1\rangle$	$\langle .7,.2,.2\rangle$	$\langle .7,.2,.1\rangle$	$\langle .7,.4,.3\rangle$
	A_2	$\langle .8,.2,.0\rangle$	$\langle .8,.2,.1\rangle$	$\langle .7,.3,.2\rangle$	$\langle .7,.1,.3\rangle$	$\langle .7,.3,.2\rangle$	$\langle .6,.4,.3\rangle$	$\langle .7,.2,.2\rangle$	$\langle .7,.3,.3\rangle$
$D_4=$	A_3	$\langle .8,.1,.2\rangle$	$\langle .8,.2,.2\rangle$	$\langle .7,.3,.3\rangle$	$\langle .7,.3,.2\rangle$	$\langle .7,.2,.2\rangle$	$\langle .6,.3,.2\rangle$	$\langle .7,.3,.3\rangle$	$\langle .7,.3,.3\rangle$
	A_4	$\langle .8,.1,.0\rangle$	$\langle .8,.2,.3\rangle$	$\langle .7,.3,.3\rangle$	$\langle .7,.1,.2\rangle$	$\langle .7,.2,.2\rangle$	$\langle .7,.2,.2\rangle$	$\langle .7,.2,.3\rangle$	$\langle .7,.2,.4\rangle$
	A_5	$\langle .8,.2,.2\rangle$	$\langle .8,.3,.0\rangle$	$\langle .7,.3,.3\rangle$	$\langle .7,.2,.2\rangle$	$\langle .7,.1,.3\rangle$	$\langle .7,.1,.1\rangle$	$\langle .7,.1,.2\rangle$	$\langle .7,.2,.3\rangle$

Table 5. Hybrid score accuracy matrix for D_1

$Y_1=$

.	C_1	C_2	C_3	C_4	C_5	C_6	C_7	C_8
A_1	1.7667	1.7167	1.6000	1.5167	1.5333	1.4500	1.5667	1.3667
A_2	1.6000	1.6833	1.4833	1.4000	1.4833	1.3667	1.5167	1.3167
A_3	1.6333	1.6500	1.3667	1.5667	1.4333	1.3167	1.4667	1.4000
A_4	1.8000	1.5167	1.3167	1.5500	1.5167	1.5167	1.4333	1.3500
A_5	1.6000	1.4833	1.3167	1.5167	1.4667	1.6333	1.5500	1.4667

Table 6. Hybrid score accuracy matrix for D_2

$Y_2=$

.	C_1	C_2	C_3	C_4	C_5	C_6	C_7	C_8
A_1	1.6833	1.7167	1.5167	1.5500	1.4500	1.4500	1.4833	1.4000
A_2	1.6000	1.6000	1.4000	1.4000	1.5167	1.2833	1.4833	1.2833
A_3	1.6000	1.4833	1.4000	1.4833	1.4000	1.3167	1.4333	1.4333
A_4	1.8000	1.6000	1.3167	1.5500	1.4833	1.5167	1.4000	1.3167
A_5	1.6333	1.5167	1.4000	1.5167	1.4333	1.5500	1.5167	1.4333

Table 7. Hybrid score accuracy matrix for D_3

$Y_3=$

.	C_1	C_2	C_3	C_4	C_5	C_6	C_7	C_8
A_1	1.8000	1.7167	1.5167	1.6000	1.5667	1.4833	1.4833	1.4000
A_2	1.6833	1.6833	1.4833	1.4333	1.4833	1.2000	1.4833	1.4000
A_3	1.6000	1.6000	1.4000	1.4833	1.5167	1.3500	1.4333	1.3167
A_4	1.8000	1.6000	1.4833	1.5500	1.5167	1.5167	1.4333	1.4333
A_5	1.6333	1.5167	1.3500	1.5500	1.4667	1.5500	1.5167	1.4333

Table 8. Hybrid score accuracy matrix for D_4

$Y_4=$

.	C_1	C_2	C_3	C_4	C_5	C_6	C_7	C_8
A_1	1.6833	1.6833	1.6000	1.5167	1.5667	1.5167	1.6000	1.3667
A_2	1.7333	1.6833	1.4833	1.4667	1.4833	1.2833	1.5167	1.4000
A_3	1.6333	1.6000	1.4000	1.4833	1.5167	1.4000	1.4000	1.4000
A_4	1.8000	1.5167	1.4000	1.5500	1.5167	1.5167	1.4333	1.3500
A_5	1.6000	1.7333	1.4000	1.5167	1.4667	1.6333	1.5500	1.4333

Table 9. The average matrix

$Y^*=$

.	C_1	C_2	C_3	C_4	C_5	C_6	C_7	C_8
A_1	1.7208	1.7084	1.5584	1.5459	1.5292	1.4750	1.5333	1.3834
A_2	1.6417	1.6500	1.4625	1.4375	1.4917	1.2833	1.5000	1.3625
A_3	1.6167	1.5833	1.3917	1.5042	1.4792	1.3459	1.4333	1.3875
A_4	1.8000	1.5584	1.3792	1.5500	1.5084	1.5167	1.4250	1.3625
A_5	1.6167	1.5625	1.3667	1.3450	1.4584	1.5917	1.5334	1.4417

Table 10. Collective hybrid score accuracy- matrix

$Y=$

.	C_1	C_2	C_3	C_4	C_5	C_6	C_7	C_8
A_1	1.7209	1.7085	1.5584	1.5459	1.5292	1.4751	1.5334	1.3834
A_2	1.6417	1.6500	1.4624	1.4375	1.4918	1.2833	1.5000	1.3624
A_3	1.6168	1.5834	1.3917	1.5043	1.4792	1.3458	1.4332	1.3875
A_4	1.8001	1.5584	1.3793	1.5500	1.5085	1.5167	1.4250	1.3626
A_5	1.6167	1.5626	1.3667	1.3451	1.4584	1.5918	1.5334	1.4417

From the equations. (5) and (6), we determine the weights of the three decision makers as follows: λ_1=0.2505, λ_2=0.2510, λ_3=0.2491, λ_3=0.2494.

Hence, the hybrid score-accuracy values of the different decision makers' evaluations are aggregated [48] by equation (7) and the following collective hybrid score-accuracy matrix can be obtained as shown in Table 10.

Assume that the information about attribute weights is incompletely known weight vectors,

$0.1 \leq W_1 \leq 0.2$, $0.1 \leq W_2 \leq 0.2$,

$0.1 \leq W_3 \leq 0.2$, $0.1 \leq W_4 \leq 0.2$, $0.1 \leq W_5 \leq 0.2$,

$0.1 \leq W_6 \leq 0.2$, $0.1 \leq W_7 \leq 0.2$, $0.1 \leq W_8 \leq 0.2$

given by the decision makers,

By using the linear programming model (8), we obtain the weight vector of the attributes as:

$W=[0.2, 0.2, 0.1, 0.1, 0.1, 0.1, 0.1, 0.1]^T$.

We can calculate the overall hybrid score-accuracy values $M(A_i)$ (i=1, 2, 3, 4, 5):

$M(A_1)$=1.58842,

$M(A_2)=1.51208$,

$M(A_3)=1.49421$,

$M(A_4)=1.54591$,

$M(A_5)=1.50957$.

According to the above values of $M(A_i)$ (i= 1, 2, 3, 4, 5), the ranking order of the alternatives is

$A_1 > A_4 > A_2 > A_5 > A_3$.

Then, the alternative A_1 is the best teacher.

Application of Cosine Similarity Measure for Interval Valued Neutrosophic Numbers to Pattern Recognition

In order to demonstrate the application of the proposed cosine similarity measure for interval valued neutrosophic numbers to pattern recognition, we discuss the medical diagnosis problem as follows:

For example the patient reported temperature claiming that the patient has temperature between 0.5 and 0.7 severity /certainty, some how it is between 0.2 and 0.4 indeterminable if temperature is cause or the effect of his current disease. And it between 0.1 and 0.2 sure that temperature has no relation with his main disease.

This piece of information about one patient and one symptom may be written as:

(patient, Temperature) = $\langle[0.5, 0.7], [0.2, 0.4], [0.1, 0.2]\rangle$,

(patient, Headache) = $\langle[0.2, 0.3], [0.3, 0.5], [0.3, 0.6]\rangle$,

(patient, Cough) = $\langle[0.4, 0.5], [0.6, 0.7], [0.3, 0.4]\rangle$

Then,

$$P = \left\{ \begin{matrix} \langle x_1, [0.5,\ 0.7], [0.2\ , 0.4], [0.1,\ 0.2] \rangle, \\ \langle x_2, [0.2,\ 0.3], [0.3,\ 0.5], [0.3,\ 0.6] \rangle, \\ \langle x_3, [0.4,\ 0.5], [0.6\ , 0.7], [0.3,\ 0.4] \rangle \end{matrix} \right\}.$$

And each diagnosis A_i (i=1, 2, 3) can also be represented by interval valued neutrosophic numbers with respect to all the symptoms as follows:

$$A_1 = \left\{ \begin{matrix} \langle x_1, [0.5, 0.6], [0.2, 0.3], [0.4, 0.5] \rangle, \\ \langle x_2, [0.2\ , 0.6\ ], [0.3, 0.4\ ], [0.6, 0.7] \rangle, \\ \langle x_3, [0.1, 0.2\ ], [0.3, 0.6\ ], [0.7, 0.8] \rangle \end{matrix} \right\},$$

$$A_2 = \left\{ \begin{matrix} \langle x_1, [0.4, 0.5], [0.3, 0.4], [0.5, 0.6] \rangle, \\ \langle x_2, [0.3, 0.5\ ], [0.4, 0.6], [0.2, 0.4] \rangle, \\ \langle x_3, [0.3, 0.6\ ], [0.1, 0.2], [0.5, 0.6] \rangle \end{matrix} \right\},$$

$$A_3 = \left\{ \begin{matrix} \langle x_1, [0.6, 0.8], [0.4, 0.5], [0.3, 0.4] \rangle, \\ \langle x_2, [0.3, 0.7\ ], [0.2, 0.3], [0.4, 0.7] \rangle, \\ \langle x_3, [0.3, 0.5\ ], [0.4, 0.7\ ], [0.2, 0.6] \rangle \end{matrix} \right\}.$$

Our aim is to classify the pattern P in one of the classes A_1, A_2, A_3. According to the recognition principle of maximum degree of similarity measure between interval valued neutrosophic numbers, the process of diagnosis A_k to patient P is derived according to k = arg Max$\{C_N(A_i,P)\}$.

We can compute the cosine similarity between A_i (i=1, 2, 3) and P as follows;

$C_N(A_1,P)$ =0.8988,

$C_N(A_2,P)$=0.8560,

$C_N(A_3,P)$ =0.9654

Then, we can assign the patient to diagnosis A_3 (Typoid) according to recognition of principal.

CONCLUSION

Neutrosophic set is a mathematical framework which handles uncertain, incomplete, inconsistent, false, indeterminate information. Several hybrid structures have been proposed which based on neutrosophic sets. In this chapter, the authors presented the study on neutrosophic sets which is a generalization of fuzzy sets and intuitionistic fuzzy sets. Some set theoretic operations and properties are studied in this chapter. The authors also studied the hybrid structures associated with neutrosophic sets such as neutrosophic crisp sets and their related properties. Further, interval valued neutrosophic sets have been presented under discussion in this chapter. At the end, some applications of neutrosophic sets presented to show the applicability of neutrosophic sets in the real life problems.

REFERENCES

Atanassov, K. (1986). Intuitionistic fuzzy sets. *Fuzzy Sets and Systems*, *20*(1), 87–96. doi:10.1016/S0165-0114(86)80034-3

Bhowmik, M., & Pal, M. (2009). Intuitionistic neutrosophic set. *Journal of Information and Computing Science*, *2*(4), 142–152.

Broumi, S., & Smarandache, F. (2014). On Neutrosophic Implications. *Neutrosophic Sets and Systems*, *2*, 9–17.

Broumi, S., & Smarandache, F. (2015). Cosine Similarity Meas-ure of Interval Valued Neutrosophic Set. *Neutrosophic Sets and Systems*, *05*, 15–20.

Mondal, K., & Pramanik, S. (2015). Multi-criteria Group Decision Making Approach for Teacher Recruitment in Higher Education under Simplified Neutrosophic Environment. *Neutrosophic Sets and Systems*, *06*, 28–34.

Salama, A. A. (2015). Basic Structure of Some Classes of Neutrosophic Crisp Nearly Open Sets and Possile Application to GIS Topology. *Neutrosophic Sets and Systems*, *7*, 18–22.

Salama, A. A., & Smarandache, F. (2015). Neutrosophic Crisp Set Theory. *Neutrosophic Sets and Systems*, *05*, 27–35.

Smarandache, F. (1998). *Neutrosophy*. Rehoboth: Neutrosophic Probability, Set, and Logic, Amer. Res. Press.

Smarandache, F. (1999). *A Unifying Field in Logics. Neutrosophy: Neutrosophic Probability, Set and Logic*. Rehoboth: American Research Press.

Smarandache, F. (2005). Neutrosophic set, a generalisation of the intuitionistic fuzzy sets. *International Journal of Pure and Applied Mathematics*, *24*, 287–297.

Turksen, I. (1986). Interval valued fuzzy sets based on normal forms. *Fuzzy Sets and Systems*, *20*(2), 191–210. doi:10.1016/0165-0114(86)90077-1

Zadeh, L. A. (1965). Fuzzy sets. *Information and Control*, *8*(3), 338–353. doi:10.1016/S0019-9958(65)90241-X

Zadeh, L. A. (1975). The concept of a linguistic variable and its application to approximate reasoning-Part I. *Information Sciences*, *7*(3), 199–249. doi:10.1016/0020-0255(75)90036-5

KEY TERMS AND DEFINITIONS

Cosine Similarity Measure: Given two vectors of attributes, X= $(x_1, x_2, \ldots, x_n)$ and Y=$(y_1, y_2, \ldots, y_n)$, the cosine similarity, cosθ, is represented using a dot product and magnitude as Cosθ= $\frac{\sum_{i=}^{n} x_i y_i}{\sqrt{\sum_{i=}^{n} x_i^2}\sqrt{\sum_{i=}^{n} y_i^2}}$.

In vector space, a cosine similarity measure between two fuzzy set $\mu_A(x_i)$ and $\mu_B(x_i)$defined as follows:

$$C_F(A,B) = \frac{\sum_{i=}^{n} \mu_A(x_i)\mu_B(x_i)}{\sqrt{\sum_{i=}^{n} \mu_A(x_i)^2}\sqrt{\sum_{i=}^{n} \mu_B(x_i)^2}}$$

. The cosine of the angle between the vectors is within the values between 0 and 1. In 2-D vector space, cosine similarity measure between IFS as follows:

$$C_{IFS}(A,B) = \frac{\sum_{i=}^{n} \mu_A(x_i)\mu_B(x_i) + \nu_A(x_i)\nu_B(x_i)}{\sqrt{\sum_{i=}^{n} \mu_A(x_i)^2 + \nu_A(x_i)^2}\sqrt{\sum_{i=}^{n} \mu_B(x_i)^2 + v_B(x_i)^2}}.$$

Fuzzy Set: Let X be a non-empty collection of objects denoted by x. Then a fuzzy set A in X is a set of ordered pairs having the form $A = \{(x, \mu_A(x)) : x \in X\}$, where the function μ_A: $X \to [0,1]$ is called the membership function or grade of membership (also degree of compatibility or degree of truth) of x in A. The interval M = [0,1] is called membership space.

Interval Valued Fuzzy Set: Let D[0, 1] be the set of closed sub-intervals of the interval [0, 1]. An *interval-valued fuzzy set* in X, $X \neq \phi$ and Card(X) = n, is an expression A given by $A = \{(x, M_A(x)) : x \in X\}$, where M_A: $X \to D[0,1]$.

Intuitionistic Fuzzy Set: Let X be a non-empty set. Then an intuitionistic fuzzy set A is a set having the form $A=\{(x, \mu_A(x), \gamma_A(x)): x \in X\}$ where the functions μ_A: $X \to [0,1]$ and γ_A: $X \to [0,1]$ represents the degree ofmembership and the degree of non-membership respectively of each element $x \in X$ and $0 \leq \mu_A(x)+\gamma_A(x) \leq 1$ for each $x \in X$.

s-Norm: The function *s*: $[0,1]\times[0,1]\to[0,1]$ is called an *s-norm* if it satisfies the following four axioms: Axiom 1. $s(x,y)=s(y,x)$ (commutative condition). Axiom 2. s(s(x, y), z) = s(x, s(y, z)) (associative condition). Axiom 3. If $x_1 \geq x_2$ and $y_1 \geq y_2$, then $s(x_1,y_1) \geq s(x_2,y_2)$ (nondecreasing condition). Axiom 4. s(1, 1) = 1, s(x, 0) = s(0, x) = x (boundary condition).

t-Norm: The function *t*: $[0,1]\times[0,1]\to[0,1]$ is called a *t-norm* if it satisfies the following four axioms: Axiom t1. t(x, y) = t(y, x) (commutative condition). Axiom t2. t(t(x, y), z) = t(x, t(y, z)) (associative condition). Axiom t3. If $x_1 \geq x_2$ and $y_1 \geq y_2$, then $t(x_1,y_1) \geq t(x_2,y_2)$ (nondecreasing condition). Axiom t4 t(x, 1) = x (boundary condition).

Chapter 3
Interval-Valued Intuitionistic Fuzzy Partition Matrices

Amal Kumar Adak
Jafuly Deshpran High School, India

ABSTRACT

If in an interval-valued intuitionistic fuzzy matrix each element is again a smaller interval-valued intuitionistic fuzzy matrix then the interval-valued intuitionistic fuzzy matrix is called interval-valued intuitionistic fuzzy partion matrix (IVIFPMs). In this paper, the concept of interval-valued intuitionistic fuzzy partion matrices (IVIFPMs) are introduced and defined different types of interval-valued intuitionistic fuzzy partion matrices (IVIFPMs). The operations like direct sum, Kronecker sum, Kronecker product of interval-valued intuitionistic fuzzy matrices are presented and shown that their resultant matrices are also interval-valued intuitionistic fuzzy partion matrices (IVIFPMs).

INTRODUCTION

Atanassov (1986) introduced the concept of intuitionistic fuzzy sets (IFSs), which is a generalization of fuzzy subsets. Later on much research works have done with this concept by Atanasov and others. The term fuzzy matrix has important role in fuzzy algebra. For definition of fuzzy matrix we follow the definition of Duobois and Prade (1980), i.e. a matrix with fuzzy member as its element. This class of fuzzy matrices consist of applicable matrices which can model uncertain aspects and the works on them are limited. Some of the most interesting works on these matrices done by Tan(2005). Xin (1992). Thomson (1977) defined convergence of a square fuzzy matrix. Pal and Shyamal (2002) introduced two new operators on fuzzy matrices and shown several properties of them. By the concept of IFSs, first time Pal (2001) introduced intuitionistic fuzzy determinant. Latter on Pal *et al.* (2002) introduced intuitionistic fuzzy matrices (IFMs) and distance between intuitionistic fuzzy matrices. Bhowmik and Pal (2008) presented some results on intuitionistic fuzzy matrices, intuitionistic circulant fuzzy matrices and generalized intuitionistic fuzzy matrices. Adak *et al.* investigated some interesting properties of interval-valued intuitionistic fuzzy sets and matrices (2011, 2012)

DOI: 10.4018/978-1-5225-0914-1.ch003

The general rectangular or square array of the numbers are known as matrix and if the elements are interval-valued intuitionistic fuzzy then the matrix is called interval-valued intuitionistic fuzzy matrix. If we delete some rows or some columns or both or neither then the interval-valued intuitionistic fuzzy matrix is called interval-valued intuitionistic fuzzy submatrix. The concept of non-empty subset in set theory and the principle of combination are used for the construction and calculation of the number interval-valued intuitionistic fuzzy submatrices of a given interval-valued intuitionistic fuzzy matrix.

Again, if an interval-valued intuitionistic fuzzy matrix is divided or partitioned into smaller interval-valued intuitionistic fuzzy matrices called cells or blocks with consecutive rows and columns by drawing dotted horizontal lines of full width between rows and vertical lines of full height between columns, then the interval-valued intuitionistic fuzzy matrix is called interval-valued intuitionistic fuzzy block matrix. There are lots of advantages noted in partitioning an interval-valued intuitionistic fuzzy matrix A into blocks or cells. It simplifies the writing or printing of an IFM A in compact form and thus save space. It exhibits some smaller structure of A. It also simplifies computation.

The structure of this chapter is organized as follows. In Section 2, the preliminaries and some definitions are given. In Section 3, different kinds of interval-valued intuitionistic fuzzy submatrices and block matrices are given. Section 4 deals with direct sum, Kronecker sum and Kronecker product of interval-valued intuitionistic fuzzy block matrix. Finally, at the end of this paper a conclusion is given.

PRELIMINARIES

In this section, the concept of interval arithmetics are recalled. Let $[I]$ be the set of all closed subintervals of the interval [0,1]. An interval on $[I]$, say $\overline{a}$, is a closed subinterval of $[I]$ i.e., $\overline{a} = [a^-, a^+]$ where a^- and a^+ are lower and upper limits of $\overline{a}$ respectively and satisfy the condition $0 \leq a^- \leq a^+ \leq 1$. For any two interval $\overline{a}$ and $\overline{b}$ where $\overline{a} = [a^-, a^+]$ and $\overline{b} = [b^-, b^+]$ then:

1. $\overline{a} = \overline{b} \Leftrightarrow a^- = b^-, a^+ = b^+$,
2. $\overline{a} \leq \overline{b} \Leftrightarrow a^- \leq b^-, a^+ \leq b^+$ and
3. $\overline{a} < \overline{b} \Leftrightarrow a^- < b^-, a^+ < b^+$ and $\overline{a} \neq \overline{b}$.

Definition (Interval-Valued Intuitionistic Fuzzy Sets (IVIFSs)): An IVIFS A over X (universe of discourse) is an object having the form

$$A = \{\langle x, M_A(x), N_A(x)\rangle \mid x \in X\},$$

where $M_A(x): X \to [I]$ and $N_A(x): X \to [I]$.

The intervals $M_A(x)$ and $N_A(x)$ denote the intervals of the degree of membership and degree of non-membership of the element x to the set A, where

$$M_A(x) = [M_{AL}(x), M_{AU}(x)]$$

and

$$N_A(x) = [N_{AL}(x), N_{AU}(x)],$$

for all $x \in X$, with the condition

$$0 \le M_{AU}(x) + N_{AU}(x) \le 1.$$

For simplicity, we denote

$$A = \{\langle x, [A^-(x), A^+(x)], [B^-(x), B^+(x)] \rangle \mid x \in X\}.$$

Definition (Intuitionistic Fuzzy Matrix (IFM)): An intuitionistic fuzzy matrix (IFM) of order $m \times n$ is defined as $A = [\langle a_{ij\mu}, a_{ij\nu} \rangle]$ where $a_{ij\mu}$ and $a_{ij\nu}$ are the membership and non-membership values of the *ij*-th element in *A* satisfying the condition $0 \le a_{ij\mu} + a_{ij\nu} \le 1$ for all *i*, *j*.

Definition (Interval-Valued Intuitionistic Fuzzy Matrix (IVIFM)): An Interval-valued intuitionistic fuzzy matrix (IVIFM) of order $m \times n$ is denoted by *A* and is defined by

$$A = \left(\left\langle x_{ij}, M_{A_{ij}}, N_{A_{ij}} \right\rangle \right)_{m \times n},$$

where

$$M_{A_{ij}}(x) : x \to [I]$$

and

$$N_{A_{ij}}(x) : x \to [I].$$

The interval $M_{A_{ij}} = [a_{ij\mu L}, a_{ij\mu U}]$, where $a_{ij\mu L}$ and $a_{ij\mu U}$ are lower and upper membership values of the *ij*-th element of IVIFM *A* respectively. Similarly, the interval $N_{A_{ij}} = [a_{ij\nu L}, a_{ij\nu U}]$, where $a_{ij\nu L}$ and $a_{ij\nu U}$ are lower and upper non-membership values of the *ij*-th element of IVIFM *A* respectively.

Therefore, an IVIFM *A* can be written as

$$A = (\langle x_{ij}, [a_{ij\mu L} + a_{ij\mu U}], [a_{ij\nu L} + a_{ij\nu U}] \rangle),$$

satisfying the condition $0 \le a_{ij\mu U} + a_{ij\nu U} \le 1$.

In short, an IVIFM *A* is denoted as

$$A = \left(\left\langle [a_{ij\mu L} + a_{ij\mu U}], [a_{ij\nu L} + a_{ij\nu U}] \right\rangle\right),$$

satisfying the condition $0 \leq a_{ij\mu U} + a_{ij\nu U} \leq 1$.

Some Operations of IVIFMs

Here, we represent some important operations of IVIFMs, which are used to prove several results of this chapter.

Let A and B be two IVIFMs, such that

$$A = \left(\left\langle [a_{ij\mu L} + a_{ij\mu U}], [a_{ij\nu L} + a_{ij\nu U}] \right\rangle\right)$$

and

$$B = \left(\left\langle [b_{ij\mu L} + b_{ij\mu U}], [b_{ij\nu L} + b_{ij\nu U}] \right\rangle\right).$$

Then,

1. $A + B = \left(\left\langle \left[\max\{M_{AL_{ij}}, M_{BL_{ij}}\}, \max\{M_{AU_{ij}}, M_{BU_{ij}}\}\right], \left[\min\{N_{AL_{ij}}, N_{BL_{ij}}\}, \min\{N_{AU_{ij}}, N_{BU_{ij}}\}\right] \right\rangle\right).$
2. $A \bullet B = \left(\left\langle \left[\min\{M_{AL_{ij}}, M_{BL_{ij}}\}, \min\{M_{AU_{ij}}, M_{BU_{ij}}\}\right], \left[\max\{N_{AL_{ij}}, N_{BL_{ij}}\}, \max\{N_{AU_{ij}}, N_{BU_{ij}}\}\right] \right\rangle\right).$

$$AB = \left(\left\langle \left[\max_k\left\{\min\left\{M_{AL_{ik}}, M_{BL_{kj}}\right\}\right\}, \max_k\left\{\min\left\{M_{AU_{ik}}, M_{BU_{kj}}\right\}\right\}\right], \right.\right.$$
$$\left.\left. \left[\min_k\left\{\max\left\{N_{AL_{ik}}, N_{BL_{kj}}\right\}\right\}, \min_k\left\{\max\left\{N_{AU_{ik}}, N_{BU_{kj}}\right\}\right\}\right] \right\rangle\right)$$
$$= (\langle \sum_{k=1}^{n} \min\{M_{A_{ik}}, M_{B_{kj}}\}, \prod_{k=1}^{n} \max\{N_{A_{ik}}, N_{B_{kj}}\} \rangle).$$

The product AB is defined if and only if the number of columns of A is the same as the number of rows B, then A and B are said to be conformable for multiplication.

DIFFERENT KINDS OF INTERVAL-VALUED INTUITIONISTIC FUZZY SUBMATRIX AND PARTION MATRIX

In this section, the concept of interval-valued intuitionistic fuzzy submatrix and block matrices are introduced and presented some properties of them. We begin this section with some definitions:

Definition (Interval-Valued Intuitionistic Fuzzy Submatrix): An interval-valued intuitionistic fuzzy submatrix of an IVIFM of order ≥1 is obtained by deleting some rows or some columns or both (not necessarily consecutive) or neither.

- The IVIFM itself is its interval-valued intuitionistic fuzzy submatrix.

Definition (Interval-Valued Intuitionistic Fuzzy Principal Submatrix): The interval-valued intuitionistic fuzzy principal submatrix of order $(n–r)$ obtained by deleting r rows and columns of a square IVIFM of order n, is called interval-valued intuitionistic fuzzy principal submatrix.

The first order principal interval-valued intuitionistic fuzzy submatrices obtained from the following third order IVIFM

$$\begin{bmatrix} \langle[a_{11\mu L}, a_{11\mu U}][a_{11\nu L}, a_{11\nu U}]\rangle & \langle[a_{12\mu L}, a_{12\mu U}][a_{12\nu L}, a_{12\nu U}]\rangle & \langle[a_{13\mu L}, a_{13\mu U}][a_{13\nu L}, a_{13\nu U}]\rangle \\ \langle[a_{21\mu L}, a_{21\mu U}][a_{21\nu L}, a_{21\nu U}]\rangle & \langle[a_{22\mu L}, a_{22\mu U}][a_{22\nu L}, a_{22\nu U}]\rangle & \langle[a_{23\mu L}, a_{23\mu U}][a_{23\nu L}, a_{23\nu U}]\rangle \\ \langle[a_{31\mu L}, a_{31\mu U}][a_{31\nu L}, a_{31\nu U}]\rangle & \langle[a_{32\mu L}, a_{32\mu U}][a_{32\nu L}, a_{32\nu U}]\rangle & \langle[a_{33\mu L}, a_{33\mu U}][a_{33\nu L}, a_{33\nu U}]\rangle \end{bmatrix}$$

are

$$[\langle[a_{11\mu L}, a_{11\mu U}][a_{11\nu L}, a_{11\nu U}]\rangle], \quad [\langle[a_{12\mu L}, a_{12\mu U}][a_{12\nu L}, a_{12\nu U}]\rangle]$$

and

$$[\langle[a_{13\mu L}, a_{13\mu U}][a_{13\nu L}, a_{13\nu U}]\rangle].$$

Second order interval-valued intuitionistic fuzzy submatrices are

$$\begin{bmatrix} \langle[a_{11\mu L}, a_{11\mu U}][a_{11\nu L}, a_{11\nu U}]\rangle & \langle[a_{12\mu L}, a_{12\mu U}][a_{12\nu L}, a_{12\nu U}]\rangle \\ \langle[a_{21\mu L}, a_{21\mu U}][a_{21\nu L}, a_{21\nu U}]\rangle & \langle[a_{22\mu L}, a_{22\mu U}][a_{22\nu L}, a_{22\nu U}]\rangle \end{bmatrix},$$

$$\begin{bmatrix} \langle[a_{22\mu L}, a_{22\mu U}][a_{22\nu L}, a_{22\nu U}]\rangle & \langle[a_{23\mu L}, a_{23\mu U}][a_{23\nu L}, a_{23\nu U}]\rangle \\ \langle[a_{32\mu L}, a_{32\mu U}][a_{32\nu L}, a_{32\nu U}]\rangle & \langle[a_{33\mu L}, a_{33\mu U}][a_{33\nu L}, a_{33\nu U}]\rangle \end{bmatrix},$$

and

$$\begin{bmatrix} \langle[a_{11\mu L}, a_{11\mu U}][a_{11\nu L}, a_{11\nu U}]\rangle & \langle[a_{13\mu L}, a_{13\mu U}][a_{13\nu L}, a_{13\nu U}]\rangle \\ \langle[a_{31\mu L}, a_{31\mu U}][a_{31\nu L}, a_{31\nu U}]\rangle & \langle[a_{33\mu L}, a_{33\mu U}][a_{33\nu L}, a_{33\nu U}]\rangle \end{bmatrix}.$$

Third order interval-valued intuitionistic fuzzy principal submatrix is the matrix itself.

Definition (Interval-Valued Intuitionistic Fuzzy Partition Matrix): If an IVIFM is divided or partitioned into smaller IVIFMs called blocks or cells with consecutive rows and columns by separated by dotted horizontal lines of full width between rows and vertical lines of full height between columns, then the IVIFM is called intuitionistic fuzzy partition matrix.

- The elements of interval-valued intuitionistic fuzzy partition matrix are smaller IVIFMs.
- It is also called the interval-valued intuitionistic fuzzy block matrix.

Definition (Conformal Partition): Two IFMs of same order are said to be conformably or identically partitioned if

- Both the IVIFMs are partitioned in such way that the number of columns of two interval-valued intuitionistic fuzzy partition matrices are same,
- The corresponding blocks are of same order.

INTERVAL-VALUED INTUITIONISTIC FUZZY BLOCK MATRIX

Definition (Interval-Valued Intuitionistic Fuzzy Block Matrix): The IVIFM, whose elements are blocks obtained by partitioning is called interval-valued intuitionistic fuzzy block matrix.

Thus,

$$A = \begin{bmatrix} \langle [a_{11\mu L}, a_{11\mu U}][a_{11\nu L}, a_{11\nu U}] \rangle & \langle [a_{12\mu L}, a_{12\mu U}][a_{12\nu L}, a_{12\nu U}] \rangle & \vdots & \langle [a_{13\mu L}, a_{13\mu U}][a_{13\nu L}, a_{13\nu U}] \rangle \\ \cdots & \cdots & \vdots & \cdots \\ \langle [a_{21\mu L}, a_{21\mu U}][a_{21\nu L}, a_{21\nu U}] \rangle & \langle [a_{22\mu L}, a_{22\mu U}][a_{22\nu L}, a_{11\nu U}] \rangle & \vdots & \langle [a_{23\mu L}, a_{23\mu U}][a_{23\nu L}, a_{23\nu U}] \rangle \\ \langle [a_{31\mu L}, a_{31\mu U}][a_{31\nu L}, a_{31\nu U}] \rangle & \langle [a_{32\mu L}, a_{32\mu U}][a_{32\nu L}, a_{32\nu U}] \rangle & \vdots & \langle [a_{33\mu L}, a_{33\mu U}][a_{33\nu L}, a_{33\nu U}] \rangle \end{bmatrix},$$

$$= \begin{bmatrix} P_{11} & P_{12} \\ P_{21} & P_{22} \end{bmatrix}$$

where

$$P_{11} = \begin{bmatrix} \langle [a_{11\mu L}, a_{11\mu U}][a_{11\nu L}, a_{11\nu U}] \rangle & \langle [a_{12\mu L}, a_{12\mu U}][a_{12\nu L}, a_{12\nu U}] \rangle \end{bmatrix},$$

$$P_{12} = \begin{bmatrix} \langle [a_{13\mu L}, a_{13\mu U}][a_{13\nu L}, a_{13\nu U}] \rangle \end{bmatrix},$$

$$P_{21} = \begin{bmatrix} \langle [a_{21\mu L}, a_{21\mu U}][a_{21\nu L}, a_{21\nu U}] \rangle & \langle [a_{22\mu L}, a_{22\mu U}][a_{22\nu L}, a_{11\nu U}] \rangle \\ \langle [a_{31\mu L}, a_{31\mu U}][a_{31\nu L}, a_{31\nu U}] \rangle & \langle [a_{32\mu L}, a_{32\mu U}][a_{32\nu L}, a_{32\nu U}] \rangle \end{bmatrix}$$

and

$$P_{22} = \begin{bmatrix} \langle [a_{23\mu L}, a_{23\mu U}][a_{23\nu L}, a_{23\nu U}] \rangle \\ \langle [a_{33\mu L}, a_{33\mu U}][a_{33\nu L}, a_{33\nu U}] \rangle \end{bmatrix}.$$

The IFM

$$A = \begin{bmatrix} P_{11} & \vdots & P_{12} \\ \cdots & \cdots & \cdots \\ P_{21} & \vdots & P_{22} \end{bmatrix}$$

is an example of interval-valued intuitionistic fuzzy block matrix.

Definition (Transpose of Intuitionistic Fuzzy Block Matrix): The transpose of intuitionistic fuzzy block matrix is the transpose of both blocks and constituents blocks.

$$A^T = \begin{bmatrix} P_{11}^T & P_{21}^T \\ P_{12}^T & P_{22}^T \end{bmatrix}.$$

Definition (Diagonal Blocks): The blocks along the diagonal of the interval-valued intuitionistic fuzzy block matrix are called diagonal blocks. The blocks P_{ij} for which $i=j$ are diagonal blocks. Thus P_{11} and P_{22} diagonal blocks of the interval-valued intuitionistic fuzzy block matrix

$$A = \begin{bmatrix} P_{11} & P_{12} \\ P_{21} & P_{22} \end{bmatrix}.$$

Definition (Diagonal Interval-Valued Intuitionistic Fuzzy Block Matrix): If a square interval-valued intuitionistic fuzzy block matrix is such that the blocks $A_{ij} = [\langle [0,0][1,1] \rangle]$ for all $i \neq j$, the IVIFM A is said to be a diagonal intuitionistic fuzzy block matrix.

Note that IVIFM A needs not be square but it must be partitioned as a square interval-valued intuitionistic fuzzy block matrix. Thus,

$$\begin{pmatrix} A_{11} & 0 & 0 \\ 0 & A_{22} & 0 \end{pmatrix} where\ 0 = [\langle 0,1 \rangle]$$

is a diagonal interval-valued intuitionistic fuzzy block matrix.

Definition (Triangular Interval-Valued Intuitionistic Fuzzy Block Matrix): If the square or rectangular blocks above (or below) the square diagonal blocks of a square interval-valued intuitionistic fuzzy block matrix are all $\langle[0,0][1,1]\rangle$, then the IVIFM is said to be the lower (or upper) triangular interval-valued intuitionistic fuzzy block matrix.

Definition (Quasidiagonal Interval-Valued Intuitionistic Fuzzy Block Matrix): It is a interval-valued intuitionistic fuzzy block matrix whose diagonal blocks are square IVIFMs of different order and off diagonal blocks are zero interval-valued intuitionistic fuzzy matrices.

Thus,

$$A=\begin{pmatrix} D_1 & 0 & \cdots & 0 \\ 0 & D_2 & \cdots & 0 \\ \vdots & \vdots & \cdots & \vdots \\ 0 & 0 & \cdots & D_r \end{pmatrix}$$

is a quasidiagonal matrix whose diagonal blocks D_i, $i=1,2,\ldots,s$ are square IVIFMs of different orders.

The IVIFM A is also called decomposable interval-valued intuitionistic fuzzy block matrix or pseudo-diagonal interval-valued intuitionistic fuzzy block matrix or direct sum of IVIFMs D_1, $D_2,\ldots,D_s$ taken in this order.

Theorem

If

$$A=\left[\langle[a_{ij\mu L},a_{ij\mu U}],[a_{ij\nu L},a_{ij\nu U}]\rangle\right]_{m\times n}$$

and

$$B=\left[\langle[b_{ij\mu L},b_{ij\mu U}],[b_{ij\nu L},b_{ij\nu U}]\rangle\right]_{n\times p}$$

are two IVIFMs such that

$$AB=C=\left[\langle[c_{ij\mu L},c_{ij\mu U}],[c_{ij\nu L},c_{ij\nu U}]\rangle\right]_{m\times p}$$

then the j-th column of C is $AB_{j\cdot}$, where

$$B_{j\cdot}=\begin{bmatrix} \langle[b_{1j\mu L},b_{1j\mu U}],[b_{1j\nu L},b_{1j\nu U}]\rangle \\ \langle[b_{2j\mu L},b_{2j\mu U}],[b_{2j\nu L},b_{2j\nu U}]\rangle \\ \vdots \\ \langle[b_{nj\mu L},b_{nj\mu U}],[b_{nj\nu L},b_{nj\nu U}]\rangle \end{bmatrix}$$

are the column partition of IFM *B*.

Proof

Let IVIFM *B* of order $n \times p$ be partition into *p* column vectors ($n \times 1$) IVIFMs as

$$B = \begin{bmatrix} B_1 & B_2 & \cdots & B_j & \cdots & B_p \end{bmatrix} \text{where}$$

$$B_{j\cdot} = \begin{bmatrix} \langle [b_{1j\mu L}, b_{1j\mu U}], [b_{1j\nu L}, b_{1j\nu U}] \rangle \\ \langle [b_{2j\mu L}, b_{2j\mu U}], [b_{2j\nu L}, b_{2j\nu U}] \rangle \\ \vdots \\ \langle [b_{nj\mu L}, b_{nj\mu U}], [b_{nj\nu L}, b_{nj\nu U}] \rangle \end{bmatrix}, j = 1, 2, \cdots, p$$

to find a column of the product *AB*. From the product rule of the IVIFMs, the elements of the product is

$$c_{ij} = \left[\left\langle \sum_k \left[\min\left\{a_{ik\mu L}, b_{kj\mu L}\right\}, \min\left\{a_{ik\mu U}, b_{kj\mu U}\right\}\right], \prod_k \left[\max\left\{a_{ik\nu L}, b_{kj\nu L}\right\}, \max\left\{a_{ik\nu U}, b_{kj\nu U}\right\}\right] \right\rangle \right],$$

$i=1,2,\ldots,m$ and $j=1,2,\ldots,n$

where *A* be an IVIFM of order $m \times n$ and $C=AB$.

Therefore *j*-th column of *C* is obtained by giving the values $1,2,\ldots,m$ to *i* and it is

$$\begin{aligned} C_{j\cdot} &= \begin{bmatrix} \langle \sum_k [\min\{a_{1k\mu L}, b_{kj\mu L}\}, \min\{a_{1k\mu U}, b_{kj\mu U}\}], \prod_k [\max\{a_{1k\nu L}, b_{kj\nu L}\}, \max\{a_{1k\nu U}, b_{kj\nu U}\}] \rangle \\ \langle \sum_k [\min\{a_{2k\mu L}, b_{kj\mu L}\}, \min\{a_{2k\mu U}, b_{kj\mu U}\}], \prod_k [\max\{a_{2k\nu L}, b_{kj\nu L}\}, \max\{a_{2k\nu U}, b_{kj\nu U}\}] \rangle \\ \langle \sum_k [\min\{a_{mk\mu L}, b_{kj\mu L}\}, \min\{a_{mk\mu U}, b_{kj\mu U}\}], \prod_k [\max\{a_{mk\nu L}, b_{kj\nu L}\}, \max\{a_{mk\nu U}, b_{kj\nu U}\}] \rangle \end{bmatrix} \\ &= AB_j, j = 1, 2, \cdots, p \end{aligned}$$

Hence the theorem.

Theorem

Let *A* be an $m \times n$ IVIFM and *B* be an $n \times p$ IVIFM. Let *B* (or *A*) be partitioned into two blocks by column partitioning only. Then the product *AB* is also partitioned into two blocks of same column (row) partitioning.

Proof

Let $B=[B_1 B_2]$ where B_1 is of order $n \times t$ and B_2 is of order $n \times (p-t)$ IFM. Then

$$AB = A\left[b_1 \quad b_2 \quad \cdots \quad b_t \;\vdots\; b_{(t+1)} \quad \cdots \quad \cdots \quad b_p\right]$$

where

$$b_j = \begin{bmatrix} \langle [b_{1j\mu L}, b_{1j\mu U}], [b_{1j\nu L}, b_{1j\nu U}] \rangle \\ \langle [b_{2j\mu L}, b_{2j\mu U}], [b_{2j\nu L}, b_{2j\nu U}] \rangle \\ \vdots \\ \langle [b_{nj\mu L}, b_{nj\mu U}], [b_{nj\nu L}, b_{nj\nu U}] \rangle \end{bmatrix}$$

$$= \left[Ab_{1\cdot} \quad Ab_{2\cdot} \quad \cdots \quad Ab_{t\cdot} \;\vdots\; Ab_{(t+1)\cdot} \quad \cdots \quad \cdots \quad Ab_{p\cdot}\right]$$
$$= \left[AB_1 \;\vdots\; AB_2\right]$$

Hence the theorem.

OPERATIONS ON INTERVAL-VALUED INTUITIONISTIC FUZZY BLOCK MATRIX

- **Addition:** The conformal intuitionistic fuzzy matrices can be added by block as addition of two intuitionistic fuzzy matrices of the same dimensions.

$$A + B = \begin{pmatrix} A_{11} + B_{11} & A_{12} + B_{12} & \cdots & A_{1q} + B_{1q} \\ A_{21} + B_{21} & A_{22} + B_{22} & \cdots & A_{2q} + B_{2q} \\ \cdots & \cdots & \cdots & \cdots \\ A_{p1} + B_{p1} & A_{p2} + B_{p2} & \cdots & A_{pq} + B_{pq} \end{pmatrix}$$

- **Scalar Multiplication:** As in scalar multiplication of an IVIFM by a scalar, each block of partition is multiplied by scalar.

Thus,

$$\alpha A = \begin{bmatrix} \alpha A_{11} & \alpha A_{12} & \cdots & \alpha A_{1q} \\ \alpha A_{21} & \alpha A_{22} & \cdots & \alpha A_{2q} \\ \cdots & \cdots & \cdots & \cdots \\ \alpha A_{p1} & \alpha A_{p2} & \cdots & \alpha A_{pq} \end{bmatrix}$$

- **Multiplication of Interval-Valued Intuitionistic Fuzzy Partition Matrices:** Let A and B be two IVIFMs of order $m\times n$ and $n\times p$, conformable for multiplication. Let A_{ij} and B_{ij} denote blocks of A and B.

For IVIFM multiplication AB by partition to be conformable, the number of column partitioning of A must be equal to that of row partitioning of B and in addition blocks must be conformable for multiplication of IVIFM and

$$AB = [\langle [c_{ik\mu L}, c_{ik\mu U}], [c_{ik\nu L}, c_{ik\nu U}]\rangle]_{r\times t} = \left[\sum_{j=1}^{s} A_{ij} B_{jk}\right]$$

which is again a partition IFM with r horizontal and t vertical dotted lines.

Theorem

If $AB=C$ the intuitionistic fuzzy submatrix containing rows $i_1, i_2,\ldots,i_r$ and columns $j_1, j_2,\ldots,j_s$ of C is equal to the product of the interval-valued intuitionistic fuzzy submatrix with these rows of A and the interval-valued intuitionistic fuzzy submatrix with these columns of B.

Proof

Let

$$A = [\langle [a_{ij\mu L}, a_{ij\mu U}], [a_{ij\nu L}, a_{ij\nu U}]\rangle]_{m\times n}$$

and

$$B = [\langle [b_{ij\mu L}, b_{ij\mu U}], [b_{ij\nu L}, b_{ij\nu U}]\rangle]_{n\times p}$$

be two IVIFMs. Then

$$C = [\langle [c_{ij\mu L}, c_{ij\mu U}], [c_{ij\nu L}, c_{ij\nu U}]\rangle] = \left[\left\langle \sum_{j=1}^{n} \min\{a_{ij\mu}, b_{jk\mu}\}, \prod_{j=1}^{n} \max\{a_{ij\mu}, b_{jk\mu}\}\right\rangle\right]$$

where $i=1,.,\ldots,m$ and $k=1,2,\ldots,p$. Now the intuitionistic fuzzy submatrix C_{ik} of IFM C with rows $i_1, i_2,\ldots,i_r$ and columns $j_1, j_2,\ldots,j_s$ is obtained by replacing row i and column k of C by these rows and columns. It is

$$C_{ik} = \left[\left\langle \sum_{j=1}^{n}\{\min\{a_{ij\mu L}, b_{jk\mu L}\}, \min\{a_{ij\mu U}, b_{jk\mu U}\}\}\prod_{j=1}^{n}\{\max\{a_{ij\nu L}, b_{jk\nu L}\}, \max\{a_{ij\nu U}, b_{jk\nu U}\}\}\right\rangle\right] \quad (1)$$

where $i= i_1, i_2,\ldots,i_r$ and columns $k=j_1,j_2,\ldots j_s$ Again the product of the given interval-valued intuitionistic fuzzy submatrices A_i and B_k of IFM A and B respectively is

$$(A_i)_{r\times n}(B_k)_{n\times s}=\left[\left\langle\sum_{j=1}^{n}\{\min\{a_{ij\mu L},b_{jk\mu L}\},\min\{a_{ij\mu U},b_{jk\mu U}\}\}\prod_{j=1}^{n}\{\max\{a_{ij\nu L},b_{jk\nu L}\},\max\{a_{ij\nu U},b_{jk\nu U}\}\}\right\rangle\right]_{r\times s} \quad (2)$$

where $i= i_1, i_2,\ldots,i_r$ and columns $k= j_1, j_2,\ldots j_s$

Therefore the relation (1) and (2) together give the results.

Theorem

If the $m\times n$ IFM A is partitioned by consecutive groups of rows into blocks A_i, $i=1,2,\ldots,r$ and $n\times p$ IFM B is partitioned by consecutive groups of columns into blocks B_j, $j=1,2,\ldots,s$. Then the product $AB=C$ of order $m\times p$ is partitioned into blocks by row groups exactly as A and column groups exactly as B. The ik-th block C_{ik} of C is given by $C_{ik}=A_iB_k$.

Proof

The proof of the theorem follows from definition.

SOME ALGEBRAIC OPERATIONS OF INTUITIONISTIC FUZZY MATRICES

In this section, the direct sum, Kronecker product and Kronecker sum of the IVIFMs are defined and studied some useful properties with the help of interval-valued intuitionistic fuzzy partition matrix.

Direct Sum

Definition: Let $A_1, A_2,\ldots,A_r$ be square IFMs of orders $m_1, m_2,\ldots,m_r$ respectively. The diagonal IVIFM

$$diag(A_1,A_2,\cdots,A_r)=\begin{bmatrix} A_1 & 0 & \cdots & 0\\ 0 & A_2 & \cdots & 0\\ \vdots & \vdots & \vdots & \cdots\\ 0 & 0 & \cdots & A_r\end{bmatrix}_{(m_1+m_2+\cdots+m_r)}$$

is called the direct sum of the square IVIFMs $A_1, A_2,\ldots,A_r$ and is expressed by $A_1\oplus A_2\oplus\cdots\oplus A_r$ of order $(m_1+m_2+\ldots+m_r)$. It is also called the block diagonalize form.

Properties of Direct Sum

Direct sum of IFMs possesses the following algebric properties:

1. **Commutative Property:** Commutative property does not hold of the square intuitionistic fuzzy matrices.

Let A and B be two square intuitionistic fuzzy matrices. Then the direct sum of A and$B$ are

$$A \oplus B = \begin{bmatrix} A & 0 \\ 0 & B \end{bmatrix} and\ B \oplus A = \begin{bmatrix} B & 0 \\ 0 & A \end{bmatrix}$$

It is obvious that, $A \oplus B \neq B \oplus A$.

2. **Associative Property:** Let A, B and C be three square intuitionistic fuzzy matrices. Then

$$A \oplus B = \begin{pmatrix} A & 0 \\ 0 & B \end{pmatrix} = D$$

Now,

$$(A \oplus B) \oplus C = D \oplus C = \begin{pmatrix} D & 0 \\ 0 & C \end{pmatrix} = \begin{pmatrix} A & 0 & 0 \\ 0 & B & 0 \end{pmatrix}$$

Similarly,

$$B \oplus C = \begin{pmatrix} B & 0 \\ 0 & C \end{pmatrix} = E$$

Now,

$$A \oplus (B \oplus C) = A \oplus E = \begin{pmatrix} A & 0 \\ 0 & E \end{pmatrix} = \begin{pmatrix} A & 0 & 0 \\ 0 & B & 0 \end{pmatrix}$$

Therefore,

$$(A \oplus B) \oplus C = A \oplus (B \oplus C).$$

Hence, the associative law holds for direct sum of the intuitionistic fuzzy block matrix.

3. **Mixed Sum:** $(A+B)\oplus(C+D)=(A\oplus B)+(C\oplus D)$, if the addition are conformable corresponding intuitionistic fuzzy block matrices.

By the definition of direct sum of the intuitionistic fuzzy block matrix and intuitionistic fuzzy matrix addition,

$$\begin{aligned}(A+B)\oplus(C+D) &= \begin{bmatrix}(A+B) & 0\\ 0 & (C+D)\end{bmatrix}\\ &= \begin{bmatrix}A & 0\\ 0 & C\end{bmatrix}+\begin{bmatrix}B & 0\\ 0 & D\end{bmatrix}\\ &= (A\oplus C)+(B\oplus D).\end{aligned}$$

4. **Intuitionistic Fuzzy Matrix Multiplication of Direct Sum:** $(A\oplus B)(C\oplus D)=(AC)\oplus(BD)$ if the multiplication is conformable for intuitionistic fuzzy matrix .

$$(A\oplus B)(C\oplus D)=\begin{bmatrix}A & 0\\ 0 & B\end{bmatrix}\begin{bmatrix}C & 0\\ 0 & D\end{bmatrix}$$

since intuitionistic fuzzy matrix multiplication is conformable

$$=\begin{bmatrix}AC & 0\\ 0 & BD\end{bmatrix}$$
$$=(AC)\oplus(BD).$$

5. **Transposition:** $(A\oplus B)^T=A^T\oplus B^T$.

Since,

$$A\oplus B=\begin{bmatrix}A & 0\\ 0 & B\end{bmatrix}$$

therefore,

$$(A\oplus B)^T=\begin{bmatrix}A & 0\\ 0 & B\end{bmatrix}^T=\begin{bmatrix}A^T & 0\\ 0 & B^T\end{bmatrix}=A^T\oplus B^T.$$

Kronecker Product of Intuitionistic Fuzzy Matrices

Let

$$A = \left[\langle [a_{ij\mu L}, a_{ij\mu U}], [a_{ij\nu L}, a_{ij\nu U}] \rangle\right]_{m\times n}$$

and

$$B = \left[\langle [b_{ij\mu L}, b_{ij\mu U}], [b_{ij\nu L}, b_{ij\nu U}] \rangle\right]_{p\times q}$$

be two rectangular IVIFMs. Then the Kronecker product of *A* and *B*, denoted by $A \otimes B$ is defined as the partitioned interval-valued intuitionistic fuzzy matrix

$$A \otimes B = \begin{bmatrix} a_{11}B & a_{12}B & \cdots & a_{1n}B \\ a_{21}B & a_{22}B & \cdots & a_{2n}B \\ \vdots & \vdots & \vdots & \vdots \\ a_{m1}B & a_{m2}B & \cdots & a_{mn}B \end{bmatrix}_{mp\times nq},$$

where

$$a_{ij} = \langle [a_{ij\mu L}, a_{ij\mu U}], [a_{ij\nu L}, a_{ij\nu U}] \rangle$$

for i=1,2,…,m and j=1,2,…,n. It has mn blocks. The ijth blocks $a_{ij}B$ of order p×q.

Note: The difference between the product of intuitionistic fuzzy matrices and Kronecker product of intuitionistic fuzzy matrices is that in product of IFM product *AB* requires equality of the number of columns in *A* and the number of rows in *B* while in Kronecker product it is free from such restriction.

Kronecker Product of Two Intuitionistic Fuzzy Column Vectors

Let

$$x = \left[\langle [x_{1\mu L}, x_{1\mu U}], [x_{1\nu L}, x_{1\nu U}] \rangle \quad \langle [x_{2\mu L}, x_{2\mu U}], [x_{2\nu L}, x_{2\nu U}] \rangle \quad \cdots \quad \langle [x_{n\mu L}, x_{n\mu U}], [x_{n\nu L}, x_{n\nu U}] \rangle\right]^T$$

and

$$y = \left[\langle [y_{1\mu L}, y_{1\mu U}], [y_{1\nu L}, y_{1\nu U}] \rangle \quad \langle [y_{2\mu L}, y_{2\mu U}], [y_{2\nu L}, y_{2\nu U}] \rangle \quad \cdots \quad \langle [y_{m\mu L}, y_{m\mu U}], [y_{m\nu L}, y_{m\nu U}] \rangle\right]^T$$

be two column intuitionistic fuzzy vectors. Then by definition of Kronecker product, we have

$$x \otimes y = \begin{bmatrix} \langle [x_{1\mu L}, x_{1\mu U}], [x_{1\nu L}, x_{1\nu U}] \rangle y \\ \langle [x_{2\mu L}, x_{2\mu U}], [x_{2\nu L}, x_{2\nu U}] \rangle y \\ \vdots \\ \langle [x_{n\mu L}, x_{n\mu U}], [x_{n\nu L}, x_{n\nu U}] \rangle y \end{bmatrix}_{nm \times 1}$$

$$= \begin{bmatrix} \langle [x_{1\mu L}, x_{1\mu U}], [x_{1\nu L}, x_{1\nu U}] \rangle \langle [y_{1\mu L}, y_{1\mu U}], [y_{1\nu L}, y_{1\nu U}] \rangle \\ \vdots \\ \langle [x_{1\mu L}, x_{1\mu U}], [x_{1\nu L}, x_{1\nu U}] \rangle \langle [y_{m\mu L}, y_{m\mu U}], [y_{m\nu L}, y_{m\nu U}] \rangle \\ \langle [x_{2\mu L}, x_{2\mu U}], [x_{2\nu L}, x_{2\nu U}] \rangle \langle [y_{1\mu L}, y_{1\mu U}], [y_{1\nu L}, y_{1\nu U}] \rangle \\ \vdots \\ \langle [x_{2\mu L}, x_{2\mu U}], [x_{2\nu L}, x_{2\nu U}] \rangle \langle [y_{m\mu L}, y_{m\mu U}], [y_{m\nu L}, y_{m\nu U}] \rangle \\ \vdots \\ \langle [x_{n\mu L}, x_{n\mu U}], [x_{n\nu L}, x_{n\nu U}] \rangle \langle [y_{1\mu L}, y_{1\mu U}], [y_{1\nu L}, y_{1\nu U}] \rangle \\ \vdots \\ \langle [x_{n\mu L}, x_{n\mu U}], [x_{n\nu L}, x_{n\nu U}] \rangle \langle [y_{m\mu L}, y_{m\mu U}], [y_{m\nu L}, y_{m\nu U}] \rangle \end{bmatrix}_{nm \times 1}$$

Properties of Kronecker Product

1. **Commutative:** The Kronecker product is not commutative, $A \otimes B \neq B \otimes A$.
2. **Distributive:** If *B* and *C* are conformable for addition, then

$$A \otimes (B + C) = A \otimes B + A \otimes C, [\textit{left distribution}]$$

$$(B + C) \otimes A = B \otimes A + C \otimes A, [\textit{right distribution}]$$

3. **Associative:** $A \otimes (B \otimes C) = (A \otimes B) \otimes C$.
4. **Transposition:** $(A \otimes B)^T = A^T \otimes B^T$.
5. **Trace:** $Tr(A \otimes B) = (TrA)(TrB)$.
6. Two column vectors α and β, not necessarily of the same order:

$$\alpha^T \otimes \beta = \beta \alpha^T = \beta \otimes \alpha^T$$

Kronecker Sum

The Kronecker sum of two square intuitionistic fuzzy matrices $A_{n \times n}$ and $B_{m \times m}$ is defined by

$$A \dagger B = A \otimes I_m + I_n \otimes B,$$

which is an $nm \times nm$ intuitionistic fuzzy matrix.

CONCLUSION

In this paper, we divide or partition an intuitionistic fuzzy matrix into an intuitionistic fuzzy block matrix. Also, introduce different types of intuitionistic fuzzy submatrices and intuitionistic fuzzy block matrix. Also we derive the operations direct sum, Kronecker sum and Kronecker product of intuitionistic fuzzy matrix. Some relational operation on intuitionistic fuzzy matrix and intuitionistic fuzzy block matrix are presented. In the next paper, we should try prove regularity, symmetricity, convergency and some other related properties of intuitionistic fuzzy block matrices.

REFERENCES

Adak, A. K., Bhowmik, M., & Pal, M. (2011). Semiring of interval-valued intuitionistic fuzzy matrices. *Global Journal of Computer Application and Technology*, *1*(3), 340–347.

Adak, A. K., Bhowmik, M., & Pal, M. (2011). Application of generalized intuitionistic fuzzy matrix in multi-criteria decision making problem. *Journal of Mathematical and Computational Science*, *1*(1), 19–31.

Adak, A. K., Bhowmik, M., & Pal, M. (2012). Some properties of generalized intuitionistic fuzzy nilpotent matrices over distributive lattice. *International Journal of Fuzzy Information and Engineering*, *4*(4), 371–387. doi:10.1007/s12543-012-0121-1

Adak, A. K., Bhowmik, M., & Pal, M. (2013). Distributive Lattice over Intuitionistic Fuzzy Matrices. *The Journal of Fuzzy Mathematics*, *21*(2), 401–416.

Adak, A. K., Bhowmik, M., & Pal, M. (2014). *Decomposition Theorem of Generalized Interval-Valued Intuitionistic Fuzzy Sets. In Contemporary Advancements in Information Technology Development in Dynamic Environments* (pp. 212–219). Information Resources Management Association.

Atanassov, K. (1986). Intuitionistic fuzzy sets. *Fuzzy Sets and Systems*, *20*(1), 87–96. doi:10.1016/S0165-0114(86)80034-3

Bhowmik, M., & Pal, M. (2008). Some results on intuitionistic fuzzy matrices and intuitionistic circulant fuzzy matrices. *International Journal of Mathematical Sciences*, *7*(1-2), 177–192.

Dubois, D., & Prade, H. (1980). *Theory and applications, Fuzzy Sets and Systems*. Academic Press.

Giveon, Y. (1964). Lattice matrices. *Information and Control*, *7*(3), 477–484. doi:10.1016/S0019-9958(64)90173-1

Hasimoto, H. (1982). Reduction of a nilpotent fuzzy matrix. *Information Sciences*, (27): 223–243.

Kim, K.H. & Roush, F.W. (1980). Generalised fuzzy matrices. *Fuzzy Sets and System*, (4), 293-315.

Moussavi, A., & Omit, S., & Ahmadi, A. (2011). A note on nilpotent lattice matrices. *International Journal of Algebra*, *5*(2), 83–89.

Pal, M. (2001). Intuitionistic fuzzy determinant. *V.U.J. Physical Sciences*, (7), 87-93.

Pal, M., Khan, S. K., & Shyamal, A. K. (2002). Intuitionistic fuzzy matrices. *Notes on Intuitionistic Fuzzy Sets*, *8*(2), 51–62.

Pal, M., & Shyamal, A. K. (2004). Two new operators on fuzzy matrices, *J. Applied Mathematics and Computation*, (15), 91–107.

Sriram, S., & Murugadas, P. (2010). On semiring of intuitionistic fuzzy matrices. *Applied Mathematical Sciences*, *4*(23), 1099–1105.

Tan, Y. J. (2005). On nilpotent matrices over distributive lattices. *Fuzzy Sets and Systems*, *151*(2), 421–433. doi:10.1016/j.fss.2004.06.009

Thomason, M. G. (1977). Convergence of powers of a fuzzy matrix. *Journal of Mathematical Analysis and Applications*, *57*(2), 476–480. doi:10.1016/0022-247X(77)90274-8

Xin, L. J. (1992). Controllable fuzzy matrices. *Fuzzy Sets and Systems*, (45): 313–319.

Zadeh, L. A. (1965). Fuzzy sets. *Information and Control*, *8*(8), 338–353. doi:10.1016/S0019-9958(65)90241-X

Chapter 4
P-F Fuzzy Rings and Normal Fuzzy Ring:
Fuzzy Ring

Manoj Kumar
International Engineering Services, India

ABSTRACT

In 1965, Zadeh introduced the concept of fuzzy subset. Since that time many papers were introduced in different mathematical scopes of theoretical and practical applications. In 1982, Liuformulated the term of fuzzy ring and fuzzy ideal of a ring R. In 2004, Hadi and Abou-Draeb, introduced and studied P-F fuzzy rings and normal fuzzy rings and now we are complete it. In this chapter, the concepts P-F fuzzy rings and normal fuzzy rings have been investigated. Several basic results related to these concepts have given and studied. The relationship between them has also been given. Moreover, some properties of t-pure fuzzy ideal of a fuzzy ring have been given which need it later.

1. INTRODUCTION

The present paper study P-F fuzzy rings and normal fuzzy rings. In section one, some basic definitions and results are recalled which will be needed later. In section two, several results about t-pure fuzzy ideals of a fuzzy ring, are given which are necessary in proving some results in the following sections. Section three is devoted for studying P-F fuzzy rings, where a fuzzy ring X is called P-F fuzzy ring if (a_t) is a t-pure fuzzy ideal of X, for all $a_t \subseteq X$. Next, in the fourth section, normal fuzzy rings are introduced, where a fuzzy ring X is called normal if every fuzzy ideal of X is t-pure. Many properties about this concept are given. Its relationship with P-F fuzzy ring is also given. Throughout this chapter R is commutative ring with unity, and every fuzzy ideal A of a fuzzy ring X is a finite valued, that is Im(A) is finite set. Finally, A(0) =X(0), for any fuzzy ideal A of a fuzzy ring X .

DOI: 10.4018/978-1-5225-0914-1.ch004

Basic Concepts

This section contains some definitions and properties of fuzzy subset, fuzzy ring, fuzzy ideal which we will be used in the next section.

Preliminary Concepts

Let $(R,+,\cdot)$ be a commutative ring with identity. A fuzzy subset of R is a function from R into [0,1], (Zadeh, 1965; Liu, 1982].

Let A and B be fuzzy subset of R. We write

$\mathbf{A} \subseteq \mathbf{B}$ if $A(x) \leq B(x)$,

for all $x \in R$. If $A \subseteq B$ and there exists $x \in R$ such that $A(x) < B(x)$, then we write $\mathbf{A} \subset \mathbf{B}$ and we say that A is a proper fuzzy subset of B, (Liu, 1982). Note that $\mathbf{A} = \mathbf{B}$ if and only if $A(x) = B(x)$, for all $x \in R$, (Zadeh, 1965).

Let R, R' be any sets and f: R→ R' be any function, A and B be two fuzzy subsets of R and R' respectively, the fuzzy subset f(A) of R' defined by:

$f(A)(y) = \sup A(y)$ if $f(y) \neq 0$, $y \in R'$

and $f(A)(y) = 0$, otherwise. It is called the image of A under f and denoted by f(A). The fuzzy subset $f^{-1}(B)$ of R defined by:

$f^{-1}(B)(y) = B(f(x))$, for all $x \in R$.

is called the inverse image of B and denoted by $f^{-1}(B)$, (Liu, 1982).

Let R, R' be any sets and f: R→ R' be any function. A fuzzy subset A of R is called **f-invariant** if $f(x) = f(y)$ implies $A(x) = A(y)$, where $x, y \in R$, (Dixit, Kumar R. and Ajmal, 1991).

For each $t \in [0,1]$, the set

$A_t = \{x \in R \mid A(x) \geq t\}$

is called a level subset of R and the set

$A_* = \{x \in R \mid A(x) = A(0)\}$,

and A=B if and only if $A_t = B_t$ for all $t \in [0,1]$ (Liu, 1982; Khamees and Mordeson, 1998).

Let λ_R denote the characteristic function of R defined by

$\lambda_R(x) = 1$ if $x \in R$

and

λ_R (x) = 0 if $x \notin R$, (Dixit *et al.*, 1991; Khamees and Mordeson, 1998).

Let $x \in R$ and $t \in [0,1]$, let x_t denote the fuzzy subset of R defined by $x_t(y) = 0$ if $x \neq y$ and $x_t(y) = t$ if $x = y$ for all $y \in R$. x_t is called a fuzzy singleton, (Khamees and Mordeson, 1998).

If x_t and y_s are fuzzy singletons, then

$$x_t + y_s = (x + y)_\lambda$$

and

$$x_t \circ y_s = (x.\ y)_\lambda,$$

where $\lambda = \min\{\ t, s\ \}$, (Zadeh, 1965; Khamees and Mordeson, 1998).

Let

$$I^R = \{A_i \mid i \in \Lambda\}$$

be a collection of fuzzy subset of R. Define the fuzzy subset of R (intersection) by

$$(\bigcap_{i\in\Lambda} A_i)(x) = \inf\{A_i(x) \mid i \in \Lambda\},$$

for all $x \in R$,(Liu W.J., 1982). Define the fuzzy subset of R (union) by

$$(\bigcup_{i\in\Lambda} A_i)(x) = \sup\{A_i(x) \mid i \in \Lambda\},$$

for all $x \in R$, (Liu, 1982; Khamees & Mordeson, 1998).

Let ϕ denote $\phi(x) = 0$ for all $x \in R$, the empty fuzzy subset of R, (Zadeh, 1965; Martines, 1995).

Note that throughout chapter any fuzzy subset is a nonempty fuzzy subset.

Let A and B be a fuzzy subsets of R, the product A∘B define by:

$$A\circ B\ (x) = \sup\{\min\{A(y), B(z)\} \mid x = y \cdot z\}\ y, z \in R,$$

for all $x \in R$, (Mukherjee and Sen, 1987).

The addition A + B define by

$$(A + B)(x) = \sup\{\min\{A(y), B(z) \mid x = y + z\}\ y, z \in R,$$

for all $x \in R$, (Mukherjee & Sen, 1987).

Let A be a fuzzy subset of R, A is called a fuzzy subgroup of R if for all

$$x, y \in R,\ A(x + y) \geq \min\{A(x), A(y)\}$$

and $A(x) = A(-x)$, (Mukherjee & Sen, 1987).

Let A be a fuzzy subset of R, A is called a fuzzy ring of R if for all

$x, y \in R, A(x - y) \geq \min \{A(x), A(y)\}$

and

$A(x \cdot y) \geq \min \{A(x), A(y)\}$, (Martines,1995; Mukherjee & Sen, 1987).

A fuzzy subset A of R is called a fuzzy ideal of R if and only if for all

$x, y \in R, A(x - y) \geq \min \{A(x), A(y)\}$

and

$A(x \cdot y) \geq \max \{A(x), A(y)\}$, (Martines, 1995; Mukherjee & Sen, 1987).

Let X be a fuzzy ring of R and A be a fuzzy ideal of R such that $A \subseteq X$. Then A is a fuzzy ideal of the fuzzy ring X (Khamees & Mordeson, 1998).

But let X be a fuzzy ring of R and A be a fuzzy subset. A is called a fuzzy ideal of the fuzzy ring

X if $A \subseteq X$ (that is $A(a) \leq X(a)$, for all $a \in R$),

$A(b-c) \geq \min \{A(b), A(c)\}$

and

$A(bc) \geq \min \{A(b), A(c)\}$,

for all $b, c \in R$, (Martines, 1995).

And A is a fuzzy ideal of the fuzzy ring X of R if

$A(b-c) \geq \min \{A(b), A(c)\}$

and

$A(bc) \geq \min \{\max\{A(b), A(c)\}, X(bc)\}$, (Dixit *et al.*, 1991; Martines, 1995).

Let X is a fuzzy ring of R. A be a fuzzy subset of X is a fuzzy ideal of X if and only if At is an ideal of X_t, for all $t \in [0, A(0)]$, (Martines, 1995).

Let A be a fuzzy ideal of R. If for all $t \in [0, A(0)]$, then A_t is an ideal of R and A_* is an ideal of R, (Dixit *et al.,* 1991; Khamees & Mordeson, 1998).

Let $\{A_i | i \in \Lambda\}$ be a family of fuzzy ideals of R. Then $\bigcap_{i\in\Lambda} A_i$ is a fuzzy ideal of R and $(\bigcup_{i\in\Lambda} A_i)$ is a fuzzy ideal of R, (Martines, 1995; Khamees & Mordeson, 1998).

Let A and B are fuzzy ideals of R, then $A\circ B$ is a fuzzy ideal of R, (Martines, 1995]. Let A and B are fuzzy ideals of R, then $A \cap B$, $A + B$ are fuzzy ideals of R, (Martinez, 1999; Abou-Draeb, 2000).

Now, we give definition and some result about the fuzzy direct sum of X and Y as a definition of the direct sum by (Kash, 1982).

Definition 1.1 (Abou-Draeb, 2000)

Let X be a fuzzy ring of a ring R_1 and Y be a fuzzy ring of a ring R_2. Let

$f: R_1 \oplus R_2 \rightarrow [0,1]$

definite by

$T(a, b) = \min \{X(a), Y(b)\}$

for all $(a, b) \in R_1 \oplus R_2$. T is called a fuzzy external direct sum of denoted by $X \oplus Y = T$.

Proposition 1.2 (Abou-Draeb, 2000)

If X and Y are fuzzy rings of rings R_1 and R_2 respectively, then $T = X \oplus Y$ is a fuzzy ring of $R_1 \oplus R_2$.

Proposition 1.3 (Abou-Draeb, 2000)

If X and Y are fuzzy rings of R_1 and R_2 respectively, then $T = X\oplus Y$ is a fuzzy ring of $R_1 \oplus R_2$. A be a fuzzy ideal of R_1 such that $A \subseteq X$ and B be a fuzzy ideal of R_2 such that $B \subseteq Y$. Then:

1. $A \oplus B$ is a fuzzy ideal of $R_1 \oplus R_2$.
2. $(A \oplus B)_t = A_t \oplus B_t$, for all $t \in (0, (A \oplus B)(0, 0)]$.
3. $A \oplus B$ is a fuzzy ideal of T, such that $(A \oplus B) \subseteq (X \oplus Y) = T$, where

$(A \oplus B)(a, b) = \min \{A(a), B(b)\}$, for all $(a, b) \in R_1 \oplus R_2$.

Proposition 1.4 (Abou-Draeb, 2000)

If X and Y are fuzzy rings of R_1 and R_2 respectively such that $T = X \oplus Y$. If A is a fuzzy ideal of $R_1 \oplus R_2$ such that $A \subseteq T$, then there exist B_1 and B_2 fuzzy ideals of R_1 and R_2 respectively such that $B_1 \subseteq X$ and $B_2 \subseteq Y$ and $A = B_1 \oplus B_2$.

Corollary 1.5 (Abou-Draeb, 2000)

If X and Y are fuzzy rings of R_1 and R_2 respectively. If A, C are fuzzy ideals of X and B, D are fuzzy ideals of Y. Then $A \oplus B = C \oplus D$ if and only if A=C, B=D.

Proposition 1.6

Let A and B be two fuzzy subsets of a ring R. Then:

1. $A \circ B \subseteq A \cap B$.
2. $(A \circ B)_t = A_t \bullet B_t$, $t \in [0,1]$.
3. $(A \cap B)_t = A_t \cap B_t$, $t \in [0,1]$.

Proof

1. To prove $A \circ B \subseteq A \cap B$, let $x \in R$,

$(A \circ B)(x) = \sup\{\min\{A(y), B(z)\} \mid x = y \,.\, z\}$ $y, z \in R$

$= \sup\{\min\{A(x), B(1)\}, \min\{B(x), A(1)\}, \{\min\{A(y), B(z)\} \mid x = y \,.z\}\}$.

$\leq \min\{\max\{A(x), B(x)\}, \max\{A(1), B(1)\}, \min\{A(y), B(z)\} \mid x = y \,.z\}\}$ by (Abou-Draeb, 2000).

$\leq \min\{\min\{A(x), B(x)\}, \min\{A(1), B(1)\}, \min\{A(y), B(z)\} \mid x = y \,.z\}$

$\leq \min\{A(x), B(x)\}$

$= (A \cap B)(x)$. Hence $A \circ B \subseteq A \cap B$.

2. $(A \circ B)_t = A_t \bullet B_t$, $t \in [0,1]$, (Hadi and Abou-Draeb, 2004).
3. To prove

$(A \cap B)_t = A_t \cap B_t$, $t \in [0,1]$,

since

$A_t = \{x : x \in R \mid A(x) \geq t\}$, $B_t = \{x : x \in R \mid B(x) \geq t\}$.

$(A \cap B)_t = \{x : x \in R \mid (A \cap B)(x) \geq t\}$.

$= \{x : x \in R \mid \min\{A(x), B(x)\} \geq t\}$.

$= \{x : x \in R \mid A(x) \geq t, B(x) \geq t\}$.

$= \min\{\{x : x \in R \mid A(x) \geq t\}, \{x : x \in R \mid B(x) \geq t\}\}$.

$= A_t \cap B_t$. Hence $(A \cap B)_t = A_t \cap B_t$, $t \in [0,1]$.

Proposition 1.7 [Martines, 1995]

Let

$X: R \to [0,1]$, $Y: R' \to [0,1]$

are fuzzy rings $f: R \to R'$ be homomorphism between them and $A: R \to [0,1]$ a fuzzy ideal of X, $B: R' \to [0,1]$ a fuzzy ideal of Y, then:

1. $f(A)$ is a fuzzy ideal of Y.
2. $f^{-1}(B)$ is a fuzzy ideal of X.

Proposition 1.8

Let A and B be two fuzzy subsets of a ring R and $f: R \to R'$ is inverse image function of B. Then:

1. $f(A) \cap f(B) = f(A \cap B)$.
2. $f(A) \circ f(B) = f(A \circ B)$.
3. $f(A_t) = (f(A))_t$.
4. $f^{-1}(A_t) = (f^{-1}(A))_t$.

Proof

1. To prove

$f(A) \cap f(B) = f(A \cap B)$,

let

$x \in R$, $f(A \cap B)(x) = f[(A \cap B)(x)]$

$= f[\min\{A(x), B(x)\}] = \min\{f(A(x)), f(B(x))\} = f(A) \cap f(B)$.

2. To prove

$f(A) \circ f(B) = f(A \circ B)$,

let

$x \in R$, $f(A \circ B)(x) = f[(A \circ B)(x)]$

$= f\,[\sup\{\min\{A(y),B(z)\} \mid x=y \,.\, z\}]\ y, z\in R$

$= \sup\{\min\{f(A)(y), f(B)(z)\} \mid x=y \,.\, z\} = [f(A) \circ f(B)](x)$ by (Martines, 1995).

Hence, $f(A) \circ f(B) = f(A \circ B)$.
Note that

$A(f^{-1}(x)) = f(A(x))$

and

$A(f(x)) = f^{-1}(A(x))$

for each $x\in R$ since f is inverse image function.

3. To prove $f(A_t) = (f(A))_t$, let $x \in f(A_t)$ if and only if $f^{-1}(x) \in A_t$ if and only if $A(f^{-1}(x)) \geq t$ if and only if $f(A(x)) \geq t$ if and only if $x \in (f(A))_t$.
4. To prove $f^{-1}(A_t) = (f^{-1}(A))_t$, let $x \in f^{-1}(A_t)$ if and only if $f(x) \in A_t$ if and only if $A(f(x)) \geq t$ if and only if $f^{-1}(A(x)) \geq t$ if and only if $x \in (f^{-1}(A))_t$.

We give definition and some properties of quatient fuzzy ring.

Definition 1.9 (Abou-Draeb, 2000)

Let X be a fuzzy ring of R and A is a fuzzy ideal in X.
Define $X / A: R / A_* \to [0,1]$ such that:

$$X / A(a + A_*) = \begin{cases} 1 & if\ a \in A_* \\ \sup\{X(a+b)\} & if\ a \notin A_*, b \in A_* \end{cases}$$

For all $a + A_* \in R / A_*$, X / A is called a quatient fuzzy ring of X by A.

Proposition 1.10 (Abou-Draeb, 2000)

Let X be a fuzzy ring of R and A is a fuzzy ideal in X, then:

X / A is a fuzzy ring of R / A_*.

Proposition 1.11 (Abou-Draeb, 2000)

Let X be a fuzzy ring of R and A is a fuzzy ideal in X, then $X / A\,(0 + A_*) = 1$, $[0 + A_* = A_*]$.

Proposition 1.12 (Abou-Draeb, 2000)

Let X is a fuzzy ring of R. A and B are fuzzy ideals in X such that A$\subseteq$ B. Then B / A: R / A_* $\rightarrow$ [0,1] such that:

$$B / A(a + A_*) = \begin{cases} 1 & if\ a \in A_* \\ \sup\{B(a + b)\} & if\ a \notin A_*, b \in A_* \end{cases}$$

For all a + A_* $\in$ R / A_*, B / A is a fuzzy ideal in X / A.

Proposition 1.13

Let X be a fuzzy ring of R and A be a fuzzy ideal of X. Then:

1. $x_t + A_* = (x + A_*)_t$, $x_t \subseteq X$.
2. $a_t + A_* \subseteq b_k + A_*$ if and only if $a_t \subseteq b_k$, a_t, $b_k \subseteq X$.

Proof

1. Since A_t = {x: x $\in$ R l A(x) $\geq$ t} and A_*= { x: x $\in$ R l A(x) = A(0) }, implies that

$(A_*)_t$ ={x: x $\in$ R lA(x) =A(0) $\geq$ t } ={ x: x $\in$ R l A(x) =A(0)} =A_*.

Then $x_t + A_* = x_t + (A_*)_t$.

2. It is easy.

Proposition 1.14

Let X be a fuzzy ring of R and A, B, C be fuzzy ideals of X. Then:

1. (A$\cap$ B) / C = (A / C) $\cap$ (B / C).
2. (A$\circ$B) / C = (A / C) $\circ$ (B / C).

Proof

1. Let a+$C_*$$\in$R/$C_*$,

$$\begin{aligned} [(A \cap B) / C](a + C_*) &= \begin{cases} 1 & if\ a \in C_* \\ \sup\{A \cap B(a + b)\} & if\ a \notin C_*, b \in C_* \end{cases} \\ &= \begin{cases} 1 & if\ a \in C_* \\ \sup\{\min A(a + b), B(a + b)\} & if\ a \notin C_*, b \in C_* \end{cases} \end{aligned} \quad (1)$$

$$[(A/C)\cap(B/C)](a+C_*)=\min\{A/C(a+C_*),B/C(a+C_*)\}$$
$$=\begin{cases}1 & if\ a\in C_*\\ \min\{\sup\{A(a+b),B(a+b)\} & if\ a\notin C_*, b\in C_*\end{cases} \qquad (2)$$
$$=\begin{cases}1 & if\ a\in C_*\\ \sup\{\min A(a+b),B(a+b)\} & if\ a\notin C_*, b\in C_*\end{cases}$$

From (1) and (2), (A∩B) / C =(A/ C)∩ (B/C).

2. Let $a + C_* \in R / C_*$,

$$[(A\circ B)/C](a+C_*)=\begin{cases}1 & if\ a\in C_*\\ \sup\{A\circ B(a+b)\} & if\ a\notin C_*, b\in C_*\end{cases} \qquad (3)$$

$[(A / C)\circ(B/ C)]\ (a + C_*)$

$= \sup \{\inf \{\min \{A / C(d_i + C_*), B/ C\ (e_i + C_*)\} \mid d_i e_i \in R\} \mid a + C_*$

$= \sum_{i=1}^{n} (d_i + C_*)(e_i + C_*)\}.$

$[(A / C) \circ(B/ C)]\ (a + C_*)$

$= \sup \{\inf \{\min \{A / C(d_i + C_*), B/ C\ (e_i + C_*)\} \mid d_i e_i \in R\} \mid a + C_*$

$= \sum_{i=1}^{n} (d_i e_i + C_*)\}.$

But

$$(A/C)\ (d_i+C_*)=\begin{cases}1 & if\ d_i\in C_*\\ \sup\{\min A(d_i+b)\} & if\ d_i\notin C_*, b\in C_*\end{cases}$$

$$(B/C)\ (e_i+C_*)=\begin{cases}1 & if\ e_i\in C_*\\ \sup\{\min B(e_i+b)\} & if\ e_i\notin C_*, b\in C_*\end{cases}$$

Thus $[(A / C)\circ (B / C)](a+C_*) =$

$$\begin{cases} 1 & \text{if } d_i \in C_* \text{ or } e_i \in C_* \\ \sup\{\inf\{\min\{\sup\{A(d_i + b)\}, \sup\{B(e_i + b)\}\}\}\} & \text{if } d_i \text{ and } e_i \notin C_*, b \in C_* \end{cases}$$

$$= \begin{cases} 1 & \text{if } d_i \in C_* \text{ or } e_i \in C_* \\ \sup\{\inf\{\min\{\sup\{A(d_i + b)\}, \sup\{B(e_i + b)\}\}\}\} & \text{if } d_i \text{ and } e_i \notin C_*, b \in C_*, a = \sum_{i=1}^{n} d_i e_i \end{cases}$$

$$= \begin{cases} 1 & \text{if } d_i \in C_* \text{ or } e_i \in C_* \\ \sup\{A \circ B(\sum_{i=1}^{n} (d_i + b)(e_i + b))\}\}\}\} & \text{if } d_i \text{ and } e_i \notin C_*, b \in C_* a = \sum_{i=1}^{n} d_i e_i \end{cases}$$

$$= \begin{cases} 1 & \text{if } a \in C_* \\ \sup\left\{A \circ B\left[\sum_{i=1}^{n} d_i e_i + b\sum_{i=1}^{n} d_i + b\sum_{i=1}^{n} e_i + b^2\right]\right\} & \text{if } a \notin C_*, b \in C_* \end{cases}$$

$$= \begin{cases} 1 & \text{if } a \in C_* \\ \sup\{A \circ B(a + b_1)\} & \text{if } a \notin C_*, b_1 \in C_* \end{cases}, b_1 = b\, \Sigma i_{=1}\, di + b\, \Sigma i_{=1}\, e_i + b^2 \quad (4)$$

From (1) and (2), (A∘B) / C = (A / B) ∘ (B / C).

Proposition 1.15 (Abou-Draeb, 2010)

Let X be a fuzzy ring of R and A, B, C be fuzzy ideals of X. Then B / A = C / A if and only if B = C.

2. T-PURE FUZZY IDEALS

Recall that an ideal I of a ring R is called a t-pure ideal if for each ideal J of R, I∩J = I•J, (Kash F., 1982).

A fuzzy ideal A of R is called t-pure fuzzy ideal of R if for each fuzzy ideal B of R, A ∩ B= A o B, (Hadi and Abou-Draeb, 2004).

We shall give the definition and some properties for t-pure fuzzy ideals which will be needed later.

Lemma 2.1 (Hadi & Abou-Draeb, 2004)

Let X be a fuzzy ring of R and A, B are fuzzy ideals of X. Then: for all t ∈ [0, A(0)],

1. $(A \circ B)_t = A_t \bullet B_t$.
2. $(A \cap B)_t = A_t \cap B_t$.

Definition 2.2 (Hadi & Abou-Draeb, 2004)

If X is a fuzzy ring of a ring R, a fuzzy ideal A of X is called a t-pure fuzzy ideal of X if for each fuzzy ideal B of X, $A \cap B = A \circ B$.

Proposition 2.3 (Hadi & Abou-Draeb, 2004)

Let X be a fuzzy ring of R. Then $0_{X(0)}$ is a t-pure fuzzy ideal of X .

Proposition 2.4

Let A be a fuzzy ideal of R. Then A is a t-pure fuzzy ideal if and only if A_t is a t-pure ideal of R, for all $t \in (0,A(0)]$.

Proof

Suppose A is a t-pure fuzzy ideal of R. To prove A_t is a t-pure ideal of R, for all $t \in (0, A(0)]$.

We must show that $A_t \cap I = A_t \bullet I$, for any ideal I of R.

Let $B:R \rightarrow [0,1]$ defined by $B(x)=1$ if $x \in I$, $B(x)=0$ otherwise .

It can be easily shown that B is a fuzzy ideal of R and $I = (B)_t$, for all $t \in (0, A(0)]$. However $A \cap B = A \circ B$, since A is a t-pure fuzzy ideal of R.

Hence

$(A \cap B)_t = (A \circ B)_t$,

for all

$t \in (0, A(0)]$.

But

$(A \cap B)_t = A_t \cap B_t = A_t \cap I$

and

$(A \circ B)_t = A_t \bullet B_t = A_t \bullet I$,

by lemma (2.1). Then $A_t \cap I = A_t \bullet I$.

Thus $A_t \cap I = A_t \bullet I$ and so A_t is a t-pure ideal of R, for all $t \in (0,A(0)]$.

Conversely, if A_t is a t-pure ideal of R, for all $t \in (0, A(0)]$. To prove A is a t-pure fuzzy ideal of R.

Let B be any fuzzy ideal of R, then B_t is a ideal of R, for all

$t \in (0, A(0)]$

and so

$A_t \cap B_t = A_t \bullet B_t$.

Hence

$(A \cap B)_t = A_t \cap B_t$

and

$A_t \bullet B_t = (A \text{ o } B)_t$,

for all $t \in (0,A(0)]$, by lemma (2.1) .
Thus

$(A \cap B)_t = (A \text{ o } B)_t$,

for all $t \in (0, A(0)]$, which implies $A \cap B = A \text{ o } B$. Therefore A is a t-pure fuzzy ideal of R.

Corollary 2. 5

Let I be an ideal of R. Then I is a t-pure ideal if and only if B is a t-pure fuzzy ideal of R where B(x)=1 if $x \in I$ and B(x)=0 otherwise .

Proof

It follows directly by proposition (2.4) and in fact $B_t = I$, for all $t \in [0,B(0)]$.

Proposition 2.6

Let X be a fuzzy ring of R, A be a fuzzy ideal of X. Then A is a t-pure fuzzy ideal of X if and only if At is a t-pure ideal of X_t, for all $t \in (0, X(0)]$.

Proof

The proof is similarly.

Proposition 2.7 [Hadi and Abou-Draeb, 2004]

Let X be a fuzzy ring of R such that X(0) = 1,for all $a \in R$ and let I be ideal of R .I is t-pure ideal of R if and only if

$$A(x)=\begin{cases}1 & if\ x\in I\\ c & otherwise\end{cases}$$

is a t-pure fuzzy ideal of X, when c ∈ (0,1].

Proposition 2.8 [Hadi and Abou-Draeb, 2004]

Let X and Y be fuzzy rings of R_1 and R_2 respectively and A and C be fuzzy ideals of X and B and D be fuzzy ideals of Y respectively. Then:

1. $(A \oplus B) \cap (C \oplus D) = (A \cap C) \oplus (B \cap D)$.
2. $(A \oplus B)\ o\ (C \oplus D) = (A\ o\ C) \oplus (B\ o\ D)$.

Proposition 2.9

Let X and Y be fuzzy rings of R_1 and R_2 respectively and A and B be fuzzy ideals of X and Y respectively. Then A and B are t-pure fuzzy ideals if and only if $A \oplus B$ is t-pure fuzzy ideal of $X \oplus Y$.

Proof

(→) Let $C\oplus D$ be any fuzzy ideal of $X \oplus Y$. We must prove

$(A \oplus B) \cap (C \oplus D) = (A \oplus B)\ o\ (C \oplus D)$.

It is enough to prove

$(A \oplus B)\cap (C \oplus D) \subseteq (A \oplus B)\ o\ (C \oplus D)$.

But C is a fuzzy ideal of X and D is a fuzzy ideal of Y implies that

$A\cap C= A\ o\ C$ and $B \cap D = B\ o\ D$

since A and B are t-pure fuzzy ideals.

$(A \oplus B)\cap (C \oplus D) = (A \cap C) \oplus (B \cap D)$

by proposition (2.8).

$= (A\ o\ C) \oplus (B\ o\ D = (A \oplus B)\ o\ (C\oplus D)$

by proposition (2.8)

Hence $A \oplus B$ is t-pure fuzzy ideal of $X \oplus Y$.

Conversely, to prove A and B are t-pure fuzzy ideals of X and Y respectively.

Let C be any fuzzy ideal of X and D be any fuzzy ideal of Y.
To prove

$A \circ C = A \cap C$ and $B \circ D = B \cap D$.

but

$(A \oplus B) \cap (C \oplus D) = (A \oplus B) \circ (C \oplus D)$.

Since $(A \oplus B)$, $(C \oplus D)$ are fuzzy ideals of $X \oplus Y$ and $(A \oplus B)$ is t-pure fuzzy ideal of $X \oplus Y$.
Note

$(A \oplus B) \cap (C \oplus D) = (A \cap C) \oplus (B \cap D)$

by proposition (2.8) and

$(A \oplus B) \cap (C \oplus D) = (A \circ C) \oplus (B \circ D)$

by defined (2.5).
Thus

$(A \circ C) \oplus (B \circ D) = (A \cap C) \oplus (B \cap D)$

implies that

$A \circ C = A \cap C$ and $B \circ D = B \cap D$

by corollary (1.5).
Hence A and B are t-pure fuzzy ideals of X and Y respectively.

Proposition 2.10

Let $X: R_1 \rightarrow [0,1]$, $Y: R_2 \rightarrow [0,1]$ are fuzzy rings $f: R_1 \rightarrow R_2$ be epimorphism function and $A: R_1 \rightarrow [0,1]$ is a fuzzy ideal of R_1 and $B: R_2 \rightarrow [0,1]$ is a fuzzy ideal of Y, then:

1. If A is t-pure fuzzy ideal of R_1, then f(A) is t-pure fuzzy ideal of R_2.
2. If B is t-pure fuzzy ideal of R_2, then $f^{-1}(B)$ is t-pure fuzzy ideal of R_1.

Proof

To prove the first, see (Hadi and Abou-Draeb, 2004).
To prove the second, let D be fuzzy ideal of R_1. To prove $f^{-1}(B)$ is t-pure fuzzy ideal of R_1, that mean $f^{-1}(B) \cap D = f^{-1}(B) \circ D$.
It is enough prove

$f^{-1}(B) \cap D \subseteq f^{-1}(B) \circ D$

Consider

$f(f^{-1}(B) \cap D) = f(f^{-1}(B)) \cap f(D)$

$= B \cap f(D)$

$= B \circ f(D)$, since B is t-pure fuzzy ideal.

Hence

$f^{-1}[f(f^{-1}(B) \cap D)] = f^{-1}[B \circ f(D)]$

$f^{-1}(B) \cap D = f^{-1}(B) \circ f^{-1}(f(D))$

$f^{-1}(B) \cap C = f^{-1}(B) \circ D$

Then $f^{-1}(B)$ is t-pure fuzzy ideal of R_1.

Corollary 2. 11

Let X: $R_1 \rightarrow [0,1]$, Y: $R_2 \rightarrow [0,1]$ are fuzzy rings f: $R_1 \rightarrow R_2$ be homomorphism function between them and onto and A: $R_1 \rightarrow [0,1]$ is a fuzzy ideal of X and B: $R_2 \rightarrow [0,1]$ is a fuzzy ideal of Y, then:

1. If A is t-pure fuzzy ideal of X, then f(A) is t-pure fuzzy ideal of Y.
2. If B is t-pure fuzzy ideal of Y, then $f^{-1}(B)$ is t-pure fuzzy ideal of X.

Proposition 2.12

Let X be a fuzzy ring of R. A, B are fuzzy ideals of X such that $A \subseteq B$ .X / A is a fuzzy ring of R / A_* and B / A is a fuzzy ideal in X / A. B/ A is a t-pure fuzzy ideal in X / A if and only if B is t-pure fuzzy ideal of X.

Proof

Suppose B / A is a t-pure fuzzy ideal in X / A, to prove B is t-pure fuzzy ideal of X.
Let C be fuzzy ideal of X, C/ A is fuzzy ideal in X / A.

$(B / A) \cap (C / A) = (B / A) \circ (C / A)$

if and only if

$(B \cap C) / A = (B \circ C) / A$

by proposition (1.14) if and only if $(B\cap C) = (B \circ C)$ by proposition (1.15). Then B is t-pure fuzzy ideal of X.

Conversely, if B is t-pure fuzzy ideal of X, to prove B / A is a t-pure fuzzy ideal in X / A.

Let C/ A is fuzzy ideal in X / A, C be fuzzy ideal of X.

$(B / A)\cap (C / A) = (B\cap C) / A$

by proposition (1.14)

$= (B \circ C) / A$

by definition (2.2).

$= (B / A) \circ (C / A)$

by proposition (1.14).

Then B / A is a t-pure fuzzy ideal in X / A.

3. P-F FUZZY RINGS

In this section, we will fuzzify the concept of P-F ring into P-F fuzzy ring. Then we will investigate some basic results about P-F fuzzy rings.

Recall that any ring R is called a P-F ring if $ann_R(a)$ is a t-pure ideal of R, for all $a\in R$, (Kash, 1982).

Before giving the definition of P-F fuzzy ring, we have:

Definition 3.1 (Abou-Draeb, 2000)

Let A be a nonempty fuzzy ideal of R. The Annihilator of A denoted by (F-Ann A) is defined by

$\{xt: x \in R, x_t \circ A \subseteq 0_1\}, t \in [0, A(0)]$.

Note that

$(F\text{-}Ann\ A)(a) = \sup \{t: t \in [0, A(0)], a_t \circ A \subseteq 0_1\}, a\in R$.

$= (0_1: A)$.

Proposition 3.2 (Abou-Draeb, 2000)

Let X be fuzzy ring of R and $a\in R$, $[F\text{-}Ann\ (a_t)]_k = ann\ (a)$ for all t, k (0, X (0)].

Proposition 3.3 (Abou-Draeb, 2000)

The Annihilator of a fuzzy ideal A of R (F-Ann A) is a fuzzy ideal of R.

Proposition 3.4

Let X be a fuzzy ring of R and a $\in$R, t $\in$ [0, X(0)], then:
F-Ann (a_t) is a fuzzy ideal of a fuzzy ring X of a ring R, when F-Ann (a_t) $\subseteq$ X.

Proof

Let b, c $\in$R, to prove the following:

1. F-Ann (a_t) (b-c) $\geq$ min {F-Ann (a_t) (b), F-Ann (a_t) (c)}.
2. F-Ann (a_t) (b.c) $\geq$ min {max {F-Ann (a_t) (b), F-Ann (a_t) (c)},X(b.c)}.

Now, let F-Ann (a_t) (b) = h and F-Ann (a_t) (c) = k, where h, k $\in$ (0,X(0)].
Let F-Ann (a_t) (b-c) = r, to prove r $\geq$ min {h,k} = λ.
Since

$b_h \text{ o } a_t \subseteq 0_{X(0)}$

and

$c_k \text{ o } a_t \subseteq 0_{X(0)}$

and

$b_h \subseteq b_\lambda$, $c_k \subseteq c_\lambda$,

then

$b_\lambda \text{ o } a_t \subseteq b_h \text{ o } a_t$, $c_\lambda \text{ o } a_t \subseteq c_k \text{ o } a_t$, (Hameed, 2000),

implies that

$b_\lambda \text{ o } a_t \subseteq 0_{X(0)}$, $c_\lambda \text{ o } a_t \subseteq 0_{X(0)}$, (Abou-Draeb, 2000).

Hence

$(b_\lambda \text{ o } a_t) - (c_\lambda \text{ o } a_t) \subseteq 0_{X(0)} - 0_{X(0)} = 0_{X(0)}$, (Abou-Draeb, 2000),

implies that

$(b_\lambda - c_\lambda)\, a_t \subseteq 0_{X(0)}$

and

$(b - c)_\lambda\, a_t \subseteq 0_{X(0)}$.

Then $(b - c)_\lambda \subseteq$ F-Ann (a_t).
But

F-Ann $(a_t)(b\text{-}c)= \sup \{ \beta: \beta \in (0,X(0)],\ (b - c)_\beta \text{ o } a_t \subseteq 0_{X(0)}\} = r \geq \lambda$.

The first condition is true.
Now, to prove the second condition. Let F-Ann $(a_t)(bc) = r$ and $X(bc) = q$.
To prove

$r \geq \min\{\max\{h, k\}, q\}$.

Suppose that

$\max \{h, k\} = h,\ (bc)_r \text{ o } a_t \subseteq 0_{X(0)}$.

But

$(bc)_h \text{ o } a_t \subseteq ((bc)\, a)_\lambda \subseteq (c\, (ba))_\lambda \subseteq (c_h \text{ o } (b_h \text{ o } a_t) \subseteq c_h \text{ o } 0_{X(0)} \subseteq 0_{X(0)}$

where $\lambda = \min \{h, t\}$. Since

F-Ann $(a_t)(bc)= \sup \{\beta: \beta \in (0,X(0)],\ (bc)_\beta \text{ o } a_t \subseteq 0_{X(0)}\} = r \geq h$.

Similarly, if $\max \{h, k\} = k$, then $r \geq k$.
Hence $r \geq \max \{h, k\}$, then F-Ann (a_t) is a fuzzy ideal of R.
Since

F-Ann $(a_t)(bc) \subseteq X(bc)$,

then

F-Ann $(a_t)(bc) \geq \min\{\max\{$F-Ann$(a_t)(b)$, F-Ann $(a_t)\ (c)\}, X(bc)\}$.

Thus F-Ann (a_t) is a fuzzy ideal of a fuzzy ring X of a ring R.
We shall the definition as follows:

Definition 3.5 (Hadi and Abou-Draeb, 2004)

Let X be a fuzzy ring of R. X is called P-F fuzzy ring if F-Ann (a_t) is a t-pure fuzzy ideal of X, for each $a_t \subseteq X$ and $t \in (0,X(0)]$.

That mean: if A is a fuzzy ideal of X, then F-Ann (a_t) o A$\subseteq$ F-Ann (a_t)$\cap$ A.

Now, we give some properties and Theorems about this concept.

Theorem 3.6

Let X be a fuzzy ring of R and $x_t \subseteq X$, for all $t\in (0,X(0)]$. X is a P-F fuzzy ring if and only if X_t is a P-F ring, for all $t \in (0,X(0)]$.

Proof

If X is a P- F fuzzy ring, to prove X_t is a P-F ring, for all $t \in (0, X(0)]$.

Let $a \in X_t$, then $a_t \subseteq X$. Since X is P- F fuzzy ring, then F-ann (a_t) is a t-pure fuzzy ideal of X by definition (3.5). That mean

F-ann (a_t) o B= F-ann (a_t)$\cap$ B

for each B fuzzy ideal of X.

To prove ann (a) is t-pure ideal in X_t, for all $t \in (0,X(0)]$. Let I be any ideal of X_t, for all $t \in (0,X(0)]$, we must prove

ann(a)$\cap$ I = ann(a) o I.

It is enough to show that

ann(a)$\cap$ I$\subseteq$ ann(a) o I.

Define B: R $\rightarrow$ [0, 1] such that

$B(y) = X(y)$ if $y\in I$

and B(y)= 0 otherwise. B is a fuzzy ideal of X by (Swamy and Swamy, 1988).

Let x$\in$ ann(a) $\cap$ I, then x $\in$ ann(a) and

$x \in I$, let $X(x) = r$, $r \in (0,X(0)]$

implies that x a = 0 and B(x) = X(x) = r implies that

$x_r\, a_t \subseteq 0_{X(0)}$

and

$x_r \subseteq B$,

then

$x_r \subseteq$ F-ann (a_t)

and

$x_r \subseteq B$.

Hence

$x_r \subseteq$ F-ann $(a_t) \cap B =$ F-ann (a_t) o B.

Since

(F-ann $(a_t) \cap B)(x) = \min\{$ F-ann (a_t) (x), B(x) $\} \geq r$,

then $x \in$ F-ann (a_t) o B.

Let

F-ann $(a_t) = c$, c $B(x) \geq r$

and

$\sup\{\inf\{\min\{c(b_i),B(d_i)\} | x=\sum b_i d_i\}\} \geq r$.

Note that

$\min\{c(b_i),B(d_i)\} \geq r$

for all i= 1,2,--,n., then $c(b_i) \geq r$ and $B(d_i) \geq r$. Hence

$(b_i)_r \subseteq$ F-ann $(a_t) = c$,

then

$(b_i)_r a_t \subseteq 0_{X(0)}$

for all i= 1,2,--,n. b_i a =0 for all i= 1,2,--,n ., then $b_i \subseteq$ ann (a) for all i= 1,2,--,n.

Also,

$B(d_i)$ r = X(x), $d_i \in I$

for all i= 1,2,--,n. Hence

$x=\sum b_i d_i \in \text{ann}(a) \circ I$,

thus

$\text{ann}(a) \cap I \subseteq \text{ann}(a) \circ I$

and X_t is a P- F ring, for all $t \in (0,X(0)]$.

Conversely, since X_t is a P- F ring, for all $t \in (0, X(0)]$, then to prove X is a P-F fuzzy ring.

Let $a_t \subseteq X$, then $a \in X_t$, since X_t is a P- F ring, for all $t \in (0,X(0)]$, then ann (a) is t-pure ideal of X_t, that mean $\text{ann}(a) \circ I = \text{ann}(a) \cap I$, for all I ideal of X_t .

To prove F-ann (a_t) is a t-pure fuzzy ideal of X, let B is a fuzzy ideal of X. We must prove

F-ann $(a_t) \cap B=$ F- ann (a) o B.

It is enough to show that

F-ann $(a_t) \cap B \subseteq$ F-ann (a_t) o B.

Let

$x \in R$, $t \in (0,X(0)]$,

note that B_t is ideal of

X_t and $x_t \subseteq$ (F-ann $(a_t) \cap B$), $x_t \subseteq$ F-ann (a_t)

and $x_t \subseteq B$, then

$x_t \circ a_t \subseteq 0_{X(0)}$

and

$B(x) \geq t$ x a =0

and $x \in B_t$, then $x \in \text{ann}(a)$ and $x \in B_t$.

Hence

$x \in \text{ann}(a) \cap B_t = \text{ann}(a) \circ B_t$.

There exists

$b_i \in \text{ann}(a)$ and $d_i \in B_t$

such that

$x=\sum b_i d_i$, $b_i \in ann (a) = (F\text{-}ann (a_t))_t$

by proposition (3.2)

$(b_i)_t \subseteq F\text{- } ann (a_t)$

and $d_i \in B_t$, then $(d_i)_t \subseteq B$, for all i= 1,2,--,n. Such that

$B(d_i) \geq t$ andb$(F\text{-}ann (a_t) (b_i)) \geq t$.

Then

$\min\{F\text{-}ann (a_t) (b_i), B(d_i)\} \geq t$,

for all i= 1,2,--,n.

And

$\inf \{\min\{F\text{-}ann (a_t) (b_i), B(d_i)\} \mid x=\sum b_i d_i\}\} \geq t$.

Also,

$\sup\{\inf \{\min\{F\text{-}ann (a_t) (b_i), B(d_i)\} \mid x=\sum b_i d_i\}\}\} \geq t$.

Hence

$(F\text{-}ann (a_t) \circ B)(x) = \sup\{\inf \{\min\{F\text{-}ann (a_t) (b_i), B(d_i)\} \mid x=\sum b_i d_i\}\}\} \geq t$,

then

$x_t \subseteq F\text{-}ann (a_t) \circ B$.

$F\text{-}ann (a_t) \cap B \subseteq F\text{-}ann (a_t) \circ B$.

Thus X is a P-F fuzzy ring.

Remark 3.7 [Hadi & Abou-Draeb, 2004]

Let X be a fuzzy ring of R. If X is a P- F fuzzy ring of R, then R is not necessary P- F ring.

Example

Let X: $Z_{12} \rightarrow [0,1]$ defined by X(a) = 1 if a {0,4,8} and X(a) = 0 otherwise.

Then for all $t > 0$, $x_t = \{0,4,8\}$ which is a P-F ring. Hence X is a P-F ring of Z_{12} by theorem (3.6). However Z_{12} is not a P-F ring.

Proposition 3.8

Let X be a fuzzy ring over field F, then X is a P-F fuzzy ring of F.

Proof

Let a_t X and $a \neq 0$, let

$r_k \in$ F-ann (a_t) $r_k \circ a_t \subseteq 0_{X(0)}$,

then a. r= 0 and r = 0. Then F-ann $(a_t) = 0_{X(0)}$ is t-pure fuzzy ideal of X by proposition (2.3).

Hence X is a P-F fuzzy ring of F.

Note that, if X is a fuzzy ring over an integral domain R, then X is a P-F fuzzy ring of R.

Proposition 3.9

Let X be a fuzzy ring of R and A be a fuzzy ideal of X. If X is a P-F fuzzy ring of R, then (F-Ann A) is a t-pure fuzzy ideal of X.

Proof

Since If X is a P-F fuzzy ring of R and A be a fuzzy ideal of X, then (F-Ann A) is a fuzzy ideal of X by proposition (3.3).

To prove (F-Ann A) is a t-pure. That mean

(F-Ann A) $\cap$ B = (F-Ann A) o B,

for any B fuzzy ideal of X.

If $X(0) = 1$ and $a_t \subseteq A$, then F-ann (a_t) = F-Ann A by (Swamy and Swamy, 1988; Abou-Draeb, 2010).

[F-ann (a_t) o B = F-ann (a_t) $\cap$B] = [F-Ann A o B = F-Ann A $\cap$ B]

by (Abou-Draeb, 2000). Then (F-Ann A) is a t-pure fuzzy ideal of X

Lemma 3.10

Let R be a P-F ring, then every subring of R is P-F ring.

Theorem 3.11 (Hadi & Abou-Draeb, 2004)

Let X and Y be fuzzy rings of R_1 and R_2 respectively. Then X and Y are P-F fuzzy rings if and only if $X \oplus Y$ is a P-F fuzzy ring of $R_1 \oplus R_2$.

Theorem 3.12

Let X be a fuzzy ring of R and A be a fuzzy ideal in X .X is a P- F fuzzy ring if X/A is a P-F fuzzy ring of R/ A_*.

Proof

If X/A is a P-F fuzzy ring of R/ A_*, we must prove X is a P- F fuzzy ring, that mean F-ann (a_t) is t-pure fuzzy ideal of X, for all

$a_t \subseteq X$, $t \in (0,X(0)]$.

We must prove

F-ann (a_t) $\cap$ B= F- ann (a) o B

for every fuzzy ideal of X. It is enough to show that

F-ann (a_t) $\cap$ B $\subseteq$ F-ann (a_t) o B.

Since X/A is P-F fuzzy ring of R/ A_*, then F-ann (a_t) / A and B/ A are fuzzy ideals of X/A. And

(F-ann (a_t)/A) $\cap$(B/ A) =(F-ann (a_t)/ A) o (B/ A) $\leftrightarrow$(F-ann (a_t) $\cap$ B) / A=(F-ann (a_t) o B) / A

by proposition (1.14).

$\leftrightarrow$ (F-ann (a_t) $\cap$ B = F-ann (a_t) o B

by proposition (1.15).
Hence F-ann (a_t) is t-pure fuzzy ideal of X $\leftrightarrow$ X is a P-F fuzzy ring of R.

Remark 3.13

The converse of theorem (3.12) is not true as the following example shows.

Example

Let X: Z$\rightarrow$[0,1] such that:

$$X(a) = \begin{cases} 1 & if\ a \in 2Z \\ 0 & otherwise \end{cases}$$

X is a fuzzy ring of Z and fuzzy ideals A, B in X such that:

$$A_a = \begin{cases} 1 & if\ a \in 4Z \\ 1/2 & if\ a \in Z/4Z \end{cases}$$

Note that $A_* = 4Z$. And

$$B(a) = \begin{cases} 1 & if\ a \in 4Z \\ 1/2 & if\ a \in 2Z/4Z \end{cases}$$

and B(a) =0 otherwise.

Then $X/A:Z/4Z \to [0,1]$ such that:

$$X(a + A_*) = \begin{cases} 1 & if\ a \in 4Z \\ \sup(a+b) & if\ b \in 4Z, a \notin 4Z \end{cases}$$

$$= \begin{cases} 1 & if\ a + A* = A* \\ 1/2 & if\ a + A* = 2 + A* \end{cases} \quad X(a + A_*) = 0$$

otherwise.

X is a P-F fuzzy ring and F- ann (2+ A)=B, B is not t-pure fuzzy ideal of X/A, since $B \cap B = B$ and $B \circ B = 0_{X/A}$.

4. NORMAL FUZZY RINGS

In this section, we introduce the concept of a Normal fuzzy ring and we state some properties and Theorems about it. Also we shall give its relationship with P-F fuzzy ring.

As a generalization of definition in (Kash, 1982), a ring R is called a normal if every ideal of R is t-pure ideal.

Definition 4.1 (Abou-Draeb, 2010)

Let X be a fuzzy ring of R .X is called a Normal fuzzy ring if every fuzzy ideal of X is t-pure fuzzy ideal.

Now, we give the following properties:

Proposition 4.2 (Hadi & Abou-Draeb, 2004)

Let X be a fuzzy ring of R .X is a Normal fuzzy ring of R if and only if X_t is a normal ring, for all t ∈ (0,X(0)] .

Remark 4.3 (Hadi & Abou-Draeb, 2004)

Let X be a fuzzy ring of a ring R. If R is a normal ring, then X $_{is}$ not necessarily that Normal fuzzy ring.

Example

Let R =Q is a normal ring and

$$X(a) = \begin{cases} 1 & if\ a \in Z \\ 0 & otherwise \end{cases}$$

X is a fuzzy ring of Q. But X_t=Z for all t = 0 and Z is not normal ring.
Hence X is not Normal fuzzy ring by proposition (4.2).

Remark 4.4

The converse of proposition (4.3) is not true as the following example shows.

Example

Let R =Z_{12} is not normal ring and

$$X(a) = \begin{cases} 1 & if\ a \in \{0,4,8\} \\ 0 & otherwise \end{cases}$$

But X is a Normal fuzzy ring.

Proposition 4.5

Let X: $R_1 \rightarrow [0,1]$, Y: $R_2 \rightarrow [0,1]$ are fuzzy rings. f: $R_1 \rightarrow R_2$ be epimorphism function. Then:

1. If X is Normal fuzzy ring, then Y is Normal fuzzy ring.
2. If Y is Normal fuzzy ring, then X is Normal fuzzy ring, where every fuzzy ideal of X is f-invariant.

Proof

The proof follows directly by proposition (2.11) and definition (4.1).

Proposition 4. 6

Let X and Y be fuzzy rings of R_1 and R_2 respectively. X and Y are Normal if and only if X⊕Y is Normal fuzzy ring of $R_1 \oplus R_2$.

Proof

Let X and Y are Normal fuzzy rings, to prove X ⊕ Y is Normal fuzzy ring.

Since X and Y be fuzzy rings of R_1 and R_2 respectively, then (X ⊕ Y) is fuzzy ring, by (Abou-Draeb, 2000).

Let (C ⊕ D) be a fuzzy ideal of (X ⊕ Y), then C is fuzzy ideal of X and D is a fuzzy ideal of Y.

Since X and Y are Normal, then C and D are t-pure fuzzy ideals of X and Y respectively $\Longrightarrow$ (C ⊕ D) is a t-pure fuzzy ideal of X ⊕ Y by proposition (2.9).

Hence X ⊕ Y is Normal fuzzy ring of $R_1 \oplus R_2$.

Conversely, X ⊕ Y is Normal fuzzy ring, we must prove X and Y are Normal fuzzy rings of R_1 and R_2 respectively.

Let A and B be fuzzy ideals of X and Y respectively, then (A ⊕ B) is a fuzzy ideal of (X ⊕ Y).

Since X ⊕ Y is Normal, then (A ⊕ B) is a t-pure fuzzy ideal $\Longrightarrow$ A and B are t-pure fuzzy ideals of X and Y respectively by proposition (2.9)

Hence X and Y are Normal fuzzy rings of R_1 and R_2 respectively.

Proposition 4.7

Let X be a fuzzy ring of a ring R and A be a fuzzy ideal in X. Then X is a Normal fuzzy ring if and only if X/A is a Normal fuzzy ring of R/A_*.

Proof

Let X be a Normal fuzzy ring, to prove X/A is a Normal fuzzy ring of R/A_*. By (Abou-Draeb, 2000), X/A is a fuzzy ring of R/A_*.

We must prove X/A is a Normal fuzzy ring of R/A_*. Let B is a fuzzy ideal of X, then B is t-pure by definition (4.1) implies that B/A is t-pure fuzzy ideal by proposition (2.12) that mean

$$(B/A) \cap (C/A) = (B/A) \circ (C/A)$$

for all C/A fuzzy ideal of X/A.

Hence X/A is Normal fuzzy ring

Conversely, we must prove X is Normal fuzzy ring. Let B be any fuzzy ideal of X, to prove B is t-pure fuzzy ideal that mean

$$B \cap C = B \circ C$$

for all C fuzzy ideal of X.

But B/A, C/A are fuzzy ideals of X/A and X/A is Normal fuzzy ring, then

(B/A) ∩ (C/A) = (B/A) o (C/A).

By proposition (1.14),

(B/A) ∩ (C/A) = (B∩ C) /A

and

(B/A) o (C/A) = (B o C) /A,

then

(B∩ C) /A = (B o C) /A.

Thus B ∩ C =B o C by proposition (1.15), then B is t-pure fuzzy ideal.
Hence X is Normal fuzzy ring of R.
We give the relation about Normal fuzzy ring and P-F fuzzy ring.

Proposition 4.8

Let X be a fuzzy ring of a ring R. If X is a Normal fuzzy ring, then X is P-F fuzzy ring of R.

Proof

Since X is a fuzzy ring of a ring R, that mean any fuzzy ideal of X is t-pure, then F-ann (a_t) is t-pure fuzzy ideal of X, for each $a_t \subseteq X \Longrightarrow$ X is a P-F fuzzy ring of R.

Remark 4.9

The converse of proposition (4.8) is not true as the following example shows.

Example

Let R =Q is a normal ring and

$$X(a) = \begin{cases} 1 & \text{if } a \in Z \\ 0 & \text{otherwise} \end{cases}$$

X is a fuzzy ring of Q. But X_t=Z for all t ∈ (0,1] and Z is not normal ring.
Hence X is not Normal fuzzy ring by proposition (4.2).

$[\text{F-ann}(a_t)]_k$ = ann(a) for all k ∈ (0,1].
= {0}

is pure ideal of $Z = X_t$ for all $k \in (0,1]$.

Then F-ann (a_t) is t-pure fuzzy ideal of X.

Hence X is a P-F fuzzy ring of R.

REFERENCES

Abou-Draeb, A. T. (2000). *On Almost Quasi–Frobenius Fuzzy Rings* (M.Sc. Thesis). University of Baghdad, College of Education Ibn-AL-Haitham.

Abou-Draeb, A.T. (2010). *Fuzzy Quotient Rings and Fuzzy Isomorphism Theorem*. Academic Press.

Al-Khamees, Y., & Mordeson, J. N. (1998). Fuzzy Principal Ideals and Simple Field Extensions. *Fuzzy Sets and Systems*, (96): 247–253.

Dixit, V. N., Kumar, R., & Ajmal, N. (1991). Fuzzy Ideals and Fuzzy Prime Ideals of a Ring. *Fuzzy Sets and Systems*, *44*(1), 127–138. doi:10.1016/0165-0114(91)90038-R

Hadi, I.M.A., & Abou-Draeb, A.T. (2004). P-F Fuzzy Rings and Normal Fuzzy Rings. *Ibn-Al-Haitham J. for Pure & Appl. Sci.,* (17), 111 – 120.

Kash, F. (1982). *Modules and Rings*. New York: Academic Press.

Liu, W. J. (1982). Fuzzy Invariant Subgroups and Fuzzy Ideal. *Fuzzy Sets and Systems*, *8*(8), 133–139. doi:10.1016/0165-0114(82)90003-3

Martines, L. (1995). Fuzzy Subgroup of Fuzzy Groups and Fuzzy Ideals of Fuzzy Rings. *The Journal of Fuzzy Mathematics*, (3), 833 – 849.

Martinez, L. (1999). Prime and Primary L– Fuzzy Ideals of L– Fuzzy Rings. *Fuzzy Sets and Systems*, *101*(3), 489–494. doi:10.1016/S0165-0114(97)00114-0

Mukherjee, T. K., & Sen, M. K. (1987). On Fuzzy Ideals of a Ring I. *Fuzzy Sets and Systems*, *21*(1), 99–104. doi:10.1016/0165-0114(87)90155-2

Swamy, U.M., & Swamy, K. L. N. (1988). Fuzzy Prime Ideals of Rings. *The Journal of Fuzzy Mathematics*, (134), 94 – 103.

Zadeh, L. A. (1965). Fuzzy Sets. *Information and Control*, *8*(8), 338–353. doi:10.1016/S0019-9958(65)90241-X

Chapter 5
Intutionistic Fuzzy Difference Equation

Sankar Prasad Mondal
National Institute of Technology Agartala, India

Dileep Kumar Vishwakarma
National Institute of Technology Agartala, India

Apu Kumar Saha
National Institute of Technology Agartala, India

ABSTRACT

In this chapter we solve linear difference equation with intuitionistic fuzzy initial condition. All possible cases are defined and solved them to obtain the exact solutions. The intuitionistic fuzzy numbers are also taken as trapezoidal intuitionistic fuzzy number. The problems are illustrated by two different numerical examples.

INTRODUCTION

Fuzzy Sets and Intuitionistic Fuzzy Sets

Lotfi A. Zadeh (1965) published the paper on his new theory of Fuzzy Sets and Systems in the year 1965. Since the 1980s, this mathematical theory of "uncertain ammount" has been applied with great success in many different areas. Chang and Zadeh (1972) introduced the concept of fuzzy numbers in 1972. A lot of mathematicians have been studying the concept (one-dimension or n-dimension) fuzzy numbers, see for example Diamond and Kloeden (1994), Dubois and Prade (1978), Goetschel and Voxman (1986), Kaleva (1987). With the development of theories and applications of fuzzy numbers, this concept becomes more and more important.

Generalizations of fuzzy sets theory are considered to be one of Intuitionistic fuzzy set (IFS) theory. Out of several higher-order fuzzy sets, IFS was first introduced by Atanassov (1983) and have been found to be suitable to deal with unexplored areas. The fuzzy set considers only the degree of belong-

DOI: 10.4018/978-1-5225-0914-1.ch005

ingness. Fuzzy set theory does not incorporate the degree of hesitation (i.e., degree of non-determinacy defined as, 1- sum of membership function and non-membership function. To handle such situations, Atanassov (1983) explored the concept of fuzzy set theory by intuitionistic fuzzy set (IFS) theory. The degree of acceptance in Fuzzy Sets is only considered, otherwise IFS is characterized by a membership function and a non-membership function so that the sum of both values is less than one (see Atanassov (1986)). Now-a-days, IFSs are being studied extensively and being used in different fields of Science and Technology.

Necessity for Difference Equation and Fuzzy Difference

In modeling of real natural phenomena, difference equations play an important role in many areas of discipline, exemplary in economics, biomathematics, sciences and engineering. Many experts in such areas widely use difference equations in order to make some problems under study more comprehensible.

Difference Equation

Recently the study of the behavior of difference equation and difference equation system is a topic of a great interest. A difference equation is an equation specifying the change in a variable between two periods. By using the difference equation we can study the concerning factors, which cause the change in the value of the given functions in different time periods. It is known that difference equation appears naturally as discrete system which has many applications in computer science, control engineering, ecology, population dynamics, queuing problems, statistical problems, stochastic time sires, geometry, psychology, sociology physics economics engineering etc. The theory of difference equations developed greatly during last three decays. The theory of difference equation occupies an important position in different fields. No doubt the theory of difference equation is play important role in mathematics as well as its applications.

Fuzzy Difference Equation and Intuitionistic Fuzzy Difference Equation

There exist several research papers where difference equation is solved with fuzzy environment. Now we concentrate some published paper:

Deeba et.al. (1996) solve a fuzzy difference equation with an application. The model of CO2 level in blood is modeled with fuzzy difference equation and solved by Deeba et. al. (1999). Lakshmikantham and Vatsala (2002) discuss the basic theory of fuzzy difference equations. Papaschinopoulos et.al. (2002a, 2002b). Papaschinopoulos and Schinas (2000) discuss the behavior and solution of some different type of fuzzy difference equations. Papaschinopoulos and Stefanidou (2003) give a description on boundedness and asymptotic behavior of the solutions of a fuzzy difference equation. Umekkan et.al. (2014) give an application of finance in fuzzy difference equation. Stefanidou et.al. (2010) give brief discussion on an exponential type fuzzy difference equation. The asymptotic behavior of a second order fuzzy difference equation is delivered by Din (2015). The behavior of solution to a fuzzy non linear difference equations are treated by Zhang et.al. (2012). Memarbashi and Ghasemabadi (2013) solved fuzzy difference equation of volterra type. A fuzzy difference equation of rational form was solved by Stefanidou and Papaschinopoulos (2005). The application of fuzzy difference equation in finance is consider by Konstantinos et.al. (2008).

Motivation

Many authors consider fuzzy difference equation. But no one solve difference equation in intuitionistic fuzzy environment. But the point is that they considered the fuzzy numbers which only define the membership i.e., the acceptance or, belongingness. For reality if membership functions define the belongingness then there exists a non belongingness which can be defined by non membership function. In this paper we consider intuitionistic fuzzy number with difference equation. Here we solve the problem using -cut sets of intuitionistic fuzzy number and intuitionistic fuzzy function.

Novelties

In spite the above mention developments, few developments can still be done by our self which are:

1. Difference equation is solved in intuitionistic fuzzy environment.
2. The intuitionistic fuzzy numbers are taken as trapezoidal intutionistic fuzzy number.
3. The possible all cases are discussed with numerical examples.

Structure of the Chapter

The structure of the chapter is as follows: In first section we introduce the previous work on fuzzy and intuitionistic fuzzy sets, fuzzy and intuitionistic fuzzy difference equation. Second section goes to preliminary concept. We define fuzzy and intuitionistic fuzzy number here. In third section we introduce difference and intuitionistic fuzzy difference equation. Forth section goes the solution for different cases. In fifth section the numerical examples are illustrated. The conclusion is done in sixth section.

PRELIMINARIES

Basic Concept of Fuzzy and Intuitionistic Fuzzy Set Theory

Definition 2.1: Fuzzy Set

A fuzzy set $\tilde{A}$ is defined by

$$\tilde{A} = \left\{\left(x, \mu_{\tilde{A}}\left(x\right)\right) : x \in A, \mu_{\tilde{A}}\left(x\right) \in \left[0,1\right]\right\}.$$

In the pair $\left(x, \mu_{\tilde{A}}\left(x\right)\right)$ the first element x belong to the classical set A, the second element $\mu_{\tilde{A}}\left(x\right)$, belong to the interval [0,1], called Membership function.

Definition 2.2: α-Cut of a Fuzzy Set

The α-level set (or interval of confidence at level α or α -cut) of the fuzzy set $\tilde{A}$ of X is a crisp set A_α that contains all the elements of X that have membership values in $\tilde{A}$ greater than or equal to α i.e.,

$$\tilde{A} = \left\{x : \mu_{\tilde{A}}\left(x\right) \geq \alpha, x \in X, \alpha \in \left[0,1\right]\right\}$$

Definition 2.3: Fuzzy Number (Zadeh (2005))

A fuzzy number is fuzzy set like u: $R \rightarrow I=[0,1]$ which satisfies

1. u is upper semi-continuous.
2. $u(x)=0$ outside the interval $[c,d]$
3. There are real numbers a,b such $c \leq a \leq b \leq d$ and
   a. $u(x)$ is monotonic increasing on $[c,a]$,
   b. $u(x)$ is monotonic decreasing on $[b,d]$,
   c. $u(x)=1$, $a \leq x \leq b$

Let E^1 be the set of all real fuzzy numbers which are normal, upper semi-continuous, convex and compactly supported fuzzy sets.

Definition 2.4: Fuzzy Number (Parametric Form) (Chang and Zadeh (1972))

A fuzzy number u in a parametric form is a pair (u_1,u_2) of function $u_1(r)$, $u_2(r)$, $0 \leq r \leq 1$, which satisfies the following requirements:

1. $u_1(r)$ is a bounded monotonic increasing left continuous function,
2. $u_2(r)$ is a bounded monotonic decreasing left continuous function,
3. $u_1(r) \leq u_2(r)$, $0 \leq r \leq 1$.

A crisp number x is simply represented by

$$\left(u_1\left(r\right), u_2\left(r\right)\right) = \left(x, x\right), 0 \leq r \leq 1.$$

By appropriate definitions, the fuzzy number space $\left\{\left(u_1\left(r\right), u_2\left(r\right)\right)\right\}$ becomes a convex cone E^1 which could be embedded isomorphically and isometrically into a Banach space.

Definition 2.5: Intuitionistic Fuzzy Number

An IFN A^i is defined as follows:

1. An intuitionistic fuzzy subject of real line
2. Normal i.e., there is any $x_0 \in R$ such that $\mu_{A^i}(x_0) = 1$ (so $\upsilon_{A^i}(x_0) = 0$)
3. A convex set for the membership function $\mu_{A^i}(x)$, i.e.,

$$\mu_{A^i}(\lambda x_1 + (1-\lambda)x_2) \geq \min(\mu_{A^i}(x_1), \mu_{A^i}(x_2)) \forall x_1, x_2 \in R, \lambda \in [0,1]$$

4. A concave set for the non-membership function $\upsilon_{A^i}(x)$, i.e.,

$$\upsilon_{A^i}(\lambda x_1 + (1-\lambda)x_2) \geq \max(\upsilon_{A^i}(x_1), \upsilon_{A^i}(x_2)) \forall x_1, x_2 \in R, \lambda \in [0,1]$$

Definition 2.6: Trapezoidal Intuitionistic Fuzzy Number

A ITrFN A^i is a subset of IFN in R with following membership function and non membership function as follows:

$$\mu_{\tilde{A}}(x) = \begin{cases} \dfrac{x - a_1}{a_2 - a_1}, & a_1 < x < a_2 \\ 1, & a_2 \leq x \leq a_3 \\ \dfrac{a_3 - x}{a_4 - a_3}, & a_3 < x < a_4 \\ 0, & otherwise \end{cases}$$

and

$$\upsilon_{\tilde{A}}(x) = \begin{cases} \dfrac{a_2 - x}{a_2 - a_1'}, & a_1' < x < a_2 \\ 0, & a_2 \leq x \leq a_3 \\ \dfrac{x - a_3}{a_4' - a_3}, & a_3 < x < a_4' \\ 1, & otherwise \end{cases}$$

where

$$a_1' \leq a_1 \leq a_2 \leq a_3 \leq a_4 \leq a_4'$$

and TrIFN is denoted by

$$A^i_{TrIFN} = (a_1, a_2, a_3, a_4; a_1', a_2, a_3, a_4')$$

Definition 2.7: α-Cut Set

A α-cut set of

$$A^i_{TrIFN} = (a_1 \le a_2 \le a_3; a_1' \le a_2 \le a_3')$$

is a crisp subset of *R* which is defined as follows

$$A_\alpha = \{x : \mu_{A^i}(x) \ge \alpha, \forall \alpha \in [0,1]\} = [A_1(\alpha), A_2(\alpha)] = [a_1 + \alpha(a_2 - a_1), a_4 - \alpha(a_4 - a_3)]$$

Definition 2.8: β-Cut Set

A β-cut set of

$$A^i_{TrIFN} = (a_1, a_2, a_3, a_4; a_1', a_2, a_3, a_4')$$

is a crisp subset of *R* which is defined as follows

$$A_\beta = \{x : v_{A^i}(x) \le \beta, \forall \beta \in [0,1]\} = [A_1'(\beta), A_2'(\beta)] = [a_2 - \beta(a_2 - a_1'), a_3 + \beta(a_4' - a_3)]$$

Definition 2.9: (α, β)-Cut Set

A (α,β) -cut set of

$$A^i_{TrIFN} = (a_1 \le a_2 \le a_3, a_4; a_1' \le a_2 \le a_3 \le a_4')$$

is a crisp subset of *R* which is defined as follows

$$A_{(\alpha,\beta)} = \{[A_1(\alpha), A_2(\alpha)]; [A_1'(\beta), A_2'(\beta)]\}, \alpha + \beta \le 1, \alpha \in [0,1], \beta \in [0,1]$$

Theorem 2.1

The sum of membership and non-membership function at any particular point is between 0 and 1, i.e., if for a non-linear intutionistic fuzzy number

$$A^i_{TrIFN} = (a_1 \le a_2 \le a_3, a_4; a_1' \le a_2 \le a_3 \le a_4')$$

(see above figure) membership and non-membership function is denoted by $\mu_{A^i}(x)$ and $v_{A^i}(x)$ then

$$0 < \mu_{A^i}(x) + v_{A^i}(x) \le 1 .$$

DIFFERENCE EQUATION AND INTUITIONISTIC FUZZY DIFFERENCE EQUATION

A qth order linear difference equation (synonymously, a linear recurrence relation) is a set of equations of the form

$$x_n - \left(a_{n-1}x_{n-1} + a_{n-2}x_{n-2} + \ldots + a_{n-q}x_{n-q}\right) = r_n \tag{1}$$

for $n=q,q+1,\ldots$.

If $r_n=0$, for all n, the equation is said to be a homogeneous difference equation otherwise it is non homogeneous difference equation (r_n is called the forcing factor).

Now if $a_i(i=1,2,\ldots,n)$ do not depend on n then the equation said to have constant coefficients.

Intuitionistic Fuzzy Difference Equation

Consider the linear difference equation of the form

$$a_0 u_{n+1} + a_1 u_n = f(n)$$

with initial condition $u_{n=0} = u_0$

The above difference equation is called intutionistic fuzzy difference equation if u_0 is an intuitionistic fuzzy number.

Let

$$u_0^i = (u_1, u_2, u_3, u_4; u_1', u_2, u_3, u_4')$$

Then the intutionistic fuzzy equation becomes

$$a_0 u_{n+1} + a_1 u_n = f(n)$$

with

$$u_0^i = (u_1, u_2, u_3, u_4; u_1', u_2, u_3, u_4') .$$

Here four cases arise

Case 1: $a_0>0$ and $a_1>0$
Case 2: $a_0<0$ and $a_1>0$
Case 3: $a_0>0$ and $a_1<0$

Case 4: $a_0<0$ and $a_1<0$

SOLUTION OF INTUITIONISTIC FUZZY DIFFERENCE EQUATION

Transforming Intuitionistic Fuzzy Difference Equation to System of Difference Equation

Case 1: When $a_0>0$ and $a_1>0$

Taking (α,β)-cut of the given equation we have

$$a_0[u_{n+1,1}(\alpha), u_{n+1,2}(\alpha); u'_{n+1,1}(\beta), u'_{n+1,2}(\beta)] + a_1[u_{n,1}(\alpha), u_{n,2}(\alpha); u'_{n,1}(\beta), u'_{n,2}(\beta)]$$
$$= [f(n), f(n); f(n), f(n)]$$

i.e.,

$$a_0 u_{n+1,1}(\alpha) + a_1 u_{n,1}(\alpha) = f(n)$$

$$a_0 u_{n+1,2}(\alpha) + a_1 u_{n,2}(\alpha) = f(n)$$

$$a_0 u'_{n+1,1}(\beta) + a_1 u'_{n,1}(\beta) = f(n)$$

$$a_0 u'_{n+1,2}(\beta) + a_1 u'_{n,2}(\beta) = f(n)$$

with initial condition

$$u_{0,1}(\alpha) = u_{01}(\alpha)$$

$$u_{0,2}(\alpha) = u_{02}(\alpha)$$

$$u'_{0,1}(\beta) = u'_{01}(\beta)$$

$$u'_{0,2}(\beta) = u'_{02}(\beta)$$

Solution

The above equation is system of difference equation. For particular examples we can easily find its solution.

Case 2: When a_0<0 and a_1>0

Taking (α,β)-cut of the given equation we have

$$a_0[u_{n+1,2}(\alpha), u_{n+1,1}(\alpha); u'_{n+1,2}(\beta), u'_{n+1,1}(\beta)] + a_1[u_{n,1}(\alpha), u_{n,2}(\alpha); u'_{n,1}(\beta), u'_{n,2}(\beta)] \\ = [f(n), f(n); f(n), f(n)]$$

i.e.,

$$a_0 u_{n+1,2}(\alpha) + a_1 u_{n,1}(\alpha) = f(n)$$

$$a_0 u_{n+1,1}(\alpha) + a_1 u_{n,2}(\alpha) = f(n)$$

$$a_0 u'_{n+1,2}(\beta) + a_1 u'_{n,1}(\beta) = f(n)$$

$$a_0 u'_{n+1,1}(\beta) + a_1 u'_{n,2}(\beta) = f(n)$$

with initial condition

$$u_{0,1}(\alpha) = u_{01}(\alpha)$$

$$u_{0,2}(\alpha) = u_{02}(\alpha)$$

$$u'_{0,1}(\beta) = u'_{01}(\beta)$$

$$u'_{0,2}(\beta) = u'_{02}(\beta)$$

Solution

The above equation is system of difference equation. For particular examples we can easily find its solution.

Case 3: When a_0>0 and a_1<0

Taking (α,β)-cut of the given equation we have

$$a_0[u_{n+1,1}(\alpha), u_{n+1,2}(\alpha); u'_{n+1,1}(\beta), u'_{n+1,2}(\beta)] + a_1[u_{n,2}(\alpha), u_{n,1}(\alpha); u'_{n,2}(\beta), u'_{n,1}(\beta)] \\ = [f(n), f(n); f(n), f(n)]$$

i.e.,

$$a_0 u_{n+1,1}(\alpha) + a_1 u_{n,2}(\alpha) = f(n)$$

$$a_0 u_{n+1,2}(\alpha) + a_1 u_{n,1}(\alpha) = f(n)$$

$$a_0 u'_{n+1,1}(\beta) + a_1 u'_{n,2}(\beta) = f(n)$$

$$a_0 u'_{n+1,2}(\beta) + a_1 u'_{n,1}(\beta) = f(n)$$

with initial condition

$$u_{0,1}(\alpha) = u_{01}(\alpha)$$

$$u_{0,2}(\alpha) = u_{02}(\alpha)$$

$$u'_{0,1}(\beta) = u'_{01}(\beta)$$

$$u'_{0,2}(\beta) = u'_{02}(\beta)$$

Solution

The above equation is system of difference equation. For particular examples we can easily find its solution.

Case 4: When a_0<0 and a_1<0

Taking (α,β)-cut of the given equation we have

$$a_0[u_{n+1,2}(\alpha), u_{n+1,1}(\alpha); u'_{n+1,2}(\beta), u'_{n+1,1}(\beta)] + a_1[u_{n,2}(\alpha), u_{n,1}(\alpha); u'_{n,2}(\beta), u'_{n,1}(\beta)]$$
$$= [f(n), f(n); f(n), f(n)]$$

i.e.,

$$a_0 u_{n+1,2}(\alpha) + a_1 u_{n,2}(\alpha) = f(n)$$

$$a_0 u_{n+1,1}(\alpha) + a_1 u_{n,1}(\alpha) = f(n)$$

$$a_0 u'_{n+1,2}(\beta) + a_1 u'_{n,2}(\beta) = f(n)$$

$$a_0 u'_{n+1,1}(\beta) + a_1 u'_{n,1}(\beta) = f(n)$$

with initial condition

$$u_{0,1}(\alpha) = u_{01}(\alpha)$$

$$u_{0,2}(\alpha) = u_{02}(\alpha)$$

$$u'_{0,1}(\beta) = u'_{01}(\beta)$$

$$u'_{0,2}(\beta) = u'_{02}(\beta)$$

Solution

The above equation is system of difference equation. For particular examples we can easily find its solution.

Rules for Finding the Particular Solution

Let us consider the difference equation

$$u_{n+r} + a_1 u_{n+r-1} + \ldots + a_r u_n = f(n)$$

which can be written as $F(E)u=f(n)$ where

$$F(E) = E^r + a_1 E^{r-1} + \ldots + a_r$$

The particular solution is given by,

$$\text{P.S.} = \frac{1}{F(E)} f(n)$$

Now for different types of the function the particular solution is different. We refer some particular solution of some well known function as follows:

Case I: When $f(n)=a^n$.

$$\text{P.S}=\frac{1}{F(E)}a^{n}=\frac{1}{F(a)}a^{n},$$

provided $F(a)\neq 0$.

If $F(a)=0$, then for the equation $(E-a)u=a^n$ the

$$\text{P.S}=\frac{1}{E-a}a^{n}=na^{n-1}$$

Case II: When $f(n)=\sin kn$.

$$\text{P.S}=\frac{1}{F(E)}\sin kn=\frac{1}{F(E)}\left(\frac{e^{ikn}-e^{-ikn}}{2i}\right)=\frac{1}{2i}\left[\frac{1}{F(E)}a^{n}-\frac{1}{F(E)}b^{n}\right]$$

and proceed as before where $a=e^{ikn}$ and $b=e^{-ikn}$. Similar for $f(n)=\cos kn$

Case III: When $f(n)=n^p$.

$$\text{P.S}=\frac{1}{F(E)}n^{p}=\frac{1}{F(1+\Delta)}n^{p}$$

Now,

1. Expand $\dfrac{1}{F(1+\Delta)}$ in ascending power of Δ by Binomial theorem as far as the term in Δ^p.
2. Expand n^p in the fractional form and operate on it with each term of the expansion.

Case 4: When $f(n)=a^nW(n)$, where $W(n)$ is a polynomial of degree n.

$$\text{P.S}=\frac{1}{F(E)}a^{n}W(n)=a^{n}\frac{1}{F(aE)}W(n)$$

NUMERICAL EXAMPLE

Example 5.1

Consider the difference equation $u_{n+1}-4u_{n}=0$ with $u_{0}{}^{i}=(2,4,6,9;1,4,6,8)$

Solution

Taking (α,β) -cut of the given equation we have

$$[u_{n+1,1}(\alpha), u_{n+1,2}(\alpha); u'_{n+1,1}(\beta), u'_{n+1,2}(\beta)] - 4[u_{n,2}(\alpha), u_{n,1}(\alpha); u'_{n,2}(\beta), u'_{n,1}(\beta)]$$
$$= [0,0;0,0]$$

i.e.,

$$u_{n+1,1}(\alpha) - 4u_{n,2}(\alpha) = 0 \quad (5.1)$$

$$u_{n+1,2}(\alpha) - 4u_{n,1}(\alpha) = 0 \quad (5.2)$$

$$u'_{n+1,1}(\beta) - 4u'_{n,2}(\beta) = 0 \quad (5.3)$$

$$u'_{n+1,2}(\beta) - 4u'_{n,1}(\beta) = 0 \quad (5.4)$$

with initial condition

$$u_{0,1}(\alpha) = 2 + 2\alpha$$

$$u_{0,2}(\alpha) = 9 - 3\alpha$$

$$u'_{0,1}(\beta) = 4 - 3\beta$$

$$u'_{0,2}(\beta) = 6 + 2\beta$$

From (5.1) we can write

$$u_{n+2,1}(\alpha) - 4u_{n+1,2}(\alpha) = 0 \quad (5.5)$$

Now from (5.5) using (5.2) we can write

$$u_{n+2,1}(\alpha) - 4.4u_{n,2}(\alpha) = 0 \text{ i.e., } u_{n+2,1}(\alpha) - 16u_{n,2}(\alpha) = 0 \quad (5.6)$$

The general solution is written as

$$u_{n,1}(\alpha) = c_1(4)^n + c_2(-4)^n \quad (5.7)$$

(since the particular solution is 0).

Now from (5.1) we have

$$c_1\left(4\right)^{n+1}+c_2\left(-4\right)^{n+1}-4u_{n,2}(\alpha)=0$$

or,

$$u_{n,2}(\alpha)=c_1\left(4\right)^{n}-c_2\left(-4\right)^{n} \qquad (5.8)$$

Using initial condition using (5.7) and (5.8) we get

$$u_{n,1}(\alpha)=\left(\frac{11}{2}-\frac{1}{2}\alpha\right)\left(4\right)^{n}+\left(-\frac{7}{2}+\frac{5}{2}\alpha\right)\left(-4\right)^{n}$$

$$u_{n,1}(\alpha)=\left(\frac{11}{2}-\frac{1}{2}\alpha\right)\left(4\right)^{n}-\left(-\frac{7}{2}+\frac{5}{2}\alpha\right)\left(-4\right)^{n}$$

Similarly we can find

$$u'_{n,1}(\beta)=\left(5-\frac{1}{2}\beta\right)\left(4\right)^{n}+\left(-1-\frac{5}{2}\beta\right)\left(-4\right)^{n}$$

$$u_{n,1}(\alpha)=\left(5-\frac{1}{2}\beta\right)\left(4\right)^{n}-\left(-1-\frac{5}{2}\beta\right)\left(-4\right)^{n}$$

Table 1. Solution for n=2

α,β	$u_{n,1}(\alpha)$	$u_{n,2}(\alpha)$	$u'_{n,1}(\beta)$	$u'_{n,2}(\beta)$
0	32.0000	144.0000	64.0000	96.0000
0.1	35.2000	139.2000	59.2000	99.2000
0.2	38.4000	134.4000	54.4000	102.4000
0.3	41.6000	129.6000	49.6000	105.6000
0.4	44.8000	124.8000	44.8000	108.8000
0.5	48.0000	120.0000	40.0000	112.0000
0.6	51.2000	115.2000	35.2000	115.2000
0.7	54.4000	110.4000	30.4000	118.4000
0.8	57.6000	105.6000	25.6000	121.6000
0.9	60.8000	100.8000	20.8000	124.8000
1	64.0000	96.0000	16.0000	128.0000

Figure 1. Graph of $u_{n,1}(\alpha)$, $u_{n,2}(\alpha)$, $u'_{n,1}(\beta)$ *and* $u'_{n,2}(\beta)$ *for n=2*

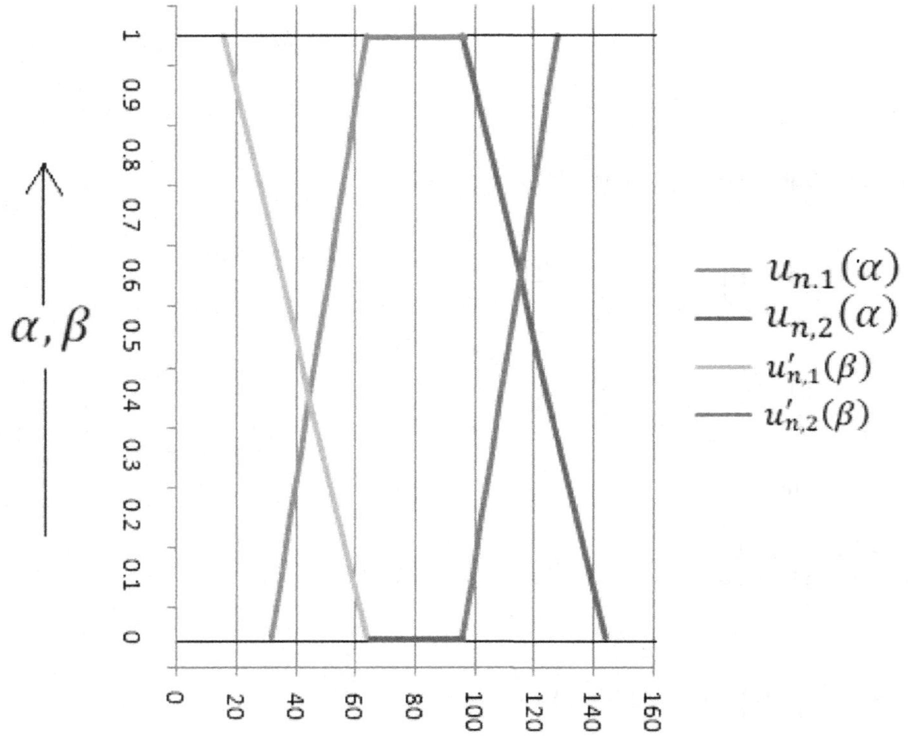

Remarks 1

Clearly from the above table and graph we see that $u_{n,1}(\alpha)$ is increasing and $u_{n,2}(\alpha)$ is decreasing as α goes to zero to one and other side $u'_{n,1}(\beta)$ is decreasing and $u'_{n,2}(\beta)$ is increasing as β goes to zero to one, which conclude that the solution is also a intuitionistic fuzzy solution.

Example 5.2

Consider the difference equation

$$u_{n+1} + 2u_n = 4^n$$

with

$$u_0^{\,i} = (350, 400, 500, 600; 300, 400, 500, 650)$$

Solution

Taking (α,β)-cut of the given equation we have

$$[u_{n+1,1}(\alpha),u_{n+1,2}(\alpha);u'_{n+1,1}(\beta)(\beta),u'_{n+1,2}(\beta)]+2[u_{n,1}(\alpha),u_{n,2}(\alpha);u'_{n,1}(\beta),u'_{n,2}(\beta)]$$
$$=[4^n,4^n;4^n,4^n]$$

i.e.,

$$u_{n+1,1}(\alpha)+2u_{n,1}(\alpha)=4^n$$

$$u_{n+1,2}(\alpha)+2u_{n,2}(\alpha)=4^n$$

$$u'_{n+1,1}(\beta)+2u'_{n,1}(\beta)=4^n$$

$$u'_{n+1,2}(\beta)+2u'_{n,2}(\beta)=4^n$$

with initial condition

$$u_{0,1}(\alpha)=350+50\alpha$$

$$u_{0,2}(\alpha)=600-100\alpha$$

$$u'_{0,1}(\beta)=400-100\beta$$

$$u'_{0,2}(\beta)=500+150\beta$$

In similar way as above we can find the solution as

$$u_{n,1}(\alpha)=\left(\frac{2099}{6}+50\alpha\right)(-2)^n+\frac{1}{6}(4)^n$$

$$u_{n,1}(\alpha)=\left(\frac{3599}{6}-100\alpha\right)(-2)^n+\frac{1}{6}(4)^n$$

$$u_{n,2}(\alpha)=\left(\frac{3599}{6}-100\alpha\right)\left(-2\right)^{n}+\frac{1}{6}\left(4\right)^{n}$$

$$u'_{n,2}(\beta)=\left(\frac{2999}{6}+150\beta\right)\left(-2\right)^{n}+\frac{1}{6}\left(4\right)^{n}$$

Remarks 2

Clearly from the above table and graph we see that $u_{n,1}(\alpha)$ is increasing and $u_{n,2}(\alpha)$ is decreasing as α goes to zero to one and other side $u'_{n,1}(\beta)$ is decreasing and $u'_{n,2}(\beta)$ is increasing as β goes to zero to one, which conclude that the solution is also a intuitionistic fuzzy solution.

CONCLUSION

Difference equations are very important for modeling various problems in different fields. It is more important if it is studied in intuitionistic fuzzy environment. In the present chapter, we have solved a difference equation with intuitionistic fuzzy initial value. We have showed that different sign of coefficient can change the nature of intuitionistic fuzzy difference equations. In other words, we have got

Table 2. Solution for n=2

α,β	$u_{n,1}(\alpha)$	$u_{n,2}(\alpha)$	$u'_{n,1}(\beta)$	$u'_{n,2}(\beta)$
0	5640.0000	9640.0000	6440.0000	8040.0000
0.1	5720.0000	9480.0000	6280.0000	8280.0000
0.2	5800.0000	9320.0000	6120.0000	8520.0000
0.3	5880.0000	9160.0000	5960.0000	8760.0000
0.4	5960.0000	9000.0000	5800.0000	9000.0000
0.5	6040.0000	8840.0000	5640.0000	9240.0000
0.6	6120.0000	8680.0000	5480.0000	9480.0000
0.7	6200.0000	8520.0000	5320.0000	9720.0000
0.8	6280.0000	8360.0000	5160.0000	9960.0000
0.9	6360.0000	8200.0000	5000.0000	10200.0000
1	6440.0000	8040.0000	4840.0000	10440.0000

Figure 2. Graph of $u_{n,1}(\alpha)$, $u_{n,2}(\alpha)$, $u'_{n,1}(\beta)$ *and* $u'_{n,2}(\beta)$ *for n=2*

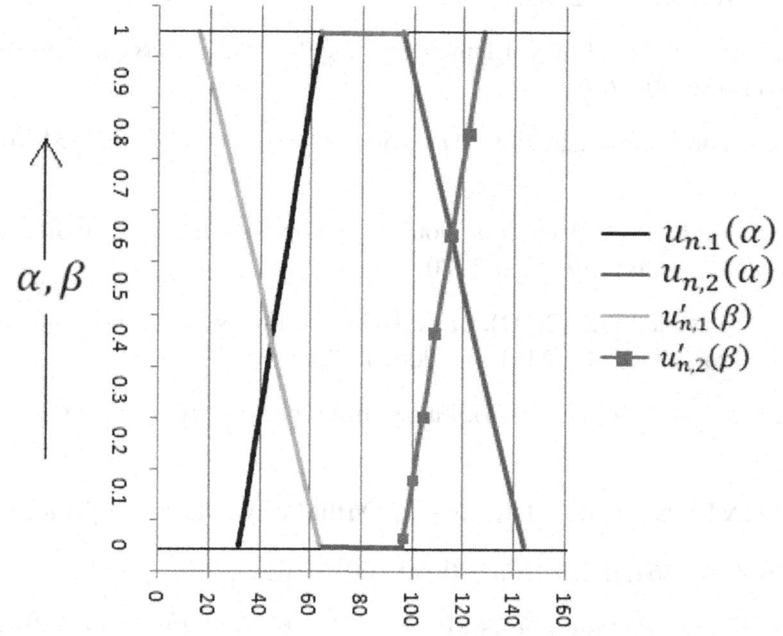

different types of solutions when the sign of coefficient are different in different cases. We have defined and solved all possible cases. The general theory is illustrated by two numerical examples. The theory and results are surely very important for researcher.

REFERENCES

Atanassov, K. T. (1983). *Intuitionistic fuzzy sets, VII ITKR's Session*. Sofia: Bulgarian.

Atanassov, K. T. (1986). Intuitionistic fuzzy sets. *Fuzzy Sets and Systems*, *20*(1), 87–96. doi:10.1016/S0165-0114(86)80034-3

Chang, S. S. L., & Zadeh, L. A. (1972). On fuzzy mappings and control. *IEEE Transactions on Systems, Man, and Cybernetics*, *2*(1), 30–34. doi:10.1109/TSMC.1972.5408553

Deeba, E. Y., & de Korvin, A. (1999). Analysis by Fuzzy Difference Equations of a model of CO2 Level in the Blood. *Applied Mathematics Letters*, *12*(3), 33–40. doi:10.1016/S0893-9659(98)00168-2

Deeba, E. Y., Korvin, A. D., & Koh, E. L. (1996). A Fuzzy Difference Equation with an application. *J.Diff. Equa. Appl.*, *2*(4), 365–374. doi:10.1080/10236199608808071

Diamond, P., & Kloeden, P. (1994). *Metric Space of Fuzzy Sets*. Singapore: World Scientific.

Din, Q. (2015). Asymptotic behavior of a second –order fuzzy rational difference equations. *Journal of Discrete Mathematics*.

Dubois, D., & Prade, H. (1978). Operations on fuzzy numbers. *International Journal of Systems Science, 9*(6), 613–626. doi:10.1080/00207727808941724

Goetschel, R. Jr, & Voxman, W. (1986). Elementary calculus. *Fuzzy Sets and Systems, 18*(1), 31–43. doi:10.1016/0165-0114(86)90026-6

Kaleva, O. (1987). Fuzzy differential equations. *Fuzzy Sets and Systems, 24*(3), 301–317. doi:10.1016/0165-0114(87)90029-7

Konstantios, A. C., Basil, K. P., & Papaschinopoulos, G. (2008). On the fuzzy difference equations of finance. *Fuzzy Sets and Systems, 159*, 3259-3270.

Lakshmikatham, V., & Vatsala, A. S. (2002). Basic Theory of Fuzzy Difference Equations. *J. Diff.Equa. Appl, 8*(11), 957–968. doi:10.1080/1023619021000048850

Memarbashi, R., & Ghasemabadi, A. (2013). Fuzzy difference equations of volterra type. *Int. J. Nonlinear Anal.Appl, 4*, 74–78.

Papaschinopoulos, G., & Papadopoulos, B. K. (2002a). On the fuzzy difference equation $x_{n+1} = A + B/x_n$. *Soft Computing, 6*(6), 456–461. doi:10.1007/s00500-001-0161-7

Papaschinopoulos, G., & Papadopoulos, B. K. (2002b). On the fuzzy difference equation $x_{n+1} = A + x_n/x_{n-m}$. *Fuzzy Sets and Systems, 129*(1), 73–81. doi:10.1016/S0165-0114(01)00198-1

Papaschinopoulos, G., & Schinas, C. J. (2000). On the fuzzy difference equation $x_{n+1}\sum_{k=0}^{k=1} Ai/x_{n-i}^{\ pi} + 1/x_{n-k}^{\ pk}$. *J. Difference Equation Appl, 6*(7), 85–89.

Papaschinopoulos, G., & Stefanidou, G. (2003). Boundedness and asymptotic behavior of the Solutions of a fuzzy difference equation. *Fuzzy Sets and Systems, 140*(3), 523–539. doi:10.1016/S0165-0114(03)00034-4

Stefanidou, G., Papaschinopoulos, G., & Schinas, C. J. (2010). On an exponential –type fuzzy Difference equation. *Advanced in Difference Equations.*

Stfanidou,G., & Papaschinopoulos, G .(2005). A fuzzy difference equation of a rational form. *Journal of Nonlinear Mathematical Physics, 12*(S2), 300-315.

Umekkan, S. A., Can, E., & Bayrak, M. A. (2014). Fuzzy difference equation in finance. *IJSIMR, 2*(8), 729–735.

Zadeh, L. A. (1965). Fuzzy sets. *Information and Control, 8*(3), 338–353. doi:10.1016/S0019-9958(65)90241-X

Zhang, Q. H., Yang, L. H., & Liao, D. X. (2012). Behaviour of solutions of to a fuzzy nonlinear difference equation. *Iranian Journal of Fuzzy Systems, 9*(2), 1-12.

KEY TERMS AND DEFINITIONS

Intuitionistic Fuzzy Difference: The intuitionistic fuzzy number is not like crisp number. So the intuitionistic fuzzy difference is not same as crisp difference.

Intuitionistic Fuzzy Difference Equation: The difference equation associated with intuitionistic fuzzy number.

Intuitionistic Fuzzy Number: The element of intuitionistic fuzzy sets is called intuitionistic fuzzy number.

Intuitionistic Fuzzy Sets: A set which is a collection of object with graded membership and non membership function.

Chapter 6
Semiring of Generalized Interval-Valued Intuitionistic Fuzzy Matrices

Debashree Manna
Damda Jr. High School, India

ABSTRACT

In this paper, the concept of semiring of generalized interval-valued intuitionistic fuzzy matrices are introduced and have shown that the set of GIVIFMs forms a distributive lattice. Also, prove that the GIVIFMs form an generalized interval valued intuitionistic fuzzy algebra and vector space over [0, 1]. Some properties of GIVIFMs are studied using the definition of comparability of GIVIFMs.

INTRODUCTION

In 1965, Zadeh(1965) introduced the concept of fuzzy subsets. Atanassov (1989, 1994) introduced the concept of intuitionistic fuzzy sets (IFSs), which is a generalization of fuzzy subsets. Later on much fundamental works have done with this concept by Attanasov and others. Mondal and Samanta (2002) give some results on generalized intuitionistic fuzzy sets. Thomson (1977) give some results on convergence of powers of a fuzzy matrix and Kim (1980) defined adjoint of a square fuzzy matrix. Kim and Roush (1988) studied the canonical form of an idempotent matrix. Pal and Shyamal (2005a) introduced interval-valued fuzzy matrices and shown several properties of them. By the concept of IFSs, first time Pal (2001) introduced intuitionistic fuzzy determinant. Latter on Pal and Shyamal (2005b) introduced intuitionistic fuzzy matrices and distance between intuitionistic fuzzy matrices. Bhowmik and Pal (2008) introduced some results on intuitionistic fuzzy matrices and intuitionistic circulant fuzzy matrices and generalized intuitionistic fuzzy matrices. Lattice matrices are useful tools in various domains like the theory of switching, automata theory and theory of finite graphs. The notions of nilpotent lattice matrices seem to be appeared first in the work of Give'on (1964).

The structure of this chapter is organized as follows. At first, contains the preliminaries and some backgrounds in this study. Then, define distributive lattice over GIVIFMs and some results are given. After that some algebric structure of GIVIFMs are defined followed by some properties of GIVIFMs.

DOI: 10.4018/978-1-5225-0914-1.ch006

PRELIMINARIES

Here some preliminaries, definitions of IVIFMs and GIVIFMs are recalled and presented some operations on GIVIFMs.

Definition 1

A semiring is an algebraic structure $(R,+,.)$ such that $(R,+)$ is an abelian monoid (identity 0), $(R,.)$ is a monoid (identity 1). distributes over + from either side, $r0=0r=0$ for all $r\in R$ and $0\neq 1$.

Definition 2

A fuzzy matrix (FM) of order $m\times n$ is defined as $A = \langle a_{ij}, a_{ij\mu} \rangle$ where $a_{ij\mu}$ is the membership value of the ij-element in A. Let $F_{m\times n}$ denote the set of all fuzzy matrices of order $m\times n$. If $m=n$, in short, we write F_n, the set of all square matrices of order n.

Definition 3

An intuitionistic fuzzy matrix (IFM) of order $m\times n$ is defined as $A = [\langle a_{ij}, a'_{ij} \rangle]$ where a_{ij}, and a'_{ij} are the membership value and non membership value of the ij-element in A satisfying the condition $0 \leq a_{ij} + a'_{ij} < 1$ for all i,j.

Definition 4

An interval-valued intuitionistic fuzzy matrix (IVIFM) of order $m\times n$ is denoted by A and is defined by

$$A = [\langle x_{ij}, [M_{A_{ij}}, N_{A_{ij}}] \rangle]$$

where

$$M_{A_{ij}}(x) : x \to [I] \text{and } N_{A_{ij}}(x) : x \to [I],$$

$[I]$ be the set of all closed sub interval of [0,1]. The interval

$$M_{A_{ij}} = [M_{AL_{ij}}, M_{AU_{ij}}]$$

$$M_{AL_{ij}} \text{ and } M_{AU_{ij}}$$

are lower and upper membership value respectively of the ijth element of IVIFM A. Similarly the interval

$$N_{A_{ij}} = [N_{AL_{ij}}, N_{AU_{ij}}]$$

where $N_{AL_{ij}}$ and $N_{AU_{ij}}$ are lower and upper non-membership value respectively of the *ij*th element of IVIFM A. Therefore, an IVIFM A can be written as

$$A = [\langle x_{ij}, [M_{AL_{ij}}, M_{AU_{ij}}], [N_{AL_{ij}}, N_{AU_{ij}}]\rangle)$$

satisfying the condition

$$0 \leq M_{AU_{ij}} + N_{AU_{ij}} \leq 1.$$

In short an IVIFM A is denoted as

$$A = [\langle [M_{AL_{ij}}, M_{AU_{ij}}], [N_{AL_{ij}}, N_{AU_{ij}}]\rangle]$$

satisfying the condition

$$0 \leq M_{AU_{ij}} + N_{AU_{ij}} \leq 1.$$

Definition 5

A generalized interval-valued intuitionistic fuzzy matrix (GIVIFM) of order *m*×*n* is denoted by *A* and is defined by

$$A = [\langle x_{ij}, [M_{A_{ij}}, N_{A_{ij}}]\rangle]$$

where

$$M_{A_{ij}}(x) : x \to [I] \text{and } N_{A_{ij}}(x) : x \to [I],$$

the set of all closed sub interval of [0,1], satisfying the condition

$$M_{AU_{ij}} \wedge N_{AU_{ij}} \leq 0.5.$$

The condition

$$M_{AU_{ij}} \wedge N_{AU_{ij}} \leq 0.5$$

is called generalized interval valued intuitionistic fuzzy condition. The maximum value $M_{AU_{ij}}$ and $N_{AU_{ij}}$ is 1.0. Therefore GIVIFC imply that

$$0 \leq M_{AU_{ij}} + N_{AU_{ij}} \leq 1.5 .$$

SOME OPERATIONS OF GIVIFMS

1. Let A and B be two GIVIFMs, then the matrix addition is given by

$$A + B = [\langle[\max\{M_{AL_{ij}}, M_{BL_{ij}}\}, \max\{M_{AU_{ij}}, M_{BU_{ij}}\}], [\min\{N_{AL_{ij}}, N_{BL_{ij}}\}, \min\{N_{AU_{ij}}, N_{BU_{ij}}\}]\rangle]$$

2. Let A and B be two GIVIFMs, then the componentwise multiplication as

$$A \in B = [\langle[\min\{M_{AL_{ij}}, M_{BL_{ij}}\}, \min\{M_{AU_{ij}}, M_{BU_{ij}}\}], [\max\{N_{AL_{ij}}, N_{BL_{ij}}\}, \max\{N_{AU_{ij}}, N_{BU_{ij}}\}]\rangle].$$

3. Also let

$$A = [\langle[M_{AL_{ij}}, M_{AU_{ij}}], [N_{AL_{ij}}, N_{AU_{ij}}]\rangle] \in F_{m\times n}$$

and

$$B = [\langle[M_{BL_{ij}}, M_{BU_{ij}}], [N_{BL_{ij}}, N_{BU_{ij}}]\rangle] \in F_{n\times p},$$

then matrix multiplication is defined as follows:

$$AB = [\langle[\max_k\{M_{AL_{ik}}, M_{BL_{kj}}\}, \max_k\{M_{AU_{ik}}, M_{BU_{kj}}\}], [\min_k\{N_{AL_{ik}}, N_{BL_{kj}}\}, \min_k\{N_{AU_{ik}}, N_{BU_{kj}}\}]\rangle] \in F_{m\times n}$$

where $i=1,2,\ldots,m$, $k=1,2,\ldots,n$, $j=1,2,\ldots,p$. The product AB is defined if and only if the number of columns of A is the same as the number of rows B, then A and B are said to be conformable for multiplication.

4. Let $A = \in F_{m\times n}$ and $c = \langle[c_1, c_2], [d_1, d_2]\rangle \in F$, and $[c_1,c_2]$, $[d_1,d_2] \in [I]$ then the interval valued intuitionistic fuzzy scalar multiplication is defined as

$$cA = [\langle[\min\{c_1, M_{AL_{ij}}\}, \min\{c_2, M_{AU_{ij}}\}], [\max\{d_1, N_{AL_{ij}}\}, \max\{d_2, N_{AU_{ij}}\}]\rangle] \in F_{m\times n}.$$

For the universal matrix J we have from definition

$$cJ = [\langle[\min\{c_1, 1\}, \min\{c_2, 1\}], [\max\{d_1, 0\}, \max\{d_2, 0\}]\rangle] = [\langle[c_1, c_2], [d_1, d_2]\rangle]$$

Under component wise multiplication

$$cJeA = [\langle[\min\{c_1, M_{AL_{ij}}\}, \min\{c_2, M_{AU_{ij}}\}], [\max\{d_1, N_{AL_{ij}}\}, \max\{d_2, N_{AU_{ij}}\}]\rangle] = cA.$$

DIFFERENT TYPES OF GIVIFMS

Definition 6: Zero Matrix

The $m\times n$ interval-valued intuitionistic fuzzy zero matrix O is the matrix all of whose entries are $\langle[0,0],[1,1]\rangle$.

Definition 7: Identity Matrix

The $n\times n$ interval-valued intuitionistic fuzzy indentity matrix I_n is defined by $(\langle\delta_{ij}, \delta'_{ij}\rangle)$ such that δ_{ij}=[1.1], $\delta'_{ij} = [0,0]$ for $i=j$ and δ_{ij}=[0,0], $\delta'_{ij} = [1,1]$ for $i\neq j$.

Definition 8: Universal Matrix

The $m\times n$ interval-valued intuitionistic fuzzy universal matrix J is the matrix all of whose entries are $(\langle[1,1],[0,0]\rangle)$.

Definition 9: Comparable GIVIFMs

Let $A, B \in F_{m\times n}$ such that

$$A = [\langle[M_{AL_{ij}}, M_{AU_{ij}}], [N_{AL_{ij}}, N_{AU_{ij}}]\rangle]$$

and

$$B = [\langle[M_{BL_{ij}}, M_{BU_{ij}}], [N_{BL_{ij}}, N_{BU_{ij}}]\rangle],$$

then we write $A\leq B$ if

$$M_{AL_{ij}} \leq M_{BL_{ij}}, \;\; M_{AU_{ij}} \leq M_{BU_{ij}},$$

and

$$N_{AL_{ij}} \geq N_{BL_{ij}}, \;\; N_{AL_{ij}} \geq N_{BL_{ij}}$$

for all *i,j*.

Note: For any GIVIFM *A*, it is obvious that $O \leq A \leq J$.

POSET OF FUZZY SETS AND GIVIFMS

Lemma 1: (Poset of GIVIFMs)

Let F_n be the set of all $n \times n$ GIVIFMs and '≤ ' be comparable fuzzy matrix relation, then $(F_n, \leq)$ is a poset.

$A \leq A$ is true since

$$M_{AL_{ij}} \leq M_{AL_{ij}}, \;\; M_{AU_{ij}} \leq M_{AU_{ij}}$$

and

$$N_{AL_{ij}} \leq N_{AL_{ij}}, \;\; N_{AL_{ij}} \leq N_{AL_{ij}}.$$

Hence the relation '≤' is reflexive.

$A \leq B$ and $B \leq A$ possible only when $A = B$, since $A \leq B$ when

$$M_{AL_{ij}} \leq M_{AL_{ij}}, \;\; M_{AU_{ij}} \leq M_{AU_{ij}}$$

and

$$N_{AL_{ij}} \leq N_{AL_{ij}}, \;\; N_{AL_{ij}} \leq N_{AL_{ij}}$$

and $B \leq A$ when

$$M_{BL_{ij}} \leq M_{BL_{ij}}, \quad M_{BU_{ij}} \leq M_{BU_{ij}}$$

and

$$N_{BL_{ij}} \leq N_{BL_{ij}}, \quad N_{BL_{ij}} \leq N_{BL_{ij}}.$$

Combining above results give $A=B$. Therefore the relation '$\leq$' is anti-symmetric.

$A \leq B$ and $B \leq C$ when

$$M_{AL_{ij}} \leq M_{BL_{ij}}, \quad M_{AU_{ij}} \leq M_{BU_{ij}}$$

and

$$N_{AL_{ij}} \geq N_{BL_{ij}}, \quad N_{AL_{ij}} \geq N_{BL_{ij}}$$

and $B \leq C$ when

$$M_{BL_{ij}} \leq M_{CL_{ij}}, \quad M_{BU_{ij}} \leq M_{CU_{ij}}$$

and

$$N_{BL_{ij}} \leq N_{CL_{ij}}, \quad N_{BL_{ij}} \leq N_{CL_{ij}}.$$

Then it is obvious that $A \leq C$ since

$$M_{AL_{ij}} \leq M_{CL_{ij}}, \quad M_{AU_{ij}} \leq M_{CU_{ij}}$$

and

$$N_{AL_{ij}} \geq N_{CL_{ij}}, \quad N_{AL_{ij}} \geq N_{CL_{ij}}.$$

Hence the relation '$\leq$' is transitive.

Lattice of Fuzzy Sets

Definition 11: (Lattice of Fuzzy Sets)

A lattice is a partial ordered set $(L, ^\circ)$ in which every two elements have a unique least upper bound and a greatest lower bound.

For any two elements *a* and *b* in *L*, the least upper bound and greatest lower bound will be denoted by $a \vee b$ and $a \wedge b$.

Lattice is also denoted by $(L, ^\circ, \wedge, \vee)$.

Definition 12 (Distributive Lattice of FSs)

A lattice $(L, ^\circ, \vee, \wedge)$ is said to be distributive lattice if the operations $\vee$ and $\wedge$ are distributive with respect to each other i.e.,

1. $a \vee (b \wedge c) = (a \vee b) \wedge (a \vee c)$
2. $a \wedge (b \vee c) = (a \wedge b) \vee (a \wedge c)$, where *a*, *b* and $c \in (L, ^\circ)$, a poset.

An important special case of a distributive lattice is the real unit interval [0,1] with 'max' and 'min' is called fuzzy algebra.

Distributive Lattice of GIVIFMs

In this section we introduce the concept of distributive lattice of IMFs and give some properties of GIVIFMs over distributive lattice. We begin this section with some definitions:

Lattice of GIVIFMs

A non-empty poset $(F_n, \leq)$ with two binary operation + and e is called a lattice if the following axioms hold:

1. **Closure:** $A, B \in F_n$ then $A+B \in F_n$ and $AeB \in F_n$.
2. **Commutative:** $A, B \in F_n$ then $A+B=B+A$ and $AeB=BeA$.
3. **Associative:** $A, B, C \in F^n$ then $(A+B)+C=A+(B+C)$ and $(AeB)eC=Ae(BeC)$
4. **Absorption:** $A, B \in F_n$ then $Ae(A+B)=A$ and $A+(AeB)=A$.

Therefore, the poset $(F_n, \leq)$ with two binary operation matrix addition and componentwise matrix multiplication of GIVIFMs form lattice.

It should be noted that the poset $(F_n, \leq)$ with two binary operation matrix addition and matrix product of GIVIFMs does not form lattice since matrix product is not commutative.

Idempotent Law

Let A be an $n \times n$ GIVIFMs over distributive lattice $(F_n(L),\leq,+,e)$, then A satisfy idempotent law i.e.,

1. $A+A=A$ and
2. $AeA=A$

Theorem 1

Let A, B be two square GIVIFMs of $n \times n$ over distributive lattice $(F_n(L),\leq,+,e)$ then $AeB=A$ if and only if $A+B=B$.

Proof: Let $AeB=A$ where $A, B \in F_n(L)$.

Therefore,

$$\min\{M_{AL_{ij}}, M_{BL_{ij}}\} = M_{AL_{ij}}, \quad \min\{M_{AU_{ij}}, M_{BU_{ij}}\} = M_{AU_{ij}}$$

and

$$\max\{N_{AL_{ij}}, N_{BL_{ij}}\} = N_{AL_{ij}}, \quad \max\{N_{AU_{ij}}, N_{BU_{ij}}\} = N_{AU_{ij}}.$$

Hence,

$$\max\{M_{AL_{ij}}, M_{BL_{ij}}\} = M_{BL_{ij}}, \quad \max\{M_{AU_{ij}}, M_{BU_{ij}}\} = M_{BU_{ij}}$$

and

$$\min\{N_{AL_{ij}}, N_{BL_{ij}}\} = N_{BL_{ij}}, \quad \min\{N_{AU_{ij}}, N_{BU_{ij}}\} = N_{BU_{ij}}.$$

Now,

$$\begin{aligned} A + B &= [\langle[\max\{M_{AL_{ij}}, M_{BL_{ij}}\}, \max\{M_{AU_{ij}}, M_{BU_{ij}}\}], [\min\{N_{AL_{ij}}, N_{BL_{ij}}\}, \min\{N_{AL_{ij}}, N_{BL_{ij}}\}]\rangle] \\ &= [\langle[M_{BL_{ij}}, M_{BU_{ij}}], [N_{BL_{ij}}, N_{BU_{ij}}]\rangle] = B \end{aligned}.$$

Similarly, it can be proved the converse part of the theorem.

Theorem 2

Let $(F_n(L),\leq,+,e)$ be the lattice of GIVIFMs and A, B, $C\in F_n$. If $A\leq B$ and $A\leq C$ then

1. $A\leq B+C$,
2. $A\leq BeC$.

Proof: If $A\leq B$ then

$$M_{AL_{ij}} \leq M_{BL_{ij}},\quad M_{AU_{ij}} \leq M_{BU_{ij}}$$

and

$$N_{AL_{ij}} \geq N_{BL_{ij}},\quad N_{AU_{ij}} \geq N_{BU_{ij}}.$$

Again, $A\leq C$ then

$$M_{AL_{ij}} \leq M_{CL_{ij}},\quad M_{AU_{ij}} \leq M_{CU_{ij}}$$

and

$$N_{AL_{ij}} \geq N_{CL_{ij}},\quad N_{AU_{ij}} \geq N_{CU_{ij}}.$$

Hence,

$$M_{AL_{ij}} \leq \max\{M_{BL_{ij}}, M_{CL_{ij}}\},\quad M_{AU_{ij}} \leq \max\{M_{BU_{ij}}, M_{CU_{ij}}\}$$

and

$$N_{AL_{ij}} \leq \min\{N_{BL_{ij}}, N_{CL_{ij}}\},\quad N_{AU_{ij}} \leq \min\{N_{BU_{ij}}, N_{CU_{ij}}\}.$$

Therefore,

$$A = [\langle [M_{AL_{ij}}, M_{AU_{ij}}], [N_{AL_{ij}}, N_{AU_{ij}}]\rangle]$$
$$\leq [\langle [\max\{M_{BL_{ij}}, M_{CL_{ij}}\}, \max\{M_{BL_{ij}}, M_{CL_{ij}}\}], [\min\{N_{BL_{ij}}, N_{CL_{ij}}\}, \min\{N_{BL_{ij}}, N_{CL_{ij}}\}]\rangle] = B + C.$$

Similarly, it can be proved the second part of the theorem.

Theorem 3

Let $(F_n(L),\leq,+,e)$ be a lattice over GIVIFMs and A, B, C, $D\in F_n$. If $A\in B$ and $C\leq D$ then

1. $A+C\leq B+D$ and
2. $AeC\leq BeD$.

Proof: If $A\leq B$ then

$$M_{AL_{ij}} \leq M_{BL_{ij}},\quad M_{AU_{ij}} \leq M_{BU_{ij}}$$

and

$$N_{AL_{ij}} \geq N_{BL_{ij}},\quad N_{AU_{ij}} \geq N_{BU_{ij}}.$$

Again, $C\leq D$ then

$$M_{CL_{ij}} \leq M_{DL_{ij}},\quad M_{CU_{ij}} \leq M_{DU_{ij}}$$

and

$$N_{CL_{ij}} \geq N_{DL_{ij}},\quad N_{CU_{ij}} \geq N_{DU_{ij}}.$$

Hence,

$$\max\{M_{AL_{ij}}, M_{CL_{ij}}\} \leq \max\{M_{BL_{ij}}, M_{DL_{ij}}\},\quad \max\{M_{AU_{ij}}, M_{CU_{ij}}\} \leq \max\{M_{BU_{ij}}, M_{DU_{ij}}\}$$

and

$$\min\{M_{AL_{ij}}, M_{CL_{ij}}\} \leq \min\{M_{BL_{ij}}, M_{DL_{ij}}\},\quad \min\{M_{AU_{ij}}, M_{CU_{ij}}\} \leq \min\{M_{BU_{ij}}, M_{DU_{ij}}\}.$$

Therefore,

$$A + C = [\langle[\max\{M_{AL_{ij}}, M_{CL_{ij}}\}, \max\{M_{AU_{ij}}, M_{CU_{ij}}\}], [\min\{N_{AL_{ij}}, N_{CL_{ij}}\}, \min\{N_{AU_{ij}}, N_{CU_{ij}}\}]$$
$$= [\langle[\max\{M_{BL_{ij}}, M_{DL_{ij}}\}, \max\{M_{BU_{ij}}, M_{DU_{ij}}\}], [\min\{N_{BL_{ij}}, N_{DL_{ij}}\}, \min\{N_{BU_{ij}}, N_{DU_{ij}}\}] = B + D.$$

Proof is similar for $AeC\leq BeD$.

Distributive Lattice of GIVIFMs

Let A, B, $C \in F_n$ then the lattice of GIVIFMs $(F_n(L), \leq, +, e)$ is said to be distributive lattice of GIVIFMs if

1. $Ae(B+C)=(AeB)+(AeC)$
2. $A+(BeC)=(A+B)e(A+C)$.

Example 1

We shown by means of example of the distributive property of GIVIFMs. Let A, B, C be three 3x3 GIVIFMs where

$$A = \begin{bmatrix} \langle [0.2,0.4],[0.5,0.9] \rangle & \langle [0.3,0.5],[0.6,0.8] \rangle & \langle [0.2,0.4],[0.5,0.6] \rangle \\ \langle [0.3,0.5],[0.5,0.6] \rangle & \langle [0.2,0.3],[0.5,0.9] \rangle & \langle [0.2,0.4],[0.6,0.8] \rangle \\ \langle [0.3,0.4],[0.5,0.7] \rangle & \langle [0.1,0.5],[0.4,0.7] \rangle & \langle [0.3,0.5],[0.4,0.8] \rangle \end{bmatrix},$$

$$B = \begin{bmatrix} \langle [0.3,0.4],[0.4,0.8] \rangle & \langle [0.4,0.6],[0.4,0.5] \rangle & \langle [0.3,0.5],[0.4,0.6] \rangle \\ \langle [0.4,0.6],[0.4,0.5] \rangle & \langle [0.3,0.4],[0.5,0.8] \rangle & \langle [0.3,0.5],[0.5,0.7] \rangle \\ \langle [0.4,0.5],[0.4,0.6] \rangle & \langle [0.2,0.6],[0.3,0.5] \rangle & \langle [0.4,0.7],[0.3,0.5] \rangle \end{bmatrix}$$

and

$$C = \begin{bmatrix} \langle [0.4,0.6],[0.3,0.4] \rangle & \langle [0.5,0.6],[0.2,0.3] \rangle & \langle [0.4,0.7],[0.3,0.5] \rangle \\ \langle [0.5,0.7],[0.2,0.4] \rangle & \langle [0.4,0.6],[0.2,0.5] \rangle & \langle [0.4,0.6],[0.3,0.4] \rangle \\ \langle [0.5,0.8],[0.3,0.5] \rangle & \langle [0.3,0.7],[0.1,0.4] \rangle & \langle [0.5,0.8],[0.2,0.3] \rangle \end{bmatrix}.$$

Now,

$$B + C = \begin{bmatrix} \langle [0.4,0.6],[0.3,0.4] \rangle & \langle [0.5,0.6],[0.2,0.3] \rangle & \langle [0.4,0.7],[0.3,0.5] \rangle \\ \langle [0.5,0.7],[0.2,0.4] \rangle & \langle [0.4,0.6],[0.2,0.5] \rangle & \langle [0.4,0.6],[0.3,0.4] \rangle \\ \langle [0.5,0.8],[0.3,0.5] \rangle & \langle [0.3,0.7],[0.1,0.4] \rangle & \langle [0.5,0.8],[0.2,0.3] \rangle \end{bmatrix},$$

$$Ae(B + C) = \begin{bmatrix} \langle [0.2,0.4],[0.5,0.9] \rangle & \langle [0.3,0.5],[0.6,0.8] \rangle & \langle [0.2,0.4],[0.5,0.6] \rangle \\ \langle [0.3,0.5],[0.5,0.6] \rangle & \langle [0.2,0.3],[0.5,0.9] \rangle & \langle [0.2,0.4],[0.6,0.8] \rangle \\ \langle [0.3,0.4],[0.5,0.7] \rangle & \langle [0.1,0.5],[0.4,0.7] \rangle & \langle [0.3,0.5],[0.4,0.8] \rangle \end{bmatrix},$$

$$AeB = \begin{bmatrix} \langle[0.2,0.4],[0.5,0.9]\rangle & \langle[0.3,0.5],[0.6,0.8]\rangle & \langle[0.2,0.4],[0.5,0.6]\rangle \\ \langle[0.3,0.5],[0.5,0.6]\rangle & \langle[0.2,0.3],[0.5,0.9]\rangle & \langle[0.2,0.4],[0.6,0.8]\rangle \\ \langle[0.3,0.4],[0.5,0.7]\rangle & \langle[0.1,0.5],[0.4,0.7]\rangle & \langle[0.3,0.5],[0.4,0.8]\rangle \end{bmatrix},$$

$$AeC = \begin{bmatrix} \langle[0.2,0.4],[0.5,0.9]\rangle & \langle[0.3,0.5],[0.6,0.8]\rangle & \langle[0.2,0.4],[0.5,0.6]\rangle \\ \langle[0.3,0.5],[0.5,0.6]\rangle & \langle[0.2,0.3],[0.5,0.9]\rangle & \langle[0.2,0.4],[0.6,0.8]\rangle \\ \langle[0.3,0.4],[0.5,0.7]\rangle & \langle[0.1,0.5],[0.4,0.7]\rangle & \langle[0.3,0.5],[0.4,0.8]\rangle \end{bmatrix},$$

$$AeB + AeC = \begin{bmatrix} \langle[0.2,0.4],[0.5,0.9]\rangle & \langle[0.3,0.5],[0.6,0.8]\rangle & \langle[0.2,0.4],[0.5,0.6]\rangle \\ \langle[0.3,0.5],[0.5,0.6]\rangle & \langle[0.2,0.3],[0.5,0.9]\rangle & \langle[0.2,0.4],[0.6,0.8]\rangle \\ \langle[0.3,0.4],[0.5,0.7]\rangle & \langle[0.1,0.5],[0.4,0.7]\rangle & \langle[0.3,0.5],[0.4,0.8]\rangle \end{bmatrix}.$$

Therefore, $A\mathrm{e}(B+C)=(A\mathrm{e}B)+(A\mathrm{e}C)$.

Similarly, it can be proved that $A+(B\mathrm{e}C)=(A+B)\mathrm{e}(A+C)$.

Theorem 4

In a distributive lattice of GIVIFMs $(F_n(L),\leq,+,\mathrm{e})$ if $A, B, C\in F_n(L)$, $A+B=A+C$ and $A\mathrm{e}B=A\mathrm{e}C$, then $B=C$.

Proof

Since, $A, B, C\in(F_n(L),\leq,+,\mathrm{e})$ we have

$$B = [\langle[\min\{M_{BLij},\max\{M_{ALij},M_{BLij}\}\},\min\{M_{BUij},\max\{M_{AUij},M_{BUij}\}\}],$$

$$[\max\{N_{BLij},\min\{N_{ALij},N_{BLij}\}\},\max\{N_{BUij},\min\{N_{AUij},N_{BUij}\}\}]\rangle]\;[\mathit{By\ absorption\ property}]$$

$$= B\mathrm{e}[\langle[\max\{M_{ALij},M_{CLij}\},\max\{M_{AUij},M_{CUij}\}],[\min\{N_{ALij},N_{CLij}\},\min\{N_{AUij},N_{CUij}\}]\rangle]$$

[Since $A+B=A+C$]

$$= [\langle[\min\{M_{BLij},M_{ALij}\}\},\min\{M_{BUij},M_{AUij}\}\}],[\max\{N_{BLij},N_{ALij}\}\},\max\{N_{BUij},N_{AUij}\}\}]\rangle]$$

$$+[\langle[\min\{M_{BLij},M_{ALij}\}\},\min\{M_{BUij},M_{AUij}\}\}],[\max\{N_{BLij},N_{CLij}\}\},\max\{N_{BUij},N_{CUij}\}\}]\rangle]$$

[By distributive law]

$$= [\langle[\min\{M_{CLij},M_{ALij}\}\},\min\{M_{CUij},M_{AUij}\}\}],[\max\{N_{BLij},N_{ALij}\}\},\max\{N_{BUij},N_{AUij}\}\}]\rangle]$$

$$+[\langle[\min\{M_{BLij}, M_{CLij}\}\}, \min\{M_{BUij}, M_{CUij}\}\}], [\max\{N_{BLij}, N_{CLij}\}\}, \max\{N_{BUij}, N_{CUij}\}\}]\rangle]$$

$[BeA{=}CeA]$

$$= [\langle[\min\{M_{CLij}, M_{ALij}\}\}, \min\{M_{CUij}, M_{AUij}\}\}], [\max\{N_{CLij}, N_{ALij}\}\}, \max\{N_{CUij}, N_{AUij}\}\}]\rangle]$$

$$+[\langle[\min\{M_{CLij}, M_{BLij}\}\}, \min\{M_{CUij}, M_{BUij}\}\}], [\max\{N_{CLij}, N_{BLij}\}\}, \max\{N_{CUij}, N_{BUij}\}\}]\rangle]$$

[By commutative law]

$$= Ce[\langle[\max\{M_{ALij}, M_{BLij}\}\}, \max\{M_{AUij}, M_{BUij}\}\}], [\min\{N_{ALij}, N_{BLij}\}\}, \min\{N_{AUij}, N_{BUij}\}\}]\rangle]$$

[By distributive law]

$$= Ce(A + C) = C[By\ absorption\ property]$$

Hence the theorem.

SOME ALGEBRIC OPERATIONS ON GIVIFMS

In this section we prove that F_n is an interval valued intuitionistic fuzzy albebra and form a vector space under component wise addition, component wise multiplication and scalar multiplication.

Theorem 5

F_n, the set of all square matrices of order n, is an interval valued intuitionistic fuzzy algebra under componentwise addition and multiplication (+,e).

Proof

It is obvious that $A+O=A$ and $AeJ=A$ for all $A \in F_n$. Hence zero matrix O, is the additive identity element and the universal matrix J is the multiplicative identity element. Thus the identity element relative to the operation + and e exit. Also, $A+J=J$ and $AeO=O$. Hence bound exit for all $A \in F_n$

For

$$A = [\langle[M_{AL_{ij}}, M_{AU_{ij}}], [N_{AL_{ij}}, N_{AU_{ij}}]\rangle],$$

$$B = [\langle[M_{BL_{ij}}, M_{BU_{ij}}], [N_{BL_{ij}}, N_{BU_{ij}}]\rangle]$$

and

$$C = [\langle [M_{CL_{ij}}, M_{CU_{ij}}], [N_{CL_{ij}}, N_{CU_{ij}}] \rangle] \in F_n$$

then

$$A + (B + C) = [\langle [M_{AL_{ij}}, M_{AU_{ij}}], [N_{AL_{ij}}, N_{AU_{ij}}] \rangle] +$$

$$[\langle [\max\{M_{BL_{ij}}, M_{CL_{ij}}\}, \max\{M_{BU_{ij}}, M_{CU_{ij}}\}], [\min\{N_{BL_{ij}}, N_{CL_{ij}}\}, \min\{N_{BU_{ij}}, N_{CU_{ij}}\}] \rangle]$$

$$= [\langle [\max\{M_{AL_{ij}}, M_{BL_{ij}}, M_{CL_{ij}}\}, \max\{M_{AU_{ij}}, M_{BU_{ij}}, M_{CU_{ij}}\}],$$

$$[\min\{N_{AL_{ij}}, N_{BL_{ij}}, N_{CL_{ij}}\}, \min\{N_{AU_{ij}}, N_{BU_{ij}}, N_{CU_{ij}}\}] \rangle] \quad (1)$$

$$(A + B) + C = [\langle [\max\{M_{AL_{ij}}, M_{BL_{ij}}\}, \max\{M_{AU_{ij}}, M_{BU_{ij}}\}],$$

$$[\min\{N_{AL_{ij}}, N_{BL_{ij}}\}, \min\{N_{AU_{ij}}, N_{BU_{ij}}\}] \rangle] + [\langle [M_{CL_{ij}}, M_{CU_{ij}}], [N_{CL_{ij}}, N_{CU_{ij}}] \rangle)$$

$$= (\langle [\max\{M_{AL_{ij}}, M_{BL_{ij}}, M_{CL_{ij}}\}, \max\{M_{AU_{ij}}, M_{BU_{ij}}, M_{CU_{ij}}\}],$$

$$[\min\{N_{AL_{ij}}, N_{BL_{ij}}, N_{CL_{ij}}\}, \min\{N_{AU_{ij}}, N_{BU_{ij}}, N_{CU_{ij}}\}] \rangle]. \quad (2)$$

From (1) and (2) we have $A+(B+C)=(A+B)+C$.
Similarly we can prove that $Ae(BeC)=(AeB)eC$.
Hence associativity law under + and e is satisfied.
Further,

$$A + (AeB) = [\langle [M_{AL_{ij}}, M_{AU_{ij}}], [N_{AL_{ij}}, N_{AU_{ij}}] \rangle] +$$

$$[\langle [\min\{M_{AL_{ij}}, M_{BL_{ij}}\}, \min\{M_{AU_{ij}}, M_{BU_{ij}}\}], [\max\{N_{AL_{ij}}, N_{BL_{ij}}\}, \max\{N_{AU_{ij}}, N_{BU_{ij}}\}] \rangle]$$

$$= [\langle [\max\{M_{AL_{ij}}, \min\{M_{AL_{ij}}, M_{BL_{ij}}\}\}, \max\{M_{AU_{ij}}, \min\{M_{AU_{ij}}, M_{BU_{ij}}\}\}],$$

$$(\langle[\min\{M_{AL_{ij}}, \max\{M_{AL_{ij}}, M_{BL_{ij}}\}\}, \min\{M_{AU_{ij}}, \max\{M_{AU_{ij}}, M_{BU_{ij}}\}\}]\rangle]$$

$$= [\langle[M_{AL_{ij}}, M_{AU_{ij}}], [N_{AL_{ij}}, N_{AU_{ij}}]\rangle] = A.$$

Similarly, we can prove $Ae(A+B)=A$.

Therefore, the condition of absorption is satisfied. Assume $A\leq B$ or C

$$Ae(B+C) = [\langle[M_{AL_{ij}}, M_{AU_{ij}}], [N_{AL_{ij}}, N_{AU_{ij}}]\rangle]e$$

$$[\langle[\max\{M_{BL_{ij}}, M_{CL_{ij}}\}, \max\{M_{BU_{ij}}, M_{CU_{ij}}\}], [\min\{N_{BL_{ij}}, N_{CL_{ij}}\}, \min\{N_{BU_{ij}}, N_{CU_{ij}}\}]\rangle]$$

$$= [\langle[\min\{M_{AL_{ij}}, \max\{M_{BL_{ij}}, M_{CL_{ij}}\}\}, \min\{M_{AU_{ij}}, \max\{M_{BU_{ij}}, M_{CU_{ij}}\}\}],$$

$$[\max\{M_{AL_{ij}}, \min\{M_{BL_{ij}}, M_{CL_{ij}}\}\}, \max\{M_{AU_{ij}}, \min\{M_{BU_{ij}}, M_{CU_{ij}}\}\}]\rangle]$$

$$= [\langle[M_{AL_{ij}}, M_{AU_{ij}}], [N_{AL_{ij}}, N_{AU_{ij}}]\rangle] = A. \quad (3)$$

Also, $(AeB)+(AeC)$

$$= [\langle[min\{M_{AL_{ij}}, M_{BL_{ij}}\}, min\{M_{AU_{ij}}, M_{BU_{ij}}\}], [max\{N_{AL_{ij}}, N_{BL_{ij}}\}, max\{N_{AU_{ij}}, N_{BU_{ij}}\}]\rangle] +$$

$$[\langle[min\{M_{AL_{ij}}, M_{CL_{ij}}\}, min\{M_{AU_{ij}}, M_{CU_{ij}}\}], [max\{N_{AL_{ij}}, N_{CL_{ij}}\}, max\{N_{AU_{ij}}, N_{CU_{ij}}\}]\rangle]$$

$$= [\langle[\max\{\min\{M_{AL_{ij}}, M_{BL_{ij}}\}, \min\{M_{AL_{ij}}, M_{CL_{ij}}\}\}, \max\{\min\{M_{AU_{ij}}, M_{BU_{ij}}\}, \min\{M_{AU_{ij}}, M_{CU_{ij}}\}\}]$$

$$[\min\{\max\{M_{AL_{ij}}, M_{BL_{ij}}\}, \max\{M_{AL_{ij}}, M_{CL_{ij}}\}\}, \min\{\max\{M_{AU_{ij}}, M_{BU_{ij}}\}, \max\{M_{AU_{ij}}, M_{CU_{ij}}\}\}]\rangle]$$

$$= [\langle[M_{AL_{ij}}, M_{AU_{ij}}], [N_{AL_{ij}}, N_{AU_{ij}}]\rangle] = A \quad (4)$$

from (3) and (4) $Ae(B+C)=(AeB)+(AeC)$ if, $A\geq B$ and C, then we have two cases $A\geq B\geq C$ or $A\geq C\geq B$ for, $A\geq B\geq C$ from (3) and (4) $Ae(B+C)=B=(AeB)+(AeC)$ $A\geq C\geq B$ from (3) and (4) $Ae(B+C)=C=(AeB)+(AeC)$.

Therefore, $Ae(B+C)=(AeB)+(AeC)$.

Similarly, we can prove $A+(BeC)=(A+B)e(A+C)$.

Thus the property of distributivity holds.

Hence, F_n is an interval valued intuitionistic fuzzy algebra under the operation + and e.

The algebric structure $(F_{m\times n}, +, \mathrm{e})$ such that $(F_{m\times n}, +)$ is an abelian monoid (with identity element as null matrix), $(F_{m\times n}, \mathrm{e})$ is a monoid (with identity matrix as a identity element), e distributes over + from either side. Therefore $F_{m\times n}$ is a semiring.

Theorem 6

The set $F_{m\times n}$ is an interval-valued intuitionistic fuzzy vector space under the operation GIVIFM addition and scalar multiplication.

Proof

Let any three GIVIFMs A, B, $C \in F_{m\times n}$, then

$$A + B = [\langle[\max\{M_{AL_{ij}}, M_{BL_{ij}}\}, \max\{M_{AU_{ij}}, M_{BU_{ij}}\}],$$

$$[\min\{N_{AL_{ij}}, N_{BL_{ij}}\}, \min\{N_{AU_{ij}}, N_{BU_{ij}}\}]\rangle]$$

$$= [\langle[\max\{M_{BL_{ij}}, M_{AL_{ij}}\}, \max\{M_{BU_{ij}}, M_{AU_{ij}}\}], [\min\{N_{BL_{ij}}, N_{AL_{ij}}\}, \min\{N_{BU_{ij}}, N_{AU_{ij}}\}]\rangle] = B + A$$

Therefore, commutative law holds in $F_{m\times n}$.

Again, in earlier we prove that associative law holds in $F_{m\times n}$.

Also, for all $A \in F_{m\times n}$, there exit an element $O \in F_{m\times n}$ such that $A+O=A$.

Again, for $c \in IVIFS$ we have

$$c(A + B) = cJ\mathrm{e}(A + B) = cJ\mathrm{e}A + cJ\mathrm{e}B = cA + cB$$

For

$$c_1, c_2 \in F(c_1 + c_2)A = (c_1 + c_2)J\mathrm{e}A = (c_1 J + c_2 J)\mathrm{e}A = c_1 J\mathrm{e}A + c_2 J\mathrm{e}A = c_1 A + c_2 A$$

Hence, $F_{m\times n}$ is an interval-valued intuitionistic vector space over F.

SOME PROPERTIES OF GIVIFMS

In this section we prove matrix multiplication is associative and distributive in F_n.

Theorem 7

For any three GIVIFMs A, B, C of order $m\times n$, $n\times p$, $p\times q$, respectively $(AB)C=A(BC)$

Proof

Both $(AB)C$ and $A(BC)$ are defined and are of type mxq. Let

$$A = [\langle[M_{AL_{ij}}, M_{AU_{ij}}], [N_{AL_{ij}}, N_{AU_{ij}}]\rangle],$$

$$B = [\langle[M_{BL_{ij}}, M_{BU_{ij}}], [N_{BL_{ij}}, N_{BU_{ij}}]\rangle]$$

and

$$C = [\langle[M_{CL_{ij}}, M_{CU_{ij}}], [N_{CL_{ij}}, N_{CU_{ij}}]\rangle]$$

such that the ranges of the suffixes i, j, k, l are 1 to m, 1 to n, 1 to p, 1 to q respectively. Now, $(i,k)^{th}$ element of the product

$$AB = (\langle \sum_{j=1}^{n}(M_{A_{ij}}.M_{B_{jk}}), \prod_{j=1}^{n}(N_{A_{ij}} + N_{B_{jk}})\rangle)$$

The $(i,l)^{th}$ element of the product $(AB)C$ is the sum of the corresponding element in the ith row of AB, l^{th} column of C with k common. Thus $(i,l)^{th}$ element of

$$\begin{aligned}(AB)C &= [\langle \sum_{k=1}^{p}(\sum_{j=1}^{n}(M_{A_{ij}}.M_{B_{jk}}).M_{C_{kl}}), \prod_{k=1}^{p}(\prod_{j=1}^{n}(N_{A_{ij}} + N_{B_{jk}}) + N_{C_{kl}})\rangle] \\ &= [\langle \sum_{k=1}^{p}\sum_{j=1}^{n}M_{A_{ij}}.M_{B_{jk}}.M_{C_{kl}}, \prod_{k=1}^{p}\prod_{j=1}^{n}N_{A_{ij}} + N_{B_{jk}} + N_{C_{kl}}\rangle]\end{aligned} \tag{5}$$

Again the $(i,l)^{th}$ element of the element $A(BC)$ is sum of products of the correspondig elements in the ith row of A and l^{th} column of (BC). $(i,l)^{th}$ element of

$$\begin{aligned}A(BC) &= [\langle \sum_{j=1}^{n}M_{A_{ij}}.\sum_{k=1}^{p}(M_{B_{jk}}.M_{C_{kl}}), (\prod_{j=1}^{n}N_{A_{ij}} + \prod_{k=1}^{p}(N_{B_{jk}} + N_{C_{kl}})\rangle] \\ &= [\langle \sum_{k=1}^{p}\sum_{j=1}^{n}M_{A_{ij}}.M_{B_{jk}}.M_{C_{kl}}, \prod_{k=1}^{p}\prod_{j=1}^{n}N_{A_{ij}} + N_{B_{jk}} + N_{C_{kl}}\rangle]\end{aligned} \tag{6}$$

Hence from (5) and (6) we have $(AB)C=A(BC)$.

Theorem 8

For any three GIVIFMs *A*, *B*, *C* of order $m\times n$, $n\times p$, $p\times q$, respectively in $F_{m\times n}$, $A(B+C)=AB+AC$.

Proof

Let

$$A=[\langle[M_{AL_{ij}},M_{AU_{ij}}],[N_{AL_{ij}},N_{AU_{ij}}]\rangle],$$

$$B=[\langle[M_{BL_{jk}},M_{BU_{jk}}],[N_{BL_{jk}},N_{BU_{jk}}]\rangle]$$

and

$$C=[\langle[M_{CL_{jk}},M_{CU_{jk}}],[N_{CL_{jk}},N_{CU_{jk}}]\rangle]$$

such that the ranges of the suffixes i, j, k are 1 to m, 1 to n, 1 to p respectively. Now $(j,k)^{th}$ element of

$$B+C=[\langle[\max\{M_{BL_{jk}},M_{CL_{jk}}\},\max\{M_{BU_{jk}},M_{CU_{jk}}\}],[\min\{N_{BL_{jk}},N_{CL_{jk}}\},\min\{N_{BU_{jk}},N_{CU_{jk}}\}]\rangle]$$

and $(i,k)^{th}$ element in the product of *A* and $(B+C)$ is the sum of the products of the corresponding elements in the ith of *A* and k^{th} column of $B+C$ i.e.

$$A(B+C)=[\langle[\max_j\{\min\{M_{AL_{ij}},\max\{M_{BL_{jk}},M_{CL_{jk}}\}\}\},\max_j\{\min\{M_{AU_{ij}},\max\{M_{BU_{jk}},M_{CU_{jk}}\}\}\}],$$

$$[\min_j\{\max\{M_{AL_{ij}},\min\{M_{BL_{jk}},M_{CL_{jk}}\}\}\},\min_j\{\max\{M_{AU_{ij}},\min\{M_{BU_{jk}},M_{CU_{jk}}\}\}\}]\rangle]$$

$$=[\langle\sum_{j=1}^{n}M_{A_{ij}}(M_{B_{jk}}+M_{C_{jk}}),\prod_{j=1}^{n}(N_{A_{ij}}+N_{B_{jk}}N_{C_{jk}})\rangle] \tag{7}$$

Now, $(i,k)^{th}$ element of $(AB+AC$ is

$$\begin{aligned}AB+AC&=[\langle\sum_{j=1}^{n}M_{A_{ij}}M_{B_{jk}},\prod_{j=1}^{n}(N_{A_{ij}}+N_{B_{jk}})\rangle]+[\langle\sum_{j=1}^{n}M_{A_{ij}}M_{C_{jk}},\prod_{j=1}^{n}(N_{A_{ij}}+N_{C_{jk}})\rangle]\\&=[\langle\sum_{j=1}^{n}M_{A_{ij}}(M_{B_{jk}}+M_{C_{jk}}),\prod_{j=1}^{n}(N_{A_{ij}}+N_{B_{jk}}N_{C_{jk}})\rangle]\end{aligned} \tag{8}$$

Therefore, from (7) and (8) we have $A(B+C)=AB+AC$.

Theorem 9

For any three GIVIFMs A, B of order $m \times n$, $n \times p$ respectively in $F_{m\times n}$, if $A \leq B$ then for any $C \in F_{np}$, $AC \leq BC$ and for any $D \in F_{pm}$, $DA \leq DB$.

Proof

If $A \leq B$ then $M_{A_{ij}} \leq M_{B_{ij}}$ and $N_{A_{ij}} \geq N_{B_{ij}}$ for all $i=1$ to m and $j=1$ to n. By generalized interval valued intuitionistic fuzzy matrix multiplication we have

$$AC = (\langle \sum_{j=1}^{n} M_{A_{ij}} M_{C_{jk}}, \prod_{j=1}^{n} (N_{A_{ij}} + N_{C_{jk}}) \rangle)$$

$$BC = (\langle \sum_{j=1}^{n} M_{B_{ij}} M_{C_{jk}}, \prod_{j=1}^{n} (N_{B_{ij}} + N_{C_{jk}}) \rangle)$$

Since

$$M_{A_{ij}} \leq M_{B_{ij}}$$

therefore

$$\sum_{j=1}^{n} M_{A_{ij}} M_{C_{jk}} \leq \sum_{j=1}^{n} M_{B_{ij}} M_{C_{jk}}$$

and

$$\prod_{j=1}^{n} N_{A_{ij}} + N_{C_{jk}} \geq \prod_{j=1}^{n} N_{B_{ij}} + N_{C_{jk}}$$

Thus $AC \leq BC$.
Similarly, it can be prove that $DA \leq DB$.

CONCLUSION

We introduce the concept of semiring of generalized interval-valued intuitionistic fuzzy matrices and proved that GIVIFMs forms distributive lattice and an interval-valued intuitionistic fuzzy algebra and proved some properties of GIVIFMs using component wise addition and fuzzy multiplication. In the next paper we should try to prove some related properties generalized interval-valued intuitionistic fuzzy subgroups and ideals.

REFERENCES

Adak, A. K., & Bhowmik, M. (2011). Application of Generalized Intuitionistic Fuzzy Matrix in Multi-Criteria Decision Making Problem. *Journal of Mathematical and Computational Science*, *1*(1), 1–13.

Atanassov, K. (1994). Operations over interval valued fuzzy set. *Fuzzy Sets and Systems*, (64): 159–174. doi:10.1016/0165-0114(94)90331-X

Atanassov, K., & Gargo, G. (1989). Interval-valued intuitionistic fuzzy sets. *Fuzzy Sets and Systems*, *31*(1), 343–349. doi:10.1016/0165-0114(89)90205-4

Bhowmik, M., & Pal, M. (2008). Generalized intuitionistic fuzzy matrices. *Far East Journal of Mathematical Sciences*, *29*(3), 533–554.

Bhowmik, M., & Pal, M. (2010). Generalized interval-valued intuitionistic fuzzy sets. *The Journal of Fuzzy Mathematics*, *18*(2), 357–371.

Giveon, Y. (1964). Lattice matrices. *Information and Control*, *7*(3), 477–484. doi:10.1016/S0019-9958(64)90173-1

Kim. (1988). Determinant theory for fuzzy and boolean matrices. *Congressus Numerantium*, 273-276.

Kim & Roush. (1980). Generalised fuzzy matrices. *Fuzzy Sets and System*, (4), 293-315.

Mondal, T. K., & Samanta, S. K. (2002). Generalized intuitionistic fuzzy sets. *The Journal of Fuzzy Mathematics*, *10*(4), 839–862.

Pal. (2001). Intuitionistic fuzzy determinant. *V.U.J. Physical Sciences*, (7), 87-93.

Panigrahi, M., & Nanda, S. (2006). A comparison betwen intuitionistic fuzzy sets and generalized intuitionistic fuzzy sets. *The Journal of Fuzzy Mathematics*, *14*(2), 407–421.

Shyamal & Pal. (2005a). Distance between fuzzy matrices and its applications. *Acta Siencia Indica*, *31*(1), 199-204.

Shyamal, , & Pal, . (2006). Interval-valued fuzzy matrices. *The Journal of Fuzzy Mathematics*, *14*(3) 583-604.

Shyamal, A. K., & Pal, M. (2005b). Distance between fuzzy matrices and its applications-I. *J. Nature. Physical Science (London)*, *19*(1), 39–58.

Sriram, S., & Murugadas, P. (2010). On semiring of intuitionistic fuzzy matrices. *Applied Mathematical Sciences*, *4*(23), 1099–1105.

Thomson, M. G. (1977). Convergence of powers of a fuzzy matrix. *Journal of Mathematical Analysis and Applications*, *57*(55), 476–480. doi:10.1016/0022-247X(77)90274-8

Zadeh, L. A. (1965). Fuzzy sets. *Information and Control*, *8*(8), 338–353. doi:10.1016/S0019-9958(65)90241-X

Chapter 7
Classification Techniques in Data Mining:
Classical and Fuzzy Classifiers

Ali Hosseinzadeh
Comprehensive Imam Hossein University, Iran

S. A. Edalatpanah
Ayandegan Institute of Higher Education, Tonekabon, Iran

ABSTRACT

Learning is the ability to improve behavior based on former experiences and observations. Nowadays, mankind continuously attempts to train computers for his purpose, and make them smarter through trainings and experiments. Learning machines are a branch of artificial intelligence with the aim of reaching machines able to extract knowledge (learning) from the environment. Classical, fuzzy classification, as a subcategory of machine learning, has an important role in reaching these goals in this area. In the present chapter, we undertake to elaborate and explain some useful and efficient methods of classical versus fuzzy classification. Moreover, we compare them, investigating their advantages and disadvantages.

INTRODUCTION

Our level of learning depends on the perfection degree of our former knowledge (Alpayden, 2010). Learning is an important human behavior and very close to artificial intelligence which makes mankind able to boost his knowledge in relation to the environment. Received information through senses, are processed by brain, extracting knowledge from the received information and further preserving them (Nilsson, 2005). Learning is the ability to improve behavior based on former experiences and observations. Thus, learning ability must be regarded as a potential tool (Mitchell, 1997; Bishop 2006; Natarajan 1991). Development of computer technologies and automatic learning techniques can result in easier, more efficient. Numerous approaches of decision making techniques exist in machine learning domain where computers decide or make suggestions for the decision. The aim of machine learning is producing smart systems with high levels of flexibility and intelligence able to extract knowledge (learning) from

DOI: 10.4018/978-1-5225-0914-1.ch007

the environment, and simulating human behavior, use former experiences in solving a problem. Machine learning is in three forms of supervised, unsupervised, and semi supervised of which we have focused on the supervised form (Nilsson, 2005; Mitchell, 2006). In recent decades, advances in data collection and conserving capabilities have resulted in high sum of information in many sciences. Advanced-databases management technology can contain different types of data. Therefore, statistical techniques and traditional management tools are not sufficient for the analysis of these data, and extracting knowledge from this amount is a true difficulty (Bishop, 2006). Data mining is an attempt to obtain useful information out of these data which has become even more significant with overdue growth of data (Jing He, 2009).

Nowadays, data mining, as a subcategory of machine learning, plays a vital role in retrieving information for the classification of large collections of textual or non-textual documents. Basically, the most important knowledge mankind has achieved is classification. Classification is a process which divides data sets into determined parts, making organizations able to discover patterns in particular problems in complex, large sets (Heikki, 1996; Han & Kamber, 2001).

Data classification is a 2-phase process. First, a model is generated based on train data sets existing in the database. Train data sets consist of records, samples, examples, and or objects which include a set of features or aspects. Second, every sample has a label of predetermined class verified in one feature named 'class level'. When 'class level' is determined, the learning phase is called supervised learning (Nilsson, 2005; Bishop, 2006). In classification process, objects are assigned to distinct classes with distinguished attributes, and are introduced as a model. Subsequently, having considered features of each category, the new object is dedicated to them, and its label and type is predicted. Some of common, important methods used nowadays for data mining in classification, supervised problems are listed below (Han & Kamber, 2001):

- Support vector machine,
- Linear regression,
- Decision tree,
- K- nearest neighbor.

In real-world environment data are irresolute and vague, and in these classifiers, error-value importance is the same for different train sample, while it should not logically be so (Zadeh, 1965; Zadeh, 1968; Baldwin, 1981; Zadeh, 1984). (Since some data are defected by noise confusions of filter,) fuzzy classification methods were proposed for this difficulty (Joachims, 2002). Since quantitative data can be classified, and these techniques can be used for detecting and eliminating noise and intruder, these methods are useful for contracting amount of data. These methods include:

- Fuzzy support-vector machine,
- Fuzzy linear regression,
- Fuzzy decision tree,
- Fuzzy nearest neighbor.

In this chapter, we aim at clarification, description, and comparison of different classical versus fuzzy classification methods of data as an important branch of machine learning.

BACKGROUND

Acquiring knowledge is regarded as a crucial strait in knowledge-engineering process today. Machine learning algorithms are a method to overcome this difficulty, aiming at extracting knowledge from data.

A common approach in machine learning is decision tree induction for decision making or classification. Decision trees can attribute symbolic decisions to new samples. Decision tree is a method for proposing law base, and in fact, a method of representing knowledge (Clark & Niblett, 1987). Traditional decision trees are a powerful approach in machine learning, but they have little efficiency in the instances of confusion, lack of values of attributes in sample description, high cardinality of an attribute, insufficient set of training samples, inadequate partition of the value space for some attributes,as well as when there is a need for numeral decisions. Combining fuzzy-logic capabilities with decision trees is a good idea. This trend of thought has led to emergence of fuzzy decision trees.

Another approach in machine learning is support vector machine. Theory of support vector machine (SVMs) is a new classifying technique attended lately (Burges, 1998). SVMs is an efficient classifier especially when there is little data and no commonality between classes (Abe, 2001). The first algorithm for classification of the patterns was proposed by Fisher in 1936, and its optimization criterion was reducing train data classification error. SVM's approach tries to select decision edge with maximum distance from each category in the training phase. SVM method is based on structural idea of minimum risk (SRM) (Burges, 1998). In classification problems, often a number of train samples have more importance than others. We need to classify train data accurately, avoiding protection of some data as noise or wrong classification i.e. when each train sample does not exactly to a class. Fuzzy support vector was proposed with respect to the membership of every datum in relation to its belonging to each class (Lin & Wang, 2002).

Other common approaches in machine learning are regression vector machine and nearest neighbor. Nearest neighbor K is one of best and most used classifiers, due to being simple and non-parametric (Duda et al. 2001). This classifier classifies data by comparison with their neighbors. Verifying K, we determine the number of comparison. For attributing label, classical KNN considers all nearest neighbors of the sample test with the same importance degree. Therefore, Keller et al. proposed fuzzy KNN by giving membership to every sample (Keller, Grey, & Givens, 1985). Fuzzy KNN results from combination of classical KNN and fuzzy sets (Zadeh, 1965).

Another support vector machine useful in regression is support vector regression which is specific to continuous data (Smola et al. 1998; Chang & Lin, 2002; Smola & Scholkopf, 1997). Actually, it is a generalization of SVM. We use SVM to estimate function values, approximation function, or curve fitting. Fuzzy regression has been proposed for special time occasions when decisions are often based on inaccurate data, or data is produced by skeptical measurements. In fact, fuzzy regression is generalization of classical regression used for calculating functional relation between independent and dependent variables in a fuzzy environment (Draper & Smith, 1980).

MAIN FOCUS OF THE CHAPTER

Decision Tree

A decision tree consists of tree-like structure in addition to some inference procedures based on the tree. Due to their potential understandability, decision trees have been welcomed lately. The understandability is significant from diverse viewpoints: understanding the domain, perception of classifying capabilities, decision justification, and finally, symbolic laws which are extractable from the tree and can be put in a decision system based on the laws (Quinlan, 1993).

Decision trees were first introduced by Quinlan as ID3 (Quinlan, 1986). Employing systems of learning based on decision trees like CRT, C4.5, and …, were given, each of them dealing with certain aspects of learning. Decision trees have been successfully employed in areas like classification, regression, support vector system, etc (Friedman et al. 1984).

CART and ID3 are particular algorithms for producing decision trees (Jang, 1994). Induction is one common method for symbolic learning, developed first by Quinlan as ID3 algorithm. ID3 is both widespread and effective in categorizing symbolic data, but not appropriate for dealing with numerical data (Sushmita et al. 2002).

Using Matlab software, decision tree is shown below:

Figure 1. ClassificationTree
PredictorNames: {'x1' 'x2' 'x3' 'x4'}
ResponseName: 'Y'
ClassNames: {'setosa' 'versicolor' 'virginica'}
ScoreTransform: 'none'
CategoricalPredictors: []
NObservations: 150

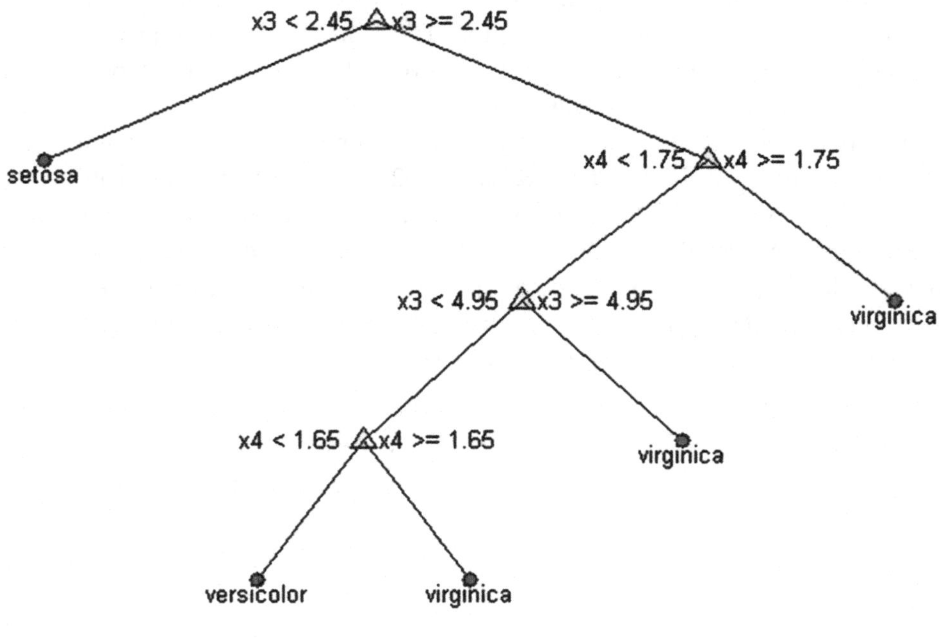

Decision Tree ID3

This algorithm has been comprehensively accounted for by Quinlan (1986) and (1993). ID3, and generally speaking, every method of decision-tree induction has a function based on recursive splitting: partition of the sample's space in a data-driven method, and subsequently representation of the partition as a tree. This classification is performed in a step-by-step and top-down manner. First, all training samples are placed at the root of decision tree. Then, every node is broken down recursively, by partition of its samples. A node is regarded as a leaf if all its samples belong to a single class, or all attributes are used on the route and the root origin of the node. When it is decided for this node to be further divided, one of the remaining attributes is selected (i.e. that which has not appeared on the route). The values of this Attribute's area are used for the conditions leading to offspring nodes. The samples within this node, depending on the conditions of the branches they meet, are divided among offspring nodes, and this procedure continues. The manner of attribute selection directly affects size and output of produced tree. Generally, all decision-tree induction algorithms, while at the same time optimizing an attribute's quality criterion (locally), try to minimize the size of the tree to the utmost possible extent (Mingers, 1989a).

A prevalent attribute-selection mechanism is selecting that which maximizes information interest (Mingers, 1989b). Other criteria could be namely Gini index, uncertainty criterion U- and so forth (Mitchell, 2005). Inference from decision tree in ID3 is so performed that in case of deciding for a new sampl e, its attributes are blended with the condition of the tree, beginning from the root. If there is a leaf node which meets the attributes of the new sample, it is assigned to the class with same conditions. In case of a situation other than this. Appropriate decisions should be made.

It has been stated by Guoxiu (2005) that the best attribute is that which contains highest level of information.

Even though applying ID3 in symbolic areas with small cardinality has been thriving, in practice, in cases of confusion, lack of values of attributes in sample description, high cardinality of an attribute, insufficient setoff training samples, inadequate partition of the value space for some attributes, content

Table 1. Executive algorithm of decision tree ID3

(features, target attributes, samples) ID3
Samples: are training samples
Target attributes: that attribute whose value is predicted by the tree
Attributes; are other attributes which may be tested by the decision tree

- Generate root node
- If all samples are positive, we will have a one-node tree with the mark (+)
- If all samples are negative, we will have a one-node tree with the mark (-)
- If there is no attribute for the development of the tree, refer to the one-node root marked by the most prevalent attribute.

Otherwise begin

- Label the best classifying attribute as A
- Put A as decision attribute for the root
- For each possible quantity OF V_i from A
    - o Add the new branch under the root according to test attribute V_i=A
    - o Put (V_i) examples in subset of A examples with V_i quantity
    - o If examples are empty:

      add leaf node below the new branch marked by prevalent, target attribute in samples,
      otherwise, the new branch is added below the tree
      ({A}-attributes, target attribute/samples) ID3

- Finished.
- get back to the root

overlap, inaccuracy of language in representing samples, and lack of enough attributes they lead to problems like unknown attribute, imperfect tree, incompatibility, etc.

Numerous researches have been performed on altering inference procedures from imperfect or incompatible tree (Quinlan, 1984; Quinlan, 1987; Quinlan, 1986; Mingers, 1989a; Mingers, 1989b; Clark and Niblett, 1987). Nonetheless, no method is predominant.

Furthermore, another shortcoming in traditional decision trees is that a slight change in data collection may upset the structure of the decision tree and in instances where numeral decisions are needed, they become ineffective. To overcome this problem, some researchers have proposed fuzzy decision trees (Guoxiu, 2005).

In these cases, traditional decision trees are useless (Janikow, 1998); appropriate solution for this method, as indicated in different resources, is using fuzzy decision tree.

Fuzzy Decision Tree

The aim of developing fuzzy decision trees is fusion of fuzzy representation and its proximate reasoning capabilities with traditional decision trees such that preserves the advantages of the both: dealing with uncertainty and gradual processing which are characteristics of fuzzy logic, and understandability, generality, and ease of application which characterize decision trees (Breiman et al. 1984). Among substantial developments in theoretical fusion of fuzzy logic with decision trees we can name fuzzy CART and UR for reasoning uncertainty in ID3 (Breiman et al. 1984; Mitchell, 2005; Maher and Clair, 1993). The former is the method which uses CART algorithm to generate the tree. Nevertheless, the tree is not the ultimate result. Instead, it is employed for determining features of the effective branch and offering fuzzy sets of continuous, numeral fields. Then, another algorithm is used as a neural-multilayered network for learning fuzzy laws which as a result optimizes generated knowledge by primary CART and produces more understandable, fuzzy laws. A similar method has been proposed in (Guoxiu, 2005). In fact, both of them use methods of decision-tree production for pre-processing and not generating fuzzy decision tree. On the other hand, UR-ID3 begins with generating traditional decision tree, and subsequently makes the tree conditions fuzzy. Besides, there is a large category of induction of fuzzy decision-tree methods, and based on ID3 induction (Quinlan, 1986; Quinlan, 1993; Sushmita et al. 2002; Ningers, 1989; Mitchell, 2005; Chang and Pavlidis, 1977; Koen et al. 1999; Zeidler et al. 1996). These methods fall mainly into 2 different groups: some of them build the tree according to crisp data. These methods employ fuzzy-language conditions in order to optimize the generalization feature, aiming at avoiding inappropriate, dramatic changes of the class resulting from change in the value of classified-data features. Other methods are those which build the structure of the tree from fuzzy data. FDT structuring method suggested by Quinlan (1986), Yuan and Shaw (1995) is designed for classification issue in which attributes and classes are represented by fuzzy language conditions, and in fact, fuzzy membership functions. Quinlan (1993) presented a fuzzy method of fuzzy decision-tree induction for generating the tree from a set of crisp data where all the attributes are continuous, numeral type and accurate in terms of value. Breiman et al. (2002) developed a fuzzy decision-tree induction method which produces trees useful both for classification and regression. In this method, train data can contain fuzzy values, but fuzzy language conditions used in the tree should be already defined by experts or other pre-processing procedures. Mitchell (2005) proposed a method in which attributes with nominal, discrete domains are determined by accurate values, range values, and fuzzy numbers. Every train datum has a specific class and confidence interval. This induction of fuzzy decision tree automatically generates fuzzy membership functions for continuous, numeral attributes. After the production of the tree, we can attribute descriptive, language conditions to the resulting fuzzy membership functions in order to improve understandability of the tree.

Other methods of generating fuzzy decision trees are relatively similar to the already- mentioned methods. In the next section, we will comprehensively explain how to learn ID3-based fuzzy decision trees.

Fuzzy ID3

The investigated methods for generating fuzzydecision trees could be categorized collectively as ID3. The methods share the characteristic of being based on modified ID3. Here, the main algorithm for generating fuzzy decision tree, according to this method, is presented. It is a given here that all attributes have a fuzzy domain on a universal set of accurate values or discrete nominal and fuzzy language conditions have already been defined. Every sample from data has sets of value-attribute pairs and a confidence interval of belonging to the class. First, every sample belongs to the set of root-node samples with a membership degree equal to its confidence interval. As in regressive ID3, every node is broken down by division of its samples. Nevertheless, contrary to ID3, here the samples can make their way to more than one offspring node since we are dealing with fuzzy and not accurate sets. When it is decided for a node to divide, one of the remaining attributes is selected. Once again the values of this attribute's domain is used for generating conditions leading to offspring nodes, but here, these conditions contain fuzzy constraints. As in ID3, a feature is selected which would optimize a quality criterion. After attribute selection, offspring nodes are generated and labeled with fuzzy language terms. The conformity degree of each sample within the current node to each fuzzy constraint determines if it is a member of that offspring node, to what degree. Usually, a T-norm like minimum operator or multiplication is used to combine degree of membership within the current node and degree of fuzzy constraint fulfillment of the particular fuzzy node to reach membership degree in offspring node. Similar to ID3, this dividing procedure is repeatedly enacted until there remain leaf nodes. A node is regarded as leaf node if the number of its samples is from one threshold, or all of the attributes are used on the path and origin of the root. As it was mentioned, we need optimization of a quality criterion for attribute selection. Entropy criterion in ID3 is based on probability theory. Here we need criteria compatible with fuzzy sets. "Fuzzy Entropy", which is a criterion for representing the level of fuzziness of asset, is used. However, other criteria like the least classification ambiguity and highest degree of importance (Wang et al. 2001) have been employed as well.

In contrast to symbolic decision tree, in fuzzy decision tree every sample can belong to the nodes with varying membership degrees. Inference methods in these trees are necessarily different from traditional decision trees. Diverse inference methods have been proposed for fuzzy decision trees. These methods are inspired with either inference principles in symbolic decision trees or approximate reason-

Table 2. Fuzzy decision tree executive algorithm

1. Generates the root node.
2. Tests the leaf node (see section 2 for three conditions).
3. Finds a test attribute.
a. Divides the data according to this attribute.
b. Generates new nodes for fuzzy subsets.
4. Makes recursion of the process for the new nodes from point 2.

(Kazemi & Mehrzadegan, 2011)

ing ideas (Mitchell, 2005; Breiman et al. 1984). After performing inference, the sample is assigned a membership degree in every target class. To reach this goal, classification information of all leaf nodes are put together. In its simplest form, membership degree of the sample in each node can be multiplied by the membership degree of that node in a target class, and select the maximum value from the resulting values as membership degree in the particular class (Mitchell, 2005). Additionally, dependent on inference method and structure of the target classes, a numeral value may be considered as the output (Breiman et al. 1984).

Regardless of its generating method, fuzzy decision tree can convert onto a set of fuzzy laws, and consequently, a fuzzy inference system. Moreover, by applying pruning methods, we may be able to extend its generalizability.

Comparing Fuzzy Decision Trees with Traditional Decision Trees

Generally, it can be argued that fuzzy decision tree has attracted attention due to following reasons. The crucial privilege of fuzzy decision tree is its similarity of its generation to traditional decision trees. It makes it have an understandable structure for analyzing information as in traditional decision trees. Fuzzy decision tree can manage data with symbolic and numeral values as well as fuzzy conditions. Since fuzzy constraints are assessed by fuzzy membership functions, this procedure makes a relation between continuous domain and definite features. Using fuzzy set and approximate reasoning, we can process confused, contrasting and imperfect data. Therefore we have higher degree of accuracy compared to decision tree. On the other hand, besides mentioned advantages, there are shortcomings in FDT as well (Wernick et al. 2012; Bishop, 2006; Breiman et al. 1984; Quinlan, 1993).

With regards to calculation, this method is slower than traditional DT. The lower speed is the expense for extension of accuracy in a manner that interpretability is not affected. From pruning perspective, if the tree is larger than the condition of selecting the best attribute or the main attributes of the samples are not duly used, the generated fuzzy tree needs pruning algorithm in order to be smaller in size. Fuzzy DT has a low level of flexibility for the change in input data, and for the purpose of learning new data, the structure of the tree must change altogether, or a part of it must be regenerated. In general, its advantages can be summed up as follows (Quinlan, 1993; Breiman et al. 1984; Mitchell, 2005):

1. Numeral decisions
2. Norm division
3. More generalizability
4. More understandability

Support Vector Machine Theory

Support vector machine theory (SVMS) is a new classifying technique which has been given considerable attention in the recent years (Corte and Vapnik, 1995; Abe, 2001; Burges, 1998; Vapnik, 1995; Poggio et al. 2002; Schölkopf et al. 1999; Pontil and Verri, 1998; Joachims, 2002; Lin, 2002; Wu et al. 2008; Fatai and Abdulazeez, 2011; Zhang, 1999; Van Gestel et al. 2002; Thomas, 2003; Stecking, and schebesch, 2003).

Support vector machine is an efficient classifier, especially when there is little data and no commonality between classes (Abe, 2001). The first algorithm for classification of the patterns was proposed by

Fisher in 1936, and its optimization criterion was reducing train data classification error. Continuing this, Russian researcher Vapnik made an important step in designing classifiers, and established statistical learning theory more firmly proposing SVM based on it (Joachims, 2002). SVM's approach tries to select decision edge with maximum distance from each category in the training phase.

SVM method is based on structural idea of minimum risk (SRM) (Burges, 1998). With respect to many of the functions, SVMs provide higher efficiency than traditional learning machines, and are a powerful tool for solving classification problems.

There are a lot of functions in using SVM. However, in many functions, a number of input points cannot be exactly appropriated by either of the two classes.

That number of data is significant which is appropriated into a class. Thus, SVM can be more accurate in discriminating the points. Some data points are damaged by noise or data confusion that SVM should be able to eliminate them. Fuzzy SVM in SVM training phase engages importance of every sample among class samples compared to digressed, non-significant data, using fuzzy membership function, and makes the decision (Lin & Wang, 2002).

Separable Support Vector Machine

In this section, we provide a brief account of SVM classification problems (Abe, 2001; Burges, 1998; Vapnik, 1995; Poggio et al. 2002; Schölkopf et al. 1999).

Suppose we have number of train data as $X = \{x_1, x_2, ..., x_i, ..., x_N\}$ each of which has an attribute vector with d dimensions and labeled by $y_i \in \{-1,1\}$, the aim is solving and optimizing a two-class classification problem. Suppose we undertake to discriminate the two classes with distinguish function of *f*(*x*) and an H hyper plane using following equation:

$$\begin{aligned} &w^T x + b = 0 \\ &f(x) = sign(w.x + b) \end{aligned} \tag{1}$$

W weight vector is upright to the hyper plane, *w.x* means the inner product and b is the value of bias. Vapnik in 1995, showed that VC dimension for canonical hyper plane classifiers is upper-bounded, which is positive correlate of second power of norm vector $\|w\|^2$. In fact if we minimize and limit $\|w\|^2$, we have minimized VC dimension, and our estimate of actual risk in terms of probability has been more accurate, and the generalizability of classification will increase.

$$\left\| w \right\| = (\sum_{i=1}^{N} w_i^2)^{\frac{1}{2}} \tag{2}$$

The relation between classifier and weight norm vector $\|w\|$ can be justified differently: suppose the data of the two classes are distinguishable, and edge attribute vector of the first class are placed on the optimized H^+ hyper plane, and the second edge attribute vector is placed on H^- hyper plane. H^+ and H^- hyper planes are defined as follows:

$$\begin{cases} H^{+} = w.x + b = +1, \\ H^{-} = w.x + b = -1. \end{cases} \tag{3}$$

The patterns on H^{-} and H^{+} hyper planes are called support vectors. The area between these planes is the edge area or margin. Additionally, the distance between two hyper planes equals maximum $\frac{2}{\left\| w \right\|}$ and $\|w\|$ Or $\|w\|^2$ are minimized. The aim is the correct classification of the patterns, secondly being placed on or outside edge area, i.e. $y_i(w.x_i + b) \geq 0 \ , \quad i = 1,2,\ldots,N.$

Therefore, design of a hyper plane classifier by optimized edge area will be as following problem:

$$\begin{cases} mnimize & \frac{\left\| w \right\|^2}{2} \\ s.t & y_i(w.x_i + b) \geq 0 \ , \quad i = 1,2,\ldots,N \end{cases} \tag{4}$$

Which is an optimization constraint problem of type convex and quadratic. For solving this problem we form following Lagrangin function and obtain the coefficient.

$$L(w,b,a) = \frac{1}{2} w.w - \sum_{i=1}^{N} \alpha_i (y_i (w.x_i + b) - 1). \tag{5}$$

If (w, a, b) are supposed to be the product of the problem, the product should be true to KKT method that is, for the obtained product, L derivation to w, a, b should equal zero. If we put the derivation equal to zero we will have:

$$\begin{cases} w = \sum_{i=1}^{N} \alpha_i y_i x_i \\ \sum_{i=1}^{N} \alpha_i y_i = 0 \end{cases} \tag{6}$$

By putting the value of w out of above equation, we reach dual problem for constraint optimization.

$$\begin{cases} \max imize & -\frac{1}{2}\sum_{i=1}^{N} \alpha_i \alpha_j y_i y_j x_i x_j + \sum_{i=1}^{N} \alpha_i \\ S.t \quad \alpha_i \geq 0 & i = 1,2,\ldots,N, \\ \sum_{i=1}^{N} \alpha_i y_i = 0. \end{cases} \tag{7}$$

After solving the dual problem, we obtain Lagrangin coefficients $\alpha_i \geq 0$. In fact, every α_i coefficient corresponds to one of x_i patterns. Corresponding x_i patterns, with (positive) coefficients are called sv_i. The value for b and w is obtained through following equations:

$$\begin{cases} w = \sum_{i=1}^{N_{sv}} \alpha_i y_i sv_i, \\ b_j = y_j - \sum_{i=1}^{N_{sv}} \alpha_i y_i sv_i sv_j, \\ b = \frac{1}{N_{sv}} \sum_{i=1}^{N_{sv}} b_j. \end{cases} \tag{8}$$

Distinguish function for input pattern classification will be as follows

$$f(x) = sign(\sum_{i=1}^{N_{sv}} \alpha_i y_i sv_i sv_j) \tag{9}$$

Therefore, if $f(x) \geq 0$, x belongs to class one, and if $f(x) \leq 0$, x belongs to class 2.
In Figure 2, hyper plane is shown in its separable form using Matlab software.

Figure 2.

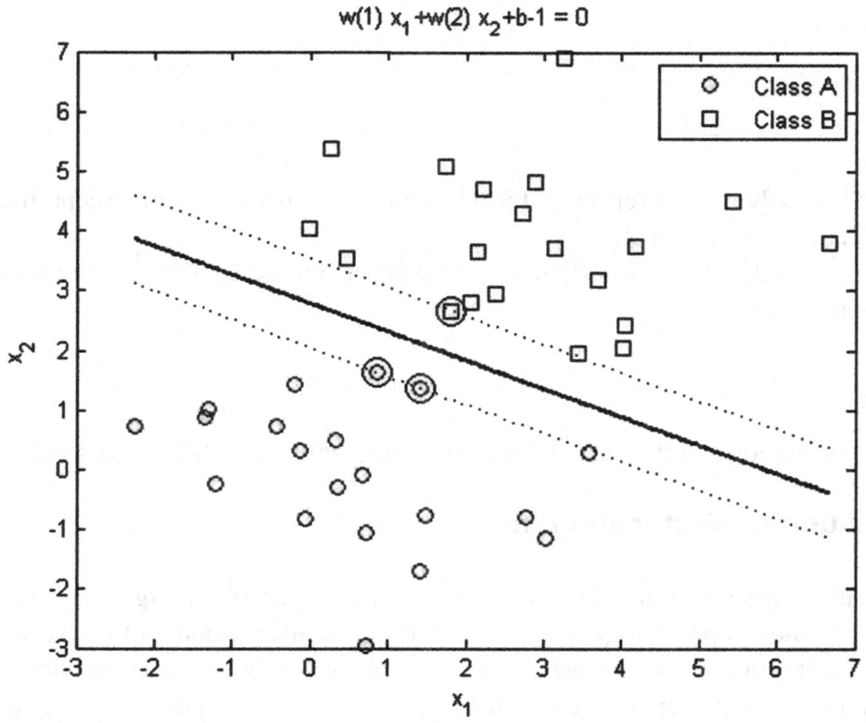

Support Vector Machine in Inseparable Form

In the previous section, SVM problem was solved for separable form, in practice, however, all problems are solved in inseparable form. For inseparable form we define a category of $\in_i$ Variables named loss function, with following conditions:

$$\begin{aligned} & y_i(w.x_i + b) \geq 1 - \in_i \\ & \in_i \geq 0 \quad , \ for\, i = 1,2,\ldots,N \end{aligned} \tag{10}$$

It is obvious that the higher the sum of $\in_i$ Variables' values, less optimization will be achieved, and error will increase. Thus c, constraint optimization problem is defined as follows:

$$\begin{cases} \min imize & \frac{1}{2} w.w + C\sum_{i=1}^{N} \in_i \\ S.t & y_i(w.x_i + b) \geq 1 - \in_i \\ \in_i \geq 0 & , \ for\, i = 1,2,\ldots,N \end{cases} \tag{11}$$

KKT conditions are formed for this problem and we reach following dual problem:

$$\begin{cases} \max imize & -\frac{1}{2}\sum_{i=1}^{N} \alpha_i \alpha_j y_i y_j x_i x_j + \sum_{i=1}^{N} \alpha_i \\ S.t & 0 \leq \alpha_i \leq C, \\ \sum_{i=1}^{N} \alpha_i y_i = 0 & i = 1,2,\ldots,N. \end{cases} \tag{12}$$

As we see, SVM solving in inseparable form is similar to separable form, except that the area of α_i Lagrangin coefficients are different.

Having obtained α_i Lagrangin coefficients, the patterns whose coefficients are true to the below equation are support vector:

$$0 \leq \alpha_i \leq C \tag{13}$$

The value of w and form of distinguish function is similar to separable form as well.

Non-Linear Support Vector Machine

Support vector machines mentioned in former sections use linear separating edges and a hyper plane for classifying a two-class problem patterns, and in fact, the inner product of the vector is calculated by each support vector in input d-dimension space. Using the concept of inner product in Hilbert space and Hilbert Schmitt theorem Vapnik showed that first we can move x input vector to a space with many dimensions by a non-linear transformation and perform the inner product in that space, showing that if a symmetric core meets Mercer theorem conditions, applying this core in input space with few dimensions can be regarded as inner production a Hilbert space with high dimensions and decrease the calculations considerably (Cortes and Vapnik, 1995). Core functions can be in following forms:

Polynomial: $K(x_i, x_j) = (1 + x_i^T x_j)^p$

Gaussian: $K(x_i, x_j) = \exp(-\frac{1}{2\sigma^2}\|x_i - x_j\|)$

Mlp or Tangent: $K(x_i, x_j) = \tanh(\beta_0 + \beta_1 x_i^T x_j)$

Dual optimization problem in inseparable form and non-linear will be as follows:

$$\begin{aligned} & Min\ \frac{1}{2}\sum_i\sum_j \alpha_i\alpha_j y_i y_j \phi(x_i)^T \phi(x_j) - \sum_i \alpha_i \\ & s.t \\ & \sum_i \alpha_i y_i = 0 \\ & 0 \le \alpha_i \le C \quad \forall i \end{aligned} \tag{14}$$

Support vectors are pattern, the Lagrangin coefficients of which are true in 0< $\alpha_i \le C$. A number of support vectors whose corresponding Lagrangin coefficients are true in 0< $\alpha_i < C$and it is their number, are used for the calculation:

$$b_j = y_j - \sum_{i=1}^{N_{sv}} \alpha_i y_i k(sv_i, sv_j) \tag{15}$$

$$b = \frac{1}{N}\sum_{j=1}^{N_b} b_j \tag{16}$$

Decision function will be as follows:

$$f(x) = sign\,(\sum_{i=1}^{N_{sv}} \alpha_i y_i k(x, sv_i) + b) \tag{17}$$

Showing support vector in non-linear form and using Matlab software is shown in Figure 3:

Figure 3.

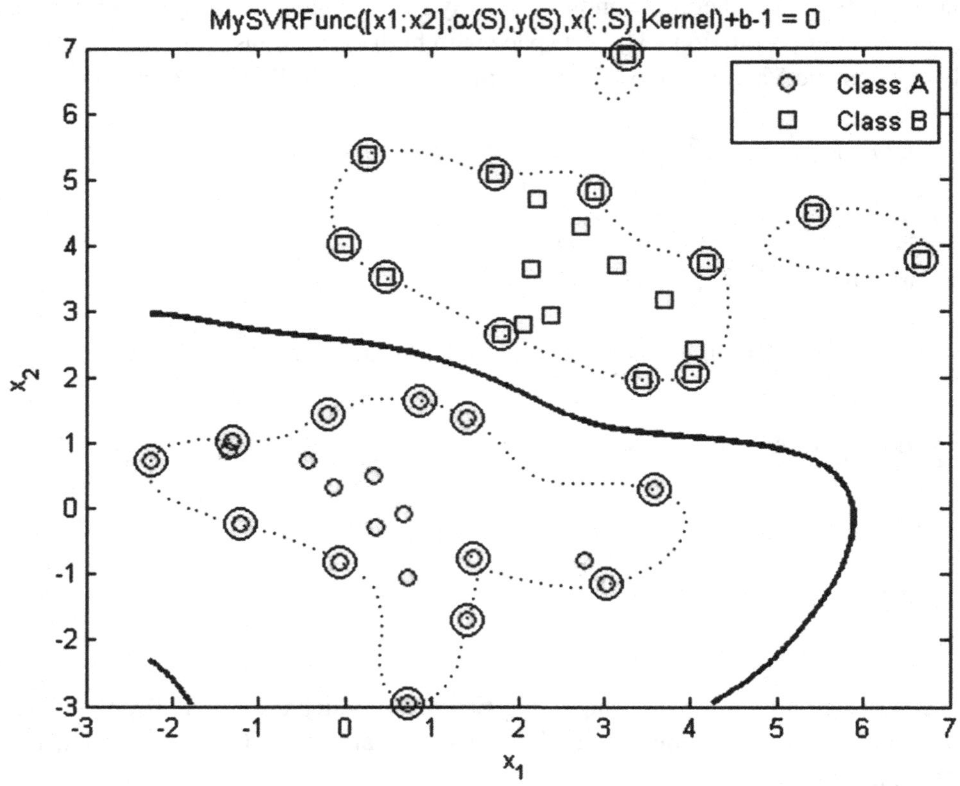

Fuzzy Support Vector Machine

Although SVMs are appropriate tools for data classification, there are limitations too (Mitchell, 1997). In data input of $(y_1,x_1),\ldots,(y_l,x_l)$ or it belongs to a single class or another class, and more accurately put, it belongs to neither of the two classes. In many of real-world functions, the importance of train points differ; in classification problems, often a number of train samples are more significant. We need to classify train samples accurately, and not to keep some of the data as noise, or classify inaccurately, i.e each train sample does not belong exactly to a class. It can belong to a class with 90% probability, 10% undetermined, which can increase to 20%. Differently put, there is a fuzzy membership function $0\leq \mu_i \leq 1$ attributed to every x_i train data. This μ_i fuzzy membership can be considered as belonging or inclination toward a class in classification problem, and $(1-\mu_i)$ can be considered as being meaningless. But the difficulty arises when want to assign new data, with regards to train data, to a class (Joachims, 2002).

In standard SVM classification, significance of error value is the same for different train samples, while it should not be so logically speaking. Using fuzzy logic, we can engage significance of each sample in training phase.

Engaging Importance Value of the Samples

Standard SVM considers train sample as (x_i, y_i) pairs and $y_i \in \{-1,1\}$. Now, in order to engage importance value of each sample, samples are considered as (y_i, x_i, μ_i) triples. In fact, μ_i is the value of membership degree of x_i sample to its class. To engage significance of each sample, we change SVM formula as follows (Lin and Wang, 2002):

$$\begin{aligned}
&Minimize\ \frac{1}{2} w.w^T + C\sum_{i=1}^{l} \mu_i \in_i \\
&s.t \quad y_i(w.x_i + b) \geq 1 - \in_i \qquad i = 1,\ldots N \\
&\in_i \geq 0 \qquad i = 1,\ldots N
\end{aligned} \tag{18}$$

With this alteration the optimization dual problem will be as follows:

$$\begin{cases}
\max imize & -\frac{1}{2}\sum_{i=1}^{N}\sum_{j=1}^{N} \alpha_i \alpha_j y_i y_j x_i x_j + \sum_{i=1}^{N} \alpha_i \\
S.t \quad 0 \leq \alpha_i \leq \mu_i C, & \\
\sum_{i=1}^{N} \alpha_i y_i = 0 & i = 1,2,\ldots,N.
\end{cases} \tag{19}$$

In fact, the difference between fuzzy and standard SVM is that the upper limit of α_i Lagrange coefficients equals $\mu_i C$. Whereas in standard SVM this limit equals C. support vectors will be patterns the corresponding Lagrange coefficients of which will be true in equation $0 \leq \alpha_i \leq \mu_i C$. A number of support vectors with corresponding Lagrange coefficients true to the equation $0 \leq \alpha_i \leq \mu_i C$ are used for calculating b.

Showing fuzzy support vector by determining its membership in Matlab software is as it is shown in Figure 4.

K-NN Classifying Method

One of best classifiers is nearest neighbor K classifier (Duda et al. 2001). This algorithm is simple and without any parameter (Cover and Hart, 1967). It assigns the test sample to the class with maximum votes among its nearest neighbor K. To obtain sample's nearest neighbors, Euclidean distance is often used (Cover and Hart, 1967):

$$d_{eucl}(x,t) = \sqrt{\sum_{i=1}^{m} d_{eucl}^{i}(x,t)} \tag{20}$$

If the values of attributes are numeral and continuous d_{eucl}^{i} is obtained from below equation:

Figure 4.

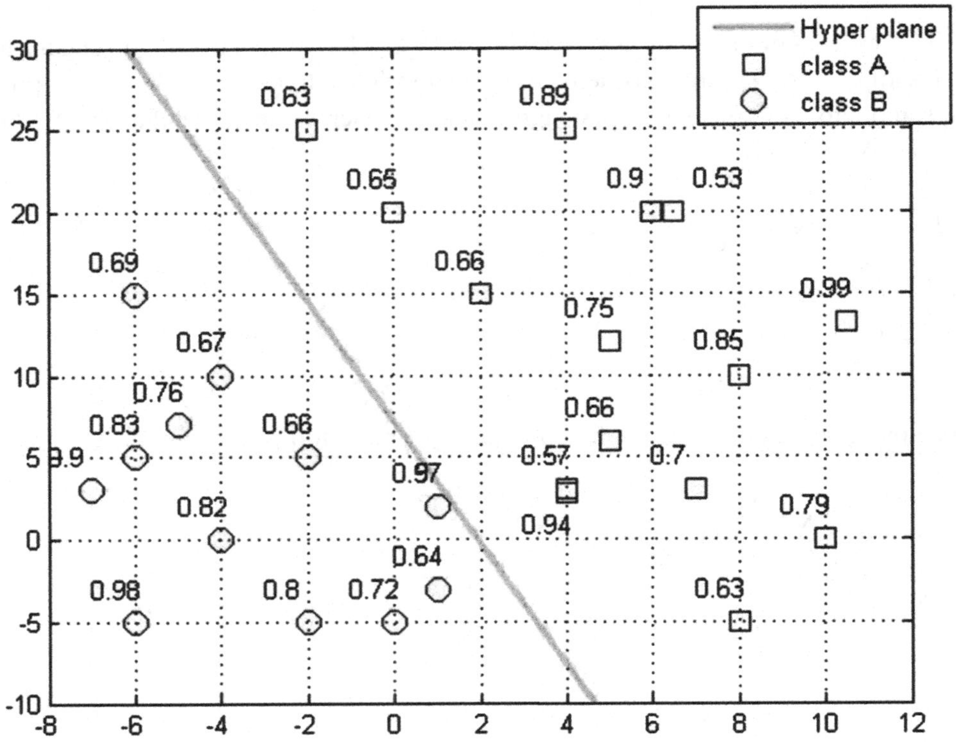

$$d^{i}_{eucl}(x,t) = (a_i(x) - a_i(t))^2 \qquad (21)$$

And if the attributes have nominal values, the equation will accordingly be altered as follows:

$$d^{i}_{eucl}(x,t) = \begin{cases} 1 & if\ a_i(x) \neq a_i(t) \\ 0 & if\ a_i(x) = a_i(t) \end{cases} \qquad (22)$$

If we want to classify data by this method we have to find out special similarities. We have, for instance, a series of Data in a two-dimensional space, and then take the account of a new datum. We try to know what class the new datum belongs to. We suppose neighborhood as 3NN. Thus, we find the three nearest data. 2 data belong to red class and 1 datum belongs to blue class. Therefore, our datum belongs to the red class too. It should be remembered that when neighbor data exist in 2 classes, the target class will be that which contains most of the data.

Understanding K-NN is easy when predicting variables are few. They are also useful for models with types of non-standard data as in text.

Figure 5.

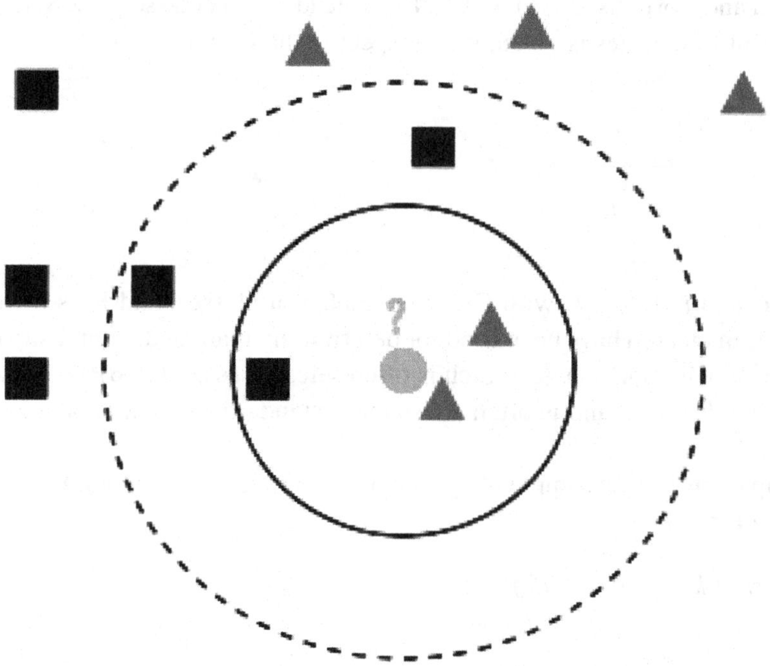

A K-NN example using Matlab software

Input:
Load fisheriris
x=meas;
y=species;
c=ClassificationTree.fit(x,y);
Output:
c =
ClassificationKNN
PredictorNames: {'x1' 'x2' 'x3' 'x4'}
ResponseName: 'Y'
ClassNames: {'setosa' 'versicolor' 'virginica'}
ScoreTransform: 'none'
NObservations: 150
Distance: 'euclidean'
NumNeighbors: 2

Fuzzy K-Nearest Neighbor

One of shortcomings of classical K-NN is that in attributing labels, it considers all test-sample nearest neighbor with same importance degree. To overcome this, Keller et al. (1985) proposed fuzzy nearest neighbor. FKNN is an optimized version of fuzzy sets combinations and KNN (Shang et al. 2006; Sarkar, 2007; Jensen and Cornelis, 2011). In FKNN, instead of Odd classes in KNN, fuzzy membership of samples to different Categories is given, with respect to the formula:

$$u_i(x) = \frac{\sum_{j=1}^{k} u_{ij}(1 / \left\|x - x_j\right\|^{2/(m-1)})}{\sum_{j=1}^{k}(1 / \left\|x - x_j\right\|^{2/(m-1)})} \tag{23}$$

Here, $i=1,2,\ldots,C$ and $j=1,2,\ldots,k$, with C as the number of classes, and K as the number of nearest neighbors. Fuzzy parameters m have been used for determining manner and intensity of distance weight when calculating each neighbor's share, which is often selected as $m\in(1,\infty)$.

$\|x-x_i\|$ is Euclidean distance, and is often chosen as a standard (here, it is between x sample and its jth nearest neighbor).

u_{ij} is membership degree of jth sample of x_j from train set in ith class among KNN of x sample which is calculated by (42) formula:

$$u_{ij}(x_k) = \begin{cases} 0.51 + (n_j / k) * 0.49, & if\ j = i \\ (n_j / k) * 0.49 & if\ j \neq i \end{cases} \tag{24}$$

where x_k, is the KNN of each train sample, and u_{ij} is membership degree of x_k in each class. n_j, is the number of found neighbors which belong to jth class.

The calculated membership degree in (42) formula should be based on below conditions:

$$\begin{aligned} &\sum_{i=1}^{c} u_{ij} = 1, \quad j = 1,2,\ldots n \\ &0 < \sum_{j=1}^{n} u_{ij} < n \\ &u_{ij} \in [0,1] \end{aligned} \tag{25}$$

At the end, having calculated all membership degree for an X sample, with regards to (44) formula, the sample is placed in a class which contains most membership.

$$C(x) = \arg\max_{i=1}^{c}(u_i(x)) \tag{26}$$

Regression (SVR)

Another type of support vector machines is support vector regression which is used in regression and is specific to continuous data (Smola et al. 1998; Chang and Lin, 2002; Smola and Scholkopf, 1997; Van Gestel et al. 2002; Van Gestel et al. 2003).

In fact, it is generalization of SVM (there, the inputs were in n-dimension space but the output were either -1 or +1, but here the outputs have more than 2 values).

We use SVR to estimate function values of approximation function for curve fitting (Vapnik et aal. 1997) as well as in modeling and time series (Scholkopf et al. 1999). Regression is similar to binary SVMs with some changes, and generally, is not much different from them in terms of mathematical logic, and its functions are close to SM (Stanevski and Tsvetkov, 2005).

We suppose that we want to proximate such a model $t_i \cong y_i = w^T x_i + b$ (we want to perform linear regression).

- **Point:** To minimize operation risk or simplify model, if w=0 it reaches its simplest form. Therefore, the smaller the w, the less complex the model will be.

We will elaborate on this method by (Vapnik et al. 1997; Scholkopf et al. 1999; Drucker et al. 1997; Smola and Scholkopf, 1998; Cherkassky and Ma and, 2002; Cherkassky Ma, 2004; Niklasson et al. 1998).

After some investigations, Vapnik stated that suppose line $y=w^T x+b$ for data fitting in a 1-dimensional space. The error of the model could be tolerated to some extent. The data are acceptable as far as they exist between two bounds, but the data outside the bound must be forfeited. Actually, the value of forfeit is obtained by a function given below:

$$L_\varepsilon(t_i, y_i) = \begin{cases} 0 & \left|t_i - y_i\right| \le \varepsilon \\ t & other\ wise \end{cases} \tag{27}$$

Therefore, $|t_i - y_i| \le \varepsilon$ is our acceptable space.

Figure 6.

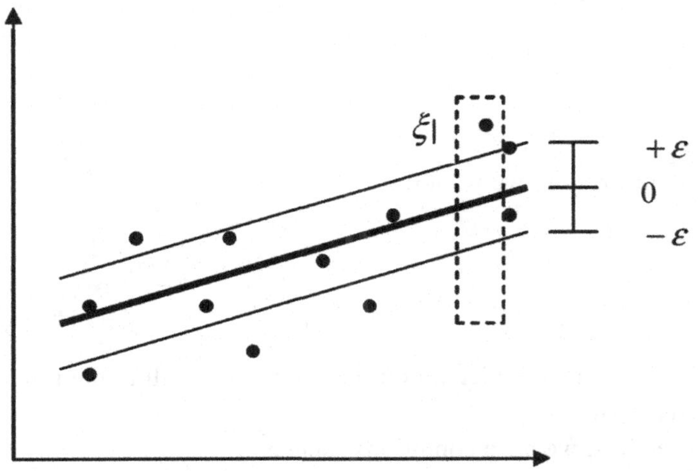

Figure 7.

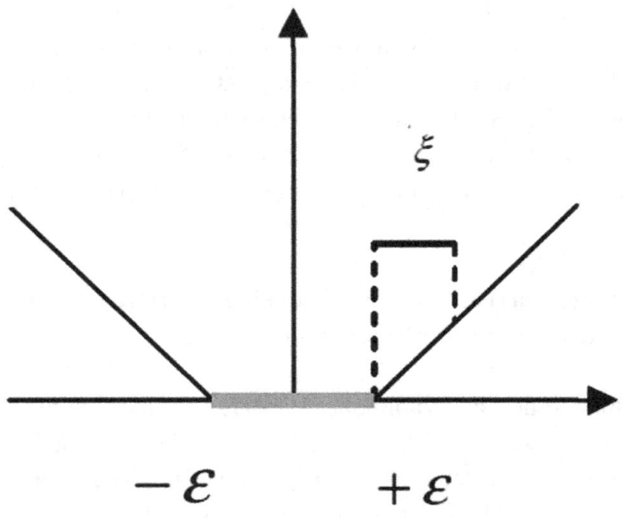

Defining Loss Function

Between ε and –ε the function is fixed; if it gets smaller or larger, the function also becomes smaller or larger as a consequence.

If σ_i is a value larger than ε that $\sigma_i=|t_i-y_i|-\varepsilon$. Therefore:

$$L_\varepsilon(t_i, y_i) = \begin{cases} 0 & |t_i - y_i| \le \varepsilon \\ |t_i - y_i| & other\ wise \end{cases} \tag{28}$$

Thus $|t_i-y_i|$ Must be true, if it is not true to what extent? Which is the same $|t_i-y_i|\le\varepsilon$, here we define an operational risk for our purpose (to optimize L value for all data).

$$R_{emp} = \frac{1}{N}\sum_{i=1}^{N} L_\varepsilon(t_i, y_i) \tag{29}$$

In addition to risk minimization, we want to:

$$Min\left\| w\right\| \rightarrow Min\frac{1}{2}w^T w \tag{30}$$

The aim of this minimization is model simplification i.e. w small to the utmost extent if the model is to remain close to fixed form.

With regards to above aims, we have conditions such as:

$$-\varepsilon < t_i - y_i < +\varepsilon$$
$$-\varepsilon + \sigma^{-}_{i} < t_i - y_i < \varepsilon + \sigma^{+}_{i} \tag{31}$$

Point 1:

$$\begin{cases} \sigma^{+}_{i} + \sigma^{-}_{i} = L_{\varepsilon}(t_i, y_i) \\ \sigma^{+}_{i}\sigma^{-}_{i} = 0 \end{cases} \tag{32}$$

Thus, based on point (1) and Equation (45) we have:

$$R_{emp} = \frac{1}{N}\sum_{i=1}^{N} L_{\varepsilon}(t_i, y_i) \tag{33}$$

Therefore, generally the problem will be:

$$\begin{aligned} & Min\ \frac{1}{2}w^T w + C\sum_{\substack{i=1 \\ i}}^{N} (\sigma^{+}_{i} + \sigma^{-}_{i}) \\ & s.t \quad -t_i + y_i + \varepsilon + \sigma^{+}_{i} \geq 0 \\ & \qquad t_i - y_i + \varepsilon + \sigma^{-}_{i} \geq 0 \\ & \sigma^{+}_{i} \geq 0 \quad \forall i \\ & \sigma^{-}_{i} \geq 0 \quad \forall i \end{aligned} \tag{34}$$

therefore:

$$\begin{aligned} LP: & \frac{1}{2}w^T w + C\sum_{\substack{i=1 \\ i}}^{N} (\sigma_i^{+} + \sigma_i^{-}) - \sum_{i=1}^{N} \alpha_i^{+}(-t_i + y_i + \varepsilon + \sigma_i^{+}) \\ & - \sum_{i=1}^{N} \alpha_i^{-}(t_i - y_i + \varepsilon + \sigma_i^{-}) - \sum_{i=1}^{N} \alpha_i^{-}(t_i - y_i + \varepsilon + \sigma_i^{-}) - \sum_{i=1}^{N} \mu_i^{+}(t_i - y_i + \varepsilon + \sigma_i^{-}) \end{aligned} \tag{35}$$

Now by derivation and placing, the main problem converts to below dual problem:

$$\begin{aligned} & L_D : -\frac{1}{2}\sum_i \sum_j (\alpha_i^{+} - \alpha_i^{-})(\alpha_i^{+} - \alpha_i^{-})x_i^{T} + \sum_i (\alpha_i^{+} - \alpha_i^{-})t_i - \varepsilon\sum_i (\alpha_i^{+} - \alpha_i^{-}) \\ & s.t \quad \sum_i (\alpha_i^{+} - \alpha_i^{-}) \\ & 0 \leq \alpha_i^{+} \leq c \\ & 0 \leq \alpha_i^{-} \leq c \end{aligned} \tag{36}$$

By solving dual problem we obtain $\alpha_i^-, \alpha_i^+ \begin{cases} w \\ s \end{cases} \rightarrow \ b \ \rightarrow y = w^T + b$.

By applying KKT conditions (Jing, 2009) we have:

$$\begin{aligned}
&1)\ \alpha_i^+(-t_i + y_i + \varepsilon + \sigma_i^+) = 0 \\
&2)\ \alpha_i^-(-t_i + y_i + \varepsilon + \sigma_i^-) = 0 \\
&3)\ \mu_i^+\sigma_i^+ = (c - \alpha_i^+)\sigma_i^+ = 0 \\
&4)\ \mu_i^-\sigma_i^- = (c - \alpha_i^-)\sigma_i^- = 0
\end{aligned} \tag{37}$$

In order to analyze the conditions, we should consider different edge forms and observe the results

$$if \quad \alpha_i^+ = 0 \xrightarrow{3} \mu_i^+ = c \xrightarrow{3} \sigma_i^+ = 0 \xrightarrow{1} -t_i + y_i + \varepsilon \geq 0 \ \rightarrow \ -t_i + y_i \leq \varepsilon$$

$$if \quad \alpha_i^- = 0 \xrightarrow{4} \mu_i^- = c \xrightarrow{4} \sigma_i^- = 0 \xrightarrow{1} t_i - y_i + \varepsilon \geq 0 \ \rightarrow \ t_i - y_i \geq -\varepsilon$$

and

$$0 \leq \alpha_i^+ \leq c \ \rightarrow 0 \leq \mu_i^+ \leq c \rightarrow \sigma_i^+ \ \rightarrow \ -t_i + y_i + \varepsilon = 0 \ \rightarrow \ \underline{t_i - y_i = \varepsilon}$$

and

$$\begin{aligned}
&\alpha_i^- = 0 \\
&\qquad \begin{cases} \alpha_i^- = 0 \xleftarrow{2} t_i - y_i \geq \varepsilon \\ \mu_i^+ > 0 \longleftarrow \sigma_i^- = 0 \end{cases} \\
&\mu_i^+ = c
\end{aligned}$$

therefore:

$$\begin{aligned}
&\alpha_i^-\alpha_i^+ = 0 \\
&1)\ \alpha_i^- = \alpha_i^+ = 0 \\
&2)\ 0 \leq \alpha_i^+ \leq c, \alpha_i^- = 0 \\
&3)\ 0 \leq \alpha_i^- \leq c, \alpha_i^+ = 0 \\
&4)\ \alpha_i^+ = c, \alpha_i^- = 0 \\
&5)\ \alpha_i^- = c, \alpha_i^+ = 0
\end{aligned}$$

Finally, what we obtain as support vector must fall into one of conditions 2 or 3:

$$S = \{i | 0 \le \alpha_i^+ \le c \ or \ 0 \le \alpha_i^- \le c\}$$
$$S = \{i | 0 \le \alpha_i^+ + \alpha_i^- \le c\} \quad (38)$$

Another conclusion could be drawn:

$$0 \le \alpha_i^+ \le c \Rightarrow \alpha_i^- = 0$$
$$t_i - y_i = \varepsilon \Rightarrow t_i = y_i + \varepsilon$$

and

$$0 \le \alpha_i^- \le c \Rightarrow \alpha_i^+ = 0$$
$$t_i - y_i = -\varepsilon \Rightarrow t_i = y_i - \varepsilon$$

thus

$$t_i = y_i + sign(\alpha_i^+ - \alpha_i^-)\varepsilon = w^T x_i + b + sign(\alpha_i^+ - \alpha_i^-)\varepsilon$$
$$b = t_i - w^T x_i + sign(\alpha_i^+ - \alpha_i^-)\varepsilon$$
$$b = \frac{1}{N}\sum_i (t_i - w^T x_i + sign(\alpha_i^+ - \alpha_i^-)\varepsilon)$$

therefore, this general form of linear SVR is:

$$Input : \{x_i, y_i\}$$
$$output : y = w^T + b$$
$$\xrightarrow{\alpha_i^+, \alpha_i^-} S = \{i | 0 \le \alpha_i^+ + \alpha_i^- \le c\}$$
$$Then : w = \sum_i (\alpha_i^+ + \alpha_i^-) x_i$$
$$Then : b = \frac{1}{N}\sum_i (t_i - w^T x_i + sign(\alpha_i^+ - \alpha_i^-)\varepsilon)$$

Showing support vector regression by determining its membership in Matlab software is as it is shown in Figure 8.

Fuzzy Regression

Linear regression models are widely used in engineering economy and many other fields nowadays. Fuzzy regression is a type of regression proposed for special occasions when decision has to be according to inaccurate data, or when data is produced by skeptical evaluations.

Figure 8.

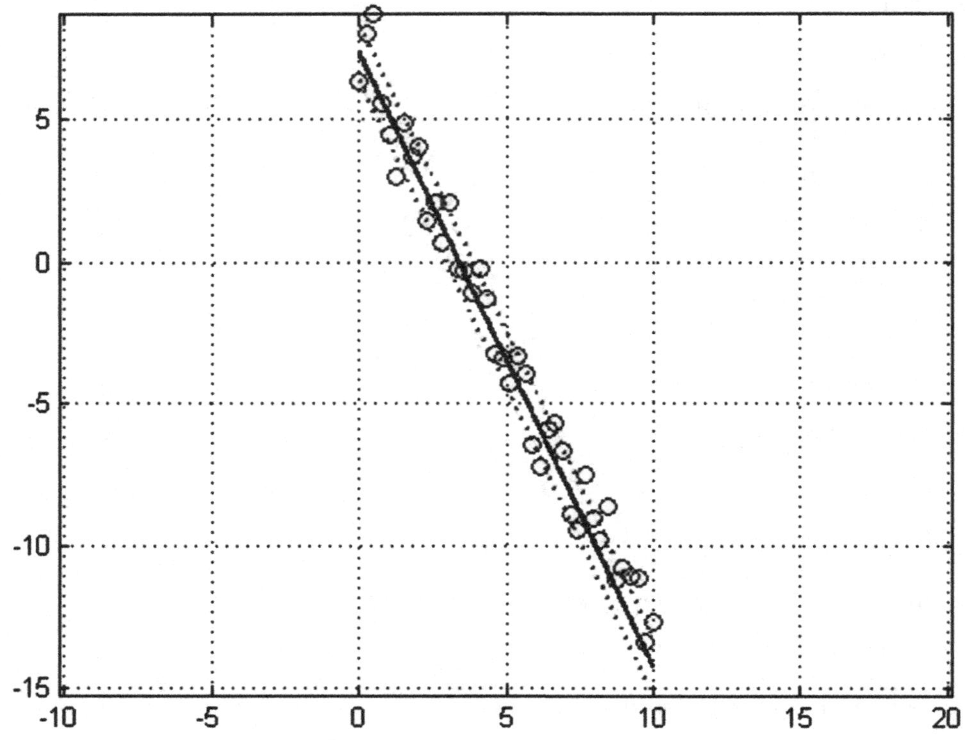

In fact, fuzzy regression is a generalization of classical regression used for calculating functional relation among dependent and independent variables in a fuzzy environment when fuzzy regression-model parameters can be categorized in 3 groups, with respect to the conditions of input and output variables:

1. Input data are non-fuzzy parameters and output data are fuzzy
2. Input data are fuzzy output data are fuzzy but parameters are non-fuzzy
3. Input data, output data, and parameters are fuzzy

Generally, two different types have been used more frequently:
Tanaka method which minimizes output wide
Fuzzy least squares method which minimizes output error square

Fuzzy sets were first introduced by Zadeh (1965). Subsequently, Tanaka et al., in 1982 investigated fuzzy regression. Tanaka has supposed that data are supposed triangle numbers, and beta minimizing of a fuzzy scale has produced regression coefficients. The base of Tanaka's work had been mathematical programming methods (Tanaka et al. 1982). In the same year, Yager (1982) investigated the simplest form of fuzzy regression, and predicted the value of dependent variable. Chang and Lee (1994) pointed out some shortcomings of Tanaka's proposed model, particularly showing that analysis of Tanaka fuzzy regression does not always result in virtual products. (Sakawa and Yano, 1992) stated 3 criteria for equality of fuzzy numbers, and formulated 3 types of multi-objective programming problems to estimate parameters. Peters (1994) introduced fuzzy linear-regression model based on Tanaka's method, using fuzzy linear-programming methods. Kim and Bishu (1998) based their work on minimizing difference between observed and estimated fuzzy-numbers membership-functions. From models of new methods of mathematical programming, we can mention Hojati et al. model (2005), and Hassanpour et al. model (2009)

In 1986, Jajuga calculated linear regression coefficients using a generalized version of least squares. Diamond (1998) introduced a meter for fuzzy-number sets and used it for defining least squares. Chang and Lee (1996) proposed a technique of fuzzy regression based on least squares method to estimate the value of centers and wide of L_R fuzzy numbers. Yang and Lin (2002) proposed a method of least squares for models with fuzzy input. In the same year, Chang (2001) presented a method for regression of least fuzzy squares, defining weighted fuzzy account, and using least squared fitting criterion, Kao and Chyo (2002) presented a least squares method using membership function of error squares sum. Coppi et al. (2006) proposed a method of least squares to estimate a linear-regression model with L-R fuzzy response, and Wang et al. (2007) proposed a method for fuzzy non-parametric regression with non-fuzzy input and L-R, non-fuzzy output based on local linear smoothing technique. Works within this area may also include Tata and Arabpour's method (2008).

Recently fuzzy regression-model fitting has been moving towards numeral methods. Abdalla and Buckley (2007) applied Monte Carlo method in fuzzy regression. Broadly speaking, 3 methods have been proposed for analyzing fuzzy linear-regression models:

1. Mathematical programming method
2. Least fuzzy squares method
3. Numeral methods

MATHEMATICAL PROGRAMMING METHODS

In these methods, ambiguity minimization of model is as fitting criterion. Advantage of mathematical methods is easy calculations and their disadvantage is that the estimated values are too wide, since the concept of least squares is not used. Moreover, addition of an observation to data multiplies constraints of the problem. In this section, several models based on mathematical programming methods are mentioned.

Tanaka and Watada Model

Tanaka and Watada (1988) took the fuzzy linear-regression model with non-fuzzy (accurate) input, fuzzy parameters, and fuzzy output as it is shown below:

$$\tilde{y}_i = \tilde{\beta}_0 + \tilde{\beta}_1 x_{ik} + \dots + \tilde{\beta}_k x_{ik} + \varepsilon_i \qquad i = 1, \dots, n \tag{39}$$

In which independent variable in ith observation, and parameters are symmetrical, triangular, fuzzy numbers shown respectively

$$\begin{aligned} \tilde{y}_i &= (y_i, e_i) \quad , \quad i = 1, \dots, n \\ \tilde{\beta}_j &= (\beta_i, \alpha_j) \quad , \quad j = 1, \dots, k \end{aligned} \tag{40}$$

Model (58) can be rewritten as follows:

$$\tilde{y}_i = (\underline{\beta}\underline{x}_i, \underline{\alpha}|\underline{x}_i|) \quad , \quad i = 1,\dots,n \tag{41}$$

in which

$$\begin{aligned} &\underline{\beta} = (\beta_0,\dots,\beta_k), \\ &\underline{\alpha} = (\alpha_0,\dots,\alpha_k), \\ &\underline{x}_i = (1, x_{i1},\dots,x_{ik})', \quad i = 1,\dots,n. \end{aligned} \tag{42}$$

Tanaka and Watada determined such that the model ambiguity defined below is minimized.

$$j(\alpha) = \sum_{i=1}^{n} \underline{\alpha}|\underline{x}_i|. \tag{43}$$

Such that for certain values –*h*,*h* of cut of estimated values covers –*h* cut of observed values

$$[\tilde{y}_i]^h \subseteq [\hat{\tilde{y}}_i]^h \tag{44}$$

i.e.

$$[y_i - L^{-1}(h)e_i, y_i + L^{-1}(h)e_i] \subseteq [\underline{\beta}\underline{x}_i - L^{-1}(h)\underline{\alpha}|\underline{x}_i|, \underline{\beta}\underline{x}_i + L^{-1}(h)\underline{\alpha}|\underline{x}_i|] \tag{45}$$

Stated analyses lead to formulation of linear programming problem

$$\begin{cases} \min j(\alpha) = \sum_{i=1}^{n} \underline{\alpha}|\underline{x}_i|, \\ s.t. \\ \underline{\beta}\underline{x}_i - L^{-1}(h)\underline{\alpha}|\underline{x}_i| \leq y_i - L^{-1}(h)e_i \ , \qquad i = 1,\dots,n \\ \underline{-\beta}\underline{x}_i - L^{-1}(h)\underline{\alpha}|\underline{x}_i| \leq -y_i - L^{-1}(h)e_i \ , \qquad i = 1,\dots,n \\ \alpha_j \geq 0 \quad , \alpha_j \in R \qquad for\ j = 0,\dots,k \qquad 0 \leq h \leq 1. \end{cases} \tag{46}$$

Where the value of h is selected by decision maker. There are several methods for solving fuzzy linear programming problems; for more details see(Zimmermann (1978), Zimmermann (1987), Tanaka et al.

(1987), Buckley and Feuring (2000), MishmastNehi et al. (2004), Dehghan et al. (2006), Jimenez (2007), Kashyap and Raol (2008), Lotfi et al. (2009), Kumar et al. (2011), Edalatpanah and Shahabi (2012), Ezzati et al. (2013), Najafi and Edalatpanah (2013), Shamooshaki et al. (2014)and Shamooshaki et al. (2015).

Hojati et al., Model

Hojati et al. [72] presented a method for estimating regression coefficients, and used their method for two models given below: HBS1 and HBS2 respectively.

Fuzzy Independent Variables (Accurate) and Fuzzy Dependent Variables (HBS1)

In this condition, regression coefficients are calculated such that the sum of upper points' deviations, $-h$ cuts of predicted values and corresponding observed $-h$ lower points' deviations predicted values' cuts and corresponding observed values are minimized. It has been presumed, in this model, that observed values and regression coefficients of fuzzy numbers are symmetrical triangular. This method is presented as linear programming problem given below:

$$\begin{cases} \min \sum_{i=1}^{n} d_{iU}^{+} + d_{iU}^{-} + d_{iL}^{+} + d_{iL}^{-} \\ s.t. \\ \sum_{j=0}^{k} (\beta_j + (1-h)\alpha_j)x_{ij} + d_{iU}^{+} - d_{iU}^{-} = y_i + (1-h)e_i, \qquad i = 1,\ldots,n \\ \sum_{j=0}^{k} (\beta_j - (1-h)\alpha_j)x_{ij} + d_{iL}^{+} - d_{iL}^{-} = y_i - (1-h)e_i, \qquad i = 1,\ldots,n \\ d_{iU}^{+}, d_{iL}^{-}, d_{iL}^{+}, d_{iL}^{-} \geq 0 \quad , \qquad i = 1,\ldots,n \\ \alpha_j \geq 0 \quad ,\beta_j \in R \qquad for\ j = 0,1,\ldots,k \qquad 0 \leq h \leq 1 \ . \end{cases} \tag{47}$$

In which for every i, i=1,2…,n, at best one of d_{iU}^{-}, d_{iU}^{+} will be positive as well as in d_{iL}^{-}, d_{iL}^{+}. As a matter of fact, $[d_{iU}^{+} - d_{iU}^{-}]$ is the cross distance, $-h$ upper points is predicted value cut, and $-h$ upper points is observed value cut. The target function is indeed minimizing these two distances

Fuzzy Independent Variables and Fuzzy Dependent Variable (HBS2)

In this condition, regression coefficients are calculated such that the sum of $-h$ Upper points' deviations, predicted values' cuts and $-h$ lower points' deviations, predicted values' cuts and corresponding observed values in every lower p[point (left) and upper point (right), and every value of independent variable (except X_0) are minimized. Linear programming problem given below is formulated for the instances when there is only one independent variable (in addition to X_0).

$$\begin{cases} \min \sum_{i=1}^{n} (d_{ilU}^{+} + d_{ilU}^{-} + d_{ilL}^{+} + d_{ilL}^{-} + d_{irU}^{+} + d_{irU}^{-} + d_{irL}^{+} + d_{irL}^{-}) \\ s.t. \\ \sum_{j=0}^{k} (\beta_j + (1-h)\alpha_j)(x_{ij} - (1-h)f_{ij}) + d_{iU}^{+} - d_{iU}^{-} = y_i + (1-h)e_i, \qquad i = 1,\dots,n \\ \sum_{j=0}^{k} (\beta_j - (1-h)\alpha_j)(x_{ij} - (1-h)f_{ij}) + d_{irU}^{+} - d_{irU}^{-} = y_i - (1-h)e_i, \qquad i = 1,\dots,n \\ \sum_{j=0}^{k} (\beta_j - (1-h)\alpha_j)(x_{ij} - (1-h)f_{ij}) + d_{ilL}^{+} - d_{ilL}^{-} = y_i - (1-h)e_i, \qquad i = 1,\dots,n, \\ \sum_{j=0}^{k} (\beta_j - (1-h)\alpha_j)(x_{ij} - (1-h)f_{ij}) + d_{irL}^{+} - d_{irL}^{-} = y_i - (1-h)e_i, \qquad i = 1,\dots,n, \\ d_{ilU}^{+}, d_{ilU}^{-}, d_{ilL}^{+}, d_{ilL}^{-}, d_{irU}^{-}, d_{irL}^{-}, d_{irL}^{-} \geq 0 \quad , \qquad i = 1,\dots,n, \\ \alpha_j \geq 0 \quad , \beta_j \in R \qquad for\ j = 0,1,\dots,k \qquad 0 \leq h \leq 1\ . \end{cases} \tag{48}$$

In indexes of deviation variables (d_is), "l" indicates left point and r indicates right point (upper) of independent variable processing ranges, the two "U"s indicate upper points and "L" indicates lower points of predicted and observed ranges in this model $\tilde{x}_{ij} = (x_{ij}, f_{ij})$, $\tilde{y} = (y_i, e_i)$ and $\tilde{\beta}_j = (\beta_i, \alpha_i)$ for *j*=0,1,…,*k*.

Hassanpour et al. Model

Hassanpour et al. (2009) presented a mathematical programming model to estimate linear-regression model parameters with non-fuzzy input and fuzzy output in which $\tilde{y}_i = (y_i, e_{il}, e_{ir})$, *i*=1,..,*n* fuzzy output

$$\tilde{\beta}_j = (\beta_i, \alpha_{jl}, \alpha_{jr}) \quad , \ i = 1,\dots,n \tag{49}$$

Are fuzzy parameters, and without decrease in the overall problem, it has been supposed that $x_{ij}>0$ $\forall i,j$. The main aim of this method is drawing near the membership function of each estimated, response variable to membership function of corresponding observed, response variable which has been considered in this method by drawing near the wides (and centers) to the possible extent.

Estimating parameters has been formulated as a linear programming problem:

$$\begin{cases} \min \sum_{i=1}^{n} (n_{il} + p_{il} + n_{ic} + p_{ic} + n_{ir} + p_{ir}) \\ s.t. \\ \sum_{j=0}^{k} \beta_j x_{ij} + n_{ic} - p_{ic} = y_i, \qquad i = 1,\dots,n \\ \sum_{j=0}^{k} \alpha_{jl} x_{ij} + n_{il} - p_{il} = e_{il}, \qquad i = 1,\dots,n, \\ \sum_{j=0}^{k} \alpha_{jr} x_{ij} + n_{ir} - p_{ir} = e_{ir}, \qquad i = 1,\dots,n, \\ n_{ik}, p_{ik} \geq 0 \quad , \qquad i = 1,\dots,n \quad , k = l,c,r \\ n_{ik} p_{ik} = 0 \quad , \qquad i = 1,\dots,n \quad , k = l,c,r \\ \alpha_{jl}, \alpha_{jr} \geq 0 \quad , \beta_j \in R \quad for\ j = 0,1,\dots,k \qquad 0 \leq h \leq 1 \ . \end{cases} \tag{50}$$

In which for every i, p_{ic} and n_{ic} positive and negative deviations are estimated and observed between response centers respectively.

Moreover, n_{il}, p_{ic} and (p_{ir}, n_{ir}) are negative and positive deviations between left wides (right) of observed responses and estimated respectively. If model input are fuzzy numbers a $\tilde{x}_{ij} = (x_{ij}, f_{ijl}, f_{ijr})$. The subsequent programming problem is formulated by Hassanpour et.al for the instances when there is only one independent variable (in addition to x_0).

Fuzzy linear programming has different solving methods illustrated comprehensively in:

$$\begin{cases} \min \sum_{i=1}^{n} (n_{il} + p_{il} + n_{ic} + p_{ic} + n_{ir} + p_{ir}) \\ \text{s.t.} \\ \sum_{j=0}^{k} \beta_j (x_{ij} - f_{ijl}) + n_{icL} - p_{icL} = y_i, \qquad i = 1,\dots,n \\ \sum_{j=0}^{k} \beta_j (x_{ij} + f_{ijr}) + n_{icU} - p_{icU} = y_i, \qquad i = 1,\dots,n \\ \sum_{j=0}^{k} \alpha_{jl} (x_{ij} - f_{ijl}) + n_{ilL} - p_{ilL} = e_{il}, \qquad i = 1,\dots,n, \\ \sum_{j=0}^{k} \alpha_{jl} (x_{ij} + f_{ijr}) + n_{ilU} - p_{ilU} = e_{il}, \qquad i = 1,\dots,n, \\ \sum_{j=0}^{k} \alpha_{jr} (x_{ij} - f_{ijl}) + n_{irL} - p_{irL} = e_{ir}, \qquad i = 1,\dots,n, \\ \sum_{j=0}^{k} \alpha_{jr} (x_{ij} + f_{ijr}) + n_{irU} - p_{irU} = e_{ir}, \qquad i = 1,\dots,n, \\ n_{ikL}, p_{ikL}, n_{ikU}, p_{ikU} \geq 0, \qquad i = 1,\dots,n, \quad k = l,c,r \\ n_{ikL}, p_{ikL} = 0, \quad n_{ikU} p_{ikU} = 0, \qquad i = 1,\dots,n, \quad k = l,c,r \\ \alpha_{jl}, \alpha_{jr} \geq 0, \ \beta_j \in R \ for\ j = 0,1,\dots,k \qquad 0 \leq h \leq 1 \end{cases} \tag{51}$$

Where in deviation variables indexes (n_l, p_i), "r" indicates upper points, "l" indicates lower points, and "C" indicates predicted and observed values' centers, and "L" indicates left point (lower) and "U" indicates right point (upper) of independent variable values.

Role of Classification

Classification is one of basic, important topics, and subcategory of machine learning, which can be useful in many sciences such as medicine, psychology, economy, statistics, and engineering sciences. Basically, the most important knowledge mankind has achieved is classification (Jing, 2009; Wernik et al. 2012; Bishop, 2006). Some of its functions could be named

- Pattern recognition: face recognition and its forms, fingerprint, handwriting, and photo processing
- Anomality detection: detecting signal malfunction, and misusing credit cards
- Controlling robots
- Controlling and preventing diseases
- Bioinformatics

CONCLUSION

In this chapter, different methods of classification have been investigated as one of most important machine learning methods. In addition to introducing different classical classification methods where train sample sets are insufficient and partition of value space of some attributes are inadequate, and noise and confusion exist in the data, as well as when numeral decisions are needed, fuzzy classification is being proposed and compared to classical methods.

REFERENCES

Abdalla, A., & Buckley, J. J. (2007). Monte Carlo methods in fuzzy linear regression. *Soft Computing*, *11*(10), 991–996. doi:10.1007/s00500-006-0148-5

Abe, A. A. (2001). *Pattern Classification: Neuro-fuzzy Methods and Their Comparison*. London, UK: Springer-Verlag. doi:10.1007/978-1-4471-0285-4

Alpayden, A. A. (2010). *Introduction to Machine Learning*. The MIT Press.

Arabpour, A. R., & Tata, M. (2008). It estimating the parameters of a fuzzy linear regression model. *Iranian Journal of Fuzzy Systems*, *5*(2), 1–19.

Baldwin, J. F. (1981). Fuzzy logic and fuzzy reasoning. In E. H. Mamdani & B. R. Gaines (Eds.), *Fuzzy Reasoning and Its Applications*. London: Academic Press.

Bishop, A. A. (2006). Pattern Recognition and Machine Learning. Springer.

Breiman, A. A., Friedman, B. B., Olshen, C. C., & Stone, E. E. (1984). *Classification and Regression Tree*. Wadsworth and Brooks.

Buckley, J., & Feuring, T. (2000). Evolutionary Algorithm Solution to Fuzzy Problems: Fuzzy Linear Programming. *Fuzzy Sets and Systems*, *109*(1), 35–53. doi:10.1016/S0165-0114(98)00022-0

Burges, C. (1998). A tutorial on support vector machines for pattern recognition. *Data Mining and Knowledge Discovery*, *2*(2), 121–167. doi:10.1023/A:1009715923555

Chang, C. C., & Lin, C. J. (2002). Training V-support Vector Regression. *Theory and Neural Computation*, *14*(8), 1959–1977. doi:10.1162/089976602760128081 PMID:12180409

Chang, P. T., & Lee, E. S. (1996). A generalized fuzzy weighted least-squares regression. *Fuzzy Sets and Systems*, *82*(3), 289–298. doi:10.1016/0165-0114(95)00284-7

Chang, R. L. P., & Pavlidis, T. (1977). Fuzzy Decision Tree Algorithms. *IEEE Transactions on Systems, Man, and Cybernetics*, *7*(1), 28–35. doi:10.1109/TSMC.1977.4309586

Chang, Y. O. (2001). Hybrid fuzzy least-squares regression analysis and its reliability measures. *Fuzzy Sets and Systems*, *119*(2), 225–246. doi:10.1016/S0165-0114(99)00092-5

Cherkassky, V., & Ma, Y. (2002). Comparison of Model Selection for Regression. *Neural Computation*, *15*(7), 1691–1714. doi:10.1162/089976603321891864 PMID:12816572

Cherkassky, V., & Ma, Y. (2004). Practical Selection of SVM Parameters and Noise Estimation for SVM Regression. *Neural Networks*, *17*(1), 113–126. doi:10.1016/S0893-6080(03)00169-2 PMID:14690712

Clark, P., & Niblett, T. (1987). Induction in Noisy Domains. In I. Bratko & N. Lavrac (Eds.), Progress in Machine Learning. Sigma Press.

Coppi, R., DUrso, P., Giordani, P., & Santoro, A. (2006). It Least squares estimation of a linear regression model with LR fuzzy response. *Computational Statistics & Data Analysis*, *51*(1), 267–286. doi:10.1016/j.csda.2006.04.036

Cortes, C., & Vapnik, V. (1995). Support-Vector Networks. *Machine Learning*, *20*(3), 273–297. doi:10.1007/BF00994018

Cover, T., & Hart, P. (1967). Nearest neighbor pattern classification. *IEEE Transactions on Information Theory*, *13*(1), 21–27. doi:10.1109/TIT.1967.1053964

Dehghan, M., Hashemi, B., & Ghatee, M. (2006). Computational methods for solving fully fuzzy linear systems. *Applied Mathematical Modelling*, *179*, 328–343.

Diamond, P. (1988). Fuzzy least squares. *Information Sciences*, *46*(3), 141–157. doi:10.1016/0020-0255(88)90047-3

Draper, N. R., & Smith, H. (1980). *Applied Regression Analysis*. New York: Wiley.

Drucker, H., Burges, C. J. C., Kaufman, L., Smola, A., & Vapnik, V. (1997). Support vector regression machines. *Advances in Neural Information Processing Systems*, *9*, 155–161.

Duda, A. A., Hart, B. B., & Stork, C. C. (2001). *Pattern Classification*. Wiley.

Edalatpanah, S. A., & Shahabi, S. (2012). A new two-phase method for the fuzzy primal simplex algorithm. *International Review of Pure and Applied Mathematics*, *8*, 157-164.

Ezzati, R., Khorram, E., & Enayati, R. (2013). A New Algorithm to Solve Fully Fuzzy Linear Programming Problems Using the MOLP Problem. *Applied Mathematical Modelling*, *39*(12), 3183–3193. doi:10.1016/j.apm.2013.03.014

Fatai, A., & Abdulazeez, A. (2011). Fuzzy logic-driven and SVM-driven hybrid computational intelligence models applied to oil and gas reservoir characterization. *Journal of Natural Gas Science and Engineering*, *3*(3), 505–517. doi:10.1016/j.jngse.2011.05.002

Guoxiu, L. (2005). *A comparative study of three decision Tree algorithms: ID3, Fuzzy ID3 and probabilistic fuzzy ID3* (Bachelor thesis). Informatics & Economics, Erasmus University, Rotterdam, The Netherlands.

Han, A. A., & Kamber, B. B. (2001). *Data mining: Concepts and techniques*. San Diego, CA: Academic Press.

Hassanpour, H., Maleki, H. R., & Yaghoobi, M. A. (2009). It a goal programming approach to fuzzy linear regression with non-fuzzy input and fuzzy output data. *Asia-Pacific Journal of Operational Research*, *26*(5), 587–604. doi:10.1142/S0217595909002420

Heikki, A. A., & Mannila, B. B. (1996). *Data mining: machine learning, statistics, and databases*. IEEE.

Hojati, M., Bector, C. R., & Smimou, K. (2005). It A simple method for computation of fuzzy linear regression. *European Journal of Operational Research*, *166*(1), 172–184. doi:10.1016/j.ejor.2004.01.039

Jajuga, K. (1986). Linear fuzzy regression. *Fuzzy Sets and Systems*, *20*(3), 343–353. doi:10.1016/S0165-0114(86)90045-X

Jang, J. (1994). Structure determination in fuzzy modeling: A fuzzy CART approach. In *Proc.IEEE Conf. Fuzzy Systems*, (pp. 480-485). doi:10.1109/FUZZY.1994.343738

Janikow, C. Z. (1998). Fuzzy Decision Trees: Issues and Methods. *IEEE Trans. on Systems. Man, and Cybernetics – Part B*, *28*(1), 1–14. doi:10.1109/3477.658573

Jensen, R., & Cornelis, C. (2011). Fuzzy-rough nearest neighbour classification. *Lecture Notes in Computer Science*, *6499*, 56–72. doi:10.1007/978-3-642-18302-7_4

Jimenez, M., Arenas, M., Bilbao, A., & Rodrguez, M. V. (2007). Linear Programming with Fuzzy Parameters: An Interactive Method Resolution. *European Journal of Operational Research*, *177*(3), 1599–1609. doi:10.1016/j.ejor.2005.10.002

Jing He, A. A. (2009). Advances in Data Mining: History and Future. *Third international Symposium on Information Technology Application*, *1*, 634 – 636.

Joachims, A. A. (2002). *Learning to Classify Text Using Support Vector Machines* (Dissertation). Kluwer.

Kao, C., & Chyu, C. (2002). A fuzzy linear regression model with better explanatory power. *Fuzzy Sets and Systems*, *126*(3), 401–409. doi:10.1016/S0165-0114(01)00069-0

Kashyap, S. K., & Raol, J. R. (2008). Fuzzy Logic Applications in Filtering and Fusion for Target Tracking. *Defence Science Journal*, *58*(1), 120–135. doi:10.14429/dsj.58.1630

Kazemi, A., & Mehrzadegan, E. (2011). A New Algorithm for Optimization of Fuzzy Decision Tree in Data Mining. *Journal of Optimization in Industrial Engineering*, *7*(2), 29–35.

Keller, J. M., Gray, M. R., & Givens, J. A. (1985). A fuzzy k-nearest neighbour algorithm. *IEEE Transactions on Systems, Man, and Cybernetics*, *15*(4), 580–585. doi:10.1109/TSMC.1985.6313426

Kim, N., & Bishu, R. R. (1998). Evaluation of fuzzy linear regression models by comparing membership functions. *Fuzzy Sets and Systems*, *100*(1-3), 343–353. doi:10.1016/S0165-0114(97)00100-0

Koen, M. L., Kyung, M. L., Jee, H. L., & Lee, K. H. (1999). A fuzzy decision tree induction method for fuzzy data. In *Proc. of 8th IEEE Inter. Conference on Fuzzy Systems*.

Kumar, A., Kaur, J., & Singh, P. (2011). A new method for solving fully fuzzy linear programming problems. *Applied Mathematical Modelling*, *35*(2), 817–823. doi:10.1016/j.apm.2010.07.037

Li, B., Lu, Q., & Yu, S. (2004). An Adaptive k-Nearest Neighbor Text Categorization Strategy. *ACM Transactions on Asian Language Information Processing*, *3*(4), 215–226. doi:10.1145/1039621.1039623

Lin, C. F., & Wang, S. D. (2002). Fuzzy Support Vector Machines. *IEEE Transactions on Neural Networks*, *13*(2), 464–471. doi:10.1109/72.991432 PMID:18244447

Lotfi, F. H., Allahviranloo, M., Jondabeha, A., & Alizadeh, L. (2009). Solving A Fully Fuzzy Linear Programming Using Lexicography Method and Fuzzy Approximate Solution. *Applied Mathematical Modelling*, *33*(7), 3151–3156. doi:10.1016/j.apm.2008.10.020

Maher, P. E., & St. Clair, D. C. (1993). Uncertain reasoning in an ID3 machine learning framework. In *Proc. 2nd IEEE Int. Conf. Fuzzy Systems*. doi:10.1109/FUZZY.1993.327472

Mingers, J. (1989a). An empirical comparision of selection measures for decision trees induction. *Machine Learning*, *3*(4), 319–342. doi:10.1007/BF00116837

Mingers, J. (1989b). An empirical comparision of pruning methods for decision tree induction. *Machine Learning*, *4*(2), 227–243. doi:10.1023/A:1022604100933

MishmastNehi, H., Maleki, H. R., & Mashinchi, M. (2004). Solving fuzzy number linear programming problem by lexicographic ranking function. *International Journal of Pure and Applied Mathematics*, *15*, 9–20.

Mitchell, A. A. (1997). *Machine learning*. McGraw Hill.

Mitchell, A. A. (2005). *Machine Learning*. The McGraw-Hill Co.

Mitchell, A. A. (2006). *The Discipline of Machine Learning*. School of Computer Science, Carnegie Mellon University.

Natarajan, A. A. (1991). *Machine Learning: A Theoretical Approach*. Academic Press.

Niklasson, L., Boden, M., & Ziemke, T. (Eds.). (1998). *Proceedings of the 8th International Conference on Artificial Neural Networks*. Springer Verlag.

Nilsson, A. A. (2005). *Introduction to Machine Learning*. Robotics Laboratory Department of Computer Science Stanford University Stanford.

Peters, G. (1994). Fuzzy linear regression with fuzzy intervals. *Fuzzy Sets and Systems*, *63*(1), 45–55. doi:10.1016/0165-0114(94)90144-9

Poggio, T., Pontil, M., & Verri, A. (2002). Regularization and statistical learning theory for data analysis. *Computational Statistics & Data Analysis - Nonlinear Methods and Data Mining*, *38*(4), 421 – 432.

Pontil, M., & Verri, A. (1998). Properties of support vector machines. Massachusetts Institute of Technology.

Quinlan, A. A. (1993). *C4.5: Programs for Machine Learning*. San Mateo, CA: Morgan Kaufmann.

Quinlan, J. R. (1984). Unknown attribute-values in induction. In *Proc. 6th Int. Workshop Machine Learning*, (pp. 164-168).

Quinlan, J. R. (1986). Induction on Decision Trees. *Machine Learning*, *1*(1), 81–106. doi:10.1007/BF00116251

Quinlan, J. R. (1987). Decision trees as probabilistic classifiers. In *Proc. 4th Int. Workshop Machine Learning*, (pp. 31-37). doi:10.1016/B978-0-934613-41-5.50007-6

Saberi Najafi, H., & Edalatpanad, S. A. (2013). A note on A new method for solving fully fuzzy linear programming problems. *Applied Mathematical Modelling*, *37*(14-15), 7865–7867. doi:10.1016/j.apm.2013.02.039

Sakawa, M., & Yano, H. (1992). Multi-objective fuzzy linear regression analysis for fuzzy input-output data. *Fuzzy Sets and Systems*, *47*(2), 173–181. doi:10.1016/0165-0114(92)90175-4

Sarkar, M. (2007). Fuzzy-rough nearest neighbor algorithms in classification. *Fuzzy Sets and Systems*, *158*(19), 2134–2152. doi:10.1016/j.fss.2007.04.023

Schölkopf, A. A., Burges, B. B., & Smola, C. C. (1999). *Advances in Kernel Methods: Support Vector Learning*. Cambridge, MA: MIT Press.

Schölkopf, B., Bartlett, P. L., Smola, A., & Williamson, R. (1999). Shrinking the tube: A new support Vector regression algorithm. *Advances in Neural Information Processing Systems*, *11*, 330–336.

Shamooshaki, M. M., Hosseinzadeh, A., & Edalatpanah, S. A. (2014). A New Method for Solving Fully Fuzzy Linear Programming with LR- type Fuzzy Numbers. *International Journal of Data Envelopment Analysis and Operations Research*, *1*, 53–55.

Shamooshaki, M. M., Hosseinzadeh, A., & Edalatpanah, S. A. (2015). A New Method for Solving Fully Fuzzy Linear Programming Problems by Using the Lexicography Method. *Applied and Computational Mathematics*, *1*, 53–55.

Shang, W., Huang, H., Zhu, H., & Lin, Y. (2006). An improved kNN algorithm: Fuzzy kNN. In *Proceedings of international conference on computational intelligence and security*, (pp. 741–746).

Smola, A. & Scholkopf, B. (1997). On a Kernel-based Method for Pattern Recognition, Regression. *Approximation and Operator Inversion*, 211 – 231.

Smola, A., Schölkopf, B., & Müller, K. R. (1998). General cost functions for support vector regression. In *Proc. of the Ninth Australian Conf. on Neural Networks*. Brisbane, Australia: University of Queensland.

Smola, A. J., & Schölkopf, B. (1998). *A Tutorial on Support Vector Regression*. Technical Report NC-TR-98-030. Royal Holloway College, University of London.

Stanevski, N., & Tsvetkov, D. (2005). Using Support Vector Machine as a Binary Classifier. *International Conference on Computer Systems and Technologies –CompSysTech.*

Stecking, R., & Schebesch, K. B. (2003). Support vector machines for credit scoring: Comparing to and combining with some traditional classification methods. In M. Schader, W. Gaul, & M. Vichy (Eds.), *Between Data Science and Applied Data Analysis* (pp. 604–612). Berlin, Germany: Springer- Verlag. doi:10.1007/978-3-642-18991-3_69

Sushmita, M., Kishorim. K., & Sankar. K.P. (2002). Fuzzy decision tree, linguistic rules and fuzzy knowledge basednetwork: Generation and Evaluation. *IEEE Transaction on Systems, 32*(4).

Tanaka, H., Okuda, T., & Asai, K. (1973). On Fuzzy Mathematical Programming. *Journal of Cybernetics and Systems*, 37-46.

Tanaka, H., Vejima, S., & Asai, K. (1982). Linear regression analysis with fuzzy model. *IEEE Transactions on Systems, Man, and Cybernetics, 12*(6), 903–907. doi:10.1109/TSMC.1982.4308925

Tanaka, H., & Watada, J. (1988). Possibilistic systems and their application to the linear regression model. *Fuzzy Sets and Systems, 27*(3), 275–289. doi:10.1016/0165-0114(88)90054-1

Thomas, L. C. (2002). A survey of credit and behavioral scoring: Forecasting financial risk of lending to consumers. *International Journal of Forecasting, 16*(2), 149–172. doi:10.1016/S0169-2070(00)00034-0

Van Gestel, T., Baesens, B., Suykens, J. A. K., De Espinoza, M., Baestaens, J., Vanthienen, D., & Moor, B. (2003). Bankruptcy prediction with least squares support vector machine classifiers. In *Proc. IEEE Int. Conf. Computational Intelligence for Financial Engineering*. doi:10.1109/CIFER.2003.1196234

Van Gestel, T., Suykens, J. A. K., Lanckriet, G., Lambrechts, A., DeMoor, B., & Vandewalle, J. (2002). Bayesian framework for least squares support vector machine classifiers, Gaussian processes and kernel Fisher discriminant analysis. *Neural Computation, 15*(5), 1115–1148. doi:10.1162/089976602753633411 PMID:11972910

Vapnik, A. A. (1995). *The Nature of Statistical Learning Theory*. New York: Springer-Verlag. doi:10.1007/978-1-4757-2440-0

Vapnik, V., Golowich, S., & Smola, A. (1997). Support Vector Method for Function Approximation, Regression Estimation, and Signal Processing. In M. Mozer, M. Jordan, & T. Petsche (Eds.), *Neural Information Processing Systems, 9*. Cambridge, MA: MIT Press.

Wang, N., Zhang, W. X., & Mei, C. L. (2007). It Fuzzy nonparametric regression based on local linear smoothing technique. *Information Sciences, 177*(18), 3882–3900. doi:10.1016/j.ins.2007.03.002

Wang, X. Z., Yeung, D. S., & Tsang, E. C. C. (2001). A comparative study on heuristic algorithms for generating fuzzy decision trees. *IEEE Transactions on Systems, 31*(2), 215–226. PMID:18244783

Wernick, Y., & Yourganov, B. (2012). Machine Learning in Medical Imaging. *IEEE Signal Processing Magazine*, *27*(4), 25–38. doi:10.1109/MSP.2010.936730 PMID:25382956

Wu, X. et al.. (2008). Top ten algorithms in data mining (Support vector machines). *Knowledge and Information Systems*, *14*, 1–37. doi:10.1007/s10115-007-0114-2

Yager, R. R. (1982). Fuzzy prediction based on regression model, *Information Sciences*. 26, 45-63. Chang, P. T., Lee, E. S. (1994). Fuzzy linear regression whit spreads unrestricted in sign. *Computers & Mathematics with Applications (Oxford, England)*, *28*(4), 61–70.

Yang, M., & Lin, T. (2002). Fuzzy least-squares linear regression analysis for fuzzy input-output data. *Fuzzy Sets and Systems*, *126*(3), 389–399. doi:10.1016/S0165-0114(01)00066-5

Yuan, Y., & Shaw, M. J. (1995). Induction of fuzzy decision trees. *Fuzzy Sets and Systems*, *69*(2), 125–139. doi:10.1016/0165-0114(94)00229-Z

Zadeh, L. A. (1965). Fuzzy sets. *Information and Control*, *8*(3), 69–78. doi:10.1016/S0019-9958(65)90241-X

Zadeh, L. A. (1968). Fuzzy algorithms. *Information and Control*, *12*(2), 94–102. doi:10.1016/S0019-9958(68)90211-8

Zadeh L. A. (1984). Making computers think like people. *Spectrum, IEEE, 21*(8), 26-32.

Zeidler, J., Schlosser, M., Ittner, A., & Posthoff, C. (1996). Fuzzy Decision Trees and Numerical Attributes. *Proc. of 5th IEEE Inter. Conference on Fuzzy Systems*, 2,985-990. doi:10.1109/FUZZY.1996.552312

Zhang, X. (1999). Using class-center vectors to build support vector machines. In *Proc. IEEE NNSP*, (pp. 3–11).

Zimmerman, H. J. (1978). Fuzzy Programming and Linear Programming with Several Objective Functions. *Fuzzy Sets and Systems*, *1*(1), 45–55. doi:10.1016/0165-0114(78)90031-3

Zimmermann, H. J. (1987). *Fuzzy Sets, Decision Making and Expert Systems*. Boston: Kluwer. doi:10.1007/978-94-009-3249-4

Chapter 8
Multiobjective Optimization of Solar-Powered Irrigation System with Fuzzy Type-2 Noise Modelling

T. Ganesan
Tenaga Nasional Berhad - Research (TNBR), Malaysia

Pandian Vasant
Universiti Teknologi Petronas, Malaysia

I. Elamvazuthi
Universiti Teknologi Petronas, Malaysia

ABSTRACT

Design optimization has been commonly practiced for many years across various engineering disciplines. Optimization per se is becoming a crucial element in industrial applications involving sustainable alternative energy systems. During the design of such systems, the engineer/decision maker would often encounter noise factors (e.g. solar insolation and ambient temperature fluctuations) when their system interacts with the environment. Therefore, successful modelling and optimization procedures would require a framework that encompasses all these uncertainty features and solves the problem at hand with reasonable accuracy. In this chapter, the sizing and design optimization of the solar powered irrigation system was considered. This problem is multivariate, noisy, nonlinear and multiobjective. This design problem was tackled by first using the Fuzzy Type II approach to model the noise factors. Consequently, the Bacterial Foraging Algorithm (BFA) (in the context of a weighted sum framework) was employed to solve this multiobjective fuzzy design problem. This method was then used to construct the approximate Pareto frontier as well as to identify the best solution option in a fuzzy setting. Comprehensive analyses and discussions were performed on the generated numerical results with respect to the implemented solution methods.

DOI: 10.4018/978-1-5225-0914-1.ch008

INTRODUCTION

Diesel generators, gas turbines and other fossil-fuel based power systems have been widely employed for driving conventional irrigation systems. Currently, various issues related to the utilization of fossil fuel in power systems have surfaced (e.g. price fluctuations, environmental concerns and efficiency). Hence in recent studies, the harnessing of solar energy to power irrigation pumps have become popular (Helikson *et al.*, 1991; Wong & Sumathy, 2001; Jasim *et al.*, 2014; Dhimmar *et al.*, 2014). The design and sizing of solar power systems greatly impacts the system's reliability, emissions and efficiency (Al-Ali *et al.*, 2001). Thus challenges in effective sizing of this system falls into the realm of optimization. Here the optimal sizing and design are obtained such that the following targets are achieved (Shivrath *et al.*, 2012; Carroqino *et al.*,2009):

- Increased savings
- Low emissions
- Good system efficiency
- High power output

Efforts in the optimization of solar powered irrigation systems have been performed via the implementation of metaheuristics such as: genetic algorithms (GA) and particle swarm optimization (PSO) (Gouws & Lukhwareni, 2012). However, due to the complexity of the system, the design needs to be carried out in such a way that it takes into account multiple aims simultaneously (i.e. multiobjective optimization) (Chen *et al.*, 1995).

Real-world optimization problems often contain large degrees of uncertainties. To effectively handle such problems, higher order fuzzy logic (FL) such type-2 FL approaches are often employed in tandem with optimization techniques (Castillo & Melin, 2012; Ontoseno *et al.*, 2013; Sánchez *et al.*, 2015). Most existing research works involving the application of type-2 FL systems revolve around control theory and control system design (Fayek *et al.*, 2014; Martinez *et al.*, 2011; Bahraminejad *et al.*, 2014; Oh *et al.*, 2011; Linda and Manic, 2011). For instance in Wu and Tan (2004), the authors investigated the effectiveness of evolutionary type-2 FL controllers for uncertainty modelling in liquid-level processes. In that work, the authors employed the genetic algorithm (GA) to evolve the type-2 FL controller. This approach was found to perform very well for modelling uncertainties in complex plants compared to conventional type-1 FL frameworks. In Bahraminejad *et al.*, (2014), a type-2 FL controller was employed for pitch control in wind turbines. Pitch control in wind turbines are critical for power regulation and reduction of fatigue load in the components of the turbine. In Bahraminejad *et al.*, (2014), the type-2 FL controller was shown to significantly improve the adjustment of the pitch angle, rotor speed and power output of the wind turbine generator. Similarly, in Allawi (2014), a type-2 FL controller was utilized for controlling robots involved in cooperation and target achieving tasks in multi-robot navigation systems. In that work, the controllers were optimized using the Particle Swarm Optimization (PSO) and the Hybrid Reciprocal Velocity Obstacles techniques. The author discovered that the optimized type-2 FL controller performed very well for controlling such robots.

Besides control theory and engineering, type-2 FL has also been employed for modelling systems endowed with high levels of uncertainty. For instance in Paricheh and Zare (2013), a type-2 FL system was used to predict long-term traffic flow volume. In Paricheh and Zare (2013), the traffic flow data was heavily influenced by various time-dependent uncertainties and nonlinearities. In that work, the authors employed a type-2 FL system in combination with genetic algorithm and neural net-based approaches. Another interesting implementation of type-2 FL was presented in the work of Qiu *et al.*, (2013). In that research, the authors focused on developing a general interval type-2 fuzzy C-means algorithm. The proposed fuzzy algorithm was employed for medical image segmentation in magnetic-resonance images (MRI). These MRIs are usually noisy and highly inhomogeneous. The works of Castillo and Melin (2012) and Dereli *et al.*, (2011) provides a more comprehensive review on type-2 FL systems applied in industrial settings.

Swarm intelligence (SI) stands as one of the most favored strategies for solving complex optimization problems due to its effectiveness during search operations and in terms of computational cost (Liu *et al.*, 2002). Some of the most popular SI-based techniques are, cuckoo search (CS) (Yildiz, 2013), ant colony optimization (ACO) (El-Wahed, 2008), PSO (Kennedy & Eberhart, 1995) and bacterial foraging algorithm (BFA) (Passino, 2002). In many past research works, PSO has been implemented extensively for solving nonlinear optimization problems. Recently, alternative optimization strategies such as BFA has become attractive to be implemented for such purposes. BFA's computational performance has been demonstrated to be as good as and sometimes better than other SI-based techniques (Al-Hadi & Hashim, 2011). BFA is inspired by the natural behavior of the E. Coli bacterium. This behaviour involves the search mechanisms utilized by the bacteria during nutrient foraging. These mechanism were then employed by Passino (2002) to design the BFA for solving complex optimization problems. The central principle of the BFA framework is as follows:

Each bacteria in the swarm tries to maximize its energy per unit time spent during the foraging for nutrients while simultaneously evading noxious substances

In recent times, BFA has been seen applied in many engineering applications (e.g. economic dispatch, engineering design, manufacturing technology, power systems and control systems). In the research work by Mezura-Montes and Hernandez-Ocana (2009), specific adjustments to the BFA approach was performed to enhance its optimization capability. This enhanced-BFA was then effectively implemented for engineering design. In Mezura-Montes *et al.*, (2014), the design optimization of a crank-rocker-slider (variable transmission) system was performed using BFA.

The design optimization problem in Mezura-Montes *et al.*, (2014) was formulated in two forms (single-objective and bi-objective). The authors then restructured the conventional BFA for multiobjective optimization. The conventional and multiobjective techniques were successfully implemented to optimize the mechanical design of the crank-rocker-slider system. BFA has also been applied in cellular manufacturing systems (Nouri and Hong, 2013). In these systems, the cell formation issue is tackled while considering the number of exceptional elements and cell load variations. In Nouri and Hong (2013), using the BFA approach, part families and machine cells were generated by the authors. In Panda *et al.*, (2009), the BFA was seen to aid the manufacturing process of rapid prototyping. In that work, the BFA was used for optimizing the process parameters employed for fused deposition modeling (FDM).

Besides manufacturing, BFA has also been widely applied by engineers/researchers in power engineering and distribution. In such applications the BFA is utilized for optimizing economic load dispatch. In economic load dispatch, the target is to obtain the most optimal load dispatch for the power generating units while taking into account variable load demands and load constraints (Vijay, 2012). In addition, BFA has been utilized for obtaining optimal power flow (i.e. economic and efficient) in flexible alternating current transmission system (FACTS) devices (Ravi *et al.*, 2014).

This chapter is organized as follows: Section 2 presents an overview of type-2 fuzzy logic while Section 3 discusses some fundamentals involving the application of type-2 fuzzy logic for noise modeling. Section 4 contains information on solar-powered irrigation system design followed by the BFA approach give in Section 5. Section 6 provides some details regarding the sigma diversity metric employed in this work while Section 7 presents the computational results and analyses. Finally, this chapter ends with some conclusions and recommendations for future research works.

OVERVIEW OF TYPE-2 FUZZY LOGIC

Type-2 fuzzy sets are generalizations of the conventional or type-1 fuzzy sets (Zadeh, 1975). The primary feature of the Type-1 fuzzy set is its membership function, $\eta_F(x)\in[0,1]$ and $x\in X$. Type-2 FL employs a membership function of a second order, $\mu_F(y,\eta_F(x))\in[0,1]$ such that $y\in Y$. Therefore, $\mu_F(y,\eta_F(x))$ is a membership function that requires three-dimensional inputs. The type-2 fuzzy set is defined as follows:

$$\tilde{F} = \left\{(y, \eta_F(x)), \mu_F(y, \eta_F(x)) : \forall x \in X, \forall y \in Y, \eta_F(x) \in [0,1]\right\} \tag{1}$$

The type-2 membership function has two membership grades: primary and secondary memberships. Thus, a crisp set (or function) undergoes fuzzification twice such that the first fuzzification transforms it to a type-1 fuzzy set (via the primary membership function). Using the secondary membership function the type-1 fuzzy set is transformed to a type-2 fuzzy set. In simple terms, type-2 fuzzy set results from the fuzzification of a type-1 fuzzy set. This operation aims to improve its efficacy and accuracy in capturing uncertainties. The region covered by the type-1 fuzzy sets in type-2 FL systems is represented by the footprint of uncertainty (FOU). This region of uncertainty is contained by the uppermost and lowermost type-1 membership functions $\eta_F^U(x)$ and $\eta_F^L(x)$ respectively. A type-2 FL system usually consists of four subcomponents: fuzzifier, inference engine, type reducer and defuzzifier. The fuzzifier directly transforms the crisp set into a type-2 fuzzy set. The inference engine functions to combine rules to map the type-2 fuzzy set from crisp inputs. Therefore each rule is interpreted as a type-2 fuzzy implication in the inference engine. In this work, all the consequent and antecedent sets are generalized type-2 fuzzy sets. The rule, R_i from a type-2 FL system could be generally represented as follows:

$$R_i\text{: IF } x_1 \text{ is } \tilde{M}_1 \text{ AND....AND } x_j \text{ is } \tilde{M}_j \text{ THEN } y_1 \text{ is } \tilde{N}_1,\ldots, y_k \text{ is } \tilde{N}_k \text{ such that } i\in[1,Z] \tag{2}$$

where j is the number of fuzzy inputs, k is the number of fuzzy outputs and i is the number of rules. The type reducer functions to transform (or reduce) the type-2 fuzzy set to a type-1 fuzzy set. Various type-reduction approaches have been developed in the past. For instance: centroid type reduction (Mendel and John, 2002) vertical slice-centroid type reduction (Lucas *et al.*, 2007), alpha cuts/planes (Hamrawi & Coupland, 2009) and the random sampling technique (Greenfield *et al.*, 2005). Defuzzification on the other hand reduces the type-1 fuzzy set to a crisp output similar to operations in conventional type-1 FL systems. There are various defuzzification techniques which are employed selectively to suit specific data representations and applications (Rao & Saraf, 1996).

TYPE-2 FUZZY LOGIC FOR NOISE MODELLING

Energy systems that rely on their surroundings are often difficult to design if the surroundings are noisy. In solar-powered systems, weather-dependent variables such as insolation and ambient temperature are often found to be irregular and noisy. Thus, when designing such systems, the model utilized should be able to account for such irregularities. In this work, equipped with meteorological data, type-2 FL is employed to model and incorporate insolation and ambient temperature into the optimization formulation. The meteorological data for Santa Rosa Station at California was retrieved from the weather database of the University of California Agriculture and Natural Resources. The daily average insolation (in W/m^2) and ambient temperature (in K) was obtained for every month of the year 2014. Table 1 provides the monthly ambient temperature and insolation data:

The primary membership function, $\eta_F(x)$ was employed to model the monthly data while the secondary membership function, $\mu_F(y,\eta_F(x))$ was used to model the overall annual data. This way the noisy monthly fluctuations in the data is taken into consideration via the type-2 FL approach. The overall type-2 fuzzy modelling strategy is given in Figure 1:

The S-curve function is employed as the primary and secondary membership functions ($\eta_F(x)$and $\mu_F(y,\eta_F(x))$). Therefore type-2 fuzzification is performed on the ambient temperature (Z_a) and insolation, (Z_b) using the S-curve membership function. This is carried out by determining the average, maximum and minimum values of insolation and ambient temperature from the meteorological data. The S-curve membership function is as follows:

Table 1. Monthly average ambient temperature and insolation taken at Santa Rosa Station, California in 2014

Month, m	Ambient Temperature, Za (K)			Average Solar Radiation, Zb (W/m2)		
	MAX	MIN	AVERAGE	MAX	MIN	AVERAGE
1 (Jan)	297.4	265.2	281.3	146	43	104.71
2 (Feb)	295.8	266.3	281.05	186	16	107.11
3 (Mac)	301.9	272.4	287.15	236	41	169.16
4 (April)	304.7	273.6	289.15	295	77	240.03
5 (May)	305.8	275.2	290.5	335	30	286.52
6 (Jun)	306.3	276.3	291.3	336	211	306.20
7 (July)	308	279.1	293.55	330	102	255.16
8 (Aug)	306.9	279.7	293.3	282	62	220.71
9 (Sept)	308	278.6	293.3	252	92	196.13
10 (Oct)	309.1	273.6	291.35	216	27	149.87
11 (Nov)	301.3	271.9	286.6	146	18	99.67
12 (Dec)	293.6	270.8	282.2	115	14	62.45

Figure 1. Type2 fuzzy modelling strategy

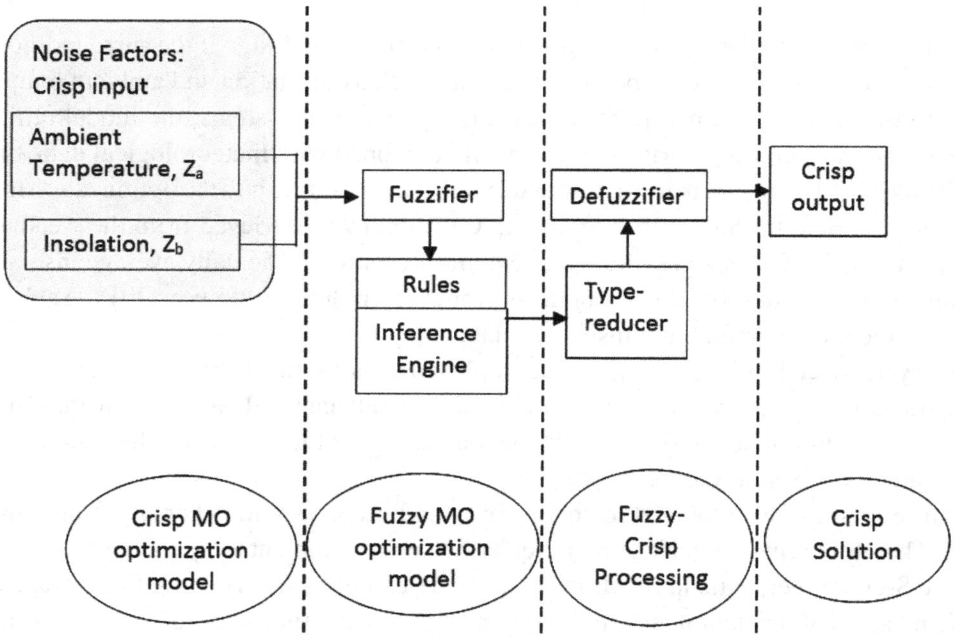

$$\mu_{\bar{b}_i} = \begin{cases} 1 & \text{if } b_i \leq b_i^a \\ \dfrac{B}{1 + Ce^{\alpha\left(\frac{b_i - b_i^a}{b_i^b - b_i^a}\right)}} & \text{if } b_i^a \leq b_i \leq b_i^b \\ 0 & \text{if } b_i \geq b_i^b \end{cases} \tag{3}$$

where B and C are parameters which are tuned heuristically such that the membership fits the meteorological data effectively. Using Zadeh's extension principle, all crisp variables (ambient temperature (Z_a) and insolation (Z_b)) and their respective constraints are transformed via type-2 fuzzification. Assuming a credibility level ε, ($0 < \varepsilon < \frac{B}{1+C}$) chosen by the Decision Maker (DM), as he/she takes a risk and ignores all the membership degrees smaller than the ε levels (Rommelfanger, 1989). The FOU is the union of all the primary memberships (Mo *et al.*, 2014). In this case, the union of all the primary S-curve memberships, $\eta_F(x)$ for each month depicts the FOU:

Let $\eta_F^i(x) \in \left(J_x^i \subseteq [0,1]\right)$ such that i=[L, U], THEN

$$FOU = \bigcup_{x \in X} J_x^i \tag{4}$$

where J_x^i is the fuzzy set, L is the lower bound and U is the upper bound. A graphical depiction of the FOU generated by the primary S-curve memberships in this work is given in Figure 2:

Figure 2. FOU generated by the primary S-curve memberships

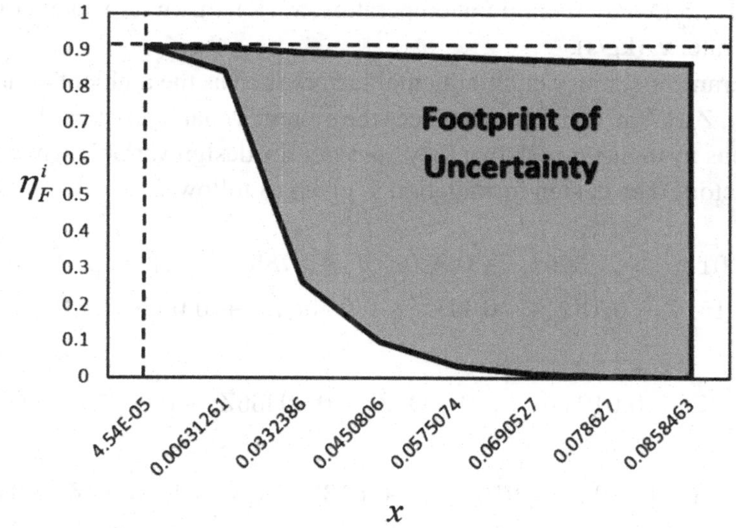

There are many readily available techniques for type-reduction and defuzzification. In this work, the alpha-plane approach (Hamrawi & Coupland, 2009; Liu 2006) was employed for type-reduction while the conventional alpha-cut approach (Klir & Yuan, 1995) was used for the defuzzification. An alpha cut can be defined on a fuzzy set, $\tilde{F}$ via its decomposed form as follows:

$$\tilde{F} = \bigcup_{\alpha \in [0,1]} \alpha \cdot F_{\alpha} \tag{5}$$

where F_α is an α-level set. Similarly, an alpha-cut on a type-2 fuzzy set could performed via the decomposition theorem. Since this operation is performed on a type-2 fuzzy set, it is defined as an alpha-plane instead of an alpha cut:

$$\tilde{\tilde{F}} = \bigcup_{\tilde{\alpha} \in [0,1]} \tilde{\alpha} \cdot \tilde{F}_{\tilde{\alpha}} \tag{6}$$

where $\tilde{F}_{\tilde{\alpha}}$ is a type-2 α-level set. It should be noted that by using Zadeh's extension principle, the alpha-planes could be utilized to execute type-2 fuzzy operations using interval type-2 fuzzy sets. This is analogous to implementations in type-1 fuzzy sets since the extension principle could be evoked to extend functions that interrelate crisp, type-1 fuzzy as well as type-2 fuzzy sets.

SOLAR-POWERED IRRIGATION SYSTEM

The design of the solar-powered irrigation system significantly affects its system characteristics. In Chen *et al.* (1995), the system characteristics which were given emphasis were the pump load/power output, f_1 (kW), overall efficiency, f_2 (%) and the fiscal savings, f_3 (USD). The design variables were: the maximum pressure, x_a (MPa), maximum temperature, x_b (K), maximum solar collector temperature, x_c (K), the fluid flowrate, x_d (kg/s).

Besides design parameters, noisy environmental factors such as the ambient temperature, Z_a (K) and the level of insolation, Z_b (W/m^2) greatly influences the system's characteristics. The objective functions and constraints are thus formulated such that they consider the design variable while taking into account the environmental factors. The design formulation is given as follows:

$$f_1 = -(24.947 + 16.011x_d + 1.306x_b + 0.820x_b x_d - 0.785Z_a - 0.497x_d Z_a + 0.228x_a x_b + 0.212x_a - 0.15x_b^2 + 0.13x_a x_d - 0.11x_a^2 - 0.034x_b Z_a + 0.002x_a Z_a)10^{-3.24} \quad (7)$$

$$f_2 = -43.4783(0.18507 + 0.01041x_a + 0.0038Z_b - 0.00366Z_a - 0.0035x_c - 0.00157x_b) \quad (8)$$

$$f_3 = -(174695.73 + 112114.69x_d + 9133.8x_b + 5733.05x_b x_d - 5487.76Z_a - 3478.84x_d Z_a + 1586.48x_a x_b + 1486.84x_a - 1067.42x_b^2 + 916.26x_a x_d - 768.9x_a^2 - 242.88x_b Z_a + 152.4x_a Z_a)10^{-3.23} \quad (9)$$

$$x_a \in [0.3,3];\ x_b \in [450,520];\ x_c \in [520,800];\ x_d \in [0.01,0.2];\ Z_a \in [293,303];\ Z_b \in [800,1000] \quad (10)$$

As mentioned in previous sections, to accurately account for the uncertainties arising from the noisy environment, the fuzzy type-2 approach is incorporated into the system design. Taking this view, the ambient temperature, Z_a (K) and the level of insolation, Z_b (W/m^2) is fuzzified. By implication, the target objectives and the constraints that bound the environmental factors (Z_a and Z_b) in the model above is transformed to a fuzzy form. The type-1 fuzzy constraints for the environmental factors are as follows:

$$\tilde{Z}_a^m \in [Z_{a,\min}^m, Z_{a,\max}^m] \qquad \tilde{Z}_b^m \in [Z_{b,\min}^m, Z_{b,\max}^m] \quad (11)$$

where m represents the months in the year as in Table 1 while $Z_{a,\max}^m$ and $Z_{b,\max}^m$ are the maximum monthly average and $Z_{b,\max}^m$ and $Z_{b,\max}^m$ are the minimum monthly average. The type-2 fuzzy constraint for the whole year is represented as follows:

$$\tilde{\tilde{Z}}_a \in [\tilde{Z}_{a,\min}, \tilde{Z}_{a,\max}] = [265.2, 309.1] \qquad \tilde{\tilde{Z}}_b \in [\tilde{Z}_{b,\min}, \tilde{Z}_{b,\max}] = [14, 336] \quad (12)$$

Therefore, the MO design optimization of the solar-powered irrigation system is effectively transformed to a Fuzzy MO optimization problem:

$$Maximize \rightarrow (\tilde{\tilde{f}}_1, \tilde{\tilde{f}}_2, \tilde{\tilde{f}}_3)$$

subject to

Crisp Design Constraints & Type-2 Fuzzy Environmental Constraints (13)

BACTERIA FORAGING ALGORITHM

The dynamics of bacteria foraging is directly influenced by evolutionary biology. Thus, bacteria with successful foraging strategies would stand a better chance in propagating their genetic makeup as compared to bacteria with poor strategies. This way bacteria at successive generations always contain improved foraging strategies relative to past generations and the strategies continually improves as they go along reproducing. Due to such progressive behavior, many researches were targeted to model bacteria foraging dynamics as an optimization process. The central theme of foraging viewed from this perspective is that the organisms conduct the search in such a way that they maximize the energy they obtained from the nutrients at minimal time during foraging.

Foraging efforts vary according to the species of the organism and the environment where the foraging is taking place. For instance, herbivores would find it easier to locate food as compared to carnivores in any habitat. As for the environmental factor, the distribution of nutrients in desert or tundra conditions are sparser in contrast with the nutrient-rich tropical jungles. Design of effective and efficient search strategies for nutrient foraging which respects the previous constraints is critical for the long-term well-being of any organism. Another important factor to be considered for the design of effective search strategies is the type of nutrient. The type of nutrient will influence the fractionalization and planning of the strategy (O'Brien *et al.*, 1990). For instance, consider a case where the nutrient is stationary but hidden in a hard shell (e.g. eggs). Then the organism would have design the foraging strategy in such a way that it searches for the shell (1), evades the nutrients parent (2), breaks the shell (3), consumes the nutrient (4) then escapes the nutrient location or nest before it gets attacked/killed (5).

In many organisms, synergetic foraging strategies are observed to emerge in nature (e.g. ants, bees and thermites). These organisms create communication mechanisms that enable them to share information about the foraging efforts led by each individual in the group. Such mechanisms provide the capability of the organisms to conduct 'group/swarm foraging'. Group foraging provides these organisms with a plethora of advantages such as increased protection against predators and enhanced hunting/foraging strategies. These advantageous traits increases the organism's chances for finding nutrients in good time. Besides synergetic strategies for foraging, other strategies such as cooperative building (Turner, 2011), group defense (Schneider & McNally, 1992) and other cooperative group behaviors are common in nature.

In the BFA, four main levels of loops are present in the technique (chemotaxis, swarming, reproduction and elimination-dispersal loops). These loops manage the main functional capabilities of the BFA. Each of the mentioned loops are designed according to bacteria foraging strategies and principles from evolutionary biology. These loops are executed iteratively until the total number of iterations, N_T is satisfied. Each of the main loops may be iterated until some fitness condition is satisfied or until a user-defined loop cycle limit (chemotaxis (N_c), swarming (N_s), reproduction (N_r) and elimination-dispersal (N_{ed})) is reached. In chemotaxis, the bacteria with the use of its flagellum, swims and tumbles towards the nutrient source. The tumbling mode allows bacterium motion in a fixed direction while the tumbling mode enables the bacterium to augment its search direction accordingly. Applied in tandem, these two modes gives the bacterium capability to stochastically move towards a sufficient source of nutrient. Thus, computationally chemotaxis is presented as follows:

$$\theta^i(j+1,k,l,m) = \theta^i(j,k,l,m) + C(i)\frac{\Delta(i)}{\sqrt{\Delta(i)\Delta^T(i)}} \tag{14}$$

where $\theta^i(j+1,k,l,m)$ is the ith bacterium at the jth chemotactic step, k^{th} swarming step and l^{th} reproductive step and m^{th} elimination-dispersal step. $C(i)$ is the size of the step taken in a random direction which is fixed by the tumble, and $\Delta\in[-1,1]$ is the random vector.

In the swarming phase, the bacterium communicates to the entire swarm regarding the nutrient profile it mapped during its movement. The communication method adopted by the bacterium is cell-to-cell signaling. In *E.Coli* bacteria, aspartate is released by the cells if it is exposed to high amounts of succinate. This causes the bacteria to conglomerate into groups and hence move in a swarm of high bacterial density. The swarming phase is mathematically presented as follows:

$$J(\theta, P(j,k,l,m)) = \sum_{i=1}^{S}\left[-D_{att}\exp(-W_{att}\sum_{m=1}^{P}\left(\theta_m - \theta_m^i\right)^2\right] + \sum_{i=1}^{S}\left[-H_{rep}\exp(-W_{rep}\sum_{m=1}^{P}\left(\theta_m - \theta_m^i\right)^2\right] \quad (15)$$

where $J(\theta,P(j,k,l,.))$ is the computed dynamic objective function value (not the real objective function in the problem), S is the total number of bacteria, P is the number of variables to be optimized (embedded in each bacterium), H_{rep}, W_{rep}, H_{att}, and W_{att} are user-defined parameters.

During reproduction, the healthy bacteria or the bacteria which are successful in securing a high degree of nutrients are let to reproduce asexually by splitting into two. Bacteria which do not manage to perform according to the specified criteria are eliminated from the group and thus not allowed to reproduce causing their genetic propagation (in this case their foraging strategies) to come to a halt. Due to this cycle, the amount of individual bacterium in the swarm remains constant throughout the execution of the BFA. Catastrophic events in an environment (such as a sudden change in physical/chemical properties or rapid decrease in nutrient content) can effect in death to a population of bacteria. Such events can cause bacteria to be killed and some to be randomly dispersed to different locations in the objective space. These events which are set to occur in the elimination/dispersal phase help to maintain swarm diversity to make sure the search operation is efficient. Figure 3 shows the workflow of the BFA technique. The pseudo-code for the BFA approach is provided below:

Box 1.

START PROGRAM
Initialize all input parameters (S, P, H_{rep}, W_{rep}, H_{att}, W_{att}, N_T, N_c, N_r, N_s, N_{ed})
Generate a randomly located swarm of bacteria throughout the objective space
Evaluate bacteria fitness in the objective space
For $i=1\rightarrow N_T$ **do**
For $l=1\rightarrow N_r$ **do**
For $m=1\rightarrow N_{ed}$ **do**
For $j=1\rightarrow N_c$ **do**
For $k=1\rightarrow N_s$ **do**
Perform *chemotaxis* – bacterium swim and tumble until maximum fitness/loop cycle limit is reached
Perform *swarming* – bacterium swarm until maximum fitness/loop cycle limit is reached
End For
End For
If bacterium healthy/maximally fit **then** split and *reproduce*
Else *eliminate* remaining bacterium
End For
Execute catastrophic *elimination* by assigning some probability of elimination to the swarm. Similarly *disperse* the remaining swarm randomly.
End For
End For
END PROGRAM

Figure 3. The workflow of the BFA

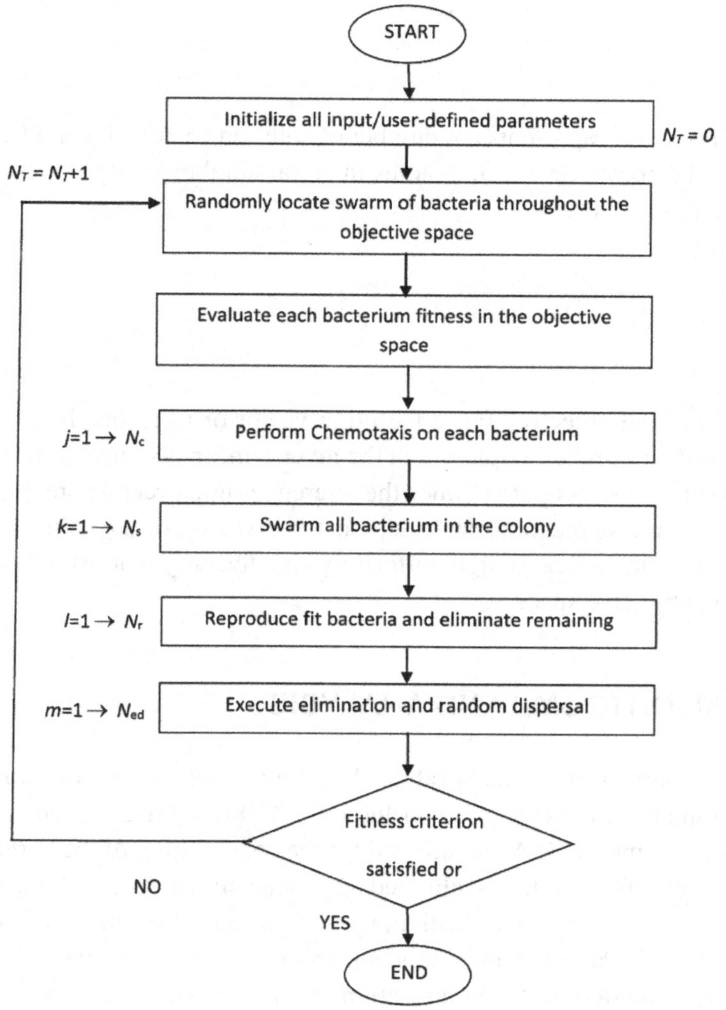

SIGMA DIVERSITY METRIC

The diversity measure used in this work is the sigma diversity metric (Mostaghim and Teich, 2003). The Sigma Diversity Metric (SDM) evaluates the locations of the solution vectors in the objective space relative to the sigma vectors. For lower dimensional objective spaces ($n<3$), metrics that are based on spherical and polar coordinates could be used. However, as the dimensions increase beyond three ($n \geq 3$), the mentioned coordinate systems do not define the distribution of the solution vectors well (Mostaghim and Teich, 2005). In such scenarios, the SDM is highly effective for computing the solution distribution. To begin the computation of the SDM, two types of sigma lines would have to be constructed. First the sigma lines that represent the solution vectors, σ' and the sigma lines that represent the reference lines, σ. The sigma lines that represent the solution vectors can be computed as the following:

$$\sigma'_k(ij) = \frac{f_i^2 - f_j^2}{\sum_{l=1}^{n} f_l^2} \text{ such that } \forall i \neq j \tag{16}$$

where k denotes the index that represents the number of solution vectors, i, j and l denotes the index that represents the number of objectives and n denotes the total number of objectives. Then the magnitude sigma $\left|\sigma'_k\right|$ is computed as follows:

$$\left|\sigma'_k\right| = \sqrt{\sum_{i=1}^{m} \sum_{j=1}^{m} \sigma'_k(ij)} \tag{17}$$

Thus, for each line in the objective space (solution vector or reference line), there exists a unique sigma value. The central working principle is that the inverse mean distance of the solution vectors from the reference sigma vectors are computed. Since the reference sigma vectors are distributed evenly along the objective space, the inverse mean distance depicts the diversity of the solution spread. High values of the sigma diversity metric, indicates high uniformity and diversity in terms of the distributions of the solution vectors in the objective space.

COMPUTATIONAL OUTCOME AND ANALYSIS

In this work, all computational procedures (algorithms and metrics) were developed using the Visual C++ Programming Language on a PC with an Intel i5-3470 (3.2 GHz) Processor. The compromised solutions were obtained using the BFA and utilized for the construction of the Pareto frontier. The fuzzy MO design problem was converted to a scalarized aggregate single-objective form using the weighted sum framework. Hence for various scalarization, the compromised solutions to the MO problem were obtained. In this work, each Pareto frontier was constructed using a cumulative of 35 solution points. The fuzzified ambient temperature, Z_a and insolation, Z_b is shown in Figures 4 and 5 respectively:

As in Equations 3 and 4, the $\mu_{F,S}$ and $\mu_{F,T}$ are the primary membership grades while $\eta_{F,S}$ and $\eta_{F,T}$ are the secondary membership grades. The S and T subscripts denote the insolation and ambient temperature respectively. When performing type-2 fuzzy modeling, the number of membership grades are often large. Thus, data acquisition may become rather complicated as compared to data acquisition with fuzzy type-1 systems. To reduce the complexity of data acquisition, some approximate symmetry properties of the fuzzy membership grades are exploited. Thus, data acquisition could be performed by fixing the insolation membership grades and letting the ambient temperature membership grades vary. The other scenario being fixing the ambient temperature membership grade and varying the insolation grades. Due to the symmetrical properties of the membership grades, the final results should mirror each other in both scenarios. Evoking the symmetry property, the mapping of the objectives to the membership grades are represented in terms of membership grades of the ambient temperature while the membership grades of the insolation are let to vary in the following ranges:

$$\mu_{F,S}=[0.25264,0.39913];\ \eta_{F,S}=[0.02907,0.92274] \tag{18}$$

Figure 4. Fuzzy Ambient Temperature (Z_a) versus Membership grades

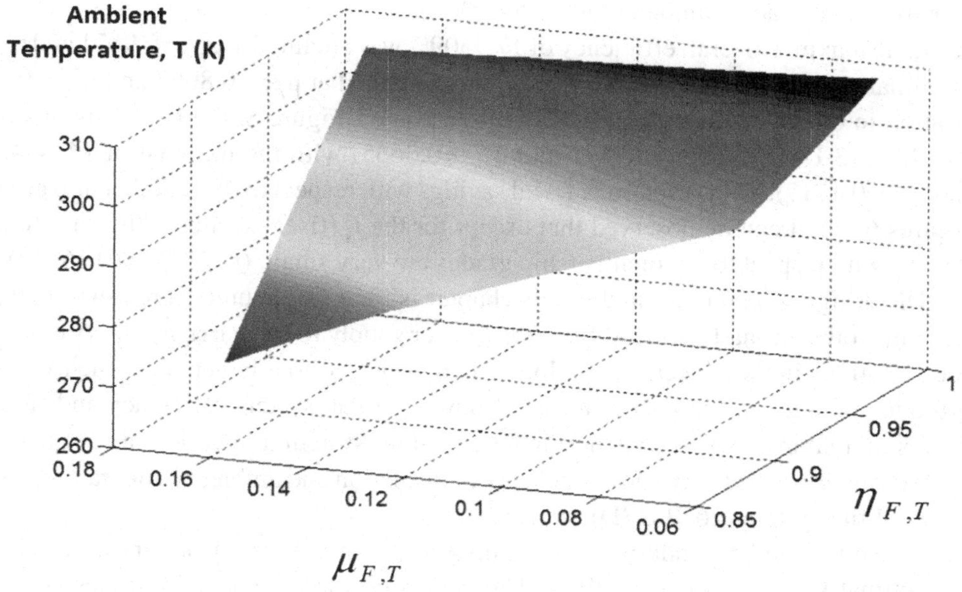

Figure 5. Fuzzy Insolation (Z_b) versus Membership grades

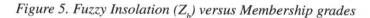

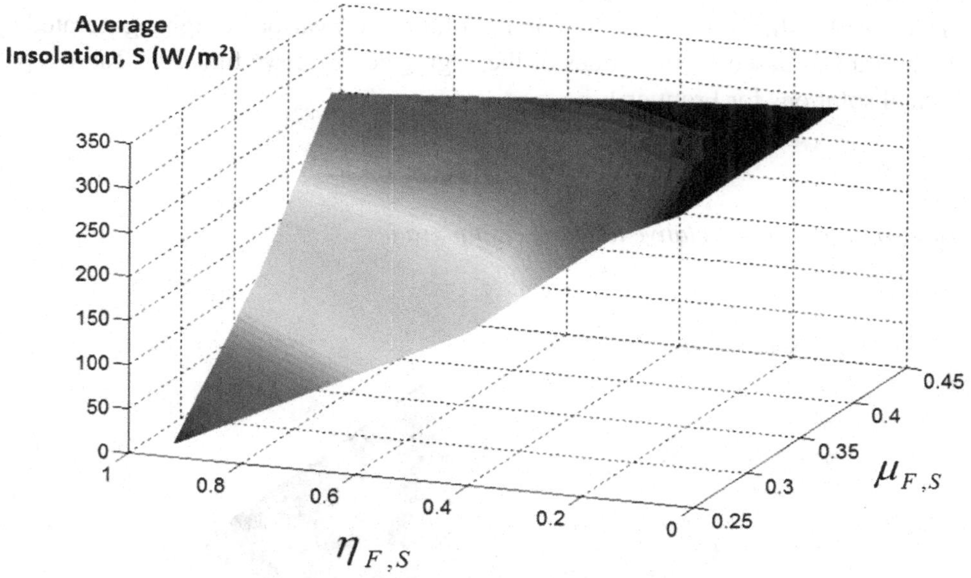

The mapping of the power output, f_1 (kW) to various primary and secondary membership grades (of ambient temperature) are depicted in Figure 6:

Referring to Figure 6, the maximal variation of power outputs at all membership grades is 0.3671 kW. A maximum power output of 20.1267 kW was obtained at $\mu_{F,T}$ =0.9871 and $\eta_{F,T}$ =0.0665. The minimal power output at $\mu_{F,T}$ =0.8967 and $\eta_{F,T}$ =0.1717 was 19.7596 kW. Figure 7 and 8 show the mapping of the overall efficiency, f_2 (%) and the fiscal savings, f_3 (USD) respectively relative to the primary and secondary membership grades (ambient temperature):

In Figure 7, the maximal overall efficiency of 17.9509% was obtained at $\mu_{F,T}$=0.9871 and $\eta_{F,T}$=0.0665 while the minimal overall efficiency of 16.7487% was obtained at $\mu_{F,T}$ =0.8967 and $\eta_{F,T}$ =0.1717 . The highest variation in overall efficiency is 1.022%. Referring to Figure 8, the fiscal savings reaches the maximum of 144113 USD (at $\mu_{F,T}$ =0.9871 and $\eta_{F,T}$ =0.0665) with the minimal of 141434 USD ($\mu_{F,T}$ =0.8967 and $\eta_{F,T}$=0.1717). The variation in fiscal savings with respect to the membership grades is 2679 USD. In Figures 6 – 8, it can be observed that except for the f_3 (fiscal savings), the variation in values of the objectives with respect to the membership grades are very small, (f_1, f_2, f_3) = (0.3671kW, 1.022%, 2679 USD). The design model presented in this chapter is for a single unit. In real-world applications, multiple units are conventionally utilized for stable power supply to large irrigation systems. Therefore, although the variations in the objectives are low, when projected to a larger scale such variations may compound producing a greater impact in terms of power output, system efficiency and fiscal savings. It should be noted, that even when considering a single-unit system, the variations in the membership grades (which spring from the noisy and uncertainty in insolation and ambient temperature) significantly affects the cost of the system (2679 USD).

For specific primary and secondary membership grades, three Pareto frontiers were selected based on the most optimal values of the objectives. The details on the membership grades are specified to construct these frontiers are given in Table 2:

Referring to Table 2, it is seen that the ambient temperature memberships are specified while the insolation memberships are left to vary in their ranges. This is done via the utilization of the symmetry properties in the membership grades. The individual solutions for various weights generated by the BFA were gauged and ranked based on the values of the aggregate objective function. Table 3 provides the ranked individual solutions for Frontier 1.

Figure 6. Power output, f_1(kW) relative to membership grades

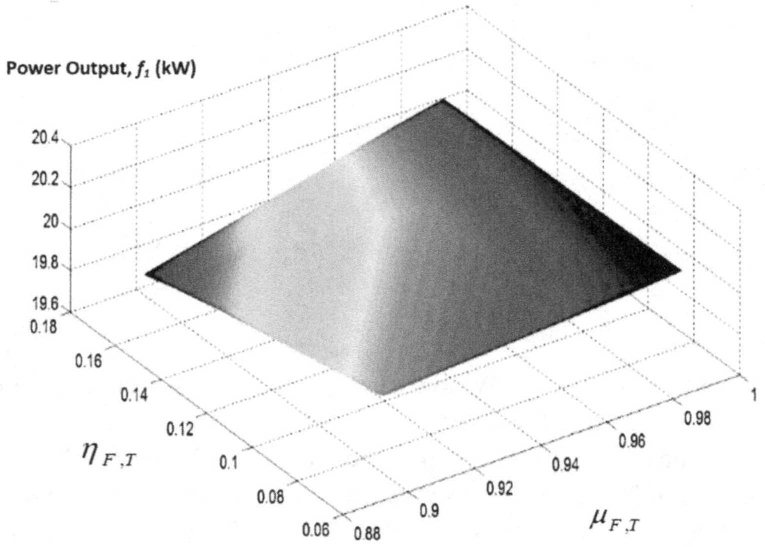

Figure 7. Overall efficiency, f_2(%) relative to membership grades

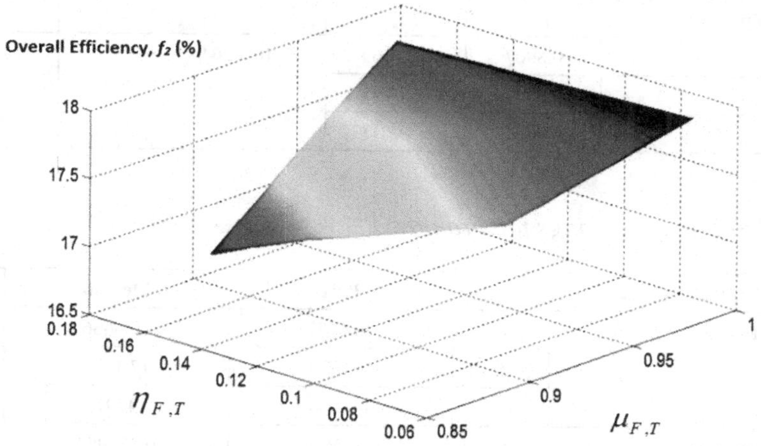

Figure 8. Fiscal savings, f_3 (USD) relative too membership grades

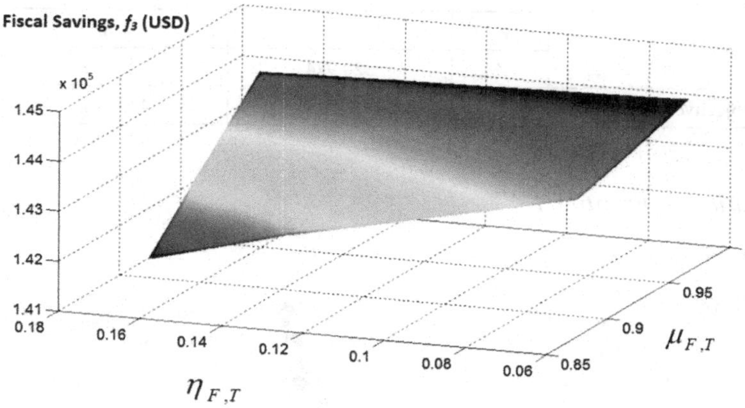

In Table 1, the best individual solution was obtained at the weights (0.1, 0.1, 0.8) while the worst solution was attained at (0.6, 0.3, 0.1). The weight assignment for the median solution was (0.3, 0.4, 0.3). The scattered solutions in the objective space approximating the Pareto Frontier 1 is shown in Figure 9. The ranked individual solutions along with their respective aggregate objective functions and parameters for Frontier 2 is given in Table 4.

The best, worst and median individual solutions presented in Table 4 are associated with the weights ((0.1, 0.1, 0.8), (0.1, 0.8, 0.1) and (0.1, 9.6, 0.3) respectively. The graphical representation of the Pareto frontier 2 is depicted in Figure 10.

Table 5 gives the ranked individual solutions for frontier 3 along with its respective parameters, noise factors and objective values.

The best and worst individual solutions are associated with the weights (0.1, 0.1, 0.8) and (0.5, 0.4, 0.1) respectively. The median solution has the weights (0.2, 0.5, 0.3). The Pareto Frontier 3 is shown in Figure 11.

Table 2. Pareto frontiers and their membership grades

Description	$\mu_{F,T}$	$\eta_{F,T}$	$\mu_{F,S}$	$\eta_{F,S}$
Frontier 1	0.8967	0.17169	0.25264 - 0.39913	0.02907 - 0.92274
Frontier 2	0.9565	0.15725		
Frontier 3	0.9871	0.06648		

Table 3. Individual Solution Rankings for Frontier 1

Description		Best	Median	Worst
Objective Function	f_1	20.6787	20.6666	20.6466
	f_2	17.1771	17.1173	17.0407
	f_3	148004	147917	147774
Decision Parameters	x_a	0.355846	0.354952	0.353833
	x_b	460.647	460.504	460.267
	x_c	677.284	674.784	671.6
	x_d	0.030827	0.030491	0.030037
Noise Factors	Z_a	251.838	251.837	251.835
	Z_b	328.974	328.972	328.97
Aggregate Objective	F	118407	44388.1	14794.9

Figure 9. Approximation of Frontier 1

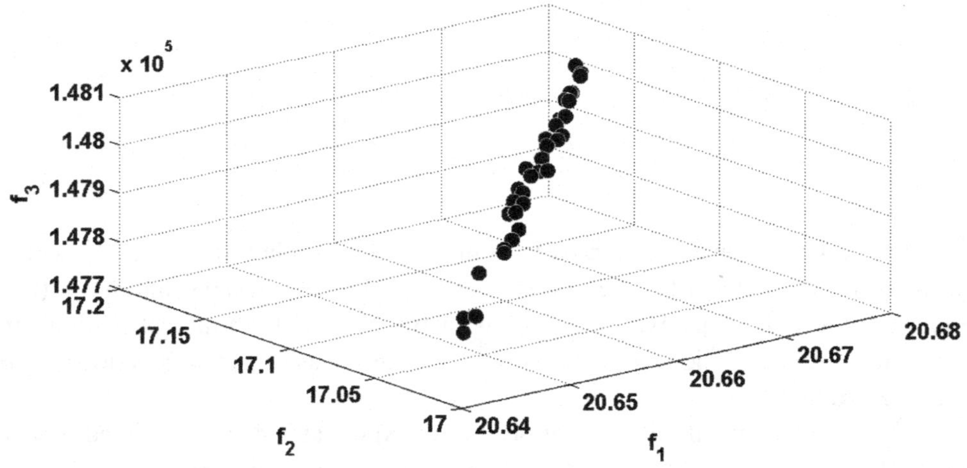

The three frontiers generated by the BFA technique was obtained at various weights for three different membership grades (refer to Table 2). In this chapter, the overall dominance of the Pareto frontier is measured by taking the average value of the aggregate objective function, F across the entire frontier. Frontier 3 outranks Frontier 2 followed by Frontier 1. The average value of the objective function across the entire frontier for Frontier 1, 2 and 3 are: 50305.86, 50911.64 and 51237.71 respectively. Similarly

Table 4. Individual Solution Rankings for Frontier 2

Description		Best	Median	Worst
Objective Function	f1	20.9103	20.9103	20.8872
	f2	17.7455	17.7506	17.6432
	f3	149696	149696	149531
Decision Parameters	xa	0.354758	0.354881	0.353615
	xb	460.473	460.473	460.202
	xc	674.513	674.732	670.244
	xd	0.030421	0.030458	0.029886
Noise Factors	Za	277.854	277.854	277.852
	Zb	328.972	328.972	328.969
Aggregate Objective	F	119761	44921.7	14969.3

Figure 10. Approximation of Frontier 2

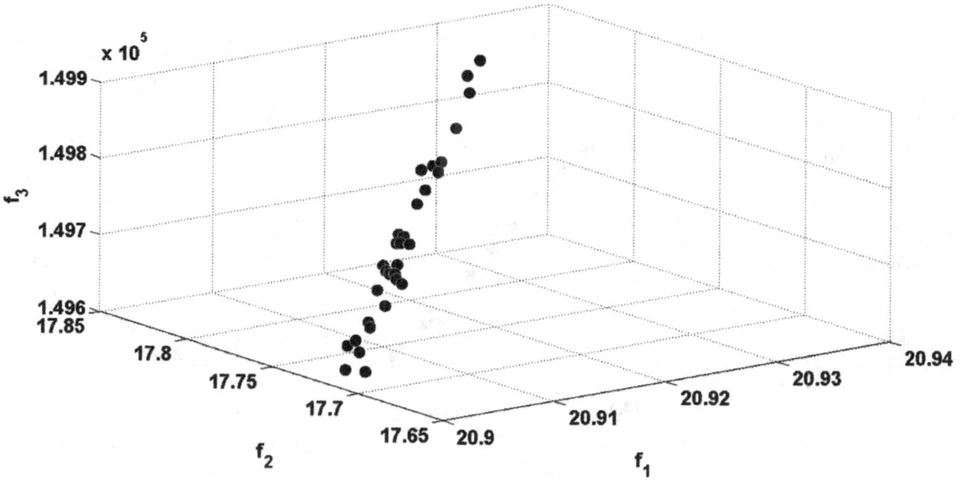

in Tables 3-5, it can be observed that the value of the aggregate objective function for the best individual solution follows a similar trend as compared to the entire Pareto frontiers in terms of ranking. The Pareto frontier were also gauged using the SDM as presented in the previous section. The diversity levels obtained for each of the frontiers are presented in Figure 12.

In MO optimization, the capability of the solution technique to continuously produce solutions with high diversity is crucial. This is so that the solution technique (algorithm) does not stagnate at certain locations in objective space or the local optima. Such stagnations may inhibit the algorithm from exploring other regions in the objective space which may contain other local optima which are much closer to the global optima. Therefore, measuring the diversity of the solution spread across the Pareto frontier provides the user/decision maker with information about the performance of the algorithm during its search operations. The BFA employed in this work seem to generate a highly diverse solution spread which constructs the Pareto Frontier 3 (Figure 12). Frontier 2 has lower diversity that Frontier 3 fol-

Table 5. Individual Solution Rankings for Frontier 3

Description		Best	Median	Worst
Objective Function	f1	21.034	21.0524	21.0335
	f2	18.0657	18.1411	18.0577
	f3	150600	150731	150596
Decision Parameters	xa	0.354785	0.355775	0.354627
	xb	460.435	460.65	460.428
	xc	674.234	677.372	673.892
	xd	0.030391	0.030815	0.030349
Noise Factors	Za	291.26	291.262	291.26
	Zb	328.972	328.974	328.971
Aggregate Function	F	120484	45232.6	15077.3

Figure 11. Approximation of Frontier 3

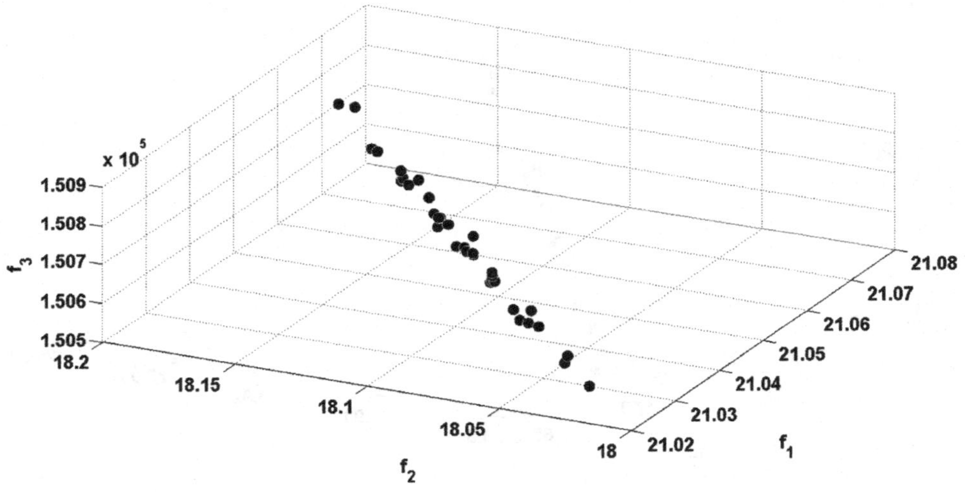

lowed by Frontier 1 which has the lowest diversity as compared to all the frontiers generated using the BFA technique.

Since diverse solution generation provides the algorithm with the ability to overcome stagnation, the degree of frontier dominance closely relates to the diversity of the solution spread across the concerned frontier. In this work, it is seen that the diversity levels follow the ranking of the dominance measured by using the average aggregate objective function value. Therefore, the BFA approach generated diverse solutions during its execution which resulted in the construction of highly dominant Pareto frontiers.

One of the most vital issues in green energy engineering is the design of low-cost and efficient systems which could match (or surpass) its fossil-fuel counterparts. However, these design efforts are often faced with challenges due to the system's interactions with noisy and uncertain environments. Identification and classification of the type of uncertainty is essential for the conception of suitable design frameworks. Using such frameworks, uncertainty-tolerant systems could be optimally designed and manufactured.

Figure 12. Diversity levels for the Pareto Frontiers

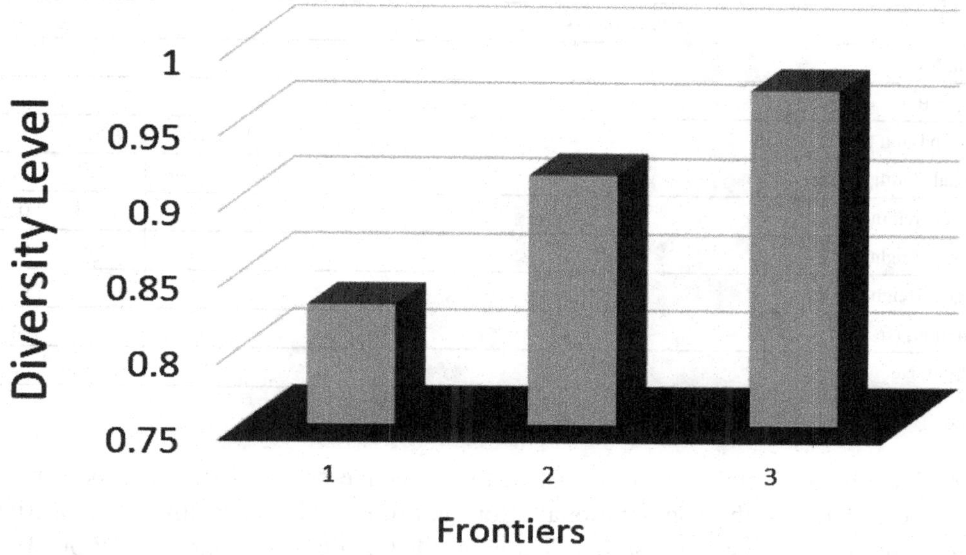

In view of this idea, the data consisting of environmental factors presented in Table 1 could be seen to have two levels of division: monthly average data and annual average. Thus, modeling this data using a fuzzy type-1 system is clearly inadequate and may lead to inaccurate approximations to the solar-powered irrigation system's design characteristics. It could be observed that the reformulation of the problem in a fuzzy type-2 MO programming setting offers various new information such as the system tolerance limits and its behaviour when under the influence of uncertainties. The three frontiers in Figures 9-11 were extracted because they contain the most significant variations in the target objectives when exposed to the uncertainties in the environmental factors. The maximal variation in the power output when faced with uncertainties (represented by the membership grades of the frontiers) is 0.3548 kW. The highest variation of the overall efficiency and the fiscal savings considering the mentioned uncertainties are 0.8806% and 2592 USD respectively. Therefore, in a large-scale solar irrigation system, uncertainties in the environmental factor (specifically: insolation levels and ambient temperature) does significantly affect the design properties of these systems.

The BFA technique like most metaheuristic approaches is a stochastic optimization technique. Therefore due to tis random nature, multiple runs are required during execution for result consistency. In this work, each individual solution is obtained after 5 program executions which adds up to 175 runs per frontier. The parameter setting of the BFA were heuristically determined and were not varied in this work. The parameter setting for the BFA is as in Table 6:

Referring to Figure 3, it can be observed that the BFA has one overall loop plus four primary loops: chemotaxis, swimming, reproduction and elimination/dispersal. Due to its rigor in solution discrimination portrayed by the cascaded loops, the BFA has high algorithmic complexity. The BFA code employed in this work contains multiple subroutines to account for the BFAs complexity. This significantly influences the computational time of the BFA during execution. The BFA program employed in this work takes an average of 4.217 seconds to compute each individual solution per run with an average of 1500 iterations. Therefore to construct the entire frontier for this application, the BFA takes approximately 12.3 minutes.

Table 6. Initial parameters for the BFA

Parameters	Values
Total Iteration, NT	200
Population Size, P	25
Swimming Loop limit, NS	5
Repellent Signal Width, Wrep	10
Attractant Signal Width, Watt	0.2
Repellent Signal Height, Hrep	0.1
Attractant Signal Height, Hatt	0.1
Reproduction limit, Nr	5
Elimination limit, Ne	5

Besides the algorithmic complexity of the BFA, the objective space of the solar-powered irrigation problem also contributes to the computational effort and time. This is because, the objective space in this problem contains multiple local optima that misleads the algorithm into stagnation. To overcome these local optima and proceed with the computation, the BFA takes additional computational time.

Another important feature of a MO optimization approach is the fitness assignment. The fitness assignment in the computational approach affects the way the algorithm is driven during the search process. In this work, all three target objectives are maximized and no objectives are minimized. Therefore, the aggregate objective function is used as a fitness criterion for the BFA algorithm during the search. The fitness of swarm is considered improved if the aggregate objective function is maximized during the current iteration as compared to the previous iteration. It is important to note that although the diversity metric is employed to measure the diversity of the solutions in the frontier, the diversity metric was not assigned as a fitness criterion in the algorithm. The diversity metric was employed in an offline manner from time to time to ensure that the algorithm is producing a diverse population during execution.

Diversity preservation is crucial when it comes to dealing with MO programming algorithms. In this work, two diversity preservation mechanism were utilized. The first one as mentioned previously is the offline implementation of the diversity metric. The second approach is the in-built diversification mechanism of the BFA. The in-built mechanism of the BFA consists of the two subcomponents which are the initial randomization and the random dispersal components (see Figure 3). The initial randomization component, randomly locates each of the bacterium at various locations in the objective space prior to the search. The random dispersal component, spreads the bacteria which survived elimination randomly throughout the objective space. This random spreading diversifies the bacteria population preparing it for the next program iteration. These two subcomponents randomizes the BFA during execution such that the bacterium population is sufficiently diverse during the search.

In the BFA, solution elitism could be readily ensured by the process of elimination (refer to Figure 3). In this process, bacteria which does not perform improvements based on the fitness assignment (which in this case is the maximization of the aggregate objective function) is eliminated from the population pool. This elitism mechanism ensures that only the elite bacteria is allowed to swarm during the consequent program cycles. Throughout the execution, the BFA algorithm performed in a stable manner and managed to successfully converge to a solution during each run. Besides, none of the fuzzy constraints were violated by solutions generated by the BFA. Therefore, the BFA reliably produces feasible solutions for all the associated weights. This in effect enables the BFA to capture solutions in the objective space which are close to the global optima.

CONCLUSION

The MO design of the solar-powered irrigation system was completed using type-2 fuzzy modeling to represent uncertain environmental factors. Using the BFA in tandem with the weighted-sum approach, dominant Pareto frontiers were constructed using individual solutions (with various weights). The dominance of the three generated Pareto frontiers were evaluated and ranked. The design problem was successfully reformulated using type-2 fuzzy logic to depict uncertainty in the environmental data (as shown in Table 1). As seen in Tables 3-5, new optimal individual solutions were obtained. In addition, information regarding the effects of uncertainties on the variations in the target objectives were ascertained and analyzed. This knowledge would prove to be very useful for designers dealing with solar-powered irrigation systems which operate in uncertain (or noisy) environments. In addition, using the diversity metric and the aggregate objective function, the quality of the solutions as well as the behaviour of the algorithm was analyzed in detail. The operations and the mechanisms of the BFA related to the solar-powered irrigation problem is presented. Characteristics such as algorithmic complexity and execution time was also presented and discussed.

It can be concluded that although the BFA consumes high computational resources, it compensates in terms rigor in solution scrutiny. This in turn provides the engineer/decision maker with high quality solutions. Based on the results obtained in this work, it can be seen that if a multi-unit (large-scale) solar-powered irrigation system were to designed for operation in an uncertain environment, its key properties such as efficiency, cost and power output would be greatly affected.

FUTURE RESEARCH DIRECTIONS

In the future, to address the issue of algorithmic uncertainty, the BFA should be implemented to this design problem however by varying its initialization parameters. This way, the optimal parameters could be identified for solving this design problem with uncertain environmental factors. Besides, other conventional fuzzy-based approaches (Vasant *et al.*, 2010; Ganesan *et al.*, 2014) could be upgraded to a type-2 fuzzy framework and implemented to this problem. Other forms of metaheuristic approaches such using evolutionary strategies could be implemented to this design problem (Ganesan *et al.*, 2015). Other measurement metrics such as the hypervolume indicator could be employed for gauging the degree of dominance of the generated Pareto frontiers (Zitzler & Thiele, 1998). A study on rigorously determining the fuzzy parameters (Equation (3)) could be done to obtain better modeling accuracy. This would be very useful for future researchers attempting to optimize the design of this system.

ACKNOWLEDGMENT

The authors are very grateful to the reviewers for their efforts in providing useful and constructive insights that has been overlooked by the author during the preparation of the manuscript. The authors would also like to thank Universiti Teknologi Petronas for their support during progress of this work. Special thanks to our friends, colleagues and students who continuously inspire and support us throughout the phases of our research.

REFERENCES

Al-Ali, A. R., Rehman, S., Al-Agili, S., Al-Omari, M. H., & Al-Fayezi, M. (2001). Usage of photovoltaic in an automated irrigation system. *Renewable Energy*, *23*(1), 17–26. doi:10.1016/S0960-1481(00)00110-5

Al-Hadi, I. A. A., & Hashim, S. I. M. (2011). Bacterial Foraging Optimization Algorithm For Neural Network Learning Enhancement. *International Journal of Innovative Computing*, *1*(1), 8–14.

Allawi, Z. T. (2014). A PSO-optimized type-2 fuzzy logic controller for navigation of multiple mobile robots. *19th International Conference on Methods and Models in Automation and Robotics (MMAR)*. doi:10.1109/MMAR.2014.6957321

Bahraminejad, B., Iranpour, M. R., & Esfandiari, E. (2014). Pitch Control of Wind Turbines Using IT2FL Controller versus T1FL Controller. *International Journal Of Renewable Energy Research*, *4*(4), 1065–1077.

Castillo, O., & Melin, P. (2012). A review on the design and optimization of interval type-2 fuzzy controllers. *Applied Soft Computing*, *12*(4), 1267–1278. doi:10.1016/j.asoc.2011.12.010

Chen, W., Kwok-Leung, T., Allen, J. K., & Mistree, F. (1995). Integration of the Response Surface Methodology with the compromise decision support problem in developing a general robust design procedure. *Advances in Design Automation*, *82*(2).

Dereli, T., Baykasoglu, A., Altun, K., Durmusoglu, A., & Türksen, I. B. (2011). Industrial applications of type-2 fuzzy sets and systems: A concise review. *Computers in Industry*, *62*(2), 125–137. doi:10.1016/j.compind.2010.10.006

Dhimmar, V., Prajapti, J., Patel, M., Patel, D., Mistry, B., & Parmar, J. (2014). Design of Solar Steam Irrigation Pump. *International Journal of Engine Research*, *3*(5), 315–317. doi:10.17950/ijer/v3s5/504

El-Wahed, W. F. A., Mousa, A. A., & Elsisy, M. A. (2008). Solving Economic Emissions Load Dispatch problem by using Hybrid ACO-MSM approach. *The Online Journal on Power and Energy Engineering*, *1*, 31–35.

Fayek, H. M., Elamvazuthi, I., Perumal, N., & Venkatesh, B. (2014). A controller based on Optimal Type-2 Fuzzy Logic: Systematic design, optimization and real-time implementation. *ISA Transactions*, *53*(5), 1583–1591. doi:10.1016/j.isatra.2014.06.001 PMID:24962934

Ganesan, T., Elamvazuthi, I., & Vasant, P. (2015). Multiobjective Design Optimization of a Nano-CMOS Voltage-Controlled Oscillator Using Game Theoretic-Differential Evolution. *Applied Soft Computing*, *32*, 293–299. doi:10.1016/j.asoc.2015.03.016

Ganesan, T., Vasant, P., & Elamvazuthi, I. (2014). Hopfield neural networks approach for design optimization of hybrid power systems with multiple renewable energy sources in a fuzzy environment. *Journal of Intelligent and Fuzzy Systems*, *26*(5), 2143–2154.

Gouws, R., & Lukhwareni, T. (2012). Factors influencing the performance and efficiency of solar water pumping systems: A Review. *International Journal of Physical Sciences*, *7*(48), 6169–6180.

Greenfield, S., John, R., & Coupland, S. (2005). A novel sampling method for type-2 defuzzification. In *Proc. UKCI*.

Hamrawi, H., & Coupland, S. (2009). Type-2 fuzzy arithmetic using Alpha-planes.*Proceedings of the Joint 2009 International Fuzzy Systems Association World Congress and 2009 European Society of Fuzzy Logic and Technology conference*, (pp. 606-611).

Helikson, H. J., Haman, D. Z., & Baird, C. D. (1991). *Pumping water for irrigation using solar energy, Fact Sheet (EES-63)*. University of Florida.

Jasim, K. K., Kadhum, J. A., & Ali, M. (2014). Design and Construction of Hybrid Solar-Wind System used for Irrigation Projects. *Indian Journal of Applied Research*, *4*(7), 518–522. doi:10.15373/2249555X/July2014/163

Kennedy, J., & Eberhart, R. (1995). Particle Swarm Optimization. *IEEE Proceedings of the International Conference on Neural Networks*.

Klir, G. J., & Yuan, B. (1995). *Fuzzy Sets and Fuzzy Logic: Theory and Applications*. Upper Saddle River, NJ: Prentice Hall.

Linda, O., & Manic, M. (2011). Evaluating Uncertainty Resiliency of Type-2 Fuzzy Logic Controllers for Parallel Delta Robot. *4th International Conference on Human System Interactions (HSI)*, Yokohama. doi:10.1109/HSI.2011.5937349

Liu, F. (2006). *An efficient centroid type reduction strategy for general type-2 fuzzy logic systems. Walter J. Karplus Summer Research Grant Report*. IEEE Computational Intelligence Society.

Liu, Y., Passino, K. M., & Simaan, M. A. (2002). Biomimicry of social foraging bacteria for distributed optimization: Models, principles, and emergent behaviors. *Journal of Optimization Theory and Applications*, *115*(3), 603–628. doi:10.1023/A:1021207331209

Lucas, L., Centeno, T., & Delgado, M. (2007). General type-2 fuzzy inference systems: Analysis, design and computational aspects. In *Proceedings of IEEE International Conference of Fuzzy Systems*. doi:10.1109/FUZZY.2007.4295522

Martinez, R., Castillo, O., Aguilar, L. T., & Rodriguez, A. (2011). Optimization of Type-2 Fuzzy Logic Controllers Using PSO Applied to Linear Plants, Soft Computing for Intelligent Control and Mobile Robotics. *Studies in Computational Intelligence*, *318*, 181–193.

Mendel, J., & John, R. (2002). Type-2 fuzzy sets made simple. *IEEE Transactions on Fuzzy Systems*, *10*(2), 117–127. doi:10.1109/91.995115

Mezura-Montes, E., & Hern'andez-Ocana, B. (2009). Modified bacterial foraging optimization for engineering design. In *Proceedings of the Artificial Neural Networks in Engineering Conference* (ANNIE'2009). St. Louis, MO: ASME Press.

Mezura-Montes, E., Portilla-Flores, E. A., & Hernández-Ocaña, B. (2014). Optimum synthesis of a four-bar mechanism using the modified bacterial foraging algorithm. *International Journal of Systems Science*, *45*(5), 1080–1100. doi:10.1080/00207721.2012.745023

Mo, H., Wang, F. Y., Zhou, M., Li, R., & Xiao, Z. (2014). Footprint of uncertainty for type-2 fuzzy sets. *Information Sciences*, *272*, 96–110.

Mostaghim, S., & Teich, J. (2003). Strategies for finding good local guides in multiobjective particle swarm optimization. In *IEEE Swarm Intelligence Symposium*, (pp. 26-33).

Mostaghim, S., & Teich, J. (2005). A New Approach on Many Objective Diversity Measurement. *Dagstuhl Seminar Proceedings 04461, Practical Approaches to Multi-Objective Optimization.*

Nouri, H., & Hong, T. S. (2013). Development of bacteria foraging optimization algorithm for cell formation in cellular manufacturing system considering cell load variations. *Journal of Manufacturing Systems*, *32*(1), 20–31. doi:10.1016/j.jmsy.2012.07.014

Nurcahyo, G. W. (2003). Selection of Defuzzification Method to Obtain Crisp Value for Representing Uncertain Data in a Modified Sweep Algorithm. JCS&T, 3(2).

O'Brien, W., Browman, H., & Evans, B. (1990). Search strategies of foraging animals. *American Scientist*, *78*, 152–160.

Oh, S. K., Jang, H. J., & Pedrycz, W. (2011). A comparative experimental study of type-1/type-2 fuzzy cascade controller based on genetic algorithms and particle swarm optimization. *Expert Systems with Applications*, *38*(9), 11217–11229. doi:10.1016/j.eswa.2011.02.169

Ontoseno, P., Abdillah, M., Wibowo, R., & Soeprijanto, A. (2013). Optimal Design of Photovoltaic–Battery Systems Using Interval Type-2 Fuzzy Adaptive Genetic Algorithm. *Engineering*, *5*(01No. 1B), 50–55. doi:10.4236/eng.2013.51B009

Panda, S. K., Padhee, S., Kumar Sood, A., & Mahapatra, S. S. (2009). Optimization of Fused Deposition Modelling (FDM) Process Parameters Using Bacterial Foraging Technique. *Intelligent Information & Management*, *1*, 89–97.

Paricheh, M., & Zare, A. (2013). Traffic Flow Prediction Based on Optimized Type-2 Neuro-Fuzzy Systems. *International Journal of Engineering and Computer Science*, *2*(8), 2434–2439.

Passino, K. (2002). Biomimicry of bacterial foraging for distributed optimization and control. *IEEE Control Systems Magazine*, *22*(3), 52–67. doi:10.1109/MCS.2002.1004010

Qiu, C., Xiao, J., Yu, L., Han, L., & Iqbal, M. N. (2013). A modified interval type-2 fuzzy C-means algorithm with application in MR image segmentation. *Journal of Pattern Recognition Letters*, *34*(12), 1329–1338. doi:10.1016/j.patrec.2013.04.021

Rao, D. H., & Saraf, S. S. (1996). Study of defuzzification methods of fuzzy logic controller for speed control of a DC motor. *Proceedings of the 1996 International Conference on Power Electronics, Drives and Energy Systems for Industrial Growth*. doi:10.1109/PEDES.1996.535878

Ravi, K., Shilaja, C., Chitti Babu, B., & Kothari, D. P. (2014). Solving Optimal Power Flow Using Modified Bacterial Foraging Algorithm Considering FACTS Devices. *Journal of Power and Energy Engineering*, *2*(04), 639–646. doi:10.4236/jpee.2014.24086

Rommelfanger, H. (1989). Interactive decision making in fuzzy linear optimization problems. *European Journal of Operational Research*, *41*(2), 210–217.

Sánchez, D., Melin, P., & Castillo, O. (2015). Fuzzy System Optimization Using a Hierarchical Genetic Algorithm Applied to Pattern Recognition. *Advances in Intelligent Systems and Computing*, *323*, 713–720. doi:10.1007/978-3-319-11310-4_62

Schneider, S. S., & McNally, L. C. (1992). Colony Defense in the African Honey Bee In Africa. *Environmental Entomology*, *21*(6), 1362–1370. doi:10.1093/ee/21.6.1362

Turner, J. S. (2011). Termites as models of swarm cognition. *Swarm Intelligence*, *5*(1), 19–43. doi:10.1007/s11721-010-0049-1

Vasant, P., Elamvazuthi, I., Ganesan, T., & Webb, J. F. (2010). Iterative fuzzy optimization approach for crude oil refinery industry. *Scientific Annals of Computer Science*, *8*(2), 261–280.

Vijay, R. (2012). Intelligent Bacterial Foraging Optimization Technique to Economic Load Dispatch Problem. *International Journal of Soft Computing and Engineering*, *1*(2), 2231–2307.

Wong, Y. W., & Sumathy, K. (2001). Thermodynamic analysis and optimization of a solar thermal water pump. *Applied Thermal Engineering*, *21*(5), 613–627. doi:10.1016/S1359-4311(00)00065-X

Wu, D., & Tan, W. W. (2004). A type-2 fuzzy logic controller for the liquid-level process. *Proceedings of 2004 IEEE International Conference on Fuzzy Systems*. doi:10.1109/FUZZY.2004.1375536

Yildiz, A. R. (2013). Cuckoo search algorithm for the selection of optimal machining parameters in milling operations. *International Journal of Advanced Manufacturing Technology*, *64*(1-4), 55–61. doi:10.1007/s00170-012-4013-7

Zadeh, L. (1975). The concept of a linguistic variable and its application to approximate reasoning—I. *Information Sciences*, *8*(3), 199–249. doi:10.1016/0020-0255(75)90036-5

Zitzler, E., & Thiele, L. (1998). Multiobjective Optimization Using Evolutionary Algorithms - A Comparative Case Study. In *Conference on Parallel Problem Solving from Nature* (PPSN V), (pp. 292–301).

ADDITIONAL READING

Beume, N., Naujoks, B., & Emmerich, M. (2007). SMS-EMOA: Multiobjective selection based on dominated hypervolume. *European Journal of Operational Research*, *181*(3), 1653–1669. doi:10.1016/j.ejor.2006.08.008

Ganesan, T., & Elamvazuthi, I. K.Z.K., Shaari and Vasant, P., (2013), Hypervolume-driven analytical programming for solar-powered irrigation system optimization, Nostradamus 2013: Prediction, Modeling and Analysis of Complex Systems, pp. 147-154.

Igel, C., Hansen, N., & Roth, S. (2007). Covariance matrix adaptation for multi-objective optimization. *Evolutionary Computation*, *15*(1), 1–28. doi:10.1162/evco.2007.15.1.1 PMID:17388777

Knowles, J., & Corne, D. (2003). Properties of an adaptive archiving algorithm for storing nondominated vectors. *IEEE Transactions on Evolutionary Computation*, *7*(2), 100–116. doi:10.1109/TEVC.2003.810755

Varacha, P. (2011). *Neural Network Synthesis via Asynchronous Analytical Programming*. Recent Researches in Neural Networks, Fuzzy Systems, Evolutionary Computing and Automation.

Zelinka, I. (2002), Analytic programming by Means of Soma Algorithm. Mendel '02, In: *Proceeding of the 8th International Conference on Soft Computing Mendel'02, Brno, Czech Republic,* 93-101.

KEY TERMS AND DEFINITIONS

Bacteria Foraging Algorithms (BFA): A type of swarm algorithm that uses the dynamics of bacteria foraging to search for optimal solutions in the objective space.

Metaheuristics: A framework consisting of a class of algorithms employed to find good solutions to optimization problems by iterative improvement of solution quality.

Multiobjective Optimization: Optimization problems which are represented with more than one objective functions.

Solar-Powered Irrigation System: Systems which harness solar energy to power irrigation pumps.

Swarm Intelligence: A group or collective behavior of natural or artificial individuals in a system towards some target.

Type-2 Fuzzy Logic: Type-2 fuzzy logic is generalization of the conventional or type-1 fuzzy logic for handling high levels of uncertainty.

Chapter 9
Non-Linear Intuitionistic Fuzzy Number and Its Application in Partial Differential Equation

Sankar Prasad Mondal
National Institute of Technology Agartala, India

ABSTRACT

In this chapter the concept of non linear intuitionistic fuzzy number is addressed. Mainly the construction of non linear intuitionistic fuzzy number whose membership function is non linear function is taken here. Finally the number is taken with partial differential equation and solve the problem.

INTRODUCTION

Fuzzy Sets and Intuitionistic Fuzzy Sets

Generalizations of fuzzy sets theory (see Zadeh (1965)) is considered to be one of Intuitionistic fuzzy set (IFS). Out of several higher-order fuzzy sets, IFS was first introduced by Atanassov (1983) have been found to be suitable to deal with unexplored areas. The fuzzy set considers only the degree of belongingness and non belongingness. Fuzzy set theory does not incorporate the degree of hesitation (i.e., degree of non-determinacy defined as, 1- sum of membership function and non-membership function. To handle such situations, Atanassov (1983) explored the concept of fuzzy set theory by intuitionistic fuzzy set (IFS) theory. The degree of acceptance in Fuzzy Sets is only considered, otherwise IFS is characterized by a membership function and a non-membership function so that the sum of both values is less than one (see Atanassov (1986)). Now-a-days, IFSs are being studied extensively and being used in different fields of Science and Technology.

Fuzzy Differential Equation and Intuitionistic Fuzzy Differential Equation

The topic "fuzzy differential equation"(FDE) has been rapidly developing in recent years. The appliance of fuzzy differential equations is a inherent way to model dynamic systems under possibilistic uncertainty

DOI: 10.4018/978-1-5225-0914-1.ch009

(Zadeh (2005)). The concept of the fuzzy derivative was first induced by Chang and Zadeh (1972). It was followed up by Dubois and Prade (1982). Other methods have been discussed by Puri and Ralescu (1983) and Goetschel and Voxman (1986). The concept of differential equations in a fuzzy environment was first formulated by Kaleva (1987). In fuzzy differential equation all derivative is deliberated as either Hukuhara or generalized derivatives. The Hukuhara differentiability has a imperfection (see Bede and Gal (2005)). The solution turns fuzzier as time goes by. Bede (2006) exhibited that a large class of BVPs has no solution if the Hukuhara derivative is used. To overcome this difficulty, the concept of a generalized derivative was developed (see Chalco-Cano and Roman-Flores (2008)) and fuzzy differential equations were discussed using this concept (see Bede et.al. (2007)). Khastan and Nieto (2010) found solutions for a large enough class of boundary value problems using the generalized derivative. Bede (2013) discussed the generalized differentiability for fuzzy valued functions. Pointedly the disadvantage of strongly generalized differentiability of a function in comparison H-differentiability is that, a fuzzy differential equation has no unique solution. Recently, Stefanini and Bede (2005) by the concept of generalization of the Hukuhara difference for compact convex set, introduced generalized Hukuhara differentiability (see Stefanini and Bede (2009)) for fuzzy valued function and they demonstrated that, this concept of differentiability have relationships with weakly generalized differentiability and strongly generalized differentiability. Recently Gasilov et. al. (2014) solve the fuzzy initial value problem by a new technique where Barros et. al. (2013) solve fuzzy differential equation via fuzzification of the derivative operator.

Intuitionistic FDE is very rare. Melliani and Chadli (2001) solve partial differential equation with intuitionistic fuzzy number. S. Abbasbandy, T. Allahviranloo (2002) discussed numerical Solution of fuzzy differential equations by Runge-Kutta and the Intuitionistic treatment. Lata and Kumar (2012) solve time-dependent intuitionistic fuzzy differential equation and its application to analyze the intuitionistic fuzzy reliability of industrial system. First order homogeneous ordinary differential equation with initial value as triangular intuitionistic fuzzy number is described by Mondal and Roy (2014). System of Differential Equation with Initial Value as Triangular Intuitionistic Fuzzy Number and its Application is solved by Mondal and Roy (2015).

Fuzzy Partial Differential Equation

Partial differential equations are important for modeling many real world problems. When it's comes with uncertainty then the solution procedure become complicated. Many works done is completed in fuzzy partial differential equation. Bertone et. al. (2013) found the deterministic solution of fuzzy PDE and defuzzify the solution. Buckley and Feuring (1999) find the solution by extension principle method. Tapaswini and Chakraverty (2014) find dynamic response of imprecisely defined beam subject to various loads using Adomian decomposition method. For an application non-probabilistic solution of uncertain vibration equation of large membranes using adomian decomposition methods is addressed by Tapaswini and Chakraverty (2014). iNumerical Solution of Uncertain Beam Equations Using Double Parametric Form of Fuzzy Numbers is illustrated by Tapaswini and Chakraverty (2013). Chen et.al. (2009) use adaptive approach for finding the solution of fuzzy PDE whereas Ahmadi and Kiani (2011) use differential transformation method. Fuzzy numerical schemes for Hyperbolic differential equations is addressed by Breuss and Dietrich (2009). An implicit method for solving Fuzzy PDE with nonlocal boundary conditions is considered by Orouji et.al. (2014). Allahviranloo (2002) use difference method where as Farajzadeh and Pour (2010) used explicit method. Solution of Poisson equation with fuzzy data is found by Sakia (2011). Numerical methods for fuzzy linear partial differential equations under new definition for derivative are developed by Allahviranloo and Kermani (2010). Numerical solution of fuzzy elliptic PDEs by means of polynomial response surfaces are treated by Corveleyn and Vandewalle (2010). Salahshour and Haghi (2010) develop Laplace transform for fuzzy partial derivative and apply this for finding the solution of fuzzy heat equation. Application of fuzzy Laplace transforms for solving fuzzy partial Volterra integro-differential equations by Ullah et.al. (2014).

Motivation

Many authors consider intuitionistic fuzzy number for different article any apply different fields. But the point is that they considered the intutionistic fuzzy number with linear membership and non membership function. It is need not necessary to consider linear membership. In this chapter the consideration of intutionistic fuzzy number with non-linear membership and non membership function are derived and apply it in partial differential equation.

Novelties

In spite the above mention development few developments can still be done which are as:

1. Non-linear intutionistic fuzzy number is defined i.e., a intuitionistic fuzzy number with non linear membership and non membership function.
2. We apply this number in partial differential equation problem.
3. Partial differential equation are defined in intuitionistic fuzzy environment i.e., initial and coefficients are both taken as intutionistic fuzzy number.
4. The necessity for taking intuitionistic fuzzy number with non linear membership and non membership function is expressed briefly.

Structure of the Chapter

The structure of the chapter is as follows: In first section we introduce the previous work on fuzzy and intuitionistic fuzzy set theory, fuzzy and intutionistic fuzzy differential equation. Second section goes to preliminary concept. In third section introduce non-linear intuitionistic fuzzy number i.e., an intuitionistic fuzzy number with non linear membership and non membership function. In fourth section intuitionistic fuzzy difference and derivative is addressed. In fifth section we use the number in partial differential equation and solve them. The conclusion is done in sixth section.

PRELIMINARIES

Basic Concept of Fuzzy and Intuitionistic Fuzzy Set Theory

Definition 2.1: Fuzzy Set: A fuzzy set $\tilde{A}$ is defined by $\tilde{A} = \left\{ \left(x, \mu_{\tilde{A}}\left(x \right) \right) : x \in A, \mu_{\tilde{A}}\left(x \right) \in \left[0,1 \right] \right\}$. In the pair $\left(x, \mu_{\tilde{A}}\left(x \right) \right)$ the first element *x* belong to the classical set *A*, the second element $\mu_{\tilde{A}}\left(x \right)$, belong to the interval [0,1], called Membership function.

Definition 2.2: Height: The height $h(\tilde{A})$, of a fuzzy set $\tilde{A}=\left\{\left(x,\mu_{\tilde{A}}\left(x\right)\right):x\in X\right\}$, is the largest membership grade obtained by any element in that set i.e., $h(\tilde{A})=\sup\mu_{\tilde{A}}\left(x\right)$.

Definition 2.3: Support of Fuzzy Set: The support of fuzzy set $\tilde{A}$ is the set of all points x in X such that $\mu_{\tilde{A}}\left(x\right)>0$ i.e., $support(\tilde{A})=\left\{x\mid\mu_{\tilde{A}}\left(x\right)>0\right\}$.

Definition 2.4: Convex Fuzzy sets: A fuzzy set $\tilde{A}=\left\{\left(x,\mu_{\tilde{A}}\left(x\right)\right):x\in X\right\}\subseteq X$ is called convex fuzzy set if all A_α for every $\alpha\in[0,1]$ are convex sets i.e. for every element $x_1\in A_\alpha$ and $x_2\in A_\alpha$ and $\lambda x_1+(1-\lambda)x_2\in A_\alpha\ \forall\lambda\in[0,1]$. Otherwise the fuzzy set is called non-convex fuzzy set.

Definition 2.5: α-cut of a fuzzy set: The α -level set (or interval of confidence at level α or α-cut) of the fuzzy set $\tilde{A}$ of X is a crisp set A_α that contains all the elements of X that have membership values in $\tilde{A}$ greater than or equal to α i.e.,

Definition 2.6: Strong α -cut of a fuzzy set: Strong α-cut is denoted by $A_\alpha^{strong}=\left\{x:\mu_{\tilde{A}}\left(x\right)>0\right\}$ $\forall\lambda\in[0,1]$.

Definition 2.7: Fuzzy Number: (Zadeh (2005)) A fuzzy number is fuzzy set like u: $R\rightarrow I=[0,1]$ which satisfies

1. u is upper semi-continuous.
2. $u(x)=0$ outside the interval $[c,d]$
3. There are real numbers a,b such $c\leq a\leq b\leq d$ and
    a. (3.1) $u(x)$ is monotonic increasing on $[c,a]$,
    b. (3.2) $u(x)$ is monotonic decreasing on $[b,d]$,
    c. (3.3) $u(x)=1$, $a\leq x\leq b$

Let E^1 be the set of all real fuzzy numbers which are normal, upper semi-continuous, convex and compactly supported fuzzy sets.

Definition 2.8: Positive and Negative Fuzzy Number: A fuzzy number $\tilde{A}$ is called positive (or negative), denoted by $\tilde{A}>0$ (or, $\tilde{A}<0$), if its membership function $\mu_{\tilde{A}}\left(x\right)$ satisfies $\mu_{\tilde{A}}\left(x\right)=0$, $\forall x<0$ ($x>0$).

Definition 2.9: Fuzzy Number (Parametric Form): (Chang and Zadeh (1972)) A fuzzy number u in a parametric form is a pair (u_1,u_2) of function $u_1\left(r\right),u_2\left(r\right),0\leq r\leq 1$, which satisfies the following requirments:

1. $u_1\left(r\right)$ is a bounded monotonic increasing left continuous function,
2. $u_2\left(r\right)$ is a bounded monotonic decreasing left continuous function,
3. $u_1\left(r\right)\leq u_2\left(r\right),0\leq r\leq 1$.

A crisp number x is simply represented by $\left(u_1\left(r\right),u_2\left(r\right)\right)=\left(x,x\right),0\leq r\leq 1$. By appropriate definitions, the fuzzy number space $\{\left(u_1\left(r\right),u_2\left(r\right)\right)\}$ becomes a convex cone E^1 which could be embedded isomorphically and isometrically into a Banach space.

Definition 2.10: Intuitionistic Fuzzy Set: Let a set X be fixed. An IFS A^i in X is an object having the form $A^i = \left\{\left(x, \mu_{A^i}\left(x\right), \upsilon_{A^i}\left(x\right)\right) : x \in X\right\}$, where the $\mu_{A^i}\left(x\right) : X \to [0,1]$ and $\upsilon_{A^i}\left(x\right) : X \to [0,1]$ define the degree of membership and degree of non-membership respectively, of the element $x \in X$ to the set A^i which is a subset of X, for every element of $x \in X$, $0 \le \mu_{A^i}\left(x\right) + \upsilon_{A^i}\left(x\right) \le 1$.

Definition 2.11: Intuitionistic Fuzzy Number: An IFN A^i is defined as follows:

1. An intuitionistic fuzzy subject of real line
2. Normal i.e., there is any $x_0 \in R$ such that $\mu_{A^i}(x_0) = 1$ (so $\upsilon_{A^i}(x_0) = 0$)
3. A convex set for the membership function $\mu_{A^i}(x)$, i.e.,

$$\mu_{A^i}(\lambda x_1 + (1-\lambda)x_2) \ge \min(\mu_{A^i}(x_1), \mu_{A^i}(x_2)) \quad \forall x_1, x_2 \in R, \lambda \in [0,1]$$

4. A concave set for the non-membership function $\upsilon_{A^i}(x)$, i.e.,

$$\upsilon_{A^i}(\lambda x_1 + (1-\lambda)x_2) \ge \max(\upsilon_{A^i}(x_1), \upsilon_{A^i}(x_2)) \quad \forall x_1, x_2 \in R, \lambda \in [0,1]$$

Definition 2.12: Triangular Intuitionistic Fuzzy Number: A TIFN A^i is a subset of IFN in R with following membership function and non membership function as follows:

$$\mu_{A^i}\left(x\right) = \begin{cases} \dfrac{x - a_1}{a_2 - a_1}, & a_1 \le x < a_2 \\ 1, & x = a_2 \\ \dfrac{a_3 - x}{a_3 - a_2}, & a_2 < x \le a_3 \\ 0, & otherwise \end{cases} \quad \text{and} \quad \upsilon_{A^i}\left(x\right) = \begin{cases} \dfrac{a_2 - x}{a_2 - a_1'}, & a_1' \le x < a_2 \\ 0, & x = a_2 \\ \dfrac{x - a_2}{a_3' - a_2}, & a_2 < x \le a_3' \\ 1, & otherwise \end{cases}$$

where $a_1' \le a_2 \le a_3'$ and $a_1 \le a_2 \le a_3$.

The TIFN is denoted by $A_{TIFN}{}^i = (a_1 \le a_2 \le a_3; a_1' \le a_2 \le a_3')$.

NON LINEAR INTUITIONISTIC FUZZY NUMBER

Definition 3.1: A NIFN A^{ni} is a subset of IFN in R with following membership function and non membership function as follows:

$$\mu_{A^{ni}}\left(x\right) = \begin{cases} \left(\dfrac{x - a_1}{a_2 - a_1}\right)^p, & a_1 \le x < a_2 \\ 1, & x = a_2 \\ \left(\dfrac{a_3 - x}{a_3 - a_2}\right)^q, & a_2 < x \le a_3 \\ 0, & otherwise \end{cases} \quad \text{and} \quad \upsilon_{A^{ni}}\left(x\right) = \begin{cases} \left(\dfrac{a_2 - x}{a_2 - a_1'}\right)^r, & a_1' \le x < a_2 \\ 0, & x = a_2 \\ \left(\dfrac{x - a_2}{a_3' - a_2}\right)^s, & a_2 < x \le a_3' \\ 1, & otherwise \end{cases}$$

where $a_1^{'} \le a_2 \le a_3^{'}$ and $a_1 \le a_2 \le a_3$.

The NIFN is denoted by $A_{NIFN}^{ni} = (a_1 \le a_2 \le a_3; a_1^{'} \le a_2 \le a_3^{'})$. Where p, q, r and s are suitable chosen constant.

Definition 3.2: α-Cut Set: A α-cut set of $A_{NIFN}^{ni} = (a_1 \le a_2 \le a_3; a_1^{'} \le a_2 \le a_3^{'})$ is a crisp subset of R which is defined as follows

$$A_\alpha = \left\{x : \mu_{A^{ni}}(x) \ge \alpha, \forall \alpha \in [0,1]\right\} = [A_1(\alpha), A_2(\alpha)] = [a_1 + \alpha^{\frac{1}{p}}(a_2 - a_1), a_3 - \alpha^{\frac{1}{q}}(a_3 - a_2)]$$

Definition 3.3: β-Cut Set: A β-cut set of $A_{NIFN}^{ni} = (a_1 \le a_2 \le a_3; a_1^{'} \le a_2 \le a_3^{'})$ is a crisp subset of R which is defined as follows

$$A_\beta = \left\{x : \upsilon_{A^{ni}}(x) \le \beta, \forall \beta \in [0,1]\right\} = [A_1^{'}(\beta), A_2^{'}(\beta)] = [a_2 - \beta^{\frac{1}{r}}(a_2 - a_1^{'}), a_2 + \beta^{\frac{1}{s}}(a_3^{'} - a_2)]$$

Definition 3.4: (α,β) -Cut Set: A (α,β) -cut set of $A_{NIFN}^{ni} = (a_1 \le a_2 \le a_3; a_1^{'} \le a_2 \le a_3^{'})$ is a crisp subset of R *which* is defined as follows

$$A_{(\alpha,\beta)} = \left\{[A_1(\alpha), A_2(\alpha)]; [A_1^{'}(\beta), A_2^{'}(\beta)]\right\}, \alpha + \beta \le 1, \alpha \in [0,1], \beta \in [0,1]$$

Theorem 3.1: The sum of membership and non-membership function at any particular point is between 0 and 1.

i.e., if for a non-linear intuitionistic fuzzy number $A_{NIFN}^{ni} = (a_1 \le a_2 \le a_3; a_1^{'} \le a_2 \le a_3^{'})$ membership and non-membership function is denoted by $\mu_{A^{ni}}(x)$ and $\upsilon_{A^{ni}}(x)$ then'

$$0 < \mu_{A^{ni}}(x) + \upsilon_{A^{ni}}(x) \le 1.$$

INTUITIONISTIC DIFFERENCE AND INTUITIONISTIC PARTIAL DERIVATIVE

Generalized Hukuhara Derivative on Intuitionistic Fuzzy Valued Function

Definition 4.1: The Hausdorff distance between intuitionistic fuzzy number is given by $D : R_F \times R_F \to R^+ \cup \{0\}$ as

$$D(u,v;p,q) = \sup_{\alpha,\beta \in [0,1]} d([u]_\alpha, [v]_\alpha; [p]_\beta, [q]_\beta)$$
$$= \sup_{\alpha,\beta \in [0,1]} \max\left\{\left|u_1(\alpha) - v_1(\alpha)\right|, \left|u_2(\alpha) - v_2(\alpha)\right|; \left|p_1(\beta) - q_1(\beta)\right|, \left|p_2(\beta) - q_2(\beta)\right|\right\}$$

Definition 4.2: The generalized Hukuhara difference of two intuitionistic fuzzy numbers $a,b\in R_{iF}$ is defined as follows

$$a -_{igH} b = k \Leftrightarrow \begin{cases} a = b + k \\ b = a + (-1)k \end{cases}$$

In terms of (α,β) -cut set we have

$$[a -_{igH} b]_{\alpha,\beta} = [\min\{r_1(\alpha), r_2(\alpha)\}, \max\{r_1(\alpha), r_2(\alpha)\}; \max\{s_1(\beta), s_2(\beta)\}, \min\{s_1(\beta), s_2(\beta)\}]$$

where, $r_1(\alpha) = a_1(\alpha) - b_2(\alpha)$, $r_2(\alpha) = a_2(\alpha) - b_1(\alpha)$, $s_1(\beta) = a_1^{'}(\beta) - b_2^{'}(\beta)$ and $s_2(\beta) = a_2^{'}(\beta) - b_1^{'}(\beta)$

Let $e = a -_{igH} b$

The conditions for which the existence of $a -_{igH} b$ exists

1. $e_1(\alpha) = a_1(\alpha) - b_2(\alpha)$, $e_2(\alpha) = a_2(\alpha) - b_1(\alpha)$, $e_1^{'}(\beta) = a_1^{'}(\beta) - b_2^{'}(\beta)$ and $e_2^{'}(\beta) = a_2^{'}(\beta) - b_1^{'}(\beta)$ with $e_1(\alpha)$, $e_2^{'}(\beta)$ are increasing and $e_2(\alpha)$, $e_1^{'}(\beta)$ are decreasing function for α,β∈[0,1], $e_1(\alpha) \le e_2(\alpha)$ and $e_1^{'}(\beta) \ge e_2^{'}(\beta)$.
2. $e_2(\alpha) = a_1(\alpha) - b_2(\alpha)$, $e_1(\alpha) = a_2(\alpha) - b_1(\alpha)$, $e_2^{'}(\beta) = a_1^{'}(\beta) - b_2^{'}(\beta)$ and $e_1^{'}(\beta) = a_2^{'}(\beta) - b_1^{'}(\beta)$ with $e_2(\alpha)$, $e_1^{'}(\beta)$ are increasing and $e_1(\alpha)$, $e_2^{'}(\beta)$ are decreasing function for all α,β∈[0,1] and $e_2(\alpha) \le e_1(\alpha)$, $e_2^{'}(\beta) \ge e_1^{'}(\beta)$.

Remark 4.1: Throughout the paper, we assume that $a -_{igH} b \in R_{iF}$.

Definition 4.3: Generalized Hukuhara Derivative: The generalized Hukuhara derivative of an intuitionistic fuzzy valued function *f*: (*a,b*)→R_{iF} at t_0 is defined as

$$f^{'}(t_0) = \lim_{h\to 0} \frac{f(t_0 + h) -_{igH} f(t_0)}{h} \tag{2.1}$$

If $f^{'}(t_0) \in R_{iF}$ satisfying (2.1) exists, we say that *f*(*t*) is generalized Hukuhara differentiable at t_0. Also we say that *f*(*t*) is (i)-igH differentiable at t_0 if

$$[f^{'}(t_0)]_{\alpha,\beta} = [f_1^{'}(t_0,\alpha), f_2^{'}(t_0,\alpha); g_1^{'}(t_0,\alpha), g_2^{'}(t_0,\alpha)] \tag{2.2}$$

and *f*(*t*) is (ii)-igH differentiable at t_0 if

$$[f^{'}(t_0)]_{\alpha,\beta} = [f_2^{'}(t_0,\alpha), f_1^{'}(t_0,\alpha); g_2^{'}(t_0,\alpha), g_1^{'}(t_0,\alpha)] \tag{2.3}$$

where (α,β)-cut of *f*(*t*) is $[f_1(t_0,\alpha), f_2(t_0,\alpha); g_1(t_0,\alpha), g_2(t_0,\alpha)]$

Remarks 4.2: In whole paper we consider (i)-igH derivative.

Generalized Hukuhara Partial Differentiation on Intuitionistic Fuzzy Valued Function

Definition 4.4: Let $f(x,t)$ is a intuitionistic fuzzy valued function of two variable. Let $(x_0,t_0)\in D$, then the first order generalized Hukuhara partial derivative of the said intuitionistic fuzzy valued function with respect to the variable x and t are denoted by $\partial_{x_{igH}} f(x_0,t_0)$ and $\partial_{t_{igH}} f(x_0,t_0)$ and is derived by the formulae

$$\partial_{x_{igH}} f(x_0,t_0) = \lim_{h\to 0} \frac{f(x_0+h,t_0) -_{igH} f(x_0,t_0)}{h}$$

$$\partial_{t_{igH}} f(x_0,t_0) = \lim_{k\to 0} \frac{f(x_0,t_0+k) -_{igH} f(x_0,t_0)}{k}$$

Provided that $\partial_{x_{igH}} f(x_0,t_0)$ and $\partial_{t_{igH}} f(x_0,t_0) \in R_{iF}$.

PARTIAL DIFFERENTIAL EQUATION IN INTUITIONISTIC FUZZY ENVIRONMENT

Intuitionistic Fuzzy Partial Differential Equation

Consider the boundary value problem

$$\varphi(D_x, D_y)U(x,y) = F(x,y,k)$$

subject to the boundary condition

$$U(0,y) = c_1,\quad U(x,0) = c_2,\quad U(M_1,y) = c_3,\ldots$$

or,

$$U(0,y) = g_1(y;c_4),\quad U(x,0) = f_1(x;c_5),\ldots$$

or,

$$U_x(x,0) = f_2(x,c_6),\quad U_y(0,y) = g_2(y;c_7,c_8),\ldots$$

The above differential equation is said to be intuitionistic fuzzy partial differential equation if

1. Any one of or all or some of $c_1,c_2,c_3,c_4,\ldots$ are intuitionistic fuzzy number.
2. Only the coefficient k is intuitionistic fuzzy number.
3. Both the coefficient k and any one of or all or some of $c_1,c_2,c_3,c_4,\ldots$ are intuitionistic fuzzy number.

Here $\varphi(D_x,D_y)$ is the polynomial with constant coefficients in D_x and D_y.
Let the (α,β) -cut of $U(x,y)$ be

$$U(x,y)[\alpha,\beta]=[U_1(x,y;\alpha),U_2(x,y;\alpha);U_1'(x,y;\beta),U_2'(x,y;\beta)]$$

Condition for Existence for Solution Partial Differential Equation

Consider the intuitionistic fuzzy Partial Differential Equation

$$\varphi(D_x,D_y)U(x,y)=F(x,y,k)$$

Let the solution of the above IFPDE be $U(x,y)$ and its (α,β)-cut be
$U(x,y)[\alpha,\beta]=[U_1(x,y;\alpha),U_2(x,y;\alpha);U_1'(x,y;\beta),U_2'(x,y;\beta)]$
The solution is a strong solution if

1. $\dfrac{\partial U_1(x,y;\alpha)}{\partial\alpha}>0,\dfrac{\partial U_2(x,y;\alpha)}{\partial\alpha}<0\forall\alpha\in[0,1],U_1(x,y;1)\le U_2(x,y;1)$
2. $\dfrac{\partial U_1'(x,y;\beta)}{\partial\beta}<0,\dfrac{\partial U_2'(x,y;\beta)}{\partial\beta}>0\forall\beta\in[0,1],U_1'(x,y;0)\ge U_2'(x,y;0)$

Otherwise the solution is week solution.

Solution of Intutionistic Fuzzy Partial Differential Equation

Problem 5.1: Consider the partial differential equation $\dfrac{\partial U(x,y)}{\partial x}=a^2\dfrac{\partial U(x,y)}{\partial y}$ with initial condition $U(0,y)=ce^{-py}$, where a and c are intuitionistic fuzzy numbers.
Solution: Taking (α,β)-cut of the partial differential equation we have

$$\frac{\partial U_1(x,y;\alpha)}{\partial x}=a_1(\alpha)\frac{\partial U_1(x,y;\alpha)}{\partial y}$$

$$\frac{\partial U_2(x,y;\alpha)}{\partial x}=a_2(\alpha)\frac{\partial U_2(x,y;\alpha)}{\partial y}$$

$$\frac{\partial U_1'(x,y;\beta)}{\partial x}=a_1'(\beta)\frac{\partial U_1'(x,y;\beta)}{\partial y}$$

$$\frac{\partial U_2'(x,y;\beta)}{\partial x} = a_2'(\beta)\frac{\partial U_2'(x,y;\beta)}{\partial y}$$

where the (α,β)-cut of the solution $U(x,y)$ is $[U_1(x,y;\alpha), U_2(x,y;\alpha); U_1'(x,y;\beta), U_2'(x,y;\beta)]$ and a^2 is $[a_1(\alpha), a_2(\alpha); a_1'(\beta), a_2'(\beta)]$.

The(α,β)-cutofinitialcondition $U_1(0,y;\alpha) = c_1(\alpha)e^{-py}$, $U_2(0,y;\alpha) = c_2(\alpha)e^{-py}$, $U_1'(0,y;\beta) = c_1'(\beta)e^{-py}$ and $U_2'(0,y;\beta) = c_2'(\beta)e^{-py}$.

The general solution of the partial differential equation is

$$U_1(x,y;\alpha) = c_1(\alpha)e^{-(a_1(\alpha)x+y)p}$$

$$U_2(x,y;\alpha) = c_2(\alpha)e^{-(a_2(\alpha)x+y)p}$$

$$U_1'(x,y;\beta) = c_1'(\beta)e^{-(a_1'(\beta)x+y)p}$$

$$U_2'(x,y;\beta) = c_2'(\beta)e^{-(a_2'(\beta)x+y)p}$$

The above solution is strong solution if $U_1(x,y;\alpha)$, $U_2'(x,y;\beta)$ is increasing function and $U_2(x,y;\alpha)$, $U_1'(x,y;\beta)$ is decreasing function. Otherwise it is week solution.

Example 5.1: a=(2,4,6; 1,4,8) and c=(7,8,10; 5,8,11)$^{-3y}$ with p, q, r, s=2

The (α,β)-cut of a is $[2+2\alpha^{\frac{1}{2}}, 6-2\alpha^{\frac{1}{2}}; 4-3\beta^{\frac{1}{2}}, 4+4\beta^{\frac{1}{2}}]$ and c is $[7+\alpha^{\frac{1}{2}}, 10-2\alpha^{\frac{1}{2}}; 8-3\beta^{\frac{1}{2}}, 8+3\beta^{\frac{1}{2}}]e^{-3y}$

Now α -cut of a^2 is

$$[\min\left\{\left(2+2\alpha^{\frac{1}{2}}\right)^2, \left(2+2\alpha^{\frac{1}{2}}\right)\left(6-2\alpha^{\frac{1}{2}}\right), \left(6-2\alpha^{\frac{1}{2}}\right)^2\right\}, \max\left\{\left(2+2\alpha^{\frac{1}{2}}\right)^2, \left(2+2\alpha^{\frac{1}{2}}\right)\left(6-2\alpha^{\frac{1}{2}}\right), \left(6-2\alpha^{\frac{1}{2}}\right)^2\right\}]$$

and β -cut of a^2 is

$$[\max\left\{\left(4-3\beta^{\frac{1}{2}}\right)^2, \left(4-3\beta^{\frac{1}{2}}\right)\left(4+4\beta^{\frac{1}{2}}\right), \left(4+4\beta^{\frac{1}{2}}\right)^2\right\}, \min\left\{\left(4-3\beta^{\frac{1}{2}}\right)^2, \left(4-3\beta^{\frac{1}{2}}\right)\left(4+4\beta^{\frac{1}{2}}\right), \left(4+4\beta^{\frac{1}{2}}\right)^2\right\}]$$

Table 1. Possible value of α-cut of a^2 for different α

α	$\left(2+2\alpha^{\frac{1}{2}}\right)^2$	$\left(2+2\alpha^{\frac{1}{2}}\right)\left(6-2\alpha^{\frac{1}{2}}\right)$	$\left(6-2\alpha^{\frac{1}{2}}\right)^2$
0	4.0000	12.0000	36.0000
0.1	6.9298	14.1298	28.8105
0.2	8.3777	14.7777	26.0669
0.3	9.5818	15.1818	24.0547
0.4	10.6596	15.4596	22.4211
0.5	11.6569	15.6569	21.0294
0.6	12.5968	15.7968	19.8097
0.7	13.4933	15.8933	18.7202
0.8	14.3554	15.9554	17.7337
0.9	15.1895	15.9895	16.8316
1	16.0000	16.0000	16.0000

Figure 1. Possible plot of α-cut of a^2 for α∈[0,1]

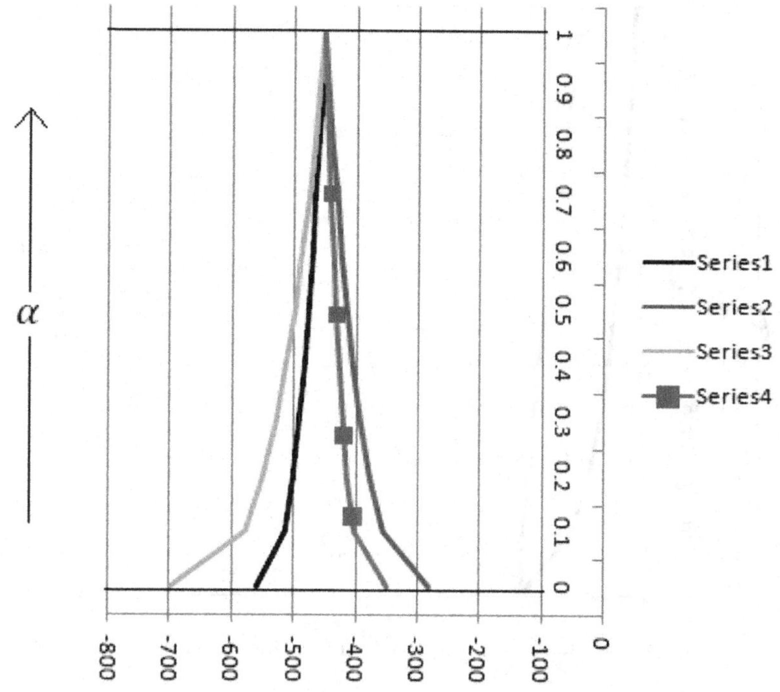

Table 2. Possible value of β-cut of $a^2$for different β

β	$\left(4-3\beta^{\frac{1}{2}}\right)^2$	$\left(4-3\beta^{\frac{1}{2}}\right)\left(4+4\beta^{\frac{1}{2}}\right)$	$\left(4+4\beta^{\frac{1}{2}}\right)^2$
0	16.0000	16.0000	16.0000
0.1	9.3105	16.0649	26.0544
0.2	7.0669	15.3889	30.9220
0.3	5.5547	14.5909	34.9362
0.4	4.4211	13.7298	38.5088
0.5	3.5294	12.8284	41.7990
0.6	2.8097	11.8984	44.8887
0.7	2.2202	10.9466	47.8265
0.8	1.7337	9.9777	50.6440
0.9	1.3316	8.9947	53.3631
1	1.0000	8.0000	56.0000

Figure 2. Possible plot of β-cut of a^2 for β∈[0,1]

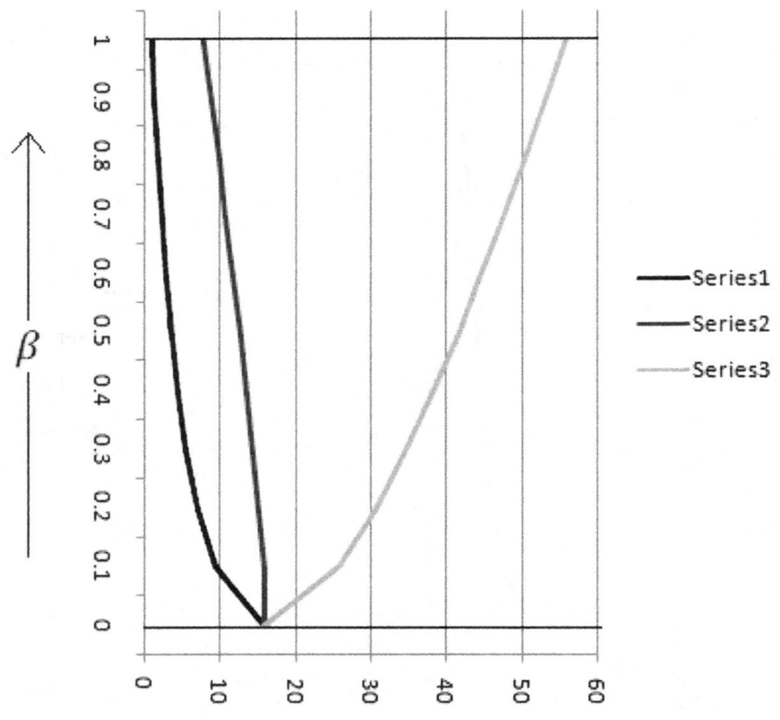

Now we check what is the α-cut and β-cut of the number a^2. We should check the maximum and minimum function from the above results.

From the above table and graph we conclude that the (α,β) -cut of a^2 is defined as

$$\left[\left(2+2\alpha^{\frac{1}{2}}\right)^2,\left(6-2\alpha^{\frac{1}{2}}\right)^2;\left(4-3\beta^{\frac{1}{2}}\right)^2,\left(4+4\beta^{\frac{1}{2}}\right)^2\right]$$

So the solution is given by

$$U_1(x,y;\alpha)=\left(7+\alpha^{\frac{1}{2}}\right)e^{-3\left(\left(2+2\alpha^{\frac{1}{2}}\right)^2x+y\right)}$$

$$U_2(x,y;\alpha)=\left(10-2\alpha^{\frac{1}{2}}\right)e^{-3\left(\left(6-2\alpha^{\frac{1}{2}}\right)^2x+y\right)}$$

$$U_1'(x,y;\beta)=\left(8-3\beta^{\frac{1}{2}}\right)e^{-3\left(\left(4-3\beta^{\frac{1}{2}}\right)^2x+y\right)}$$

Table 3. Value of $U_1(x,y;\alpha)$, $U_2(x,y;\alpha)$, $U_1'(x,y;\beta)$ and $U_2'(x,y;\beta)$ at x=2, y=3 for different α,β

α,β	$U_1(x,y;\alpha)$	$U_2(x,y;\alpha)$	$U_1'(x,y;\beta)$	$U_2'(x,y;\beta)$
0	7.0000	10.0000	8.0000	8.0000
0.1	7.3162	9.3675	7.0513	8.9487
0.2	7.4472	9.1056	6.6584	9.3416
0.3	7.5477	8.9046	6.3568	9.6432
0.4	7.6325	8.7351	6.1026	9.8974
0.5	7.7071	8.5858	5.8787	10.1213
0.6	7.7746	8.4508	5.6762	10.3238
0.7	7.8367	8.3267	5.4900	10.5100
0.8	7.8944	8.2111	5.3167	10.6833
0.9	7.9487	8.1026	5.1540	10.8460
1	8.0000	8.0000	5.0000	11.0000

Figure 3. Plot of $U_1(x,y;\alpha)$, $U_2(x,y;\alpha)$, $U_1'(x,y;\beta)$ and $U_2'(x,y;\beta)$ at x=2, y=3 for $\alpha,\beta\in[0,1]$

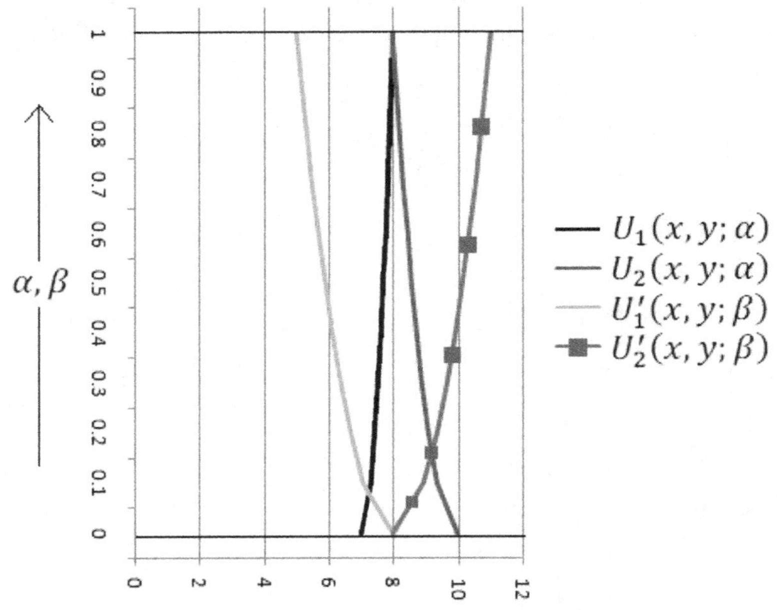

$$U_2'(x,y;\beta) = \left(8 + 3\beta^{\frac{1}{2}}\right) e^{-3\left(\left(4+4\beta^{\frac{1}{2}}\right)^2 x + y\right)}$$

Remark 5.1: Clearly from graph and table we see that $U_1(x,y;\alpha), U_2'(x,y;\beta)$ is increasing function and $U_2(x,y;\alpha)$, $U_1'(x,y;\beta)$ is decreasing function at $x=2$, $y=3$. Hence for the particular point the solution is a strong solution.

Problem 5.2: Consider the partial differential equation $\frac{\partial V(x,y)}{\partial x \partial y} = k$ with initial condition $V(0,y)=c$ sin y and $\frac{\partial V(x,1)}{\partial x} = dx^2$, where k, c and d are intutionistic fuzzy number.

Solution: Taking (α,β) -cut of the partial differential equation we have

$$\frac{\partial^2 V_1(x,y;\alpha)}{\partial x \partial y} = k_1(\alpha)$$

$$\frac{\partial^2 V_2(x,y;\alpha)}{\partial x \partial y} = k_2(\alpha)$$

$$\frac{\partial^2 V_1'(x,y;\beta)}{\partial x \partial y} = k_1'(\beta)$$

$$\frac{\partial^2 V_2^{'}(x,y;\beta)}{\partial x \partial y} = k_2^{'}(\beta)$$

With boundary condition $V_1(0,y;\alpha)=c_1(\alpha)\sin y$, $V_2(0,y;\alpha)=c_2(\alpha)\sin y$, $V_1^{'}(0,y;\beta) = c_1^{'}(\beta)\sin y$, $V_2^{'}(0,y;\beta) = c_2^{'}(\beta)\sin y$

and

$$\frac{\partial V_1(x,1;\alpha)}{\partial x} = d_1(\alpha)x^2$$

$$\frac{\partial V_2(x,1;\alpha)}{\partial x} = d_2(\alpha)x^2$$

$$\frac{\partial V_1^{'}(x,1;\beta)}{\partial x} = d_1^{'}(\beta)x^2$$

$$\frac{\partial V_2^{'}(x,1;\beta)}{\partial x} = d_2^{'}(\beta)x^2$$

The solution is

$$V_1(x,y;\alpha) = k_1(\alpha)x(y-1) + \frac{d_1(\alpha)}{3}x^3 + c_1(\alpha)\sin y$$

$$V_2(x,y;\alpha) = k_2(\alpha)x(y-1) + \frac{d_2(\alpha)}{3}x^3 + c_2(\alpha)\sin y$$

$$V_1^{'}(x,y;\beta) = k_1^{'}(\beta)x(y-1) + \frac{d_1^{'}(\beta)}{3}x^3 + c_1^{'}(\beta)\sin y$$

$$V_2^{'}(x,y;\beta) = k_2^{'}(\beta)x(y-1) + \frac{d_2^{'}(\beta)}{3}x^3 + c_2^{'}(\beta)\sin y$$

The above solution is a strong solution if $V_1(x,y;\alpha)$, $V_2^{'}(x,y;\beta)$ is increasing function and $V_2(x,y;\alpha)$, $V_1^{'}(x,y;\beta)$ is decreasing function, otherwise it is a week solution.

Example 5.2: Solve $\frac{\partial^2 V(x,y)}{\partial x \partial y} = k$ with initial condition $V(0,y)=c\sin y$ and $\frac{\partial V(x,1)}{\partial x} = dx^2$, where $k=(5,7,8;4,7,10)$, $c=(0.75,1,1.25;0.65,1,1.35)$ and $d=(0.50,0.70,0.80;0.60,0.70,0.90)$, $p,q,r,s = \frac{1}{3}$.

Solution: Here

$$(k)_{\alpha,\beta} = \left[5 + 2\alpha^{\frac{1}{3}}, 8 - \alpha^{\frac{1}{3}}; 7 - 3\beta^{\frac{1}{3}}, 7 + 3\beta^{\frac{1}{3}}\right]$$

$$(c)_{\alpha,\beta} = \left[0.75 + 0.25\alpha^{\frac{1}{3}}, 1.25 - 0.25\alpha^{\frac{1}{3}}; 1 - 0.35\beta^{\frac{1}{3}}, 1 + 0.35\beta^{\frac{1}{3}}\right]$$

$$(d)_{\alpha,\beta} = \left[0.50 + 0.20\alpha^{\frac{1}{3}}, 0.80 - 0.10\alpha^{\frac{1}{3}}; 0.70 - 0.10\beta^{\frac{1}{3}}, 0.70 + 0.20\beta^{\frac{1}{3}}\right]$$

The solution is

$$V_1(x,y;\alpha) = \left(5 + 2\alpha^{\frac{1}{3}}\right)x(y-1) + \frac{1}{3}\left(0.50 + 0.20\alpha^{\frac{1}{3}}\right)x^3 + \left(0.75 + 0.25\alpha^{\frac{1}{3}}\right)\sin y$$

$$V_2(x,y;\alpha) = \left(8 - \alpha^{\frac{1}{3}}\right)x(y-1) + \frac{1}{3}\left(0.80 - 0.10\alpha^{\frac{1}{3}}\right)x^3 + \left(1.25 - 0.25\alpha^{\frac{1}{3}}\right)\sin y$$

Table 4. Value of $V_1(x,y;\alpha)$, $V_2(x,y;\alpha)$, $V_1'(x,y;\beta)$, $V_2'(x,y;\beta)$ at x=5 and y=8 for different α,β

α,β	$V_1(x,y;\alpha)$	$V_2(x,y;\alpha)$	$V_1'(x,y;\beta)$	$V_2'(x,y;\beta)$
0	196.5754	314.5700	275.1560	275.1560
0.1	233.0493	296.2757	224.3246	327.9214
0.2	242.5296	291.5206	211.1125	341.6363
0.3	249.1798	288.1850	201.8445	351.2569
0.4	254.4741	285.5295	194.4662	358.9159
0.5	258.9449	283.2871	188.2355	365.3836
0.6	262.8529	281.3270	182.7892	371.0371
0.7	266.3474	279.5742	177.9190	376.0926
0.8	269.5232	277.9813	173.4932	380.6868
0.9	272.4442	276.5162	169.4224	384.9125
1	275.1560	275.1560	165.6431	388.8356

Figure 4. Plot of $V_1(x,y;\alpha)$, $V_2(x,y;\alpha)$, $V_1'(x,y;\beta)$ and $V_2'(x,y;\beta)$ at x=5 and y=8 for $\alpha,\beta\in[0,1]$

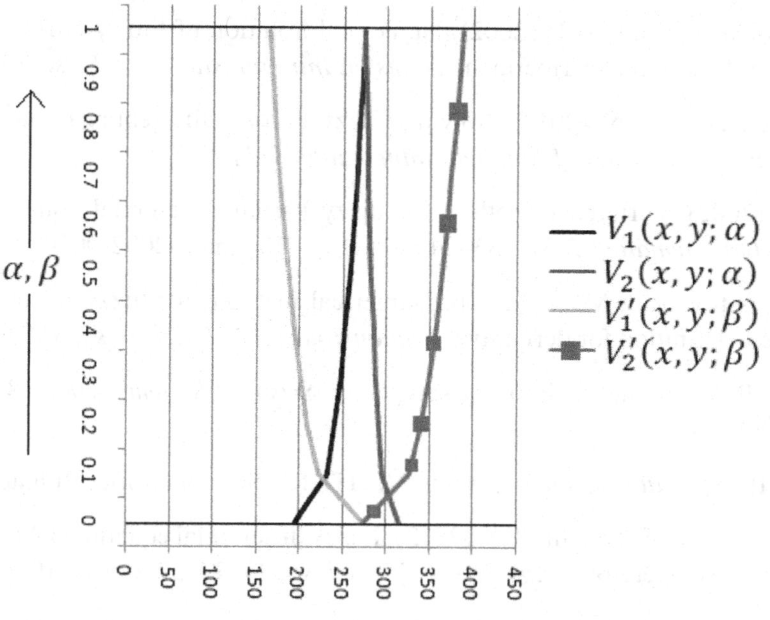

$$V_1'(x,y;\beta)=\left(7-3\beta^{\frac{1}{3}}\right)x(y-1)+\frac{1}{3}\left(0.70-0.10\beta^{\frac{1}{3}}\right)x^3+\left(1-0.35\beta^{\frac{1}{3}}\right)\sin y$$

$$V_2'(x,y;\beta)=\left(7+3\beta^{\frac{1}{3}}\right)x(y-1)+\frac{1}{3}\left(0.70+0.20\beta^{\frac{1}{3}}\right)x^3+\left(1+0.35\beta^{\frac{1}{3}}\right)\sin y$$

Remark 5.2: Clearly from graph and table we see that $V_1(x,y;\alpha)$, $V_2'(x,y;\beta)$ is increasing function and $V_2(x,y;\alpha)$, $V_1'(x,y;\beta)$ is decreasing function at $x=5$ and $y=8$. Hence for the particular point the solution is a strong solution.

CONCLUSION

It is not necessary that the degree of membership and non membership function of an intuitionistic fuzzy number is linear. It's may be non-linear. If its non linear then it's order may be fraction or may not. For taking the above concept we introduce non-linear intuitionistic fuzzy number (NIFN). Finally use this number in partial differential equation. The chapter help the researcher who are deal with uncertainty. In future any one can use this concept on different type fuzzy number and apply in various fields of science and engineering.

REFERENCES

Abbasbandy, S., & Allahviranloo, T. (2002). Numerical Solution of Fuzzy Differential Equations by Runge-Kutta and the Intuitionistic Treatment. *Notes on Intuitionistic Fuzzy Sets*, *8*(3), 43–53.

Ahmadi, M. B., & Kiani, N. A. (2011). Solving Fuzzy Partial Differential Equation by Differential Transformation Method. *eJournal of Applied Mathematics, 7*(4).

Allahviranloo, T. (2002). Difference method for fuzzy partial differential equation. *Computational Methods in Applied Mathematics*, *2*(3), 233–242. doi:10.2478/cmam-2002-0014

Allahviranloo, T., & Kermani, M. A. (2010). Numerical methods for fuzzy linear partial differential equations under new definition for derivative. *Iranian Journal of Fuzzy Sets and System*, *7*(3), 33–50.

Atanassov, K. T. (1986). Intuitionistic fuzzy sets. *Fuzzy Sets and Systems*, *20*(1), 87–96. doi:10.1016/S0165-0114(86)80034-3

Atanassov, K. T. (1983). *Intuitionistic fuzzy sets*. VII ITKR's Session, Sofia, Bulgarian.

Barros, L. C., Gomes, L. T., & Tonelli, P. A. (2013). Fuzzy differential equations: An approach via fuzzification of the derivative operator. *Fuzzy Sets and Systems*, *230*, 39–52. doi:10.1016/j.fss.2013.03.004

Bede, B. (2006). A note on two-point boundary value problems associated with non-linear fuzzy differential equations. *Fuzzy Sets and Systems*, *157*(7), 986–989. doi:10.1016/j.fss.2005.09.006

Bede, B., & Gal, S. G. (2005). Generalizations of the differentiability of fuzzy-number-valued functions with applications to fuzzy differential equations. *Fuzzy Sets and Systems*, *151*(3), 581–599. doi:10.1016/j.fss.2004.08.001

Bede, B., Rudas, I. J., & Bencsik, A. L. (2007). First order linear fuzzy differential equations under generalized differentiability. *Inf.Sci.*, *177*(7), 1648–1662. doi:10.1016/j.ins.2006.08.021

Bede, B., & Stefanini, L. (2013). Generalized differentiability of fuzzy-valued functions. *Fuzzy Sets and Systems*, *230*, 119–141. doi:10.1016/j.fss.2012.10.003

Bertone, A. M., Jafelice, R. M., Barros, L. C., & Bassanezi, R. C. (2013). On fuzzy solutions for partial differential equations. *Fuzzy Sets and Systems*, *219*, 68–80. doi:10.1016/j.fss.2012.12.002

Breuss, M., & Dietrich, D. (2009). *Fuzzy Numerical Schemes for Hyperbolic Differential Equations*. Springer-Verlag Berlin Heidelberg.

Buckley, J. J., & Feuring, T. (1999). Introduction to fuzzy partial differential equations. *Fuzzy Sets and Systems*, *105*(2), 241–248. doi:10.1016/S0165-0114(98)00323-6

Chalco-Cano, Y., & Román-Flores, H. (2008). On the new solution of fuzzy differential equations. *Chaos, Solitons, and Fractals*, *38*(1), 112–119. doi:10.1016/j.chaos.2006.10.043

Chang, S. L., & Zadeh, L. A. (1972). On fuzzy mapping and control. *IEEE Transactions on Systems, Man, and Cybernetics*, *2*(1), 30–34. doi:10.1109/TSMC.1972.5408553

Chen, Y. Y., Chang, Y. T., & Chen, B. S. (2009). Fuzzy Solutions to Partial Differential Equations: Adaptive Approach. *IEEE Transactions on Fuzzy Systems*, *17*(1).

Corveleyn, S., & Vandewalle, S. (2010). On the numerical solution of fuzzy elliptic PDEs by means of polynomial response surfaces. *Proceeding of ISMA 2010*.

Dubois, D., & Prade, H. (1982). Towards fuzzy differential calculus: Part 3, Differentiation. *Fuzzy Sets and Systems*, *8*(3), 225–233. doi:10.1016/S0165-0114(82)80001-8

Farajzadeh, A., & Pour, A. H. (2010). An Explicit Method for Solving Fuzzy Partial Differential Equation. *International Mathematical Forum*, *5*(21), 1025-1036.

Gasilov, N., Amrahov, S. E., Fatullayev, A. G., & Khastan, A. (2014). *A new approach to fuzzy initial value problem*. Academic Press.

Goetschel, R. Jr, & Voxman, W. (1986). Elementary fuzzy calculus. *Fuzzy Sets and Systems*, *18*(1), 31–43. doi:10.1016/0165-0114(86)90026-6

Kaleva, O. (1987). Fuzzy differential equations. *Fuzzy Sets and Systems*, *24*(3), 301–317. doi:10.1016/0165-0114(87)90029-7

Khastan, A., & Nieto, J. J. (2010). A boundary value problem for second-order fuzzy differential equations. *Nonlinear Analysis*, *72*(9-10), 3583–3593. doi:10.1016/j.na.2009.12.038

Lata, S., & Kumar, A. (2012, July). A new method to solve time-dependent intuitionistic fuzzy differential equation and its application to analyze the intutionistic fuzzy reliability of industrial system. *Concurrent Engineering: Research and Applications*, 1-8.

Melliani, S., & Chadli, L. S. (2001). Introduction to intuitionistic fuzzy partial differential Equations. *Fifth Int. Conf. on IFSs*.

Mondal, S.P., & Roy, T.K. (2014). First order homogeneous ordinary differential equation with initial value as triangular intuitionistic fuzzy number. *Journal of Uncertainty in Mathematics Science*, 1-17.

Mondal, S. P., & Roy, T. K. (2015). System of Differential Equation with Initial Value as Triangular Intuitionistic Fuzzy Number and its Application. *Int. J. Appl. Comput. Math*, *1*(1), 449–474. doi:10.1007/s40819-015-0026-x

Orouji, B., Parandin, N., Abasabadi, L., & Hosseinpour, A. (2014). *An Implicit Method for Solving Fuzzy Partial Differential Equation with Nonlocal Boundary Conditions*. Academic Press.

Puri, M. L., & Ralescu, D. A. (1983). Differentials of fuzzy functions. *Journal of Mathematical Analysis and Applications*, *91*(2), 552–558. doi:10.1016/0022-247X(83)90169-5

Saikia, R. K. (2011). Fuzzy numerical solution of Poisson equation using fuzzy data. *International Journal of Engineering Science and Technology*, *3*(12), 8450–8456.

Salahshour, S., & Haghi, E. (2010). Solving fuzzy heat equation by Fuzzy Laplace transform. *IPMU*, 512-521.

Stefanini, L. (2008). A generalization of Hukuhara difference for interval and fuzzy arithmetic. In D. Dubois, M. A. Lubiano, H. Prade, M. A. Gil, P. Grzegorzewski, & O. Hryniewicz (Eds.), *Soft Methods for Handling Variability and Imprecision, in: Series on Advances in Soft Computing, 48*. doi:10.1007/978-3-540-85027-4_25

Stefanini, L., & Bede, B. (2009). Generalized Hukuhara differentiability of interval-valued functions and interval differential equations. *Nonlinear Analysis, 71*(3-4), 1311–1328. doi:10.1016/j.na.2008.12.005

Tapaswini, S., & Chakraverty, S. (2013). iNumerical Solution of Uncertain Beam Equations Using Double Parametric Form of Fuzzy Numbers. *Applied Computational Intelligence and Soft Computing, 2013*, 1–8. doi:10.1155/2013/764871

Tapaswini, S., & Chakraverty, S. (2014). Dynamic response of imprecisely defined beam subject to variousloads using Adomian decomposition method. *Applied Soft Computing, 24*, 249–263. doi:10.1016/j.asoc.2014.06.052

Tapaswini, S., & Chakraverty, S. (2014). Non-probabilistic Solution of Uncertain Vibration Equation of Large Membranes Using Adomian Decomposition Methods. *TheScientificWorldJournal, 2014*, 1–11. doi:10.1155/2014/308205 PMID:24790562

Ullah, S., Farooq, M., Ahmad, L., & Abdullah, S. (2014). *Application of fuzzy Laplace transforms for solving fuzzy partial Volterra integro-differential equations*. arXiv:1405.1895v1 [math.GM]

Zadeh, L. (2005). Toward a generalized theory of uncertainty (GTU) – an outline. *Information Sciences, 172*(1-2), 1–40. doi:10.1016/j.ins.2005.01.017

Zadeh, L. A. (1965). Fuzzy sets. *Information and Control, 8*(3), 338–353. doi:10.1016/S0019-9958(65)90241-X

KEY TERMS AND DEFINITIONS

Intuitionistic Fuzzy Difference: The intuitionistic fuzzy number is not like crisp number. So the intuitionistic fuzzy difference is not same as crisp difference.

Intuitionistic Fuzzy Number: The element of intuitionistic fuzzy sets is called intuitionistic fuzzy number.

Intuitionistic Fuzzy Partial Differential Equation: The partial differential equation associated with intuitionistic fuzzy number.

Intuitionistic Fuzzy Sets: A set which is a collection of object with graded membership and non membership function.

Intuitionistice Fuzzy Derivative: Since intuitionistic fuzzy difference are different than crisp difference so intuitionistic fuzzy derivative are different.

Chapter 10
Use of Fuzzy Set Theory in DNA Sequence Comparison and Amino Acid Classification

Subhram Das
Narula Institute of Technology, India

Jayanta Pal
Narula Institute of Technology, India

Soumen Ghosh
Narula Institute of Technology, India

Dilip K. Bhattacharya
University of Calcutta, India

ABSTRACT

This chapter describes the use of fuzzy set theory and intuitionistic fuzzy set theory in DNA sequence comparison. It also shows an indirect application of fuzzy set theory in comparing protein sequences. In fact, protein sequences consist of 20 amino acids. The chapter shows how such amino acids can be classified in six different groups. These groups are obtained purely from theoretical considerations. These are entirely different from the known groups of amino acids based on biological considerations. Also it is known how these classified groups of amino acids help in protein sequence comparison. The results of comparison differ as the groups differ in number and their compositions. Naturally it is expected that newer results of comparison will come out from such newer classified groups of amino acids obtained theoretically. Thus fuzzy set theory is also useful in protein sequence comparison.

INTRODUCTION

This chapter highlights the importance of fuzzy set theory and intuitionistic fuzzy set theory in problems of Bioinformatics. Initially the standard Voss numerical representation of Nucleotides is interpreted by a two valued logic. While generalizing it to a polynucleotide or a whole genome, it is shown how the notion of fuzzy logic comes into play and helps in obtaining their representations finally on a 12 dimensional unit hypercube. Naturally the set of poly-nucleotides or of whole genomes may be thought of as forming a metric space under suitable metric. The metric defined this way helps in comparison of DNA sequences. Sometimes the comparison is found to be unsatisfactory. This is compensated by using intuitionistic fuzzy set theory in place of fuzzy set theory and adopting same procedure as in fuzzy

DOI: 10.4018/978-1-5225-0914-1.ch010

set theory. Next two valued logic of Voss representation is extended from Nucleotides to amino acids. Using Fuzzy set theory each amino acid is ultimately represented on a 240 dimensional hypercube. Using Euclidean measure on the set of amino acids, each having such 240 components, the amino acids are classified in different groups based on similarity measures. Such groups are finally used in protein sequence comparison. This is the general perspective behind the introduction of the chapter. However the main objective of the chapter is to show application of fuzzy set theory and intuitionistic fuzzy set theory in DNA and Protein sequence comparison.

BACKGROUND

DNA is usually presumed to be the critical macromolecular target for carcinogenesis and mutagenesis. To predict sequence changes induced by different agents, it is imperative to have quantitative measures to compare and contrast the different DNA sequences. In addition, the very rapid rise in available DNA sequence data has also made the problem more emerging and interesting too. Again the character of a whole genome is not reflected from a particular type of its gene. So for the purpose of comparison whole genomes are to be considered. But the main problem in genome sequence comparison lies in the fact that the lengths of the corresponding sequences may be too large and at the same time lengths may differ from sequence to sequence. Obviously the main target is to convert whole genome sequence of any length to a desired sequence of a manageable size. This will definitely make the process of comparison of sequences much simpler and manageable too. Let us describe how this is achieved.

Two Valued Logic in Voss Representation

It is known that DNA and RNA are made of codons, each of which is a triplet of nucleotides, having the possibility to be one of four nucleotides {T, C, A, G} in the case of DNA and {U, C, A, G} in the case of RNA (A: adenine; C: cytosine; G: guanine; T: thymine; U: uracil). In Voss representation (Voss, 1992) nucleotides T/U, C, A, G are represented as (1,0,0,0), (0,1,0,0), (0,0,1,0) and (0,0,0,1) respectively. It may be argued that when T/U is written as (1, 0, 0, 0), it is meant that T/U is understood fully but C, A, G are not understandable at all. Thus for T/U, C, A, G taken in this order T/U is given the value 1 and others are given value 0. The same argument may be given to C, A, G also. Thus a two valued logic using binary 1, 0 works well and a single codon (a combination of three nucleotides) is represented on a 12 dimensional unit hypercube and is expressed by crisp values 1 and 0. Naturally if it is polynucleotide or a whole genome consisting of n codons, it is represented on a 12n dimensional hypercube and the process becomes unmanageable if n is large. This is definitely a drawback in the representation procedure. The second and most important difficulty arises when one tries to compare two polynucleotides of different lengths. In fact, in this case, they are represented on spaces of different dimensions. So the process of comparison is no longer applicable. Obviously both types of difficulties could be avoided, had the representation been made on a single 12 dimensional hypercube. This is the reason why, for representation of a polynucleotide or a whole genome, always a 12 dimensional hypercube is chosen. As a matter of fact, necessity of introducing fuzzy set theory is realized in the process of representing a polynucleotide consisting of finite number of codons, n say, on a single 12 dimensional hypercube. This is the background of fuzzy polynucleotide space as introduced by Torres and Nieto (2003).

Table 1. Fuzzy representation of polynucleotide UACUGU

Base	No. of Nucleotides				Total no. of Nucleotides	Fraction of Nucleotides			
	U	C	A	G		U	C	A	G
1st Base	2	0	0	0	2	1	0	0	0
2nd Base	0	0	1	1	2	0	0	0.5	0.5
3rd Base	1	1	0	0	2	0.5	0.5	0	0

Use of Fuzzy Logic in Representation of Polynucleotide and Whole Genomes

Let us start with representation of a polynucleotide described by the sequence UACUGU (tyrosin/cysteine). We collect the number of nucleotides in the order U C A G in the first base i.e., at 1st, 4th positions. They are found to be 2U, 0C, 0A, 0G. Similarly we get 0U, 0C, 1A, 1G in the 2nd base, i.e., at 2nd and 5th positions and 1U, 1C, 0A, 0G in the 3rd base, i.e., at 3rd and 6th positions. The results are calculated for two codons. They are expressed by whole numbers. When they are calculated for a single codon, the results are given by fractions. These are in Table 1.

Thus for the representation of a multi-codon or a polynucleotide, two valued logic using binary 1 and 0 is no longer applicable. It is the gradation of values in [0, 1], which is now required for representation of a poly-nucleotide or for a whole genome. So it may be said that fuzzy representation of S_1= UACUGU tyrosine/cysteine is given by (1,0,0,0,0,0,.5,.5,.5,.5,0,0). Similarly one may obtain fuzzy representation of S_2 = CACUGU histidine/cysteine given by (.5,.5,0,0,0,0,.5,.5,.5,.5,0,0) and fuzzy representation of S_3 = CUCUGU leucine/cysteine given by (.5,.5,0,0,.5,0,0,.5,.5,.5,0,0).

This is how fuzzy polynucleotide space is formed. This is equally applicable to whole genome also. Later on different types of metric are introduced for measuring distances in connection with comparing poly-nucleotide or whole genome sequences.

Different Types of Metric Used on Polynucleotide Spaces

$$d\left(p,q\right)=\frac{\sum_{i=1}^{12}\left|p_i-q_i\right|}{\sum_{i=1}^{12}\max\left\{p_i,q_i\right\}},$$

$$d_1(p,q)=\frac{d(p,q)}{1+d(p,q)},$$

$$d_2(p,q)=\frac{\sqrt{\sum_{i=1}^{12}\left(p_i-q_i\right)^2}}{\sqrt{12}},$$

$$d_3(p,q)=\frac{d_2(p,q)}{1+d_2(p,q)},$$

$$d_4(p,q) = \frac{\sum_{i=1}^{12} \left| p_i - q_i \right|}{12},$$

$$d_5(p,q) = \frac{\sum_{i=1}^{12} \left| p_i - q_i \right|}{1 + \sum_{i=1}^{12} \left| p_i - q_i \right|}$$

where $p = \left(p_1,\ p_2,\ p_3, \dots ,\ p_{12}\right),\ q = \left(q_1,\ q_2,\ q_3, \dots ,\ q_{12}\right) \in I^{12}$ are two different points of the metric space.

Role of Different Types of Metric

Nieto, Torres, Georgiou, and Karakasidis (2006) prove that all the metrics d, d_1, d_2, d_3, d_4, d_5 behave identically and establish that the metrics give perfect results. In fact, using their metrics they prove that S_1 and S_2 are nearer than S_1 and S_3. Actually the results are also biologically justified as S_1 and S_2 differ only in the first base, whereas S_1 and S_3 differ in the first two bases. Naturally S_1 and S_2 are more similar than S_1 and S_3.

Fuzzy Representation of Complete Genomes and the Role of Different Types of Metric

The authors of Nieto et al. (2006) also show that the role of different metrics remains the same in cases of complete genomes also. They consider fuzzy sets of frequencies of the genomes of M. tuberculosis, E. coli. and A. Aeolicus. Using the various metrics they compute the distance between M. tuberculosis and E. coli, the distance between M. tuberculosis and A. Aeolicus and also the distance between E.coli and A. Aerolicus. These results show that for complete genomes also, the role of different metrics remains the same. In fact, those whole genomes that are known to be biologically similar from their emboss values, are also found to be nearer under the measure of all such metrics. But the results are verified only for some particular examples. So the natural query is to check whether the result is true in general. With this motivation the authors of Das, De, Dey, and Bhattacharya (2013) tried to find out some counter examples to establish that the result is not true in general. Of course they follow the same fuzzy representation and same metrics as the authors of Nieto et al. (2006) follow for their analysis.

They consider the following examples of complete genomes

1. The complete genome sequence of Corynebacterium diphtheriae NCTC 13129. It is available at http://www.ncbi.nlm.nih.gov. Its accession number is >gi|38231477|emb|BX248353.1|
2. The genome comprises of 2488679 base pairs.
3. The complete genome sequence of Haemophilus influenzae 86-028NP. It is available at http://www.ncbi.nlm.nih.gov. Its accession number is >gi|156617157|gb|CP000057.2|
4. The genome comprises of 1914526 base pairs.
5. The complete genome sequence of Halobacterium sp. NRC-1. It is available at
6. http://www.ncbi.nlm.nih.gov. Its accession number is >gi|12057215|gb|AE004437.1|
7. The genome comprises of 2014275 base pairs.

8. The complete genome sequence of Xylella fastidiosa 9a5c. It is available at
9. http://www.ncbi.nlm.nih.gov. Its accession number is>gi|12057211|gb|AE003849.1|

The genome comprises of 2679306 base pairs.

They prove the following proposition:

For the Fuzzy polynucleotide of types (a), (b), (c), (d), the metrics d, d_2, d_4 are not at all feasible for comparison; d_1 and d_5 behave identically; d_3 behaves just opposite to both d_1 and d_5.

Proof

Fuzzy set of frequencies for genome (a) is
(0.233,0.267,0.233,0.267,0.233,0.265,0.233,0.269,0.232,0.270,0.232,0.266)
Fuzzy set of frequencies for genome (b) is
(0.311,0.189,0.310,0.190,0.310,0.191,0.308,0.191,0.307,0.192,0.309,0.192)
Fuzzy set of frequencies for genome (c) is
(0.164,0.338,0.162,0.336,0.159,0.341,0.161,0.339,0.158,0.341,0.158,0.343)
Fuzzy set of frequencies for genome (d) is
(0.248,0.248,0.228,0.276,0.249,0.248,0.225,0.278,0.246,0.253,0.224,0.277)
The detailed calculations of distances under different metrics are given in Table 2.

Proposition follows from the following results on comparison

d (C.diphtheriae, H.influenzae) = d(Halobacterium.sp, X.fastidiosa)
d1 (C.diphtheriae, H.influenzae) > d1 (Halobacterium.sp, X.fastidiosa)
d2 (C.diphtheriae, H.influenzae) = d2 (Halobacterium.sp, X.fastidiosa)
d3(C.diphtheriae, H.influenzae) < d3 (Halobacterium.sp, X.fastidiosa)
d4 (C.diphtheriae, H.influenzae) = d4 (Halobacterium.sp, X.fastidiosa)
d5 (C.diphtheriae, H.influenzae) > d5 (Halobacterium.sp, X.fastidiosa).

The above proposition establishes that the conclusions of Nieto et al. (2006) are not true for all genomes.

Another interesting area where fuzzy logic can be used successfully is theoretical classification of amino acids in different groups. It may be noted that each of the codons represents an amino acid and instructs the cell machinery to produce the corresponding amino acid during the Translation phase of protein synthesis. Thus a protein is a linear chain of amino acids, which starts with a start codon ATG, which corresponds to the amino acid methionine, followed by a sequence of amino acids and ends with a stop codon. Among the numerous available amino acids only 20 are generally found in living beings. Table 3 is the list of amino acids with their abbreviated notations and their DNA codons:

Table 2. Calculated value of distances under different metrics

Genome	D	d1	d2	d3	d4	d5
C.diphtheriae, H.influenzae	0.265	0.210	0.077	0.071	0.076	0.479
Halobacterium.sp, X.fastidiosa	0.265	0.209	0.077	0.072	0.076	0.478

Table 3. List of amino acids

Amino Acid	SLC	DNA Codons
Isoleucine	I	ATT, ATC, ATA
Leucine	L	CTT, CTC, CTA, CTG, TTA, TTG
Valine	V	GTT, GTC, GTA, GTG
Phenylalanine	F	TTT, TTC
Methionine	M	ATG
Cysteine	C	TGT, TGC
Alanine	A	GCT, GCC, GCA, GCG
Glycine	G	GGT, GGC, GGA, GGG
Proline	P	CCT, CCC, CCA, CCG
Threonine	T	ACT, ACC, ACA, ACG
Serine	S	TCT, TCC, TCA, TCG, AGT, AGC
Tyrosine	Y	TAT, TAC
Tryptophan	W	TGG
Glutamine	Q	CAA, CAG
Asparagine	N	AAT, AAC
Histidine	H	CAT, CAC
Glutamic acid	E	GAA, GAG
Aspartic acid	D	GAT, GAC
Lysine	K	AAA, AAG
Arginine	R	CGT, CGC, CGA, CGG, AGA, AGG
Stop codons	Stop	TAA, TAG, TGA

The amino acids form a linear polypeptide chain by covalent linkages (Nieto et al. 2006). The amino acid sequence that makes a protein is called its primary structure. It is believed that the dynamical folding process and stable structure of a protein are determined by its primary structure. Thus the prediction of secondary and space structures of protein from its primary structure is a challenging problem. Anyway to understand primary structure of protein, knowledge of amino acid sequence is necessary. As amino acids are 20 in number, it is better to classify them in different groups as far as possible. Actually such classifications of amino acids in different groups have already been made from biological properties of amino acids. Some such known classifications of amino acids and protein sequence comparison based on such classified groups are now briefly discussed:

Classified Groups of Amino Acids and Protein Sequence Comparison

Dill (1985) and Chan and Dill (1989) proposed the following two group model known as HP model

Classification I: HP Model (2 Groups) (see Table 4)

Table 4. Classification of amino acids based on HP Model

Characteristic	Amino Aacids
Hydrophobic (H) (non-polar)	A, I, L, M, F, P, W, V
Polar (P) (hydrophilic)	D, E, N, C, Q, G, S, T, Y, R, H, K

This model has been studied extensively from 1996-2000. As Wang and Wang (2000) remark that HP model is simplistic, but lacks sufficient information on the heterogeneity and complexity of the natural set of residues, such as the interactions between the residues, so this model is not taken up further.

Brown (1998) suggests that polar class of HP model may be divided into three subclasses, positive polar, uncharged polar and negative polar. So HP model may be modified as a four group model. This model is called detailed HP model by Yu, Anh, and Lau (2004) and it gives more information than HP model.

Classification II: Detailed HP Model (4 Groups) (see Table 5)

Yu et al. (2004) has studied this model through its Chaos game representation for multifractal and correlation analysis. But it has not been used for protein sequence comparison. Also Chaos game representation could accommodate the four groups as a whole, but could not give stress on the individual members of the group in any sense whatsoever. This is the limitation of this method of analysis.

Another classified four groups of amino acids based on Hydropathy characteristic are given by Zhang and Yu (2010).

Classification III: Based on Hydropathy characteristic (4 Groups) (see Table 6)

Actually the three group model given by the first three groups of the above four group model is given by Bhasin and Ragava (2004). It is based on hydropathy scale. The symbols POL, HPO and Ambi are used in the paper of Panek, Eidhammer, and Aasland (2005). As S, T, Y, W can neither be called strongly hydrophilic, nor strongly hydrophobic, so they are ambiguous in classification. Hence they are given a separate group named ambiguous. Taylor (1986) gives the following argument against the inclusion of Proline and Glycine and Cystine in any one of the above three groups. Actually Proline and Glycine are

Table 5. Classification of amino acids based on Detailed HP Model

Characteristic	Amino Acids
Hydrophobic (H) (non-polar)	A, I, L, M, F, P, W, V
Negative polar class	D, E
Uncharged polar class	N, C, Q, G, S, T, Y
Positive polar class	R, H, K

Table 6. Classification of amino acids based on Hydropathy characteristics

Hydropathy Characteristic	Abbreviation	Amino Acids
Strongly Hydrophilic	POL	R,D,C,N,Q,K,H
Strongly Hydrophobic	HPO	L,I,V, A,M,F
Weakly Hydrophilic or weakly Hydrophobic (Ambiguous)	Ambi	S,T,Y,W
Special	None	C,G,P

not classified in any hydropathy sets because of their unique backbone properties, and Cystine is excluded from any set, because it has polarizable properties. Based on the above two observations Zhang and Yu (2010) obtain the above four group model and use it for protein sequence comparison. There is some error in the formula used and the formulae have a possible obvious generalization.

Riddle et al. (1997) try to determine exactly the different types of residues that are necessary for reproducing some useful structures and for a simplified representation of protein sequence characteristics. By using combinatorial chemistry along with a screening strategy they search and find out a subset of the natural amino acids that can be used to construct a well- ordered protein like molecule consisting of β sheets. This subset contains five amino acids I, A, G, E, K. Three years later, based on the statistical and the kinetic characteristics of the folding, and on the thermodynamic stability of the ground states of some reduced sequences, Wang and Wang (1999, 2000) prove that the suggested five letter code is valid in general and feasible for elucidating characteristics of real proteins with 20 kinds of amino acids. Following the methods of Wang and Wang (1999, 2000) the 20 amino acids can be classified in 5 groups.

Classification IV: 5 Groups (see Table 7)

For protein sequence comparison of this model Li, Xing and Wang (2008) consider the method of representation of protein sequences as is normally done with DNA sequences. The five letters are now associated with five horizontal lines. The representation is obtained in the form of a zigzag curve and taking the alley Index of L/L matrix as the descriptor and using Euclidean distance as the distance measure, the phylogenic tree of 56 corona virus spike proteins are obtained nicely.

Other classified groups are

Classification V: 6 Groups (see Table 8)
Classification VI: 7 Groups (see Table 9)

But protein sequence comparison based on such classified groups V and VI has not been attempted.

Anyway the overall observation is that there is no single approach to protein sequence analysis based on classified groups of amino acids. The methods of comparison differ from choice of classified groups.

Table 7. Classification of amino acids into 5 groups

Groups	Representative	Amino Acids
Group 1	I	C, M, F, I, L, V, W, Y
Group 2	A	A, T, H
Group 3	G	G, P
Group 4	E	D, E
Group 5	K	S, N, Q, R, K

Table 8. Classification of amino acids based on Side chain property

Side Chain Characteristic	Amino Acids
Side chain is aliphatic	G, A, V, L, I
Side chain is an organic acid	D, E, N, Q
Side chain contains a sulphur	M, C
Side chain is an alcohol	S, T, Y
Side chain is an organic base	R, K, H
Side chain is aromatic	F, W, P

Table 9. Classification of amino acids into 7groups

Characteristic	Amino acids
Amino Acids with Aliphatic R-Groups	G, A, V, L, I
Non-Aromatic Amino Acids with Hydroxyl R-Groups	S, T
Amino Acids with Sulfur-Containing R-Groups	C, M
Acidic Amino Acids and their Amides	D, N, E, Q
Basic Amino Acids	R, K, H
Amino Acids with Aromatic Rings	F, Y, W
Imino Acids	P

MAIN FOCUS OF THE CHAPTER

Issues

1. To settle the problem of non-equivalence of metrics on a poly-nucleotide space in connection with comparison of whole genome sequences.
2. To discuss the possibilities of obtaining new classification of groups of amino acids.
3. To obtain protein sequence comparison based on new classified groups of amino acids.

Controversies

1. The result of non-equivalence of different metrics on polynucleotide spaces gives a big question mark, as the above result is quite expected owing to the fact that, all the metrics are considered on a finite dimensional space.
2. In protein sequence comparison all the classifications are made only from biological properties of amino acids. But there may be possibilities to obtain such classifications theoretically by considering the similarity of members of the same group.
3. To discuss the results of protein sequence analysis based on new classified groups, which may yield some new results.

Problems

1. To avoid the result of non-equivalence of different metrics on polynucleotide spaces by replacing the fuzzy set theory by Intuitionistic fuzzy set theory and using the measure of corresponding Intuitionistic fuzzy metric and Intuitionistic fuzzy similarity in place of fuzzy metric and fuzzy similarity.
2. To try to develop new classified groups of amino acids based on theoretical considerations only for getting newer results.
3. To develop a new methodology to obtain protein sequence comparisons based on new classified groups of amino acids.

SOLUTIONS AND RECOMMENDATIONS

Solution of Problem 1

Intuitionistic Fuzzy Set and Comparison of DNA Sequences.

Intuitionistic Fuzzy Set

Intuitionistic Fuzzy Sets (Atanassov, 1986, 1989) are generalization of Fuzzy sets (Zadeh, 1965) in which non-membership values are not obtainable from the membership values, rather both of them have to be specified separately.

Definition

Let X is a non empty set. An Intuitionistic fuzzy set A on X is defined as $A = \left\{ \left\langle x, \mu_A(x), \nu_A(x) \right\rangle, x \in X \right\}$ where the functions μ_A: x→[0,1] and ν_A: x→[0,1] define respectively the degree of membership and the degree of non-membership of the element x in X to the set A, and $0 \leq \mu_A(x) + \nu_A(x) \leq 1$, for each x in X. Obviously an ordinary fuzzy set can be written as $\left\{ \left\langle x, \mu_A(x), 1 - \mu_A(x) \right\rangle, x \in X \right\}$.

In reality non-membership is always associated with some sort of hesitancy. If we fix a fraction θ of membership value as the value of hesitancy, then it is given by $\nu_A(x) = \theta \mu_A(x)$; so non-membership value equals to $\pi_A(x) = 1 - (1+\theta)\mu_A(x)$. Hence an Intuitionistic fuzzy set is written as $\left\{ \left\langle x, \mu_A(x), \nu_A(x), \pi_A(x) \right\rangle, x \in X \right\}$.

Distance Measure on Intuitionistic Fuzzy Set

The normalized hamming distance DIFS proposed for IFS by Szmidt and Kacprzyk (2000) is given by

$$D_{IFS}(A,B) = \sum_{i=1}^{n} (| \mu_A(x_i) - \mu_B(x_i) | + | \nu_A(x_i) - \nu_B(x_i) | + | \pi_A(x_i) - \pi_B(x_i) |)$$

where A and B are two IFS in $X = \{x_1, x_2, \ldots, x_n\}$. Obviously the general form of distance measure would be

$$D^{\pm}_{IFS}(A,B) = [\sum_{i=1}^{n} \{| \mu_A(x_i) - \mu_B(x_i) |^{\alpha} + | \nu_A(x_i) - \nu_B(x_i) |^{\alpha} + | \pi_A(x_i) - \pi_B(x_i) |^{\alpha}\}]^{\frac{1}{\alpha}}, \alpha$$

is a normal number.

Similarity Measures on Intuitionistic Fuzzy Set

$$S(A,B) = 1 - [1 / n \sum_{j=1}^{n} \{(| \mu_A(x_j) - \mu_B(x_j) |)^{\alpha} + (| \nu_A(x_j) - \nu_B(x_j) |)^{\alpha} + (| \Pi_A(x_j) - \Pi_B(x_j) |)^{\alpha}\}]^{\frac{1}{\alpha}}, \alpha > 0$$

Intuitionistic Fuzzy Representation of Polynucleotide on a Triplet of I^{12}

Suppose fractions of nucleotide at a point on I^{12} be given by

$$(.x_1,.x_2,.x_3,.x_4,.y_1,.y_2,.y_3,.y_4,.z_1,.z_2,.z_3,.z_4).$$

Then the Intuitionistic Fuzzy representation of the polynucleotide A is given by $\left\{\left\langle x,\mu_A(x),\nu_A(x),\pi_A(x)\right\rangle, x\in X\right\}$, where

$$\mu_A(x)=(.x_1,.x_2,.x_3,.x_4,.y_1,.y_2,.y_3,.y_4,.z_1,.z_2,.z_3,.z_4),$$

$$\nu_A(x)=(.\theta x_1,.\theta x_2,.\theta x_3,.\theta x_4,.\theta y_1,.\theta y_2,.\theta y_3,.\theta y_4,.\theta z_1,.\theta z_2,.\theta z_3,.\theta z_4)$$

and

$$\pi_A(x)=[\{1-(1+\theta)(.x_1)\},\{1-(1+\theta)(.x_2)\},\{1-(1+\theta)(.x_3)\},\{1-(1+\theta)(.x_4)\},$$
$$\{1-(1+\theta)(.y_1)\},\{1-(1+\theta)(.y_2)\},\{1-(1+\theta)(.y_3)\},\{1-(1+\theta)(.y_4)\},$$
$$\{1-(1+\theta)(.z_1)\},\{1-(1+\theta)(.z_2)\},\{1-(1+\theta)(.z_3)\},\{1-(1+\theta)(.z_4)\}]$$

Intuitionistic Fuzzy Representation, Difference, and Similarity of Polynucleotides and Whole Genome

For simplification of calculation we take $\theta=0.1$

Problem 1 is now solved completely as the Distance measures and Similarity measures for different values of α show uniform results for polynucleotides and whole genomes.

Table 10. Intuitionistic fuzzy representation of polynucleotides s_1

S_1	1	0	0	0	0	0	0.5	0.5	0.5	0.5	0	0
	0	0	0	0	0	0	0.05	0.05	0.05	0.05	0	0
	0	1	1	1	1	1	0.45	0.45	0.45	0.45	1	1

Table 11. Intuitionistic fuzzy representation of polynucleotides s_2

S_2	0.5	0.5	0	0	0	0	0.5	0.5	0.5	0.5	0	0
	0.05	0.05	0	0	0	0	0.05	0.05	0.05	0.05	0	0
	0.45	0.45	1	1	1	1	0.45	0.45	0.45	0.45	1	1

Table 12. Intuitionistic fuzzy representation of polynucleotides s_3

S_3	0.5	0.5	0	0	0.5	0	0	0.5	0.5	0.5	0	0
	0.05	0.05	0	0	0.05	0	0	0.05	0.05	0.05	0	0
	0.45	0.45	1	1	0.45	1	1	0.45	0.45	0.45	1	1

Table 13. Distance measure of Intuitionistic fuzzy representation of polynucleotides s_1, s_2 & s_3

	α=1	α=2	α=3	α=4	α=5	α=6	α=7	α=8	α=9	α=10
S_1,S_2	2.1	1.01	0.50775	0.257525	0.131282	0.067234	0.034586	0.017867	0.009268	0.004827
S_1,S_3	4.3	2.12	1.09075	0.56555	0.294439	0.153846	0.08066	0.042427	0.022385	0.011846
S_2,S_3	2.2	1.11	0.583	0.308025	0.163158	0.086611	0.046074	0.024559	0.013117	0.007019

Table 14. Similarity measure of Intuitionistic fuzzy representation of polynucleotides s_1, s_2 & s_3

	α=1	α=2	α=3	α=4	α=5	α=6	α=7	α=8	α=9	α=10
S_1,S_2	0.825	0.91625	0.93352	0.94064	0.94448	0.94686	0.94847	0.94961	0.95046	0.95111
S_1,S_3	0.64167	0.87866	0.91422	0.92773	0.93474	0.939	0.94184	0.9439	0.94536	0.94652
S_2,S_3	0.81667	0.91220	0.93038	0.93792	0.94201	0.9446	0.94631	0.94757	0.94851	0.94925

Table 15. Intuitionistic fuzzy representation of whole genome (a)

a	0.233	0.267	0.233	0.267	0.233	0.265	0.233	0.269	0.232	0.27	0.232	0.266
	0.0233	0.0267	0.0233	0.0267	0.0233	0.0265	0.0233	0.0269	0.0232	0.027	0.0232	0.0266
	0.7437	0.7063	0.7437	0.7063	0.7437	0.7085	0.7437	0.7041	0.7448	0.703	0.7448	0.7074

Table 16. Intuitionistic fuzzy representation of whole genome (b)

b	0.311	0.189	0.31	0.19	0.31	0.191	0.308	0.191	0.307	0.192	0.309	0.192
	0.0311	0.0189	0.031	0.019	0.031	0.0191	0.0308	0.0191	0.0307	0.0192	0.0309	0.0192
	0.6579	0.7921	0.659	0.791	0.659	0.7899	0.6612	0.7899	0.6623	0.7888	0.6601	0.7888

Table 17. Intuitionistic fuzzy representation of whole genome (c)

c	0.164	0.338	0.162	0.336	0.159	0.341	0.161	0.339	0.158	0.341	0.158	0.343
	0.0164	0.0338	0.0162	0.0336	0.0159	0.0341	0.0161	0.0339	0.0158	0.0341	0.0158	0.0343
	0.8196	0.6282	0.8218	0.6304	0.8251	0.6249	0.8229	0.6271	0.8262	0.6249	0.8262	0.6227

Table 18. Intuitionistic fuzzy representation of whole genome (d)

	0.248	0.248	0.228	0.276	0.249	0.248	0.225	0.278	0.246	0.253	0.224	0.277
d	0.0248	0.0248	0.0228	0.0276	0.0249	0.0248	0.0225	0.0278	0.0246	0.0253	0.0224	0.0277
	0.7272	0.7272	0.7492	0.6964	0.7261	0.7272	0.7525	0.6942	0.7294	0.7217	0.7536	0.6953

Table 19. Distance measure of Intuitionistic fuzzy representation of whole genome (a), (b), (c) & (d)

	α=1	α=2	α=3	α=4	α=5	α=6	α=7	α=8	α=9	α=10
a,b	2.0196	0.155964	0.012543	0.001015	8.24E-05	6.7E-06	5.47E-07	4.47E-08	3.66E-09	3.01E-10
a,c	1.9096	0.139554	0.01063	0.000815	6.28E-05	4.85E-06	3.76E-07	2.93E-08	2.28E-09	1.79E-10
a,d	0.3256	0.004555	7.19E-05	1.2E-06	2.09E-08	3.72E-10	6.76E-12	1.24E-13	2.32E-15	4.37E-17
b,c	3.9292	0.590183	0.092292	0.01452	0.00229	0.000362	5.74E-05	9.11E-06	1.45E-06	2.31E-07
b,d	1.914	0.144056	0.011584	0.000959	8.11E-05	6.98E-06	6.09E-07	5.38E-08	4.79E-09	4.3E-10
c,d	2.0152	0.159569	0.013492	0.001174	0.000104	9.44E-06	8.66E-07	8.05E-08	7.55E-09	7.13E-10

Table 20. Similarity measure of Intuitionistic fuzzy representation of whole genome (a), (b), (c) & (d)

	α=1	α=2	α=3	α=4	α=5	α=6	α=7	α=8	α=9	α=10
a,b	0.8317	0.96709	0.980638	0.985125	0.987295	0.988557	0.989377	0.989951	0.990373	0.990696
a,c	0.840867	0.968869	0.981677	0.985918	0.987966	0.989157	0.98993	0.99047	0.990866	0.991168
a,d	0.972867	0.994376	0.996535	0.99724	0.997574	0.997765	0.997886	0.997969	0.998029	0.998073
b,c	0.672567	0.935981	0.962341	0.971073	0.975294	0.977752	0.979349	0.980467	0.981289	0.981919
b,d	0.8405	0.968371	0.981144	0.985337	0.987336	0.988481	0.989213	0.989717	0.990082	0.990358
c,d	0.832067	0.966712	0.980161	0.984576	0.986681	0.987886	0.988656	0.989185	0.989568	0.989857

They also do work satisfactorily as is evidenced from the results of S1, S2, and S1, S3. As supported biologically distance between the first pair should be less than the next pair and consequently the similarity of the first pair should be greater than the next pair. Actually this has happened in the present case for each value of α. As α increases, distance measures increase and similarity measures decrease. This suggests that better is the result, larger is the value of α taken.

Solution of Problem 2

Use of Fuzzy Set Theory in Theoretical Classification of Amino Acids in Different Groups

While making such classified groups, the authors Ghosh, Pal, and Bhattacharya (2014) show how fuzzy set theory becomes indispensable. Just as the order T/U C A G is followed for Voss representation (Voss,

1992) in case of DNA and RNA sequences, similarly for representation of amino acids, a definite order of occurrences of amino acids as given by I L V F M C A G P T S Y W Q N H E D K R. is always followed. When one says that, one understands the amino acid Isoleucine (I) fully, it is meant that one does not understand the remaining 19 amino acids at all. So the first component is taken as 1 and the remaining 19 components as zero. This is the corresponding Voss representation (Voss, 1992) of amino acids, based on two valued logic. Again each of the amino acids is nothing but a single or a multiple of codons. So each such amino acid is fully understood by its fuzzy values on I^{12}. So in details, one may represent Isoleucine I as a 20×12 = 240 components with first 12 non zero components given by (0,0,1,0, 1,0,0,0, 0.33,0.33,0.33,0) and the remaining 19×12 = 238 components being all zero. Using 19 black zeros by 12 zeros each, the amino acid Isoleucine (I) is represented as (0,0,1,0,1,0,0,0,.33,.33,.33,0, 0, 0,0,0,0,0,0,0,0,0,0,0,0,0,0,0,0,0,0). Now the similarities amongst the 20 amino acids are determined according to the following definition:

Definition

Two amino acids are similar if the norms of the 240 component vectors of the corresponding amino acids are same. They are dissimilar or different if the norms are different.

On the basis of the above definition, all the 20 amino acids can be divided into six different groups, all the groups are different, but the components of each group are similar amongst themselves.

Theoretical Classification: 6 Groups (see Table 21)

Problem 2 is now completely solved as the above classification of amino acids in six groups is obtained from the similarity of the components, which is determined purely theoretically.

Solution of Problem 3

Methodology to Obtain Protein Sequence Analysis Based on New Classified Groups

Ghosh, Das, Pal, and Bhattacharya (in press), considered the protein sequences shown in Table 22 for comparison.

Table 21. Theoretical classification of amino acids into 6 groups

Group	Amino Acids	Length	No. of Codons
1	I	1.525352418	3
2	L,R	1.354031019	6
3	V,A,G,P,T	1.5	4
4	F,C,Y,Q,N,H,E,D,K	1.58113883	2
5	M,W	1.732050808	1
6	S	1.179491416	6

Table 22. List of 9 different species (ND5) with database source

Seq. No.	Species	ID/ACCESSION	Database	Length
Seq1	Human (Homo sapiens)	AP-000649	NCBI	603
Seq2	Gorilla(Gorilla gorilla)	NP-008222	NCBI	603
Seq3	Common Chimpanzee (Pan troglodytes)	NP-008196	NCBI	603
Seq4	Pigmy Chimpanzee (Pan paniscus)	NP-008209	NCBI	603
Seq5	Fin Whale (Balenoptera physalus)	NP-006899	NCBI	606
Seq6	Blue Whale (Balenoptera musculus)	NP-007066	NCBI	606
Seq7	Rat (Rattus norvegicus)	AP-004902	NCBI	610
Seq8	mouse (Mus musculus)	NP-904338	NCBI	607
Seq9	opossum (Didelphis virginiana	NP-007105	NCBI	602

Procedure of Analysis of Comparison

The necessary distance matrix calculated for the above classified groups and phylogenetic tree obtained by MEGA 4 software (Kumar, Nei, Dudley, and Tamura 2008) using UPGMA algorithm are given in Table 23.

The phylogenetic tree obtained above gives the full results of comparison of the protein sequences. This phylogenetic tree agrees with that obtained for the same protein sequences under different methods of comparison. Thus problem 3 is also completely solved.

FUTURE RESEARCH DIRECTIONS

As Intuitionistic fuzzy representation for multi-codons and hence for amino acids is more realistic than corresponding fuzzy representation, so Intuitionistic fuzzy set theory may be applied in place of fuzzy set theory in obtaining newer classification of groups of amino acids leading to newer results on protein sequence comparison.

Table 23. Distance matrix of 9 different species based on new classified group

	Seq1	Seq2	Seq3	Seq4	Seq5	Seq6	Seq7	Seq8	Seq9
Seq1	0	0.039520	0.021531	0.032377	0.061099	0.065155	0.115234	0.116073	0.140694
Seq2		0	0.036468	0.041304	0.065758	0.068626	0.102938	0.110177	0.132224
Seq3			0	0.023375	0.059550	0.063663	0.107149	0.111600	0.135364
Seq4				0	0.056999	0.061551	0.096271	0.104466	0.124526
Seq5					0	0.016528	0.107035	0.107391	0.123551
Seq6						0	0.108860	0.108149	0.126832
Seq7							0	0.053303	0.071680
Seq8								0	0.075308
Seq9									0

Figure 1. Phylogenetic tree of 9 different species based on new classified group

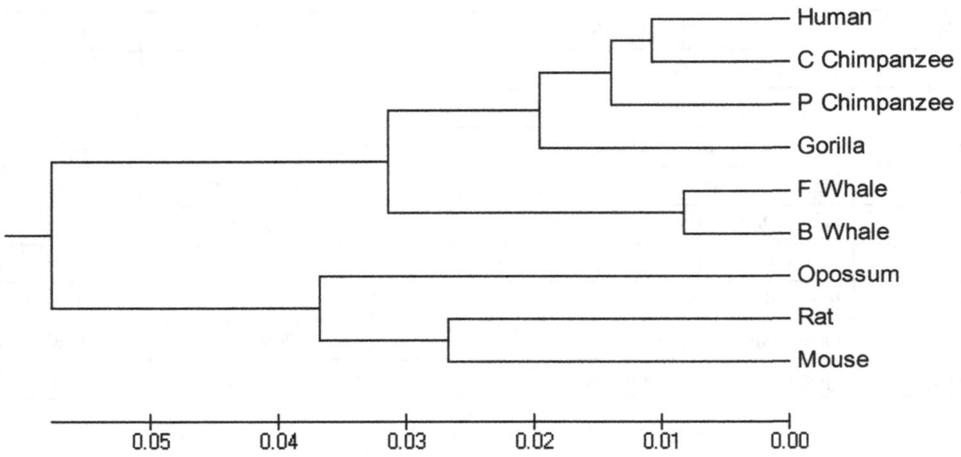

CONCLUSION

Measures of Intuitionistic fuzzy metric and fuzzy similarity do work satisfactorily as is evidenced from the results of S_1, S_2, and S_1, S_3. As supported biologically distance between the first pair should be less than the next pair and consequently the similarity of the first pair should be greater than the next pair. Actually this has happened in the present case for each value of α.The measures are of multiple choices. They vary as α varies. Again as α increases, distance measures increase and similarity measures decrease. This suggests that better is the result, larger is the value of α taken. Although the problem 1 is solved, normally it cannot be claimed that the metrics will behave equivalently for sequences other the ones used as counter examples. But as some value of the parameter θ is always involved in the calculations, so if some contradictory result appears at all, it is only apparent. It can be adjusted by choice of some suitable value of θ. Thus it can be definitely concluded that the Intuitionistic Fuzzy Set is one of the best tools in analyzing similarity of complete genomes.

Classification of amino acids in six groups obtained theoretically is completely different from other classified groups including even that of six groups obtained biologically.

The results definitely indicate that the new six group classification can also be conveniently used in protein sequence comparison. Thus finally it can be concluded that fuzzy set theory is also useful to protein sequence comparison indirectly.

REFERENCES

Atanassov, K. (1986). Intuitionistic fuzzy sets. *Fuzzy Sets and Systems*, *20*(1), 87–96. doi:10.1016/S0165-0114(86)80034-3

Atanassov, K. (1989). More on intuitionistic fuzzy sets. *Fuzzy Sets and Systems*, *33*(1), 37–45. doi:10.1016/0165-0114(89)90215-7

Bhasin, M., & Raghava, G. P. S. (2004). Analysis and prediction of affinity of TAP binding peptides using cascade SVM. *Protein Science*, *13*(3), 596–607. doi:10.1110/ps.03373104 PMID:14978300

Brown, T. A. (1998). *Genetics: A Molecular Approach* (3rd ed.). London: Chapman & Hall.

Chan, H. S., & Dill, K. A. (1989). Compact polymers. *Macromolecules*, *22*(12), 4559–4573. doi:10.1021/ma00202a031

Das, S., De, D., & Bhattacharya, D. K. (in press). Similarity and Dissimilarity of Whole Genomes using Intuitionistic Fuzzy Logic. *Notes on Intuitionistic Fuzzy Set.*

Das, S., De, D., Dey, A., & Bhattacharya, D. K. (2013). Some anomalies in the analysis of whole genome sequence on the basis of Fuzzy set theory. *International Journal of Artificial intelligence and Neural Networks, 3*(2), 38-41.

Dill, K. A. (1985). Theory for the folding and stability of globular proteins. *Biochemistry*, *24*(6), 1501–1509. doi:10.1021/bi00327a032 PMID:3986190

Ghosh, S., Das, S., Pal, J., & Bhattacharya, D. K. (in press). Differentiation of protein sequence comparison based on biological and theoretical classification of amino acids in six groups. *International Journal of Advanced Research in Computer Science and Software Engineering.*

Ghosh, S., Pal, J., & Bhattacharya, D. K. (2014). Classification of Amino Acids of a Protein on the basis of Fuzzy set theory. *International Journal of Modern Sciences and Engineering Technology*, *1*(6), 30–35.

Kumar, S., Nei, M., Dudley, J., & Tamura, K. (2008). MEGA: A biologist-centric software for evolutionary analysis of DNA and protein sequences. *Briefings in Bioinformatics*, *9*(4), 299–306. doi:10.1093/bib/bbn017 PMID:18417537

Li, C., Xing, L., & Wang, X. (2008). 2-D graphical representation of protein sequences and its application to coronavirus phylogeny. *BMB Reports, 41*(3), 217-222.

Nieto, J. J., Torres, A., Georgiou, D. N., & Karakasidis, T. E. (2006). Fuzzy Polynucleotide Spaces and Metrics. *Bulletin of Mathematical Biology*, *16*(8), 703–725. doi:10.1007/s11538-005-9020-5 PMID:16794951

Nieto, J. J., Torres, A., & Vázquez-Trasande, M. M. (2003). A metric space to study differences between polynucleotides. *Applied Mathematics Letters*, *16*(8), 1289–1294. doi:10.1016/S0893-9659(03)90131-5

Panek, J., Eidhammer, I., & Aasland, R. (2005). A new method for identification of protein (sub)families in a set of proteins based on hydropathy distribution in proteins. *Proteins*, *58*(4), 923–934. doi:10.1002/prot.20356 PMID:15645428

Riddle, D. S., Santiago, J. V., Bray-Hall, S. T., Doshi, N., Grantcharova, V. P., Yi, Q., & Baker, D. (1997). Functional rapidly folding proteins from simplified amino acid sequences. *Nature Structural Biology*, *4*(10), 805–809. doi:10.1038/nsb1097-805 PMID:9334745

Szmidt, E., & Kacprzyk, J. (2000). Intuitionistic Distances between intuitionistic fuzzy sets. *Fuzzy Sets and Systems*, *114*(3), 505–518. doi:10.1016/S0165-0114(98)00244-9

Taylor, W. R. (1986). Identification of protein sequence homology by consensus template alignment. *Journal of Molecular Biology*, *188*(2), 233–258. doi:10.1016/0022-2836(86)90308-6 PMID:3088284

Torres, A., & Nieto, J. J. (2003). The fuzzy polynucleotide space: Basic properties. *Bioinformatics (Oxford, England)*, *19*(5), 587–592. doi:10.1093/bioinformatics/btg032 PMID:12651716

Voss, R. F. (1992). Evolution of long-range fractal correlations and 1/f noise in DNA base sequences. *Physical Review Letters*, *68*(25), 3805–3808. doi:10.1103/PhysRevLett.68.3805 PMID:10045801

Wang, J., & Wang, W. (1999). A computational approach to simplifying the protein folding alphabet. *Nature Structural & Molecular Biology*, *6*(11), 1033–1038. doi:10.1038/14918 PMID:10542095

Wang, J., & Wang, W. (2000). Modeling study on the validity of a possibly simplified representation of proteins. *Physical Review E: Statistical Physics, Plasmas, Fluids, and Related Interdisciplinary Topics*, *61*(6), 6981–6986. doi:10.1103/PhysRevE.61.6981 PMID:11088391

Yu, Z. G., Anh, V., & Lau, K. S. (2004). Chaos game representation of protein sequences based on the detailed HP model and their multifractal and correlation analyses. *Journal of Theoretical Biology*, *226*(3), 341–348. doi:10.1016/j.jtbi.2003.09.009 PMID:14643648

Zadeh, L. A. (1965). Fuzzy sets. *Information and Control*, *8*(3), 338–353. doi:10.1016/S0019-9958(65)90241-X

Zhang, Y., & Yu, X. (2010). Analysis of protein sequence similarity. In *Proceedings of the IEEE Fifth International Conference on Bio-Inspired Computing: Theories and Applications* (pp. 1255-1258). Changsha, Beijing, China: Institute of Electrical and Electronics Engineers, Inc.

KEY TERMS AND DEFINITIONS

Amino Acids: Amino acids are organic compound containing a carboxyl (—COOH) and an amino (—NH2) group. Twenty different types of amino acids are normally found in living beings. Each of them is either a single codon or a multiple of codons.

Codons: A sequence of three consecutive nucleotides T,C,A,G for DNA and U,C,A,G for RNA sequence. They carry the genetic code that determines the inclusion of a specific amino acid in a polypeptide chain during protein synthesis.

Fuzzy Sets: Fuzzy sets are sets whose elements have degrees of membership. The membership values lie in [0,1].

Genomes: A genome is an organism's complete set of DNA, including all of its exons and introns. Each genome carries all of the information needed for building and maintaining the organism.

Hydrophilic: Hydrophilic molecules are also known as polar molecules. Some hydrophilic substances do not dissolve. This type of mixture is called a colloid. Those hydrophilic substances which do not dissolve are called colloids. One of the broad categories of amino acids are of hydrophilic type. They are 12 in numbers.

Hydrophobic: Hydrophobic molecules are also known as non polar molecules. They also form a broad category of amino acids. They are 8 in numbers.

Intuitionistic Fuzzy Set: Intuitionistic fuzzy sets are fuzzy sets, which consider also the hesitancy factor. Its elements have degrees of membership and non-membership. The non-membership values do not depend on membership values.

Phylogenetic Tree: A phylogenetic tree gives evolutionary relationships among various biological species. Their phylogeny is based on similarities and differences in their genetic characteristics.

Polynucleotide: A polynucleotide molecule is a biopolymer composed of 13 or more nucleotide monomers. DNA (deoxyribonucleic acid) and RNA (ribonucleic acid) are examples of polynucleotides with distinct biological function. Length of a polynucleotide is always a multiple of three.

Protein: Proteins are large biological molecules, consisting of one or more long chains of amino acid residues. The chain of amino acids forming the protein is called its primary structure. This primary structure gives sufficient information regarding the functioning of the protein.

Chapter 11
On Bipolar Fuzzy B-Subalgebras of B-Algebras

Tapan Senapati
Padima Janakalyan Banipith High School, India

ABSTRACT

Based on the concept of bipolar fuzzy set, a theoretical approach of B-subalgebras of B-algebras are established. Some characterizations of bipolar fuzzy B-subalgebras of B-algebras are given. We have shown that the intersection of two bipolar fuzzy B-subalgebras is also a bipolar fuzzy B-subalgebra, but for the union it is not always true. We have also shown that if every bipolar fuzzy B-subalgebras has the finite image, then every descending chain of B-subalgebras terminates at finite step.

INTRODUCTION

After the introduction of fuzzy set [24], many new approaches and theories treating imprecision and uncertainty have been proposed, such as the generalized theory of uncertainty (GTU) introduced by Zadeh (1965) and the intuitionistic fuzzy sets introduced by Atanassov (1999) and so on. Among these theories, a well-known extension of the classic fuzzy set is bipolar fuzzy set theory, which was pioneered by Zhang (1994). Since then, many researchers have investigated this topic and obtained some meaningful conclusions.

In traditional fuzzy sets the membership degree range is [0,1]. The membership degree is the degree of belonging ness of an element to a set. The membership degree 1 indicates that an element completely belongs to its corresponding set, the membership degree 0 indicates that an element does not belong to the corresponding set and the membership degree on the interval (0,1) indicate the partial membership to the corresponding set. Sometimes, membership degree also means the satisfaction degree of elements to some property corresponding to a set and its counter property. Bipolar-valued fuzzy sets are an extension of fuzzy sets whose membership degree range is increased from the interval [0,1] to the interval [–1,1]. In a bipolar fuzzy set the membership degree 0 means that elements are irrelevant to the corresponding property, the membership degrees on (0,1] indicate that elements somewhat satisfy the property and the membership degrees on [–1,1] indicate that elements somewhat satisfy the implicit counter-property.

DOI: 10.4018/978-1-5225-0914-1.ch011

Although bipolar fuzzy sets and intuitionistic fuzzy sets look similar to each other, they are essentially different sets [12]. In many domains, it is important to be able to deal with bipolar information. It is noted that positive information represents what is granted to be possible, while negative information represents what is considered to be impossible.

The study of *BCK*/*BCI*-algebras was initiated by Imai and Iseki in 1966 as a generalization of the concept of set-theoretic difference and propositional calculus. Neggers and Kim (2001, 2002) introduced a new notion, called a B-algebras which is related to several classes of algebras of interest such as *BCK*/*BCI* -algebras. Jun et al. (2002, 2009) applied the concept of fuzzy sets to B-algebras. Ahn and Bang [1] discussed some results on fuzzy subalgebras in B-algebras. Saeid (2006) introduced fuzzy topological B-algebras. Senapati et al. (2012, 2013) introduced fuzzy and interval-valued fuzzy closed ideals of B-algebras. They investigated fuzzy B-subalgebras with respect t-norm. They also give relationship between fuzzy dot subalgebras and fuzzy dot ideals of B-algebras.

Kim and Kim (2008) introduced the notion of *BG*-algebras, which is a generalization of B-algebras. Senapati et al. (2012, 2013, 2014) done lot of works on *BG* -algebras.

Lee (2000, 2004, 2009) introduced the notion of bipolar fuzzy subalgebras and ideals in *BCK*/*BCI* -algebras. The concept of bipolar valued fuzzy translation and bipolar valued fuzzy S-extension of a bipolar valued fuzzy subalgebra in *BCK*/*BCI* -algebra was introduced by Jun et al. (2008). Motivated by this, in this paper, the notions of bipolar fuzzy B -subalgebras of B -algebras are introduced and their properties are investigated.

PRELIMINARIES

We first recall some basic concepts which are used to present the paper.

Definition 2.1 *(B -algebra)* A non-empty set X with a constant 0 and a binary operation * is said to be B -algebra if it satisfies the following axioms

1. $x * x = 0$
2. $x * 0 = x$
3. $(x * y) * z = x * (z * (0 * y))$, for all $x, y, z \in X$.

A non-empty subset S of a B-algebra X is called a B-subalgebra [13] of X if $x * y \in S$, for all $x, y \in S$. We can define a partial ordering "$\leq$" by $x \leq y$ if and only if $x * y = 0$.

Definition 2.2: *(B -subalgebra)* A non-empty subset S of a B -algebra X is called a B -subalg ebra of X if $x * y \in S$, for all $x, y \in S$.

From this definition it is observed that, if a subset S of a B -algebra satisfies only the closer property, then S becomes a B -subalgebra.

Definition 2.3: *(Fuzzy set) Let* X be the collection of objects denoted generally by x, then a fuzzy set A in X is defined as $A = \{\langle x, \mu_A(x) \rangle : x \in X\}$, where $\mu_A(x)$ is called the membership value of x in A and $0 \leq \mu_A(x) \leq 1$.

Combined the definitions of B -subalgebra over crisp set and the idea of fuzzy set Jun et al. [7] defined fuzzy B -subalgebra, which is defined below.

Definition 2.4: *(Fuzzy B -subalgebra)* Let μ be a fuzzy set in a B -algebra. Then μ is called a fuzzy B -subalgebra of X if $\mu(x * y) \geq \min\{\mu(x), \mu(y)\}$ for all $x, y \in X$, where μ(x) is the membership value of x in X.

Definition 2.5: *(Bipolar fuzzy set) Let X* be a nonempty set. A bipolar fuzzy set ϕ in X is an object having the form $\phi = \{\langle x, \phi^+(x), \phi^-(x)\rangle : x \in X\}$ where $\phi^+ : X \to [0,1]$ and $\phi^- : X \to$ [0,1] *are mappings.*

We use the positive membership degree $\phi^+(x)$ to denote the satisfaction degree of an element x to the property corresponding to a bipolar fuzzy set ϕ and the negative membership degree $\phi^-(x)$ to denote the satisfaction degree of an element x to some implicit counter-property corresponding to a bipolar fuzzy set ϕ. If $\phi^+(x) \neq 0$ and $\phi^-(x) = 0$, it is the situation that x is regarded as having only positive satisfaction for ϕ. If $\phi^+(x) = 0$ and $\phi^-(x) \neq 0$, it is the situation that x does not satisfy the property of ϕ but somewhat satisfies the counter property of ϕ. It is possible for an element x to be such that $\phi^+(x) \neq 0$ and $\phi^-(x) \neq 0$ when the membership function of the property overlaps that of its counter property over some portion of X.

Definition 2.6: Let $\phi_1 = (\phi_1^+, \phi_1^-)$ and $\phi_2 = (\phi_2^+, \phi_2^-)$ be two bipolar fuzzy sets on X. Then the intersection and union of ϕ_1 and ϕ_2 is denoted by $\phi_1 \cap \phi_2$ and $\phi_1 \cup \phi_2$ respectively and is given by

$$\phi_1 \cap \phi_2 = (\phi_1^+ \cap \phi_2^+, \phi_1^- \cap \phi_2^-) = \{\min(\phi_1^+, \phi_2^+), \max(\phi_1^-, \phi_2^-)\}$$

$$\phi_1 \cup \phi_2 = (\phi_1^+ \cup \phi_2^+, \phi_1^- \cup \phi_2^-) = \{\max(\phi_1^+, \phi_2^+), \min(\phi_1^-, \phi_2^-)\}.$$

MAIN RESULTS

For the sake of simplicity, we shall use the symbol $\phi = (\phi^+, \phi^-)$ for the bipolar fuzzy subset $\phi = \{< x, \phi^+(x), \phi^-(x) >: x \in X\}$. Throughout this paper, X always means a B-algebra without any specification.

Definition 3.1*Let* $\phi = (\phi^+, \phi^-)$ be a bipolar fuzzy set in X, then the set ϕ is bipolar fuzzy B-subalgebra over the binary operator * if it satisfies the following conditions:

(IBS1) $\phi^+(x * y) \geq min\{\phi^+(x), \phi^+(y)\}$

(IBS2) $\phi^-(x * y) \leq max\{\phi^-(x), \phi^-(y)\}$

for all $x, y \in X$.

Table 1. Cayley table

*	0	a	b	c	d	e
0	0	e	d	c	b	a
a	a	0	e	d	c	b
b	b	a	0	e	d	c
c	c	b	a	0	e	d
d	d	c	b	a	0	e
e	e	d	c	b	a	0

We consider an example of bipolar fuzzy *B*-subalgebra below.

Example 3.2 *Let* $X = \{0, a, b, c, d, e\}$ be a *B*-algebra with the Cayley table (Table 1).

Let $\phi = (\phi^+, \phi^-)$ be a bipolar fuzzy set in *X* defined by

$$\phi^+(x) = \begin{cases} 0.56, & if\, x \in \{0, b, d\} \\ 0.44, & otherwise \end{cases} \quad \text{and} \quad \phi^-(x) = \begin{cases} -0.43, & if\, x \in \{0, b, d\} \\ -0.37, & otherwise. \end{cases}$$

All the conditions of Definition 3.1 have been satisfied by the set ϕ. Thus $\phi = (\phi^+, \phi^-)$ is a bipolar fuzzy *B*-subalgebra of *X*.

Proposition 3.3: *If* $\phi = (\phi^+, \phi^-)$ is a bipolar fuzzy *B*-subalgebra in *X*, then for all *x*∈*X*, $\phi^+(0) \geq \phi^+(x)$ and $\phi^-(0) \leq \phi^-(x)$. Thus, $\phi^+(0)$ and $\phi^-(0)$ are the upper bounds and lower bounds of $\phi^+(x)$ and $\phi^-(x)$ respectively.

Proof: Let $x \in X$. Then $\phi^+(0) = \phi^+(x * x) \geq \min\{\phi^+(x), \phi^+(x)\} = \phi^+(x)$ and $\phi^-(0) = \phi^-(x * x) \leq \max\{\phi^-(x), \phi^-(x)\} = \phi^-(x)$.

Theorem 3.4: *Let* $\phi = (\phi^+, \phi^-)$ be a bipolar fuzzy *B*-subalgebra of *X*. If there exists a sequence x_n in *X* such that $\lim_{n\to\infty} \phi^+(x_n) = 1$ and $\lim_{n\to\infty} \phi^-(x_n) = -1$, then $\phi^+(0) = 1$ and $\phi^-(0) = -1$.

Proof: By Proposition 3.3, $\phi^+(0) \geq \phi^+(x)$ for all *x*∈*X*, therefore $\phi^+(0) \geq \phi^+(x_n)$ for every positive integer *n*. Consider, $1 \geq \phi^+(0) \geq \lim_{n\to\infty} \phi^+(x_n) = 1$. Hence, $\phi^+(0) = 1$.

Again, by Proposition 3.3, $\phi^-(0) \leq \phi^-(x)$ for all *x*∈*X*, thus $\phi^-(0) \leq \phi^-(x_n)$ for every positive integer *n*. Now, $-1 \leq \phi^-(0) \leq \lim_{n\to\infty} \phi^-(x_n) = -1$. Hence, $\phi^-(0) = -1$.

Proposition 3.5:*If a bipolar fuzzy set* $\phi = (\phi^+, \phi^-)$ *in X is a bipolar fuzzy B*-subalgebra, then $\phi^+(0 * x) \geq \phi^+(x)$ and $\phi^-(0 * x) \leq \phi^-(x)$ for all *x*∈*X*.

Proof: For all $x \in X$,

$$\phi^{+}(0 * x) \geq \min\{\phi^{+}(0), \phi^{+}(x)\}$$
$$= \min\{\phi^{+}(x * x), \phi^{+}(x)\} \geq \min\{min\{\phi^{+}(x), \phi^{+}(x)\}, \phi^{+}(x)\} = \phi^{+}(x)$$

and

$$\phi^{-}(0 * x) \leq \max\{\phi^{-}(0), \phi^{-}(x)\}$$
$$= \max\{\phi^{-}(x * x), \phi^{-}(x)\} \leq \max\{\max\{\phi^{-}(x), \phi^{-}(x)\}, \phi^{-}(x)\} = \phi^{-}(x).$$

For any elements *x* and *y* of *X*, let us write $\prod^{n} x * y$ for $x * (\cdots (x * (x * y)))$ where *x* occurs *n* times.

Theorem 3.6: *Let* $\phi = (\phi^{+}, \phi^{-})$ be a bipolar fuzzy *B*-subalgebra of *X* and let $n \in N$ (the set of natural numbers). Then

1. $\phi^{+}(\prod^{n} x * x) \geq \phi^{+}(x)$, for any odd number n,
2. $\phi^{-}(\prod^{n} x * x) \leq \phi^{-}(x)$, for any odd number n,
3. $\phi^{+}(\prod^{n} x * x) = \phi^{+}(x)$, for any even number n,
4. $\phi^{-}(\prod^{n} x * x) = \phi^{-}(x)$, for any even number n.

Proof: Let $x \in X$ and assume that *n* is odd. Then $n=2p-1$ for some positive integer *p*. We prove the theorem by induction. Now $\phi^{+}(x * x) = \phi^{+}(0) \geq \phi^{+}(x)$ and $\phi^{-}(x * x) = \phi^{-}(0) \leq \phi^{-}(x)$. Suppose that $\phi^{+}(\prod^{n} x * x) \geq \phi^{+}(x)$ and $\phi^{-}(\prod^{n} x * x) \leq \phi^{-}(x)$. Then by assumption,

$$\phi^{+}(\prod^{n} x * x) = \phi^{+}(\prod^{n} x * x) = \phi^{+}(\prod^{n} x * (x * (x * x))) = \phi^{+}(\prod^{n} x * x) \geq \phi^{+}(x)$$

and

$$\phi^{-}(\prod^{n} x * x) = \phi^{-}(\prod^{n} x * x) = \phi^{-}(\prod^{n} x * (x * (x * x))) = \phi^{-}(\prod^{n} x * x) \leq \phi^{-}(x),$$

which proves (i) and (ii). Proofs are similar for the cases (iii) and (iv).

The intersection of two bipolar fuzzy *B*-subalgebras is also a bipolar fuzzy *B*-subalgebra, which is proved in the following theorem.

Theorem 3.7: *Let* $\phi_1 = (\phi_1^+, \phi_1^-)$ and $\phi_2 = (\phi_2^+, \phi_2^-)$ be two bipolar fuzzy *B*-subalgebras of *X*. Then $\phi_1 \cap \phi_2$ is a bipolar fuzzy *B*-subalgebra of X.

Proof: Let $x, y \in \phi_1 \cap \phi_2$. Then $x, y \in \phi_1$ and ϕ_2. Now,

$$\phi_1^+ \cap \phi_2^+(x * y) = \min\{\phi_1^+(x * y), \phi_2^+(x * y)\} \geq \min\{\min\{\phi_1^+(x), \phi_1^+(y)\},$$

$$\min\{\phi_2^+(x), \phi_2^+(y)\}\} = \min\{\min\{\phi_1^+(x), \phi_2^+(x)\},$$

$$\min\{\phi_1^+(y), \phi_2^+(y)\}\} = \min\{\phi_1^+ \cap \phi_2^+(x), \phi_1^+ \cap \phi_2^+(y)\}$$

and

$$\phi_1^- \cap \phi_2^-(x * y) = \max\{\phi_1^-(x * y), \phi_2^-(x * y)\} \geq \max\{\max\{\phi_1^-(x), \phi_1^-(y)\},$$

$$\max\{\phi_2^-(x), \phi_2^-(y)\}\} = \max\{\max\{\phi_1^-(x), \phi_2^-(x)\},$$

$$\max\{\phi_1^-(y), \phi_2^-(y)\}\} = \max\{\phi_1^- \cap \phi_2^-(x), \phi_1^- \cap \phi_2^-(y)\}.$$

Hence, $A_1 \cap A_2$ is a bipolar fuzzy *B*-subalgebra of X.

The above theorem can be generalized as follows.

Theorem 3.8: *Let* $\{\phi_i \mid i = 1, 2, 3, \ldots\}$ be a family of bipolar fuzzy *B*-subalgebra of *X*. Then $\bigcap \phi_i$ is also a bipolar fuzzy *B*-subalgebra of *X*, where $\bigcap \phi_i = (\min \phi_i^+(x), \max \phi_i^-(x))$.

The union of any set of bipolar fuzzy *B*-subalgebras need not be a bipolar fuzzy *B*-subalgebra which is shown in the following example.

Example 3.9: *Let* $X = \{0, a, b, c, d, e\}$ be a *B*-algebra with the Cayley table (see Table 2).

Table 2. Cayley table

*	0	a	b	c	d	e
0	0	b	a	c	d	e
a	a	0	b	d	e	c
b	b	a	0	e	c	d
c	c	d	e	0	b	a
d	d	e	c	a	0	b
e	e	c	d	b	a	0

Let $\phi = (\phi^+, \phi^-)$ and $\psi = (\psi^+, \psi^-)$ be two bipolar fuzzy sets in *X* defined by

$$\phi^+(x) = \begin{cases} 0.77, & if\, x \in \{0, d\} \\ 0.26, & if\, x \in X \setminus \{0, d\} \end{cases}, \quad \phi^-(x) = \begin{cases} -0.52, & if\, x \in \{0, c\} \\ -0.13, & if\, x \in X \setminus \{0, 3\} \end{cases},$$

$$\psi^+(x) = \begin{cases} 0.81, & if\, x \in \{0, e\} \\ 0.36, & if\, x \in X \setminus \{0, e\} \end{cases} \text{and} \quad \psi^-(x) = \begin{cases} -0.44, & if\, x \in \{0, d\} \\ -0.18, & if\, x \in X \setminus \{0, d\} \end{cases}.$$

Then $\phi = (\phi^+, \phi^-)$ and $\psi = (\psi^+, \psi^-)$ are bipolar fuzzy *B*-subalgebras of *X*. But the union of $\phi \cup \psi$ is not a bipolar fuzzy *B*-subalgebras of *X* since

$$\phi^+ \cup \psi^+(4 * 5) = 0.36 < 0.81 = \max\{\phi^+ \cup \psi^+(4), \phi^+ \cup \psi^+(5)\}$$

and

$$\phi^- \cup \psi^-(3 * 4) = -0.18 > -0.52 = \min\{\phi^- \cup \psi^-(3), \phi^- \cup \psi^-(4)\}.$$

The sets $\{x \in X : \phi^+(x) = \phi^+(0)\}$ and $\{x \in X : \phi^-(x) = \phi^-(0)\}$ are denoted by I_{ϕ^+} and I_{ϕ^-} respectively. These two sets are also *B*-subalgebra of *X*.

Theorem 3.10:*Let* $\phi = (\phi^+, \phi^-)$ be a bipolar fuzzy *B*-subalgebra of *X*, then the sets I_{ϕ^+} and I_{ϕ^-} are *B*-subalgebras of *X*.

Proof: Let $x, y \in I_{\phi^+}$. Then $\phi^+(x) = \phi^+(0) = \phi^+(y)$ and so,

$$\phi^+(x * y) \geq min\{\phi^+(x), \phi^+(y)\} = \phi^+(0).$$

By using Proposition 3.3, we know that $\phi^+(x * y) = \phi^+(0)$ or equivalently $x * y \in I_{\phi^+}$.

Again, let $x, y \in I_{\phi^-}$. Then $\phi^-(x) = \phi^-(0) = \phi^-(y)$ and so,

$$\phi^-(x * y) \leq \max\{\phi^-(x), \phi^-(y)\} = \phi^-(0).$$

Then by Proposition 3.3, we know that $\phi^-(x * y) = \phi^-(0)$ or equivalently $x * y \in I_{\phi^-}$. Hence, the sets I_{ϕ^+} and I_{ϕ^-} are *B*-subalgebras of *X*.

Theorem 3.11*Let B* be a nonempty subset of *X* and $\phi = (\phi^+, \phi^-)$ be a bipolar fuzzy set in *X* defined by

$$\phi^+(x) = \begin{cases} \lambda, & if\, x \in B \\ \tau, & otherwise \end{cases} \quad \text{and} \quad \phi^-(x) = \begin{cases} \gamma, & if\, x \in B \\ \delta, & otherwise \end{cases}$$

for all λ, τ, γ and $\delta \in [0,1]$ with $.\lambda \geq \tau$. and $\gamma \leq \delta$. Then ϕ is a bipolar fuzzy B-subalgebra of X if and only if B is a B-subalgebra of X. Moreover, $I_{\phi^+} = B = I_{\phi^-}$.

Proof: Let ϕ be a bipolar fuzzy B-subalgebra of X. Let $x,y \in X$ be such that $x,y \in B$. Then

$$\phi^+(x * y) \geq \min\{\phi^+(x), \phi^+(y)\} = \min\{\lambda, \lambda\} = \lambda$$

and

$$\phi^-(x * y) \leq \max\{\phi^-(x), \phi^-(y)\} = \max\{\gamma, \gamma\} = \gamma.$$

So $x*y \in B$. Hence, B is a B-subalgebra of X.

Conversely, suppose that B is a B-subalgebra of X. Let $x,y \in X$. Consider two cases:

Case (i): If $x,y \in B$ then $x*y \in B$, thus $\phi^+(x * y) = \lambda = \min\{\phi^+(x), \phi^+(y)\}$ and $\phi^-(x * y) = \gamma = \max\{\phi^-(x), \phi^-(y)\}$.

Case (ii): If $x \notin B$ or, $y \notin B$, then $\phi^+(x * y) \geq \tau = \min\{\phi^+(x), \phi^+(y)\}$ and $\phi^-(x * y) \leq \delta = \max\{\phi^-(x), \phi^-(y)\}$.

Hence, ϕ is a bipolar fuzzy B-subalgebra of X. Also,

$$I_{\phi^+} = \{x \in X, \phi^+(x) = \phi^+(0)\} = \{x \in X, \phi^+(x) = \lambda\} = B$$

and

$$I_{\phi^-} = \{x \in X, \phi^-(x) = \phi^-(0)\} = \{x \in X, \phi^-(x) = \gamma\} = B.$$

Definition 3.12: *Let* $\phi = (\phi^+, \phi^-)$ is a bipolar fuzzy B-subalgebra of X. For $(s,t) \in [-1,0] \times [0,1]$, *the set*

$$U(\phi^+ : t) = \{x \in X : \phi^+(x) \geq t\}$$

is called positive t-cut of ϕ and

$$L(\phi^- : s) = \{x \in X : \phi^-(x) \leq s\}$$

is called negative s-cut of ϕ.

Theorem 3.13: *If* $\phi = (\phi^{+}, \phi^{-})$ is a bipolar fuzzy *B*-subalgebra of *X*, then the positive *t*-cut and negative *s*-cut of ϕ are *B*-subalgebras of *X*.

Proof: Let $x, y \in U(\phi^{+} : t)$. Then $\phi^{+}(x) \geq t$ and $\phi^{+}(y) \geq t$. It follows that

$$\phi^{+}(x * y) \geq \min\{\phi^{+}(x), \phi^{+}(y)\} \geq t$$

so that $x * y \in U(\phi^{+} : t)$. Hence, $U(\phi^{+} : t)$ is a *B*-subalgebra of *X*.

Let $x, y \in L(\phi^{-} : s)$. Then $\phi^{-}(x) \leq s$ and $\phi^{-}(y) \leq s$. It follows that

$$\phi^{-}(x * y) \leq \max\{\phi^{-}(x), \phi^{-}(y)\} \leq s$$

so that $x * y \in L(\phi^{-} : s)$. Hence, $L(\phi^{-} : s)$ is a *B*-subalgebra of *X*.

Theorem 3.14: *Let* $\phi = (\phi^{+}, \phi^{-})$ be a bipolar fuzzy set in *X*, such that the sets $U(\phi^{+} : t)$ and $L(\phi^{-} : s)$ are *B*-subalgebras of X for every $(s,t) \in [-1,0] \times [0,1]$. Then $\phi = (\phi^{+}, \phi^{-})$ is a bipolar fuzzy *B*-subalgebra of .

Proof: Let for every $(s,t) \in [-1,0] \times [0,1]$, $U(\phi^{+} : t)$ and $L(\phi^{-} : s)$ are *B*-subalgebras of *X*. In contrary, let $x_0, y_0 \in X$ be such that $\phi^{+}(x_0 * y_0) < \min\{\phi^{+}(x_0), \phi^{+}(y_0)\}$. Let $\phi^{+}(x_0) = \theta_1$, $\phi^{+}(y_0) = \theta_2$ and $\phi^{+}(x_0 * y_0) = t$. Then $t < \min\{\theta_1, \theta_2\}$. Let us consider,

$$t_1 = \frac{1}{2}[\phi^{+}(x_0 * y_0) + \min\{\phi^{+}(x_0), \phi^{+}(y_0)\}].$$

We get that $t_1 = \frac{1}{2}(t + \min\{\theta_1, \theta_2\})$. Therefore,

$$\theta_1 > t_1 = \frac{1}{2}(t + \min\{\theta_1, \theta_2\}) > t \text{ and } \theta_2 > t_1 = \frac{1}{2}(t + \min\{\theta_1, \theta_2\}) > t.$$

Hence, $\min\{\theta_1, \theta_2\} > t_1 > t = \phi^{+}(x_0 * y_0)$, so that $x_0 * y_0 \notin U(\phi^{+} : t)$, which is a contradiction, since $\phi^{+}(x_0) = \theta_1 \geq \min\{\theta_1, \theta_2\} > t_1$ and $\phi^{+}(y_0) = \theta_2 \geq \min\{\theta_1, \theta_2\} > t_1$.

This implies $x_0, y_0 \in U(\phi^{+} : t)$. Thus $\phi^{+}(x * y) \geq \min\{\phi^{+}(x), \phi^{+}(y)\}$ for all $x, y \in X$.

Again let $x_0, y_0 \in X$ be such that $\phi^{-}(x_0 * y_0) > \max\{\phi^{-}(x_0), \phi^{-}(y_0)\}$. Let $\phi^{-}(x_0) = \eta_1$, $\phi^{-}(y_0) = \eta_2$ and $\phi^{-}(x_0 * y_0) = s$. Then $s > \max\{\eta_1, \eta_2\}$. Let us consider,

$$s_1 = \frac{1}{2}[\phi^{-}(x_0 * y_0) + \max\{\phi^{-}(x_0), \phi^{-}(y_0)\}].$$

We get that $s_1 = \frac{1}{2}(s + \max\{\eta_1, \eta_2\})$. Therefore,

$\eta_1 < s_1 = \frac{1}{2}(s + \max\{\eta_1, \eta_2\}) < s$ and $\eta_2 < s_1 = \frac{1}{2}(s + \max\{\eta_1, \eta_2\}) < s$.

Hence, $\max\{\eta_1, \eta_2\} < s_1 < s = \phi^-(x_0 * y_0)$, so that $x_0 * y_0 \notin L(\phi^- : s)$ which is a contradiction, since $\phi^-(x_0) = \eta_1 \le \max\{\eta_1, \eta_2\} < s_1$ and $\phi^-(y_0) = \eta_2 \le \max\{\eta_1, \eta_2\} < s_1$.

This implies $x_0, y_0 \in L(\phi^- : s)$. Thus $\phi^-(x * y) \le \max\{\phi^-(x), \phi^-(y)\}$ for all *x,y*∈*X*. Hence, $\phi = (\phi^+, \phi^-)$ is a bipolar fuzzy *B*-subalgebra of *X*.

Theorem 3.15: *Any B*-subalgebra of *X* can be realized as both the positive *t*-cut and negative *s*-cut of some bipolar fuzzy *B*-subalgebra of *X*.

Proof: Let *P* be a bipolar fuzzy *B*-subalgebra of *X* and $\phi = (\phi^+, \phi^-)$ be a bipolar fuzzy set on *X* defined by

$$\phi^+(x) = \begin{cases} \lambda, & if\, x \in P \\ 0, & otherwise \end{cases} \quad and \quad \phi^-(x) = \begin{cases} \tau, & if\, x \in P \\ 0, & otherwise \end{cases}$$

for all λ∈[0,1] and τ∈[–1,0]. We consider the following four cases:

Case (i): If *x,y*∈*P*, then $\phi^+(x) = \lambda$, $\phi^-(x) = \tau$ and $\phi^+(y) = \lambda$, $\phi^-(y) = \tau$. Thus,

$$\phi^+(x * y) = \lambda = \min\{\lambda, \lambda\} = \min\{\phi^+(x), \phi^+(y)\}$$

and

$$\phi^-(x * y) = \tau = \max\{\tau, \tau\} = \max\{\phi^-(x), \phi^-(y)\}.$$

Case (ii): If *x*∈*P* and $y \notin P$ then $\phi^+(x) = \lambda$, $\phi^-(x) = \tau$ and $\phi^+(y) = 0$, $\phi^-(y) = 0$. Thus,

$$\phi^+(x * y) \ge 0 = \min\{\lambda, 0\} = \min\{\phi^+(x), \phi^+(y)\}$$

and

$$\phi^-(x * y) \le 0 = \max\{\tau, 0\} = \max\{\phi^-(x), \phi^-(y)\}.$$

Case (iii): If $x \notin P$ and *y*∈*P* then $\phi^+(x) = 0$, $\phi^-(x) = 0$ and $\phi^+(y) = \lambda$, $\phi^-(y) = \tau$. Thus,

$$\phi^+(x * y) \ge 0 = \min\{0, \lambda\} = \min\{\phi^+(x), \phi^+(y)\}$$

and

$$\phi^-(x * y) \le 0 = \max\{0, \tau\} = \max\{\phi^-(x), \phi^-(y)\}.$$

Case (iv): If $x \notin P$ and $y \notin P$ then $\phi^+(x) = 0,\ \phi^-(x) = 0$ and $\phi^+(y) = 0,\ \phi^-(y) = 0$. Now

$$\phi^+(x * y) \geq 0 = \min\{0,0\} = \min\{\phi^+(x), \phi^+(y)\}$$

and

$$\phi^-(x * y) \leq 0 = \max\{0,0\} = \max\{\phi^-(x), \phi^-(y)\}.$$

Therefore $\phi = (\phi^+, \phi^-)$ is a bipolar fuzzy *B*-subalgebra of *X*.

Theorem 3.16:*Let P* be a subset of *X* and $\phi = (\phi^+, \phi^-)$ be a bipolar fuzzy set on *X* which is given in the proof of Theorem 3.15. If the positive *t*-cut and negative *s*-cut of ϕ are *B*-subalgebras of *X*, then *P* is a bipolar fuzzy *B*-subalgebra of *X*.

Proof: Let $\phi = (\phi^+, \phi^-)$ be a bipolar fuzzy *B*-subalgebra of *X*, and *x,y*∈*P*. Then $\phi^+(x) = \lambda = \phi^+(y)$ and $\phi^-(x) = \tau = \phi^-(y)$. Thus $\phi^+(x * y) \geq \min\{\phi^+(x), \phi^+(y)\} = \min\{\tau, \lambda\} = \lambda$ and $\phi^-(x * y) \leq \max\{\phi^-(x), \phi^-(y)\} = \max\{\tau, \tau\} = \tau$, which imply that *x*y*∈*P*. Hence the theorem.

Theorem 3.17:*If every bipolar fuzzy B*-subalgebras $\phi = (\phi^+, \phi^-)$ of *X* has the finite image, then every descending chain of *B*-subalgebras of *X* terminates at finite step.

Proof: Suppose there exists a strictly descending chain $S_0 \times S_1 \times S_2 \cdots$ of *B*-subalgebras of *X* which does not terminate at finite step. Define a bipolar fuzzy set $\phi = (\phi^+, \phi^-)$ in *X* by

$$\phi^+(x) = \begin{cases} \dfrac{n}{n+1} & if \quad x \in S_n \setminus S_{n+1} \\ 1 & if \quad x \in \cap_{n=0}^{\infty} S_n \end{cases} \quad \text{and} \quad \phi^-(x) = \begin{cases} -\dfrac{n}{n+1} & if \quad x \in S_n \setminus S_{n+1} \\ -1 & if \quad x \in \cap_{n=0}^{\infty} S_n \end{cases}$$

where *n*=0,1,2,... and S_0 stands for *X*. Let *x,y*∈*X*. Assume that $x \in S_n \setminus S_{n+1}$ and $y \in S_k \setminus S_{k+1}$ for *n*=0,1,2,...; *k*=0,1,2,.... Without loss of generality, we may assume that *n*≤*k*. Then obviously *x* and *y*∈S_n, so *x*y*∈S_n because S_n is a *B*-subalgebra of *X*. Hence,

$$\phi^+(x * y) \geq \frac{n}{n+1} = \min\{\phi^+(x), \phi^+(y)\}$$

$$\phi^-(x * y) \leq -\frac{n}{n+1} = \max\{\phi^-(x), \phi^-(y)\}.$$

If $x, y \in \cap_{n=0}^{\infty} S_n$, then $x * y \in \cap_{n=0}^{\infty} S_n$. Thus

$$\phi^+(x * y) = 1 = \min\{\phi^+(x), \phi^+(y)\}$$

$$\phi^-(x * y) = -1 = \max\{\phi^-(x), \phi^-(y)\}.$$

If $x \notin \cap_{n=0}^{\infty} S_n$ and $y \in \cap_{n=0}^{\infty} S_n$, then there exists a positive integer *r* such that $x \in S_r \setminus S_{r+1}$. It follows that $x*y \in S_r$ so that

$$\phi^+(x*y) \geq \frac{r}{r+1} = \min\{\phi^+(x), \phi^+(y)\}$$

$$\phi^-(x*y) \leq -\frac{r}{r+1} = \max\{\phi^-(x), \phi^-(y)\}.$$

Finally, suppose that $x \in \cap_{n=0}^{\infty} S_n$ and $y \notin \cap_{n=0}^{\infty} S_n$. Then $y \in S_s \setminus S_{s+1}$ for some positive integer *s*. It follows that $x*y \in S_s$, and hence

$$\phi^+(x*y) \geq \frac{s}{s+1} = \min\{\phi^+(x), \phi^+(y)\}$$

$$\phi^-(x*y) \leq -\frac{s}{s+1} = \max\{\phi^-(x), \phi^-(y)\}.$$

This proves that $\phi = (\phi^+, \phi^-)$ is a bipolar fuzzy *B*-subalgebras with an infinite number of different values, which is a contradiction. This completes the proof.

CONCLUSION

In this paper, notion of bipolar fuzzy *B*-subalgebras of *B*-algebras are introduced and investigated some of their useful properties. It is our hope that this work would other foundations for further study of the theory of *B*-algebras. In our future study of fuzzy structure of *B*-algebras, may be the following topics should be considered: (i) to find bipolar fuzzy closed ideals of *B*-algebra, (ii) to find the relationship between bipolar fuzzy *B*-subalgebras and closed ideals of *B*-algebras, (iii) to find bipolar fuzzy translation of *B*-algebras.

REFERENCES

Ahn, S. S., & Bang, K. (2003). On fuzzy subalgebras in B. *Commun. Korean Math. Soc.*, *18*(3), 429–437. doi:10.4134/CKMS.2003.18.3.429

Atanassov, K. T. (1999). *Intuitionistic Fuzzy Fets: Theory and Applications*. Heidelberg, Germany: Studies in Fuzziness and Soft Computing, Physica-Verl. doi:10.1007/978-3-7908-1870-3

Cho, J. R., & Kim, H. S. (2001). On B-algebras and quasigroups. *Quasigroups and Related Systems*, *7*, 1–6.

Dubois, D., & Prade, H. (2008). An introduction to bipolar representations of information and preference. *International Journal of Intelligent Systems*, *23*(8), 866–877. doi:10.1002/int.20297

Dubois, D., & Prade, H. (2012). Gradualness, uncertainty and bipolarity: Making sense of fuzzy sets. *Fuzzy Sets and Systems*, *192*(8), 3–24. doi:10.1016/j.fss.2010.11.007

Huang, Y. (2006). BCI-algebra. Science Press.

Jun, Y. B., Kim, H. S., & Lee, K. J. (2009). Bipolar fuzzy translation in *BCK/BCI*-algebra. J. of the Chungcheong Math.*Soc.*, *22*(3), 399–408.

Jun, Y. B., Roh, E. H., & Kim, H. S. (2002). On fuzzyB. *Czechoslovak Mathematical Journal*, *52*(127), 375–384. doi:10.1023/A:1021739030890

Kim, C. B., & Kim, H. S. (2008). On BG-algebras. *Demonstratio Mathematica*, *41*, 497–505.

Lee, K. J. (2009). Bipolar fuzzy subalgerbas and bipolar fuzzy ideals of *BCK/BCI*-algerbas. *Bull. Malays. Math. Sci. Soc.*, *32*(3), 361–373.

Lee, K. M. (2000). Bipolar-valued fuzzy sets and their operations. *Proc. Int. Conf. on Intelligent Technologies*.

Lee, K. M. (2004). Comparison of interval-valued fuzzy sets, intuitionistic fuzzy sets, and bipolar- valued fuzzy sets, *J. Fuzzy Logic Intelligent Systems*, *14*(2), 125–129.

Neggers, J., & Kim, H. S. (2002). On B-algebras. *Math. Vensik*, *54*, 21–29.

Saeid, A. B. (2006). Fuzzy topological B-algebra. *International Journal of Fuzzy Systems*, *8*(3), 160–164.

Senapati, Bhowmik, & Pal. (2013). Fuzzy closed ideals of *B*-algebras with interval-valued membership function. *Int. J. of Fuzzy Mathematical Archive*, (1), 79-91.

Senapati, T., Bhowmik, M., & Pal, M. (2011). Fuzzy closed ideals of B-algebras. Int. J. of Computer Science*Engineering and Technology*, *1*(10), 669–673.

Senapati, T., Bhowmik, M., & Pal, M. (2012a). Interval-valued intuitionistic fuzzy BG-subalgebras. *J. Fuzzy Math.*, *20*(3), 707–720.

Senapati, T., Bhowmik, M., & Pal, M. (2012b)n Fuzzy B-subalgebras of B-algebra with respect to t-norm. Journal of Fuzzy Set Valued Analysis.

Senapati, T., Bhowmik, M., & Pal, M. (2012c). Intuitionistic fuzzifications of ideals in BG-algebras. *Mathematica Aeterna*, *2*(9), 761–778.

Senapati, T., Bhowmik, M., & Pal, M. (2012d). Interval-valued intuitionistic fuzzy closed ideals ofBG. *Int. J. of Fuzzy Logic Systems*, *2*(2), 27–44. doi:10.5121/ijfls.2012.2203

Senapati, T., Bhowmik, M., & Pal, M. (2013). Atanassov's intuitionistic fuzzy translations of intuitionistic fuzzy H-ideals in BCK/BCI-algebras. *Notes on Intuitionistic Fuzzy Sets*, *19*, 32–47.

Senapati, T., Bhowmik, M., & Pal, M. (2014). Fuzzy dot subalgebras and fuzzy dot ideals of B-algebras. *Journal of Uncertain Systems*, *8*(1), 22–30.

Senapati, T., Bhowmik, M., & Pal, M. (2016). Intuitionistic *L BG*. *Afrika Matematika*, *27*(1-2), 187–199. doi:10.1007/s13370-015-0330-y

Zadeh, L. A. (1965). Fuzzy sets. *Information and Control*, *8*(3), 338–353. doi:10.1016/S0019-9958(65)90241-X

Zadeh, L. A. (2005). Toward a generalized theory of uncertainty (GTU)-an outline. *Inform. Sci.*, *172*(1-2), 1–40. doi:10.1016/j.ins.2005.01.017

Zadrozny, S., & Kacprzyk, J. (2012). Bipolar queries: An aggregation operator focused perspective. *Fuzzy Sets and Systems*, *196*, 69–81. doi:10.1016/j.fss.2011.10.013

Zhang, W. R. (1994). Bipolar fuzzy sets and relations: a computational framework for cognitive modeling and multiagent decision analysis. *Proceedings of IEEE Conf.*, (pp. 305-309).

Zhang, W. R., & Zhang, L. (2004). Bipolar logic and bipolar fuzzy logic. *Inform. Sci.*, *165*(3-4), 265–287. doi:10.1016/j.ins.2003.05.010

Chapter 12
Decision Making by Using Intuitionistic Fuzzy Rough Set

T. K. Das
VIT University, India

ABSTRACT

This chapter begins with a brief introduction of the theory of rough set. Rough set is an intelligent technique for handling uncertainty aspect in the data. This theory has been hybridized by combining with many other mathematical theories. In recent years, much decision making on rough set theory has been extended by embedding the ideas of fuzzy sets, intuitionistic fuzzy sets and soft sets. In this chapter, the notions of fuzzy rough set and intuitionistic fuzzy rough (IFR) sets are defined, and its properties are studied. Thereafter rough set on two universal sets has been studied. In addition, intuitionistic fuzzy rough set on two universal sets has been extensively studied. Furthermore, we would like to give an application, which shows that intuitionistic fuzzy rough set on two universal sets can be successfully applied to decision making problems.

INTRODUCTION

In our day to day life, most of the situations and associated data we come across are of not certain due to presence of uncertainties in the physical world. Uncertainty exists almost everywhere, even in the most idealized circumstances. Data set from real-life applications like medical, business, economics, etc. is not crisp and has uncertainties. In addition, uncertainty is an attribute of information and usually decision-relevant information is uncertain and imprecise. It is imperative to model these day to day problems involving uncertainties mathematically.

To this end, theories like probability theory, fuzzy set theory, intuitionistic fuzzy set theory, rough set theory, etc. to deal with problems involving uncertainties. However each theory has their limitations. In fact, the inadequacy of the parameterization tool in these theories does not allow them to handle vagueness properly.

In 1999, Molodtsov introduced the concept of soft sets and established the fundamental results of the new theory. Soft set theory somehow is free from the difficulties present in fuzzy set theory, rough

DOI: 10.4018/978-1-5225-0914-1.ch012

set theory, probability theory, etc. In 2002, P.K. Maji studied the theory of soft sets and exhibited some results of the soft set in decision making tasks. Further, researchers redefined complement of a soft set and showed that the axioms of exclusion and contradiction are satisfied by the soft sets also.

This chapter begins with a brief introduction of soft set and then describes generalizations of it. This chapter endeavors to forge a connection between fuzzy set and soft set and depicts a new model fuzzy soft set to address the challenges of vagueness and impreciseness. Furthermore, an attempt has been made to hybridize soft set with intuitionistic fuzzy set. We present a brief overview on intuitionistic fuzzy sets, which cuts across some definitions, operations, algebra, modal operators and normalization on intuitionistic fuzzy set.

FOUNDATIONS OF ROUGH COMPUTING

At the present age of internet, a huge repository of the data is available across various domains. Therefore, it is very hard to extract useful information from voluminous data available in the universe. So, information retrieval and knowledge representation has become one of the most popular areas of recent research. Information retrieval and acquisition of knowledge is one of the important components of an information system. But, the real challenge lies in converting voluminous data into knowledge and to use this knowledge to make proper decisions. In order to transform the processed data into useful information and knowledge, there is a need of new techniques and tools. Rough set theory developed by Pawlak (1982) used to process uncertain and incomplete information is a tool to the above mentioned problem. One of its strength is the attribute dependencies, their significance among inconsistent data. At the same time, it does not need any preliminary or additional information about the data. Therefore, it classifies imprecise, uncertain or incomplete information expressed in terms of data acquired from experience.

Rough Sets

In this section we recall the definitions of basic rough set theory developed by Pawlak (1991). Let U be a finite nonempty set called the universe. Suppose $R \subseteq (U \times U)$ is an equivalence relation on U. The equivalence relation R partitions the set U into disjoint subsets. Elements of same equivalence class are said to be indistinguishable. Equivalence classes induced by R are called elementary concepts. Every union of elementary concepts is called a definable set. The empty set is considered to be a definable set, thus all the definable sets form a Boolean algebra and (U,R) is called an approximation space. Given a target set X, we can characterize X by a pair of lower and upper approximations. We associate two subsets $\underline{R}X$ and $\overline{R}X$ called the R-lower and R-upper approximations of X respectively and are given by

$$\underline{R}X = \cup\{Y \in U / R : Y \subseteq X\}$$

$$\overline{R}X = \cup\{Y \in U / R : Y \cap X \neq \phi\}$$

The R-boundary of X, $BN_R(X)$ is given by $BN_R(X) = \overline{R}X - \underline{R}X$. We say X is rough with respect to R if and only if $\overline{R}X \neq \underline{R}X$, equivalently $BN_R(X) \neq \phi$. X is said to be R- definable if and only if $\overline{R}X = \underline{R}X$ or $BN_R(X) = \phi$. So, a set is rough with respect to R if and only if it is not R- definable.

Rough Set on Fuzzy Approximation Space

To unfold the article, we present the definitions, notions and results of rough set on fuzzy approximation spaces as studied by Acharjya and Tripathy (2008, 2010). We first define the following concepts leading to the introduction of rough set on fuzzy approximation space. We use the standard notation μ(x) for membership functions associated with fuzzy set.

Let U be universe of discourse. A fuzzy relation on U is a fuzzy subset of $(U \times U)$. A fuzzy relation R on U is said to be a fuzzy proximity relation if $\mu_R(x,x) = 1$ for all $x \in U$ and $\mu_R(x; y) = \mu_R(y; x)$ for all $x; y \in U$. For a given $\alpha \in [0,1]$, the α -cut of R is given by $R_\alpha = \mu_R(x,y) \geq \alpha$. We say that two elements x and y are α -similar with respect to R if $(x,y) \in R_\alpha$ and we write $xR_\alpha y$. We say that two elements x and y are α -identical with respect to R if either x is α -similar to y or x is transitively α -similar to y with respect to R, i.e., there exists a sequence of elements $(u_1, u_2, u_3, \ldots, u_n)$ in U such that $xR_\alpha u_1, u_1R_\alpha u_2, u_2R_\alpha u_3, \ldots, u_nR_\alpha y$. If x and y are α -identical with respect to fuzzy proximity relation R, then we write $(x; y) \in R(\alpha)$. It is easy to see that for any $\alpha \in [0,1]$, $R(\alpha)$ is an equivalence relation on U. We use R_α^* to denote the set of equivalence classes generated by the equivalence relation $R(\alpha)$ for any $\alpha \in [0,1]$. We denote the $R(\alpha)$-equivalence class of an element x in U by $[x]_\alpha$. The pair (U,R) is called fuzzy approximation space.

Let $X \subseteq U$, the rough set on fuzzy approximation space of X in the generalized approximation space $(U,R(\alpha))$ is denoted by $(\underline{X}_\alpha, \overline{X}_\alpha)$ where

$$\underline{X}_\alpha = \cup\{Y: Y \in R_\alpha^* \text{ and } Y \subseteq X\}$$

$$\overline{X}_\alpha = \cup\{Y: Y \in R_\alpha^* \text{ and } Y \cap X \neq \phi\}$$

The α boundary of X with respect to R is defined as $BN_{R_\alpha} = \overline{X}_\alpha - . \underline{X}_\alpha$ The set X is said to be α -discernible with respect to R if and only if $\overline{X}_\alpha = \underline{X}_\alpha$ and α -rough set with respect to R if and only if $\overline{X}_\alpha \neq \underline{X}_\alpha$. If $\alpha = 1$ then rough set on fuzzy approximation space reduces to Pawlak's rough sets.

An Example

We discuss how the above concept can be applied to real life problems. We consider an example in which we establish the relation between resource persons working in a project. We consider the number of hours of work over a period of week. We define the relation between any two resources as

$$s(x,y) = 1 - \frac{|x - y|}{40}$$

The information about the small universe $U = \{x_1, x_2, x_3, x_4, x_5, x_6, x_7, x_8\}$ is of the eight resource persons and the number of hours of work over a week in a project is presented in Table 1.

The fuzzy proximity relation R on $U$is given in Table 2.

Table 1. Resource persons and number of hours worked

Resource Persons	x_1	x_2	x_3	x_4	x_5	x_6	x_7	x_8
Number of Hours	40	36	40	32	36	38	40	34

Table 2. Fuzzy proximity relation R

R	x_1	x_2	x_3	x_4	x_5	x_6	x_7	x_8
x_1	1	0.9	1	0.8	0.9	0.95	1	0.85
x_2	0.9	1	0.9	0.9	1	0.95	0.9	0.95
x_3	1	0.9	1	0.8	0.9	0.95	1	0.85
x_4	0.8	0.9	0.8	1	0.9	0.85	0.8	0.95
x_5	0.9	1	0.9	0.9	1	0.95	0.9	0.95
x_6	0.95	0.95	0.95	0.85	0.95	1	0.95	0.9
x_7	1	0.9	1	0.8	0.9	0.95	1	0.85
x_8	0.85	0.95	0.85	0.95	0.95	0.9	0.85	1

For α= 0.95, we get $U / R = \{\{x_1, x_2, x_3, x_5, x_6, x_7, x_8\}, \{x_4\}\}$

Rough Set on Intuitionistic Fuzzy Approximation Space

To unfold the chapter, the definitions, notions and results of rough set on intuitionistic fuzzy approximation spaces discussed in chapter 1 and chapter 2 are presented here. In real time environment we face a lot of problem while studying information retrieval from large databases. This is because of inconsistent and ambiguous dataset that are precise in character. The basic rough set philosophy for information retrieval developed by Pawlak (1991) depends upon equivalence relations. However, such types of relations are rare in practice while studying information system containing numerical values. Therefore, the equivalence relation is generalized to fuzzy proximity relation and it leads to rough sets on fuzzy approximation spaces (De, 1999). The fuzzy proximity relation is further generalized to intuitionistic fuzzy proximity relation (Atanasov, 1986). Thus rough set on fuzzy approximation spaces is generalized to rough set on intuitionistic fuzzy approximation spaces (Tripathy, 2006). Further it is observed that, rough set on intuitionistic fuzzy approximation spaces is a better model over rough set and rough set on fuzzy approximation space (Acharjya, 2009). However, for completeness of the paper we provide the basic notions of rough sets on intuitionistic fuzzy approximation spaces. We use standard notation μ for membership and ν for non-membership functions associated with an intuitionistic fuzzy set.

An intuitionistic fuzzy relation R on a universal set U is an intuitionistic fuzzy set defined on $(U \times U)$. An intuitionistic fuzzy relation R on U is said to be an intuitionistic fuzzy proximity relation if the following properties hold.

$\mu_R(x,x)=1$ and $\nu_R(x,x)=0$ for all $x \in U$

$\mu_R(x,y)= \mu_R(y,x)$ and $\nu_R(x,y)= \nu_R(y,x)$ for all $x,y \in U$

Then for any (α,β)∈*J*, where $J = \{(\alpha, \beta) : \alpha, \beta \in [0,1] \text{ and } 0 \le (\alpha + \beta) \le 1\}$ (α,β) -cut, $R_{\alpha,\beta}$, of R is given by

$$R_{\alpha,\beta} = \{(x, y) : \mu_R(x,y) \ge \alpha \text{ and } \nu_R(x,y) \le \beta\}$$

We say that two elements *x* and *y* are (α,β)-similar with respect to R if $(x,y) \in R_{\alpha,\beta}$ and we write $xR_{\alpha,\beta}y$. In addition, we say that two elements x and y are (α,β)-identical with respect to R for (α,β)∈*J*, written as $xR(\alpha,\beta)y$ if and only if $xR_{\alpha,\beta}y$ or there exists a sequence of elements $u_1, u_2, u_3, \cdots, u_n$ in U such that $xR_{\alpha,\beta}u_1, u_1R_{\alpha,\beta}u_2, u_2R_{\alpha,\beta}u_3, \cdots, u_nR_{\alpha,\beta}y$. In the last case, we say that x is transitively (α,β)-similar to y with respect to R.

It is also easy to see that for any (α,β)∈*J*, *R*(α,β) is an equivalence relation on U. We denote $R^*_{\alpha,\beta}$ the set of equivalence classes generated by the equivalence relation *R*(α,β) for each fixed (α,β)∈*J*. The pair (U, R) generated in this way is an intuitionistic fuzzy approximation space (IF-approximation space). An IF-approximation space (U, R) generates usual approximation space (U, *R*(α,β)) of Pawlak for every (α,β)∈*J*. The rough set on X in the generalized approximation space (U, *R*(α,β)) is denoted by $(\underline{X}_{\alpha,\beta}, \overline{X}_{\alpha,\beta})$ where

$$\underline{X}_{\alpha,\beta} = \cup\{Y : Y \in R^*_{\alpha,\beta} \text{ and } Y \subseteq X\}$$

and

$$\overline{X}_{\alpha,\beta} = \cup\{Y : Y \in R^*_{\alpha,\beta} \text{ and } Y \cap X \ne \phi\}$$

Let X be a rough set in the generalized approximation space (U, *R*(α,β)). Then we define the (α,β)-boundary of X with respect to R denoted by $BNR_{\alpha,\beta}(X)$ as $BNR_{\alpha,\beta}(X) = \overline{X}_{\alpha,\beta} - \underline{X}_{\alpha,\beta}$. The target set X is (α,β)-discernible with respect to R if and only if $\overline{X}_{\alpha,\beta} = \underline{X}_{\alpha,\beta}$ and X is (α,β)-rough with respect to R if and only if $\overline{X}_{\alpha,\beta} \ne \underline{X}_{\alpha,\beta}$.

Almost Indiscernibility Relation

An information system provides all available information and knowledge about the objects under certain consideration. Objects are only perceived or measured by using a finite number of properties without considering any semantic relationship between attribute values of a particular attribute. Therefore, in general one uses the trivial equality relation on values of an attribute as discussed in Pawlak's rough set theory. However, in many real life applications it is observed that the attribute values are not exactly identical but almost identical (Tripathy & Acharjya, 2010). At this point we generalize Pawlak's approach of indiscernibility. Keeping view to this, the almost indiscernibility relation is generated and is the basis of rough set on intuitionistic fuzzy approximation space as discussed in the previous section.

Let U be the universe and A be a set of attributes. With each attribute *a*∈*A*, we associate a set of its values V_a, called the domain of a. The pair *S*=(*U*,*A*) will be called an information system. Let $B \subseteq A$. For a chosen (α,β)∈[0,1] we denote a binary relation $R_B(\alpha,\beta)$ on U defined by $xR_B(\alpha,\beta)y$ if and only if

$x(a)\ R_B(\alpha,\beta)\ y(a)$ for all $a \in B$, where $x(a) \in V_a$ denotes the value of attribute x in a. Obviously, it can be proved that the relation $R_B(\alpha,\beta)$ is an equivalence relation on U. Also, we notice that $R_B(\alpha,\beta)$ is not exactly the indiscernibility relation defined by Pawlak (1991); rather it can be viewed as an almost indiscernibility relation on U. For $\alpha=1$, $\beta=0$ the almost indiscernibility relation, $R_B(\alpha,\beta)$ reduces to the indiscernibility relation. Thus, it generalizes the Pawlak's indiscernibility relation. The family of all equivalence classes of $R_B(\alpha,\beta)$ i.e., the partition generated by B for $(\alpha,\beta) \in [0,1]$, will be denoted by $U/R_B(\alpha,\beta)$. If $(x,y) \in R_B(\alpha,\beta)$, then we will say that x and y are (α,β) -indiscernible. Blocks of the partition $U/R_B(\alpha,\beta)$ are referred as $B_{\alpha,\beta}$-elementary concepts. These are the basic concepts of our knowledge in the theory of rough set on intuitionistic fuzzy approximation space.

ROUGH SET BASED ON TWO UNIVERSAL SETS

An information system provides a means to describe a finite set of objects called a universe with a finite set of attributes thereby represents all the available information and knowledge. But in many real life situations an information system sets up relation with more than one universe. This extends the concept of rough set on single universal set to rough sets on two universal sets. This eventually extends the scope of rough sets to extract knowledge. Liu (2010) generalized the rough set models using two distinct universal sets. Let U and V be two universal sets and $R \subseteq (U \times V)$ be a binary relation. A relational system (U, V, R) denotes an approximation space. For an element $x \in U$, right neighborhood or the R-relative set of x in U is defined as $r(x) = \cup\{y \in V : (x,y) \in R\}$. Similarly, for an element $y \in V$, the left neighborhood or the R-relative set of y in V is defined as $l(y) = \cup\{x \in U : (x,y) \in R\}$.

For any two elements $x_1,x_2 \in U$, x_1 and x_2 are equivalent if $r(x_1)=r(x_2)$. Thus, $(x_1,x_2) \in E_U$ if and only if $r(x_1)=r(x_2)$, where E_U denotes the equivalence relation on U. Hence, E_U partitions the universal set U into disjoint subsets. Similarly for any two elements $y_1,y_2 \in V$, we say y_1 and y_2 are equivalent if $l(y_1)=l(y_2)$. Thus, $(y_1,y_2) \in E_V$ if and only if $l(y_1)=l(y_2)$, where E_V denotes the equivalence relation on V and partitions the universal set V into disjoint subsets. Therefore for the approximation space (U, V, R), it is clear that $E_V \circ R = R = R \circ E_U$, where $E_V \circ R$ is the composition of R and E_V. For any $Y \subseteq V$ and the binary relation R, we associate two subsets $\underline{R}Y$ and $\overline{R}Y$ called the R-lower and R-upper approximations of Y respectively, which are given by:

$$\underline{R}Y = \cup\{x \in U : r(x) \subseteq Y\}$$

and

$$\overline{R}Y = \cup\{x \in U : r(x) \cap Y \neq \phi\}$$

The R-boundary of Y is denoted as $BN_R(Y) = \overline{R}Y - \underline{R}Y$. The pair $(\overline{R}Y, \underline{R}Y)$ is called as the rough set of $Y \subseteq V$ if $\overline{R}Y \neq \underline{R}Y$ or equivalently $BN_R(Y) \neq \phi$. Further, if U and V are finite sets, then the binary relation R from U to V can be represented as $R(x,y)$, where

$$R(x,y) = \begin{cases} 1 & \text{if } (x,y) \in R \\ 0 & \text{if } (x,y) \notin R \end{cases}$$

The characteristic function of $X \subseteq U$ is defined for each $x \in U$ as follows:

$$\chi(x) = \begin{cases} 1 & \text{if } x \in X \\ 0 & \text{if } x \notin X \end{cases}$$

Therefore, the R- lower and R- upper approximations can also be presented in an equivalent form as shown below. Here $\bigwedge$ and $\bigvee$ denote the minimum and the maximum operators respectively.

$$(\underline{R}Y)x = \bigwedge_{y \in V} ((1 - R(x, y)) \vee Y(y))$$

and

$$(\overline{R}Y)x = \bigvee_{y \in V} (R(x, y) \wedge Y(y))$$

Definition 6.1 Let U and V be two universal sets. Let R be a binary relation from U to V. If $x \in U$ and $r(x)=\phi$, then we call x is a solitary element with respect to R. The set of all solitary elements with respect to the relation R is called as solitary set and is denoted as S. Mathematically,

$$S = \{x \in U : r(x) = \phi\}$$

Topological Characterization of Rough Set on Two Universal Sets

In this section, we state an interesting topological characterization of rough set on two universal sets employing the notion of the lower and upper approximation. It results four important and different types of rough sets on two universal sets as discussed by Acharjya, Tripathy and Ezhilarsi (2012).

Type 1: If $\underline{R}Y \neq \phi$ and $\overline{R}Y \neq U$, then we say that Y is roughly R-definable on two universal sets.
Type 2: If $\underline{R}Y = \phi$ and $\overline{R}Y \neq U$, then we say that Y is internally R-undefinable on two universal sets.
Type 3: If $\underline{R}Y \neq \phi$ and $\overline{R}Y = U$, then we say that Y is externally R-undefinable on two universal sets.
Type 4: If $\underline{R}Y = \phi$ and $\overline{R}Y = U$, then we say that Y is totally R-undefinable on two universal sets.

Approximation of Classification of Rough Set on Two Universal Sets

Real time data contains uncertainties. Therefore, paying no attention to it often leads to the failure of system. Traditional statistical tools overlook these uncertainties and, therefore, lack in accuracy. Computational intelligence techniques such as artificial neural networks, evolutionary algorithms, fuzzy sets, rough sets etc. consider these uncertainties and deal with them specifically. The notion of rough set (Pawlak, 1982) was classifications and categories in knowledge base. Some categories must be defined in a knowledge base otherwise the objects of our interest can not be defined approximately in a knowledge base. The basic idea of rough set is based upon the approximation of sets by a pair of sets known as the lower approximation and upper approximation of the set which are based on equivalence relation. However, to overcome the limitation of equivalence relation; the concept of binary relation is introduced and rough sets on two universal sets is studied by Liu (2010). Also, the approximation of classification in rough set on two universal sets is studied by Tripathy and Acharjya (2012). These are important in the context of knowledge representation. Because we are interested in generalized characterization for types of classifications in rough set on two universal sets, it is essential to state the notions and results of approximation of classifications as discussed by Tripathy and Acharjya (2012). Now, we formally state these notions and important results as below.

Definition: Let $F = \{Y_1, Y_2, \cdots, Y_n\}$, where $n>1$ be a family of non empty sets defined over V. We say that F is a classification of V if and only if $(Y_i \cap Y_j) = \phi$ for $i \neq j$ and $\sum_{k=1}^{n} Y_k = V$.

Definition: Let $F = \{Y_1, Y_2, \cdots, Y_n\}$ be a family of non empty classification of V and let R be a binary relation from $U \to V$. Then the R-lower and R-upper approximation of the family F is given as $\underline{R}F = \{\underline{R}Y_1, \underline{R}Y_2, \underline{R}Y_3, \cdots, \underline{R}Y_n\}$ and $\overline{R}F = \{\overline{R}Y_1, \overline{R}Y_2, \overline{R}Y_3, \cdots, \overline{R}Y_n\}$ respectively.

Theorem: Let R be a binary relation from $U \to V$ and let $F = \{Y_1, Y_2, \cdots, Y_n\}$, where $n>1$ be a classification of V. For any $i \in \{1,2,3,\ldots,n\}$, $\overline{R}(\bigcup_i Y_i) = U$ if and only if $\underline{R}(\bigcup_j Y_j) = \phi$ for $j \neq i$ and $j \in \{1,2,3,\ldots,n\}$.

Corollary: Let R be a binary relation from $U \to V$ and let $F = \{Y_1, Y_2, \cdots, Y_n\}$, where $n>1$ be a classification of V. For any $i \in \{1,2,3,\ldots,n\}$, if $\overline{R}(\bigcup_i Y_i) = U$, then $\underline{R}Y_j = \phi$ for each $j \neq i$ and $j \in \{1,2,3,\ldots,n\}$.

Corollary: Let R be a binary relation from $U \to V$ and let $F = \{Y_1, Y_2, \cdots, Y_n\}$, where $n>1$ be a classification of V. For each $i \in \{1,2,3,\ldots,n\}$, $\overline{R}Y_i = U$ if and only if $\underline{R}(\bigcup_j Y_j) = \phi$ for each $j \neq i$ and $j \in \{1,2,3,\ldots,n\}$.

Corollary: Let R be a binary relation from $U \to V$ and let $F = \{Y_1, Y_2, \cdots, Y_n\}$, where $n>1$ be a classification of V. For each $i \in \{1,2,3,\ldots,n\}$, $\underline{R}Y_i = \phi$ if and only if $\overline{R}(\bigcup_j Y_j) = U$, for each $j \neq i$ and $j \in \{1,2,3,\ldots,n\}$.

Corollary: Let R be a binary relation from $U \to V$ and let $F = \{Y_1, Y_2, \cdots, Y_n\}$, where $n>1$ be a classification of V. If there exists $i \in \{1,2,3,\ldots,n\}$ such that $\overline{R}Y_i = U$, then for each $j \neq i$ and $j \in \{1,2,3,\ldots,n\}$; $\underline{R}Y_j = \phi$.

Corollary: Let R be a binary relation from $U \to V$ and let $F = \{Y_1, Y_2, \cdots, Y_n\}$, where $n>1$ be a classification of V. If $\overline{R}Y_i = U$ for all $i \in \{1,2,3,\ldots,n\}$, then $\underline{R}Y_i = \phi$ for all $j \in \{1,2,3,\ldots,n\}$.

Theorem: Let R be a binary relation from $U \to V$ and let $F = \{Y_1, Y_2, \cdots, Y_n\}$, where $n>1$ be a classification of V. For any $i \in \{1,2,3,\ldots,n\}$, $\underline{R}(\bigcup_i Y_i) \neq \phi$ if and only if $\bigcup_j \overline{R}Y_j \neq U$ for $j \neq i$ and $j \in \{1,2,3,\ldots,n\}$.

Corollary: Let R be a binary relation from $U \to V$ and let $F = \{Y_1, Y_2, \cdots, Y_n\}$, where $n>1$ be a classification of V. For any $i \in \{1,2,3,\ldots,n\}$, if $\underline{R}(\bigcup_i Y_i) \neq \phi$ then $\overline{R}Y_j \neq U$ for each $j \neq i$ and $j \in \{1,2,3,\ldots,n\}$.

Corollary: Let R be a binary relation from $U \to V$ and let $F = \{Y_1, Y_2, \cdots, Y_n\}$, where $n>1$ be a classification of V. For any $i \in \{1,2,3,\ldots,n\}$, $\underline{R}Y_i \neq \phi$ if and only if $\bigcup_j \overline{R}Y_j \neq U$ for $j \neq i$ and $j \in \{1,2,3,\ldots,n\}$.

Corollary: Let R be a binary relation from $U \to V$ and let $F = \{Y_1, Y_2, \cdots, Y_n\}$, where $n>1$ be a classification of V. For all i, $i \in \{1,2,3,\ldots,n\}$, $\overline{R}Y_i \neq U$ if and only if $\underline{R}(\bigcup_j Y_j) \neq \phi$ for $j \neq i$ and $j \in \{1,2,3,\ldots,n\}$.

Corollary: Let R be a binary relation from $U \to V$ and let $F = \{Y_1, Y_2, \cdots, Y_n\}$, where $n>1$ be a classification of V. If there exists $i \in \{1,2,3,\ldots,n\}$ such that $\underline{R}Y_i \neq \phi$, then $\overline{R}Y_j \neq U$ for each $j \neq i$ and $j \in \{1,2,3,\ldots,n\}$.

Corollary: Let R be a binary relation from $U \to V$ and let $F = \{Y_1, Y_2, \cdots, Y_n\}$, where $n>1$ be a classification of V. If for all $i \in \{1,2,3,\ldots,n\}$, $\underline{R}Y_i \neq \phi$ holds then $\overline{R}Y_j \neq U$ for all $j \in \{1,2,3,\ldots,n\}$.

Intuitionistic Fuzzy Rough Set on Two Universal Sets

A fuzzy relation is an extension of the concept of binary relation on any set U. Therefore, fuzzy rough sets by Dubois and Prade (1990) generalize the concepts of Pawlak rough sets. Further it is generalized to fuzzy rough sets in two universal sets by Liu (2010). In fuzzy set theory it is taken into consideration that there exist a membership value for all the elements of the set and we do not consider non membership values of the elements of the set. However, it is not true in many real life problems due to the presence of hesitation. In fuzzy set theory, if $\mu(x)$ be the degree of membership of an element x, then the degree of non membership of x is calculated using mathematical formula $(1-\mu(x))$ with the assumption that full part of the degree of membership is determinism and in-deterministic part is zero. This is not always applicable in real life and hence intuitionistic fuzzy set theory is better. At the same time, intuitionistic fuzzy set theory reduces to fuzzy set theory if in-deterministic part is zero. It indicates that intuitionistic fuzzy set model is a generalized model over fuzzy set model. Therefore, intuitionistic fuzzy rough set on two universal sets is a better model than fuzzy rough set on two universal sets.

Now, we present the definitions, notations and results of intuitionistic fuzzy rough set on two universal sets as established and introduced by Tripathy and Acharjya (2012). We define the basic concepts leading to intuitionistic fuzzy rough set on two universal sets in which we denote μ for membership and ν for non membership functions that are associated with an intuitionistic fuzzy rough set on two universal sets.

Definition: (Atanasov, 1986) Let U be a universe of discourse and x is a particular element of U. An intuitionistic fuzzy set X of U is defined as $\langle x, \mu_X(x), \nu_X(x) \rangle$, where the function $\mu_X(x)$: $U \to [0,1]$ and $\nu_X(x)$: $U \to [0,1]$ define the degree of membership and non membership respectively of the element $x \in U$. For every element $x \in U$, $0 \leq \mu_X(x) + \nu_X(x) \leq 1$. The amount $1-(\mu_X(x) + \nu_X(x))$ is called the hesitation part, which may cater either membership value or non membership value or the both. For simplicity we will use $(\mu_X\ \nu_X)$ to denote the intuitionistic fuzzy set X. The family of all intuitionistic fuzzy subsets of U is denoted by $IF(U)$. The complement of an intuitionistic fuzzy set X is denoted by

$$X' = \{< x, \nu_X(x), \mu_X(x) > | \; x \in U\}$$

Definition: (Atanasov, 1986) Let U and V be two non empty universal sets. An intuitionistic fuzzy relation R_{IF} from $U \rightarrow V$ is an intuitionistic fuzzy set of $(U \times V)$ characterized by the membership function $\mu_{R_{IF}}$ and non-membership function $\nu_{R_{IF}}$ where

$$R_{IF} = \{ \langle (x,y), \mu_{R_{IF}}(x,y), \nu_{R_{IF}}(x,y) \rangle \mid x \in U, \, y \in V\}$$

with $0 \leq \mu_{R_{IF}}(x,y) + \nu_{R_{IF}}(x,y) \leq 1$ for every $(x,y) \in U \times V$.

Definition: (Acharjya & Tripathy, 2012) Let U and V be two non empty universal sets and R_{IF} is a intuitionistic fuzzy relation from U to V. If for $x \in U$, $\mu_{R_{IF}}(x, y) = 0$ and $\nu_{R_{IF}}(x, y) = 1$ for all $y \in V$, then x is said to be a solitary element with respect to R_{IF}. The set of all solitary elements with respect to the relation R_{IF} is called the solitary set S. That is,

$$S = \{x \mid x \in U, \; \mu_{R_{IF}}(x, y) = 0, \; \nu_{R_{IF}}(x, y) = 1 \; \forall \; y \in V\}$$

Definition: (Acharjya & Tripathy, 2012) Let U and V be two non empty universal sets and R_{IF} is a intuitionistic fuzzy relation from U to V. Therefore, (U, V, R_{IF}) is called a intuitionistic fuzzy approximation space. For $Y \in IF(V)$, an intuitionistic fuzzy rough set is a pair $(\underline{R_{IF}}Y, \overline{R_{IF}}Y)$ of intuitionistic fuzzy set on U such that for every $x \in U$

$$\underline{R_{IF}}Y = \{\langle x, \mu_{\underline{R_{IF}}(Y)}(x), \nu_{\underline{R_{IF}}(Y)}(x)\rangle \mid x \in U\}$$

$$\overline{R_{IF}}Y = \{\langle x, \mu_{\overline{R_{IF}}(Y)}(x), \nu_{\overline{R_{IF}}(Y)}(x)\rangle \mid x \in U\}$$

where

$$\mu_{\underline{R_{IF}}(Y)}(x) = \bigwedge_{y \in V} [\nu_{R_{IF}}(x,y) \vee \mu_Y(y)]$$

$$\nu_{\underline{R_{IF}}(Y)}(x) = \bigvee_{y \in V} [\mu_{R_{IF}}(x,y) \wedge \nu_Y(y)]$$

$$\mu_{\overline{R_{IF}}(Y)}(x) = \bigvee_{y \in V} [\mu_{R_{IF}}(x,y) \wedge \mu_Y(y)]$$

and

$$\nu_{\overline{R_{IF}}(Y)}(x) = \bigwedge_{y \in V} [\nu_{R_{IF}}(x,y) \vee \nu_Y(y)]$$

The pair $(\underline{R_{IF}}Y,\ \overline{R_{IF}}Y)$ is called the intuitionistic fuzzy rough set of Y with respect to (U,V,R_{IF}), where $\underline{R_{IF}},\ \overline{R_{IF}} : IF(U) \rightarrow IF(V)$ are referred as lower and upper intuitionistic fuzzy rough approximation operators on two universal sets.

Algebraic Properties of Intuitionistic Fuzzy Rough Set on Two Universal Sets

This section discusses the algebraic properties of intuitionistic fuzzy rough set on two universal sets through solitary set as established by Tripathy and Acharjya (2012). These are interesting and valuable in the study of intuitionistic fuzzy rough sets on two universal sets and are useful in finding knowledge from the information system that establishes relation between two universes.

Let U and V be two universal sets. Let R_{IF} be an intuitionistic fuzzy relation from U to V and further let S be the solitary set with respect to R_{IF}. Then for $X, Y \in IF(V)$, the following properties holds:

1. $\underline{R_{IF}}(V) = U$ and $\overline{R_{IF}}(\phi) = \phi$
2. If $X \subseteq Y$, then $\underline{R_{IF}}(X) \subseteq \underline{R_{IF}}(Y)$ and $\overline{R_{IF}}(X) \subseteq \overline{R_{IF}}(Y)$
3. $\underline{R_{IF}}(X) = (\overline{R_{IF}}(X'))'$ and $\overline{R_{IF}}(X) = (\underline{R_{IF}}(X'))'$
4. $\underline{R_{IF}}\phi \supseteq S$ and $\overline{R_{IF}}V \subseteq S'$, where S' denotes the complement of S in U.
5. For any given index set J, $X_i \in IF(V)$, $\underline{R_{IF}}(\bigcup_{i\in J} X_i) \supseteq \bigcup_{i\in J} \underline{R_{IF}}X_i$ and $\overline{R_{IF}}(\bigcap_{i\in J} X_i) \subseteq \bigcap_{i\in J} \overline{R_{IF}}X_i$.
6. For any given index set J, $X_i \in IF(V)$, $\underline{R_{IF}}(\bigcap_{i\in J} X_i) = \bigcap_{i\in J} \underline{R_{IF}}X_i$ and $\overline{R_{IF}}(\bigcup_{i\in J} X_i) = \bigcup_{i\in J} \overline{R_{IF}}X_i$.

Approximation of Classification of Intuitionistic Fuzzy Rough Set on Two Universal Sets

In an information system, the understanding of the objects and their attributes influencing the objects with a depicted value are of major concern. The basic philosophy of rough set is based upon the approximation of sets by lower and upper approximation of the set. Here, the lower and upper approximation operators are based on equivalence relation. But, the requirement of an equivalence relation is restrictive and may limit the application of rough set model. Therefore, rough set is generalized by G. Liu (2010) to rough set on two universal sets. Further, Acharjya and Tripathy (2012) generalized the concepts to intuitionistic fuzzy rough set on two universal sets. Because we are interested in classifications based on intuitionistic fuzzy relation, it is interesting to have the idea of approximation of classifications. It is because classifications of universes play central roles in rough set theory. In this section, we introduce the approximation of classification formally.

Definition: Let $F = \{Y_1, Y_2, Y_3, \cdots, Y_n\}$, where $n>1$ be a family of non empty sets defined over V. We say that F is a classification of V if and only if $(Y_i \cap Y_j) = \phi$ for $i \neq j$ and $\sum_{k=1}^{n} Y_k = V$.

Definition: Let $F = \{Y_1, Y_2, Y_3, \cdots, Y_n\}$ be a family of non-empty classification of V and let R_{IF} be a intuitionistic fuzzy relation from $U \rightarrow V$. Then the R_{IF} -lower and R_{IF} -upper approximation of the family F is given as $\underline{R}_{IF}F = \{\underline{R}_{IF}Y_1, \underline{R}_{IF}Y_2, \underline{R}_{IF}Y_3, \cdots, \underline{R}_{IF}Y_n\}$ and $\overline{R}_{IF}F = \{\overline{R}_{IF}Y_1, \overline{R}_{IF}Y_2, \overline{R}_{IF}Y_3, \cdots, \overline{R}_{IF}Y_n\}$ respectively.

Measures of Uncertainty in Intuitionistic Fuzzy Rough Set on Two Universal Sets

This section introduces the concept of measures of uncertainty such as accuracy and quality of approximation employing the intuitionistic fuzzy relation R_{IF}. We denote the number of objects in a set V by card(V). Let $F = \{Y_1, Y_2, \cdots, Y_n\}$ be a family of non-empty classifications. Then the R_{IF} -lower and R_{IF} -upper approximation of the family F are given as $\underline{R}_{IF}F = \{\underline{R}_{IF}Y_1, \underline{R}_{IF}Y_2, \underline{R}_{IF}Y_3, \cdots, \underline{R}_{IF}Y_n\}$ and $\overline{R}_{IF}F = \{\overline{R}_{IF}Y_1, \overline{R}_{IF}Y_2, \overline{R}_{IF}Y_3, \cdots, \overline{R}_{IF}Y_n\}$ respectively. Now we define accuracy of approximation and quality of approximation of the family F employing the intuitionistic fuzzy relation R_{IF} as follows:

Definition: The accuracy of approximation of F that expresses the percentage of possible correct decisions when classifying objects employing the intuitionistic fuzzy relation R_{IF} is defined as

$$\alpha_{R_{IF}}(F) = \frac{\sum card\,(\underline{R}_{IF}Y_i)}{\sum card\,(\overline{R}_{IF}Y_i)} \text{ for } i=1,2,3,\ldots,n$$

Definition: The quality of approximation of F that expresses the percentage of objects which can be correctly classified to classes of F by the intuitionistic fuzzy relation R_{IF} is defined as

$$\nu_{R_{IF}}(F) = \frac{\sum card\,(\underline{R}_{IF}Y_i)}{card\,(V)} \text{ for } i=1,2,3,\ldots,n$$

Definition: We say that $F = \{Y_1, Y_2, \cdots, Y_n\}$ is R_{IF} -definable if and only if $\underline{R}_{IF} = \overline{R}_{IF}$; that is $\underline{R}_{IF}Y_i = \overline{R}_{IF}Y_i$ for i=1,2,3,…,n.

APPLICATIONS TO MULTI CRITERION DECISION MAKING

This section depicts a real life application of intuitionistic fuzzy rough set on two universal sets to multi criterion decision making. The model application is explained as intuitionistic fuzzy rough set upper approximation. Let us consider the multi criteria decision making in the case of supermarkets in a particular city. However, it is observed that due to several factors such as best possible value for customer's money, quality of the product, style and the behaviour of supporting staff, customers depend on more than one supermarket. Therefore, from customer behaviour it is clear that they are not happy with one supermarket. Hence, intuitionistic fuzzy relation better depicts the relation between the customers and supermarkets.

Let us set the criteria $V = \{y_1, y_2, y_3, y_4, y_5, y_6\}$, in which y_1 denotes best possible value of customer's money; y_2 denotes quality of the product; y_3 denotes the behavior of supporting staff; y_4 denotes the location of supermarket; y_5 denotes availability of items; and y_6 denotes offers. Let us consider the decisions $U = \{d_1, d_2, d_3, d_4, d_5\}$, in which d_1 denotes outstanding; d_2 denotes most welcome; d_3 denotes more welcome; d_4 denotes much welcome; and d_5 denotes least welcome. Several variety of customers and professionals are invited to the survey that only focuses on the criterion of best possible value of customers money in a supermarket. Therefore, (U, V, R_{IF}) be an intuitionistic fuzzy approximation space, where $U = \{d_1, d_2, d_3, d_4, d_5\}$ and $V = \{y_1, y_2, y_3, y_4, y_5, y_6\}$.

If 15% people select "outstanding" and 10% people select "not outstanding"; 25% select "most welcome" and 20% select not "most welcome"; 35% select "more welcome" and 5% select "not more welcome"; 10% select "much welcome" and 20% select "not much welcome"; and 15% select "least welcome" and 10% select not "least welcome", then the vector can be obtained as $(0.15,0.1; 0.25,0.2; 0.35,0.5; 0.1,0.2; 0.15,0.1)^t$, where t represents the transpose. Similarly, the decisions based on other criteria are obtained as follows: $(0.1,0.2; 0.35,0.21; 0.25,0.15; 0.1,0.8; 0.2,0.7)^t$, $(0.55,0.1; 0.15,0.45; 0.2,0.15; 0,0.6; 0.1,0.3)^t$, $(0.1,0.7; 0.1,0.4; 0.4,0.2; 0.2,0.3; 0.2,0.1)^t$, $(0,0.6; 0,0.5; 0.15,0.3; 0.35,0.1; 0.5,0.15)^t$, and $(0.25,0.1; 0.25,0.2; 0.2,0.4; 0.1,0.4; 0.2,0.3)^t$. Based on the decision vectors, the intuitionistic fuzzy relation R_{IF} from U to V is presented by the following matrix. We define the intuitionistic fuzzy relation $R_{IF} \in IF(U \times V)$ by the following matrix.

$$R_{IF} = \begin{array}{c} \\ d_1 \\ d_2 \\ d_3 \\ d_4 \\ d_5 \end{array} \begin{array}{cccccc} y_1 & y_2 & y_3 & y_4 & y_5 & y_6 \\ \end{array}$$

$$R_{IF} = \begin{matrix} & y_1 & y_2 & y_3 & y_4 & y_5 & y_6 \\ d_1 & 0.15, 0.1 & 0.1, 0.2 & 0.55, 0.1 & 0.1, 0.7 & 0, 0.6 & 0.25, 0.1 \\ d_2 & 0.25, 0.2 & 0.35, 0.21 & 0.15, 0.45 & 0.1, 0.4 & 0, 0.5 & 0.25, 0.2 \\ d_3 & 0.35, 0.05 & 0.25, 0.15 & 0.2, 0.15 & 0.4, 0.2 & 0.15, 0.3 & 0.2, 0.4 \\ d_4 & 0.1, 0.2 & 0.1, 0.8 & 0, 0.6 & 0.2, 0.3 & 0.35, 0.1 & 0.1, 0.4 \\ d_5 & 0.15, 0.1 & 0.2, 0.7 & 0.1, 0.3 & 0.2, 0.1 & 0.5, 0.15 & 0.2, 0.3 \end{matrix}$$

It is assumed that there are two categories of customers, where right weights for each criterion in V are

$$Y_1 = \left(\langle d_1, 0.35, 0.15\rangle, \langle d_2, 0.15, 0.3\rangle, \langle d_3, 0.2, 0.3\rangle, d\langle_4, 0.1, 0.5\rangle, \langle d_5, 0.1, 0.4\rangle, \langle d_6, 0.1, 0.2\rangle\right)$$

and

$$Y_2 = \left(\langle d_1, 0.2, 0.3\rangle, \langle d_2, 0.4, 0.1\rangle, \langle d_3, 0.15, 0.4\rangle, \langle d_4, 0.1, 0.3\rangle, \langle d_5, 0.1, 0.3\rangle, \langle d_6, 0.05, 0.5\rangle\right)$$

respectively. Thus, by using upper approximation we have:

$$\begin{aligned}\mu_{\overline{R_{IF}}(Y_1)}(d_1) &= \vee_{y\in V}[\mu_{R_{IF}}(d_1,y)\wedge\mu_{Y_1}(y)]\\ &= [0.15\wedge0.35]\vee[0.1\wedge0.15]\vee[0.55\wedge0.2]\vee[0.1\wedge0.1]\vee[0\wedge0.1]\vee[0.25\wedge0.1]\\ &= 0.15\vee0.1\vee0.2\vee0.1\vee0\vee0.1\\ &= 0.2\end{aligned}$$

$$\begin{aligned}\nu_{\overline{R_{IF}}(Y_1)}(d_1) &= \wedge_{y\in V}[\nu_{R_{IF}}(d_1,y)\vee\nu_{Y_1}(y)]\\ &= [0.1\vee0.15]\wedge[0.2\vee0.3]\wedge[0.1\vee0.3]\wedge[0.7\vee0.5]\wedge[0.6\vee0.4]\wedge[0.1\vee0.2]\\ &= 0.15\wedge0.3\wedge0.3\wedge0.7\wedge0.6\wedge0.2\\ &= 0.15\end{aligned}$$

$$\begin{aligned}\mu_{\overline{R_{IF}}(Y_1)}(d_2) &= \vee_{y\in V}[\mu_{R_{IF}}(d_2,y)\wedge\mu_{Y_1}(y)]\\ &= [0.25\wedge0.35]\vee[0.35\wedge0.15]\vee[0.15\wedge0.2]\vee[0.1\wedge0.1]\vee[0\wedge0.1]\vee[0.25\wedge0.1]\\ &= 0.25\vee0.15\vee0.15\vee0.1\vee0\vee0.1\\ &= 0.25\end{aligned}$$

$$\begin{aligned}\nu_{\overline{R_{IF}}(Y_1)}(d_2) &= \wedge_{y\in V}[\nu_{R_{IF}}(d_2,y)\vee\nu_{Y_1}(y)]\\ &= [0.2\vee0.15]\wedge[0.21\vee0.3]\wedge[0.45\vee0.3]\wedge[0.4\vee0.5]\wedge[0.5\vee0.4]\wedge[0.2\vee0.2]\\ &= 0.2\wedge0.3\wedge0.45\wedge0.5\wedge0.5\wedge0.2\\ &= 0.2\end{aligned}$$

$$\begin{aligned}\mu_{\overline{R_{IF}}(Y_1)}(d_3) &= \vee_{y\in V}[\mu_{R_{IF}}(d_3,y)\wedge\mu_{Y_1}(y)]\\ &= [0.35\wedge0.35]\vee[0.25\wedge0.15]\vee[0.2\wedge0.2]\vee[0.4\wedge0.1]\vee[0.15\wedge0.1]\vee[0.2\wedge0.1]\\ &= 0.35\vee0.15\vee0.2\vee0.1\vee0.1\vee0.1\\ &= 0.35\end{aligned}$$

$$\begin{aligned}\nu_{\overline{R_{IF}}(Y_1)}(d_3) &= \wedge_{y\in V}[\nu_{R_{IF}}(d_3,y)\vee\nu_{Y_1}(y)]\\ &= [0.05\vee0.15]\wedge[0.15\vee0.3]\wedge[0.15\vee0.3]\wedge[0.2\vee0.5]\wedge[0.3\vee0.4]\wedge[0.4\vee0.2]\\ &= 0.15\wedge0.3\wedge0.3\wedge0.5\wedge0.4\wedge0.4\\ &= 0.15\end{aligned}$$

$$\begin{aligned}\mu_{\overline{R_{IF}}(Y_1)}(d_4) &= \vee_{y\in V}[\mu_{R_{IF}}(d_4,y)\wedge\mu_{Y_1}(y)]\\ &= [0.1\wedge0.35]\vee[0.1\wedge0.15]\vee[0\wedge0.2]\vee[0.2\wedge0.1]\vee[0.35\wedge0.1]\vee[0.1\wedge0.1]\\ &= 0.1\vee0.1\vee0\vee0.1\vee0.1\vee0.1\\ &= 0.1\end{aligned}$$

$$\begin{aligned}\nu_{\overline{R_{IF}(Y_1)}}(d_4) &= \bigwedge_{y \in V}[\nu_{R_{IF}}(d_4, y) \vee \nu_{Y_1}(y)] \\ &= [0.2 \vee 0.15] \wedge [0.8 \vee 0.3] \wedge [0.6 \vee 0.3] \wedge [0.3 \vee 0.5] \wedge [0.1 \vee 0.4] \wedge [0.4 \vee 0.2] \\ &= 0.2 \wedge 0.8 \wedge 0.6 \wedge 0.5 \wedge 0.4 \wedge 0.4 \\ &= 0.2\end{aligned}$$

$$\begin{aligned}\mu_{\overline{R_{IF}(Y_1)}}(d_5) &= \bigvee_{y \in V}[\mu_{R_{IF}}(d_5, y) \wedge \mu_{Y_1}(y)] \\ &= [0.15 \wedge 0.35] \vee [0.2 \wedge 0.15] \vee [0.1 \wedge 0.2] \vee [0.2 \wedge 0.1] \vee [0.5 \wedge 0.1] \vee [0.2 \wedge 0.1] \\ &= 0.15 \vee 0.15 \vee 0.1 \vee 0.1 \vee 0.1 \vee 0.1 \\ &= 0.15\end{aligned}$$

$$\begin{aligned}\nu_{\overline{R_{IF}(Y_1)}}(d_5) &= \bigwedge_{y \in V}[\nu_{R_{IF}}(d_5, y) \vee \nu_{Y_1}(y)] \\ &= [0.1 \vee 0.15] \wedge [0.7 \vee 0.3] \wedge [0.3 \vee 0.3] \wedge [0.1 \vee 0.5] \wedge [0.15 \vee 0.4] \wedge [0.3 \vee 0.2] \\ &= 0.15 \wedge 0.7 \wedge 0.3 \wedge 0.5 \wedge 0.4 \wedge 0.3 \\ &= 0.15\end{aligned}$$

Hence, the upper approximation for Y_1 is given as:

$$\overline{R_{IF}}Y_1 = \left\{d\left\langle_1, 0.2, 0.15\right\rangle, \left\langle d_2, 0.25, 0.2\right\rangle, \left\langle d_3, 0.35, 0.15\right\rangle, \left\langle d_4, 0.1, 0.2\right\rangle, \left\langle d_5, 0.15, 0.15\right\rangle\right\}^t$$

Similarly, for the set Y_2 we get the following:

$$\begin{aligned}\mu_{\overline{R_{IF}(Y_2)}}(d_1) &= \bigvee_{y \in V}[\mu_{R_{IF}}(d_1, y) \wedge \mu_{Y_2}(y)] \\ &= [0.15 \wedge 0.2] \vee [0.1 \wedge 0.4] \vee [0.55 \wedge 0.15] \vee [0.1 \wedge 0.1] \vee [0 \wedge 0.1] \vee [0.25 \wedge 0.05] \\ &= 0.15 \vee 0.1 \vee 0.15 \vee 0.1 \vee 0 \vee 0.05 \\ &= 0.15\end{aligned}$$

$$\begin{aligned}\nu_{\overline{R_{IF}(Y_2)}}(d_1) &= \bigwedge_{y \in V}[\nu_{R_{IF}}(d_1, y) \vee \nu_{Y_2}(y)] \\ &= [0.1 \vee 0.3] \wedge [0.2 \vee 0.1] \wedge [0.1 \vee 0.4] \wedge [0.7 \vee 0.3] \wedge [0.6 \vee 0.3] \wedge [0.1 \vee 0.5] \\ &= 0.3 \wedge 0.2 \wedge 0.4 \wedge 0.7 \wedge 0.6 \wedge 0.5 \\ &= 0.2\end{aligned}$$

$$\begin{aligned}\mu_{\overline{R_{IF}(Y_2)}}(d_2) &= \bigvee_{y \in V}[\mu_{R_{IF}}(d_2, y) \wedge \mu_{Y_2}(y)] \\ &= [0.25 \wedge 0.2] \vee [0.35 \wedge 0.4] \vee [0.15 \wedge 0.15] \vee [0.1 \wedge 0.1] \vee [0 \wedge 0.1] \vee [0.25 \wedge 0.05] \\ &= 0.2 \vee 0.35 \vee 0.15 \vee 0.1 \vee 0 \vee 0.05 \\ &= 0.35\end{aligned}$$

$$\nu_{\overline{R_{IF}(Y_2)}}(d_2) = \bigwedge_{y \in V}[\nu_{R_{IF}}(d_2, y) \vee \nu_{Y_2}(y)]$$
$$= [0.2 \vee 0.3] \wedge [0.21 \vee 0.1] \wedge [0.45 \vee 0.4] \wedge [0.4 \vee 0.3] \wedge [0.5 \vee 0.3] \wedge [0.2 \vee 0.5]$$
$$= 0.3 \wedge 0.21 \wedge 0.45 \wedge 0.4 \wedge 0.5 \wedge 0.5$$
$$= 0.21$$

$$\mu_{\overline{R_{IF}(Y_2)}}(d_3) = \bigvee_{y \in V}[\mu_{R_{IF}}(d_3, y) \wedge \mu_{Y_2}(y)]$$
$$= [0.35 \wedge 0.2] \vee [0.25 \wedge 0.4] \vee [0.2 \wedge 0.15] \vee [0.4 \wedge 0.1] \vee [0.15 \wedge 0.1] \vee [0.2 \wedge 0.05]$$
$$= 0.2 \vee 0.25 \vee 0.15 \vee 0.1 \vee 0.1 \vee 0.05$$
$$= 0.25$$

$$\nu_{\overline{R_{IF}(Y_2)}}(d_3) = \bigwedge_{y \in V}[\nu_{R_{IF}}(d_3, y) \vee \nu_{Y_2}(y)]$$
$$= [0.05 \vee 0.3] \wedge [0.15 \vee 0.1] \wedge [0.15 \vee 0.4] \wedge [0.2 \vee 0.3] \wedge [0.3 \vee 0.3] \wedge [0.4 \vee 0.5]$$
$$= 0.3 \wedge 0.15 \wedge 0.4 \wedge 0.3 \wedge 0.3 \wedge 0.5$$
$$= 0.15$$

$$\mu_{\overline{R_{IF}(Y_2)}}(d_4) = \bigvee_{y \in V}[\mu_{R_{IF}}(d_4, y) \wedge \mu_{Y_2}(y)]$$
$$= [0.1 \wedge 0.2] \vee [0.1 \wedge 0.4] \vee [0 \wedge 0.15] \vee [0.2 \wedge 0.1] \vee [0.35 \wedge 0.1] \vee [0.1 \wedge 0.05]$$
$$= 0.1 \vee 0.1 \vee 0 \vee 0.1 \vee 0.1 \vee 0.05$$
$$= 0.1$$

$$\nu_{\overline{R_{IF}(Y_2)}}(d_4) = \bigwedge_{y \in V}[\nu_{R_{IF}}(d_4, y) \vee \nu_{Y_2}(y)]$$
$$= [0.2 \vee 0.3] \wedge [0.8 \vee 0.1] \wedge [0.6 \vee 0.4] \wedge [0.3 \vee 0.3] \wedge [0.1 \vee 0.3] \wedge [0.4 \vee 0.5]$$
$$= 0.3 \wedge 0.8 \wedge 0.6 \wedge 0.3 \wedge 0.3 \wedge 0.5$$
$$= 0.3$$

$$\mu_{\overline{R_{IF}(Y_2)}}(d_5) = \bigvee_{y \in V}[\mu_{R_{IF}}(d_5, y) \wedge \mu_{Y_2}(y)]$$
$$= [0.15 \wedge 0.2] \vee [0.2 \wedge 0.4] \vee [0.1 \wedge 0.15] \vee [0.2 \wedge 0.1] \vee [0.5 \wedge 0.1] \vee [0.2 \wedge 0.05]$$
$$= 0.15 \vee 0.2 \vee 0.1 \vee 0.1 \vee 0.1 \vee 0.05$$
$$= 0.2$$

$$\nu_{\overline{R_{IF}(Y_2)}}(d_5) = \bigwedge_{y \in V}[\nu_{R_{IF}}(d_5, y) \vee \nu_{Y_2}(y)]$$
$$= [0.1 \vee 0.3] \wedge [0.7 \vee 0.1] \wedge [0.3 \vee 0.4] \wedge [0.1 \vee 0.3] \wedge [0.15 \vee 0.3] \wedge [0.3 \vee 0.5]$$
$$= 0.3 \wedge 0.7 \wedge 0.4 \wedge 0.3 \wedge 0.3 \wedge 0.5$$
$$= 0.3$$

Hence, the upper approximation for Y_2 is given as:

$$\overline{R_{IF}}Y_2 = \left\{ \left\langle d_1, 0.15, 0.2 \right\rangle, \left\langle d_2, 0.35, 0.21 \right\rangle, \left\langle d_3, 0.25, 0.15 \right\rangle, \left\langle d_4, 0.1, 0.3 \right\rangle, \left\langle d_5, 0.2, 0.3 \right\rangle \right\}^t$$

From the above analysis, according to the principle of maximum membership, the decision for the first category of customers is "more welcome" whereas the decision for the second category of customers is "most welcome".

CONCLUSION

In this chapter, we have discussed the theory of rough computing. Pawlak's rough set is based on the equivalence relation, but equivalence class is not feasible in most practical scenarios. To handle this, we have defined almost indiscernibility relation. Hence rough set on fuzzy approximation space has been discussed which works as the basis of almost indiscernibility relation. Afterward rough set on intuitionistic fuzzy approximation space has been discussed. Subsequently we have defined rough set on two universal sets. The concept of intuitionistic fuzzy rough sets has been extended on two universal sets. We have elaborated a real life application on multi-criterion decision making employing intuitionistic fuzzy rough set on two universal sets. The main objective is to furnish the concept application of intuitionistic fuzzy rough set on two universal sets in decision making problems.

REFERENCES

Acharjya, D. P., & Ezhilarasi, L. (2011). A Knowledge Mining Model for Ranking Institutions using Rough Computing with Ordering Rules and Formal Concept Analysis. *International Journal of Computer Science Issues*, *8*(2), 417–425.

Acharjya, D.P., & Bhattacharjee, D. (2013). A Rough Computing based Performance Evaluation approach for Educational Institutions. *International Journal of Software Engineering and its Applications*, *7*(4), 331-348.

Acharjya, D. P. (2013). Rough computing based Information Retrieval in Knowledge Discovery Databases. In Information and Knowledge Management-Tools, Techniques and Practices (pp. 123 - 153). New Delhi: New India Publishing Company.

Busse, J. G. (1988). Knowledge acquisition under uncertainty – a rough set approach. *Journal of Intelligent & Robotic Systems*, *1*(1), 3–16. doi:10.1007/BF00437317

Chen, D., Zhang, W., Yeung, D., & Tsang, E. C. C. (2006). Rough Approximations on a Complete Completely Distributive Lattice with Applications to Generalized Rough Sets. *Information Sciences*, *176*(13), 1829–1848. doi:10.1016/j.ins.2005.05.009

Kondo, M. (2005). Algebraic Approach to Generalized Rough Sets. *Lecture Notes in Artificial Intelligence*, *3641*, 132–140.

Kondo, M. (2006). On the Structure of Generalized Rough Sets. *Information Sciences*, *176*(5), 589–600. doi:10.1016/j.ins.2005.01.001

Kryszkiewlcz, M. (1998). Rough Set Approach to Incomplete Information Systems. *Information Sciences*, *112*(1-4), 39–49. doi:10.1016/S0020-0255(98)10019-1

Kumar, K. S., Acharjya, D. P., & Thangavelu, A. (2013). Trust Evaluation using Fuzzy Proximity Relation with ordering for MANET. *International Journal of Trust Management in Computing Communications*, *1*(2), 105–120. doi:10.1504/IJTMCC.2013.053259

Lin, T. Y. (2005). Granular Computing: Examples, Intuitions and Modeling. *IEEE International Conference on Granular Computing*(pp. 40– 44).

Lin, T. Y. (1989). Neighborhood Systems and Approximation in Database and Knowledge Base Systems. *Proceedings of the fourth International Symposium on Methodologies of Intelligent Systems* (pp. 75–86).

Liu, G. L. (2005). Rough Sets over the Boolean Algebras. *Lecture Notes in Artificial Intelligence*, *3641*, 24–131.

Liu, G. L. (2008). Generalized Rough Sets over Fuzzy Lattices. *Information Sciences*, *178*(6), 1651–1662. doi:10.1016/j.ins.2007.11.010

Liu, G. L. (2010). Rough set theory based on two universal sets and its applications. *Knowledge-Based Systems*, *23*(2), 110–115. doi:10.1016/j.knosys.2009.06.011

Molodtsov, D. (1999). Soft Set Theory-First Results. *Computers & Mathematics with Applications (Oxford, England)*, *37*(4-5), 19–31. doi:10.1016/S0898-1221(99)00056-5

Maji, P. K., Roy, A. R., & Biswas, R. (2002). An Application of Soft Sets in A Decision Making Problem. *Computers & Mathematics with Applications (Oxford, England)*, *44*(8-9), 1077–1083. doi:10.1016/S0898-1221(02)00216-X

Pawlak, Z. (2004). Decision rules and flow networks. *European Journal of Operational Research*, *154*(1), 184–190. doi:10.1016/S0377-2217(03)00004-3

Pawlak, Z. (1982). Rough Sets. *International Journal of Computer and Information Sciences*, *11*(5), 341–356. doi:10.1007/BF01001956

Pawlak, Z. (1983). Rough Classification. *International Journal of Man-Machine Studies*, *20*(5), 469–483. doi:10.1016/S0020-7373(84)80022-X

Pawlak, Z. (1991). *Rough Sets, Theoretical aspect of Reasoning about Data*. Kluwer Academic Publishers.

Pawlak, Z., & Skowron, A. (2007a). Rough sets some extensions. Information Science. *International Journal (Toronto, Ont.)*, *177*(1), 28–40.

Pawlak, Z., & Skowron, A. (2007b). Rough sets and Boolean reasoning, *Information Science*. *International Journal (Toronto, Ont.)*, *177*(1), 41–73.

Tripathy, B. K., & Acharjya, D. P. (2012). Approximation of Classification and Measures of Uncertainty in Rough Set on Two Universal Sets. *International Journal of Advanced Science and Technology*, *40*, 77–90.

Tripathy, B. K., Acharjya, D. P., & Ezhilarasi, L. (2012). Topological Characterization of Rough Set on Two Universal Sets and Knowledge Representation. In Global Trends in Information Systems and Software Applications, Proceedings of 4th ObCom 2011, (vol. 270, pp. 70–83). Vellore, India: Springer CCIS. doi:10.1007/978-3-642-29216-3_9

Zadeh, L. (1965). Fuzzy Sets. *Information and Control*, *8*(3), 338–353. doi:10.1016/S0019-9958(65)90241-X

Zhu, W. (2007). Generalized Rough Sets based on Relations. *Information Sciences*, *177*(22), 4997–5011. doi:10.1016/j.ins.2007.05.037

Zhong, N. & Skowron, A. (2001). A Rough Set-Based Knowledge Discovery Process. *International Journal of Applied Mathematics.*

Chapter 13
An Efficient Method for Forecasting Using Fuzzy Time Series

Pritpal Singh
CHARUSAT University, India

ABSTRACT

Forecasting using fuzzy time series has been applied in several areas including forecasting university enrollments, sales, road accidents, financial forecasting, weather forecasting, etc. Recently, many researchers have paid attention to apply fuzzy time series in time series forecasting problems. In this paper, we present a new model to forecast the enrollments in the University of Alabama and the daily average temperature in Taipei, based on one-factor fuzzy time series. In this model, a new frequency based clustering technique is employed for partitioning the time series data sets into different intervals. For defuzzification function, two new principles are also incorporated in this model. In case of enrollments as well daily temperature forecasting, proposed model exhibits very small error rate.

1. INTRODUCTION

Forecasting using fuzzy time series has been applied in several areas including forecasting university enrollments, sales, road accidents, financial forecasting, weather forecasting, etc. In a conventional time series, the recorded values of a special dynamic process are represented by crisp numerical values. However, in a fuzzy time series concept, the recorded values of a special dynamic process are represented by linguistic values. Based on fuzzy time series concept, first forecasting model was introduced by Song and Chissom (Song & Chissom, 1993,1994,1993). They presented the fuzzy time series model by means of fuzzy relational equations involving max-min composition operation and applied the model to forecast the enrollments in the University of Alabama. Chen (1996) used simplified arithmetic operations avoiding the complicated max-min operations and their method produced better results. Later, many studies provided some improvements to the existing methods in terms of effective lengths of intervals, fuzzification and defuzzification techniques used.

DOI: 10.4018/978-1-5225-0914-1.ch013

Hwang et al. (1998) used the differences of the available historical data as fuzzy time series instead of direct usage of raw numeric values. Sah and Degtiarev also used a similar approach in this article (Sah & Konstantin, 2005). Huarng tried to improve the forecasting accuracy based on the determination of effective length of intervals (Huarng, 2001a), and heuristic approaches (Huarng, 2001b). In this article (Lee& Chou, 2004), authors forecasted the university enrollments with the average error rate less than Chen's method (Chen, 1996) by defining the supports of the fuzzy numbers that represent the linguistic values of the linguistic variables more appropriately.

Cheng et al. (2006)used entropy minimization to create the intervals. They also used trapezoidal membership functions in the fuzzification process. Chang et al. (2007) presented cardinality-based fuzzy time series forecasting model, which builds weighted fuzzy rules by calculating the cardinality of fuzzy relations. To enhance the performance of fuzzy time series models, Chen et al. (2007) incorporates the concept of the Fibonacci sequence in the existing models as proposed by Song and Chissom (Song & Chissom, 1993,1994,1993), and Yu (Yu, 2005). To obtain less number of intervals, Cheng et al. (2008) proposed a model using fuzzy clustering technique to partition the data effectively. The k-means clustering algorithm has been applied to partition the universe of discourse in fuzzy time series modeling approach (Kai et al. 2010). Chou et al. (2010) forecasted the tourism demand based on hybridization of rough set with fuzzy time series. In this article (Singh & Borah, 2011), authors forecasted the university enrollments with the help of new proposed algorithm by dividing the universe of discourse of the historical time series data into different length of intervals.

To enhance the accuracy in forecasted values, many researchers recently proposed various one-factor fuzzy time series models. For example, Chen et el. (2007) proposed a new fuzzy time series model for stock price forecasting by employing the concept of fibonacci sequence. In these articles (Chen, 2002; Chen & Tanuwijaya, 2011; Chen et al., 2008; Gangwar & Kumar, 2012; Singh, 2009; Singh, 2016), researchers proposed computational methods of forecasting based on the high-order fuzzy logical relations (FLRs) to overcome the drawback of fuzzy first-order forecasting model. More recent advancement in fuzzy time series forecasting modeling approach can be found in these articles (Singh, 2015; Singh & Borah, 2014a; Singh & Borah, 2013a; Singh & Borah, 2014b; Singh & Borah, 2013b).

This paper is organized as follows. In Section 2, research objectives have been discussed. In Section 3, some basic concepts of fuzzy set theory has been explained with an overview of fuzzy time series. In Section 4, a technique is presented for partitioning one-factor time series data set into different length of intervals. Application of fuzzy time series concept for designing the proposed model has been discussed in Section 5. The performance of the model has been assessed and presented in the results Section 6. Another application of proposed model for forecasting the daily average temperature has been shown in Section 7. The conclusions and future works are discussed in Section 8.

2. RESEARCH OBJECTIVE

Forecasting of events like temperature, rainfall, stock price, population growth, economy growth, *etc.* are major scientific issues in the field of data analysis. Forecasting of all these events are tedious tasks because of their dynamic nature. Forecasting of these events with 100% accuracy may not be possible, but the forecasting accuracy and the speed of forecasting process can be improved. Traditional linear forecasting methods such as Auto Regressive (AR), Moving Average (MA), Auto Regressive Moving Average (ARMA), and Auto Regressive Integrated Moving Average (ARIMA), *etc.* require a large amount of historical data for modeling purpose. These linear statistical methods sometimes can not fit the highly non-linear and non-stationary time series data very well.

To avoid the problems associated with these methods, a model that can deal with one-factor time series data set is proposed using fuzzy time series modeling approach. This model is entitled as "One-Factor Fuzzy Time Series Forecasting Model". The main purpose of designing such a model is explained next.

For fuzzification of time series data set, the determination of length of intervals is very important. In case of most of the above discussed models (Chen, 1996; Huarng, 2001b; Hwang et al.,1998; Song & Chissom, 1993; Song & Chissom, 1994), the lengths of the intervals were kept same. No specific reason is mentioned for using the fixed lengths of intervals. Huarng (2001a) shows that effective lengths of intervals always affect the results of forecasting. Therefore, for the creation of effective length of intervals of the historical time series data set, we have proposed new clustering technique, which is entitled as "Frequency Based Re-Partitioning Clustering Technique". After generating the intervals, the historical time series data set is fuzzified based on fuzzy time series concept. Each fuzzified time series values are then used to create the fuzzy relationships. Yu (2005) proposed weighted fuzzy time series model to resolve issues of recurrence and weighting in fuzzy time series forecasting. He proposed improved fuzzy time series forecasting model by assigning different weights to various fuzzy relationships. Similarly, authors (Wang & Liu, 2010) assigned weights on fuzzy relationships based on trend variations of fuzzified time series values. Most of the fuzzy time series models as discussed earlier rejected the repeated fuzzy relationships. So, if we assign weights on them, then there may be a chance of information lose. Therefore, in this proposed model, author gives more emphasis on creating effective length of intervals, and assigning weights on intervals based on their frequencies rather than assigning weights on fuzzy relationships.

Authors (Song & Chissom, 1993a) adopted the following method to forecast enrollments of the University of Alabama:

$$Y(t) = Y(t-1) \circ R \tag{1}$$

where $Y(t-1)$ is the fuzzified enrollment of year $(t-1)$, $Y(t)$ is the forecasted enrollment of year t represented by fuzzy set, $\circ$ is the max-min composition operator, and R is the union of fuzzy relations. The computation time of this method (Equation 1) is very high due to computing the union of fuzzy relation, R. If the number of fuzzy relation "R" is more in Equation 1, then the max-min composition operations will also take lots of time for computation. Therefore, for defuzzification function, the author proposes the"Interval-Frequency Based Defuzzification Technique".

In this model, the author tries to improve the fuzzification and defuzzification processes as well to enhance forecasting accuracy of one-factor time series data sets. To evaluate the performance of the proposed model, two different types of one-factor time series data sets are used as:

1. University enrollments data set of Alabama (Song & Chissom, 1993b), and
2. Daily average temperature data set of Taipei (Singh & Borah, 2013b).

3 . FUZZY SETS AND FUZZY TIME SERIES

3.1 Basic Concepts

In 1965, Zadeh (1965) introduced the concepts of fuzzy sets involving continuous set membership for processing data in presence of uncertainty. He also presented fuzzy arithmetic theory and its application (Zadeh, 1973, 1971, 1975). Here, we briefly reviewed some concepts of fuzzy time series from these articles (Song & Chissom, 1993a, 1994, 1993b).

A fuzzy set is a class with varying degrees of membership in the set. Let U be the universe of discourse, which is discrete and finite, then fuzzy set A can be defined as follows:

$$A = \{\mu_A(x_1) / x_1 + \mu_A(x_2) / x_2 + \ldots\} = \Sigma_i \mu_A(x_i) / x_i \quad (2)$$

where μ_A is the membership function of A, μ_A: $U \rightarrow [1,0]$, and $\mu_A(x_i)$ is the degree of membership of the element x_i in the fuzzy set A. Here, the symbol + indicates the operation of union and the symbol / indicates the separator rather than the commonly used summation and division in algebra respectively.

When U is continuous and infinite, then the fuzzy set A of U can be defined as:

$$A = \{\int \mu_A(x_i) / x_i\}, \forall x_i \in U \quad (3)$$

where the integral sign stands for the union of the fuzzy singletons, $\mu_A(x_i)/x_i$.

Fuzzy time series concept was proposed in these articles (Song & Chissom, 1993a, 1994, 1993b), and the main difference between the traditional time series and the fuzzy time series is that the values of the former are crisp numerical values, while the values of the latter are fuzzy sets. The crisp numerical values can be represented by real numbers whereas in fuzzy sets, the values of observations are represented by linguistic values. The definitions of fuzzy time series are briefly reviewed as follows.

Let $Y(t)(t=0,1,2,\ldots)$ is a subset of R and is the universe of discourse on which fuzzy sets $\mu_i(t)(i=1,2,\ldots)$ are defined and let $F(t)$ be a collection of $\mu_i(t)(i=1,2,\ldots)$. Then, $F(t)$ is called a fuzzy time series on $Y(t)$ $(t=0,1,2,\ldots)$.

From the above definition, we can see that $F(t)$ is a function of time t, and $\mu_i(t)$ are linguistic values of $F(t)$, where $\mu_i(t)(i=1,2,\ldots)$ are represented by fuzzy sets, and the values of $F(t)$ can be different at different times because the universe of discourse can be different at different times. Fuzzy time series can be divided into two categories which are the time-invariant fuzzy time series and the time-variant fuzzy time series.

If $F(t)$ is caused by $F(t-1)$, *i.e.*, $F(t-1) \rightarrow F(t)$, then this relationship can be represented as follows:

$$F(t) = F(t-1) \circ R(t, t-1) \quad (4)$$

where $R(t,t-1)$ is fuzzy relationship between $F(t)$ and $F(t-1)$. Here, R is the union of fuzzy relations and $\circ$ is max-min composition operator. It is also called the first-order model of $F(t)$.

Let $F(t)$ be a fuzzy time series, and $R(t,t{-}1)$ is a first--order model of $F(t)$. If $R(t,t{-}1)=R(t{-}1,t{-}2)$ for any time t, and $F(t)$ only has finite elements, then $F(t)$ is referred as a time-invariant fuzzy time series. Otherwise, it is referred as a time-variant fuzzy time series.

Assume that $F(t{-}1)=A_i$ and $F(t)$-A_j. The relationship between $F(t)$ and $F(t{-}1)$ is referred as a fuzzy logical relationship (FLR) (Chen, 1996; Song & Chissom, 1993a, 1994, 1993b), which can be represented as:

$$A_i \rightarrow A_j,$$

where A_i and A_j refer to the left-hand side (LHS) and right-hand side (RHS) of the FLR respectively.

Assume the following FLRs:

$$A_i \rightarrow A_{k1},$$
$$A_i \rightarrow A_{k2},$$
$$\ldots$$
$$A_i \rightarrow A_{km}$$

Chen (1996) suggested that FLRs having same fuzzy sets on LHS can be grouped into a same fuzzy logical relationship group (FLRG). So, based on Chen's model (Chen, 1996), these FLRs can be grouped into same FLRG as:

$$A_i \rightarrow A_{k1}, A_{k2}, \ldots, A_{km}.$$

3.2 Basic Steps of Fuzzy Time Series Forecasting Models

Most of the existing fuzzy time series forecasting models as discussed in previous section use the following steps to handle forecasting problems (Chen, 1996; Song & Chissom, 1993a, 1994, 1993b):

Step 1: Divide the universe of discourse into intervals.
Step 2: Fuzzify the historical data.
Step 3: Build FLRs and obtain FLRGs.
Step 4: Calculate the forecasted values.

Various applications of fuzzy time series are based on these four steps. For example, in the University enrollments forecasting of Alabama, Song and Chissom (Chen, 1996; Song & Chissom, 1993a, 1994, 1993b) apply Steps 1-4 to obtain the forecasted values. Chou et al. (2010) proposed improved fuzzy time series model to forecast tourism demand. In this model, they generate rules from FLRs by rough set rule induction method. Teoh et al. (2008) proposed hybrid time series forecasting model, in which time series data set is fuzzified based on fuzzy time series, and generate rules (FLRs) from them by rough set rule induction algorithm. In this article (Huarng & Yu, 2006) proposed improved fuzzy time series model for forecasting enrollments as well stock index. In this model, a ratio based method is adopted for determination of effective length of intervals.

Table 1. The data set of the enrollments of the University of Alabama

Year	Actual Enrollments	Year	Actual Enrollments
1971	13055	1982	15433
1972	13563	1983	15497
1973	13867	1984	15145
1974	14696	1985	15163
1975	15460	1986	15984
1976	15311	1987	16859
1977	15603	1988	18150
1978	15861	1989	18970
1979	16807	1990	19328
1980	16919	1991	19337
1981	16388	1992	18876

4. FREQUENCY BASED RE-PARTITIONING CLUSTERING TECHNIQUE

In this section, the proposed Frequency Based Re-Partitioning Clustering Technique is presented. Here, the author uses the enrollments data set of the University of Alabama, as an example for explaining the steps. This data set is shown in Table 1. Each step of the proposed technique is explained next.

Step 1: *Determine the universe of discourse of time series data set.*

[Explanation:] Define the universe of discourse U of time series data set. Assume that $U=[L_B, U_B]$, where L_B=13000 and U_B=20000. In universe of discourse U, the length of the intervals is 1000, which gives us seven intervals $a_0, a_1, \ldots, a_6$. Here, a_0=[13000,14000], a_1=[14000,15000], a_2=[15000,16000], a_3=[16000,17000], a_4=[17000,18000], a_5=[18000,19000], and a_6=[19000,20000].

Step 2: *Determine the frequency of each interval.*

[Explanation:]The frequency is recorded by counting the number of element belong to each interval. The result is shown in Table 2.

Table 2. Frequency table for enrollments data set.

Partition	Frequency
[13000,14000]	3
[14000,15000]	1
[15000,16000]	9
[16000,17000]	4
[17000,18000]	0
[18000,19000]	3
[19000,20000]	2

Step 3: *Determine the median of the frequencies.*

[Explanation:]For this purpose, rearrange the frequencies as shown in second column of Table 2 in ascending order as: 0, 1, 2, 3, 3, 4, 9. Now, obtain the median of frequencies as:

$$Median = \frac{(n+1)}{2} \tag{5}$$

Based on Formula 5, $Median = \frac{7+1}{2} = \frac{8}{2} = 4$ (Here, *n*=7), *i.e.*, the median is the 4th element, which is 3.

Step 4:*Determine the mid-value of the frequencies.*

[Explanation:]From Table 2, we have the minimum frequency (F_{min})=0 and the maximum frequency (F_{max})=9. Therefore, the mid-value $(F_{mid}) = \frac{(F_{min} + F_{max})}{2} = \frac{(0+9)}{2} = 4.5$

Step 5:*Determine the factor based on median and mid-value.*

[Explanation:]The factor is determined by taking the ratio of median to mid-value, *i.e.*, $Factor = \frac{Median}{F_{mid}} = \frac{3}{4.5} = 0.6667$

Step 6:*Obtain the new partition interval based on the factor and the old partition interval.*

[Explanation:]The new partition interval can be obtained as:

$$New\ partition\ interval\ (PI){=}Factor{\times}Old\ partition\ interval$$
$$= 0.6667 \times 1000 = 666.7;666$$

[*Note: In time series data set, if the length of interval is in unit or fraction, then the floating point value should also be considered, because it may impact the results of forecasting as in the case of daily temperature forecasting (Section 7)*].

The universe of discourse *U* is now partition into *n* intervals (*i.e.*, a_0, a_1,…, and a_n) based on PI. Each interval of time series data set is defined as:

$$a_i = [L_B + (i-1)\times PI, L_B + i \times PI], \tag{6}$$

for *i*=1,2,…,9.

The newly determined intervals with their corresponding elements are shown in Table 3. In this table, the mid-point of each newly determined interval is also shown along with the frequency. We have removed the interval [16996,17662] from Table 3, since it does not contain any historical value.

Table 3. New intervals and their corresponding elements

Interval	Corresponding Element	Mid-point	Frequency
[13000,13666]	13055,13563	13,333	2
[13666,14322]	13867	13,994	1
[14322,14988]	14696	114,655	1
[14988,15664]	15460,15311,15603,15433,15497,15145,15163	15,326	7
[15664,16330]	15861,15984	15,997	2
[16330,16996]	16807,16919,16388,16859	16,663	4
[17662,18328]	18150	17,995	1
[18328,18994]	18970,18876	18,661	2
[18994,19660]	19328,19337	19,327	2

5. PROPOSED FUZZY TIME SERIES MODEL

In this section, we propose a new model for forecasting using fuzzy time series. The proposed model takes the time series data set as the input and the output is computed for any particular year/day. For verification purpose of the model, the data set as shown in Table 1, is considered as an example. The functionality of each phases are explained in step-wise as follows.

Phase 1: *Define the universe of discourse* U and partition it into equal length of intervals.

[Explanation:]Based on technique proposed in Section 4, we have divided the universe of discourse U of the historical time series data set [32] into equal length of intervals. For each interval, the mid-point is calculated and stored for future consideration. Each interval bears a frequency equal to the number of elements in the interval. The experimental results are already presented in Table 3.

Phase 2: *Define linguistic terms for each of the interval.*

[Explanation:]The universe of discourse U of time series data set is divided into 9 intervals (*i.e.*, a_0, a_1,..., and a_8). Therefore, total 9 linguistic variables (*i.e.*, A_0,A_1,..., A_8) are defined. All these linguistic variables can be represented by fuzzy sets as shown below:

$$A_0 = 1/a_1 + 0.5/a_2 + 0/a_3 + \ldots + 0/a_{n-2} + 0/a_{n-1} + 0/a_8,$$
$$A_1 = 0.5/a_1 + 1/a_2 + 0.5/a_3 + \ldots + 0/a_{n-2} + 0/a_{n-1} + 0/a_8,$$
$$A_2 = 0/a_1 + 0.5/a_2 + 1/a_3 + \ldots + 0/a_{n-2} + 0/a_{n-1} + 0/a_8,$$
$$\vdots$$
$$A_8 = 0/a_1 + 0/a_2 + 0/a_3 + \ldots + 0/a_{n-2} + 0.5/a_{n-1} + 1/a_8.$$

For ease of computation, the degree of membership values of fuzzy set A_j(j=0,1,...,8) are considered as either 0, 0.5 or 1. Then, obtain the degree of membership of each year's enrollment belonging to each A_j. The maximum degree of membership of fuzzy set A_i occurs at interval a_i and $1 \leq i \leq j$.

Phase 3: *Fuzzify the time series data sets.*

[Explanation:]If one year's enrollment value belongs to the interval a_i, then the fuzzified enrollment value for that year is considered as A_i. For example, if enrollment value of year 1971 belongs to the interval a_0, then it is fuzzified to A_0. In this way, we have fuzzified historical time series data set. The fuzzified enrollments of the time series data set are shown in Table 4.

Phase 4: *Establish the fuzzy logical relations (FLRs) between the fuzzified data values.*

[Explanation:] We can establish FLRs between two consecutive fuzzified enrollment values. For example, in Table 4, fuzzified enrollment values for Years 1973 and 1974 are A_1 and A_2, respectively. So, we can establish a FLR between A_1 and A_2 as: $A_1 \rightarrow A_2$. In this way, we have obtained all FLRs for fuzzified enrollment values, which are presented in Table 5.

The left hand side and right hand side of FLR, $A_i \rightarrow A_j$, are called the *previous state* and *current state* respectively.

Phase 5: *Create the fuzzy logical relationship groups (FLRGs).*

Table 4. Fuzzified enrollments data set of the University of Alabama

Year	Actual Enrollment	Fuzzified Enrollment
1971	13055	A_0
1972	13563	A_0
1973	13867	A_1
1974	14696	A_2
1975	15460	A_3
1976	15311	A_3
1977	15603	A_3
1978	15861	A_4
1979	16807	A_5
1980	16919	A_5
1981	16388	A_5
1982	15433	A_3
1983	15497	A_3
1984	15145	A_3
1985	15163	A_3
1986	15984	A_4
1987	16859	A_5
1988	18150	A_6
1989	18970	A_7
1990	19328	A_8
1991	19337	A_8
1992	18876	A_7

[Explanation:] The FLRs of Table 5 can be clustered into FLRGs based on same LHS of FLRs. All these FLRGs are shown in Table 6. In our model, if the same FLR appears more than once, it is included only once.

Phase 6: *Defuzzify and compute the forecasted values from the fuzzified time series data sets.*

Principle 1: For forecasting year $Y(t)$, the fuzzified enrollment for year $Y(t-1)$ is required, where t is the current year which we want to forecast. The Principle 1 is applicable only if there are more than one fuzzified enrollment values available in the current state. The steps under Principle 1 are explained next.

- Obtain the fuzzified enrollment for year $Y(t-1)$ as $A_i(i=0,1,2,\ldots,n)$.
- Obtain the FLRG whose previous state is $A_i(i=0,1,2,\ldots,n)$ and the current state is $A_k, A_s, \ldots, A_n$, *i.e.*, the FLRG is in the form of $A_i \rightarrow A_k, A_s, \ldots, A_n$.
- Find the intervals where the maximum membership value of the fuzzy sets $A_k, A_s, \ldots, A_n$ occurs. Let these intervals be $a_k, a_s, \ldots, a_n$. All these intervals has the corresponding interval mid-points $(C_k, C_s, \ldots, C_n)$ and corresponding frequencies $(F_k, F_s, \ldots, F_n)$.

Apply the following Equation 7 to calculate the forecasted value for year, $Y(t)$:

$$Forecast(t) = \frac{\sum_{i=1}^{n} F_k W_k + F_s W_s + \ldots + F_n W_n}{\sum_{i=1}^{n} F_k + F_s + \ldots + F_n} \tag{7}$$

Principle 2: This rule is applicable if there is only one fuzzified enrollment value in the current state. The steps under Principle 2 are explained next.

Table 5. FLRs of the enrollments data set of the University of Alabama

FLR
$A_0 \rightarrow A_0$
$A_0 \rightarrow A_1$
$A_1 \rightarrow A_2$
$A_2 \rightarrow A_3$
$A_3 \rightarrow A_3$
$A_3 \rightarrow A_4$
$A_4 \rightarrow A_5$
$A_5 \rightarrow A_5$
$A_5 \rightarrow A_3$
$A_5 \rightarrow A_6$
$A_6 \rightarrow A_7$
$A_7 \rightarrow A_8$
$A_8 \rightarrow A_8$
$A_8 \rightarrow A_7$

Table 6. FLRGs of the enrollments data set of the University of Alabama

Group	FLRs of the enrollments
Group 1:	$A_0 \rightarrow A_0, A_0 \rightarrow A_1$
Group 2:	$A_1 \rightarrow A_2$
Group 3:	$A_2 \rightarrow A_3$
Group 4:	$A_3 \rightarrow A_3, A_3 \rightarrow A_4$
Group 5:	$A_4 \rightarrow A_5$
Group 6:	$A_5 \rightarrow A_5, A_5 \rightarrow A_3, A_5 \rightarrow A_6$
Group 7:	$A_6 \rightarrow A_7$
Group 8:	$A_7 \rightarrow A_8$
Group 9:	$A_8 \rightarrow A_8, A_8 \rightarrow A_7$

- Obtain the fuzzified enrollment for year $Y(t-1)$ as $A_i(i=0,1,\ldots,n)$.
- Find the FLRG whose previous state is A_i and the current state is A_j, *i.e.*, the FLRG is in the form of $A_i \rightarrow A_j$.
- Find the interval where the maximum value of the fuzzy set A_j occurs. Let this interval be a_j. This interval a_j has the corresponding interval mid-point C_j. For forecasting year, $Y(t)$, this mid-point C_j is the forecasted value.

6. EMPIRICAL ANALYSIS: THE UNIVERSITY ENROLLMENTS FORECASTING

The proposed model is verified using the University enrollments data set of Alabama from the period 1972 to 1992. While verifying the model, 9 number of intervals are considered. The results of the forecasted enrollments are provided in Table 7. The performance of the model is evaluated with the help of average forecasting error rate (AFER), which can be defined as:

Table 7. Forecasting results of the University enrollments with the help of proposed model

Year	Actual Enrollment	Forecasted Enrollment
1971	13055	--
1972	13563	13666
1973	13867	13666
1974	14696	14665
1975	15460	15331
1976	15311	15664
1977	15603	15664
1978	15861	15664
1979	16807	16663
1980	16919	16663
1981	16388	16663
1982	15433	16663
1983	15497	15664
1984	15145	15664
1985	15163	15664
1986	15984	15664
1987	16859	16663
1988	18150	16663
1989	18970	18661
1990	19328	19327
1991	19337	18994
1992	18876	18994
AFER		2.02%

$$AFER = \frac{\sum_{i=1}^{n}(F_i - A_i) / A_i}{n} \times 100, \tag{8}$$

where, F_i and A_i is the forecasted and actual value of year/day i respectively, n is the total number of years/days to be forecasted.

To assess the forecasting performance of our model, it is compared with existing models (Chen, 1996; Cheng et al., 2008; Cheng et al. 2006; Lee & Chou, 2004; Song & Chissom, 1993). Table 8 conveys a comparison of the obtained results in terms of *AFER* with existing models (Chen, 1996; Cheng et al., 2008; Cheng et al. 2006; Lee & Chou, 2004; Song & Chissom, 1993). In Table 8, it could be observed that *AFER* value for the proposed model is much smaller than those of considered models, which depicts the superiority of the proposed model.

Table 8. A comparison of the existing models with the proposed model

Year	Actual	(Song & Chissom, 1993)	(Chen, 1996)	(Lee & Chou, 2004)	(Cheng et al.,2006)	(Cheng et al., 2006)	(Cheng et al., 2008)	Proposed
	Enrollment				(MEPA)	(TFA)		Model
19771	13055	–	–	–	–	–	–	–
1972	13563	14000	14000	14025	15430	14230	14242.0	13666
1973	13867	14000	14000	14568	15430	14230	14242.0	13666
1974	14696	14000	14000	14568	15430	14230	14242.0	14665
1975	15460	15500	15500	15654	15430	15541	15474.3	15331
1976	15311	16000	16000	15654	15430	15541	15474.3	15664
1977	15603	16000	16000	15654	15430	15541	15474.3	15664
1978	15861	16000	16000	15654	15430	16196	15474.3	15664
1979	16807	16000	16000	16197	16889	16196	16146.5	16663
1980	16919	16813	16833	17283	16871	16196	16988.3	16663
1981	16388	16813	16833	17283	16871	17507	16988.3	16663
1982	15433	16789	16833	16197	15447	16196	16146.5	16663
1983	15497	16000	16000	15654	15430	15541	15474.3	15664
1984	15145	16000	16000	15654	15430	15541	15474.3	15664
1985	15163	16000	16000	15654	15430	15541	15474.3	15664
1986	15984	16000	16000	15654	15430	15541	15474.3	15664
1987	16859	16000	16000	16197	16889	16196	16146.5	16663
1988	18150	16813	16833	17283	16871	17507	16988.3	16663
1989	18970	19000	19000	18369	19333	18872	19144.0	18661
1990	19328	19000	19000	19454	19333	18872	19144.0	19327
1991	19337	19000	19000	19454	19333	18872	19144.0	18997
1992	18876	–	19000	–	19333	18872	19144.0	18997
AFER		3.22%	3.11%	2.67%	2.75%	2.66%	2.40%	2.02%

7. DAILY TEMPERATURE FORECASTING: A CASE STUDY

For the validation purpose, the proposed model is applied on average daily temperature data sets from June (1996) to September (1996) in Taipei (Singh & Borah, 2013a). All these data sets are analyzed under the same conditions and criteria as used in the forecasting of enrollments of the University of Alabama.

7.1 Performance Analysis

In case of daily temperature forecasting, the performance of the model is evaluated with the help of root mean square error (RMSE), average forecasting error rate (AFER) (Equation 8), evaluation parameter (δ_r), correlation coefficient (R), coefficient of determination (R^2), performance parameter (PP) and tracking signal (TS). All these parameters are defined as follows:

1. The RMSE can be defined as:

$$RMSE = \sqrt{\frac{\sum_{i=1}^{n}(F_i - A_i)^2}{n}} \tag{9}$$

2. The δ_r can be defined (Chakraverty & Gupta, 2008) as:

$$\delta_r = \frac{|F_i - A_i|}{\sigma} \tag{10}$$

3. The R can be defined as:

$$R = \frac{n\sum A_i F_i - (\sum A_i)(\sum F_i)}{\sqrt{n(\sum A_i^2) - (\sum A_i)^2}\sqrt{n(\sum F_i^2) - (\sum F_i)^2}} \tag{11}$$

4. The PP can be defined (Wilks, 2011) as:

$$PP=1-(RMSE/\sigma) \tag{12}$$

5. The steps involve in determining the TS can be explained as (Chase et al., 2006; Wang& Liu, 2010): Compute the mean absolute deviation (M_{ad}).

$$M_{ad} = \frac{\sum_{i=1}^{n}|(F_i - A_i)|}{n} \tag{13}$$

6. Compute the running sum of forecast errors (R_{sfe}).

$$R_{sfe} = \sum_{i=1}^{n}(F_i - A_i) \tag{14}$$

7. Compute the TS.

$$TS = \frac{R_{sfe}}{M_{ad}} \tag{15}$$

Here, each F_i and A_i is the forecasted and actual value of day i respectively, n is the total number of days to be forecasted. In Equation 10, σ is the standard deviation of the data sets. A value of δ_r less than 1 indicates good forecasting. In Equation 11, the value of R is such that $-1<R<+1$. The + and – indicate the positive linear correlations and negative linear correlations between the forecasted and actual value of daily temperature respectively. A correlation coefficient (R) greater than equal to 0.5 is generally considered as strong. The R^2 lies between $0<R^2<1$, and indicates the strength of the linear association between A_i and F_i. In Equation 12, the PP value greater than zero indicates good forecasting and vice-versa.

In Equation 13, a$M_{ad}>0$ indicates that forecasting model tends to under-forecast, whereas $M_{ad}<0$ indicates that forecasting model tends to over-forecast. In Equation 14, the R_{sfe} indicates the bias in the forecasting. A value of R_{sfe} equal to 0 indicates that positive errors are equaled to the negative errors. Based on Equation 15, TS value is determined which is used to measure how well different time series forecasting models are performed individually. A TS value between –4 and +4 indicates that the model is working correctly.

7.2 Empirical Analysis: Daily Temperature Forecasting

The empirical results of daily temperature forecasting are shown against the actual temperature in Table 9. The results of forecasting in terms of *AFER* and *RMSE* indicate very small error rate.

The computed values of δ_r (mean values are shown) are less than 1 as shown in Table 9. The R values between actual and forecasted temperature also indicate the efficiency of our model. The R^2 values exhibit

Table 9. The daily average temperature forecasting from June (1996) to September (1996) in Taipei (Unit: °C)

Day	Actual	Fore. June	Actual	Fore. July	Actual	Fore. Aug	Actual	Fore. Sep
	June		July		Aug		Sep	
		(I=7)		(I=6)		(I=5)		(I=7)
1	26.1	--	29.9	--	27.1	--	27.5	--
2	27.6	27.9	28.4	29.3	28.9	28.5	26.8	26.2
3	29.0	28.7	29.2	28.9	28.9	28.5	26.4	27.1
4	30.5	29.3	29.4	28.9	29.3	28.5	27.5	27.1
5	30.0	29.2	29.9	28.9	28.8	28.85	26.6	26.2
6	29.5	29.6	29.6	29.3	28.7	28.5	28.2	27.1
7	29.7	29.3	30.1	29.3	29.0	28.5	29.2	28.2
8	29.4	29.6	29.3	29.3	28.2	28.77	29.0	29.1
9	28.8	29.3	28.1	28.9	27.0	28.5	30.3	28.2

continued on following page

Table 9. Continued

Day	Actual June	Fore. June (I=7)	Actual July	Fore. July (I=6)	Actual Aug	Fore. Aug (I=5)	Actual Sep	Fore. Sep (I=7)
10	29.4	28.5	28.9	28.9	28.3	28.5	29.9	29.1
11	29.3	29.3	28.4	28.9	28.9	28.5	29.9	29.1
12	28.5	29.3	29.6	28.9	28.1	28.5	30.5	29.1
13	28.7	28.5	27.8	29.3	29.9	28.5	30.2	29.7
14	27.5	28.5	29.1	28.9	27.6	28.6	30.3	29.1
15	29.5	28.8	27.7	28.9	26.8	28.5	29.5	29.1
16	28.8	29.3	28.1	28.3	27.6	27.1	28.3	29.1
17	29.0	28.5	28.7	28.9	27.9	28.5	28.6	28.2
18	30.3	29.3	29.9	28.9	29.0	28.5	28.1	28.2
19	30.2	29.6	30.8	29.3	29.2	28.5	28.4	28.2
20	30.9	29.6	31.6	29.8	29.8	28.5	28.3	28.2
21	30.8	29.2	31.4	31.0	29.6	28.6	26.4	28.2
22	28.7	29.2	31.3	31.0	29.3	29.27	25.7	27.1
23	27.8	28.5	31.3	29.8	28.0	28.5	25.0	27.1
24	27.4	28.7	31.3	29.8	28.3	28.5	27.0	25.6
25	27.7	28.8	28.9	29.8	28.6	28.5	25.8	26.2
26	27.1	28.7	28.0	28.9	28.7	28.5	26.4	27.1
27	28.4	28.8	28.6	28.9	29.0	28.5	25.6	27.1
28	27.8	28.5	28.0	28.9	27.7	28.5	24.2	25.6
29	29.0	28.7	29.3	28.9	26.2	28.5	23.3	23.9
30	30.2	29.2	27.9	28.9	26.0	27.1	23.5	23.8
31	--		26.9	28.9	27.7	27.1	--	--
AFER		2.4%		2.7%		2.5%		3.1%
RMSE		0.8252		0.9024		0.7520		1.0277
δ_r		0.6625		0.6323		0.9091		0.4075
R		0.6695		0.6619		0.4655		0.8776
R^2		0.4482		0.4381		0.2167		0.7702
PP		0.22		0.2459		0.0012		0.5085
M_{ad}		0.7069		0.1367		0.6845		0.8517
TS		0.0537		1.0000		1.0000		0.0364

the strong linear association between actual and forecasted temperature. The *PP* values in Table 9 also indicate the efficiency of the model. The M_{ad} values indicates that model tends to slightly under-forecast. In Table 9, it could be observed that TS values for each of the forecasted value lies between the range ±4, which indicate that the model is working correctly. The performance analyses of daily temperature indicate that this model can also be applied for forecasting the daily temperature.

8. CONCLUSION AND THE WAY AHEAD

This paper presents a novel approach based on Type-1 fuzzy time series concept for building a one-factor time series forecasting expert system. For verification purpose, the University enrollments data set of Alabama is used; whereas for validation purpose, the daily average temperature data sets of Taipei are considered as the forecasting target. The proposed model is an improvement over the original models presented by Song and Chissom (Song & Chissom, 1993),and later modification by Chen (1996). In this model, for determination of effective length of intervals, the proposed Frequency Based Re-Partitioning Clustering Technique have been employed. To reduce the time complexity and to enhance the performance of the model, two new defuzzification principles (Principle 1 and Principle 2) are also incorporated in this model. All these improvement in the existing models(Chen, 1996; Cheng et al., 2008; Cheng et al. 2006; Lee & Chou, 2004; Song & Chissom, 1993) lead to our model at the higher accuracy level. The proposed model also show satisfactory performance for forecasting the daily average temperature in Taipei.

A significant drawback of fuzzy time series forecasting model is that increase in the number of intervals of time series data set increases the accuracy rate of forecasting, but decreases the fuzziness of time series data sets. In order to deal with this problem, in this study, we tried to obtain the results with minimum number of intervals. So, there is a scope to test this model with different number of intervals. Work is underway to apply the proposed model on financial, stocks and marketing data sets, etc.

REFERENCES

Chakraverty, S., & Gupta, P. (2008). Comparison of neural network configurations in the long-range forecast of southwest monsoon rainfall over India. *Neural Computing & Applications*, *17*(2), 187–192. doi:10.1007/s00521-007-0093-y

Chang, J. R., Lee, Y. T., Liao, S. Y., & Cheng, C. H. (2007). Cardinality-based fuzzy time series for forecasting enrollments. In New trends in applied artificial intelligence (pp. 735-744). Springer Berlin Heidelberg. doi:10.1007/978-3-540-73325-6_73

Chase, R. B., Aquilano, N. J., & Jacobs, F. R. (2006). *Operations management for competitive advantage*. McGraw-Hill.

Chen, S. M. (1996). Forecasting enrollments based on fuzzy time series. *Fuzzy Sets and Systems*, *81*(3), 311–319. doi:10.1016/0165-0114(95)00220-0

Chen, S. M. (2002). Forecasting enrollments based on high-order fuzzy time series. *Cybernetics and Systems*, *33*(1), 1–16. doi:10.1080/019697202753306479

Chen, S. M., & Tanuwijaya, K. (2011). Fuzzy forecasting based on high-order fuzzy logical relationships and automatic clustering techniques. *Expert Systems with Applications*, *38*(12), 15425–15437. doi:10.1016/j.eswa.2011.06.019

Chen, T. L., Cheng, C. H., & Teoh, H. J. (2007). Fuzzy time-series based on Fibonacci sequence for stock price forecasting. *Physica A: Statistical Mechanics and its Applications, 380*, 377-390.

Chen, T. L., Cheng, C. H., & Teoh, H. J. (2008). High-order fuzzy time-series based on multi-period adaptation model for forecasting stock markets. *Physica A: Statistical Mechanics and its Applications, 387*(4), 876-888.

Cheng, C. H., Chang, J. R., & Yeh, C. A. (2006). Entropy-based and trapezoid fuzzification-based fuzzy time series approaches for forecasting IT project cost. *Technological Forecasting and Social Change, 73*(5), 524–542. doi:10.1016/j.techfore.2005.07.004

Cheng, C. H., Cheng, G. W., & Wang, J. W. (2008). Multi-attribute fuzzy time series method based on fuzzy clustering. *Expert Systems with Applications, 34*(2), 1235–1242. doi:10.1016/j.eswa.2006.12.013

Chou, H. L., Chen, J. S., Cheng, C. H., & Teoh, H. J. (2010). Forecasting tourism demand based on improved fuzzy time series model. In *Intelligent Information and Database Systems* (pp. 399–407). Springer Berlin Heidelberg. doi:10.1007/978-3-642-12145-6_41

Gangwar, S. S., & Kumar, S. (2012). Partitions based computational method for high-order fuzzy time series forecasting. *Expert Systems with Applications, 39*(15), 12158–12164. doi:10.1016/j.eswa.2012.04.039

Huarng, K. (2001a). Effective lengths of intervals to improve forecasting in fuzzy time series. *Fuzzy Sets and Systems, 123*(3), 387–394. doi:10.1016/S0165-0114(00)00057-9

Huarng, K. (2001b). Heuristic models of fuzzy time series for forecasting. *Fuzzy Sets and Systems, 123*(3), 369–386. doi:10.1016/S0165-0114(00)00093-2

Huarng, K., & Yu, T. H. K. (2006). Ratio-based lengths of intervals to improve fuzzy time series forecasting. *Systems, Man, and Cybernetics, Part B: Cybernetics. IEEE Transactions on, 36*(2), 328–340.

Hwang, J. R., Chen, S. M., & Lee, C. H. (1998). Handling forecasting problems using fuzzy time series. *Fuzzy Sets and Systems, 100*(1), 217–228. doi:10.1016/S0165-0114(97)00121-8

Kai, C., Fang-Ping, F., & Wen-Gang, C. (2010, March). Notice of Retraction A Novel Forecasting Model of Fuzzy Time Series Based on K-means Clustering. In *Education Technology and Computer Science (ETCS), 2010 Second International Workshop on* (Vol. 1, pp. 223-225). IEEE.

Lee, H. S., & Chou, M. T. (2004). Fuzzy forecasting based on fuzzy time series. *International Journal of Computer Mathematics, 81*(7), 781–789. doi:10.1080/00207160410001712288

Sah, M., & Konstantin, Y. (2005). Forecasting enrollment model based on first-order fuzzy time series. *In World Academy of Science. Engineering and Technology, 1*, 375–378.

Singh, P. (2015). A brief review of modeling approaches based on fuzzy time series. *International Journal of Machine Learning and Cybernetics*, 1-24.

Singh, P. (2016). High-order fuzzy-neuro-entropy integration-based expert system for time series forecasting. *Neural Computing & Applications*, 1–18.

Singh, P., & Borah, B. (2011). *An efficient method for forecasting using fuzzy time series. In Machine Intelligence* (pp. 67–75). Narosa.

Singh, P., & Borah, B. (2013a). An efficient time series forecasting model based on fuzzy time series. *Engineering Applications of Artificial Intelligence, 26*(10), 2443–2457. doi:10.1016/j.engappai.2013.07.012

Singh, P., & Borah, B. (2013b). High-order fuzzy-neuro expert system for time series forecasting. *Knowledge-Based Systems*, *46*, 12–21. doi:10.1016/j.knosys.2013.01.030

Singh, P., & Borah, B. (2014a). An effective neural network and fuzzy time series-based hybridized model to handle forecasting problems of two factors. *Knowledge and Information Systems*, *38*(3), 669–690. doi:10.1007/s10115-012-0603-9

Singh, P., & Borah, B. (2014b). Forecasting stock index price based on M-factors fuzzy time series and particle swarm optimization. *International Journal of Approximate Reasoning*, *55*(3), 812–833. doi:10.1016/j.ijar.2013.09.014

Singh, S. R. (2009). A computational method of forecasting based on high-order fuzzy time series. *Expert Systems with Applications*, *36*(7), 10551–10559. doi:10.1016/j.eswa.2009.02.061

Song, Q., & Chissom, B. S. (1993a). Forecasting enrollments with fuzzy time series-part I. *Fuzzy Sets and Systems*, *54*(1), 1–9. doi:10.1016/0165-0114(93)90355-L

Song, Q., & Chissom, B. S. (1993b). Fuzzy time series and its models. *Fuzzy Sets and Systems*, *54*(3), 269–277. doi:10.1016/0165-0114(93)90372-O

Song, Q., & Chissom, B. S. (1994). Forecasting enrollments with fuzzy time series-part II. *Fuzzy Sets and Systems*, *62*(1), 1–8. doi:10.1016/0165-0114(94)90067-1

Teoh, H. J., Cheng, C. H., Chu, H. H., & Chen, J. S. (2008). Fuzzy time series model based on probabilistic approach and rough set rule induction for empirical research in stock markets. *Data & Knowledge Engineering*, *67*(1), 103–117. doi:10.1016/j.datak.2008.06.002

Wang, J. W., & Liu, J. W. (2010). Weighted fuzzy time series forecasting model. In *Intelligent Information and Database Systems* (pp. 408–415). Springer Berlin Heidelberg. doi:10.1007/978-3-642-12145-6_42

Wilks, D. S. (2011). *Statistical methods in the atmospheric sciences* (Vol. 100). Academic press.

Yu, H. K. (2005). Weighted fuzzy time series models for TAIEX forecasting. *Physica A: Statistical Mechanics and its Applications, 349*(3), 609-624.

Zadeh, L. A (1965). *Fuzzy sets, information and control*. Academic Press.

Zadeh, L. A. (1971). Similarity relations and fuzzy orderings. *Information Sciences*, *3*(2), 177–200. doi:10.1016/S0020-0255(71)80005-1

Zadeh, L. A. (1973). Outline of a new approach to the analysis of complex systems and decision processes. *Systems, Man and Cybernetics, IEEE Transactions on*, (1), 28-44.

Zadeh, L. A. (1975). The concept of a linguistic variable and its application to approximate reasoning-I. *Information Sciences*, *8*(3), 199–249. doi:10.1016/0020-0255(75)90036-5

Chapter 14
A Three-Level Supply Chain Model with Necessity Measure

Barun Das
Sidho-Kanho-Birsha University, India

ABSTRACT

In this chapter, a vertical information sharing in terms of inventory replenishment / requirement from the customer(s)→ retailer(s)→ producer→ supplier(s) has been done. The constant imprecise fuzzy demands of the goods are made to the retailers by the customers. These goods are produced (along with defectiveness, which decreases due to learning effects) from the raw materials in the producer's production center with a constant production rate (to be determined). Producer stores these raw materials in a warehouse by purchasing these from a supplier and the suppliers collect these raw materials from open markets at a constant collection rate (to be determined). The whole system is considered in a finite time horizon with fuzzy demand for finished products and fuzzy inventory costs. Here shortages are allowed and fully backlogged. The fuzzy chance constraints on the available space of the producer and transportation costs for both producer, retailers are defuzzified using necessity approach. Results indicate the efficiency of proposed approach in performance measurement. This paper attempts to provide the reader a complete picture of supply chain management through a systematic literature review.

INTRODUCTION

A supply chain model (SCM) is a network of supplier, producer, distributor and customer which synchronizes a series of inter-related business process in order to:

1. Optimal procurement of raw materials from nature;
2. Transportation of raw materials into warehouse;
3. Production of the goods in the production center;
4. Distribution of these finished goods to retailer for sale to the customers.

With a recent paradigm shift to the supply chain (SC), the ultimate success of a firm may depend on its ability to link supply chain members seamlessly. One of the earliest efforts to create an integrated

DOI: 10.4018/978-1-5225-0914-1.ch014

supply chain model dates back to Cachon and Zipkin [1999], Cohen and Lee [1988], Nair et.al. [2006]. They developed a production, distribution and inventory (PDI) planning system that integrated three supply chain segments comprised of supply, storage / location and customer demand planning. The core of the PDI system was a network model and diagram that increased the decision maker's insights into supply chain connectivity. The model, however was confined to a single-period and single-objective problem. Viswanathan and Piplani [2001] concerned an integrated inventory model through common replenishment in the SC. Hill. et.al. [2007] discussed the SCM with lost sale. Recently Sarmah et.al. [2008] designed a coordination of a single-manufacturer/multi-buyer supply chain. All the above SCMs are considered with constant, known demand and production rates.

Gradually the fuzzy demand over a finite planning horizon has attracted the attention of researchers (cf. Xie et,al. [2006] and others). This type of demand is observed in the case of fashionable goods, daily emerging products, etc. Moreover, the most of the product goods are breakable. Here the decrease of breakability represents by the transmission of learning justified through the experience gain in planning, organization and the familarity of the workers with their tasks. Keachie and Fontana [1966] first introduced the learning effect for a decision making problem in inventory control system. Jaber and Bonney [8] showed the learning effect of lot sizes in an economic manufacturing quantity model.

After the development of fuzzy set theory by Zadeh [1965], it has been extensively used in different field of science and technology to model complex decision making problems. Since Zimmermann [1976, 1978] first introduced fuzzy set theory into the ordinary linear programming (LP) and multi-objective linear programming (MOLP) problems, several fuzzy mathematical programming and techniques have developed by researchers to solve fuzzy production and/or distribution planing problems (cf. Liang [2011], Maiti and Maiti [2005, 2007], Liu and Iwamura [1998], Santoso, Ahmed, Goetschalckx and Shapiro[2005]). Moreover, Petrovic [2001] developed a heuristic based on fuzzy sets theory to determine the order quantities for a supply chain in the presence of uncertainties associated in the presence of uncertainties associated with customer demand,

deliveries.Das et.al [2005, 2007] designed a supply chain scheduling model as a multi-products, multi-stages and multi-periods mixed integer nonlinear programming problem with uncertain market demand, to satisfy conflict objectives. Wang and Shu [2005] presented a fuzzy supply chain model by combining possibility theory and genetic algorithm approach to provide an alternative framework to handle supply chain uncertainties and to determine inventory strategies. Xie, Petrovic and Bumham [2006] designed a two-level hierarchical method to inventory management and control in serial supply chains, in which the supply chain operated under imprecise customer demand and was modelled by fuzzy sets.

PREREQUISITE MATHEMATICS

Any fuzzy subset $\tilde{A}$ of $\mathbb{R}$ (where $\mathbb{R}$ represents the set of real numbers) with membership function $\mu_{\tilde{A}}:\mathbb{R} \to [0,1]$ is called a fuzzy number. Let $\tilde{A}$ and $\tilde{B}$ be two fuzzy numbers with membership functions $\mu_{\tilde{A}}$ and $\mu_{\tilde{B}}$ respectively. Then taking degree of uncertainty as the semantics of fuzzy number, according to Liu and Iwamura:

$$Pos\left(\tilde{A} * \tilde{B}\right) = \sup\{\min \min\left(\mu_{\tilde{A}}\left(x\right),\ \mu_{\tilde{B}}\left(y\right)\right),\ x,\ y \epsilon \mathbb{R},\ x * y\} \tag{1}$$

Where the abbreviation Pos represent possibility and * is any one of the relation >, <, =, ≥, ≤. Analogously if $\tilde{B}$ is a crisp number, say b,then

$$Pos\left(\tilde{A} * b\right) = \sup\left\{\mu_{\tilde{A}}\left(x\right),\ x \in \mathbb{R},\ x * b\right\} \tag{2}$$

On the other hand necessity measure of an event $\tilde{A} * \tilde{B}$ is a dual of possibility measure . The grade of necessity of an event is the grade of impossibility of the opposite event and is defined as:

$$Nes(\tilde{A}\ * \tilde{B}\ ) = 1 - Pos(\overline{\tilde{A} * \tilde{B}}) \tag{3}$$

Where the abbreviation Nes represent necessity measure and $(\overline{\tilde{A} * \tilde{B}})$ represents complement of the event $\tilde{A} * \tilde{B}$

If $\tilde{A}, \tilde{B} \in \mathbb{R}$ and $\tilde{C} = f(\tilde{A}, \tilde{B})$ where f: $\mathbb{R}\times\mathbb{R} \to \mathbb{R}$ be a binary operation then membership function $\mu_{\tilde{C}}$ of $\tilde{C}$ can be obtained using Fuzzy Extension Principle as:

$$\mu_{\tilde{C}}\left(z\right) = \sup\left\{\min\min\left(\mu_{\tilde{A}}\left(x\right),\ \mu_{\tilde{B}}\left(y\right)\right),\ x, y \in \mathbb{R},\ and\ z = f\left(x, y\right),\ \forall z \in \mathbb{R}\right\} \tag{4}$$

According to this principle if $\tilde{A} = \left(a_1, a_2, a_3\right)$ and $\tilde{B} = \left(b_1, b_2, b_3\right)$ be two triangular fuzzy numbers(TFNs) with positive components then $\tilde{A} + \tilde{B} = \left(a_1 + b_1, a_2 + b_2, a_3 + b_3\right)$ is a TFN. Further moreif $a_2 - a_1, a_3 - a_2,\ b_2 - b_1,\ b_3 - b_2$ aresmallthen $\tilde{A}, \tilde{B} = \left(a_1.b_1, a_2.b_2, a_3.b_3\right), \tilde{A}.\tilde{B} = \left(a_1.b_1, a_2.b_2, a_3.b_3\right)$ is approximately a TFN.

Lemma-1: If $\tilde{a} = \left(a_1, a_2, a_3\right)$ and $\tilde{b} = \left(b_1, b_2, b_3\right)$ be TFNs with $0 < a_1$ and $0 < b_1$ then

$$Nes\left(\tilde{b} > \tilde{a}\right) \geq \alpha iff \frac{a_3 - b_1}{b_2 - b_1 + a_3 - a_2} \leq 1 - \alpha.$$

Proof: Now for two fuzzy numbers $\tilde{a} = (a_1, a_2, a_3)$ and $\tilde{b} = (b_1, b_2, b_3)$,

1. If $a_2 \geq b_2$, then the relation $\tilde{b} \leq \tilde{a}$ is obviously true.
2. If $a_2 \geq b_1$ then the above relation is always false,

Otherwise the relation have a chance, calculated from Definition-1, as

$$\xi = \sup\{\min(\mu_A(x), \mu_B(y))\ , x, y \in \mathbb{R}, x \geq y\}$$

Therefore, is clear that

$$Pos(\tilde{b} \geq \tilde{a}\ ) = \begin{cases} 1 & for\ \ a_2 \geq b_2 \\ \dfrac{a_3 - b_1}{b_2 - b_1 + a_3 - a_2}\ for & a_2 \leq b_2\ and\ \ a_3 \geq b_1 \\ 0 & otherwise \end{cases}$$

Now, from the relationship of these two measures,

$$\Leftrightarrow \{1 - Pos(\tilde{b} \leq \tilde{a})\} \geq \alpha$$

$$\Leftrightarrow Pos(\tilde{b} \leq \tilde{a}) \geq 1 - \alpha$$

Hence, for $0 \leq \alpha \leq 1, Nes(\tilde{b} > \tilde{a}),\ iff\ \dfrac{(a_3 - b_1)}{(b_2 - b_1 + a_3 - a_2)} \leq 1 - \alpha$, and hence the result follows.

Lemma-2: If $\tilde{a} = (a_1, a_2, a_3)$ be a TFN with $0<a_1$ and b be a crisp number then

$$Nes(\tilde{b} > \tilde{a}) \geq \alpha \ \ iff\ \ \frac{(a_3 - b)}{(a_3 - a_2)} \leq 1 - \alpha.$$

Proof: Proof follows from Lemma-1*(Put b1 = b2 = b3 = b in Lemma-1).*

ASSUMPTIONS AND NOTATIONS

The following assumptions and notations are used in developing the proposed SCM.

Assumption

1. The model is developed for a finite time horizon.
2. Multiple suppliers, single producer and multiple retailers are considered.
3. Collection rate of raw material, production rate of the produced goods are constant.
4. Demand rate of finished goods met by the retailer is imprecise in nature.
5. The holding cost, set-up cost, purchasing cost by retailer, total warehouse space, total
6. transportation cost to transport raw materials from suppliers to production warehouse,
7. total transportation cost to transport the produced goods from producer to retailer are
8. taken as fuzzy in nature.
9. One type of raw material and finished product are considered.
10. Producer possesses two systems- a warehouse and a production center.
11. Shortages of goods are allowed and fully backlogged.
12. Multiple lot-size deliveries per order are considered instead of a single delivery per order.
13. Lot size is the same for each delivery.
14. Space constraints to the producer is allowed.
15. There is limited transportation cost.

Notation

The following notations are used for the proposed SCM.

1. T_1= length of time of each of the n equal sub intervals of order cycle(T)(a decision variable)
2. n =number of deliveries per order cycle T(a decision variable).

3. T_R= time length of having non-void stock of finished goods.
4. $\tilde{W}$ = fuzzy total space to keep the raw materials in the warehouse to keep the finished goods.
5. T_{11}=fuzzy total transportation cost to transport the raw materials from
6. $\tilde{T}_{12}$ =fuzzy total transportation cost to transport the produced goods from producer to retailer.

Instead of the above some notations are also used-

For Supplier

1. L=number of suppliers, where l=1,2,…,L.
2. $q_{al}(t)$= inventory level at time t .
3. C_1=collection rate of the supplier(a decision variable).
4. Q_{sl}=collection rate of the supplier(a decision variable).
5. $\tilde{h}_{sl}$ = fuzzy holding cost per unit quantity per unit time.
6. $\tilde{H}_s$ = total holding cost which is fuzzy in nature.
7. p_{sl}=per unit purchasing cost of goods(constant).
8. $\tilde{A}_S$ = fuzzy ordering cost per unit quantity.
9. $\widetilde{TC}_s$ = supplier's raw material cost which is fuzzy in nature.

For Producer's Warehouse

1. $q_{PW}(t)$= inventory level at time t .
2. U= production rate of the finished goods (a decision variable).
3. Q_{PW}=maximum inventory at each interval
4. $\tilde{h}_{pW}$ = fuzzy holding cost per unit quantity per unit time.
5. $\tilde{H}_{pW}$ = total holding cost which is fuzzy in nature.
6. p_{pW}= per unit production cost of goods(constant).
7. $\tilde{A}_{pW}$ = fuzzy ordering cost per unit quantity.
8. $\widetilde{TC}_{pW}$ = fuzzy total cost of raw materials for producer's warehouse.

For the Producer

1. $q_p(t)$= inventory level at time t.
2. λ= defective rate of production, $\lambda = \lambda^{-iT_1}$
3. Q_p=maximum inventory of produced goods at each interval.
4. $\tilde{h}_p$ = fuzzy holding cost per unit quantity per unit time.
5. $\tilde{H}_p$ = total holding cost which is fuzzy in nature.
6. p_p=per unit production cost of goods(constant).
7. $\tilde{A}_p$ = fuzzy ordering cost per unit quantity.
8. $\widetilde{TC}_p$ = fuzzy total cost for producer's finished goods.

For the Retailer

1. K=number of retailers,where k=1,2,...,L.
2. $q_{Rk}(t)$= inventory level at time t .
3. $\tilde{D}_k$ = demand rate of the produced goods which is fuzzy in nature.
4. Q_{Rk}=maximum inventory at each interval.
5. $\tilde{h}_{Rk}$ = fuzzy holding cost per unit quantity per unit time.
6. $\tilde{H}_R$=total holding cost which is fuzzy in nature.
7. $\tilde{p}_{Rk}$ = per unit purchasing cost of goods which is fuzzy in nature.
8. $\tilde{A}_R$ = fuzzy ordering cost per unit quantity.
9. $\tilde{C}_{3k}$ = per unit shortage cost which is fuzzy in nature.
10. $\tilde{S}_{Rk}$ = total amount of shortage which is fuzzy in nature.
11. $\widetilde{TC_R}$ = fuzzy total cost for the retailer.

MATHEMATICAL FORMULATION OF THE SUPPLY CHAIN

This paper develops a supply-chain system which consist multiple suppliers, single producer and multiple retailers. The suppliers are collect the raw material at a constant collection rate, this raw material is purchased by producer and then transported and stored in his / her warehouse, from which raw material is used for production and finished goods are produced at a production rate which is taken as control variable. Then the goods are purchased by retailers, who sells these goods in a market with imprecise demand. The system is considered over a finite time horizon and hence several cycles of procurement, production, etc are repeated within the said time period. There are some resource constraints for the producer and retailer on purchasing the raw materials and finished goods respectively. For the retailer, the model is developed with shortages which are fully-backlogged. The purpose of this study is to find the optimal collection rate, optimal production rate, the number of cycles to each partner and length of time of each of the n equal sub intervals of order cycle.

Inventory Model of Supplier's Raw Material

In this model supplier collect raw material from nature and satisfies the producers warehouse. Therefore supplier's raw material inventory quantity $q_{sl}(t)$ at any time t can be expressed as

$$\frac{dq_{sl}}{dt} = C_l, \quad iT_1 \le t \le (i+1)\ T_1, \quad i = 0,1,2,\cdots,n-2.$$

Now from the help of boundary condition $q_{sl}(iT_1) = 0$ the inventory at any time t, $q_{sl}(t)$ is given by:

$$q_{sl}(t) = C_l(t - iT_1)$$

and using the boundary condition

$$q_s((i+t)T_1) = Q_s$$

we get

$$Q_s = \sum_{l=1}^{L} Q_{sl} = C_l T_l$$

Holding cost of raw material is

$$= \widetilde{h_{sl}} \int_{iT_1}^{(i+1)T_1} q_{sl}(t)dt$$

$$= \frac{\widetilde{h_{sl}} C_l T_1^2}{2}$$

So total holding cost of raw material is

$$H_S = \sum_{l=1}^{L} \sum_{i=0}^{n-2} \frac{\widetilde{h_{sl}} C_l T_1^2}{2}$$

$$= (n-2) \sum_{l=1}^{L} \frac{\widetilde{h_{sl}} C_l T_1^2}{2}$$

Total collection cost of raw material is

$$C_S = \sum_{l=1}^{L} \sum_{i=0}^{n-2} \frac{p_{sl} C_1 T_1}{2}$$

$$= (n-2) \sum_{l=1}^{L} \sum_{i=0}^{n-2} p_{sl} C_1 T_1$$

The total raw material cost for the supplier is the sum of the set up cost, collection cost and holding cost as follows:

$$\widetilde{TC_S} = \sum_{l=1}^{L} \widetilde{A_{Sl}} + (n-2) \sum_{l=1}^{L} \sum_{i=0}^{n-2} p_{sl} C_1 T_1 + (n-2) \sum_{l=1}^{L} \frac{\widetilde{h_{sl}} C_l T_1^2}{2}$$

INVENTORY MODEL OF RAW MATERIAL IN PRODUCER'S WAREHOUSE

The inventory level of raw material at the producer's warehouse at time t, q_{pw} determine by the linear differential equation

$$\frac{dq_{PW}}{dt} = -U, (i+1)T_1 \le t \le (i+2)T_1, i = 0, 1, 2, \ldots, n-2.$$

As shown in the figure-1 the inventory conditions for the model are:

$q_{PW}((i+1)T_1) = Q_{PW}$ and $q_{PW}((i+2)T_1) = 0, i = 0,1,2,...,n-2.$

Therefore using the condition $q_{PW}((i+2)T_1) = 0$ the inventory at any time t is given by:

$$q_{PW}(t) = U\{(i+2)T_1 - t\}$$

Using the condition $q_{PW}((i+t)T_1) = Q_{PW}$ we get

$$Q_{PW} = UT_1$$

Holding cost of raw material is

$$= \widetilde{h_{PW}} \int_{(i+1)T_1}^{(i+2)T_1} q_{PW}(t)dt$$
$$= \frac{\widetilde{h_{PW}} UT_1^2}{2}$$

So total holding cost of raw material is

$$\widetilde{H_{PW}} = \sum_{i=0}^{n-2} \frac{\widetilde{h_{PW}} UT_1^2}{2}$$
$$= (n-2)\frac{\widetilde{h_{PW}} UT_1^2}{2}$$

Purchasing cost of raw material = $p_{PW}Q_{PW}$
Total purchasing cost of raw material

$$\widetilde{P_{PW}} = \sum_{i=0}^{n-2} p_{PW}Q_{PW}$$
$$= (n-2)p_{PW}Q_{PW}$$
$$= (n-2)p_{PW}UT_1$$

The total raw material cost for the producer's warehouse is the sum of the set up cost, purchasing cost of raw material and holding cost as follows:

$$\frac{dq_{Rk}}{dt} = -D_k, (i+2)T_1 \le t \le (i+3)T_1, i = 0,1,2,...,n-2.$$

INVENTORY MODEL OF PRODUCER'S FINISHED GOODS

The finished goods inventory level for the producer with unknown production rate U is described by the following differential equation

$$\frac{dq_P}{dt} = (1-\lambda^{iT_1})U, (i+1)T_1 \le t \le (i+2)T_1, i = 0,1,2,...,n-2.$$

The boundary condition are $q_P\{(i+1)T_1\} = 0$ and $q_P\{(i+2)T_1\} = Q_P$
Therefore using the condition $q_P\{(i+1)T_1\} = 0$ the inventory at any time t is given by:

$$q_P = (1-\lambda^{iT_1})U\{t-(i+2)T_1\}$$

Using the condition $q_P\{(i+2)T_1\} = Q_P$, we get,

$$q_P = (1-\lambda^{iT_1})UT_1$$

In this case holding cost is

$$= \widetilde{h_P}\int_{(i+1)T_1}^{(i+2)T_1} q_P(t)dt$$
$$= \frac{\widetilde{h_P}(1-\lambda^{iT_1})UT_1^2}{2}$$

So total holding cost of raw material is

$$\widetilde{H_P} = \sum_{i=0}^{n-2} \frac{\widetilde{h_P}(1-\lambda^{iT_1})UT_1^2}{2}$$
$$= \widetilde{h_P}\frac{UT_1^2}{2}[(n-2) - \frac{1-(\lambda^{-T_1})^{n-1}}{1-\lambda^{-T_1}}]$$

Production cost $=p_P Q_P$
Total production cost

$$\widetilde{P_P} = \sum_{i=0}^{n-2} p_P Q_P$$
$$= (n-2)1-\lambda^{-T_1} p_P Q_P$$
$$= p_P UT_1[(n-2) - \frac{1-(\lambda^{-T_1})^{n-1}}{1-\lambda^{-T_1}}]$$

The total cost for the producer due to finished goods can be expressed as the sum of the setup cost, production cost and holding cost as follows:

$$\widetilde{TC_P} = \widetilde{A_P} + p_P U T_1[(n-2) - \frac{1-(\lambda^{-T_1})^{n-1}}{1-\lambda^{-T_1}}] + \widetilde{h_P}\frac{UT_1^2}{2}[(n-2) - \frac{1-(\lambda^{-T_1})^{n-1}}{1-\lambda^{-T_1}}]$$

INVENTORY MODEL FOR THE RETAILERS FOR FINISHED GOODS

If $q_{Rk}(t)$ be the inventory of the finished goods at any time t for the retailer with imprecise demand $\tilde{D}_s$ and if t_{b_i} be the time of shortage for the k-th retailer in the i-th cycle, the governing differential equations are:

$$\frac{dq_{Rk}}{dt} = -D_k, (i+2)T_1 \le t \le (i+3)T_1, i = 0,1,2,\ldots,n-2.$$

$$q_{Rk}((i+2)T_1) = Q_{Ri}$$

$$q_{Rk}((i+2)T_1 + T_R) = 0$$

$$q_{Rk}((i+3)T_1) = S_{Rk}, i = 0,1,2,\ldots,n-2.$$

Therefore using the condition

$$q_{Rk}((i+2)T_1) = 0$$

the inventory at any time t is given by:

$$q_{Rk} = \widetilde{D_k}\{(i+2)T_1 - t\} + Q_{Rk}, (i+2)T_1 \le t \le (i+3)T_1 + T_R, i = 0,1,2,\ldots,n-2.$$

Using the condition

$$q_{Rk}((i+2)T_1 + T_R) = 0,$$

we get,

$$Q_{Rk} = \widetilde{D_k}T_R$$

Using the condition

$$q_{Rk}((i+3)T_1) = S_{Rk}$$

we get,

$$q_{Rk} = \widetilde{D_k}\{(i+3)T_1 - t\} + S_R, (i+2)T_1 + T_R \le t \le (i+3)T_1, i = 0,1,2,\ldots,n-2$$

Now using,

$$q_{Rk}((i+2)T_1 + T_R) = 0$$

we get,

$$S_{Rk} = \widetilde{D_k}\left(T_1 - T_R\right)$$

In this case holding cost is

$$= \widetilde{h_{Rk}} \int_{(i+1)T_1}^{\{(i+2)T_1 + T_R\}} q_{Rk}(t)dt$$
$$= \widetilde{h_{Rk}} \frac{Q_{Rk}T_R}{2}$$

So total holding cost of finished goods is

$$\widetilde{H_R} = \sum_{l=0}^{n-2}\sum_{k=1}^{K} \widetilde{h_{Rk}} \frac{Q_{Rk}T_R}{2}$$
$$= (n-2)\sum_{k=1}^{K} \widetilde{h_{Rk}} \frac{Q_{Rk}T_R}{2}$$

Shortage cost

$$= C_{3k} \int_{\{(i+3)T_1 + T_R\}}^{\{(i+3)T_1 + T_R\}} [\widetilde{D_k}\{(i+3)T_1 - t\} + S_R]dt$$
$$= \frac{C_{3k}S_{Rk}\left(T_1 - T_R\right)}{2}$$

Total shortage cost $\widetilde{TS_R}$

$$= \sum_{l=0}^{n-2} \sum_{k=1}^{K} C_{3k} (S_{Rk} T_R + \frac{\widetilde{D_k T_R^{\,2}}}{2})$$

$$= (n-2) \sum_{k=1}^{K} \frac{C_{3k} S_{Rk} \left(T_1 - T_R\right)}{2}$$

Purchasing cost $= \widetilde{p_{Rk}} Q_{Rk}$

Total purchasing cost

$$\widetilde{TP_R} = \sum_{k=1}^{K} \sum_{i=0}^{n-2} \widetilde{p_{Rk}} Q_{Rk}$$

$$= \sum_{k=1}^{K} (n-2) \widetilde{p_{Rk}} \widetilde{D_k} T_R$$

The total cost for the retailer due to finished goods can be expressed as the sum of the setup cost, production cost, holding cost and shortage cost as follows

$$\widetilde{TC_R} = \sum_{K=1}^{K} \widetilde{A_{Rk}} + \sum_{k=1}^{K} (n-2) \widetilde{p_{Rk}} \widetilde{D_k} T_R + (n-2) \sum_{k=1}^{K} \widetilde{h_{Rk}} \frac{Q_{Rk} T_R}{2} + (n-2) \sum_{k=1}^{K} \frac{C_{3k} S_{Rk} \left(T_1 - T_R\right)}{2}$$

INTEGRATED MODEL

Assuming the whole system is owned and managed by a single concern / management the problem reduces to a single objective minimization problem as:

$$\min imize \widetilde{TC_1} \approx \text{minimize} \{ \widetilde{TC_S} + \widetilde{TC_{PW}} + \widetilde{TC_P} + \widetilde{TC_R} \}$$

Subject to

$$\sum_{l=1}^{L} (t_0 + t_1 p_{sl}) \le \widetilde{T_{11}} \text{ (C-1)}$$

$$\sum_{l=1}^{L} (t_0' + t_1' Q_{sl}) \le \widetilde{T_{11}} \text{ (C-2)}$$

$$\sum_{k=1}^{K} (t_0'' + t_1'' Q_{Rk}) \le \widetilde{T_{21}} \text{ (C-3)}$$

Procedure for Defuzzification

Since $\widetilde{TC_1}$ is fuzzy in nature minimize $\widetilde{TC_1}$ is not well defined. So instead of minimize $\widetilde{TC_1}$ one can minimize F such that necessity of the event $\widetilde{TC_1} < F$ exceeds some predefined level $\alpha(0<\alpha<1)$ according to companies requirement. Similarly as fuzzy constraints are also npt well defined, necessity of the constraints (C-1,C-2,C-3) must exceed somne predefined level $\alpha_i(0<\alpha_i<1)(i=1,2,3)$ as proposed by Maiti and Maiti. Then the problem reduces to

Minimize F
Subject to

$$Nes(\widetilde{TC_1} < F) > \alpha$$

$$Nes(Q_P + Q_{PW} \leq \widetilde{W}) > \alpha_1$$

$$Nes(\sum_{l=1}^{L}(t_0' + t_1' Q_{Sl}) \leq \widetilde{T_{11}}) > \alpha_2$$

$$Nes(\sum_{k=1}^{K}(t_0'' + t_1'' Q_{RK}) \leq \widetilde{T_{21}}) > \alpha_3$$

Now, let us consider the fuzzy parameters as triangular fuzzy number of the form:

$$\tilde{h}_s = (h_{s1}, h_{s2}, h_{s3}),\ \tilde{h}_p = (h_{p1}, h_{p2}, h_{p3}),\ \tilde{h}_{pW} = (h_{pW1}, h_{pW2}, h_{pW3}),\ \tilde{h}_R = (h_{R1}, h_{R2}, h_{R3}),$$
$$\tilde{A}_s = (A_{s1}, A_{s2}, A_{s3}),\ \tilde{A}_p = (A_{p1}, A_{p2}, A_{p3}),\ \tilde{A}_{pW} = (A_{pW1}, A_{pW2}, A_{pW3}),\ \tilde{A}_r = (A_{r1}, A_{r2}, A_{r3}),$$
$$\tilde{D} = (D_1, D_2, D_3),\ \tilde{C}_3 = (C_{31}, C_{32}, C_{33}),\ \tilde{p}_R = (p_{R1}, p_{R2}, p_{R3}),\ \tilde{W} = (W_1, W_2, W_3),$$
$$\tilde{T}_{11} = (T_{111}, T_{112}, T_{113}),\ \tilde{T}_{21} = (T_{211}, T_{212}, T_{213}),$$

as TFNs then $\widetilde{TC_1}$ becomes a TFN $(TC_{l1}, TC_{l2}, TC_{l3})$.

Then using *Lemma-1 and Lemma-2* the above problem reduces to:

Minimize F
Subject to:

$$\frac{W_2 - (Q_P + Q_{PW})}{W_1 - W_2} \geq \alpha_1$$

$$\frac{T_{112} - \sum_{l=1}^{L}(t_0' + t_1' Q_{Sl})}{T_{112} - T_{111}} \geq \alpha_2$$

$$\frac{T_{212} - \sum_{k=1}^{K}(t_0'' + t_1'' Q_{Rk})}{T_{212} - T_{211}} \geq \alpha_3$$

Which is equivalent to

Minimize $F=\alpha TC_{I3}+(1-\alpha)TC_{I2}$

Subject to: $\frac{W_2 - (Q_P + Q_{PW})}{W_1 - W_2} \geq \alpha_1$

$$\frac{T_{112} - \sum_{l=1}^{L}(t_0' + t_1' Q_{Sl})}{T_{112} - T_{111}} \geq \alpha_2$$

$$\frac{T_{212} - \sum_{k=1}^{K}(t_0'' + t_1'' Q_{Rk})}{T_{212} - T_{211}} \geq \alpha_3$$

NUMERICAL EXAMPLE

In this section, an example to illustrate the proposed supply –chain model is considered.

Consider a SCM consisting of two suppliers (L=2), a producer and two retailers (K=2) for the respective imprecise market demands (100,112,118) and (120,125,130).The other relevant cost parameters are shown in Table 1:

Table 1. Cost parameters

SCM	Ordering Cost	Purchasing/ Prod Cost	Holding Cost	Defective Rate	Shortage Cost	Transportation Cost
Suppliers	(43,48,50) (47,52,60)	(13,15,19) (22,25,28)	(3,3.5,4.1) (4,4.5,5.0)	- -	- -	(5,0.5) (5.5,0.5)
Prod. Warehouse	(75,80,85)	(35,40,45)	(4.5,5,5.5)	-	- -	-
Prod. centre	(95,100,105)	(4.5,5,5.5)	(5.5,6,6.5)	0.02	-	
Retailers	(80,85,90) (90,95,98)	(40,45,45) (48,53,55)	(4.5,5,5.5) (4.5,5.4,5.9)	- -	(1.5,2.0,2.2) (1.8,2.2,2.5)	(5,0.4) (5.2,0.5)

In addition to this data, the following parameters are also assumed:

$\tilde{W}=(2.4,2.5,2.6)$, $\tilde{T}_{11}=(11,12,13.5)$, $\tilde{T}_{21}=(11,12,13.5)$ and predefined necessity levels $\alpha=0.9$, $\alpha_1=0.8$, $\alpha_2=0.8$, $\alpha_3=0.8$.

We used the software package LINGO 9.0(by Wolfram Research,Inc.) to obtain the optimal and heuristic solutions. The optimization option we used within the package is the Generalised Reduced Gradient (GRG) method which provides quite effectively results, such as: the optimal number of shipments is $N^{*}=8$, optimal time length of each cycle $T_1^{*}=0.1110$,$T_R^{*}=0.1022$

And the corresponding optimal rates are $C_1^{*}=(116.48,126.32)$, $U^{*}=121.42$ with optimal quantity $QS_1^{*}=(11.90,12.05)$,$QR_k^{*}=(12.05,12.72)$. The total cost under this solution is $TC_I^{*}=23071.18$ for the optimal total cost of supplier $TC_s^{*}=(2012.35,2065.46)$, for producer $TC_p^{*}=(4112.26+4502.73)$ and for retailer $TC_r^{*}=(5078.20,5299.67)$.

We used the software package LINGO 9.0(by Wolfram Research. Inc.) to obtain the optimal and heuristic solutions. The optimization option we used within the package is the Generalised Reduced Gradient (GRG) method which provides quite effectively results, such as: the optimal number of shipments is $N^{*}=10$, optimal time length of each cycle $T_1^{*}=0.1028$,$T_R^{*}=0.1000$ and the corresponding optimal rates are $C^{*}=121.21, U^{*}=121.21$ with optimal quantity $QS^{*}=12.46, QR^{*}=12.30$. The total cost under this solution is $TC_I^{*}=15990.52$ for the optimal total cost of supplier $TC_S^{*}=2064.15$ for producer $TC_P^{*}=(4091.92+4583.57)$ and for retailer $TC_r^{*}=5250.87$.

DISCUSSION

This paper addresses the optimal order quantity placed by the retailers, production rate of the producer and the collection or production rate of the suppliers to minimize the supply-chain cost. Here, it is seen that all these control variables directly or indirectly depend on the demand by the customers placed to the retailers.

From mathematical representation and numerical results, it is also observed that:

1. Producers product amount in a cycle= sum of order quantities of all the retailers for a single cycle = total demand of the customers during the cycle time to all retailers,
2. The stored amount of raw-materials by the producer= sum of the collection or production amount of all the suppliers during the cycle period,
3. The production rate of the finished goods is proportional to the decay rate of the raw-materials.

CONCLUSION

Here, fuzzy chance constraints on the transportation costs for both producer, retailers and also a space constraint for producer (to contain finished goods and different raw materials) is considered. The different supply-chain costs are imprecise in nature. The EOQ business process by the different retailer also may follow shortage of the finished goods. Considering all these real-life scenarios the supply-chain model is optimized for a finite number of sub-intervals in the finite time horizon.

REFERENCES

Cachon, G. P., & Zipkin, P. H. (1999). Competitive and cooperative inventory policies in a two-stage supply chain. *Management Science*, *45*(7), 936–953. doi:10.1287/mnsc.45.7.936

Chen, C. T., & Huang, S. F. (2006). Order fulfilment ability analysis in the supply chain system with fuzzy operation times. *International Journal of Production Economics*, *101*(1), 185–193. doi:10.1016/j.ijpe.2005.05.003

Chen, C. T., Lin, C. T., & Huang, S. F. (2006). A fuzzy approach for supplier evaluation and selection in supply chain management. *International Journal of Production Economics*, *102*, 289–301.

Cohen, M. A., & Lee, H. L. (1988). Strategic analysis of integrated production distribution systems-models and methods. *Operations Research*, *36*, 216–228.

Das, B., Maity, K., Mondal, S., & Maiti, M. (2005), A Supply-chain production control problem via genetic algorithm.*Proc, International Conference on Operation Research and Developement*.

Das, B., Maity, K., & Maiti, M. (2007). A Two Warehouse Supply-Chain Model under Possibility / Necessity / Credibility measure. *Mathematical and Computer Modelling*, *46*(3-4), 398–409. doi:10.1016/j.mcm.2006.11.017

Hill, R. M., Seifbarghy, M., & Smith, D. K. (2007). A two-echolon inventory model with lost sales. *European Journal of Operational Research*, *181*(2), 753–766. doi:10.1016/j.ejor.2006.08.017

Jaber. M. Y., & Bonney, M. (1998). The effects of learning and forgetting on the optimal lot size quantity of intermittent production runs. *Production Planning and Control*, (9), 20-27.

Keachie, E. C., & Fontana, R. J. (1966). Production lot sizes under a learning effect. *Management Science*, *13*, B102–B108. doi:10.1287/mnsc.13.2.B102

Kumar, M., Vrat, P., & Shan, R. (2004). A fuzzy goal programming approach for vendor selection problem in a supply chain. *Computers & Industrial Engineering*, *46*(1), 69–85. doi:10.1016/j.cie.2003.09.010

Liang, T. F. (2007). Applying fuzzy goal programming to production/ transportation planning decisions in supply chain. *International Journal of Systems Science*, *38*(4), 293–304. doi:10.1080/00207720601159381

Liu, B., & Iwamura, K. (1998). Chance constraint Programming with fuzzy parameters. *Fuzzy Sets and Systems*, *94*(2), 227–237. doi:10.1016/S0165-0114(96)00236-9

Maiti, M. K., & Maiti, M. (2006). Fuzzy Inventory Model with Two Warehouses under Possibility Constraints. *Fuzzy Sets and Systems*, *157*(1), 52–73. doi:10.1016/j.fss.2005.06.021

Nair, A., & Closs, D. J. (2006). An examination of the impact of coordinating supply chain policies and price markdowns on short life cycle product retail performance. *International Journal of Production Economics*, *102*(2), 379–392. doi:10.1016/j.ijpe.2005.04.009

Peidro, D., Mula, J., Polar, R., & Verdegay, J.-L. (2009). Fuzzy Optimization for supply chain planning under supply, demand and process uncertainties. *Fuzzy Sets and Systems*, *160*(18), 2640–2657. doi:10.1016/j.fss.2009.02.021

Petrovic, D. (2001). Simulation of supply chain behaviour and performance in an uncertain environment. *International Journal of Production Economics*, *71*(1-3), 429–438. doi:10.1016/S0925-5273(00)00140-7

Rau, H., Wu, M.-Y., & Wee, H.-M. (2004). Deteriorating item inventory model with shortage due to supplier in an integrated supply chain. *International Journal of Systems Science*, *35*(5), 293–303. doi: 10.1080/00207720410001714833

Sarmah, S. P., Acharya, D., & Goyal, S. K. (2008). Coordination of a singlemanufacturer/ multi-buyer supply chain with credit option. *International Journal of Production Economics*, *111*(2), 676–685. doi:10.1016/j.ijpe.2007.04.003

Santoso, T., Ahmed, S., Goetschalckx, M., & Shapiro, A. (2005). A stochastic programming approach for supply chain network design under uncertainty. *European Journal of Operational Research*, *167*(1), 96–115. doi:10.1016/j.ejor.2004.01.046

Viswanathan, S., & Piplani, R. (2001). Coordinating supply chain inventories through common replenishment epochs. *European Journal of Operational Research*, *129*(2), 277–286. doi:10.1016/S0377-2217(00)00225-3

Wang, J., & Shu, Y. F. (2005). Fuzzy decision modelling for supply chain management. *Fuzzy Sets and Systems*, *150*(1), 107–127. doi:10.1016/j.fss.2004.07.005

Xie, Y., Petrovic, D., & Bumham, K. (2006). A heuristic procedure for the two level control of serial supply chains under fuzzy customer demand. *International Journal of Production Economics*, *102*(1), 37–50. doi:10.1016/j.ijpe.2005.01.016

Zadeh, L. A. (1965). Fuzzy sets as a basis for a theory of possibility. *Fuzzy Sets and Systems*, *1*(1), 3–28. doi:10.1016/0165-0114(78)90029-5

Zimmermann, H.-J. (1976). Description and optimization of fuzzy systems. *International Journal of General Systems*, *2*(4), 209–215. doi:10.1080/03081077608547470

Zimmermann, H.-J. (1978). Fuzzy programming and linear programming with several objective functions. *Fuzzy Sets and Systems*, *1*(1), 45–56. doi:10.1016/0165-0114(78)90031-3

Chapter 15
Modified Iterative Methods for Solving Fully Fuzzy Linear Systems

S. A. Edalatpanah
Ayandegan Institute of Higher Education, Tonekabon, Iran

ABSTRACT

In the present chapter, we give an overview of computational iterative schemes for fuzzy system of linear equations. We also consider fully fuzzy linear systems (FFLS) and demonstrate a class of the existing iterative methods using the splitting approach for calculating the solution. Furthermore, the main aim in this work is to design a numerical procedure for improving this algorithm. Some numerical experiments are illustrated to show the applicability of the methods and to show the efficiency of proposed algorithm, we report the numerical results of large-scaled fuzzy problems.

INTRODUCTION

Unfailing real world problems in economics, finance, mechanics etc. can lead to solving a system of linear equations. There are many methods for solving linear systems, see(Barrett et al., 1994; Edalatpanah, 2008; Eisenstat, Elman, & Schultz, 1983; Greenbaum, 1997; Martins, Trigo, & Evans, 2007; Saad, 2003; Saberi Najafi & Edalatpanad, 2013a; Saberi Najafi & Edalatpanah, 2013b, 2013c, 2014b; Saberi Najafi & Edalatpanah, 2011; Varga, 2009; Young, 2014; Zhang, Huang, Cheng, & Wang, 2012) and the references therein. Let us consider the following linear systems

$$Ax=b, \tag{1}$$

However, when the estimation of the system coefficients is imprecise and only some vague knowledge about the actual values of the parameters is available, it may be convenient to represent some or all of them with fuzzy numbers. Fuzzy data is being used as a natural way to describe uncertain data. Fuzzy concept was introduced by Zadeh (Zadeh, 1965, 1972) and following his work, many papers and books were published in fuzzy system theory; see (Bellman & Zadeh, 1970; Bezdek, 2013; Chen, 2000; Cordón, 2001; Driankov, Hellendoorn, & Reinfrank, 2013; Hájek, 1998; Höppner, 1999; Jang & Sun,

DOI: 10.4018/978-1-5225-0914-1.ch015

1995; Kusko, 1993; Pham, Xu, & Prince, 2000; Ragin, 2000; Sheridan, 1992; Wasserman, 1993; Yager & Filev, 1994; Zadeh, 1997; Zimmermann, 2001).We refer the reader to (Kaufmann & Gupta, 1991) for more information on fuzzy numbers and fuzzy arithmetic. Fuzzy systems are used to study a variety of problems including fuzzy metric spaces (Alaca, Turkoglu, & Yildiz, 2006; Gregori, Romaguera, & Veeramani, 2006; J. H. Park, 2004), fuzzy differential equations (Bede & Gal, 2005; Buckley, Eslami, & Feuring, 2002; Kaleva, 1987; Khastan, Nieto, & Rodríguez-López, 2011; Khastan & Rodríguez-López, 2015; Malinowski, 2012; J. Y. Park & Han, 2000), particle physics (El Naschie, 2004a, 2004b), Game theory (Kacher & Larbani, 2008; Larbani, 2009; Maeda, 2000; Oliveira & Petraglia, 2014; Saberi Najafi & Edalatpanah, 2012a; Yang & Gao, 2014), optimization (Amid, Ghodsypour, & O'Brien, 2006; Edalatpanah & Shahabi, 2012; Guua & Wu, 1999; Huang, Baetz, & Patry, 1995; Inuiguchi, Ichihashi, & Kume, 1990; Lee & Li, 1993; Najafi & Edalatpanah, 2013d; Rommelfanger, 2007; Shamooshaki, Hosseinzadeh, & Edalatpanah, 2014; Słowiński, 1986; Yu, 2002), fuzzy linear systems(Allahviranloo, 2004; Asady, Abbasbandy, & Alavi, 2005; Dehghan & Hashemi, 2006b; Dehghan, Hashemi, & Ghatee, 2006, 2007; Dubois & Prade, 1980; Friedman, Ming, & Kandel, 1998; Ma, Friedman, & Kandel, 2000; Nasseri, Sohrabi, & Ardil, 2008; Saberi Najafi & Edalatpanah, 2012b), and so on.

In this chapter, we design a modified iterative method for solving fully fuzzy linear systems (FFLS). This paper is organized as follows:

In Section 2 some basic definitions and arithmetic are reviewed. In Section 3 a background for solution of fuzzy system of linear equations are presented. In Section 4 a new method is proposed for solving FFLS. In section 5 numerical results are considered to show the efficiency of the proposed method. Section 6 ends this chapter with a conclusion.

Some Basic Definition and Arithmetic Operations

In this section, an appropriate brief introduction to preliminary topics such as fuzzy numbers and fuzzy calculus will be introduced and the definition for FFLS will be provided. For details, we refer to (Abdolmaleki & Edalatpanah, 2014b; Dehghan et al., 2006, 2007).

Definition 2.1: Let X denote a universal set. Then a fuzzy subset $\tilde{A}$ of X is defined by its membership function $\mu_{\tilde{A}} : X \rightarrow [0,1]$; which assigns a real number $\mu_{\tilde{A}}(x)$ in the interval [0,1], to each element $x \in X$, where the value of $\mu_{\tilde{A}}(x)$ at x shows the grade of membership of x in $\tilde{A}$.

A fuzzy subset $\tilde{A}$ can be characterized as a set of ordered pairs of element x and grade $\mu_{\tilde{A}}(x)$ and is often written $\tilde{A} = \{(x, \mu_{\tilde{A}}(x)); x \in X\}$.The class of fuzzy sets on X is denoted with $\Gamma(X)$.

Definition 2.2 A fuzzy set with the following membership function is named a triangular fuzzy number and in this paper we will use these fuzzy numbers.

$$\mu_{\tilde{A}}(x) = \begin{cases} 1 - \dfrac{m-x}{\alpha}, & m - \alpha \leq x \leq m, \alpha > 0, \\ 1 - \dfrac{x-m}{\beta}, & m \leq x \leq m + \beta, \beta > 0, \\ 0, & else. \end{cases}$$

Definition 2.3: A fuzzy number $\tilde{A}$ is said to be positive (negative) by $\tilde{A} > 0(\tilde{A} < 0)$ if its membership function $\mu_{\tilde{A}}(x)$ satisfies $\mu_{\tilde{A}}(x) = 0, \forall x \leq 0(\forall x \geq 0)$.

Using its mean value and left and right spreads, and shape functions, such a fuzzy number $\tilde{A}$ is symbolically written $\tilde{A} = (m, \alpha, \beta)$. Obviously, $\tilde{A}$ is positive, if and only if $m - \alpha \geq 0$.

Definition 2.4: Two fuzzy numbers $\tilde{A} = (m, \alpha, \beta)$ and $\tilde{B} = (n, \gamma, \delta)$ are said to be equal, if and only if $m = n$, $\alpha = \gamma$ and $\beta = \delta$.

Definition 2.5: Let $\tilde{A} = (m, \alpha, \beta)$, $\tilde{B} = (n, \gamma, \delta)$ be two triangular fuzzy numbers then;

1. $\tilde{A} \oplus \tilde{B} = (m, \alpha, \beta) \oplus (n, \gamma, \delta) = (m + n, \alpha + \gamma, \beta + \delta)$,
2. $-\tilde{A} = -(m, \alpha, \beta) = (-m, \beta, \alpha)$,
3. if $\tilde{A}, \tilde{B}$ be a positive fuzzy number then: $(m, \alpha, \beta) \otimes (n, \gamma, \delta) \cong (mn, n\alpha + m\gamma, n\beta + m\delta)$,

For scalar multiplication we have;

$$\lambda \otimes (m, \alpha, \beta) = \begin{cases} (\lambda m, \lambda\alpha, \lambda\beta), & \lambda \geq 0, \\ (\lambda m, -\lambda\beta, -\lambda\alpha), & \lambda < 0. \end{cases}$$

Definition 2.6: A matrix $\tilde{A} = (\tilde{a}_{ij})$ is called a fuzzy matrix, if each element of $\tilde{A}$ is a fuzzy number. A fuzzy matrix $\tilde{A}$ will be positive and denoted by $\tilde{A} > 0$, if each element of $\tilde{A}$ be positive. We may represent n × n fuzzy matrix $\tilde{A} = (\tilde{a}_{ij})_{n \times n}$, such that $\tilde{a}_{ij} = (a_{ij}, \alpha_{ij}, \beta_{ij})$, with the new notation $\tilde{A} = (A, M, N)$, where $A = (a_{ij})$, $M = (\alpha_{ij})$ and $N = (\beta_{ij})$ are three n × n crisp matrices.

BACKGROUND

Fuzzy linear systems appeared at least by 1980(Dubois & Prade, 1980) . Friedman *et al.* (Friedman et al., 1998) introduced a general model for solving a fuzzy n × n linear system whose coefficient matrix is crisp and the right-hand side column is an arbitrary fuzzy number vector. They used the parametric form of fuzzy numbers and replaced the original fuzzy n × n linear system by a crisp 2n × 2n linear system. As matter of fact used left/right function(L-R functions) to embed fuzzy intervals into a Banach space with additive and multiplicative inverses for fuzzy interval numbers and solve fuzzy interval linear systems using these inverses. Briefly, they considered the n × n linear system of equations as follows:

$$\begin{cases} a_{11}x_1 + a_{12}x_2 + \cdots + a_{1n}x_n = b_1, \\ a_{21}x_1 + a_{22}x_2 + \cdots + a_{2n}x_n = b_2, \\ \vdots \\ a_{n1}x_1 + a_{n2}x_2 + \cdots + a_{nn}x_n = b_n. \end{cases} \tag{2}$$

Where the coefficient matrix A=(a_{ij}), 1≤i,j≤n is a crisp matrix and $b_i \in E^1; 1 \leq i \leq n$,is called a fuzzy linear system(FLS).And, they defined a solution of the above fuzzy linear system as:

A fuzzy number vector $X = (x_1, x_2, \ldots, x_n)^T$, given by parametric form $x_i = (\underline{x}_i(r), \overline{x}_i(r))$, $1 \le i \le n$, $0 \le r \le 1$, is called a solution of the fuzzy linear system if:

$$\begin{cases} \underline{\sum_{j=1}^{n} a_{ij} x_j} = \sum_{j=1}^{n} \underline{a_{ij} x_j} = \underline{b}_i, \\ \overline{\sum_{j-1}^{n} a_{ij} x_j} = \sum_{j=1}^{n} \overline{a_{ij} x_j} = \overline{b}_i. \end{cases} \tag{3}$$

Therefore, in order to solve the system given byEq.(3), they have solved a 2n×2n crisp linear system as:

$$SX=B \tag{4}$$

where $S=(s_{ij})$,are determined as follows:

$$\begin{cases} a_{ij} \ge 0 \rightarrow s_{ij} = a_{ij}, \quad s_{i+n,j+n} = a_{ij}, \\ a_{ij} < 0 \rightarrow s_{i,j+n} = -a_{ij}, \quad s_{i+n,j} = -a_{ij} \end{cases} \tag{5}$$

and any (s_{ij}) which is not determined by (5) is zero. Furthermore:

$$S = \begin{bmatrix} s_1 & s_2 \\ s_2 & s_1 \end{bmatrix} \& X = \begin{bmatrix} \underline{x} \\ -\overline{x} \end{bmatrix} \& B = \begin{bmatrix} \underline{b} \\ -\overline{b} \end{bmatrix} \Rightarrow \begin{cases} s_1 \underline{x} - s_2 \overline{x} = \underline{b} \\ s_2 \underline{x} - s_1 \overline{x} = -\overline{b} \end{cases} \tag{6}$$

or

$$S = \begin{bmatrix} s_1 & -s_2 \\ -s_2 & s_1 \end{bmatrix} \& X = \begin{bmatrix} \underline{x} \\ \overline{x} \end{bmatrix} \& B = \begin{bmatrix} \underline{b} \\ \overline{b} \end{bmatrix} \Rightarrow \begin{cases} s_1 \underline{x} - s_2 \overline{x} = \underline{b} \\ -s_2 \underline{x} + s_1 \overline{x} = \overline{b} \end{cases} \tag{7}$$

where s_1, $s_2 \ge 0$, $A=s_1-s_2$.

There are several numerical methods for solving fuzzy linear systems such as Jacobi(Allahviranloo, 2004), Gauss-Seidel(Allahviranloo, 2004), successive over-relaxation iterative method(Allahviranloo, 2005b), symmetric successive over-relaxation methods (Wang & Zheng, 2006b), Adomiam decomposition method(Allahviranloo, 2005a), LU decomposition method(Abbasbandy, Ezzati, & Jafarian, 2006), stationary iterative methods(Dehghan & Hashemi, 2006a), splitting iterative methods(Yin & Wang, 2009), preconditioned iterative methods(Saberi Najafi & Edalatpanah, 2012c),Conjugate gradient method (Abbasbandy, Jafarian, & Ezzati, 2005), Steepest descent method (Abbasbandy & Jafarian, 2006),GMRES method(Zhou & Wei, 2014), Block Jacobi two-stage method(Allahviranloo, Ahmady, Ahmady, & Alketaby, 2006), Block iterative methods(Miao, Zheng, & Wang, 2008; Saberi Najafi & Edalatpanah, 2012b; Wang & Zheng, 2007),homotopy perturbation methods(Saberi Najafi, Edalatpanah,

& Refahi Sheikhani, 2013); see also(Allahviranloo, Lotfi, Kiasari, & Khezerloo, 2013; Amirfakhrian, 2007; Asady & Mansouri, 2009; Behera & Chakraverty, 2012; Kumar & Bansal, 2012; Lodwick & Dubois, 2015; Malkaw, Ahmad, & Ibrahim, 2015; Saberi Najafi & Edalatpanah, 2014a; Salkuyeh, 2015; Tian, Hu, & Greenhalgh, 2010; Wang & Zheng, 2006a).In general speaking, most of above methods are based on the following strategy:

Let S in Equation (7) be nonsingular and $S=D-L-U$, where:

$$D = \begin{bmatrix} D_1 & 0 \\ 0 & D_1 \end{bmatrix}, L = \begin{bmatrix} L_1 & 0 \\ S_2 & L_1 \end{bmatrix}, U = \begin{bmatrix} U_1 & S_2 \\ 0 & U_1 \end{bmatrix}$$

$D_1=\text{diag}(S_1) \geq 0$,

$S_1=D_1-L_1-U_1$,

and L, L_1, are strictly lower triangular matrices and U, U_1 are strictly upper triangular matrices. Then for solving of Equation (4), we use the following model:

$$x^{(i+1)} = M^{-1}N x^{(i)} + M^{-1}b \quad i=0,1,\ldots \tag{8}$$

where $S=M-N$, det (M) $\neq 0$ and $x^{(0)}$ is an initial vector.

In point iterative methods for example, AOR method (Dehghan & Hashemi, 2006a) we have:

$$x^{(i+1)} = Tx^{(i)} + (D - rL)^{-1} wb, \quad i = 0,1,\cdots \tag{9}$$

where the iterative matrix is:

$$T = (D - rL)^{-1}[(1 - w)D + (w - r)L + wU] \tag{10}$$

Where (w, r) are real parameters with w≠0. By Equations (9-10) we get:

$$M = (D - rL) = \begin{pmatrix} D_1 - rL_1 & 0 \\ -rS_2 & D_1 - rL_1 \end{pmatrix} \Rightarrow M^{-1} = \begin{pmatrix} \underbrace{(D_1 - rL_1)^{-1}}_{\alpha} & \underbrace{0}_{\beta} \\ \underbrace{r(D_1 - rL_1)^{-1} S_2 (D_1 - rL_1)^{-1}}_{\eta} & \underbrace{(D_1 - rL_1)^{-1}}_{\gamma} \end{pmatrix}.$$

Now, let

$$k = (D_1 - rL_1)^{-1}$$

Therefore we have:

$$T = M^{-1}N = \begin{pmatrix} k & 0 \\ rkS_2k & k \end{pmatrix}\left\{\begin{bmatrix}\begin{pmatrix}(1-w)D_1 & 0 \\ 0 & (1-w)D_1\end{pmatrix} + \begin{pmatrix}(w-r)L_1 & 0 \\ (w-r)S_2 & (w-r)L_1\end{pmatrix} + \begin{pmatrix} wU_1 & wS_2 \\ 0 & wU_1\end{pmatrix}\end{bmatrix}\right\}$$

$$\Rightarrow T = \begin{bmatrix} \underbrace{k[(1-w)D_1 + (w-r)L_1 + wU_1]}_{\Phi} & \underbrace{wkS_2}_{\Gamma} \\ \underbrace{wkS_2k[(1-r)D_1 + rU_1]}_{\Omega} & \underbrace{k[(1-w)D_1 + (w-r)L_1 + rwS_2kS_2 + wU_1]}_{\Psi} \end{bmatrix}$$

Other methods are the same and we know that, by choosing special parameters the similar results can be obtained, for example

1. Jacobi method for w=1, r=0.
2. JOR (Jacobi Overrelaxation) method for r=0.
3. Gauss-Seidel method for r=w=1.
4. SOR method for r=w.

Now, From $x^i = \begin{bmatrix} \underline{x}^i \\ \overline{x}^i \end{bmatrix}$ we have the following Algorithms (mentioned in (Dehghan & Hashemi, 2006a) for the first time).

Algorithm 1: (iterative method for FLS)
Given an initial vector $x^{(0)}$
For i =1,2, ..., until convergence

$$\begin{cases} \underline{x}^{i+1} = \Phi \underline{x}^i + \Gamma \overline{x}^i + w(\alpha \underline{b} + \beta \overline{b}) \\ \overline{x}^{i+1} = \Psi \overline{x}^i + \Omega \underline{x}^i + w(\eta \underline{b} + \gamma \overline{b}) \end{cases}$$

And the stopping criterion with tolerance ε>0 is:

$$\frac{\left\| \overline{x}^{i+1} - \overline{x}^i \right\|}{\left\| \overline{x}^{i+1} \right\|} < \varepsilon \ \& \ \frac{\left\| \underline{x}^{i+1} - \underline{x}^i \right\|}{\left\| \underline{x}^{i+1} \right\|} < \varepsilon, \quad i = 0, 1, \ldots \tag{11}$$

Although, these methods are interesting, however these methods cannot update the approximate solution as soon as they are available. Recently, Saberi Najafi and Edalatpanah(Saberi Najafi & Edalatpanah, 2013) proposed two algorithms to solve this drawback:

Algorithm 2: (Modified iterative method for FLS)
Given an initial vector $x^{(0)}$

For i =1,2, ..., until convergence

$$\underline{x}^{i+1} = \Phi \underline{x}^{i} + \Gamma \overline{x}^{i} + wk\underline{b}$$

Gamma= $\Omega \underline{x}^{i+1}$

$$\overline{x}_{new}^{i+1} = \Psi \overline{x}^{i} + rwkS_2k\underline{b} + wk\overline{b} + Gamma$$

Algorithm 3: (Backward model of modified iterative method for FLS)
Given an initial vector $x^{(0)}$
For i =1,2, ..., until convergence

$$\overline{x}^{i+1} = \Psi \overline{x}^{i} + \Omega \underline{x}^{i} + w(\eta \underline{b} + \gamma \overline{b})$$

Lambda= $\Gamma \overline{x}^{i+1}$

$$\underline{x}^{i+1} = \Phi \underline{x}^{i} + wk\underline{b} + Lambda$$

They evaluated that for the large sparse fuzzy linear systems:

The number of iterations (Algorithm.1) $\approx$ 2 * The number of iterations (Algorithms.2-3).

All above method work good when right hand side vector for linear systems be fuzzy number. But what happens if all parameters in a fuzzy linear system be fuzzy numbers, which we call a fully fuzzy linear system (denoted by FFLS) and what is the solution of this kind of fuzzy linear systems?

Dehghan and his colleagues(Dehghan & Hashemi, 2006b; Dehghan et al., 2007) proposed the Adomian decomposition method, and other iterative methods to find the positive fuzzy vector solution of $n \times n$ fully fuzzy linear system. Dehghan *et al.* (Dehghan et al., 2006) proposed some computational methods such as Cramer's rule, Gauss elimination method, LU decomposition method and linear programming approach for finding the approximated solution of FFLS. Nasseri *et al.* (Nasseri et al., 2008) used a certain decomposition methods of the coefficient matrix for solving fully fuzzy linear system of equations. Kumar *et al.* in (Kumar, Kaur, & Singh, 2011) obtained exact solution of fully fuzzy linear system by solving a linear programming; see also (Abbasbandy & Hashemi, 2012; Abdolmaleki & Edalatpanah, 2014a, 2014c; Allahviranloo, Mikaeilvand, Kiani, & Shabestari, 2008; Babbar, Kumar, & Bansal, 2013; Dehghan et al., 2006; Ezzati, Khezerloo, Mahdavi-Amiri, & Valizadeh, 2014; Gao & Zhang, 2009; Ghanbari, 2015; Ghomashi, Salahshour, & Hakimzadeh, 2014; Gong & Liu, 2010; Kumar, Babbar, & Bansal, 2011, 2012; Kumar & Bansal, 2012; Kumar, Bansal, & Babbar, 2013; Kumar, Kaur, et al., 2011; Liu, 2010; Moloudzadeh, Allahviranloo, & Darabi, 2013; Nasseri et al., 2008; Nasseri & Zahmatkesh, 2010; Senthilkumar & Rajendran, 2011). In next section, we propose our modified iterative method for solving fully fuzzy linear systems (FFLS).

New Algorithm for FFLS

Consider Fully fuzzy linear system (FFLS) $\tilde{A} \otimes \tilde{x} = \tilde{b}$. In this study, we are going to obtain a positive solution of FFLS, where, $\tilde{A} = (A, M, N) > \tilde{0}, \tilde{b} = (b, g, h) > \tilde{0}$ and $\tilde{x} = (x, y, z) > \tilde{0}$.

So we have;

$$(A, M, N) \otimes (x, y, z) = (b, g, h). \tag{12}$$

Then by Definition 2.5 we have;

$$(Ax, Ay + Mx, Az + Nx) = (b, g, h). \tag{13}$$

And by Definition 2.4, concludes that;

$$\begin{cases} Ax = b, \\ Ay + Mx = g, \\ Az + Nx = h. \end{cases} \tag{14}$$

Then,

$$\underbrace{\begin{pmatrix} A & 0 & 0 \\ M & A & 0 \\ N & 0 & A \end{pmatrix}}_{\Lambda} \underbrace{\begin{pmatrix} x \\ y \\ z \end{pmatrix}}_{X} = \underbrace{\begin{pmatrix} b \\ g \\ h \end{pmatrix}}_{\Xi} \tag{15}$$

So, by assuming that A be a nonsingular matrix we have;

$$\begin{cases} x = A^{-1}b, \\ y = A^{-1}(g - Mx), \\ z = A^{-1}(h - Nx). \end{cases} \tag{16}$$

Dehghan *et al.* (Dehghan et al., 2007) applied some iterative techniques such as Richardson, Jacobi, Jacobi overrelaxation(JOR), Gauss–Seidel, successive overrelaxation (SOR), accelerated overrelaxation (AOR), symmetric and unsymmetric SOR (SSOR and USSOR) and extrapolated modified Aitken (EMA) for solving FFLS. First, we review their work.

Consider Equation (14) and let A=Q- P be a proper splitting of crisp matrix A and Q, called the splitting matrix, be a nonsingular crisp matrix. Thus, the iterative method for FFLS is as follows;

$$\begin{pmatrix} x^{(k+1)} \\ y^{(k+1)} \\ z^{(k+1)} \end{pmatrix} = T \begin{pmatrix} x^{(k)} \\ y^{(k)} \\ z^{(k)} \end{pmatrix} + \xi, (k \geq 0). \tag{17}$$

T is called the iteration matrix and ξ is a vector and;

$$T = \begin{pmatrix} Q^{-1}P & 0 & 0 \\ -Q^{-1}M & Q^{-1}P & 0 \\ -Q^{-1}N & 0 & Q^{-1}P \end{pmatrix}, \xi = \begin{pmatrix} Q^{-1}b \\ Q^{-1}g \\ Q^{-1}h \end{pmatrix}. \tag{18}$$

Therefore by choose special parameters in Q we can obtain the popular iterative method. For example, if $A=D-L-U$, where D is diagonal, L is lower triangular and U is upper triangular part of A, then we have;

1. Jacobi method for $Q=D$.
2. JOR(Jacobi Overrelaxation) method for $Q = \frac{1}{w}D, (w \in R)$.
3. Gauss-Seidel method for $Q=D-L$.
4. SOR method for $Q = (\frac{1}{w}D - L), (w \in R)$.

For details, we refer to (Dehghan et al., 2007).

Next, we apply our modified method called *Modified Iterative Method* (MIM) for FFLS. Our idea is based on updating of the approximate solution .

Consider Eq. (14) and let $A=Q- P$:

$$\begin{cases} Ax = b \Rightarrow x^{(i+1)} = Q^{-1}Px^{(i)} + Q^{-1}b, \\ Ay + Mx = g \Rightarrow y^{(i+1)} = Q^{-1}Py^{(i)} - Q^{-1}Mx^{(i+1)} + Q^{-1}g, \\ Az + Nx = h \Rightarrow z^{(i+1)} = Q^{-1}Pz^{(i)} - Q^{-1}Nx^{(i+1)} + Q^{-1}h. \end{cases}$$

Thus we can obtain the following matrix form:

$$\begin{pmatrix} I & 0 & 0 \\ Q^{-1}M & I & 0 \\ Q^{-1}N & 0 & I \end{pmatrix} \begin{pmatrix} x^{(k+1)} \\ y^{(k+1)} \\ z^{(k+1)} \end{pmatrix} = \begin{pmatrix} Q^{-1}P & 0 & 0 \\ 0 & Q^{-1}P & 0 \\ 0 & 0 & Q^{-1}P \end{pmatrix} \begin{pmatrix} x^{(k)} \\ y^{(k)} \\ z^{(k)} \end{pmatrix} + \begin{pmatrix} Q^{-1}b \\ Q^{-1}g \\ Q^{-1}h \end{pmatrix}, (k \geq 0).$$

And since,

$$\begin{pmatrix} I & 0 & 0 \\ Q^{-1}M & I & 0 \\ Q^{-1}N & 0 & I \end{pmatrix}^{-1} = \begin{pmatrix} I & 0 & 0 \\ -Q^{-1}M & I & 0 \\ -Q^{-1}N & 0 & I \end{pmatrix},$$

We have the following modified of the iterative method for FFLS;

$$\begin{pmatrix} x^{(k+1)} \\ y^{(k+1)} \\ z^{(k+1)} \end{pmatrix} = \tilde{T} \begin{pmatrix} x^{(k)} \\ y^{(k)} \\ z^{(k)} \end{pmatrix} + \tilde{\xi}, (k \geq 0).$$

where,

$$\tilde{T} = \begin{pmatrix} Q^{-1}P & 0 & 0 \\ -Q^{-1}MQ^{-1}P & Q^{-1}P & 0 \\ -Q^{-1}NQ^{-1}P & 0 & Q^{-1}P \end{pmatrix}, \tilde{\xi} = \begin{pmatrix} Q^{-1}b \\ -Q^{-1}MQ^{-1}b + Q^{-1}g \\ -Q^{-1}NQ^{-1}b + Q^{-1}h \end{pmatrix}.$$

Theorem 1. MIM for solving fully fuzzy linear system $\tilde{A} \otimes \tilde{x} = \tilde{b}$, converges if and only if its classical version converges for solving the crisp linear system $Ax = b$ derived from the corresponding FFLS.

Proof. By above demonstrations and based on Equation (18) it is easy to see that spectrum of $\tilde{T}$ is equal to spectrum of $Q^{-1}P$. Therefore, the proof is complete.

NUMERICAL EXPERIMENTS

In this section, we give numerical experiments to illustrate the results obtained in previous sections. All the numerical experiments presented in this section were computed in double precision using a MATLAB 7 on a PC with a 1.86GHz 32-bit processor and 1GB memory.

Example 4.1. Consider the Consider the following FFLS:

$$\tilde{A} = (A, M, N); \begin{cases} A = tridiag(1,3,1)_{m\times m}, \\ M = tridiag(0.1,1,0.1)_{m\times m}, \\ N = tridiag(0.2,1,0.1)_{m\times m}. \end{cases}$$

And,

$$\tilde{b} = (b, g, h); b_i = i, g_i = \frac{i}{m}, h_i = \frac{i}{m+1}.$$

The following tables show the numerical results of above example with the tolerance $\varepsilon=10^{-6}$ and the initial approximation zero vector. In the Table 1, we reported the number of iterations (**Iter**) and Elapsed time (**ELP**) for the *Jacobi*, *Gauss-Seidel* and *SOR* iterative method with different m.

In the Table 2, we reported the number of iterations (**Iter**) and Elapsed time (**ELP**) for the *modified iterative method* with different m.

Table 1. Shows the results of example 4.1 by Jacobi, Gauss-Seidel and SOR methods

Method	Jacobi Method		Gauss-Seidel Method		SOR Method		
m	Iter	ELP	Iter	ELP	w	Iter	ELP
50	57	0.003404	26	0.002921	1.2	24	0.002536
100	60	0.004181	27	0.003679	1.2	25	0.003482
400	65	0.013792	29	0.012011	1.2	27	0.011215
600	67	0.331068	30	0.267814	1.2	27	0.231205

Table 2. Shows the results of example 4.1 by new Jacobi, new Gauss-Seidel and new SOR methods

Method	New Jacobi Method		New Gauss-Seidel Method		New SOR Method		
m	Iter	ELP	Iter	ELP	w	Iter	ELP
50	32	0.002010	16	0.001956	1.2	16	0.001104
100	33	0.004163	17	0.002670	1.2	16	0.002459
400	37	0.045805	18	0.021951	1.2	18	0.023588
600	38	0.141011	18	0.096775	1.2	18	0.950280

From the tables, we can see that our method is superior to the basic algorithm and this modified method can be applied to large-scaled fuzzy problems.

CONCLUSION

In this chapter, we propose new technique for solving fully fuzzy linear systems of equation *i.e.*, fuzzy linear systems with fuzzy coefficients involving fuzzy variables. Furthermore, we show that our iterative method compare with some other algorithms works better. Finally, from theoretical speaking and numerical experiments, it may be concluded that this method is efficient and convenient.

REFERENCES

Abbasbandy, S., Ezzati, R., & Jafarian, A. (2006). LU decomposition method for solving fuzzy system of linear equations. *Applied Mathematics and Computation*, *172*(1), 633–643. doi:10.1016/j.amc.2005.02.018

Abbasbandy, S., & Hashemi, M. (2012). Solving fully fuzzy linear systems by using implicit Gauss–Cholesky algorithm. *Computational Mathematics and Modeling*, *23*(1), 107–124. doi:10.1007/s10598-012-9123-4

Abbasbandy, S., & Jafarian, A. (2006). Steepest descent method for system of fuzzy linear equations. *Applied Mathematics and Computation*, *175*(1), 823–833. doi:10.1016/j.amc.2005.07.036

Abbasbandy, S., Jafarian, A., & Ezzati, R. (2005). Conjugate gradient method for fuzzy symmetric positive definite system of linear equations. *Applied Mathematics and Computation*, *171*(2), 1184–1191. doi:10.1016/j.amc.2005.01.110

Abdolmaleki, E., & Edalatpanah, S. (2014a). Chebyshev Semi-iterative Method to Solve Fully Fuzzy linear Systems. *Journal of Information and Computing Science, 9*(1), 67-74.

Abdolmaleki, E., & Edalatpanah, S. (2014b). Fast iterative method (FIM) for solving fully fuzzy linear systems. *Information Sciences and Computing,* (1).

Alaca, C., Turkoglu, D., & Yildiz, C. (2006). Fixed points in intuitionistic fuzzy metric spaces. *Chaos, Solitons, and Fractals*, *29*(5), 1073–1078. doi:10.1016/j.chaos.2005.08.066

Allahviranloo, T. (2004). Numerical methods for fuzzy system of linear equations. *Applied Mathematics and Computation*, *155*(2), 493–502. doi:10.1016/S0096-3003(03)00793-8

Allahviranloo, T. (2005a). The Adomian decomposition method for fuzzy system of linear equations. *Applied Mathematics and Computation*, *163*(2), 553–563. doi:10.1016/j.amc.2004.02.020

Allahviranloo, T. (2005b). Successive over relaxation iterative method for fuzzy system of linear equations. *Applied Mathematics and Computation*, *162*(1), 189–196. doi:10.1016/j.amc.2003.12.085

Allahviranloo, T., Ahmady, E., Ahmady, N., & Alketaby, K. S. (2006). Block Jacobi two-stage method with Gauss–Sidel inner iterations for fuzzy system of linear equations. *Applied Mathematics and Computation*, *175*(2), 1217–1228. doi:10.1016/j.amc.2005.08.047

Allahviranloo, T., Lotfi, F. H., Kiasari, M. K., & Khezerloo, M. (2013). On the fuzzy solution of LR fuzzy linear systems. *Applied Mathematical Modelling*, *37*(3), 1170–1176. doi:10.1016/j.apm.2012.03.037

Allahviranloo, T., Mikaeilvand, N., Kiani, N. A., & Shabestari, R. (2008). Signed decomposition of fully fuzzy linear systems. *An International Journal of Applications and Applied Mathematics, 3*(1), 77-88.

Amid, A., Ghodsypour, S., & OBrien, C. (2006). Fuzzy multiobjective linear model for supplier selection in a supply chain. *International Journal of Production Economics*, *104*(2), 394–407. doi:10.1016/j.ijpe.2005.04.012

Amirfakhrian, M. (2007). Numerical solution of a fuzzy system of linear equations with polynomial parametric form. *International Journal of Computer Mathematics*, *84*(7), 1089–1097. doi:10.1080/00207160701294400

Asady, B., Abbasbandy, S., & Alavi, M. (2005). Fuzzy general linear systems. *Applied Mathematics and Computation*, *169*(1), 34–40. doi:10.1016/j.amc.2004.10.042

Asady, B., & Mansouri, P. (2009). Numerical solution of fuzzy linear system. *International Journal of Computer Mathematics*, *86*(1), 151–162. doi:10.1080/00207160701621206

Babbar, N., Kumar, A., & Bansal, A. (2013). Solving fully fuzzy linear system with arbitrary triangular fuzzy numbers ({m,\ alpha,\ beta}). *Soft Computing*, *17*(4), 691–702. doi:10.1007/s00500-012-0941-2

Barrett, R., Berry, M. W., Chan, T. F., Demmel, J., Donato, J., Dongarra, J., & Van der Vorst, H. (1994). *Templates for the solution of linear systems: building blocks for iterative methods* (Vol. 43). Siam. doi:10.1137/1.9781611971538

Bede, B., & Gal, S. G. (2005). Generalizations of the differentiability of fuzzy-number-valued functions with applications to fuzzy differential equations. *Fuzzy Sets and Systems*, *151*(3), 581–599. doi:10.1016/j.fss.2004.08.001

Behera, D., & Chakraverty, S. (2012). A new method for solving real and complex fuzzy systems of linear equations. *Computational Mathematics and Modeling*, *23*(4), 507–518. doi:10.1007/s10598-012-9152-z

Bellman, R. E., & Zadeh, L. A. (1970). Decision-making in a fuzzy environment. *Management Science*, *17*(4), B-141–B-164. doi:10.1287/mnsc.17.4.B141

Bezdek, J. C. (2013). *Pattern recognition with fuzzy objective function algorithms*. Springer Science & Business Media.

Buckley, J. J., Eslami, E., & Feuring, T. (2002). *Fuzzy differential equations. In Fuzzy Mathematics in Economics and Engineering* (pp. 145–163). Springer. doi:10.1007/978-3-7908-1795-9_7

Chen, C.-T. (2000). Extensions of the TOPSIS for group decision-making under fuzzy environment. *Fuzzy Sets and Systems*, *114*(1), 1–9. doi:10.1016/S0165-0114(97)00377-1

Cordón, O. (2001). *Genetic fuzzy systems: evolutionary tuning and learning of fuzzy knowledge bases* (Vol. 19). World Scientific. doi:10.1142/4177

Dehghan, M., & Hashemi, B. (2006a). Iterative solution of fuzzy linear systems. *Applied Mathematics and Computation*, *175*(1), 645–674. doi:10.1016/j.amc.2005.07.033

Dehghan, M., & Hashemi, B. (2006b). Solution of the fully fuzzy linear systems using the decomposition procedure. *Applied Mathematics and Computation*, *182*(2), 1568–1580. doi:10.1016/j.amc.2006.05.043

Dehghan, M., Hashemi, B., & Ghatee, M. (2006). Computational methods for solving fully fuzzy linear systems. *Applied Mathematics and Computation*, *179*(1), 328–343. doi:10.1016/j.amc.2005.11.124

Dehghan, M., Hashemi, B., & Ghatee, M. (2007). Solution of the fully fuzzy linear systems using iterative techniques. *Chaos, Solitons, and Fractals*, *34*(2), 316–336. doi:10.1016/j.chaos.2006.03.085

Driankov, D., Hellendoorn, H., & Reinfrank, M. (2013). *An introduction to fuzzy control*. Springer Science & Business Media.

Dubois, D., & Prade, H. (1980). Systems of linear fuzzy constraints. *Fuzzy Sets and Systems*, *3*(1), 37–48. doi:10.1016/0165-0114(80)90004-4

Edalatpanah, S. (2008). *The preconditioning AOR method for solving linear equation systems with iterative methods* (Dissertation). Lahijan Branch, Islamic Azad University.

Edalatpanah, S., & Shahabi, S. (2012). A new two-phase method for the fuzzy primal simplex algorithm. *International Review of Pure and Applied Mathematics*, *8*(2), 157–164.

Eisenstat, S. C., Elman, H. C., & Schultz, M. H. (1983). Variational iterative methods for nonsymmetric systems of linear equations. *SIAM Journal on Numerical Analysis*, *20*(2), 345–357. doi:10.1137/0720023

El Naschie, M. (2004a). The concepts of E infinity: An elementary introduction to the Cantorian-fractal theory of quantum physics. *Chaos, Solitons, and Fractals*, *22*(2), 495–511. doi:10.1016/j.chaos.2004.02.028

El Naschie, M. (2004b). A review of E infinity theory and the mass spectrum of high energy particle physics. *Chaos, Solitons, and Fractals*, *19*(1), 209–236. doi:10.1016/S0960-0779(03)00278-9

Ezzati, R., Khezerloo, S., Mahdavi-Amiri, N., & Valizadeh, Z. (2014). Approximate Nonnegative Symmetric Solution of Fully Fuzzy Systems Using Median Interval Defuzzification. *Fuzzy Information and Engineering*, *6*(3), 331–358. doi:10.1016/j.fiae.2014.12.005

Friedman, M., Ming, M., & Kandel, A. (1998). Fuzzy linear systems. *Fuzzy Sets and Systems*, *96*(2), 201–209. doi:10.1016/S0165-0114(96)00270-9

Gao, J., & Zhang, Q. (2009). *A unified iterative scheme for solving fully fuzzy linear system.* Paper presented at the Global Congress on Intelligent Systems. doi:10.1109/GCIS.2009.114

Ghanbari, R. (2015). Solutions of fuzzy LR algebraic linear systems using linear programs. *Applied Mathematical Modelling*, *39*(17), 5164–5173. doi:10.1016/j.apm.2015.03.042

Ghomashi, A., Salahshour, S., & Hakimzadeh, A. (2014). Approximating solutions of fully fuzzy linear systems: A financial case study. *Journal of Intelligent & Fuzzy Systems: Applications in Engineering and Technology*, *26*(1), 367–378.

Gong, Z.-T., & Liu, K. (2010). *Fuzzy approximate solution of general fully fuzzy linear systems based on GLR-fuzzy numbers.* Paper presented at the Machine Learning and Cybernetics (ICMLC), 2010 International Conference on. doi:10.1109/ICMLC.2010.5580538

Greenbaum, A. (1997). *Iterative methods for solving linear systems* (Vol. 17). Siam. doi:10.1137/1.9781611970937

Gregori, V., Romaguera, S., & Veeramani, P. (2006). A note on intuitionistic fuzzy metric spaces. *Chaos, Solitons, and Fractals*, *28*(4), 902–905. doi:10.1016/j.chaos.2005.08.113

Guua, S.-M., & Wu, Y.-K. (1999). Two-phase approach for solving the fuzzy linear programming problems. *Fuzzy Sets and Systems*, *107*(2), 191–195. doi:10.1016/S0165-0114(97)00304-7

Hájek, P. (1998). *Metamathematics of fuzzy logic* (Vol. 4). Springer Science & Business Media. doi:10.1007/978-94-011-5300-3

Höppner, F. (1999). *Fuzzy cluster analysis: methods for classification, data analysis and image recognition.* John Wiley & Sons.

Huang, G., Baetz, B., & Patry, G. (1995). Grey fuzzy integer programming: An application to regional waste management planning under uncertainty. *Socio-Economic Planning Sciences*, *29*(1), 17–38. doi:10.1016/0038-0121(95)98604-T

Inuiguchi, M., Ichihashi, H., & Kume, Y. (1990). A solution algorithm for fuzzy linear programming with piecewise linear membership functions. *Fuzzy Sets and Systems*, *34*(1), 15–31. doi:10.1016/0165-0114(90)90123-N

Jang, J.-S. R., & Sun, C.-T. (1995). Neuro-fuzzy modeling and control. *Proceedings of the IEEE*, *83*(3), 378–406. doi:10.1109/5.364486

Kacher, F., & Larbani, M. (2008). Existence of equilibrium solution for a non-cooperative game with fuzzy goals and parameters. *Fuzzy Sets and Systems*, *159*(2), 164–176. doi:10.1016/j.fss.2007.05.018

Kaleva, O. (1987). Fuzzy differential equations. *Fuzzy Sets and Systems*, *24*(3), 301–317. doi:10.1016/0165-0114(87)90029-7

Kaufmann, A., & Gupta, M. M. (1991). *Introduction to fuzzy arithmetic: theory and applications*. Arden Shakespeare.

Khastan, A., Nieto, J. J., & Rodríguez-López, R. (2011). Variation of constant formula for first order fuzzy differential equations. *Fuzzy Sets and Systems*, *177*(1), 20–33. doi:10.1016/j.fss.2011.02.020

Khastan, A., & Rodríguez-López, R. (2015). On periodic solutions to first order linear fuzzy differential equations under differential inclusions approach. *Information Sciences*, *322*, 31–50. doi:10.1016/j.ins.2015.06.003

Kumar, A., Babbar, N., & Bansal, A. (2011). A new approach for solving fully fuzzy linear systems. *Advances in Fuzzy Systems*, *2011*, 5. doi:10.1155/2011/943161

Kumar, A., Babbar, N., & Bansal, A. (2012). A new computational method to solve fully fuzzy linear systems for negative coefficient matrix. *International Journal of Manufacturing Technology and Management*, *25*(1-3), 19–32. doi:10.1504/IJMTM.2012.047716

Kumar, A., & Bansal, A. (2012). A new computational method for solving fully fuzzy linear systems of triangular fuzzy numbers. *Fuzzy Information and Engineering*, *4*(1), 63–73. doi:10.1007/s12543-012-0101-5

Kumar, A., Bansal, A., & Babbar, N. (2013). Fully fuzzy linear systems of triangular fuzzy numbers (a, b, c). *International Journal of Intelligent Computing and Cybernetics*, *6*(1), 21–44. doi:10.1108/17563781311301508

Kumar, A., Kaur, J., & Singh, P. (2011). A new method for solving fully fuzzy linear programming problems. *Applied Mathematical Modelling*, *35*(2), 817–823. doi:10.1016/j.apm.2010.07.037

Kusko, B. (1993). *Fuzzy thinking: the new science of fuzzy logic*. Academic Press.

Larbani, M. (2009). Non cooperative fuzzy games in normal form: A survey. *Fuzzy Sets and Systems*, *160*(22), 3184–3210. doi:10.1016/j.fss.2009.02.026

Lee, E. S., & Li, R. J. (1993). Fuzzy multiple objective programming and compromise programming with Pareto optimum. *Fuzzy Sets and Systems*, *53*(3), 275–288. doi:10.1016/0165-0114(93)90399-3

Liu, H.-K. (2010). On the solution of fully fuzzy linear systems. *International Journal of Computational and Mathematical Sciences*, *4*(1), 29–33.

Lodwick, W. A., & Dubois, D. (2015). Interval linear systems as a necessary step in fuzzy linear systems. *Fuzzy Sets and Systems*, *281*, 227–251. doi:10.1016/j.fss.2015.03.018

Ma, M., Friedman, M., & Kandel, A. (2000). Duality in fuzzy linear systems. *Fuzzy Sets and Systems, 109*(1), 55–58. doi:10.1016/S0165-0114(98)00102-X

Maeda, T. (2000). Characterization of the equilibrium strategy of the bimatrix game with fuzzy payoff. *Journal of Mathematical Analysis and Applications, 251*(2), 885–896. doi:10.1006/jmaa.2000.7142

Malinowski, M. T. (2012). Random fuzzy differential equations under generalized Lipschitz condition. *Nonlinear Analysis Real World Applications, 13*(2), 860–881. doi:10.1016/j.nonrwa.2011.08.022

Malkaw, G., Ahmad, N., & Ibrahim, H. (2015). An Algorithm for a Positive Solution of Arbitrary Fully Fuzzy Linear System. *Computational Mathematics and Modeling*, 1–30.

Martins, M. M., Trigo, M., & Evans, D. J. (2007). An iterative method for positive real systems. *International Journal of Computer Mathematics, 84*(11), 1603–1611. doi:10.1080/00207160601088456

Miao, S.-X., Zheng, B., & Wang, K. (2008). Block SOR methods for fuzzy linear systems. *Journal of Applied Mathematics and Computing, 26*(1-2), 201–218. doi:10.1007/s12190-007-0019-y

Moloudzadeh, S., Allahviranloo, T., & Darabi, P. (2013). A new method for solving an arbitrary fully fuzzy linear system. *Soft Computing, 17*(9), 1725–1731. doi:10.1007/s00500-013-0986-x

Najafi, H. S., & Edalatpanah, S. (2013d). A Note on A new method for solving fully fuzzy linear programming problems. *Applied Mathematical Modelling, 37*(14), 7865–7867. doi:10.1016/j.apm.2013.02.039

Nasseri, S., Sohrabi, M., & Ardil, E. (2008). Solving fully fuzzy linear systems by use of a certain decomposition of the coefficient matrix. *International Journal of Computational and Mathematical Sciences, 2*(1), 140–142.

Nasseri, S., & Zahmatkesh, F. (2010). Huang method for solving fully fuzzy linear system of equations. *The Journal of Mathematics and Computer Science, 1*(1), 1–5.

Oliveira, H. Jr, & Petraglia, A. (2014). Establishing Nash equilibria of strategic games: A multistart Fuzzy Adaptive Simulated Annealing approach. *Applied Soft Computing, 19*, 188–197. doi:10.1016/j.asoc.2014.02.013

Park, J. H. (2004). Intuitionistic fuzzy metric spaces. *Chaos, Solitons, and Fractals, 22*(5), 1039–1046. doi:10.1016/j.chaos.2004.02.051

Park, J. Y., & Han, H. K. (2000). Fuzzy differential equations. *Fuzzy Sets and Systems, 110*(1), 69–77. doi:10.1016/S0165-0114(98)00150-X

Pham, D. L., Xu, C., & Prince, J. L. (2000). Current methods in medical image segmentation 1. *Annual Review of Biomedical Engineering, 2*(1), 315–337. doi:10.1146/annurev.bioeng.2.1.315 PMID:11701515

Ragin, C. C. (2000). *Fuzzy-set social science*. University of Chicago Press.

Rommelfanger, H. (2007). A general concept for solving linear multicriteria programming problems with crisp, fuzzy or stochastic values. *Fuzzy Sets and Systems, 158*(17), 1892–1904. doi:10.1016/j.fss.2007.04.005

Saad, Y. (2003). *Iterative methods for sparse linear systems*. Siam. doi:10.1137/1.9780898718003

Saberi Najafi, H., & Edalatpanad, S. (2013a). On application of Liao's method for system of linear equations, Ain Shams. *Ain Shams. Eng. J, 4*, 501-505.

Saberi Najafi, H., & Edalatpanah, S. (2012a). Nash equilibrium solution of fuzzy matrix game solution of fuzzy bimatrix game. *International Journal of Fuzzy Systems and Rough Systems*, *5*(2), 93–97.

Saberi Najafi, H., & Edalatpanah, S. (2012b). The block AOR iterative methods for solving fuzzy linear systems. *The Journal of Mathematics and Computer Science*, *4*(4), 527–535.

Saberi Najafi, H., & Edalatpanah, S. (2012c). Preconditioning strategy to solve fuzzy linear systems (FLS). *International Review of Fuzzy Mathematics*, *7*(2), 65–80.

Saberi Najafi, H., & Edalatpanah, S. (2013). An improved model for iterative algorithms in fuzzy linear systems. *Computational Mathematics and Modeling*, *24*(3), 443–451. doi:10.1007/s10598-013-9189-7

Saberi Najafi, H., & Edalatpanah, S. (2013b). Comparison analysis for improving preconditioned SOR-type iterative method. *Numerical Analysis and Applications*, *6*(1), 62–70. doi:10.1134/S1995423913010084

Saberi Najafi, H., & Edalatpanah, S. (2013c). Iterative methods with analytical preconditioning technique to linear complementarity problems: Application to obstacle problems. *RAIRO-Operations Research*, *47*(01), 59–71. doi:10.1051/ro/2013027

Saberi Najafi, H., & Edalatpanah, S. (2014a). H-Matrices in Fuzzy Linear Systems. International Journal of Computational Mathematics.

Saberi Najafi, H., & Edalatpanah, S. (2014b). A new modified SSOR iteration method for solving augmented linear systems. *International Journal of Computer Mathematics*, *91*(3), 539–552. doi:10.1080/00207160.2013.792923

Saberi Najafi, H., Edalatpanah, S., & Refahi Sheikhani, A. (2013). Application of homotopy perturbation method for fuzzy linear systems and comparison with Adomian's decomposition method. Chinese Journal of Mathematics.

Saberi Najafi, H., & Edalatpanah, S. A. (2011). Some Improvements In Preconditioned Modified Accelerated Overrelaxation (PMAOR) Method For Solving Linear Systems. *Journal of Information and Computing Science, 6*(1), 15-22.

Salkuyeh, D. K. (2015). On the solution of a class of fuzzy system of linear equations. *Sadhana*, *40*(Part 2), 369–377. doi:10.1007/s12046-014-0313-y

Senthilkumar, P., & Rajendran, G. (2011). New approach to solve symmetric fully fuzzy linear systems. *Sadhana*, *36*(6), 933–940. doi:10.1007/s12046-011-0059-8

Shamooshaki, M., Hosseinzadeh, A., & Edalatpanah, S. (2014). A New Method for Solving Fully Fuzzy Linear Programming with LR-type Fuzzy Numbers. *International Journal of Data Envelopment Analysis and Operations Research*, *1*(3), 53–55.

Sheridan, T. B. (1992). *Telerobotics, automation, and human supervisory control*. MIT press.

Słowiński, R. (1986). A multicriteria fuzzy linear programming method for water supply system development planning. *Fuzzy Sets and Systems*, *19*(3), 217–237. doi:10.1016/0165-0114(86)90052-7

Tian, Z., Hu, L., & Greenhalgh, D. (2010). Perturbation analysis of fuzzy linear systems. *Information Sciences*, *180*(23), 4706–4713. doi:10.1016/j.ins.2010.07.018

Varga, R. S. (2009). *Matrix iterative analysis* (Vol. 27). Springer Science & Business Media.

Wang, K., & Zheng, B. (2006a). Inconsistent fuzzy linear systems. *Applied Mathematics and Computation*, *181*(2), 973–981. doi:10.1016/j.amc.2006.02.019

Wang, K., & Zheng, B. (2006b). Symmetric successive overrelaxation methods for fuzzy linear systems. *Applied Mathematics and Computation*, *175*(2), 891–901. doi:10.1016/j.amc.2005.08.005

Wang, K., & Zheng, B. (2007). Block iterative methods for fuzzy linear systems. *Journal of Applied Mathematics and Computing*, *25*(1-2), 119–136. doi:10.1007/BF02832342

Wasserman, P. D. (1993). *Advanced methods in neural computing*. John Wiley & Sons, Inc.

Yager, R. R., & Filev, D. P. (1994). *Essentials of fuzzy modeling and control*. New York.

Yang, X., & Gao, J. (2014). Bayesian equilibria for uncertain bimatrix game with asymmetric information. *Journal of Intelligent Manufacturing*, 1–11.

Yin, J.-F., & Wang, K. (2009). Splitting iterative methods for fuzzy system of linear equations. *Computational Mathematics and Modeling*, *20*(3), 326–335. doi:10.1007/s10598-009-9039-9

Young, D. M. (2014). *Iterative solution of large linear systems*. Elsevier.

Yu, C.-S. (2002). A GP-AHP method for solving group decision-making fuzzy AHP problems. *Computers & Operations Research*, *29*(14), 1969–2001. doi:10.1016/S0305-0548(01)00068-5

Zadeh, L. A. (1965). Fuzzy sets. *Information and Control*, *8*(3), 338–353. doi:10.1016/S0019-9958(65)90241-X

Zadeh, L. A. (1972). *A fuzzy-set-theoretic interpretation of linguistic hedges*. Academic Press.

Zadeh, L. A. (1997). Toward a theory of fuzzy information granulation and its centrality in human reasoning and fuzzy logic. *Fuzzy Sets and Systems*, *90*(2), 111–127. doi:10.1016/S0165-0114(97)00077-8

Zhang, L.-T., Huang, T.-Z., Cheng, S.-H., & Wang, Y.-P. (2012). Convergence of a generalized MSSOR method for augmented systems. *Journal of Computational and Applied Mathematics*, *236*(7), 1841–1850. doi:10.1016/j.cam.2011.10.016

Zhou, J., & Wei, H. (2014). A GMRES Method for Solving Fuzzy Linear Equations. *International Journal of Fuzzy Systems*, *16*(2), 270–276.

Zimmermann, H.-J. (2001). *Fuzzy set theory—and its applications*. Springer Science & Business Media. doi:10.1007/978-94-010-0646-0

Compilation of References

Abbasbandy, S., & Allahviranloo, T. (2002). Numerical Solution of Fuzzy Differential Equations by Runge-Kutta and the Intuitionistic Treatment. *Notes on Intuitionistic Fuzzy Sets*, *8*(3), 43–53.

Abbasbandy, S., Ezzati, R., & Jafarian, A. (2006). LU decomposition method for solving fuzzy system of linear equations. *Applied Mathematics and Computation*, *172*(1), 633–643. doi:10.1016/j.amc.2005.02.018

Abbasbandy, S., & Hashemi, M. (2012). Solving fully fuzzy linear systems by using implicit Gauss–Cholesky algorithm. *Computational Mathematics and Modeling*, *23*(1), 107–124. doi:10.1007/s10598-012-9123-4

Abbasbandy, S., & Jafarian, A. (2006). Steepest descent method for system of fuzzy linear equations. *Applied Mathematics and Computation*, *175*(1), 823–833. doi:10.1016/j.amc.2005.07.036

Abbasbandy, S., Jafarian, A., & Ezzati, R. (2005). Conjugate gradient method for fuzzy symmetric positive definite system of linear equations. *Applied Mathematics and Computation*, *171*(2), 1184–1191. doi:10.1016/j.amc.2005.01.110

Abdalla, A., & Buckley, J. J. (2007). Monte Carlo methods in fuzzy linear regression. *Soft Computing*, *11*(10), 991–996. doi:10.1007/s00500-006-0148-5

Abdolmaleki, E., & Edalatpanah, S. (2014a). Chebyshev Semi-iterative Method to Solve Fully Fuzzy linear Systems. *Journal of Information and Computing Science, 9*(1), 67-74.

Abdolmaleki, E., & Edalatpanah, S. (2014b). Fast iterative method (FIM) for solving fully fuzzy linear systems. *Information Sciences and Computing,* (1).

Abe, A. A. (2001). *Pattern Classification: Neuro-fuzzy Methods and Their Comparison.* London, UK: Springer-Verlag. doi:10.1007/978-1-4471-0285-4

Abou-Draeb, A. T. (2000). *On Almost Quasi–Frobenius Fuzzy Rings* (M.Sc. Thesis). University of Baghdad, College of Education Ibn-AL-Haitham.

Abou-Draeb, A.T. (2010). *Fuzzy Quotient Rings and Fuzzy Isomorphism Theorem.* Academic Press.

Acharjya, D. P. (2013). Rough computing based Information Retrieval in Knowledge Discovery Databases. In Information and Knowledge Management-Tools, Techniques and Practices (pp. 123 - 153). New Delhi: New India Publishing Company.

Acharjya, D.P., & Bhattacharjee, D. (2013). A Rough Computing based Performance Evaluation approach for Educational Institutions. *International Journal of Software Engineering and its Applications*, *7*(4), 331-348.

Acharjya, D. P., & Ezhilarasi, L. (2011). A Knowledge Mining Model for Ranking Institutions using Rough Computing with Ordering Rules and Formal Concept Analysis. *International Journal of Computer Science Issues*, *8*(2), 417–425.

Adak, A. K., & Bhowmik, M. (2011). Application of Generalized Intuitionistic Fuzzy Matrix in Multi-Criteria Decision Making Problem. *Journal of Mathematical and Computational Science*, *1*(1), 1–13.

Adak, A. K., Bhowmik, M., & Pal, M. (2011). Application of generalized intuitionistic fuzzy matrix in multi-criteria decision making problem. *Journal of Mathematical and Computational Science*, *1*(1), 19–31.

Adak, A. K., Bhowmik, M., & Pal, M. (2011). Semiring of interval-valued intuitionistic fuzzy matrices. *Global Journal of Computer Application and Technology*, *1*(3), 340–347.

Adak, A. K., Bhowmik, M., & Pal, M. (2012). Some properties of generalized intuitionistic fuzzy nilpotent matrices over distributive lattice. *International Journal of Fuzzy Information and Engineering*, *4*(4), 371–387. doi:10.1007/s12543-012-0121-1

Adak, A. K., Bhowmik, M., & Pal, M. (2013). Distributive Lattice over Intuitionistic Fuzzy Matrices. *The Journal of Fuzzy Mathematics*, *21*(2), 401–416.

Adak, A. K., Bhowmik, M., & Pal, M. (2014). *Decomposition Theorem of Generalized Interval-Valued Intuitionistic Fuzzy Sets. In Contemporary Advancements in Information Technology Development in Dynamic Environments* (pp. 212–219). Information Resources Management Association.

Ahmadi, M. B., & Kiani, N. A. (2011). Solving Fuzzy Partial Differential Equation by Differential Transformation Method. *eJournal of Applied Mathematics*, *7*(4).

Ahn, S. S., & Bang, K. (2003). On fuzzy subalgebras in B. *Commun. Korean Math. Soc.*, *18*(3), 429–437. doi:10.4134/CKMS.2003.18.3.429

Alaca, C., Turkoglu, D., & Yildiz, C. (2006). Fixed points in intuitionistic fuzzy metric spaces. *Chaos, Solitons, and Fractals*, *29*(5), 1073–1078. doi:10.1016/j.chaos.2005.08.066

Al-Ali, A. R., Rehman, S., Al-Agili, S., Al-Omari, M. H., & Al-Fayezi, M. (2001). Usage of photovoltaic in an automated irrigation system. *Renewable Energy*, *23*(1), 17–26. doi:10.1016/S0960-1481(00)00110-5

Al-Hadi, I. A. A., & Hashim, S. I. M. (2011). Bacterial Foraging Optimization Algorithm For Neural Network Learning Enhancement. *International Journal of Innovative Computing*, *1*(1), 8–14.

Al-Khamees, Y., & Mordeson, J. N. (1998). Fuzzy Principal Ideals and Simple Field Extensions. *Fuzzy Sets and Systems*, (96): 247–253.

Allahviranloo, T., Mikaeilvand, N., Kiani, N. A., & Shabestari, R. (2008). Signed decomposition of fully fuzzy linear systems. *An International Journal of Applications and Applied Mathematics*, *3*(1), 77-88.

Allahviranloo, T. (2002). Difference method for fuzzy partial differential equation. *Computational Methods in Applied Mathematics*, *2*(3), 233–242. doi:10.2478/cmam-2002-0014

Allahviranloo, T. (2004). Numerical methods for fuzzy system of linear equations. *Applied Mathematics and Computation*, *155*(2), 493–502. doi:10.1016/S0096-3003(03)00793-8

Allahviranloo, T. (2005a). The Adomian decomposition method for fuzzy system of linear equations. *Applied Mathematics and Computation*, *163*(2), 553–563. doi:10.1016/j.amc.2004.02.020

Allahviranloo, T. (2005b). Successive over relaxation iterative method for fuzzy system of linear equations. *Applied Mathematics and Computation*, *162*(1), 189–196. doi:10.1016/j.amc.2003.12.085

Allahviranloo, T., Ahmady, E., Ahmady, N., & Alketaby, K. S. (2006). Block Jacobi two-stage method with Gauss–Sidel inner iterations for fuzzy system of linear equations. *Applied Mathematics and Computation*, *175*(2), 1217–1228. doi:10.1016/j.amc.2005.08.047

Allahviranloo, T., & Kermani, M. A. (2010). Numerical methods for fuzzy linear partial differential equations under new definition for derivative. *Iranian Journal of Fuzzy Sets and System*, *7*(3), 33–50.

Allahviranloo, T., Lotfi, F. H., Kiasari, M. K., & Khezerloo, M. (2013). On the fuzzy solution of LR fuzzy linear systems. *Applied Mathematical Modelling*, *37*(3), 1170–1176. doi:10.1016/j.apm.2012.03.037

Allawi, Z. T. (2014). A PSO-optimized type-2 fuzzy logic controller for navigation of multiple mobile robots. *19th International Conference on Methods and Models in Automation and Robotics (MMAR)*. doi:10.1109/MMAR.2014.6957321

Alpayden, A. A. (2010). *Introduction to Machine Learning*. The MIT Press.

Amid, A., Ghodsypour, S., & OBrien, C. (2006). Fuzzy multiobjective linear model for supplier selection in a supply chain. *International Journal of Production Economics*, *104*(2), 394–407. doi:10.1016/j.ijpe.2005.04.012

Amirfakhrian, M. (2007). Numerical solution of a fuzzy system of linear equations with polynomial parametric form. *International Journal of Computer Mathematics*, *84*(7), 1089–1097. doi:10.1080/00207160701294400

Arabpour, A. R., & Tata, M. (2008). It estimating the parameters of a fuzzy linear regression model. *Iranian Journal of Fuzzy Systems*, *5*(2), 1–19.

Asady, B., Abbasbandy, S., & Alavi, M. (2005). Fuzzy general linear systems. *Applied Mathematics and Computation*, *169*(1), 34–40. doi:10.1016/j.amc.2004.10.042

Asady, B., & Mansouri, P. (2009). Numerical solution of fuzzy linear system. *International Journal of Computer Mathematics*, *86*(1), 151–162. doi:10.1080/00207160701621206

Atanassov, K. T. (1983). *Intuitionistic fuzzy sets*. VII ITKR's Session, Sofia, Bulgarian.

Atanassov, K. (1986). Intuitionistic fuzzy sets. *Fuzzy Sets and Systems*, *20*(1), 87–96. doi:10.1016/S0165-0114(86)80034-3

Atanassov, K. (1989). More on intuitionistic fuzzy sets. *Fuzzy Sets and Systems*, *33*(1), 37–45. doi:10.1016/0165-0114(89)90215-7

Atanassov, K. (1994). Operations over interval valued fuzzy sets. *Fuzzy Sets and Systems*, (64): 159–174. doi:10.1016/0165-0114(94)90331-X

Atanassov, K. T. (1983). *Intuitionistic fuzzy sets, VII ITKR's Session*. Sofia: Bulgarian.

Atanassov, K. T. (1999). *Intuitionistic Fuzzy Fets: Theory and Applications*. Heidelberg, Germany: Studies in Fuzziness and Soft Computing, Physica-Verl. doi:10.1007/978-3-7908-1870-3

Atanassov, K., & Gargo, G. (1989). Interval-valued intuitionistic fuzzy sets. *Fuzzy Sets and Systems*, *31*(1), 343–349. doi:10.1016/0165-0114(89)90205-4

Babbar, N., Kumar, A., & Bansal, A. (2013). Solving fully fuzzy linear system with arbitrary triangular fuzzy numbers ({m,\ alpha,\ beta}). *Soft Computing*, *17*(4), 691–702. doi:10.1007/s00500-012-0941-2

Bahraminejad, B., Iranpour, M. R., & Esfandiari, E. (2014). Pitch Control of Wind Turbines Using IT2FL Controller versus T1FL Controller. *International Journal Of Renewable Energy Research*, *4*(4), 1065–1077.

Baldwin, J. F. (1981). Fuzzy logic and fuzzy reasoning. In E. H. Mamdani & B. R. Gaines (Eds.), *Fuzzy Reasoning and Its Applications*. London: Academic Press.

Barrett, R., Berry, M. W., Chan, T. F., Demmel, J., Donato, J., Dongarra, J., & Van der Vorst, H. (1994). *Templates for the solution of linear systems: building blocks for iterative methods* (Vol. 43). Siam. doi:10.1137/1.9781611971538

Barros, L. C., Gomes, L. T., & Tonelli, P. A. (2013). Fuzzy differential equations: An approach via fuzzification of the derivative operator. *Fuzzy Sets and Systems*, *230*, 39–52. doi:10.1016/j.fss.2013.03.004

Bede, B. (2006). A note on two-point boundary value problems associated with non-linear fuzzy differential equations. *Fuzzy Sets and Systems*, *157*(7), 986–989. doi:10.1016/j.fss.2005.09.006

Bede, B., & Gal, S. G. (2005). Generalizations of the differentiability of fuzzy-number-valued functions with applications to fuzzy differential equations. *Fuzzy Sets and Systems*, *151*(3), 581–599. doi:10.1016/j.fss.2004.08.001

Bede, B., Rudas, I. J., & Bencsik, A. L. (2007). First order linear fuzzy differential equations under generalized differentiability. *Inf.Sci.*, *177*(7), 1648–1662. doi:10.1016/j.ins.2006.08.021

Bede, B., & Stefanini, L. (2013). Generalized differentiability of fuzzy-valued functions. *Fuzzy Sets and Systems*, *230*, 119–141. doi:10.1016/j.fss.2012.10.003

Behera, D., & Chakraverty, S. (2012). A new method for solving real and complex fuzzy systems of linear equations. *Computational Mathematics and Modeling*, *23*(4), 507–518. doi:10.1007/s10598-012-9152-z

Bellman, R. E., & Zadeh, L. A. (1970). Decision-making in a fuzzy environment. *Management Science*, *17*(4), B-141–B-164. doi:10.1287/mnsc.17.4.B141

Bertone, A. M., Jafelice, R. M., Barros, L. C., & Bassanezi, R. C. (2013). On fuzzy solutions for partial differential equations. *Fuzzy Sets and Systems*, *219*, 68–80. doi:10.1016/j.fss.2012.12.002

Bezdek, J. C. (2013). *Pattern recognition with fuzzy objective function algorithms*. Springer Science & Business Media.

Bhasin, M., & Raghava, G. P. S. (2004). Analysis and prediction of affinity of TAP binding peptides using cascade SVM. *Protein Science*, *13*(3), 596–607. doi:10.1110/ps.03373104 PMID:14978300

Bhowmik, M., & Pal, M. (2008). Generalized intuitionistic fuzzy matrices. *Far East Journal of Mathematical Sciences*, *29*(3), 533–554.

Bhowmik, M., & Pal, M. (2008). Generalized intuitionistic fuzzy matrices. *Far East Journal of Mathematics*, *29*(3), 533–554.

Bhowmik, M., & Pal, M. (2008). Some results on intuitionistic fuzzy matrices and intuitionistic circulant fuzzy matrices. *International Journal of Mathematical Sciences*, *7*(1-2), 177–192.

Bhowmik, M., & Pal, M. (2008). Some results on Intuitionistic fuzzy matrices and intuitionistic circulant fuzzy matrices. *International Journal of Mathematical Sciences*, *7*(1-2), 81–96.

Bhowmik, M., & Pal, M. (2009). Intuitionistic neutrosophic set. *Journal of Information and Computing Science*, *2*(4), 142–152.

Bhowmik, M., & Pal, M. (2010). Generalized interval-valued intuitionistic fuzzy sets. *The Journal of Fuzzy Mathematics*, *18*(2), 357–371.

Bishop, A. A. (2006). Pattern Recognition and Machine Learning. Springer.

Breiman, A. A., Friedman, B. B., Olshen, C. C., & Stone, E. E. (1984). *Classification and Regression Tree*. Wadsworth and Brooks.

Breuss, M., & Dietrich, D. (2009). *Fuzzy Numerical Schemes for Hyperbolic Differential Equations*. Springer-Verlag Berlin Heidelberg.

Broumi, S., & Smarandache, F. (2014). On Neutrosophic Implications. *Neutrosophic Sets and Systems*, *2*, 9–17.

Broumi, S., & Smarandache, F. (2015). Cosine Similarity Meas-ure of Interval Valued Neutrosophic Set. *Neutrosophic Sets and Systems*, *05*, 15–20.

Brown, T. A. (1998). *Genetics: A Molecular Approach* (3rd ed.). London: Chapman & Hall.

Buckley, J. J., Eslami, E., & Feuring, T. (2002). *Fuzzy differential equations. In Fuzzy Mathematics in Economics and Engineering* (pp. 145–163). Springer. doi:10.1007/978-3-7908-1795-9_7

Buckley, J. J., & Feuring, T. (1999). Introduction to fuzzy partial differential equations. *Fuzzy Sets and Systems*, *105*(2), 241–248. doi:10.1016/S0165-0114(98)00323-6

Buckley, J., & Feuring, T. (2000). Evolutionary Algorithm Solution to Fuzzy Problems: Fuzzy Linear Programming. *Fuzzy Sets and Systems*, *109*(1), 35–53. doi:10.1016/S0165-0114(98)00022-0

Burges, C. (1998). A tutorial on support vector machines for pattern recognition. *Data Mining and Knowledge Discovery*, *2*(2), 121–167. doi:10.1023/A:1009715923555

Busse, J. G. (1988). Knowledge acquisition under uncertainty – a rough set approach. *Journal of Intelligent & Robotic Systems*, *1*(1), 3–16. doi:10.1007/BF00437317

Bustince & Rillo. (1995). Intuitionistic fuzzy relation (part-I). *Mathware and Soft Computing*, (2), 5-38.

Cachon, G. P., & Zipkin, P. H. (1999). Competitive and cooperative inventory policies in a two-stage supply chain. *Management Science*, *45*(7), 936–953. doi:10.1287/mnsc.45.7.936

Castillo, O., & Melin, P. (2012). A review on the design and optimization of interval type-2 fuzzy controllers. *Applied Soft Computing*, *12*(4), 1267–1278. doi:10.1016/j.asoc.2011.12.010

Chakraverty, S., & Gupta, P. (2008). Comparison of neural network configurations in the long-range forecast of south-west monsoon rainfall over India. *Neural Computing & Applications*, *17*(2), 187–192. doi:10.1007/s00521-007-0093-y

Chalco-Cano, Y., & Román-Flores, H. (2008). On the new solution of fuzzy differential equations. *Chaos, Solitons, and Fractals*, *38*(1), 112–119. doi:10.1016/j.chaos.2006.10.043

Chang, J. R., Lee, Y. T., Liao, S. Y., & Cheng, C. H. (2007). Cardinality-based fuzzy time series for forecasting enrollments. In New trends in applied artificial intelligence (pp. 735-744). Springer Berlin Heidelberg. doi:10.1007/978-3-540-73325-6_73

Chang, C. C., & Lin, C. J. (2002). Training V-support Vector Regression. *Theory and Neural Computation*, *14*(8), 1959–1977. doi:10.1162/089976602760128081 PMID:12180409

Chang, P. T., & Lee, E. S. (1996). A generalized fuzzy weighted least-squares regression. *Fuzzy Sets and Systems*, *82*(3), 289–298. doi:10.1016/0165-0114(95)00284-7

Chang, R. L. P., & Pavlidis, T. (1977). Fuzzy Decision Tree Algorithms. *IEEE Transactions on Systems, Man, and Cybernetics*, *7*(1), 28–35. doi:10.1109/TSMC.1977.4309586

Chang, S. S. L., & Zadeh, L. A. (1972). On fuzzy mappings and control. *IEEE Transactions on Systems, Man, and Cybernetics*, *2*(1), 30–34. doi:10.1109/TSMC.1972.5408553

Chang, Y. O. (2001). Hybrid fuzzy least-squares regression analysis and its reliability measures. *Fuzzy Sets and Systems, 119*(2), 225–246. doi:10.1016/S0165-0114(99)00092-5

Chan, H. S., & Dill, K. A. (1989). Compact polymers. *Macromolecules, 22*(12), 4559–4573. doi:10.1021/ma00202a031

Chase, R. B., Aquilano, N. J., & Jacobs, F. R. (2006). *Operations management for competitive advantage*. McGraw-Hill.

Chen, T. L., Cheng, C. H., & Teoh, H. J. (2007). Fuzzy time-series based on Fibonacci sequence for stock price forecasting. *Physica A: Statistical Mechanics and its Applications, 380*, 377-390.

Chen, T. L., Cheng, C. H., & Teoh, H. J. (2008). High-order fuzzy time-series based on multi-period adaptation model for forecasting stock markets. *Physica A: Statistical Mechanics and its Applications, 387*(4), 876-888.

Chen, C. T., & Huang, S. F. (2006). Order fulfilment ability analysis in the supply chain system with fuzzy operation times. *International Journal of Production Economics, 101*(1), 185–193. doi:10.1016/j.ijpe.2005.05.003

Chen, C. T., Lin, C. T., & Huang, S. F. (2006). A fuzzy approach for supplier evaluation and selection in supply chain management. *International Journal of Production Economics, 102*, 289–301.

Chen, C.-T. (2000). Extensions of the TOPSIS for group decision-making under fuzzy environment. *Fuzzy Sets and Systems, 114*(1), 1–9. doi:10.1016/S0165-0114(97)00377-1

Chen, D., Zhang, W., Yeung, D., & Tsang, E. C. C. (2006). Rough Approximations on a Complete Completely Distributive Lattice with Applications to Generalized Rough Sets. *Information Sciences, 176*(13), 1829–1848. doi:10.1016/j.ins.2005.05.009

Cheng, C. H., Chang, J. R., & Yeh, C. A. (2006). Entropy-based and trapezoid fuzzification-based fuzzy time series approaches for forecasting IT project cost. *Technological Forecasting and Social Change, 73*(5), 524–542. doi:10.1016/j.techfore.2005.07.004

Cheng, C. H., Cheng, G. W., & Wang, J. W. (2008). Multi-attribute fuzzy time series method based on fuzzy clustering. *Expert Systems with Applications, 34*(2), 1235–1242. doi:10.1016/j.eswa.2006.12.013

Chen, S. M. (1996). Forecasting enrollments based on fuzzy time series. *Fuzzy Sets and Systems, 81*(3), 311–319. doi:10.1016/0165-0114(95)00220-0

Chen, S. M. (2002). Forecasting enrollments based on high-order fuzzy time series. *Cybernetics and Systems, 33*(1), 1–16. doi:10.1080/019697202753306479

Chen, S. M., & Tanuwijaya, K. (2011). Fuzzy forecasting based on high-order fuzzy logical relationships and automatic clustering techniques. *Expert Systems with Applications, 38*(12), 15425–15437. doi:10.1016/j.eswa.2011.06.019

Chen, W., Kwok-Leung, T., Allen, J. K., & Mistree, F. (1995). Integration of the Response Surface Methodology with the compromise decision support problem in developing a general robust design procedure. *Advances in Design Automation, 82*(2).

Chen, Y. Y., Chang, Y. T., & Chen, B. S. (2009). Fuzzy Solutions to Partial Differential Equations: Adaptive Approach. *IEEE Transactions on Fuzzy Systems, 17*(1).

Cherkassky, V., & Ma, Y. (2002). Comparison of Model Selection for Regression. *Neural Computation, 15*(7), 1691–1714. doi:10.1162/089976603321891864 PMID:12816572

Cherkassky, V., & Ma, Y. (2004). Practical Selection of SVM Parameters and Noise Estimation for SVM Regression. *Neural Networks, 17*(1), 113–126. doi:10.1016/S0893-6080(03)00169-2 PMID:14690712

Cho, J. R., & Kim, H. S. (2001). On B-algebras and quasigroups. *Quasigroups and Related Systems*, *7*, 1–6.

Chou, H. L., Chen, J. S., Cheng, C. H., & Teoh, H. J. (2010). Forecasting tourism demand based on improved fuzzy time series model. In *Intelligent Information and Database Systems* (pp. 399–407). Springer Berlin Heidelberg. doi:10.1007/978-3-642-12145-6_41

Clark, P., & Niblett, T. (1987). Induction in Noisy Domains. In I. Bratko & N. Lavrac (Eds.), Progress in Machine Learning. Sigma Press.

Cohen, M. A., & Lee, H. L. (1988). Strategic analysis of integrated production distribution systems- models and methods. *Operations Research*, *36*, 216–228.

Coppi, R., DUrso, P., Giordani, P., & Santoro, A. (2006). It Least squares estimation of a linear regression model with LR fuzzy response. *Computational Statistics & Data Analysis*, *51*(1), 267–286. doi:10.1016/j.csda.2006.04.036

Cordón, O. (2001). *Genetic fuzzy systems: evolutionary tuning and learning of fuzzy knowledge bases* (Vol. 19). World Scientific. doi:10.1142/4177

Cortes, C., & Vapnik, V. (1995). Support-Vector Networks. *Machine Learning*, *20*(3), 273–297. doi:10.1007/BF00994018

Corveleyn, S., & Vandewalle, S. (2010). On the numerical solution of fuzzy elliptic PDEs by means of polynomial response surfaces. *Proceeding of ISMA 2010.*

Cover, T., & Hart, P. (1967). Nearest neighbor pattern classification. *IEEE Transactions on Information Theory*, *13*(1), 21–27. doi:10.1109/TIT.1967.1053964

Das, S., De, D., Dey, A., & Bhattacharya, D. K. (2013). Some anomalies in the analysis of whole genome sequence on the basis of Fuzzy set theory. *International Journal of Artificial intelligence and Neural Networks, 3*(2), 38-41.

Das, B., Maity, K., & Maiti, M. (2007). A Two Warehouse Supply-Chain Model under Possibility / Necessity / Credibility measure. *Mathematical and Computer Modelling*, *46*(3-4), 398–409. doi:10.1016/j.mcm.2006.11.017

Das, B., Maity, K., Mondal, S., & Maiti, M. (2005), A Supply-chain production control problem via genetic algorithm. *Proc, International Conference on Operation Research and Developement.*

Das, S., De, D., & Bhattacharya, D. K. (in press). Similarity and Dissimilarity of Whole Genomes using Intuitionistic Fuzzy Logic. *Notes on Intuitionistic Fuzzy Set.*

Deeba, E. Y., & de Korvin, A. (1999). Analysis by Fuzzy Difference Equations of a model of CO2 Level in the Blood. *Applied Mathematics Letters*, *12*(3), 33–40. doi:10.1016/S0893-9659(98)00168-2

Deeba, E. Y., Korvin, A. D., & Koh, E. L. (1996). A Fuzzy Difference Equation with an application. *J.Diff. Equa. Appl.*, *2*(4), 365–374. doi:10.1080/10236199608808071

Dehghan, M., & Hashemi, B. (2006a). Iterative solution of fuzzy linear systems. *Applied Mathematics and Computation*, *175*(1), 645–674. doi:10.1016/j.amc.2005.07.033

Dehghan, M., & Hashemi, B. (2006b). Solution of the fully fuzzy linear systems using the decomposition procedure. *Applied Mathematics and Computation*, *182*(2), 1568–1580. doi:10.1016/j.amc.2006.05.043

Dehghan, M., Hashemi, B., & Ghatee, M. (2006). Computational methods for solving fully fuzzy linear systems. *Applied Mathematical Modelling*, *179*, 328–343.

Dehghan, M., Hashemi, B., & Ghatee, M. (2006). Computational methods for solving fully fuzzy linear systems. *Applied Mathematics and Computation*, *179*(1), 328–343. doi:10.1016/j.amc.2005.11.124

Dehghan, M., Hashemi, B., & Ghatee, M. (2007). Solution of the fully fuzzy linear systems using iterative techniques. *Chaos, Solitons, and Fractals*, *34*(2), 316–336. doi:10.1016/j.chaos.2006.03.085

Dereli, T., Baykasoglu, A., Altun, K., Durmusoglu, A., & Türksen, I. B. (2011). Industrial applications of type-2 fuzzy sets and systems: A concise review. *Computers in Industry*, *62*(2), 125–137. doi:10.1016/j.compind.2010.10.006

Dhimmar, V., Prajapti, J., Patel, M., Patel, D., Mistry, B., & Parmar, J. (2014). Design of Solar Steam Irrigation Pump. *International Journal of Engine Research*, *3*(5), 315–317. doi:10.17950/ijer/v3s5/504

Diamond, P. (1988). Fuzzy least squares. *Information Sciences*, *46*(3), 141–157. doi:10.1016/0020-0255(88)90047-3

Diamond, P., & Kloeden, P. (1994). *Metric Space of Fuzzy Sets*. Singapore: World Scientific.

Dill, K. A. (1985). Theory for the folding and stability of globular proteins. *Biochemistry*, *24*(6), 1501–1509. doi:10.1021/bi00327a032 PMID:3986190

Din, Q. (2015). Asymptotic behavior of a second –order fuzzy rational difference equations. *Journal of Discrete Mathematics*.

Dixit, V. N., Kumar, R., & Ajmal, N. (1991). Fuzzy Ideals and Fuzzy Prime Ideals of a Ring. *Fuzzy Sets and Systems*, *44*(1), 127–138. doi:10.1016/0165-0114(91)90038-R

Draper, N. R., & Smith, H. (1980). *Applied Regression Analysis*. New York: Wiley.

Driankov, D., Hellendoorn, H., & Reinfrank, M. (2013). *An introduction to fuzzy control*. Springer Science & Business Media.

Drucker, H., Burges, C. J. C., Kaufman, L., Smola, A., & Vapnik, V. (1997). Support vector regression machines. *Advances in Neural Information Processing Systems*, *9*, 155–161.

Dubois, D., & Prade, H. (1978). Operations on fuzzy numbers. *International Journal of Systems Science*, *9*(6), 613–626. doi:10.1080/00207727808941724

Dubois, D., & Prade, H. (1980). Systems of linear fuzzy constraints. *Fuzzy Sets and Systems*, *3*(1), 37–48. doi:10.1016/0165-0114(80)90004-4

Dubois, D., & Prade, H. (1980). *Theory and applications, Fuzzy Sets and Systems*. Academic Press.

Dubois, D., & Prade, H. (1982). Towards fuzzy differential calculus: Part 3, Differentiation. *Fuzzy Sets and Systems*, *8*(3), 225–233. doi:10.1016/S0165-0114(82)80001-8

Dubois, D., & Prade, H. (2008). An introduction to bipolar representations of information and preference. *International Journal of Intelligent Systems*, *23*(8), 866–877. doi:10.1002/int.20297

Dubois, D., & Prade, H. (2012). Gradualness, uncertainty and bipolarity: Making sense of fuzzy sets. *Fuzzy Sets and Systems*, *192*(8), 3–24. doi:10.1016/j.fss.2010.11.007

Duda, A. A., Hart, B. B., & Stork, C. C. (2001). *Pattern Classification*. Wiley.

Edalatpanah, S. (2008). *The preconditioning AOR method for solving linear equation systems with iterative methods* (Dissertation). Lahijan Branch, Islamic Azad University.

Edalatpanah, S. A., & Shahabi, S. (2012). A new two-phase method for the fuzzy primal simplex algorithm. *International Review of Pure and Applied Mathematics*, *8*, 157-164.

Edalatpanah, S., & Shahabi, S. (2012). A new two-phase method for the fuzzy primal simplex algorithm. *International Review of Pure and Applied Mathematics*, *8*(2), 157–164.

Eisenstat, S. C., Elman, H. C., & Schultz, M. H. (1983). Variational iterative methods for nonsymmetric systems of linear equations. *SIAM Journal on Numerical Analysis*, *20*(2), 345–357. doi:10.1137/0720023

El Naschie, M. (2004a). The concepts of E infinity: An elementary introduction to the Cantorian-fractal theory of quantum physics. *Chaos, Solitons, and Fractals*, *22*(2), 495–511. doi:10.1016/j.chaos.2004.02.028

El Naschie, M. (2004b). A review of E infinity theory and the mass spectrum of high energy particle physics. *Chaos, Solitons, and Fractals*, *19*(1), 209–236. doi:10.1016/S0960-0779(03)00278-9

El-Wahed, W. F. A., Mousa, A. A., & Elsisy, M. A. (2008). Solving Economic Emissions Load Dispatch problem by using Hybrid ACO-MSM approach. *The Online Journal on Power and Energy Engineering*, *1*, 31–35.

Ezzati, R., Khezerloo, S., Mahdavi-Amiri, N., & Valizadeh, Z. (2014). Approximate Nonnegative Symmetric Solution of Fully Fuzzy Systems Using Median Interval Defuzzification. *Fuzzy Information and Engineering*, *6*(3), 331–358. doi:10.1016/j.fiae.2014.12.005

Ezzati, R., Khorram, E., & Enayati, R. (2013). A New Algorithm to Solve Fully Fuzzy Linear Programming Problems Using the MOLP Problem. *Applied Mathematical Modelling*, *39*(12), 3183–3193. doi:10.1016/j.apm.2013.03.014

Farajzadeh, A., & Pour, A. H. (2010). An Explicit Method for Solving Fuzzy Partial Differential Equation. *International Mathematical Forum*, *5*(21), 1025-1036.

Fatai, A., & Abdulazeez, A. (2011). Fuzzy logic-driven and SVM-driven hybrid computational intelligence models applied to oil and gas reservoir characterization. *Journal of Natural Gas Science and Engineering*, *3*(3), 505–517. doi:10.1016/j.jngse.2011.05.002

Fayek, H. M., Elamvazuthi, I., Perumal, N., & Venkatesh, B. (2014). A controller based on Optimal Type-2 Fuzzy Logic: Systematic design, optimization and real-time implementation. *ISA Transactions*, *53*(5), 1583–1591. doi:10.1016/j.isatra.2014.06.001 PMID:24962934

Friedman, M., Ming, M., & Kandel, A. (1998). Fuzzy linear systems. *Fuzzy Sets and Systems*, *96*(2), 201–209. doi:10.1016/S0165-0114(96)00270-9

Ganesan, T., Elamvazuthi, I., & Vasant, P. (2015). Multiobjective Design Optimization of a Nano-CMOS Voltage-Controlled Oscillator Using Game Theoretic-Differential Evolution. *Applied Soft Computing*, *32*, 293–299. doi:10.1016/j.asoc.2015.03.016

Ganesan, T., Vasant, P., & Elamvazuthi, I. (2014). Hopfield neural networks approach for design optimization of hybrid power systems with multiple renewable energy sources in a fuzzy environment. *Journal of Intelligent and Fuzzy Systems*, *26*(5), 2143–2154.

Gangwar, S. S., & Kumar, S. (2012). Partitions based computational method for high-order fuzzy time series forecasting. *Expert Systems with Applications*, *39*(15), 12158–12164. doi:10.1016/j.eswa.2012.04.039

Gao, J., & Zhang, Q. (2009). *A unified iterative scheme for solving fully fuzzy linear system.* Paper presented at the Global Congress on Intelligent Systems. doi:10.1109/GCIS.2009.114

Gasilov, N., Amrahov, S. E., Fatullayev, A. G., & Khastan, A. (2014). *A new approach to fuzzy initial value problem.* Academic Press.

Gau, W. L., & Buehrer, D. J. (1993). Vague sets. *IEEE Transactions on Systems, Man, and Cybernetics*, *23*(2), 610–614. doi:10.1109/21.229476

Ghanbari, R. (2015). Solutions of fuzzy LR algebraic linear systems using linear programs. *Applied Mathematical Modelling*, *39*(17), 5164–5173. doi:10.1016/j.apm.2015.03.042

Ghomashi, A., Salahshour, S., & Hakimzadeh, A. (2014). Approximating solutions of fully fuzzy linear systems: A financial case study. *Journal of Intelligent & Fuzzy Systems: Applications in Engineering and Technology*, *26*(1), 367–378.

Ghosh, S., Das, S., Pal, J., & Bhattacharya, D. K. (in press). Differentiation of protein sequence comparison based on biological and theoretical classification of amino acids in six groups. *International Journal of Advanced Research in Computer Science and Software Engineering*.

Ghosh, S., Pal, J., & Bhattacharya, D. K. (2014). Classification of Amino Acids of a Protein on the basis of Fuzzy set theory. *International Journal of Modern Sciences and Engineering Technology*, *1*(6), 30–35.

Giveon, Y. (1964). Lattice matrices. *Information and Control*, *7*(3), 477–484. doi:10.1016/S0019-9958(64)90173-1

Goetschel, R. Jr, & Voxman, W. (1986). Elementary calculus. *Fuzzy Sets and Systems*, *18*(1), 31–43. doi:10.1016/0165-0114(86)90026-6

Gong, Z.-T., & Liu, K. (2010). *Fuzzy approximate solution of general fully fuzzy linear systems based on GLR-fuzzy numbers*. Paper presented at the Machine Learning and Cybernetics (ICMLC), 2010 International Conference on. doi:10.1109/ICMLC.2010.5580538

Gouws, R., & Lukhwareni, T. (2012). Factors influencing the performance and efficiency of solar water pumping systems: A Review. *International Journal of Physical Sciences*, *7*(48), 6169–6180.

Greenbaum, A. (1997). *Iterative methods for solving linear systems* (Vol. 17). Siam. doi:10.1137/1.9781611970937

Greenfield, S., John, R., & Coupland, S. (2005). A novel sampling method for type-2 defuzzification. In *Proc. UKCI*.

Gregori, V., Romaguera, S., & Veeramani, P. (2006). A note on intuitionistic fuzzy metric spaces. *Chaos, Solitons, and Fractals*, *28*(4), 902–905. doi:10.1016/j.chaos.2005.08.113

Guoxiu, L. (2005). *A comparative study of three decision Tree algorithms: ID3, Fuzzy ID3 and probabilistic fuzzy ID3* (Bachelor thesis). Informatics & Economics, Erasmus University, Rotterdam, The Netherlands.

Guua, S.-M., & Wu, Y.-K. (1999). Two-phase approach for solving the fuzzy linear programming problems. *Fuzzy Sets and Systems*, *107*(2), 191–195. doi:10.1016/S0165-0114(97)00304-7

Hadi, I.M.A., & Abou-Draeb, A.T. (2004). P-F Fuzzy Rings and Normal Fuzzy Rings. *Ibn-Al-Haitham J. for Pure & Appl. Sci.*, (17), 111 – 120.

Hájek, P. (1998). *Metamathematics of fuzzy logic* (Vol. 4). Springer Science & Business Media. doi:10.1007/978-94-011-5300-3

Hamrawi, H., & Coupland, S. (2009). Type-2 fuzzy arithmetic using Alpha-planes.*Proceedings of the Joint 2009 International Fuzzy Systems Association World Congress and 2009 European Society of Fuzzy Logic and Technology conference*, (pp. 606-611).

Han, A. A., & Kamber, B. B. (2001). *Data mining: Concepts and techniques*. San Diego, CA: Academic Press.

Hasimoto, H. (1982). Reduction of a nilpotent fuzzy matrix. *Information Sciences*, (27): 223–243.

Hassanpour, H., Maleki, H. R., & Yaghoobi, M. A. (2009). It a goal programming approach to fuzzy linear regression with non-fuzzy input and fuzzy output data. *Asia-Pacific Journal of Operational Research*, *26*(5), 587–604. doi:10.1142/S0217595909002420

Heikki, A. A., & Mannila, B. B. (1996). *Data mining: machine learning, statistics, and databases*. IEEE.

Helikson, H. J., Haman, D. Z., & Baird, C. D. (1991). *Pumping water for irrigation using solar energy, Fact Sheet (EES-63)*. University of Florida.

Hill, R. M., Seifbarghy, M., & Smith, D. K. (2007). A two-echolon inventory model with lost sales. *European Journal of Operational Research*, *181*(2), 753–766. doi:10.1016/j.ejor.2006.08.017

Hojati, M., Bector, C. R., & Smimou, K. (2005). It A simple method for computation of fuzzy linear regression. *European Journal of Operational Research*, *166*(1), 172–184. doi:10.1016/j.ejor.2004.01.039

Höppner, F. (1999). *Fuzzy cluster analysis: methods for classification, data analysis and image recognition*. John Wiley & Sons.

Huang, Y. (2006). BCI-algebra. Science Press.

Huang, G., Baetz, B., & Patry, G. (1995). Grey fuzzy integer programming: An application to regional waste management planning under uncertainty. *Socio-Economic Planning Sciences*, *29*(1), 17–38. doi:10.1016/0038-0121(95)98604-T

Huarng, K. (2001a). Effective lengths of intervals to improve forecasting in fuzzy time series. *Fuzzy Sets and Systems*, *123*(3), 387–394. doi:10.1016/S0165-0114(00)00057-9

Huarng, K. (2001b). Heuristic models of fuzzy time series for forecasting. *Fuzzy Sets and Systems*, *123*(3), 369–386. doi:10.1016/S0165-0114(00)00093-2

Huarng, K., & Yu, T. H. K. (2006). Ratio-based lengths of intervals to improve fuzzy time series forecasting. *Systems, Man, and Cybernetics, Part B: Cybernetics. IEEE Transactions on*, *36*(2), 328–340.

Hwang, J. R., Chen, S. M., & Lee, C. H. (1998). Handling forecasting problems using fuzzy time series. *Fuzzy Sets and Systems*, *100*(1), 217–228. doi:10.1016/S0165-0114(97)00121-8

Inuiguchi, M., Ichihashi, H., & Kume, Y. (1990). A solution algorithm for fuzzy linear programming with piecewise linear membership functions. *Fuzzy Sets and Systems*, *34*(1), 15–31. doi:10.1016/0165-0114(90)90123-N

Jaber. M. Y., & Bonney, M. (1998). The effects of learning and forgetting on the optimal lot size quantity of intermittent production runs. *Production Planning and Control*, (9), 20-27.

Jajuga, K. (1986). Linear fuzzy regression. *Fuzzy Sets and Systems*, *20*(3), 343–353. doi:10.1016/S0165-0114(86)90045-X

Jana, N. K., & Pal, M. (2006). *Some operators defined over interval-valued intuitionistic fuzzy sets.*In S. Nanda (Ed.), *Fuzzy Logic and Optimization* (pp. 113–126). New Delhi, India: Narosa Publishing House.

Jang, J. (1994). Structure determination in fuzzy modeling: A fuzzy CART approach. In *Proc.IEEE Conf. Fuzzy Systems*, (pp. 480-485). doi:10.1109/FUZZY.1994.343738

Jang, J.-S. R., & Sun, C.-T. (1995). Neuro-fuzzy modeling and control. *Proceedings of the IEEE*, *83*(3), 378–406. doi:10.1109/5.364486

Janikow, C. Z. (1998). Fuzzy Decision Trees: Issues and Methods. *IEEE Trans. on Systems. Man, and Cybernetics – Part B*, *28*(1), 1–14. doi:10.1109/3477.658573

Jasim, K. K., Kadhum, J. A., & Ali, M. (2014). Design and Construction of Hybrid Solar-Wind System used for Irrigation Projects. *Indian Journal of Applied Research*, *4*(7), 518–522. doi:10.15373/2249555X/July2014/163

Jensen, R., & Cornelis, C. (2011). Fuzzy-rough nearest neighbour classification. *Lecture Notes in Computer Science*, *6499*, 56–72. doi:10.1007/978-3-642-18302-7_4

Jimenez, M., Arenas, M., Bilbao, A., & Rodrguez, M. V. (2007). Linear Programming with Fuzzy Parameters: An Interactive Method Resolution. *European Journal of Operational Research*, *177*(3), 1599–1609. doi:10.1016/j.ejor.2005.10.002

Jing He, A. A. (2009). Advances in Data Mining: History and Future. *Third international Symposium on Information Technology Application*, *1*, 634 – 636.

Joachims, A. A. (2002). *Learning to Classify Text Using Support Vector Machines* (Dissertation). Kluwer.

Jun, Y. B., Kim, H. S., & Lee, K. J. (2009). Bipolar fuzzy translation in *BCK/BCI*-algebra. J. of the Chungcheong Math. *Soc.*, *22*(3), 399–408.

Jun, Y. B., Roh, E. H., & Kim, H. S. (2002). On fuzzyB. *Czechoslovak Mathematical Journal*, *52*(127), 375–384. doi:10.1023/A:1021739030890

Kacher, F., & Larbani, M. (2008). Existence of equilibrium solution for a non-cooperative game with fuzzy goals and parameters. *Fuzzy Sets and Systems*, *159*(2), 164–176. doi:10.1016/j.fss.2007.05.018

Kai, C., Fang-Ping, F., & Wen-Gang, C. (2010, March). Notice of Retraction A Novel Forecasting Model of Fuzzy Time Series Based on K-means Clustering. In *Education Technology and Computer Science (ETCS), 2010 Second International Workshop on* (Vol. 1, pp. 223-225). IEEE.

Kaleva, O. (1987). Fuzzy differential equations. *Fuzzy Sets and Systems*, *24*(3), 301–317. doi:10.1016/0165-0114(87)90029-7

Kao, C., & Chyu, C. (2002). A fuzzy linear regression model with better explanatory power. *Fuzzy Sets and Systems*, *126*(3), 401–409. doi:10.1016/S0165-0114(01)00069-0

Kash, F. (1982). *Modules and Rings*. New York: Academic Press.

Kashyap, S. K., & Raol, J. R. (2008). Fuzzy Logic Applications in Filtering and Fusion for Target Tracking. *Defence Science Journal*, *58*(1), 120–135. doi:10.14429/dsj.58.1630

Kaufmann, A., & Gupta, M. M. (1991). *Introduction to fuzzy arithmetic: theory and applications*. Arden Shakespeare.

Kazemi, A., & Mehrzadegan, E. (2011). A New Algorithm for Optimization of Fuzzy Decision Tree in Data Mining. *Journal of Optimization in Industrial Engineering*, *7*(2), 29–35.

Keachie, E. C., & Fontana, R. J. (1966). Production lot sizes under a learning effect. *Management Science*, *13*, B102–B108. doi:10.1287/mnsc.13.2.B102

Keller, J. M., Gray, M. R., & Givens, J. A. (1985). A fuzzy k-nearest neighbour algorithm. *IEEE Transactions on Systems, Man, and Cybernetics*, *15*(4), 580–585. doi:10.1109/TSMC.1985.6313426

Kennedy, J., & Eberhart, R. (1995). Particle Swarm Optimization. *IEEE Proceedings of the International Conference on Neural Networks*.

Khastan, A., & Nieto, J. J. (2010). A boundary value problem for second-order fuzzy differential equations. *Nonlinear Analysis*, *72*(9-10), 3583–3593. doi:10.1016/j.na.2009.12.038

Khastan, A., Nieto, J. J., & Rodríguez-López, R. (2011). Variation of constant formula for first order fuzzy differential equations. *Fuzzy Sets and Systems*, *177*(1), 20–33. doi:10.1016/j.fss.2011.02.020

Khastan, A., & Rodríguez-López, R. (2015). On periodic solutions to first order linear fuzzy differential equations under differential inclusions approach. *Information Sciences*, *322*, 31–50. doi:10.1016/j.ins.2015.06.003

Kim & Roush. (1980). Generalised fuzzy matrices. *Fuzzy Sets and System*, (4), 293-315.

Kim, K.H. & Roush, F.W. (1980). Generalised fuzzy matrices. *Fuzzy Sets and System*, (4), 293-315.

Kim. (1988). Determinant theory for fuzzy and boolean matrices. *Congressus Numerantium*, 273-276.

Kim, C. B., & Kim, H. S. (2008). On BG-algebras. *Demonstratio Mathematica*, *41*, 497–505.

Kim, N., & Bishu, R. R. (1998). Evaluation of fuzzy linear regression models by comparing membership functions. *Fuzzy Sets and Systems*, *100*(1-3), 343–353. doi:10.1016/S0165-0114(97)00100-0

Klir, G. J., & Yuan, B. (1995). *Fuzzy Sets and Fuzzy Logic: Theory and Applications*. Upper Saddle River, NJ: Prentice Hall.

Koen, M. L., Kyung, M. L., Jee, H. L., & Lee, K. H. (1999). A fuzzy decision tree induction method for fuzzy data. In *Proc. of 8th IEEE Inter. Conference on Fuzzy Systems.*

Kondo, M. (2005). Algebraic Approach to Generalized Rough Sets. *Lecture Notes in Artificial Intelligence*, *3641*, 132–140.

Kondo, M. (2006). On the Structure of Generalized Rough Sets. *Information Sciences*, *176*(5), 589–600. doi:10.1016/j.ins.2005.01.001

Konstantios, A. C., Basil, K. P., & Papaschinopoulos, G. (2008). On the fuzzy difference equations of finance. *Fuzzy Sets and Systems, 159*, 3259-3270.

Kryszkiewlcz, M. (1998). Rough Set Approach to Incomplete Information Systems. *Information Sciences*, *112*(1-4), 39–49. doi:10.1016/S0020-0255(98)10019-1

Kumar, A., Babbar, N., & Bansal, A. (2011). A new approach for solving fully fuzzy linear systems. *Advances in Fuzzy Systems*, *2011*, 5. doi:10.1155/2011/943161

Kumar, A., Babbar, N., & Bansal, A. (2012). A new computational method to solve fully fuzzy linear systems for negative coefficient matrix. *International Journal of Manufacturing Technology and Management*, *25*(1-3), 19–32. doi:10.1504/IJMTM.2012.047716

Kumar, A., & Bansal, A. (2012). A new computational method for solving fully fuzzy linear systems of triangular fuzzy numbers. *Fuzzy Information and Engineering*, *4*(1), 63–73. doi:10.1007/s12543-012-0101-5

Kumar, A., Bansal, A., & Babbar, N. (2013). Fully fuzzy linear systems of triangular fuzzy numbers (a, b, c). *International Journal of Intelligent Computing and Cybernetics*, *6*(1), 21–44. doi:10.1108/17563781311301508

Kumar, A., Kaur, J., & Singh, P. (2011). A new method for solving fully fuzzy linear programming problems. *Applied Mathematical Modelling*, *35*(2), 817–823. doi:10.1016/j.apm.2010.07.037

Kumar, K. S., Acharjya, D. P., & Thangavelu, A. (2013). Trust Evaluation using Fuzzy Proximity Relation with ordering for MANET. *International Journal of Trust Management in Computing Communications*, *1*(2), 105–120. doi:10.1504/IJTMCC.2013.053259

Kumar, M., Vrat, P., & Shan, R. (2004). A fuzzy goal programming approach for vendor selection problem in a supply chain. *Computers & Industrial Engineering*, *46*(1), 69–85. doi:10.1016/j.cie.2003.09.010

Kumar, S., Nei, M., Dudley, J., & Tamura, K. (2008). MEGA: A biologist-centric software for evolutionary analysis of DNA and protein sequences. *Briefings in Bioinformatics*, *9*(4), 299–306. doi:10.1093/bib/bbn017 PMID:18417537

Kusko, B. (1993). *Fuzzy thinking: the new science of fuzzy logic*. Academic Press.

Lakshmikatham, V., & Vatsala, A. S. (2002). Basic Theory of Fuzzy Difference Equations. *J. Diff.Equa. Appl*, *8*(11), 957–968. doi:10.1080/1023619021000048850

Larbani, M. (2009). Non cooperative fuzzy games in normal form: A survey. *Fuzzy Sets and Systems*, *160*(22), 3184–3210. doi:10.1016/j.fss.2009.02.026

Lata, S., & Kumar, A. (2012, July). A new method to solve time-dependent intuitionistic fuzzy differential equation and its application to analyze the intutionistic fuzzy reliability of industrial system. *Concurrent Engineering: Research and Applications*, 1-8.

Lee, E. S., & Li, R. J. (1993). Fuzzy multiple objective programming and compromise programming with Pareto optimum. *Fuzzy Sets and Systems*, *53*(3), 275–288. doi:10.1016/0165-0114(93)90399-3

Lee, H. S., & Chou, M. T. (2004). Fuzzy forecasting based on fuzzy time series. *International Journal of Computer Mathematics*, *81*(7), 781–789. doi:10.1080/00207160410001712288

Lee, K. J. (2009). Bipolar fuzzy subalgerbas and bipolar fuzzy ideals of *BCK/BCI*-algerbas. *Bull. Malays. Math. Sci. Soc.*, *32*(3), 361–373.

Lee, K. M. (2000). Bipolar-valued fuzzy sets and their operations. *Proc. Int. Conf. on Intelligent Technologies.*

Lee, K. M. (2004). Comparison of interval-valued fuzzy sets, intuitionistic fuzzy sets, and bipolar- valued fuzzy sets, *J. Fuzzy Logic Intelligent Systems*, *14*(2), 125–129.

Li, C., Xing, L., & Wang, X. (2008). 2-D graphical representation of protein sequences and its application to coronavirus phylogeny. *BMB Reports*, *41*(3), 217-222.

Liang, T. F. (2007). Applying fuzzy goal programming to production/ transportation planning decisions in supply chain. *International Journal of Systems Science*, *38*(4), 293–304. doi:10.1080/00207720601159381

Li, B., Lu, Q., & Yu, S. (2004). An Adaptive k-Nearest Neighbor Text Categorization Strategy. *ACM Transactions on Asian Language Information Processing*, *3*(4), 215–226. doi:10.1145/1039621.1039623

Lin, C. F., & Wang, S. D. (2002). Fuzzy Support Vector Machines. *IEEE Transactions on Neural Networks*, *13*(2), 464–471. doi:10.1109/72.991432 PMID:18244447

Linda, O., & Manic, M. (2011). Evaluating Uncertainty Resiliency of Type-2 Fuzzy Logic Controllers for Parallel Delta Robot. *4th International Conference on Human System Interactions (HSI)*, Yokohama. doi:10.1109/HSI.2011.5937349

Lin, T. Y. (1989). Neighborhood Systems and Approximation in Database and Knowledge Base Systems. *Proceedings of the fourth International Symposium on Methodologies of Intelligent Systems* (pp. 75–86).

Lin, T. Y. (2005). Granular Computing: Examples, Intuitions and Modeling. *IEEE International Conference on Granular Computing*(pp. 40– 44).

Liu, B., & Iwamura, K. (1998). Chance constraint Programming with fuzzy parameters. *Fuzzy Sets and Systems*, *94*(2), 227–237. doi:10.1016/S0165-0114(96)00236-9

Liu, F. (2006). *An efficient centroid type reduction strategy for general type-2 fuzzy logic systems. Walter J. Karplus Summer Research Grant Report*. IEEE Computational Intelligence Society.

Liu, G. L. (2005). Rough Sets over the Boolean Algebras. *Lecture Notes in Artificial Intelligence*, *3641*, 24–131.

Liu, G. L. (2008). Generalized Rough Sets over Fuzzy Lattices. *Information Sciences*, *178*(6), 1651–1662. doi:10.1016/j.ins.2007.11.010

Liu, G. L. (2010). Rough set theory based on two universal sets and its applications. *Knowledge-Based Systems*, *23*(2), 110–115. doi:10.1016/j.knosys.2009.06.011

Liu, H.-K. (2010). On the solution of fully fuzzy linear systems. *International Journal of Computational and Mathematical Sciences*, *4*(1), 29–33.

Liu, W. J. (1982). Fuzzy Invariant Subgroups and Fuzzy Ideal. *Fuzzy Sets and Systems*, *8*(8), 133–139. doi:10.1016/0165-0114(82)90003-3

Liu, Y., Passino, K. M., & Simaan, M. A. (2002). Biomimicry of social foraging bacteria for distributed optimization: Models, principles, and emergent behaviors. *Journal of Optimization Theory and Applications*, *115*(3), 603–628. doi:10.1023/A:1021207331209

Lodwick, W. A., & Dubois, D. (2015). Interval linear systems as a necessary step in fuzzy linear systems. *Fuzzy Sets and Systems*, *281*, 227–251. doi:10.1016/j.fss.2015.03.018

Lotfi, F. H., Allahviranloo, M., Jondabeha, A., & Alizadeh, L. (2009). Solving A Fully Fuzzy Linear Programming Using Lexicography Method and Fuzzy Approximate Solution. *Applied Mathematical Modelling*, *33*(7), 3151–3156. doi:10.1016/j.apm.2008.10.020

Lucas, L., Centeno, T., & Delgado, M. (2007). General type-2 fuzzy inference systems: Analysis, design and computational aspects. In *Proceedings of IEEE International Conference of Fuzzy Systems*. doi:10.1109/FUZZY.2007.4295522

Maeda, T. (2000). Characterization of the equilibrium strategy of the bimatrix game with fuzzy payoff. *Journal of Mathematical Analysis and Applications*, *251*(2), 885–896. doi:10.1006/jmaa.2000.7142

Maher, P. E., & St. Clair, D. C. (1993). Uncertain reasoning in an ID3 machine learning framework. In *Proc. 2nd IEEE Int. Conf. Fuzzy Systems*. doi:10.1109/FUZZY.1993.327472

Maiti, M. K., & Maiti, M. (2006). Fuzzy Inventory Model with Two Warehouses under Possibility Constraints. *Fuzzy Sets and Systems*, *157*(1), 52–73. doi:10.1016/j.fss.2005.06.021

Maji, P. K., Roy, A. R., & Biswas, R. (2002). An Application of Soft Sets in A Decision Making Problem. *Computers & Mathematics with Applications (Oxford, England)*, *44*(8-9), 1077–1083. doi:10.1016/S0898-1221(02)00216-X

Malinowski, M. T. (2012). Random fuzzy differential equations under generalized Lipschitz condition. *Nonlinear Analysis Real World Applications*, *13*(2), 860–881. doi:10.1016/j.nonrwa.2011.08.022

Malkaw, G., Ahmad, N., & Ibrahim, H. (2015). An Algorithm for a Positive Solution of Arbitrary Fully Fuzzy Linear System. *Computational Mathematics and Modeling*, 1–30.

Ma, M., Friedman, M., & Kandel, A. (2000). Duality in fuzzy linear systems. *Fuzzy Sets and Systems*, *109*(1), 55–58. doi:10.1016/S0165-0114(98)00102-X

Martines, L. (1995). Fuzzy Subgroup of Fuzzy Groups and Fuzzy Ideals of Fuzzy Rings. *The Journal of Fuzzy Mathematics*, (3), 833 – 849.

Martinez, L. (1999). Prime and Primary L– Fuzzy Ideals of L– Fuzzy Rings. *Fuzzy Sets and Systems*, *101*(3), 489–494. doi:10.1016/S0165-0114(97)00114-0

Martinez, R., Castillo, O., Aguilar, L. T., & Rodriguez, A. (2011). Optimization of Type-2 Fuzzy Logic Controllers Using PSO Applied to Linear Plants, Soft Computing for Intelligent Control and Mobile Robotics. *Studies in Computational Intelligence*, *318*, 181–193.

Martins, M. M., Trigo, M., & Evans, D. J. (2007). An iterative method for positive real systems. *International Journal of Computer Mathematics*, *84*(11), 1603–1611. doi:10.1080/00207160601088456

Melliani, S., & Chadli, L. S. (2001). Introduction to intuitionistic fuzzy partial differential Equations. *Fifth Int. Conf. on IFSs.*

Memarbashi, R., & Ghasemabadi, A. (2013). Fuzzy difference equations of volterra type. *Int. J. Nonlinear Anal.Appl*, *4*, 74–78.

Mendel, J., & John, R. (2002). Type-2 fuzzy sets made simple. *IEEE Transactions on Fuzzy Systems*, *10*(2), 117–127. doi:10.1109/91.995115

Mezura-Montes, E., & Hern'andez-Ocana, B. (2009). Modified bacterial foraging optimization for engineering design. In *Proceedings of the Artificial Neural Networks in Engineering Conference* (ANNIE'2009). St. Louis, MO: ASME Press.

Mezura-Montes, E., Portilla-Flores, E. A., & Hernández-Ocaña, B. (2014). Optimum synthesis of a four-bar mechanism using the modified bacterial foraging algorithm. *International Journal of Systems Science*, *45*(5), 1080–1100. doi:10.1080/00207721.2012.745023

Miao, S.-X., Zheng, B., & Wang, K. (2008). Block SOR methods for fuzzy linear systems. *Journal of Applied Mathematics and Computing*, *26*(1-2), 201–218. doi:10.1007/s12190-007-0019-y

Mingers, J. (1989a). An empirical comparision of selection measures for decision trees induction. *Machine Learning*, *3*(4), 319–342. doi:10.1007/BF00116837

Mingers, J. (1989b). An empirical comparision of pruning methods for decision tree induction. *Machine Learning*, *4*(2), 227–243. doi:10.1023/A:1022604100933

MishmastNehi, H., Maleki, H. R., & Mashinchi, M. (2004). Solving fuzzy number linear programming problem by lexicographic ranking function. *International Journal of Pure and Applied Mathematics*, *15*, 9–20.

Mitchell, A. A. (2006). *The Discipline of Machine Learning*. School of Computer Science, Carnegie Mellon University.

Mitchell, A. A. (1997). *Machine learning*. McGraw Hill.

Mitchell, A. A. (2005). *Machine Learning*. The McGraw-Hill Co.

Mo, H., Wang, F. Y., Zhou, M., Li, R., & Xiao, Z. (2014). Footprint of uncertainty for type-2 fuzzy sets. *Information Sciences*, *272*, 96–110.

Molodtsov, D. (1999). Soft Set Theory-First Results. *Computers & Mathematics with Applications (Oxford, England)*, *37*(4-5), 19–31. doi:10.1016/S0898-1221(99)00056-5

Moloudzadeh, S., Allahviranloo, T., & Darabi, P. (2013). A new method for solving an arbitrary fully fuzzy linear system. *Soft Computing*, *17*(9), 1725–1731. doi:10.1007/s00500-013-0986-x

Mondal, S.P., & Roy, T.K. (2014). First order homogeneous ordinary differential equation with initial value as triangular intuitionistic fuzzy number. *Journal of Uncertainty in Mathematics Science*, 1-17.

Mondal, K., & Pramanik, S. (2015). Multi-criteria Group Decision Making Approach for Teacher Recruitment in Higher Education under Simplified Neutrosophic Environment. *Neutrosophic Sets and Systems*, *06*, 28–34.

Mondal, S. P., & Roy, T. K. (2015). System of Differential Equation with Initial Value as Triangular Intuitionistic Fuzzy Number and its Application. *Int. J. Appl. Comput. Math*, *1*(1), 449–474. doi:10.1007/s40819-015-0026-x

Mondal, T. K., & Samanta, S. K. (2002). Generalized intuitionistic fuzzy sets. *The Journal of Fuzzy Mathematics*, *10*(4), 839–862.

Mondal, T. K., & Samanta, S. K. (2002). Generalizedintuitionistic fuzzy sets. *The Journal of Fuzzy Mathematics*, *10*(4), 839–862.

Mostaghim, S., & Teich, J. (2005). A New Approach on Many Objective Diversity Measurement. *Dagstuhl Seminar Proceedings 04461, Practical Approaches to Multi-Objective Optimization.*

Mostaghim, S., & Teich, J. (2003). Strategies for finding good local guides in multiobjective particle swarm optimization. In *IEEE Swarm Intelligence Symposium*, (pp. 26-33).

Moussavi, A., & Omit, S., & Ahmadi, A. (2011). A note on nilpotent lattice matrices. *International Journal of Algebra*, *5*(2), 83–89.

Mukherjee, T. K., & Sen, M. K. (1987). On Fuzzy Ideals of a Ring I. *Fuzzy Sets and Systems*, *21*(1), 99–104. doi:10.1016/0165-0114(87)90155-2

Nair, A., & Closs, D. J. (2006). An examination of the impact of coordinating supply chain policies and price markdowns on short life cycle product retail performance. *International Journal of Production Economics*, *102*(2), 379–392. doi:10.1016/j.ijpe.2005.04.009

Nasseri, S., Sohrabi, M., & Ardil, E. (2008). Solving fully fuzzy linear systems by use of a certain decomposition of the coefficient matrix. *International Journal of Computational and Mathematical Sciences*, *2*(1), 140–142.

Nasseri, S., & Zahmatkesh, F. (2010). Huang method for solving fully fuzzy linear system of equations. *The Journal of Mathematics and Computer Science*, *1*(1), 1–5.

Natarajan, A. A. (1991). *Machine Learning: A Theoretical Approach.* Academic Press.

Neggers, J., & Kim, H. S. (2002). On B-algebras. *Math. Vensik*, *54*, 21–29.

Nieto, J. J., Torres, A., Georgiou, D. N., & Karakasidis, T. E. (2006). Fuzzy Polynucleotide Spaces and Metrics. *Bulletin of Mathematical Biology*, *16*(8), 703–725. doi:10.1007/s11538-005-9020-5 PMID:16794951

Nieto, J. J., Torres, A., & Vâzquez-Trasande, M. M. (2003). A metric space to study differences between polynucleotides. *Applied Mathematics Letters*, *16*(8), 1289–1294. doi:10.1016/S0893-9659(03)90131-5

Niklasson, L., Boden, M., & Ziemke, T. (Eds.). (1998). *Proceedings of the 8th International Conference on Artificial Neural Networks.* Springer Verlag.

Nouri, H., & Hong, T. S. (2013). Development of bacteria foraging optimization algorithm for cell formation in cellular manufacturing system considering cell load variations. *Journal of Manufacturing Systems*, *32*(1), 20–31. doi:10.1016/j.jmsy.2012.07.014

Nurcahyo, G. W. (2003). Selection of Defuzzification Method to Obtain Crisp Value for Representing Uncertain Data in a Modified Sweep Algorithm. JCS&T, 3(2).

O'Brien, W., Browman, H., & Evans, B. (1990). Search strategies of foraging animals. *American Scientist*, *78*, 152–160.

Oh, S. K., Jang, H. J., & Pedrycz, W. (2011). A comparative experimental study of type-1/type-2 fuzzy cascade controller based on genetic algorithms and particle swarm optimization. *Expert Systems with Applications*, *38*(9), 11217–11229. doi:10.1016/j.eswa.2011.02.169

Oliveira, H. Jr, & Petraglia, A. (2014). Establishing Nash equilibria of strategic games: A multistart Fuzzy Adaptive Simulated Annealing approach. *Applied Soft Computing*, *19*, 188–197. doi:10.1016/j.asoc.2014.02.013

Ontoseno, P., Abdillah, M., Wibowo, R., & Soeprijanto, A. (2013). Optimal Design of Photovoltaic–Battery Systems Using Interval Type-2 Fuzzy Adaptive Genetic Algorithm. *Engineering*, *5*(01No. 1B), 50–55. doi:10.4236/eng.2013.51B009

Orouji, B., Parandin, N., Abasabadi, L., & Hosseinpour, A. (2014). *An Implicit Method for Solving Fuzzy Partial Differential Equation with Nonlocal Boundary Conditions*. Academic Press.

Pal, M. (2001). Intuitionistic fuzzy determinant. *V.U.J. Physical Sciences*, (7), 87-93.

Pal. (2001). Intuitionistic fuzzy determinant. *V.U.J. Physical Sciences*, (7), 87-93.

Pal. (2001). Intuitionistic fuzzy determinate. *V. U. J. Physical Sciences*, (7), 87-93.

Pal, M., Khan, S. K., & Shyamal, A. K. (2002a). Intuitionistic fuzzy matrices. *Notes on Intuitionistic Fuzzy Sets*, *8*(2), 51–62.

Pal, M., & Shyamal, A. K. (2004). Two new operators on fuzzy matrices, *J. Applied Mathematics and Computation*, (15), 91–107.

Panda, S. K., Padhee, S., Kumar Sood, A., & Mahapatra, S. S. (2009). Optimization of Fused Deposition Modelling (FDM) Process Parameters Using Bacterial Foraging Technique. *Intelligent Information & Management*, *1*, 89–97.

Panek, J., Eidhammer, I., & Aasland, R. (2005). A new method for identification of protein (sub)families in a set of proteins based on hydropathy distribution in proteins. *Proteins*, *58*(4), 923–934. doi:10.1002/prot.20356 PMID:15645428

Panigrahi, M., & Nanda, S. (2006). A comparison betwen intuitionistic fuzzy sets and generalized intuitionistic fuzzy sets. *The Journal of Fuzzy Mathematics*, *14*(2), 407–421.

Panigrahi, M., & Nanda, S. (2006a). A comparison between intuitionistic fuzzy sets and generalized intuitionistic fuzzy sets. *The Journal of Fuzzy Mathematics*, *14*(2), 407–421.

Panigrahi, M., & Nanda, S. (2006b). *Generalized intuitionistic fuzzy sets and some new operators. In Fuzzy Logic and Optimization* (pp. 155–169). New Delhi, India: Narosa Publishing House.

Papaschinopoulos, G., & Stefanidou, G. (2003). Boundedness and asymptotic behavior of the Solutions of a fuzzy difference equation. *Fuzzy Sets and Systems*, *140*(3), 523–539. doi:10.1016/S0165-0114(03)00034-4

Paricheh, M., & Zare, A. (2013). Traffic Flow Prediction Based on Optimized Type-2 Neuro-Fuzzy Systems. *International Journal of Engineering and Computer Science*, *2*(8), 2434–2439.

Park, J. H. (2004). Intuitionistic fuzzy metric spaces. *Chaos, Solitons, and Fractals*, *22*(5), 1039–1046. doi:10.1016/j.chaos.2004.02.051

Park, J. Y., & Han, H. K. (2000). Fuzzy differential equations. *Fuzzy Sets and Systems*, *110*(1), 69–77. doi:10.1016/S0165-0114(98)00150-X

Passino, K. (2002). Biomimicry of bacterial foraging for distributed optimization and control. *IEEE Control Systems Magazine*, *22*(3), 52–67. doi:10.1109/MCS.2002.1004010

Pawlak. (1982). Rough sets. *International J. Information and Computer Sciences*, (11), 341-356.

Pawlak, Z. (1982). Rough Sets. *International Journal of Computer and Information Sciences*, *11*(5), 341–356. doi:10.1007/BF01001956

Pawlak, Z. (1983). Rough Classification. *International Journal of Man-Machine Studies*, *20*(5), 469–483. doi:10.1016/S0020-7373(84)80022-X

Pawlak, Z. (1991). *Rough Sets, Theoretical aspect of Reasoning about Data*. Kluwer Academic Publishers.

Pawlak, Z. (2004). Decision rules and flow networks. *European Journal of Operational Research*, *154*(1), 184–190. doi:10.1016/S0377-2217(03)00004-3

Pawlak, Z., & Skowron, A. (2007a). Rough sets some extensions. Information Science. *International Journal (Toronto, Ont.)*, *177*(1), 28–40.

Pawlak, Z., & Skowron, A. (2007b). Rough sets and Boolean reasoning, *Information Science. International Journal (Toronto, Ont.)*, *177*(1), 41–73.

Peidro, D., Mula, J., Polar, R., & Verdegay, J.-L. (2009). Fuzzy Optimization for supply chain planning under supply, demand and process uncertainties. *Fuzzy Sets and Systems*, *160*(18), 2640–2657. doi:10.1016/j.fss.2009.02.021

Peters, G. (1994). Fuzzy linear regression with fuzzy intervals. *Fuzzy Sets and Systems*, *63*(1), 45–55. doi:10.1016/0165-0114(94)90144-9

Petrovic, D. (2001). Simulation of supply chain behaviour and performance in an uncertain environment. *International Journal of Production Economics*, *71*(1-3), 429–438. doi:10.1016/S0925-5273(00)00140-7

Pham, D. L., Xu, C., & Prince, J. L. (2000). Current methods in medical image segmentation 1. *Annual Review of Biomedical Engineering*, *2*(1), 315–337. doi:10.1146/annurev.bioeng.2.1.315 PMID:11701515

Poggio, T., Pontil, M., & Verri, A. (2002). Regularization and statistical learning theory for data analysis. *Computational Statistics & Data Analysis - Nonlinear Methods and Data Mining*, *38*(4), 421 – 432.

Pontil, M., & Verri, A. (1998). Properties of support vector machines. Massachusetts Institute of Technology.

Puri, M. L., & Ralescu, D. A. (1983). Differentials of fuzzy functions. *Journal of Mathematical Analysis and Applications*, *91*(2), 552–558. doi:10.1016/0022-247X(83)90169-5

Qiu, C., Xiao, J., Yu, L., Han, L., & Iqbal, M. N. (2013). A modified interval type-2 fuzzy C-means algorithm with application in MR image segmentation. *Journal of Pattern Recognition Letters*, *34*(12), 1329–1338. doi:10.1016/j.patrec.2013.04.021

Quinlan, A. A. (1993). *C4.5: Programs for Machine Learning*. San Mateo, CA: Morgan Kaufmann.

Quinlan, J. R. (1984). Unknown attribute-values in induction. In *Proc. 6th Int. Workshop Machine Learning*, (pp. 164-168).

Quinlan, J. R. (1986). Induction on Decision Trees. *Machine Learning*, *1*(1), 81–106. doi:10.1007/BF00116251

Quinlan, J. R. (1987). Decision trees as probabilistic classifiers. In *Proc. 4th Int. Workshop Machine Learning*, (pp. 31-37). doi:10.1016/B978-0-934613-41-5.50007-6

Ragin, C. C. (2000). *Fuzzy-set social science*. University of Chicago Press.

Rao, D. H., & Saraf, S. S. (1996). Study of defuzzification methods of fuzzy logic controller for speed control of a DC motor. *Proceedings of the 1996 International Conference on Power Electronics, Drives and Energy Systems for Industrial Growth*. doi:10.1109/PEDES.1996.535878

Rau, H., Wu, M.-Y., & Wee, H.-M. (2004). Deteriorating item inventory model with shortage due to supplier in an integrated supply chain. *International Journal of Systems Science*, *35*(5), 293–303. doi:10.1080/00207720410001714833

Ravi, K., Shilaja, C., Chitti Babu, B., & Kothari, D. P. (2014). Solving Optimal Power Flow Using Modified Bacterial Foraging Algorithm Considering FACTS Devices. *Journal of Power and Energy Engineering*, *2*(04), 639–646. doi:10.4236/jpee.2014.24086

Riddle, D. S., Santiago, J. V., Bray-Hall, S. T., Doshi, N., Grantcharova, V. P., Yi, Q., & Baker, D. (1997). Functional rapidly folding proteins from simplified amino acid sequences. *Nature Structural Biology*, *4*(10), 805–809. doi:10.1038/nsb1097-805 PMID:9334745

Rommelfanger, H. (1989). Interactive decision making in fuzzy linear optimization problems. *European Journal of Operational Research, 41*(2), 210–217.

Rommelfanger, H. (2007). A general concept for solving linear multicriteria programming problems with crisp, fuzzy or stochastic values. *Fuzzy Sets and Systems*, *158*(17), 1892–1904. doi:10.1016/j.fss.2007.04.005

Saad, Y. (2003). *Iterative methods for sparse linear systems*. Siam. doi:10.1137/1.9780898718003

Saberi Najafi, H., & Edalatpanad, S. (2013a). On application of Liao's method for system of linear equations, Ain Shams. *Ain Shams. Eng. J, 4*, 501-505.

Saberi Najafi, H., & Edalatpanah, S. (2014a). H-Matrices in Fuzzy Linear Systems. International Journal of Computational Mathematics.

Saberi Najafi, H., & Edalatpanah, S. A. (2011). Some Improvements In Preconditioned Modified Accelerated Overrelaxation (PMAOR) Method For Solving Linear Systems. *Journal of Information and Computing Science, 6*(1), 15-22.

Saberi Najafi, H., Edalatpanah, S., & Refahi Sheikhani, A. (2013). Application of homotopy perturbation method for fuzzy linear systems and comparison with Adomian's decomposition method. Chinese Journal of Mathematics.

Saberi Najafi, H., & Edalatpanad, S. A. (2013). A note on A new method for solving fully fuzzy linear programming problems. *Applied Mathematical Modelling*, *37*(14-15), 7865–7867. doi:10.1016/j.apm.2013.02.039

Saberi Najafi, H., & Edalatpanah, S. (2012a). Nash equilibrium solution of fuzzy matrix game solution of fuzzy bimatrix game. *International Journal of Fuzzy Systems and Rough Systems*, *5*(2), 93–97.

Saberi Najafi, H., & Edalatpanah, S. (2012b). The block AOR iterative methods for solving fuzzy linear systems. *The Journal of Mathematics and Computer Science*, *4*(4), 527–535.

Saberi Najafi, H., & Edalatpanah, S. (2012c). Preconditioning strategy to solve fuzzy linear systems (FLS). *International Review of Fuzzy Mathematics*, *7*(2), 65–80.

Saberi Najafi, H., & Edalatpanah, S. (2013). An improved model for iterative algorithms in fuzzy linear systems. *Computational Mathematics and Modeling*, *24*(3), 443–451. doi:10.1007/s10598-013-9189-7

Saberi Najafi, H., & Edalatpanah, S. (2013b). Comparison analysis for improving preconditioned SOR-type iterative method. *Numerical Analysis and Applications*, *6*(1), 62–70. doi:10.1134/S1995423913010084

Saberi Najafi, H., & Edalatpanah, S. (2013c). Iterative methods with analytical preconditioning technique to linear complementarity problems: Application to obstacle problems. *RAIRO-Operations Research*, *47*(01), 59–71. doi:10.1051/ro/2013027

Saberi Najafi, H., & Edalatpanah, S. (2014b). A new modified SSOR iteration method for solving augmented linear systems. *International Journal of Computer Mathematics*, *91*(3), 539–552. doi:10.1080/00207160.2013.792923

Saeid, A. B. (2006). Fuzzy topological B-algebra. *International Journal of Fuzzy Systems*, *8*(3), 160–164.

Sah, M., & Konstantin, Y. (2005). Forecasting enrollment model based on first-order fuzzy time series. *In World Academy of Science. Engineering and Technology*, *1*, 375–378.

Saikia, R. K. (2011). Fuzzy numerical solution of Poisson equation using fuzzy data. *International Journal of Engineering Science and Technology*, *3*(12), 8450–8456.

Sakawa, M., & Yano, H. (1992). Multi-objective fuzzy linear regression analysis for fuzzy input-output data. *Fuzzy Sets and Systems*, *47*(2), 173–181. doi:10.1016/0165-0114(92)90175-4

Salahshour, S., & Haghi, E. (2010). Solving fuzzy heat equation by Fuzzy Laplace transform. *IPMU*, 512-521.

Salama, A. A. (2015). Basic Structure of Some Classes of Neutrosophic Crisp Nearly Open Sets and Possile Application to GIS Topology. *Neutrosophic Sets and Systems*, *7*, 18–22.

Salama, A. A., & Smarandache, F. (2015). Neutrosophic Crisp Set Theory. *Neutrosophic Sets and Systems*, *05*, 27–35.

Salkuyeh, D. K. (2015). On the solution of a class of fuzzy system of linear equations. *Sadhana*, *40*(Part 2), 369–377. doi:10.1007/s12046-014-0313-y

Sánchez, D., Melin, P., & Castillo, O. (2015). Fuzzy System Optimization Using a Hierarchical Genetic Algorithm Applied to Pattern Recognition. *Advances in Intelligent Systems and Computing*, *323*, 713–720. doi:10.1007/978-3-319-11310-4_62

Santoso, T., Ahmed, S., Goetschalckx, M., & Shapiro, A. (2005). A stochastic programming approach for supply chain network design under uncertainty. *European Journal of Operational Research*, *167*(1), 96–115. doi:10.1016/j.ejor.2004.01.046

Sarkar, M. (2007). Fuzzy-rough nearest neighbor algorithms in classification. *Fuzzy Sets and Systems*, *158*(19), 2134–2152. doi:10.1016/j.fss.2007.04.023

Sarmah, S. P., Acharya, D., & Goyal, S. K. (2008). Coordination of a singlemanufacturer/ multi-buyer supply chain with credit option. *International Journal of Production Economics*, *111*(2), 676–685. doi:10.1016/j.ijpe.2007.04.003

Schneider, S. S., & McNally, L. C. (1992). Colony Defense in the African Honey Bee In Africa. *Environmental Entomology*, *21*(6), 1362–1370. doi:10.1093/ee/21.6.1362

Schölkopf, A. A., Burges, B. B., & Smola, C. C. (1999). *Advances in Kernel Methods: Support Vector Learning*. Cambridge, MA: MIT Press.

Schölkopf, B., Bartlett, P. L., Smola, A., & Williamson, R. (1999). Shrinking the tube: A new support Vector regression algorithm. *Advances in Neural Information Processing Systems*, *11*, 330–336.

Senapati, Bhowmik, & Pal. (2013). Fuzzy closed ideals of *B*-algebras with interval-valued membership function. *Int. J. of Fuzzy Mathematical Archive*, (1), 79-91.

Senapati, T., Bhowmik, M., & Pal, M. (2012b)n Fuzzy B-subalgebras of B-algebra with respect to t-norm. Journal of Fuzzy Set Valued Analysis.

Senapati, T., Bhowmik, M., & Pal, M. (2011). Fuzzy closed ideals of B-algebras. Int. J. of Computer Science*Engineering and Technology*, *1*(10), 669–673.

Senapati, T., Bhowmik, M., & Pal, M. (2012a). Interval-valued intuitionistic fuzzy BG-subalgebras. *J. Fuzzy Math.*, *20*(3), 707–720.

Senapati, T., Bhowmik, M., & Pal, M. (2012c). Intuitionistic fuzzifications of ideals in BG-algebras. *Mathematica Aeterna*, *2*(9), 761–778.

Senapati, T., Bhowmik, M., & Pal, M. (2012d). Interval-valued intuitionistic fuzzy closed ideals ofBG. *Int. J. of Fuzzy Logic Systems*, *2*(2), 27–44. doi:10.5121/ijfls.2012.2203

Senapati, T., Bhowmik, M., & Pal, M. (2013). Atanassov's intuitionistic fuzzy translations of intuitionistic fuzzy H-ideals in BCK/BCI-algebras. *Notes on Intuitionistic Fuzzy Sets*, *19*, 32–47.

Senapati, T., Bhowmik, M., & Pal, M. (2014). Fuzzy dot subalgebras and fuzzy dot ideals of B-algebras. *Journal of Uncertain Systems*, *8*(1), 22–30.

Senapati, T., Bhowmik, M., & Pal, M. (2016). Intuitionistic *L BG*. *Afrika Matematika*, *27*(1-2), 187–199. doi:10.1007/s13370-015-0330-y

Senthilkumar, P., & Rajendran, G. (2011). New approach to solve symmetric fully fuzzy linear systems. *Sadhana*, *36*(6), 933–940. doi:10.1007/s12046-011-0059-8

Shamooshaki, M. M., Hosseinzadeh, A., & Edalatpanah, S. A. (2014). A New Method for Solving Fully Fuzzy Linear Programming with LR- type Fuzzy Numbers. *International Journal of Data Envelopment Analysis and Operations Research*, *1*, 53–55.

Shamooshaki, M. M., Hosseinzadeh, A., & Edalatpanah, S. A. (2015). A New Method for Solving Fully Fuzzy Linear Programming Problems by Using the Lexicography Method. *Applied and Computational Mathematics*, *1*, 53–55.

Shamooshaki, M., Hosseinzadeh, A., & Edalatpanah, S. (2014). A New Method for Solving Fully Fuzzy Linear Programming with LR-type Fuzzy Numbers. *International Journal of Data Envelopment Analysis and Operations Research*, *1*(3), 53–55.

Shang, W., Huang, H., Zhu, H., & Lin, Y. (2006). An improved kNN algorithm: Fuzzy kNN. In *Proceedings of international conference on computational intelligence and security*, (pp. 741–746).

Sheridan, T. B. (1992). *Telerobotics, automation, and human supervisory control*. MIT press.

Shyamal & Pal. (2002). Distance between intuitionistics fuzzy matrices. *V.U.J. Physical Sciences*, (8), 81-91.

Shyamal & Pal. (2004). Two new operators on fuzzy matrices. *J. Applied Mathematics and Computing*, (15), 91-107.

Shyamal & Pal. (2005a). Distance between fuzzy matrices and its applications. *Acta Siencia Indica*, *31*(1), 199-204.

Shyamal, A. K., & Pal, M. (2005). Distance between fuzzy matrices and its applications–I. *J. Nature. Physical Science (London)*, *19*(1), 39–58.

Shyamal, A. K., & Pal, M. (2005b). Distance between fuzzy matrices and its applications-I. *J. Nature. Physical Science (London)*, *19*(1), 39–58.

Shyamal, , & Pal, . (2006). Interval-valued fuzzy matrices. *The Journal of Fuzzy Mathematics*, *14*(3) 583-604.

Singh, P. (2015). A brief review of modeling approaches based on fuzzy time series. *International Journal of Machine Learning and Cybernetics*, 1-24.

Singh, P. (2016). High-order fuzzy-neuro-entropy integration-based expert system for time series forecasting. *Neural Computing & Applications*, 1–18.

Singh, P., & Borah, B. (2011). *An efficient method for forecasting using fuzzy time series. In Machine Intelligence* (pp. 67–75). Narosa.

Singh, P., & Borah, B. (2013a). An efficient time series forecasting model based on fuzzy time series. *Engineering Applications of Artificial Intelligence*, *26*(10), 2443–2457. doi:10.1016/j.engappai.2013.07.012

Singh, P., & Borah, B. (2013b). High-order fuzzy-neuro expert system for time series forecasting. *Knowledge-Based Systems*, *46*, 12–21. doi:10.1016/j.knosys.2013.01.030

Singh, P., & Borah, B. (2014a). An effective neural network and fuzzy time series-based hybridized model to handle forecasting problems of two factors. *Knowledge and Information Systems*, *38*(3), 669–690. doi:10.1007/s10115-012-0603-9

Singh, P., & Borah, B. (2014b). Forecasting stock index price based on M-factors fuzzy time series and particle swarm optimization. *International Journal of Approximate Reasoning*, *55*(3), 812–833. doi:10.1016/j.ijar.2013.09.014

Singh, S. R. (2009). A computational method of forecasting based on high-order fuzzy time series. *Expert Systems with Applications*, *36*(7), 10551–10559. doi:10.1016/j.eswa.2009.02.061

Słowiński, R. (1986). A multicriteria fuzzy linear programming method for water supply system development planning. *Fuzzy Sets and Systems*, *19*(3), 217–237. doi:10.1016/0165-0114(86)90052-7

Smarandache, F. (1998). *Neutrosophy*. Rehoboth: Neutrosophic Probability, Set, and Logic, Amer. Res. Press.

Smarandache, F. (1999). *A Unifying Field in Logics. Neutrosophy: Neutrosophic Probability, Set and Logic*. Rehoboth: American Research Press.

Smarandache, F. (2005). Neutrosophic set, a generalisation of the intuitionistic fuzzy sets. *International Journal of Pure and Applied Mathematics*, *24*, 287–297.

Smola, A. & Scholkopf, B. (1997). On a Kernel-based Method for Pattern Recognition, Regression. *Approximation and Operator Inversion*, 211 – 231.

Smola, A. J., & Schölkopf, B. (1998). *A Tutorial on Support Vector Regression*. Technical Report NC-TR-98-030. Royal Holloway College, University of London.

Smola, A., Schölkopf, B., & Müller, K. R. (1998). General cost functions for support vector regression. In *Proc. of the Ninth Australian Conf. on Neural Networks*. Brisbane, Australia: University of Queensland.

Song, Q., & Chissom, B. S. (1993a). Forecasting enrollments with fuzzy time series-part I. *Fuzzy Sets and Systems*, *54*(1), 1–9. doi:10.1016/0165-0114(93)90355-L

Song, Q., & Chissom, B. S. (1993b). Fuzzy time series and its models. *Fuzzy Sets and Systems*, *54*(3), 269–277. doi:10.1016/0165-0114(93)90372-O

Song, Q., & Chissom, B. S. (1994). Forecasting enrollments with fuzzy time series-part II. *Fuzzy Sets and Systems*, *62*(1), 1–8. doi:10.1016/0165-0114(94)90067-1

Sriram, S., & Murugadas, P. (2010). On semiring of intuitionistic fuzzy matrices. *Applied Mathematical Sciences*, *4*(23), 1099–1105.

Stanevski, N., & Tsvetkov, D. (2005). Using Support Vector Machine as a Binary Classifier. *International Conference on Computer Systems and Technologies –CompSysTech.*

Stecking, R., & Schebesch, K. B. (2003). Support vector machines for credit scoring: Comparing to and combining with some traditional classification methods. In M. Schader, W. Gaul, & M. Vichy (Eds.), *Between Data Science and Applied Data Analysis* (pp. 604–612). Berlin, Germany: Springer- Verlag. doi:10.1007/978-3-642-18991-3_69

Stefanidou, G., Papaschinopoulos, G., & Schinas, C. J. (2010). On an exponential –type fuzzy Difference equation. *Advanced in Difference Equations.*

Stefanini, L. (2008). A generalization of Hukuhara difference for interval and fuzzy arithmetic. In D. Dubois, M. A. Lubiano, H. Prade, M. A. Gil, P. Grzegorzewski, & O. Hryniewicz (Eds.), *Soft Methods for Handling Variability and Imprecision, in: Series on Advances in Soft Computing, 48.* doi:10.1007/978-3-540-85027-4_25

Stefanini, L., & Bede, B. (2009). Generalized Hukuhara differentiability of interval-valued functions and interval differential equations. *Nonlinear Analysis, 71*(3-4), 1311–1328. doi:10.1016/j.na.2008.12.005

Stfanidou,G., & Papaschinopoulos, G .(2005). A fuzzy difference equation of a rational form. *Journal of Nonlinear Mathematical Physics, 12*(S2), 300-315.

Sushmita, M., Kishorim. K., & Sankar. K.P. (2002). Fuzzy decision tree, linguistic rules and fuzzy knowledge based-network: Generation and Evaluation. *IEEE Transaction on Systems, 32*(4).

Swamy, U.M., & Swamy, K. L. N. (1988). Fuzzy Prime Ideals of Rings. *The Journal of Fuzzy Mathematics*, (134), 94 – 103.

Szmidt, E., & Kacprzyk, J. (2000). Intuitionistic Distances between intuitionistic fuzzy sets. *Fuzzy Sets and Systems, 114*(3), 505–518. doi:10.1016/S0165-0114(98)00244-9

Tanaka, H., Okuda, T., & Asai, K. (1973). On Fuzzy Mathematical Programming. *Journal of Cybernetics and Systems*, 37-46.

Tanaka, H., Vejima, S., & Asai, K. (1982). Linear regression analysis with fuzzy model. *IEEE Transactions on Systems, Man, and Cybernetics, 12*(6), 903–907. doi:10.1109/TSMC.1982.4308925

Tanaka, H., & Watada, J. (1988). Possibilistic systems and their application to the linear regression model. *Fuzzy Sets and Systems, 27*(3), 275–289. doi:10.1016/0165-0114(88)90054-1

Tan, Y. J. (2005). On nilpotent matrices over distributive lattices. *Fuzzy Sets and Systems, 151*(2), 421–433. doi:10.1016/j.fss.2004.06.009

Tapaswini, S., & Chakraverty, S. (2013). iNumerical Solution of Uncertain Beam Equations Using Double Parametric Form of Fuzzy Numbers. *Applied Computational Intelligence and Soft Computing, 2013*, 1–8. doi:10.1155/2013/764871

Tapaswini, S., & Chakraverty, S. (2014). Dynamic response of imprecisely defined beam subject to variousloads using Adomian decomposition method. *Applied Soft Computing, 24*, 249–263. doi:10.1016/j.asoc.2014.06.052

Tapaswini, S., & Chakraverty, S. (2014). Non-probabilistic Solution of Uncertain Vibration Equation of Large Membranes Using Adomian Decomposition Methods. *TheScientificWorldJournal, 2014*, 1–11. doi:10.1155/2014/308205 PMID:24790562

Taylor, W. R. (1986). Identification of protein sequence homology by consensus template alignment. *Journal of Molecular Biology, 188*(2), 233–258. doi:10.1016/0022-2836(86)90308-6 PMID:3088284

Teoh, H. J., Cheng, C. H., Chu, H. H., & Chen, J. S. (2008). Fuzzy time series model based on probabilistic approach and rough set rule induction for empirical research in stock markets. *Data & Knowledge Engineering, 67*(1), 103–117. doi:10.1016/j.datak.2008.06.002

Thomas, L. C. (2002). A survey of credit and behavioral scoring: Forecasting financial risk of lending to consumers. *International Journal of Forecasting, 16*(2), 149–172. doi:10.1016/S0169-2070(00)00034-0

Thomason, M. G. (1977). Convergence of powers of a fuzzy matrix. *Journal of Mathematical Analysis and Applications, 57*(2), 476–480. doi:10.1016/0022-247X(77)90274-8

Tian, Z., Hu, L., & Greenhalgh, D. (2010). Perturbation analysis of fuzzy linear systems. *Information Sciences*, *180*(23), 4706–4713. doi:10.1016/j.ins.2010.07.018

Torres, A., & Nieto, J. J. (2003). The fuzzy polynucleotide space: Basic properties. *Bioinformatics (Oxford, England)*, *19*(5), 587–592. doi:10.1093/bioinformatics/btg032 PMID:12651716

Tripathy, B. K., Acharjya, D. P., & Ezhilarasi, L. (2012). Topological Characterization of Rough Set on Two Universal Sets and Knowledge Representation. In Global Trends in Information Systems and Software Applications, Proceedings of 4th ObCom 2011, (vol. 270, pp. 70–83). Vellore, India: Springer CCIS. doi:10.1007/978-3-642-29216-3_9

Tripathy, B. K., & Acharjya, D. P. (2012). Approximation of Classification and Measures of Uncertainty in Rough Set on Two Universal Sets. *International Journal of Advanced Science and Technology*, *40*, 77–90.

Turksen, I. (1986). Interval valued fuzzy sets based on normal forms. *Fuzzy Sets and Systems*, *20*(2), 191–210. doi:10.1016/0165-0114(86)90077-1

Turner, J. S. (2011). Termites as models of swarm cognition. *Swarm Intelligence*, *5*(1), 19–43. doi:10.1007/s11721-010-0049-1

Ullah, S., Farooq, M., Ahmad, L., & Abdullah, S. (2014). *Application of fuzzy Laplace transforms for solving fuzzy partial Volterra integro-differential equations*. arXiv:1405.1895v1 [math.GM]

Umekkan, S. A., Can, E., & Bayrak, M. A. (2014). Fuzzy difference equation in finance. *IJSIMR*, *2*(8), 729–735.

Van Gestel, T., Baesens, B., Suykens, J. A. K., De Espinoza, M., Baestaens, J., Vanthienen, D., & Moor, B. (2003). Bankruptcy prediction with least squares support vector machine classifiers. In *Proc. IEEE Int. Conf. Computational Intelligence for Financial Engineering*. doi:10.1109/CIFER.2003.1196234

Van Gestel, T., Suykens, J. A. K., Lanckriet, G., Lambrechts, A., DeMoor, B., & Vandewalle, J. (2002). Bayesian framework for least squares support vector machine classifiers, Gaussian processes and kernel Fisher discriminant analysis. *Neural Computation*, *15*(5), 1115–1148. doi:10.1162/089976602753633411 PMID:11972910

Vapnik, A. A. (1995). *The Nature of Statistical Learning Theory*. New York: Springer-Verlag. doi:10.1007/978-1-4757-2440-0

Vapnik, V., Golowich, S., & Smola, A. (1997). Support Vector Method for Function Approximation, Regression Estimation, and Signal Processing. In M. Mozer, M. Jordan, & T. Petsche (Eds.), *Neural Information Processing Systems, 9*. Cambridge, MA: MIT Press.

Varga, R. S. (2009). *Matrix iterative analysis* (Vol. 27). Springer Science & Business Media.

Vasant, P., Elamvazuthi, I., Ganesan, T., & Webb, J. F. (2010). Iterative fuzzy optimization approach for crude oil refinery industry. *Scientific Annals of Computer Science*, *8*(2), 261–280.

Vijay, R. (2012). Intelligent Bacterial Foraging Optimization Technique to Economic Load Dispatch Problem. *International Journal of Soft Computing and Engineering*, *1*(2), 2231–2307.

Viswanathan, S., & Piplani, R. (2001). Coordinating supply chain inventories through common replenishment epochs. *European Journal of Operational Research*, *129*(2), 277–286. doi:10.1016/S0377-2217(00)00225-3

Voss, R. F. (1992). Evolution of long-range fractal correlations and 1/f noise in DNA base sequences. *Physical Review Letters*, *68*(25), 3805–3808. doi:10.1103/PhysRevLett.68.3805 PMID:10045801

Wang, J. W., & Liu, J. W. (2010). Weighted fuzzy time series forecasting model. In *Intelligent Information and Database Systems* (pp. 408–415). Springer Berlin Heidelberg. doi:10.1007/978-3-642-12145-6_42

Wang, J., & Shu, Y. F. (2005). Fuzzy decision modelling for supply chain management. *Fuzzy Sets and Systems*, *150*(1), 107–127. doi:10.1016/j.fss.2004.07.005

Wang, J., & Wang, W. (1999). A computational approach to simplifying the protein folding alphabet. *Nature Structural & Molecular Biology*, *6*(11), 1033–1038. doi:10.1038/14918 PMID:10542095

Wang, J., & Wang, W. (2000). Modeling study on the validity of a possibly simplified representation of proteins. *Physical Review E: Statistical Physics, Plasmas, Fluids, and Related Interdisciplinary Topics*, *61*(6), 6981–6986. doi:10.1103/PhysRevE.61.6981 PMID:11088391

Wang, K., & Zheng, B. (2006a). Inconsistent fuzzy linear systems. *Applied Mathematics and Computation*, *181*(2), 973–981. doi:10.1016/j.amc.2006.02.019

Wang, K., & Zheng, B. (2006b). Symmetric successive overrelaxation methods for fuzzy linear systems. *Applied Mathematics and Computation*, *175*(2), 891–901. doi:10.1016/j.amc.2005.08.005

Wang, K., & Zheng, B. (2007). Block iterative methods for fuzzy linear systems. *Journal of Applied Mathematics and Computing*, *25*(1-2), 119–136. doi:10.1007/BF02832342

Wang, N., Zhang, W. X., & Mei, C. L. (2007). It Fuzzy nonparametric regression based on local linear smoothing technique. *Information Sciences*, *177*(18), 3882–3900. doi:10.1016/j.ins.2007.03.002

Wang, X. Z., Yeung, D. S., & Tsang, E. C. C. (2001). A comparative study on heuristic algorithms for generating fuzzy decision trees. *IEEE Transactions on Systems*, *31*(2), 215–226. PMID:18244783

Wasserman, P. D. (1993). *Advanced methods in neural computing*. John Wiley & Sons, Inc.

Wernick, Y., & Yourganov, B. (2012). Machine Learning in Medical Imaging. *IEEE Signal Processing Magazine*, *27*(4), 25–38. doi:10.1109/MSP.2010.936730 PMID:25382956

Wilks, D. S. (2011). *Statistical methods in the atmospheric sciences* (Vol. 100). Academic press.

Wong, Y. W., & Sumathy, K. (2001). Thermodynamic analysis and optimization of a solar thermal water pump. *Applied Thermal Engineering*, *21*(5), 613–627. doi:10.1016/S1359-4311(00)00065-X

Wu, D., & Tan, W. W. (2004). A type-2 fuzzy logic controller for the liquid-level process. *Proceedings of 2004 IEEE International Conference on Fuzzy Systems*. doi:10.1109/FUZZY.2004.1375536

Wu, X. et al.. (2008). Top ten algorithms in data mining (Support vector machines). *Knowledge and Information Systems*, *14*, 1–37. doi:10.1007/s10115-007-0114-2

Xie, Y., Petrovic, D., & Bumham, K. (2006). A heuristic procedure for the two level control of serial supply chains under fuzzy customer demand. *International Journal of Production Economics*, *102*(1), 37–50. doi:10.1016/j.ijpe.2005.01.016

Xin, L. J. (1992). Controllable fuzzy matrices. *Fuzzy Sets and Systems*, (45): 313–319.

Yager, R. R. (1982). Fuzzy prediction based on regression model, *Information Sciences*. 26, 45-63.Chang, P. T., Lee, E. S. (1994). Fuzzy linear regression whit spreads unrestricted in sign. *Computers & Mathematics with Applications (Oxford, England)*, *28*(4), 61–70.

Yager, R. R., & Filev, D. P. (1994). *Essentials of fuzzy modeling and control*. New York.

Yang, M., & Lin, T. (2002). Fuzzy least-squares linear regression analysis for fuzzy input-output data. *Fuzzy Sets and Systems*, *126*(3), 389–399. doi:10.1016/S0165-0114(01)00066-5

Yang, X., & Gao, J. (2014). Bayesian equilibria for uncertain bimatrix game with asymmetric information. *Journal of Intelligent Manufacturing*, 1–11.

Yildiz, A. R. (2013). Cuckoo search algorithm for the selection of optimal machining parameters in milling operations. *International Journal of Advanced Manufacturing Technology*, *64*(1-4), 55–61. doi:10.1007/s00170-012-4013-7

Yin, J.-F., & Wang, K. (2009). Splitting iterative methods for fuzzy system of linear equations. *Computational Mathematics and Modeling*, *20*(3), 326–335. doi:10.1007/s10598-009-9039-9

Young, D. M. (2014). *Iterative solution of large linear systems*. Elsevier.

Yu, H. K. (2005). Weighted fuzzy time series models for TAIEX forecasting. *Physica A: Statistical Mechanics and its Applications, 349*(3), 609-624.

Yuan, Y., & Shaw, M. J. (1995). Induction of fuzzy decision trees. *Fuzzy Sets and Systems*, *69*(2), 125–139. doi:10.1016/0165-0114(94)00229-Z

Yu, C.-S. (2002). A GP-AHP method for solving group decision-making fuzzy AHP problems. *Computers & Operations Research*, *29*(14), 1969–2001. doi:10.1016/S0305-0548(01)00068-5

Yu, Z. G., Anh, V., & Lau, K. S. (2004). Chaos game representation of protein sequences based on the detailed HP model and their multifractal and correlation analyses. *Journal of Theoretical Biology*, *226*(3), 341–348. doi:10.1016/j.jtbi.2003.09.009 PMID:14643648

Zadeh L. A. (1984). Making computers think like people. *Spectrum, IEEE, 21*(8), 26-32.

Zadeh, L. A (1965). *Fuzzy sets, information and control*. Academic Press.

Zadeh, L. A. (1972). *A fuzzy-set-theoretic interpretation of linguistic hedges*. Academic Press.

Zadeh, L. A. (1973). Outline of a new approach to the analysis of complex systems and decision processes. *Systems, Man and Cybernetics, IEEE Transactions on*, (1), 28-44.

Zadeh, L. (2005). Toward a generalized theory of uncertainty (GTU) – an outline. *Information Sciences*, *172*(1-2), 1–40. doi:10.1016/j.ins.2005.01.017

Zadeh, L. A. (1965). Fuzzy sets as a basis for a theory of possibility. *Fuzzy Sets and Systems*, *1*(1), 3–28. doi:10.1016/0165-0114(78)90029-5

Zadeh, L. A. (1965). Fuzzy Sets. *Information and Control*, *8*(8), 338–353. doi:10.1016/S0019-9958(65)90241-X

Zadeh, L. A. (1968). Fuzzy algorithms. *Information and Control*, *12*(2), 94–102. doi:10.1016/S0019-9958(68)90211-8

Zadeh, L. A. (1971). Similarity relations and fuzzy orderings. *Information Sciences*, *3*(2), 177–200. doi:10.1016/S0020-0255(71)80005-1

Zadeh, L. A. (1975). The concept of a linguistic variable and its application to approximate reasoning-Part I. *Information Sciences*, *7*(3), 199–249. doi:10.1016/0020-0255(75)90036-5

Zadeh, L. A. (1997). Toward a theory of fuzzy information granulation and its centrality in human reasoning and fuzzy logic. *Fuzzy Sets and Systems*, *90*(2), 111–127. doi:10.1016/S0165-0114(97)00077-8

Zadrozny, S., & Kacprzyk, J. (2012). Bipolar queries: An aggregation operator focused perspective. *Fuzzy Sets and Systems*, *196*, 69–81. doi:10.1016/j.fss.2011.10.013

Zeidler, J., Schlosser, M., Ittner, A., & Posthoff, C. (1996). Fuzzy Decision Trees and Numerical Attributes.*Proc. of 5th IEEE Inter. Conference on Fuzzy Systems*, *2*,985-990. doi:10.1109/FUZZY.1996.552312

Zhang, Q. H., Yang, L. H., & Liao, D. X. (2012). Behaviour of solutions of to a fuzzy nonlinear difference equation. *Iranian Journal of Fuzzy Systems, 9*(2), 1-12.

Zhang, L.-T., Huang, T.-Z., Cheng, S.-H., & Wang, Y.-P. (2012). Convergence of a generalized MSSOR method for augmented systems. *Journal of Computational and Applied Mathematics*, *236*(7), 1841–1850. doi:10.1016/j.cam.2011.10.016

Zhang, W. R. (1994). Bipolar fuzzy sets and relations: a computational framework for cognitive modeling and multiagent decision analysis. *Proceedings of IEEE Conf.*, (pp. 305-309).

Zhang, W. R., & Zhang, L. (2004). Bipolar logic and bipolar fuzzy logic. *Inform. Sci.*, *165*(3-4), 265–287. doi:10.1016/j.ins.2003.05.010

Zhang, X. (1999). Using class-center vectors to build support vector machines. In *Proc. IEEE NNSP*, (pp. 3–11).

Zhang, Y., & Yu, X. (2010). Analysis of protein sequence similarity. In *Proceedings of the IEEE Fifth International Conference on Bio-Inspired Computing: Theories and Applications* (pp. 1255-1258). Changsha, Beijing, China: Institute of Electrical and Electronics Engineers, Inc.

Zhong, N. & Skowron, A. (2001). A Rough Set-Based Knowledge Discovery Process. *International Journal of Applied Mathematics.*

Zhou, J., & Wei, H. (2014). A GMRES Method for Solving Fuzzy Linear Equations. *International Journal of Fuzzy Systems*, *16*(2), 270–276.

Zhu, W. (2007). Generalized Rough Sets based on Relations. *Information Sciences*, *177*(22), 4997–5011. doi:10.1016/j.ins.2007.05.037

Zimmerman, H. J. (1978). Fuzzy Programming and Linear Programming with Several Objective Functions. *Fuzzy Sets and Systems*, *1*(1), 45–55. doi:10.1016/0165-0114(78)90031-3

Zimmermann, H. J. (1987). *Fuzzy Sets, Decision Making and Expert Systems*. Boston: Kluwer. doi:10.1007/978-94-009-3249-4

Zimmermann, H.-J. (1976). Description and optimization of fuzzy systems. *International Journal of General Systems*, *2*(4), 209–215. doi:10.1080/03081077608547470

Zimmermann, H.-J. (2001). *Fuzzy set theory—and its applications*. Springer Science & Business Media. doi:10.1007/978-94-010-0646-0

Zitzler, E., & Thiele, L. (1998). Multiobjective Optimization Using Evolutionary Algorithms - A Comparative Case Study. In *Conference on Parallel Problem Solving from Nature* (PPSN V), (pp. 292–301).

About the Contributors

Amal Kumar Adak received his M.Sc. degree in Mathematics and PhD from Vidyasagar University, West Bengal, India in 2006 and 2013, respectively. He is an Assistant Teachers in Department of Mathematics of Jafuly Deshpran School (H.S.), West Bengal, India since 2007. His research interest includes fuzzy and intuitionistic fuzzy sets, intuitionistic fuzzy matrices and operations research. His papers are published in several national and international journals. He has participated and presented papers in several national and international conferences.

Debashree Manna received her MSc degree in Mathematics from Vidyasagar University, West Bengal, India in 2012. She is an Assistant Teachers in Department of Mathematics of Damda High School, West Bengal, India since 2010. Her research interest includes fuzzy and intuitionistic fuzzy matrices.

Monoranjan Bhowmik received his M.Sc. in Mathematics from Indian Institute of Technology, Kharagpur, West Bengal, India and Ph.D. from Vidyasagar University, India in 1995 and 2010, respectively. Currently, he is an Assistant Professor of VTT College, Paschim Midnapore, West Bengal, India. He is Associate-Editor of International Journal of Fuzzy Mathematical Archive. He is a reviewer of several international journals. His main scientific interest concentrates on fuzzy and intuitionistic fuzzy sets, fuzzy and intuitionistic fuzzy matrices and fuzzy algebras, Math Education and Educational Statistics. He is author of more than 30 articles published in various scholarly journals and conference proceedings and also had organized several Seminar, Conference in his institution.

* * *

Mumtaz Ali is attached with the Department of mathematics, Quaid-i-azam University Islamabad, Pakistan. His research areas are Fuzzy sets and Logic, Neutrosophic sets and Logic, Intuitionistic Fuzzy set and Logic, Complex Fuzzy set and Logic, Quantum Logic, Algebraic Coding Theory, Data Mining, Robotics, Decision Making Theory, Algebraic Structures, Soft sets. He has published more than 25 articles in these areas. He has also edited 3 books and 1 chapter. Currently he is serving as the Associate Editor-in-chief of Neutrosophic Sets and Systems.

B. Das (Gold Medalist) is an Assistant Professor in the Department of Mathematics, Sidho-Kanho-Birsha University, Purulia, West Bengal, India. He received his Ph.D. degree from Vidyasagar University, Midnapore West Bengal, India in the year 2008. He published around fifty (50) research papers in different national and international reputed journals. His area of interest is Inventory Problems, Supply Chain Managements, Fuzzy Set theory, Soft Computing, etc.

Subhram Das was born in West Bengal, India in 1979. He received the B.Tech degree in Information Technology from Kalyani University (India) in 2003 and M.Tech degree in the same discipline from Calcutta University (India) in 2005. He is working as Assistant Professor in Computer Science & Engineering department at Narula Institute of Technology, Kolkata since 2003. Presently, he is doing his research work under the supervision of Prof. D. K. Bhattacharya and Prof. D. N. Tibarewala. His research topics include Bioinformatics & Computational Biology.

T. K. Das has done his Ph.D. in the subject of Computer Science and Engineering in VIT University. He has published many research papers in the field of decision making using intelligent techniques such as fuzzy set, rough set, and soft set. In addition to this, he has used machine learning algorithms in some his works. For last 9 years, he has been teaching Artificial Intelligence to B. Tech, M. Tech and M.C.A. students in VIT. Furthermore, he has guided about 50 projects for U.G. and P.G. students in the field of Artificial Intelligence and automation. His industrial experience at Wipro Technology and CGI was in the field of data warehousing and analysis where he has worked for few Fortune 500 clients those are having business in healthcare domain.

S. A. Edalatpanah is an academic member of Islamic Azad University of Lahijan and University of Guilan. His research interests are numerical linear algebra, operation research computer science and computational mathematics. He is on the editorial boards of more than 30 refereed journals.

Irraivan Elamvazuthi obtained his PhD from Department of Automatic Control & Systems Engineering, University of Sheffield, UK in 2002. He is currently an Associate Professor at the Department of Electrical and Electronic Engineering, Universiti Teknologi PETRONAS (UTP), Malaysia. His research interests include Control, Robotics, Mechatronics, Power Systems and Bio-medical Applications.

Timothy Ganesan is a research engineer at Tenaga Nasional Berhad (Research), a power producer based in Malaysia. Holding a doctorate in Process Optimization (chemical engineering), his work focuses on Power Generation, Systems Engineering and Energy Optimization.

Soumen Ghosh was born in West Bengal, India in 1981. He received the B.Tech degree in Electronics and Communication Engineering from Dumkal Institute of Engineering and Technology under West Bengal University of Technology (India) in 2005 and M.Tech degree in the Multimedia and Software System from National Institute of Technical Teachers Training and Research (Kolkata, India) in 2007. He is working as Assistant Professor in Information Technology department at Narula Institute of Technology, Kolkata since 2008. Presently, he is doing his research work under the supervision of D. K. Bhattacharya. His research topics include Bioinformatics & Computational Biology.

Manoj Kumar received B.Tech in Production Engineering from Bihar Institute of Technology Sindri, India, M.Tech in Mechanical Engineering from Regional Institute of Technology Jamshedpur, India and Ph.D in Mechanical Engineering from Indian Institute of Technology Delhi, India. He is presently working as Director, International Engineering Services, H. No.- 87A, RZI – Block, West Sagarpur,

New Delhi – 110046, India. He has authored or coauthored over 50 research papers in Journals and Conferences. His research work appeared in International Journal of Physical Distribution and Logistics Management, International Journal of Production Economics, Computers & Industrial Engineering, International Journal of Integrated Supply Chain Management, and Advances in Industrial Engineering etc.

Sankar Prasad Mondal is an Assistant Professor in the Department of Mathematics of National Institute of Technology, Agartala, Tripura, India. He received M.Sc (Applied Mathematics) degree from Indian Institute of Engineering Science and Technology (Formally Bengal Engineering and Science University), Shibpur, West Bengal, India and Ph.D degree from Indian Institute of Engineering Science and Technology, Shibpur, West Bengal, India .His current research interest is in Fuzzy Differential Equation and its applications.

Jayanta Pal was born in West Bengal, India in 1978. He received the B.Tech degree in Computer Science and Engineering from Kalyani Govt. Engineering College under University of Kalyani (India) in 1999 and M.E degree in the Computer Science and Engineering from Jadavpur University (Kolkata, India) in 2001. He is working as Assistant Professor in Computer Science and Engineering department at Narula Institute of Technology, Kolkata since 2006. Presently, he is doing his research work under the supervision of D. K. Bhattacharya. His research topics include Bioinformatics & Computational Biology.

Apu Kumar Saha is an Assistant Professor and HOD in the Department of Mathematics of National Institute of Technology, Agartala, Tripura, India. He received M.Sc degree Tripura University, Tripura, India and Ph.D degree from National Institute of Technology, Agartala. His current research interest is Fuzzy set theory and its applications, Optimization techniques, Fluid dynamics.

Tapan Senapati received his B. Sc., M. Sc. and Ph. D. from Vidyasagar University, West Bengal, India in 2006, 2008 and 2013 respectively. He is now currently a school teacher in the Department of Mathematics, Padima Janakalyan Banipith since 2009. Dr. Senapati has published more than thirty articles in international journals. He is a reviewer of nine international journals. His research interest includes fuzzy sets, intuitionistic fuzzy sets, fuzzy algebras, triangular norms and BCK/BCI-algebras.

Priya Singh is presently working as Research Analyst, International Engineering Services. She has authored or coauthored over 5 research papers in Journals and Conferences. His research work appeared in Advances in Industrial Engineering, IUP Journal of Mechanical Engineering, etc.

Florentin Smarandache is a Mathematician, Physicist, Logician, Philosopher at the Mathematics Department in the University of New Mexico, USA. He published over 100 books and 300 articles and notes in mathematics, physics, philosophy, psychology, literature, rebus. In mathematics his research is in number theory, non-Euclidean geometry, synthetic geometry, algebraic structures, statistics, neutrosophic logic and set (generalizations of fuzzy logic and set respectively), neutrosophic probability (generalization of classical and imprecise probability). Also, small contributions to nuclear and particle physics, information fusion, neutrosophy (a generalization of dialectics), law of sensations and stimuli, etc.

Pandian Vasant is a senior lecturer at Department of Fundamental and Applied Sciences, Faculty of Science and Information technology, Universiti Teknologi PETRONAS in Malaysia. He holds PhD (All

Saints College Dublin, Republic of IRELAND) in Computational Intelligence, MSc (UMS, Malaysia, Engineering Mathematics) and BSc (Hons, UM, Malaysia) in Mathematics. His research interests include Soft Computing, Hybrid Optimization, Holistic Optimization, Innovative Computing and Applications. He has co-authored research papers and articles in national journals, international journals, conference proceedings, conference paper presentation, and special issues lead guest editor, lead guest editor for book chapters' project, conference abstracts, edited books , keynote lecture and book chapters (150 publications indexed in SCOPUS). In the year 2009, Dr. Pandian Vasant was awarded top reviewer for the journal Applied Soft Computing (Elsevier) and awarded outstanding reviewer in the year 2015 for ASOC (Elsevier) journal. He has 25 years of working experience at the various universities from 1989-2016. Currently he is Editor-in-Chief of IJCO, IJSIEC, IEM, IJEOE and Editor of GJTO.

Dileep Kumar Vishwakarma is an M.Sc student in the Department of Mathematics of National Institute of Technology, Agartala, Tripura, India.

Luige Vladareanu received his M.Sc. degree in electronics from the Polytechnic Institute Bucharest, in 1977. From 1984, scientific researcher of the Institute of Physics and Material Technology, from 1990, team leader of data acquisition systems and real time control systems of the Institute of Solid Mechanics, from 1991, President General Manager of Engineering and Technology Industrial VTC Company. In 1998 he received Ph.D. degree in electronics field from the Institute of Solid Mechanics of Romanian Academy. From 2003, Ministry of Education and Research, executive Department for Financing Superior Education and of Scientific University Research - High Level Expert Consulting for MEC/CNCSIS project, from 2003-2005, member of Engineering Science Committee of Romanian National Research Council, from 2005, Scientific Researcher Gr.I (Professor) of Romanian Academy, from 2009 Head of Mechatronics Department of Institute of Solid Mechanics, Romanian Academy. His scientific work is focused on real time control in solid mechanics applied in robot trajectory control, hybrid position – force control, multi-microprocessor systems for robot control, acquisition and processing of experimental physical data, experimental methods and signal processing, nano-micro manipulators, semi-active control of mechanical system vibrations, semi-active control of magnetorheological dissipaters systems, complex industrial automations with programmable logical controllers in distributed and decentralized structure. He has published 4 books, over 20 book chapters, 11 edited books, over 200 papers in journals, proceedings and conferences in the areas. Director and coordinator of 7 grants of national research – development programs in the last 5 years, 15 invention patents, developing 17 advanced work methods resulting from applicative research activities and more then 60 research projects. In 1985 the Central Institute of Physics Bucharest awarded his research team a price for the first Romanian industrial painting robot. He is the winner of the two Prize and Gold of Excellence in Research 2000, SIR 2000, of the Romanian Government and the Agency for Science, Technology and Innovation. 9 International Invention and Innovation Competition Awards and Gold of World's Exhibition of Inventions, Geneva 2007 - 2009, and other 9 International Invention Awards and Gold of the Brussels, Zagreb, Bucharest International Exhibition. He received "Traian Vuia" (2006) award of the Romanian Academy, Romania's highest scientific research forum, for a group of scientific papers published in the real time control in the solid mechanics. He is team leader of two ANCS (Scientific Research National Agency) funded research projects: "Fundamental and Applied Researches for Position Control of HFPC MERO Walking Robots" from CNCSIS-Exploratory Researches Program and "Complex Modular Automation Systems for Technological Flux Control AUTMPG" from AMCSIT-Innovation Program. He is a member of the International Institute of Acoustics and Vibration (IIAV), Auburn University, USA (2006), ABI/s Research Board of Advisors, American Biographical Institute (2006), World Scientific and Engineering Academy Society, WSEAS (2005), International Association for Modelling and Simulation Techniques in Enterprises-AMSE, France (2004), National Research Council from Romania(2003-2005), etc. He is a PhD advisor in the field of mechanical engineering at the Romanian Academy. He was an organizer of several international conferences such as the General Chair of four WSEAS International Conferences (http://www.wseas.org/conferences/2008/romania/amta/index.html), chaired Plenary Lectures to Houston 2009, Harvard, Boston 2010 and Penang, Malaysia 2010 to the WSEAS International Conferences, is team leader of WSEAS scientific research project: Mechanics & Robotics Systems and is serving on various other conferences and academic societies.

Index

M

N

P

R

S

T

W